Time Out

Paris

www.timeout.com/paris

Time Out Digital Ltd
4th Floor
125 Shaftesbury Avenue
London WC2H 8AD
United Kingdom
Tel: +44 (0)20 7813 3000
Fax: +44 (0)20 7813 6001
Email: guides@timeout.com
www.timeout.com

Published by Time Out Digital Ltd, a wholly owned subsidiary
of Time Out Group Ltd. Time Out and the Time Out logo are
trademarks of Time Out Group Ltd.

© Time Out Group Ltd 2015
Previous editions 1989, 1990, 1992, 1995, annually from 1997 to 2014.

10 9 8 7 6 5 4 3 2 1

This edition first published in Great Britain in 2015 by Ebury Publishing.
20 Vauxhall Bridge Road, London SW1V 2SA

Ebury Publishing is part of the Penguin Random House group of companies
whose addresses can be found at global.penguinrandomhouse.com

Distributed in the US and Latin America by Publishers Group West
(1-510-809-3700)

For further distribution details, see www.timeout.com.

ISBN: 978-1-84670-354-6

A CIP catalogue record for this book is available from the British Library.

Printed and bound in China by Leo Paper Products Ltd.

Penguin Random House is committed to a sustainable future for our
business, our readers and our planet. This book is made from Forest
Stewardship Council® certified paper.

MIX
Paper from
responsible sources
FSC® C018179

Contents

199

97

Paris's Top 20   10
Paris Today   18
Itineraries   24
Diary   30
Paris's Best   40

Explore   44

The Seine & Islands   46
Opéra to Les Halles   56
Champs-Elysées & Western Paris   88
Montmartre & Pigalle   110
Beaubourg & the Marais   122
Bastille & Eastern Paris   142
North-east Paris   158
The Latin Quarter & the 13th   172
St-Germain-des-Prés & Odéon   190
Montparnasse & Beyond   206
The 7th & Western Paris   218
Beyond the Périphérique   234

119

329

356

Arts & Entertainment 240

Children	242
Film	250
Gay & Lesbian	255
Nightlife	262
Performing Arts	280

Escapes & Excursions 294

Escapes & Excursions	296

In Context 308

History	310
Architecture	328

Essential Information 334

Hotels	336
Getting Around	365
Resources A-Z	369
Vocabulary	379
Further Reference	382
Index	383
Advertisers' Index	393

Maps 394

Métro & RER Map	396
Arrondissement Map	398
Street Maps	400
Street Index	410

Time Out **Paris**

Editorial
Editor Dominic Earle
Listings Editor Barbara Chossis
Proofreader Marion Moisy

Editorial Director Sarah Guy
Group Finance Manager Margaret Wright

Design
Senior Designer Kei Ishimaru
Designer Christie Webster
Group Commercial Senior Designer Jason Tansley

Picture Desk
Picture Editor Jael Marschner
Deputy Picture Editor Ben Rowe
Picture Researcher Lizzy Owen

Advertising
Managing Director St John Betteridge
Advertising Sales Jinga Media Ltd (www.jingamedia.com)

Marketing
Senior Publishing Brand Manager Luthfa Begum
Head of Circulation Dan Collins

Production
Production Controller Katie Mulhern-Bhudia

Time Out Group
Founder Tony Elliott
Chief Executive Officer Tim Arthur
Managing Director Europe Noel Penzer
Publisher Alex Batho

Contributors

Paris Today Alison Culliford. **Explore** Anna Brooke, Alison Culliford, Dominic Earle, Natasha Edwards. **Children** Anna Brooke. **Film** Anna Brooke. **Gay & Lesbian** Robert Vallier. **Nightlife** Anna Brooke, Julien Sauvalle. **Performing Arts** Anna Brooke, Stephen Mudge, Estelle Ricoux. **Escapes & Excursions** Anna Brooke, Alison Culliford, Dominic Earle, Julien Sauvalle. **History** Simon Cropper. **Architecture** Natasha Edwards. **Hotels** Alison Culliford, Katie Walker. **Essential Information** Barbara Chossis.

Maps JS Graphics Ltd (john@jsgraphics.co.uk).

Cover photography Brian Jannsen/Danita Delimont/AWL Images. **Back cover photography** Clockwise from top left: photogolfer/Shutterstock.com; Dmitry Brizhatyuk/Shutterstock.com; © Buddha Bar Hotel, Paris; Jean-Luc Pehau-Ricau/Moulin Rouge; S-F/Shutterstock.com.

Photography Pages 2/3, 292 (top) vvoe/Shutterstock.com; 4/5, 199 Rafal Gadomski/Shutterstock.com; 5 (bottom left), 328 Bernhard Richter/Shutterstock.com; 7 gianni triggiani/Shutterstock.com; 10 pchais/Shutterstock.com; 10/11, 91, 234/235 pio3/Shutterstock.com; 11, 285 © William Beaucardet; 12 beboy/Shutterstock.com; 13, 33 (bottom), 64, 65 (top), 80 (top), 83, 303 Kiev.Victor/Shutterstock.com; 15 (top) © Iwan Baan 2014 © Gehry partners LLP; 16 Slavko Sereda/Shutterstock.com; 16/17, 221, 255, 292 (bottom) photogolfer/Shutterstock.com; 17, 121, 156, 260, 343 (top left and top right) Olivia Rutherford; 18/19 NeydtStock/Shutterstock.com; 20 Frederic Legrand - COMEO/Shutterstock.com; 21 © Herzog & de Meuron/SCI Tour Triangle; 23 Zvonimir Atletic/Shutterstock.com; 24/25 (top), 29, 161, 178, 209, 214, 217, 257, 287, 337, 338, 357, 358, 360 Oliver Knight; 24/25 (bottom), 218 Elsa Pereira; 25 © BEAIR/JAKOB + MACFARLANE; 27 (top), 184, 291 Rrrainbow/Shutterstock.com; 27 (bottom), 56 Virginie Garnier Photography; 28, 266, 280, 293 (top) Karl Blackwell; 30/31 Christina McWilliams/Shutterstock.com; 32 (top) FashionStock.com/Shutterstock.com; 32 (bottom) Cliche Jerome Vila; 33 (top) Sergieiev/Shutterstock.com; 34 Vincent Desjardins; 35 Olga Besnard/Shutterstock.com; 36 (left) Migel/Shutterstock.com; 36 (right) Ekaterina Pokrovsky/Shutterstock.com; 37 Pascal Bouclier; 38/39 © Paul Kolnik; 40/41 (top) Nikonaft/Shutterstock.com; 40/41 (bottom) ivan bastien/Shutterstock.com; 42 (left), 298 (bottom) Huang Zheng/Shutterstock.com; 42/43 Luc Boegly; 44/45, 110/111 anshar/Shutterstock.com; 46 Eugene Sergeev/Shutterstock.com; 46/47 Samot/Shutterstock.com; 54 Botond Horvath/Shutterstock.com; 56/57 Kevin H Knuth/Shutterstock.com; 63 Jeu de Paume/Adrien Chevrot; 65 (bottom), 80 (bottom) maziarz/Shutterstock.com; 71 (top) Philippe Coutanceau; 74 Denis Kuvaev/Shutterstock.com; 84 Bernhard Winkelmann; 86 Cristina Ciochina/Shutterstock.com; 88 chrisdorney/Shutterstock.com; 88/89 Estea/Shutterstock.com; 94 hans engbers/Shutterstock.com; 96 (top) yorgda/www.flickr.com; 96 (bottom) © Florent Michel/11h45; 97 (top) Pierre Monetta; 98 (top) Edouard Sicot; 101 Pierre-Jean Durieu/Shutterstock.com; 102 Karim Daher; 103 Anton_Ivanov/Shutterstock.com; 104 lornet/Shutterstock.com; 105 Alain Gelberger; 107 kavram/Shutterstock.com; 108 meunierd/Shutterstock.com; 109 © La Pâtisserie des Rêves; 110 gabriel12/Shutterstock.com; 116 Jean-Pierre Delagarde; 122, 128 (bottom) © Manuelle Gautrand Architecture/Vincent Fillon; 122/123 Scott Norsworthy/Shutterstock.com; 126 Pack-Shot/Shutterstock.com; 128 (top) Maria Spera/CRT IdF; 130 Lelikron/Wikimedia Commons; 132 Béatrice Hatala © Musée Picasso-Paris 2014; 140 Francis Amiand; 142 Elena Dijour/Shutterstock.com; 142/143 Sergey Galyonkin/Wikimedia Commons; 150 Vincent Anceaume; 153 Aldo Sperber; 158, 237, 256, 288, 343 (bottom), 345, 353 Jean-Christophe Godet; 158/159 Alf van Beem/Wikimedia Commons; 164 Marie Genel/Picturetank; 166 Félix Vigné/Castalie/Porte 12; 169 Production Perig/Shutterstock.com; 172, 242 Elena Dijour/Shutterstock.com; 172/173 littleny/Shutterstock.com; 174, 333 Michel Denancé - Coll. Fondation Jérôme Seydoux-Pathé © 2014 – RPBW; 181 David Ionut/Shutterstock.com; 183 (top) © Annabelle Schachmes; 183 (bottom) © www.tibo.org; 186 Tangopaso/Wikimedia Commons; 188 nax; 189 JAKOB + MACFARLANE/Thibaut Vankemmel/Agence Les Barbus; 190/191 Tuul & Bruno Morandi/Corbis; 195 © AAPP Artefactory Lab; 197 Simona Belotti; 200 Marco Saracco/Shutterstock.com; 203 Maxime Montabord; 204 Elan Fleisher; 206 Viacheslav Lopatin/Shutterstock.com; 206/207 © Paris Tourist Office/David Lefranc; 225 Hélène Giansily; 226 Rina Nurra; 228 (left) Laurent Fau; 228 (right) Annabelle Schachmes; 230 (top) © Sophie Robichon/Mairie de Paris; 230 (bottom) © Paris Tourist Office/Amélie Dupont; 234 sigurcamp/Shutterstock.com; 238 Benh Lieu Song/Wikimedia Commons; 240/241 Charles Platiau; 245 Nicky Berry; 251 Vivi-1/Wikimedia Commons; 253 Rex Features; 261 Evan Bench/Wikimedia Commons; 268 © BEAIR/JAKOB + MACFARLANE; 269 Pigprox/Shutterstock.com; 271 Marie-Sophie Tekian; 272 (top) ParisSharing/Wikimedia Commons; 272 (bottom) Sunny Ripert/Wikimedia Commons; 273 MarOne/Wikimedia Commons; 275 Moonik/Wikimedia Commons; 276 © Jerome Brody; 277 © Rainer Torrado; 278 (top) Sabrina Benrehab; 278 (bottom left) Alexandra Lebon; 278 (bottom right) Svend Andersen; 279 Richard Bartz; 281 JBPellerin; 284 (top) Pat_Hastings/Shutterstock.com; 284 (bottom) posztos/Shutterstock.com; 286 Julieta Cervantes; 289 Patrick Tourneboeuf/Tendance Floue; 290 (top) Nathalie Prébende; 293 (bottom) © Yann Kgbeur; 294/295 Thomas Marchhart/Shutterstock.com; 296 Milan Vachal/Shutterstock.com; 298 (top) Jérémy-Günther-Heinz Jähnick/Wikimedia Commons; 299 Natalia Bratslavsky/Shutterstock.com; 301 Dan Breckwoldt/Shutterstock.com; 302 S-F/Shutterstock.com; 304 siete_vidas/Shutterstock.com; 305 Cloud Mine Amsterdam/Shutterstock.com; 306 Simon Patterson; 308/309 Doin Oakenhelm/Shutterstock.com; 310/311 Getty Images/The Bridgeman Art Library; 313 bensliman hassan/Shutterstock.com; 314, 315 Wikimedia Commons; 317 Oleg Golovnev/Shutterstock.com; 319 Pierre-Jean Chalencon/Photo12/UIG via Getty Images; 320 HaguardDuNord/Wikimedia Commons; 321 Everett Historical/Shutterstock.com; 323 Albert Harlingue/Roger Viollet/Getty Images; 325 Sipa Press/REX_Shutterstock; 326 360b/Shutterstock.com; 327 pixinoo/Shutterstock.com 330 (top) s74/Shutterstock.com; 330 (bottom) Luciano Morpurgo/Shutterstock.com; 332 lapas77/Shutterstock.com; 334/335 William Furniss; 342, 350 Christophe Bielsa; 355 DR; 361 Martine Houghton; 363 www.sinueserra.com; 380 (top) Michaelpuche/Shutterstock.com; 380 (bottom) Petr Jilek/Shutterstock.com; 381 (top) christinemg/Shutterstock.com; 381 (bottom) pattyphotoart/Shutterstock.com; 394/395 Ioan Panaite/Shutterstock.com

The following images were supplied by the featured establishments; 4, 5 (top and bottom right), 12/13, 15 (bottom), 22, 24 (top), 42 (right), 67, 68, 71 (bottom), 73, 77, 97 (bottom left and bottom right), 98 (bottom), 119, 135, 136, 137, 139, 145, 155, 190, 212, 233, 245 (top left and bottom left), 250, 259, 262, 263, 264, 267, 270, 290 (bottom), 307, 336, 346, 354, 364.

The Editor would like to thank all contributors to the Time Out Paris website (www.timeout.fr) and previous editions of *Time Out Paris*, whose work forms the basis for parts of this book.

About the Guide

GETTING AROUND

Each sightseeing chapter contains a street map of the area marked with the locations of sights and museums (), restaurants (❶), cafés and bars (❶), and shops (❶). There are also street maps of Paris at the back of the book, along with an overview map of the city and métro map. In addition, there is now a detachable fold-out street and métro map inside the back cover.

THE ESSENTIALS

For practical information, including visas, disabled access, emergency numbers, lost property, websites and local transport, see the Essential Information section. It begins on page 334.

THE LISTINGS

Addresses, phone numbers, websites, transport information, hours and prices are all included in our listings, along with selected other facilities. All were checked and correct at press time. However, business owners can alter their arrangements at any time, and fluctuating economic conditions can cause prices to change rapidly. The very best venues in the city, the must-sees and must-dos in every category, have been marked with a red star (★). In the sightseeing chapters, we've also marked venues with free admission with a FREE symbol.

THE LANGUAGE

Many Parisians speak a little English, but learning a few basic French phrases will go a long way. You'll find a primer on page 379 to get you started, along with some help with restaurant ordering.

PHONE NUMBERS

The area code for Paris is 01. Even if you're calling from within Paris, you'll need to use the code. From outside France, dial your country's international access code (00 from the UK, 011 from the US) or a plus symbol, followed by the French country code (33), 1 for Paris (dropping the initial zero) and the eight-digit number. So, to reach the Musée du Louvre, dial +33.1.40.20.50.50. For more on phones, see *p377*.

FEEDBACK

We welcome feedback on this guide, both on the venues we've included and on any other locations that you'd like to see featured in future editions. Please email us at guides@timeout.com.

Paris's
Top **20**

From concept stores to concert halls, we count down the capital's finest.

1 Musée du Louvre
(page 63)

If any place demonstrates the central importance of culture in French life, this is it. The world's most popular museum (it welcomed just shy of ten million visitors during 2013) is a masterpiece inside and out, and the stunning new Islamic Arts department, beneath the Cour Visconti, means the Louvre is marching boldly onwards.

2 Philharmonie de Paris
(page 284)

Tucked away in north-east Paris, the
dramatic new Philharmonie de Paris
is aiming to break down the classical
music barriers, drawing in virgins as well
as concert hall veterans with affordable
ticket prices. The rewards for making
it out to Parc de la Villette are, quite
literally, huge – the impressive 2,400-seat
concert hall (laid out so that no audience
member is sat more than 38 metres
from the conductor) was overseen
by super-composer Pierre Boulez.

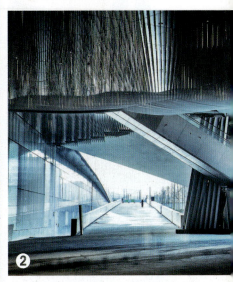

3 Musée d'Orsay
(page 224)

The revamp of the Musée d'Orsay hasn't
changed the former railway station's
exterior one iota – the wonder is all inside.
On the museum's 25th anniversary,
director Guy Cogeval finally achieved
a long-held dream to obliterate white
walls, 'the enemy of painting', and
give the Impressionist movement the
brush-up it so richly deserved. As an
extra treat, the classical concerts held
in the auditorium are always top-notch.

4 Point Ephémère
(page 267)

Housed in a former warehouse for art deco construction materials, Point Ephémère is a buzzing breeding ground for all things artistic and its location on Canal Saint-Martin makes it a summer hit. In 2004 it was an artist's squat, but today it organises everything from art exhibitions to pop, rock, electro and hip hop gigs, all within reach of youthful budgets. You can eat on the pretty terrace and the food is decent. You may jump every time a fire engine zooms out of the next-door fire station, but you'll soon settle back into the canalside vibe.

5 Eiffel Tower
(page 229)

Originally built for the 1889 World Fair, Gustave Eiffel's iconic Iron Lady strikes a pose like no other building in Paris. The radical cast-iron confection was the tallest structure in the world until it was overtaken by New York's Empire State Building in the 1930s, and views can reach 65km on a clear day. Oh, and there's now a glass floor if you fancy looking down instead.

6 Chateaubriand
(page 168)

The last few years have seen the meteoric rise of the neo-bistro scene, and Le Chateaubriand is the *coeur d'artichaut* of this new dining trend. So what are the magic ingredients? Flair, innovation and world-beating ingredients, all crafted together by chef-owner Inaki Aizpitarte in a get-what-you're-given *menu unique*.

7 Canal Saint-Martin
(page 160)

Before it harboured stalwarts of Paris's nightlife, Point Ephémère and Chez Prune, the Canal Saint-Martin served an entirely different purpose. Built between 1805 and 1825, it brought drinking water and merchandise to the capital; then, from the late 19th

8 Musée Picasso
(page 131)

Finally, after five years of building works, the Musée Picasso has reopened its doors at the Hôtel Salé in the Marais with triple the exhibition space – which means more masterpieces on show, up from 450 to 550, as well as temporary exhibitions. The revamp had its difficulties, finishing very late and horribly over budget, but the return of the Musée Picasso confirms that the Paris art scene is firmly back on track.

9 La Pagode
(page 254)

We challenge you to find a more gorgeous picturehouse than the 19th-century Japanese-style Pagode. What started out in 1896 as an eccentric present for the wife of Bon Marché department store founder François-Emile Morin is now a supremely romantic cinema for arthouse aesthetes: period touches include woven fabric on the walls, golden lights and dragon carvings over the grandiose doorways. On a warm day, treat yourself to a pre-show cup of tea in the Pagode's bamboo-speckled Japanese garden.

century onwards, it housed factories and industrial warehouses. Nowadays, many of the factories have become lofts for Paris's bobo crowd, and dozens of bars, restaurants and shops line the quaysides. Its charming footbridges and locks are ideal for a weekend stroll – especially on Sundays when the roads are reserved for walkers and cyclists.

10 Musée de la Chasse et de la Nature
(page 131)

Whether tracking deer or snaffling boar, the French adore *la chasse*, and this grand Marais mansion makes for a stunning trophy cabinet. It may be a long way from the wild forests of the Auvergne, but all manner of stuffed treats await.

LIDO

· DE PARIS ·

NEW SHOW

Paris Merveilles

CREATED AND DIRECTED BY FRANCO DRAGONE

DINNER & SHOW FROM €165
CHAMPAGNE & SHOW FROM €115

116 BIS AVENUE DES CHAMPS-ELYSÉES, 75008 PARIS
www.lido.fr · + 33 (0) 1 40 76 56 10 · reservation@lido.fr

11 Fondation Louis Vuitton
(page 107)

Like a butterfly emerging from its chrysalis, the daring glass structure housing the Fondation Louis Vuitton modern art gallery emerged in the Bois de Boulogne in October 2014.

Designed by Frank Gehry, the impressive new space is described as 'an emblematic building for the 21st century' by LMVH chairman Bernard Arnault. Visually stunning, the Fondation is shell-shaped and made up of 12 glass sails that soar above the park's green spaces. Inside is a huge auditorium and acres of exhibition space divided across 11 galleries.

12 Merci
(page 140)

At Merci – a concept store in the Haut Marais – you can pick up everything from furniture, clothes and jewellery to perfume, accessories and books. Nothing new there. What is different, though, is the fact that Merci's proceeds go to charity, so shopping here could make a real difference to people's lives. Ethics aside, the products on sale are generally gorgeous, as are the cakes in the *cantine*.

13 Boulogne-Billancourt
(page 237)

Paris's suburbs often play second fiddle to the main attractions, but you'd be wrong to ignore Boulogne-Billancourt.

There's the lovely Bois de Boulogne for a start – Paris's western lung, filled with lakes, parkland and now the Fondation Louis Vuitton as well. Then there are three museums worth an afternoon of your time. Head to the Musée Belmondo if you're into sculpture, the Musée des Années 30 for everything art deco, and the Musée Albert Kahn for its wonderful sculpted gardens and collections of 19th-century photography.

14 Les Caves Augé
(page 100)

If you want a slice of history served with your wine, head to Les Caves Augé. It has been open since 1850 and was the store where Proust used to go to stock up his cellar: the decor, awash with mouldings and panelling, has changed little since then. You can choose from thousands of bottles, the savvy *cavistes* can aid your selection, and there's an ever-increasing focus on 'natural' wines. If you fancy a *dégustation*, there's a tasting day one Saturday each month.

15 Cathédrale Notre-Dame de Paris
(page 51)

Quasimodo certainly had good taste: the views from Notre-Dame's towers are nothing short of stupendous, especially on a cloudy day when the skies spin a moody hue across the Seine. From the top, you also get the best view of the 850-year-old cathedral's famous gargoyles – cheeky little chimeras watching over the city below. They're actually not originals; architect Viollet-le-Duc added them during

the mid 19th century when he restored the cathedral to its former glory.

16 Promenade Plantée
(page 155)

Fifty years ago Bastille had a train station with a viaduct that carried trains

17 Centre Pompidou
(page 124)

As cutting-edge as ever, the Pompidou is home to modern art treasures by, among others, Braque, Dubuffet, Matisse and Ernst, plus rotating exhibitions that ensure no two visits are ever the same. Arrive at 6pm and stay until closing time at 9pm, after which Georges, the trendy rooftop bar-restaurant, serves moreish cocktails in a futuristic setting with panoramic views over the city.

18 Les Catacombes
(page 216)

Descend, if you dare, into the entrails of the city. The Catacombs are without doubt the spookiest attraction Paris has to offer, with kilometres of tunnels lined with the bones of defunct Parisians. Created in the late 18th century to stop disease from spreading from overrun inner-city cemeteries, they now make for a chilling stroll.

19 Palais Garnier
(page 284)

The 'wedding cake', as the Garnier is nicknamed, wows a highbrow crowd with some of the world's best ballet and the occasional opera. The building is an ode to opulence, dripping in marble and gold leaf. It's also fascinating, with an underground lake that inspired Gaston Leroux to write *Phantom of the Opera* and beehives on the roof that produce the honey on sale in the boutique.

20 St-Germain-des-Prés
(page 190)

Whether you're tasting st-marcellin at Fromagerie Quatrehomme or picking up a stuffed tiger at Deyrolle, shopping on the Left Bank is a sensual pleasure. Whereas we have window-shopping, the French have window-licking (*lèche-vitrine*), and a morning spent mooching around St-Germain-des-Prés' boutiques will show you why.

into the centre from Vincennes. The station is no more (the Opéra Bastille stands there now), but the viaduct is a firm fixture thanks to the Promenade Plantée – an elevated garden (like New York's High Line) that you can follow across Paris's 12th arrondissement.

Paris Today

Dark days, but a bright future.

TEXT: ALISON CULLIFORD

For one day at the beginning of 2015, Paris was all about love. This wasn't as a result of some Valentine's Day marketing special, or those ridiculous padlocks that periodically have to be cut off the city's bridges. This was a celebration of a higher love, you could say, and a more spontaneous one. You may have been there. If you weren't, your choice of media will have given you a more or less slanted view of what Sunday 11 January 2015 was really like as people gathered to remember the tragic events of the previous few days that shocked the country, and the globe. The gathering of world leaders at the head of the procession grabbed the headlines and foreign newspapers reported on a 'sea of tricolores', but for Parisians it was about reclaiming their city in all its multicultural richness.

François Hollande, Angela Merkel and Malian President Ibrahim Boubacar Keïta join the march for unity in Paris.

SEA OF LOVE

Some say that it was the largest popular gathering to have occurred in Paris's history, others say since the Liberation at the end of World War II. While Paris's regular protest marches have an ambience of old-fashioned trades union bonhomie – fuelled by margaritas from vans sporting pictures of Che – this was something completely different. Though most people didn't move more than half a kilometre, and proceeded in silence except for the waves of applause rising eerily but thrillingly – perhaps in response to the sight of a policewoman on a roof or to someone daring to hold a placard saying 'I am a Muslim, I am not a terrorist' – there was a sense of great awe on the streets of Paris that day. It is a sensation hard to describe when a city suddenly becomes more than its streets and its monuments, its neighbourhoods and green spaces: it becomes its people.

For two or three weeks afterwards the love vibe continued. Bus drivers held their doors open when they saw someone running; taxi drivers made sure to see women home safely; passers-by made a point of saying hello to the Algerian shopkeepers setting up their fruit and veg stands; the homeless probably received a few more sous. Eventually, though, Parisians started to behave like Parisians again, and dinner parties were plagued by existential questions about who, or what, is Charlie? But, writing this at the beginning of April 2015,

it still feels as though the capital has changed. It has become more aware of its past, of its present and perhaps of its future too.

PARIS DARES

The future, indeed, is where Anne Hidalgo has set her sights. Since becoming Mayor of Paris on 5 April 2014, she has put forward a number of ambitious projects with media-friendly tags. With shades of Obama's 'Yes we can' slogan, her election campaign was dubbed '*Oser Paris*' ('Paris dares'), and opened up the floor to Paris residents to have their say, via the internet or in focus groups, about making the city a better place in which to live.

Unsurprisingly, this produced some fairly leftfield ideas: a marathon along the *périphérique*; a health centre for wild animals that have made Paris their home; a giant chess game; umbrella bikes; sledging in Montmartre. But, then again, who would have dreamed 15 years ago that Paris would have its own beach? Some ideas also showed inspiration from across the Channel, such as speakers' corners or wild swimming in the Bois de Vincennes. Then, of course, there were more serious suggestions that focused on housing, the environment and inclusion. Hidalgo promised that she would put 50% of the ideas into action without raising taxes.

Another catchy phrase that the mayor has been dropping into virtually every interview is 'Le Grand Paris' – a pun on *le grand pari* or 'the big bet'. And perhaps it is just that, as the project to create a metropolitan area of Greater Paris was a Sarkozy baby that has been dogged by controversy. Long shot or not, though, it has now been reappropriated by the Socialist mayor as a way to bring a sense of inclusion to the suburbs, and it comes into being on 1 January 2016.

Her challenge is to make Le Grand Paris more than just another layer of bureaucracy, but the Mayor does seem to mean business. In late 2014, she launched an invitation to architects from around the world to 'Réinventer Paris' ('reinvent Paris'). Twenty-three sites around the city, from an electricity substation to a 16th-century mansion, have been earmarked for development in what Hidalgo has labelled an 'urban experiment of unprecedented magnitude'.

The earmarked sites are all within the 20 arrondissements of Paris, but 13 of them are on or near the périphérique, and thus part of the scheme to 'rub out this boundary'. Hidalgo also proved her feistiness by declaring null and void a Paris city council vote against the contentious Triangle Tower, a 50-storey skyscraper proposed for the edge of the périphérique at Porte de Versailles by architects Herzog & De Meuron.

CAPITAL CULTURE

The last year has shown that Paris is well on its way to reinventing itself as an exciting, modern cultural capital that no longer rests on its laurels. Having not seen a major new opening since the Musée du Quai Branly in 2006, the city is now home to the fabulous Fondation Louis Vuitton art museum in the Bois de Boulogne. The Fondation opened in October 2014 with an exhibition on the building's architect, Frank Gehry, followed by shows devoted to Icelandic conjuror of light Olafur Eliasson, and groundbreakers in 20th-century art (with masterworks loaned from the world's greatest museums). There's plenty of crossover culture, too, with concerts by Kanye West, Kraftwerk and superstar pianist Lang Lang, plus performance art and poetry. With a revolving permanent collection no less impressive and contemporary, the Fondation could well rival London's Tate Modern in its ability to gather a public looking to consume art as a social experience.

On the other side of Paris, the La Villette complex in the 19th has an equally attention-grabbing new building in the form of the Philharmonie concert hall. Designed by Jean Nouvel, it rises up next to the existing Cité de la Musique building in folds of silvery scales,

The proposed Triangle Tower.

Philharmonie de Paris.

while the acoustic moulding within its 2,400-seat auditorium billows like the clouds of a Turner sky. Most importantly for those who spent €390m on its construction, the auditorium got the thumbs-up for its acoustics from critics on the opening night, when the Orchestre de Paris played Fauré's *Requiem* for the victims of the attacks. Like the Fondation Louis Vuitton, the Philharmonie spreads its arms culturally wide: the V&A's David Bowie Is… was its first exhibition and jazz, world music and electro-pop concerts are all planned. This is all part of a desire to attract a younger audience – the average age of concertgoers in France has risen from 36 in 1981 to 61 today.

DIGITAL DARLING

Despite Bowie and electro-pop, the Philharmonie may have a hard time tearing the youth away from the compelling Gaîté Lyrique, in the hip heart of NoMa (Northern Marais), which has been a huge success thanks to its multi-faceted programme based around the digital arts – everything from animation to computer-aided design, rock concerts with spectacular VJing to training in video game architecture, debates on Google or insanity to a gay music festival ('Loud and Proud'). Kids and teenagers can't get enough of the place, often dragging their parents or grandparents along – fortunately for the grown-ups, there's a buzzing bar and guest chefs cook up decent Sunday brunches.

The idea of Paris as a digital capital may sound incongruous, but the Gaîté Lyrique is just the public face of a major behind-the-scenes movement to capitalise on one of France's lesser-known talents. Sorry London, but Paris ranked third after Stockholm and Toronto for 'intellectual capital and innovation' in a recent report, and according to Mayor Hidalgo the city is racing ahead of its cross-channel rival. It is currently home to more than 5,000 startups and 80 incubators, and the largest incubator in the world is due to open in 2016 at the Halle Freyssinet, opposite the Bibliothèque François Mitterrand in the 13th, to house 1,000 startups. Meanwhile, the old Sentier rag trade district has already been transformed into a neighbourhood of startups, bringing with them cafés, bars, restaurants and gyms where young innovators shoot the breeze. And if you want to see more concrete evidence, check out the annual Futur en Seine, Europe's biggest festival of digital innovation, which takes place in June.

So, is this Paris redefined, a 'smart' city with peripheral skyscrapers and 'intelligent bus stops', buzzing with bearded hipsters clutching MacBook Airs and sipping lattes (yes, they have finally arrived)? To a degree, yes, but the soul of the French capital can't be ripped out by a few gourmet burger joints any more than it can be by an attack on its belief in free speech. If you're in any doubt, head to Montparnasse and have coffee in La Rotonde, and pick up a copy of *Charlie Hebdo* on the way.

SLEEP TALK

Hoteliers are seething as Airbnb beds down in the capital.

When the world is at the click of a mouse, where does its largest peer-to-peer accommodation website hold its annual meet-the-public event? The City of Light, of course. In November 2015, the first Airbnb OPEN to be held outside San Francisco will take place in Paris. Earlier in the year, the company made the somewhat surprising announcement that Paris was the global capital of Airbnb, with 40,000 active listings on the site, beating New York's 34,000 and London's 23,000. Perhaps more odd still – considering the relatively small size of the capital and the widely held belief that French people holiday *chez eux* – is that Parisians are also the biggest users of the platform to travel beyond the *périph'*.

The reason behind these figures is a massive about-turn by the city authorities. Back in 2009, the Mairie de Paris decided to crack down on Parisians doing what they'd always done – renting out their apartments or pied-à-terres during the holidays – by enforcing a law against short-term rentals. The Mairie said that it was reacting to a housing shortage in the city, even though the government had previously provided tax breaks to encourage renovations for holiday lets.

Now, though, the municipal law has changed to allow Paris residents to rent out their pads for a portion of the year, with a *taxe de séjour* being levied on the rental. As a result, the Paris mayor's team was all smiles when it received Airbnb's CEO Brian Chesky at the beginning of the year and posted on its website that it was launching the world's first tourism startup incubator so Parisians could follow in his entrepreneurial footsteps. Meanwhile, Paris hoteliers are seething and have written a petition to Prime Minister Manuel Valls, railing against 'unfair' competition from Airbnb. However, given the price of many hotel rooms in the capital, their pleas may fall on unsympathetic ears.

Itineraries

*Plot out your perfect trip
to the capital with our
step-by-step Paris planner.*

10AM

NOON

Day 1

10AM If 1960s Nouvelle Vague films are anything to go by, you'd be forgiven for thinking that most Paris couples spend all day in bed. But if you're in the City of Love for a weekend only, and are too eager for sightseeing to indulge in breakfast *en lit*, then you should kick things off with some of the city's best coffee at **La Caféothèque** (*p135*). This boutique café is located on a picture-postcard stretch of the Seine, an easy stroll from beautiful 17th-century **Place des Vosges** (*p131*). The Marais is abuzz with culture, shops, bars and, in its imposing *hôtels particuliers*, important cultural institutions: take your pick from the **Musée Carnavalet** (*p129*), the **Musée d'Art et d'Histoire du Judaïsme** (*p129*), the **Maison Européenne de la Photographie** (*p129*) or the newly expanded **Musée Picasso** (*p131*). Shoppers will also find rich pickings in the streets leading off the

4PM

9PM

Clockwise from far left: **La Caféothèque; Institut du Monde Arabe; Wanderlust; Rosa Bonheur sur Seine**.

main shopping thoroughfare of rue des Francs-Bourgeois.

NOON From the Marais, head across the Seine via the Pont de Sully to the **Institut du Monde Arabe** (*p184*), which holds a fine collection of Middle Eastern art and a rooftop café with fabulous views. (Other wonderful panoramas in Paris include the summit of the Parc des Buttes-Chaumont and the Sacré-Coeur, although the latter is worth saving for dusk.) After a wander along the Left Bank, and a stop at the revamped **Monnaie de Paris** (*p195*) for a history of the *franc*, it's time for lunch in the back room at **La Palette** (*p197*) or the cosy back garden at haute treat **Le Restaurant** (*p196*). Afterwards, meander along the stone quays that border the Seine and leaf through

tatty paperbacks at the riverside *bouquinistes*, before ducking into the revamped **Musée d'Orsay** (*p224*) for an Impressionist masterclass.

4PM From here, either hop on a boat tour or explore the newly pedestrianised **Berges de Seine** (*p230*), which stretch from Quai Branly to Quai Anatole France and offer all manner of waterside fun, from teepees and climbing walls to bars and outdoor stages. Finish off with a floating Pernod on board the **Rosa Bonheur sur Seine** *péniche* (p226).

9PM Evenings start with aperitifs. Join the crowd on the terrace seats at **Le Bar du Marché** (*p197*) and watch the Left Bank people-traffic pass by over a kir. Then head along the river to party at **Wanderlust** or **Nüba** (for both, *p269*). Any post-club hunger pangs can be satiated 24/7 at **Au Pied de Cochon** (6 rue Coquillière, 1st, www. pieddecochon.com).

The Sightseeing Cruise
Get the best of Paris in 1 hour

The Parisian sightseeing cruise has to be at the top of your list of things to do when in the French Capital. Ideally located, it's charming boats enhance the pleasure of a guided cruise on the Seine.
The river banks offer you some of the most well-known monuments such as the Eiffel Tower, the Louvre, the Orsay Museum and Notre Dame Cathedral amongst others. Recorded multilingual commentary and a bar service on board.

Departures every day of the year from October to March from 11.15am to 21pm (every 45 min), from April to September from 10.30am to 22pm (every 30 min).

1 hour Sightseeing or "By Night" Cruises: Adult: **€14**; Children 4-11 y.o: €6; Free under 4 y.o

Exclusive: The Champagne Cruise
1 hr Sightseeing Cruise + 1 glass of Champagne for **19€**

*On this guide's presentation, valid for adult ticket for 2015. Terms and conditions apply. Not Cumulative offer.

At the foot of the Eiffel Tower
Port de Suffren - 75007 Paris
M° Bir Hakeim RER C Champs de Mars
+33 (0) 1 44 18 19 50
www.vedettesdeparis.com

vedettes de paris

Top: **Jardin du Luxembourg**.
Bottom: **Frenchie Bar à Vins**.

Day 2

9AM If you'd like to admire the marvels of the **Musée du Louvre** (p63), now's the time: early, before the crowds have descended (and preferably not on a weekend). Otherwise, cross over the Pont des Arts and head south through the narrow Left Bank streets to the city's oldest church, **Eglise St-Germain-des-Prés** (p192), followed by a cup of coffee at **Le Rostand** (p203). Then take a stroll down to the **Jardin du Luxembourg** (p200), pull up two green chairs (using one of them as a footrest) and size up the park life. The adjacent **Musée du Luxembourg** (p200) hosts world-class art exhibitions.

NOON From here, hop on the métro to Jacques Bonsergent. Amble along the tree-lined Canal St-Martin, crossing over its romantic bridges to explore little shops and

waterside cafés, and maybe stopping at buzzing new bistro **Les Bancs Publics** (p164) for inventive dishes and an idyllic setting, with tables outside overlooking the canal. There are plenty of boutiques to explore in the area, alongside kitsch merchants **Antoine et Lili** (p166). For a swift *demi* near the water's edge, head to bobo-friendly **Chez Prune** (p165), before catching the métro to Alma Marceau.

5PM Modern art lovers should make a point of visiting the superb collection at the **Musée d'Art Moderne de la Ville de Paris** (p95); it's a neighbour to the **Palais de Tokyo** (p96), a dynamic contemporary art space that has recently tripled in size. From here, you can walk to the Champs-Elysées and take a night-time hike up the **Arc de Triomphe** (p90) to see the lights of the avenue stretching into the city. Alternatively, head out west to the Bois de Boulogne to explore the dramatic **Fondation Louis Vuitton** art gallery (p107), a hugely ambitious Frank Gehry production that opened to great fanfare in late 2014.

8PM Head back to the Palais de Tokyo and relax with an expertly shaken cocktail at the hip bar overlooking the Seine. Then head up to Les Halles for supper at the more accessible branch of Grégory Lemarchand's loft-style bistro, **Frenchie Bar à Vins** (p86), next to rue Montorgeuil. Still got energy? Our Nightlife section awaits…

Vintage Paris

Clockwise from right: **Noir Kennedy**; **Didier Ludot**; **Bistrot Paul Bert**.

Paris is dripping in everything your vintage heart could desire, from rare 1920s Chanel accessories and art deco lighting to '60s rock LPs and '80s kitten boots. And the good news is that many of the best vintage boutiques are condensed on the Right Bank between Palais-Royal and Faidherbe Chaligny.

To look the part, and for whizzing between the shops for maximum rifling time, hire a vintage-style Vespa from **Left Bank Scooters** (www.leftbankscooters.com). There are two models to choose from, each with a handy compartment for stashing your shopping.

Park your Vespa on the corner of rue Paul Bert and rue Faidherbe, 11th. Most vintage boutiques on this tour only open in the afternoon, so start with a retro lunch on rue Paul Bert. If you're looking for old-school Paris, **Bistrot Paul Bert** (*p145*) never fails to deliver, with its zinc bar, 1930s tiles and dishes such as suckling pig with potato gratin.

After lunch, leave your Vespa and walk down rue Faidherbe, pausing to admire **Les Années Scooter** (23 rue Faidherbe, 11th, www.lesanneesscooter.com), a den of mid 20th-century scooters, table lights, clocks, jukeboxes and street signs. Philippe, the owner, can tell you the story behind every piece on display. A few doors further along, **Restaur'Bronze** (41 rue Faidherbe, www.restaur bronzeparis.com) is one of the last places in Paris to specialise in metal objects from the 1930s and '40s, including show-stopping art deco lights.

You can't scoot around town with a 1932 crystal candelabra in tow, so head back to your Vespa. Drive back down rue Faidherbe and turn left down rue de Charonne. Park up opposite the Bistrot du Peintre café (where you'll be coming back for coffee). Take a right down rue Keller, then turn left on to rue de la Roquette. **Adöm** (35 & 56 rue de la Roquette) is split into two small boutiques. Girls head to no.56 for 1970s jeans and '60s shift dresses, while boys drop into no.35 for 1950s baseball jackets, cowboy boots and sneakers.

Now retrace your steps to the art nouveau surroundings of **Le Bistro du Peintre** (116 av Ledru-Rollin, 11th, www.bistrotdupeintre.com),

where you can peruse your purchases over a coffee. Sustenance over, the boutique-filled Haut Marais beckons. Return to your Vespa and head south on av Ledru-Rollin, then right on to rue du Faubourg-St-Antoine. At place de la Bastille, take a right up bd Beaumarchais and park by St-Sébastien Froissart métro station.

During the last few years, this previously forgotten area has been transformed with numerous one-off boutiques – including the wonderful **Matières à Reflexion** (19 rue de Poitou, 3rd, www.matieresareflexion.com) – a place where old leather jackets and clothes are crafted into one-off bags and satchels fastened with aged brass hardware.

From here, hop back on the bike and whizz down rue du Pont-au-Choux, left on to rue de Turenne and then right on to rue St-Antoine. Park the bike near St-Paul métro station. Walk up rue Pavée, then left on to rue du Roi de Sicile for two vintage hotspots. For punky London retro style, try **Noir Kennedy** (22 rue du Roi de Sicile, 4th, www.noirkennedyparis. com), which is chock full of leather coats, lumberjack shirts, ripped jeans and funky 1980s T-shirts.

TWO WHEELS

All Left Bank Scooters rentals include a lock, two helmets, insurance, plus winter riding gloves and wet weather gear if needed. 50cc prices start from 70 euros per day.

If '40s fashion is more your street style, try **Mam'Zelle Swing** (35 rue du Roi de Sicile, 4th, www.mamzelle-swing.com).

Back on your Vespa, drive down rue de Rivoli, turn right up rue de l'Echelle and right down rue St-Honoré, then park wherever you can at Palais-Royal. From here, stroll to Paris's temple of luxury vintage, **Didier Ludot** (*p70*). You just have to catch a glimpse of the window displays to see there's something special about Ludot's pieces, many of which look like they could have been cast-offs from Audrey Hepburn.

Shopping over for the afternoon, head for a fittingly retro-style dinner at red- and white-checked **Astier** (44 rue Jean-Pierre Timbaud, 11th, www.restaurant-astier.com).

PARIS FOR FREE
Not everything costs the earth in the capital.

FESTIVAL FEVER
From cinema under the stars in Parc de la Villette and jazz gigs in the Bois de Vincennes to Bastille Day fireworks and Nuit Blanche's all-night arts and culture extravaganza, several of Paris's finest festivals are free to attend.

CULTURE ON THE CHEAP
Time it right and you can visit many of Paris's finest museums without spending a single cent. On the first Sunday of each month, cultural giants such as the Musée du Louvre (only Oct-Mar), Musée d'Orsay, Centre Pompidou, Musée de l'Orangerie and many more can be ticked off without reaching for your wallet.

HEAVEN SENT
Plenty of the capital's stunning churches are essential viewing, and free entry to most means you can admire everywhere from Notre-Dame's nave to St-Sulpice's Delacroix murals and the Sacré-Coeur's lavish interior without having to shell out a hefty entrance fee.

IN THE PICTURE
Timing your trip to coincide with a night of free *vernissages* (private views) gives a taste not only of the art on offer but also of the personalities who frequent the art scene, a real entrée into Paris life. The journal *L'Officiel Galeries & Musées*, which you can pick up in most galleries, has a diary of forthcoming *vernissages*.

PARK LIFE
Many of Paris's green spaces may be preened to within an inch of their life, but they're still free to all and sundry if you fancy stretching out in the sunshine. So get a picnic together and take your pick from the smart lawns of the Jardin des Tuileries, the rolling hills of the Parc des Buttes-Chaumont or the postmodern pathways of the Parc André Citroën.

Diary

Plan your perfect weekend with our year-round guide to the French capital.

Paris is positively bursting with culture and a spate of festivals have been added to the already crowded calendar in the last few years, including eco-friendly music festival We Love Green, culinary champion Fête de la Gastronomie, and Nuit Blanche-style Paris Face Cachée. During summer, many of the capital's parks turn into alfresco classical concert venues and theatrical stages. Among them is the lovely Parc Floral de Paris, which holds weekend concerts throughout the warmer months. Elsewhere, Solidays, Rock en Seine, Festival des Inrockuptibles and the Techno Parade all attract top rock acts. And if sports fans don't manage to get tickets for the Six Nations, there's always the finale of the Tour de France, which celebrated its 101st edition in 2014 with a start in Yorkshire and two Frenchmen finishing in the top three for the first time since Fignon and Hinault led the pack home in 1984.

Spring

Paris Face Cachée
Various venues (01.43.48.08.02, www.parisface cachee.fr). **Tickets** varies. **Date** early Feb.
Quirky and educational, Paris Face Cachée is in the same vein as autumn's Nuit Blanche, where the public is invited into unusual or industrial spaces for art happenings. But this new festival is not exclusively an art event. A huge variety of venues and activities lift the lid on places you might never have known existed, and give participants a chance to experience Paris at work behind the scenes.

Six Nations
Stade de France, 93210 St-Denis (www.rbs6 nations.com). RER B La Plaine Stade de France or RER D Stade de France St-Denis. **Admission** varies. **Date** Feb-Mar.
Paris hosts two massive rugby weekends in spring. Log on to the website at least three months in advance to be in with any chance of getting tickets to a match. France finished up fourth in 2014.

Fashion Week
Various venues (www.modeaparis.com). **Date** Mar, July, Oct & Jan.
Paris presents its haute couture and prêt-à-porter collections at a variety of venues across the capital, but to invited guests only. Visit the website to obtain accreditation details. *Photo p32.*

Le Printemps des Poètes
Various venues (01.53.80.08.00, www.printemps despoetes.com). **Date** Mar.
The 17th edition of this long-running national poetry festival featured 'L'Insurrection Poétique' as its theme in 2015, and included a major celebration of the work of French poet Luc Bérimont on the 100th anniversary of his birth.

Printemps du Cinéma
Various venues (www.printempsducinema.com). **Date** mid Mar.
Film tickets at a variety of cinemas all across the city are cut to a bargain €3.50 for this hugely popular three-day film bonanza.

IN THE KNOW ONLINE UPDATE

The comprehensive **Time Out Paris** website (www.timeout.fr/paris) lists everything that matters in the capital's cultural calendar; get news of key events via Facebook, Twitter and the weekly newsletter. Always confirm details well in advance – events can be cancelled and dates may change with little notice.

★ Banlieues Bleues

Various venues in Seine-St-Denis (01.49.22.10.10, www.banlieuesbleues.org). **Admission** varies. **Date** mid Mar-mid Apr.

Festival of French and international jazz, blues, R&B, soul, funk, flamenco and world music.

▶ *For more on music festivals in and around Paris, see p37.*

★ Marathon de Paris

Av des Champs-Elysées, 8th, to av Foch, 16th (01.41.33.15.68, www.parismarathon.com). **Date** early Apr.

One of the world's most picturesque marathons, with up to 40,000 runners heading off from the Champs-Elysées along the Right Bank to the Bois de Vincennes, and back along the Left Bank to the Bois de Boulogne. Registration begins in the previous September. If you're looking for something to aim at, the 2014 men's winner was Ethiopian Kenenisa Bekele in a course record 2hrs 5mins 3secs.

Le Chemin de la Croix

Square Willette, 18th. M° Abbesses or Anvers. **Date** Good Friday.

A crowd of pilgrims follows the Archbishop of Paris from the bottom of Montmartre up to Sacré-Coeur as he performs the Stations of the Cross.

Foire du Trône

Pelouse de Reuilly, 12th (www.foiredutrone.com). M° Porte Dorée. **Admission** free; rides €2-€5. **Date** Apr-June.

France's biggest funfair runs for two months, with a mix of stomach-churning rides, bungee jumping and candyfloss aplenty. Invest in a pass (around €30) in advance. At the weekends the Mairie runs a free shuttle bus from Bercy and Nation. *Photo p34.*

Fête du Travail

Date 1 May.

May Day is strictly observed. Key sights (the Eiffel Tower aside) close, and unions march in eastern Paris via Bastille. Sweet-smelling posies of lily of the valley (*muguet*) are sold on every street corner.

Foire de Paris

Paris-Expo, pl de la Porte de Versailles (01.49.09.60.00, www.foiredeparis.fr). M° Porte de Versailles. **Admission** €12; €7 reductions; free under-7s. **Date** early May.

This enormous lifestyle fair includes world crafts and foods, the latest health gizmos, plus everything you need to know about buying a swimming pool or doing up your home.

Le Printemps des Rues

Various venues (01.47.97.36.06, www. leprintempsdesrues.com). **Admission** free. **Date** mid May.

Clockwise from above: **Marathon de Paris**; **La Nuit des Musées**; **Fashion Week** (see p31).

This annual two-day street-theatre festival takes place along the Canal St-Martin and has a distinctly experimental vibe.

★ La Nuit des Musées

All over France (www.nuitdesmusees.culture.fr).
Admission free. **Date** mid May.
During this pan-European one-night culture fest, museums open their doors late for special events and entertainment, including concerts, dance, lectures, unique access and special exhibitions.

Festival Jazz à Saint-Germain-des-Prés

Various venues, St-Germain-des-Prés (www.festivaljazzsaintgermainparis.com).
Date mid-late May.
This two-week festival of jazz and blues celebrated its 15th anniversary in 2015 with everything from piano cruises along the Seine to gigs in the Eglise St-Germain-des-Prés. Many of the concerts are free.

PUBLIC HOLIDAYS

**Easter Monday
(Lundi de Pâques)**
28 Mar 2016

May Day (Fête du Travail)
1 May

VE Day (Victoire 1945)
8 May

**Ascension Day
(Jour de l'Ascension)**
5 May 2016

Whit Monday (Pentecôte)
16 May 2016

Bastille Day (Quatorze Juillet)
14 July

**Feast of the Assumption
(Fête de l'Assomption)**
15 Aug

All Saints' Day (Toussaint)
1 Nov

**Remembrance Day
(L'Armistice 1918)**
11 Nov

Christmas Day (Noël)
25 Dec

New Year's Day (Jour de l'An)
1 Jan

Left: **Foire du Trône** (see p32).
Right: **French Tennis Open**.

We Love Green Festival

Parc de Bagatelle, Bois de Bologne, 16th (www.welovegreen.fr). **Tickets** varies.
Date end May.

This three-day eco festival is held in the verdant surroundings of the Parc de Bagatelle. It's a bucolic celebration of music and nature, and the audience is positively expected to dance barefoot in the grass, wear coronets of flowers and eat nothing but vegetables for three days. Past highlights have included Norah Jones and Django Django.

Art Saint-Germain-des-Prés

Various venues (www.artsaintgermaindespres. com). **Admission** free. **Date** May.

Timing your trip to Paris to coincide with a night of *vernissages* (private views) gives a taste not only of the art on offer but also of the personalities who frequent the art scene. The big rendezvous of the year is Art St-Germain-des-Prés. Nicknamed the 'block party', it sees more than 50 galleries get together to showcase their top artists. The galleries involved are mostly concentrated on rue de Seine, rue des Beaux-Arts, rue Visconti, rue Guénégaud and rue Mazarine.

French Tennis Open

Stade Roland-Garros, 2 av Gordon-Bennett, 16th (01.47.43.48.00, www.frenchopen.org). M° Porte d'Auteuil. **Admission** see website for details.
Date late May-early June.

Paris plays host to the second event in the Grand Slam calendar and the most prestigious clay court competition in the world. Rafael Nadal and Maria Sharapova took the spoils in 2014.

Summer

Quinzaine des Réalisateurs

Forum des Images, Porte St-Eustache, Forum des Halles, 1st (01.44.76.63.00, www.quinzaine-realisateurs.com). M° Les Halles. **Admission** €5.50. **Date** June.

The Cannes Directors' Fortnight sidebar comes to Paris; 2014 was the 46th anniversary of this festival of screenings and events.

Festival de St-Denis

Various venues in St-Denis (www.festival-saint-denis.com). M° St-Denis Basilique. **Admission** €17-€60. **Date** June.

The Gothic St-Denis basilica and other historic buildings in the neighbourhood host four weeks of top-quality classical concerts.

Fête du Vélo

Across Paris (www.feteduvelo.fr). **Date** Early June.
The Fête du Vélo is a celebration of urban riding with thousands of cyclists invited to meet up at various points in the suburbs and pedal to Paris en masse. The result is what the organisation calls '*la convergence*', with a procession of two-wheelers meeting up. During the two-day festival visitors can also try in-line skating, as well as bicycles specially designed for children and people of reduced mobility.

Prix de Diane

Hippodrome de Chantilly, 16 av du Général-Leclerc, 90209 Chantilly (03.44.62.44.00, www.prix-de-diane.com). **Admission** varies.
Date mid June.

The French Derby draws the crème de la crème of high society to Chantilly, sporting silly hats and keen to have a flutter at this handsome racecourse next to the famous château and stables.

★ Fête de la Musique

All over France (01.40.03.94.70, www.fete delamusique.culture.fr). **Admission** free.
Date 21 June.
See p37 **Sounds of Summer**.

★ Marche des Fiertés (Gay Pride)

www.inter-lgbt.org. **Date** end June.
Outrageous floats and flamboyant costumes parade towards Bastille; then there's an official fête and various club and nightlife events.

Festival Chopin à Paris

Orangerie de Bagatelle, Bois de Boulogne, 16th (01.45.00.22.19, www.frederic-chopin.com). Mᵒ Porte Maillot, then bus 244. **Admission** €17-€34 (plus €5.50 park entry). **Date** mid June-mid July.
Organised by the Chopin Society, candlelit evening recitals of the composer's works are performed in the idyllic Parc de la Bagatelle.

★ Paris Jazz Festival

Parc Floral de Paris, Bois de Vincennes, 12th (www.parisjazzfestival.fr). Mᵒ Château de Vincennes. **Admission** *Park* €5.50; €2.75 reductions; free under-7s. **Date** June-July.
See p37 **Sounds of Summer**.

Solidays

Longchamp Hippodrome (www.solidays.org). Mᵒ Porte Maillot. **Admission** *Day* €39. *Weekend* €59. **Date** end June.
See p37 **Sounds of Summer**.

Paris Cinéma

Various venues (01.55.25.55.25, www.paris cinema.org). **Admission** varies. **Date** early July.

Premieres, tributes and restored films make up the diverse programme at the city's excellent summer filmgoing initiative.

Le Quatorze Juillet (Bastille Day)

All over France. **Date** 14 July.
France's national holiday commemorates the storming of the Bastille in 1789. The evening before the holiday, Parisians dance at place de la Bastille. At 10am on the 14th, crowds line up along the Champs-Elysées as the President reviews a full military parade. By night, the Champ de Mars fills for the fireworks display. *Photos p36.*

★ Le Tour de France

Av des Champs-Elysées, 8th (www.letour.fr). **Date** July.
The ultimate spectacle in cycling is reserved for the end of July. After three weeks of racing, the battle for the leader's famed yellow jersey is all but over, and the final stage usually climaxes in a mass sprint with everyone finishing together. It's an incredible spectacle as the riders propel themselves at speeds of up to 65 km/h (40mph) around nine laps of a four-mile finishing circuit that takes in the Champs-Elysées and Tuileries area.

Etés de la Danse

Théâtre du Châtelet, 1st (01.40.28.28.40, www. lesetesdeladanse.com). Mᵒ Châtelet. **Tickets** €13-€100. **Date** July.

Bastille Day (*see p35*).

Every year, the Théâtre du Châtelet brings a major dance company from overseas to the capital. Most theatres in Paris take a break over the summer, so it's a rare chance to see classical ballet in July. *Photo p38*.

Paris, Quartier d'Eté
Various venues (01.44.94.98.00, www. quartierdete.com). **Admission** free-€20. **Date** mid July-mid Aug.
Global in outlook, ambitious in scope, citywide and often free, the Quartier d'Eté festival offers a fantastic summer programme of dance, theatre, concerts and circus. Previous years have seen open-air films, gypsy music, ballet by Merce Cunningham, and an opera composed specially for the occasion by Youssou N'Dour.

★ Paris-Plages
Various venues (08.20.00.75.75, www.paris.fr). **Admission** free. **Date** mid July-mid Aug.
If there's one event that sums up Paris in the summer, this is it. Back in 2002, Bertrand Delanoë began the tradition of lining the banks of the Seine with sand, deckchairs, food stalls and volleyball nets, creating a series of city beaches for those stuck in town during the long, hot months. Since 2007, the project has extended along the length of the canal in Bassin de la Villette, making an idyllic landscape of pétanque, boules, picnicking, sunbathing and watersports.
▶ *A stretch of the Left Bank has now become a permanent park, footpath and cycle track.*

Le Cinéma en Plein Air
Parc de la Villette, 19th (01.40.03.75.75, www. villette.com). M° Porte de Pantin. **Admission** free. **Date** mid July-end Aug.

Outdoor moviegoing at its finest, with films screened for free at sundown in Parc de la Villette, the cutting-edge architectural, music and art hub that's a big part of the recent buzz around north-east Paris. Expect everything from *Fame* to Kaurismäki.

Festival Classique au Vert
Parc Floral de Paris, Bois de Vincennes, 12th (01.45.43.81.18, www.classiqueauvert.fr). M° Château de Vincennes. **Admission** *Park* €5.50; €2.75 reductions; free under-7s. **Date** Aug-Sept.
Free classical music recitals in a park setting every weekend throughout August and September.

Fête de l'Assomption
Cathédrale Notre-Dame de Paris, pl du Parvis Notre-Dame, 4th (01.42.34.56.10, www. cathedraledeparis.com). M° Cité/RER St-Michel Notre-Dame. **Admission** free. **Date** 15 Aug.
A national holiday. Notre-Dame becomes a place of religious pilgrimage for Assumption Day.

★ Rock en Seine
Domaine National de St-Cloud (www.rockenseine. com). M° Porte de St-Cloud. **Admission** *Day* €45. *3 days* €99. **Date** end Aug.
See p37 **Sounds of Summer**.

Autumn

Jazz à la Villette
Cité de la Musique & various venues (01.44.84.44.84, www.jazzalavillette.com). **Admission** €8-€35. **Date** early Sept.

SOUNDS OF SUMMER
Get in tune with the city.

Paris pulls off summer with considerable elan. The city's rooftops, terraces and riverbanks welcome *soigné* crowds with a host of summer entertainment, and more and more festivals hit the calendar every year. Celebrating dance and music from all across the world, **Le Festival de l'Imaginaire** (www.festivaldelimaginaire.com) covers everything from Balinese dance and Iraqi *maqâm* to Breton *fest noz* and lute music – the only Paris event with such a broad outlook.

The **Paris Jazz Festival** (*see p35*) is a massive hit with overheated Parisians. From the middle of June until the end of July, two jazz groups play every Saturday and Sunday in the open hall in the pretty Parc Floral de Vincennes. The free festival (you only have to pay entry to the park) makes for a brilliant outing.

Free gigs, encompassing all manner of musical genres, take place across the country – and around the world – as part of the long-running **Fête de la Musique** (*see p34*), which coincides with the summer solstice on 21 June. In the French capital, performances take place in theatres, bars, on street corners, in parks and even on balconies.

For the past 15 years, the annual **Solidays** music festival (*see p35*) has attracted huge crowds in support of HIV and AIDS charity Solidarité Sida. The 2015 line-up included sets from the likes of Clean Bandit, the Vaccines and Brigitte. Finally, the city's premier rock festival, **Rock en Seine** (*see p36; pictured*), has been held in the Domaine National de Saint-Cloud every last weekend in August since 2003. For the best experience, buy a three-day pass and pitch your tent in the historic park grounds, which include Marie Antoinette's rose garden. The 2015 line-up included Kasabian, the Libertines, Hot Chip and Tame Impala.

The first fortnight in September brings one of Paris's best jazz festivals with big-name stars such as Maceo Parker and Laura Mvula taking to the stage. There's also a series of Jazz for Kids concerts running alongside the main festival.

Festival Paris Ile-de-France

Various venues (01.58.71.01.01, www.festival-ile-de-france.com). **Tickets** varies. **Date** early Sept-mid Oct.

Each year, the Paris Ile-de-France Festival offers a brilliantly varied programme of music from classical to contemporary, traditional and folk to cutting-edge electronic, at venues ranging from central Paris to Vincennes via Fontainebleau.

Techno Parade

www.technoparade.fr. **Date** mid Sept.

The Saturday parade (which finishes up at Bastille) is followed by several late, late club nights around the capital.

Journées du Patrimoine

All over France (www.journeesdupatrimoine. culture.fr). **Date** mid Sept.

Embassies, ministries, scientific establishments and corporate headquarters open their doors to the public, allowing for some fascinating glimpses of their interiors. The festive Soirée du Patrimoine takes place on the first Journée. Get *Le Monde* or *Le Parisien* for a full programme.

★ Festival d'Automne

Various venues. Information: 156 rue de Rivoli, 1st (01.53.45.17.00, www.festival-automne.com). **Admission** €7-€45. **Date** mid Sept-mid Jan.

This major annual arts festival focuses on bringing challenging contemporary theatre, dance and modern opera to Paris. It is also intent on bringing non-Western culture into the French consciousness. As well as name-checking theatre's big players and venues, the festival also lays great emphasis on less famous names such as director Gwenaël Morin or choreographer Latifa Laâbissi, and on less well-known venues (Scène Watteau, the Nouveau Théâtre de Montreuil), making it one of the most democratic arts festivals in Europe.

Fête de la Gastronomie

Various venues (www.fete-gastronomie.fr). **Admission** varies. **Date** late Sept.

This recently launched nationwide festival is aimed at celebrating the wonders of French cuisine. The inaugural theme was 'terroir', with more than 3,000 events across the country: Michelin-starred chef Guy Martin set up market stalls in his cooking workshop L'Atelier Guy Martin, so that visitors could choose ingredients before being shown how to cook a gourmet dish with them. He also offered diners free kitchen tours around his temple of gastronomy, Le Grand Véfour, in Palais Royal.

Etés de la Danse (see p35).

Mondial de l'Automobile

Paris-Expo, pl de la Porte de Versailles (01.56.88.22.40, www.mondial-automobile. com). M° Porte de Versailles. **Admission** €14; €8 reductions; free under-10s. **Date** early Oct.

Started in 1898, the biennial Paris Motor Show features cutting-edge design from all over the world. The next show is due to pull into Paris-Expo in 2016.

★ Nuit Blanche

Various venues (http://nuitblanche.paris.fr). **Admission** free. **Date** early Oct.

Nuit Blanche is a free dusk-to-dawn carnival of arts and culture. The premise is simple: an ever-changing roster of artistic directors takes over different portions of the city every year, commissioning hundreds of works that are all about finding new ways for citizens to interact with the urban space – from clouds of paper butterflies settling on neoclassical columns to church naves sprouting enormous bejewelled skulls.

Prix de l'Arc de Triomphe

Hippodrome de Longchamp, Bois de Boulogne, 16th (www.prixarcdetriomphe.com). M° Porte d'Auteuil, then free shuttle bus. **Admission** varies. **Date** early Oct.

France's richest flat race meeting attracts the elite of horse racing for a weekend of pomp and ceremony. The big race gallops off on Sunday afternoon.

Fête des Vendanges de Montmartre

Rue des Saules, 18th (www.fetedesvendanges demontmartre.com). M° Lamarck Caulaincourt. **Date** early Oct.

of independent rock music in France, the festival also welcomes folk, soul and electronica acts. The 2014 line-up included Damon Albarn and Lykke Li.

Armistice Day
Arc de Triomphe, 8th. M° Charles de Gaulle Etoile. **Date** 11 Nov.
To commemorate French combatants who served in the World Wars, the President lays wreaths at the Tomb of the Unknown Soldier underneath the Arc de Triomphe. The *bleuet* (a cornflower) is worn.

Africolor
Various suburbs, including Montreuil, St-Denis & St-Ouen (01.47.97.69.99, www.africolor.com). **Admission** €5-€15. **Date** late Nov-late Dec.
This month-long music and dance festival has been running for more than 20 years, featuring artists from all across Africa.

Fête du Beaujolais Nouveau
Various venues (www.beaujolaisgourmand.com). **Date** late Nov.
The third Thursday in November sees cafés and wine bars buzzing in the capital as the young red *vin de primeur* Beaujolais nouveau is released on to the market. Just six to eight weeks old, the wine is intended for immediate consumption.

Noël (Christmas)
Date 24, 25 Dec.
Christmas is a family affair in France, with a dinner on Christmas Eve (*le Réveillon*), normally after mass. Usually the only bars and restaurants open are the ones in the city's main hotels.

★ New Year's Eve/New Year's Day
Date 31 Dec, 1 Jan.
Jubilant crowds swarm along the Champs-Elysées. Nightclubs and restaurants hold expensive New Year's Eve soirées, and on New Year's Day the Grande Parade de Paris brings floats, bands and dancers.

Fête des Rois (Epiphany)
Date 6 Jan.
Pâtisseries sell *galettes des rois*, cakes with a frangipane filling in which a *fève* (charm) is hidden.

Mass for Louis XVI
Chapelle Expiatoire, 29 rue Pasquier, 8th (01.42.65.35.80). M° St-Augustin. **Date** Jan.
On the Sunday closest to 21 January – the anniversary of the beheading of Louis XVI in 1793 – right-wing crackpots mourn the end of the monarchy.

Nouvel An Chinois
Around av d'Ivry & av de Choisy, 13th. M° Porte de Choisy or Porte d'Ivry. Also av des Champs Elysées, 8th. **Date** Jan/Feb.
Lion and dragon dances, and lively martial arts demonstrations to celebrate the Chinese New Year.

This is perhaps the most quintessentially Gallic of the capital's annual festivals. The event takes place in Montmartre in the vicinity of the Clos Montmartre vineyard. Although the vines cover a mere 1,560sq m and produce an average of just 1,000 bottles a year, the modest harvest is the pretext for a long weekend of Bacchanalian street parties.

FIAC (Foire Internationale d'Art Contemporain)
Various venues (01.47.56.64.20, www.fiacparis. com). **Admission** €35; €20 reductions; free under-12s. **Date** mid Oct.
The Grand Palais is the main venue for this week-long international contemporary art fair featuring more than 180 galleries, along with a series of outdoor installations in the Jardin des Tuileries.

Les Puces du Design
Bercy Village, 12th (www.pucesdudesign.com). M° Jaurès. **Admission** free. **Date** Oct & May.
This biannual weekend-long fair specialises in modern and vintage furniture, and design classics.

Winter

★ Festival des Inrockuptibles
Various venues (01.42.44.16.16, www.lesinrocks. com). **Admission** varies. **Date** mid Nov.
Famous indie cultural journal *Les InRockuptibles* has changed a lot in its 25-year history, but the annual festival has always kept its spirit alive. The champion

Paris's Best

There's something for everyone with our hand-picked highlights.

Arc de Triomphe.

Sightseeing

VIEWS

Arc de Triomphe p90
Gaze out across place Charles-de-Gaulle and its 12 arterial avenues.

Eiffel Tower p229
Brave the queues for a glimpse of Paris in panorama, and brave a peek through the new glass floor.

Institut du Monde Arabe p184
Fabulous vista from the roof of this revamped treasure.

Sacré-Coeur p116
Hilltop views as heavenly as the surroundings.

Tour Montparnasse p213
The capital laid bare from 56 floors up.

ART

Centre Pompidou p124
The largest collection of modern art in Europe.

Fondation Louis Vuitton p107
LV's luxury art showcase has landed in the Bois de Boulogne.

Musée du Louvre p63
Extravagant architecture and extraordinary art.

Musée d'Orsay p224
Gleaming after a groundbreaking revamp.

Musée Picasso p131
Bigger and brighter, Paris's Picasso showcase is finally back in the Marais.

Palais de Tokyo p96
Tripled in size and still pushing the boundaries.

Sacré-Coeur.

HISTORY

Cité Nationale de l'Histoire de l'Immigration p156
Moving tribute to more than 200 years of immigration history.
Monnaie de Paris p195
Franc discussion.
Musée Edith Piaf p168
France's greatest singer.
Musée de Montmartre p115
This 17th-century manor displays the history of the hill.
Musée de la Musique p164
Historic instruments innovatively displayed.

OUTDOORS

Bois de Vincennes p156
Space to roam in Paris's biggest park.
Jardin des Plantes p184
Botanical bliss, including a tree planted in 1636.
Parc des Buttes-Chaumont p168
Skip the Tuileries and head for the 19th instead.
Parc de la Villette p164
Postmodern paradise: themed gardens and fun activities.

CHURCHES

Cathédrale Notre-Dame de Paris p51
Glorious Gothic grandeur on the Ile de la Cité.
Eglise St-Etienne-du-Mont p181
Resting place of Pascal, Racine and Ste-Geneviève.
Eglise St-Séverin p175
The city's most charming medieval church.

DEAD FAMOUS

Cimetière de Montmartre p115
Truffaut, Berlioz and Dalida are all buried here.
Cimetière du Montparnasse p209
Literary legends, from Maupassant to Sartre.

Cimetière du Père-Lachaise p144
Home to some of France's most creative corpses.
Le Panthéon p182
Celebrity crypt, from Voltaire to Marie Curie.

CHILDREN

Cité des Sciences et de l'Industrie p161
Science can be fun at this superb museum.
Disneyland Paris p249
Mickey magic and scary rides galore.
Grande Galerie de l'Evolution p183
The natural world in all its majestic modelled glory.
Musée des Egouts p244
Take your sewer rats on a trip through Paris's tunnels.

WILDLIFE

Cinéaqua p247
Get up close and personal with sharks and sturgeon.
Parc de Thoiry p247
Suburban safari.
Parc Zoologique de Paris p247
The animals are back in style after a handsome revamp.

Eating & drinking

BISTROS

Le Bistrot Paul Bert p145
Everything you imagine from a classic bistro.
La Cantine du Troquet p213
Nose-to-tail nosh.
Le Chateaubriand p168
The leading light of Paris's neo-bistro trend.
David Toutain p232
Talented Toutain is cooking up a storm in the 7th.
Le Flamboire p119
Bavette brilliance at this flame-grilled paradise.

Frenchie p85
Grégory Marchand's
legendary loft-style eaterie.
Granterroirs p97
Terroir treats abound.
Pétrelle p120
Style and substance combine
in this quirky dining room.

BLOWOUTS
**Alain Ducasse au Plaza
Athénée** p96
Glamour guaranteed (if you
can swallow the *haute* bill).
L'Arpège p225
Lofty cuisine at Alain
Passard's Left Bank eaterie.
Lasserre p97
Lip-smacking luxury and an
illustrious history.

Candelaria p135
Tequila time at this hugely
popular taqueria.
Chez Prune p165
Bobos and beer by the
Canal Saint-Martin.
Le Crocodile p182
Mix it up with more than 300
cocktails on the menu.
Les Furieux p152
Heady mix: absinthe and rock.
Le Lock Groove p215
Vinyl rules at this retro
rock bar.
Rosa Bonheur sur Seine p226
Drink in the views from this
cool Seine-side barge.
Rouge Passion p120
Well-picked wines and free
assiettes apéros.

Jardin des Plantes. *See p41.*

La Bellevilloise.

GLOBAL
Pho 14 p187
This Vietnamese canteen is
the place to come for pho.
Rose Bakery p120
Great British classics, from
scones to sticky toffee pud.
Le Souk p150
Dream tagines.

BARS
La Bellevilloise p170
Brilliant multitasker with food,
drink, art, gigs and clubbing.
Café Charbon p170
Hugely popular bar wrapped in
belle époque surroundings.

Tape Bar p154
Affordable drinks and relaxed
vibe at this hipster hangout.
Le Trac p189
Newly opened culture hub
with a gorgeous terrace.
Le Verre Volé p165
Wondrous wine bar with
dining to match.

Shopping

CONCEPT
Colette p69
Must-have accessories from
the original concept store.

L'Eclaireur p138
Sophisticated picks.
Merci p140
Charity first at this most
generous of general stores.

FOOD & DRINK
Arnaud Delmontel p121
Legendary baguettes.
Causses p121
Deli delights and expat treats.
Chambelland p154
Baking brilliance.
**Fromagerie
Quatrehomme** p227
Seriously tasty cheeses,
from beaufort to brie.

Sonia Rykiel.

Gâteaux Thoumieux p228
Classy cakes, stunning shop.

GIFTS & SOUVENIRS
Le Bon Marché p227
Chic shopping at Paris's
oldest department store.
Diptyque p179
Divine scents, from Figuier
to Violette.

BOOKS & MUSIC
Fargo p154
A cornucopia of good
ol' country music.
Shakespeare & Co p179
An unmissable destination.
Album p179
Geek heaven at this king
of the comic scene.

FASHION
Hermès p198
Spiffing scarves.
K Jacques p140
Making sandals sexy.
Lanvin p101
Classic couture.
Olympia Le-Tan p72
Accessories and ready-to-
wear from this A-list fave.
Sonia Rykiel p198
The queen of Left Bank chic.

CHILDREN
DPAM p154
Classic kids' clothing with
a touch of French flair.
Un Zèbre O Grenier p171
Charming toy shop where
tradition rules.

MARKETS
**Marché aux Puces de
St-Ouen** p117
Probably the biggest flea
market in the world.
**Marché aux Puces
d'Aligre** p155
Junk joy at this flea market.

Nightlife
CLUBS
1936 p264
Raving in the suburbs.
Batofar p268
Seineside swaying on the
legendary lightship.
Cartel Club p265
Shabby chic and tequila galore
at this new fashionista fave.
Nüba p269
Laid-back Left Bank partying.
Rex p268
Paris's techno king.

MUSIC
Mécanique Ondulatoire p275
Rocking Bastille venue.
L'International p273
Free entry and on-the-up
bands at this indie hangout.
New Morning p278
One of the city's finest
jazz joints.

Arts
FESTIVALS
Paris Jazz Festival p35
Free summer jazz weekends
in the lovely Parc Floral.
Cinéma en Plein Air p36
Deckchair delights at this
free outdoor movie festival.
Festival d'Automne p38
Top-notch treats await at this
annual arts extravaganza.

THEATRE
Comédie Française p289
Stage classics at the gilded
mother of French theatres.
Théâtre de la Ville p292
Innovation rules at the
'City Theatre'.

FILM
Fondation Pathé p174
Movie memorabilia aplenty
at this stunning new building.
La Pagode p254
One of the loveliest cinemas
in the world.
Le Louxor p254
1920s art deco revamped.

CLASSICAL, OPERA
& BALLET
Palais Garnier p287
The jewel in the crown of Paris
music-making.
Philharmonie de Paris p284
Jean Nouvel's dramatic new
La Villette home for the
Orchestre de Paris.
Opéra Bastille p283
Hideous building, heavenly
opera classics.

Explore

The Seine & Islands

Paris owes its very existence to the Seine, and dutifully acknowledges the importance of its river on the city's coat of arms. The Seine was the transport route that brought settlers here in the first place, many millennia ago. As the city grew, so did the river's cultural importance, until it became what it still is today – the symbolic boundary between intellectual Left Bank Paris and the mercantile activities of the Right Bank. In between the two sides, like a double bullseye, are the islands. The western Ile de la Cité, home to Paris's *point zéro*, is awash with history, state machinery and religious grandeur; Notre-Dame Cathedral lords it over the area, rich with Gothic architecture and grotesque art, from chilling chimeras to Hugo's hideous Hunchback. The civilised Ile St-Louis, once a mess of marshland and islets, is now one of the most exclusive residential districts in the city, a suitable home for the capital's grande dame of *glaces*.

La Conciergerie.

Don't Miss

1 **Cathédrale Notre-Dame de Paris** 850 years of Gothic glory (p51).

2 **La Conciergerie** Forbidding fortress with a fascinating past (p51).

3 **Sainte-Chapelle** Stunning stained-glass shrine (p54).

4 **Berthillon** Naughty but very nice ice (p55).

5 **Le Sergent Recruteur** Designer dinner (p55).

ALONG THE SEINE

The banks of the Seine have always been a place for romance, exhibitionism and breathing space in a city whose parks are all too regimented and close at dusk on the dot. Novelist Edmund White has written about the frisson of being lit up by a Bateau Mouche while cruising on the quays, and for either sex the rules of social behaviour were more akin to the louche South of France than Paris once you went down the steps to the river.

When Paris-Plage was introduced in 2002, the sunbathing and picnicking on the quayside became more of a family-friendly affair, harking back to the early years of the 20th century. In those days people didn't just sunbathe by the Seine, they swam in it too – swimming, rowing and water polo events all took place on the river during the 1900 Summer Olympics. The floating Piscine Josephine Baker, which launched in 2006, is the closest you'll get to swimming in the Seine, although the water has been significantly cleaned up in recent years.

IN THE KNOW
THE SEINE DISTILLED

Length 776km
(France's second longest river)

Source Source-Seine
(30km north-west of Dijon)

Mouth Le Havre

Widest point in Paris 200m
(Pont de Grenelle)

Narrowest point in Paris 30m
(Quai de Montebello)

Speed Approx 2km/hr

Bridges in Paris 37
(two rail, four pedestrian
and 31 road)

Oldest bridge Pont Neuf (1607)

Newest bridge Passerelle Simone
de Beauvoir (2006)

Most bridges built in a year 15 (in 1870)

Goods carried per year 21.3 million tonnes

Most bodies found in a year 55 (in 2007)

Biggest flood 1910 (6.1m above average)

The bridges

From the honeyed arches of the oldest, the **Pont Neuf**, to the swooping lines of the newest, the **Passerelle Simone-de-Beauvoir**, the bridges spanning the Seine are among the best-known landmarks in the city, and enjoy fine views.

There was already a bridge on the site of the **Petit Pont** in the first century BC, when the Parisii Celts ran their river trade and toll-bridge operations. The Romans put up a cross-island thoroughfare in the form of a reinforced bridge to the south of Ile de la Cité, and another one north of it (where the **Pont Notre-Dame** now stands), thus creating a straight route all the way from Orléans through to Belgium. Since then, the city's *ponts* have been bombed, bashed by buses and boats, weather-beaten and even trampled to destruction: in 1634, the Pont St-Louis collapsed under the weight of a religious procession. In the Middle Ages, the handful of bridges linking the islands to the riverbanks were lined with shops and houses, but the flimsy wooden constructions regularly caught fire or got washed away. The Petit Pont sank 11 times before councillors decided to ban building on top of bridges.

The Pont Neuf was inaugurated in 1607 and has been standing sturdy ever since. This was the first bridge to be built with no houses to obstruct the view of the river. It had a raised stretch of road at the edge to protect walkers from traffic and horse dung (the new-fangled 'pavement' soon caught on); the alcoves that now make pit stops for lovers were once filled with tooth-pullers, peddlers and *bouquinistes*.

The 19th century was boom time for bridge-building: 21 were built in all, including the city's first steel, iron and suspension bridges. The **Pont de la Concorde** used up what was left of the Bastille after the storming of 1789; the romantic **Pont des Arts** was the capital's first solely pedestrian crossing (built in 1803 and rebuilt in the 1980s) – it hit the headlines in 2014 when part of the railings collapsed from the sheer weight of the thousands of 'love locks' attached to the bridge by amorous couples. The most exuberant bridge is the **Pont Alexandre III**, with its bronze and glass, garlanding and gilded embellishments. More practical is the **Pont de l'Alma**, with its Zouave statue that has long been a flood monitor: when the statue's toes get wet, the state raises the flood alerts; when he's up to his ankles, it's no longer possible to navigate the river by boat.

The 20th century brought some spectacular additions. **Pont Charles-de-Gaulle** stretches resplendently like the wing of a huge aeroplane, and iron **Viaduc d'Austerlitz** (1905) is striking yet elegant as it cradles métro line 5. The city's newest crossing (and its 37th in total), the Passerelle Simone-de-Beauvoir, links up the Bibliothèque Nationale to the Parc de Bercy.

EXPLORE

ILE DE LA CITE

In the 1st & 4th arrondissements.

The Ile de la Cité is where Paris was born around 250 BC, when the Parisii, a tribe of Celtic Gauls, founded a settlement on this convenient bridging point of the Seine. Romans, Merovingians and Capetians followed, in what became a centre of political and religious power into the Middle Ages: royal authority at one end, around the Capetian palace; the Church at the other, by Notre-Dame.

When Victor Hugo wrote *Notre-Dame de Paris* in 1831, the Ile de la Cité was a bustling quarter of narrow streets and tall houses: 'the head, heart and very marrow of Paris'. Baron Haussmann performed a marrow extraction when he supervised the expulsion of around 25,000 people from the island, razing tenements and some 20 churches – the law courts, the **Conciergerie**, Hôtel-Dieu hospital, the police headquarters and the cathedral. The lines of the old streets are traced into the parvis in front of **Notre-Dame**.

Sainte-Chapelle, Pierre de Montreuil's masterpiece of stained glass and slender Gothic columns, stands among the nearby law courts. Enveloping the chapel, the Palais de Justice was built alongside the Conciergerie. Behind elaborate railings, most of the present buildings around the fine neoclassical entrance courtyard date from the 1780s reconstruction by Desmaisons and Antoine. After passing through security, you can visit the **Salle des Pas Perdus**, busy with plaintiffs and barristers, and sit in on cases in the civil and criminal courts. The Palais is still the centre of the French legal system.

Across boulevard du Palais, behind the Tribunal du Commerce, place Louis-Lépine is occupied by the Marché aux Fleurs. The Hôtel-Dieu, east of the market place, was founded in the seventh century. During the Middle Ages, your chances of survival here were, at best, slim. The hospital originally stood on the other side of the island facing the Latin Quarter, but after a series of fires in the 18th century it was rebuilt here in the 1860s.

Notre-Dame cathedral dominates the eastern half of the island. On the parvis in front of the cathedral is the bronze 'Kilomètre Zéro' marker, the point from which distances between Paris and the rest of France are measured. The **Crypte Archéologique** hidden under the parvis gives a sense of the island's multi-layered past, when it was a tangle of alleys, houses, churches and cabarets. Notre-Dame is still a place of worship, and holds its Assumption Day procession, Christmas Mass and Nativity scene on the parvis.

Walk through the garden by the cathedral to appreciate its flying buttresses. To the north-east, a medieval feel persists in the few streets untouched by Haussmann, such as rue Chanoinesse, rue de la Colombe and rue des Ursins, though the crenellated medieval remnant on the corner of rue des Ursins and rue des Chantres was redone in the 1950s for the Aga Khan. The capital's oldest love story unfolded in the 12th century at 9 quai aux Fleurs, where Héloïse lived with her uncle Canon Fulbert, who had her tutor and lover, the scholar Abélard, castrated. Héloïse was sent to a nunnery. Behind the cathedral, at the eastern end of the island, is the **Mémorial des Martyrs de la Déportation**, remembering people sent to Nazi concentration camps.

Sights & Museums

★ FREE Cathédrale Notre-Dame de Paris

Pl du Parvis-Notre-Dame, 4th (01.42.34.56.10, www.cathedraledeparis.com). M° Cité/RER St-Michel. **Open** 8am-6.45pm Mon-Fri; 8am-7.15pm Sat, Sun. *Towers* Apr-Sept 10am-6.30pm daily (June-Aug until 11pm Sat, Sun). Oct-Mar 10am-5.30pm daily. **Admission** free. *Towers* €8.50; €5.50 reductions; free under-18s, under-26s (EU citizens). PMP. **Map** p49 C4 ❶

Notre-Dame was constructed between 1163 and 1334, and the amount of time and money spent on it reflected the city's growing prestige. The west front remains a high point of Gothic art for the balanced proportions of its twin towers and rose window, and the three doorways with their rows of saints and sculpted tympanums: the *Last Judgement* (centre), *Life of the Virgin* (left) and *Life of St Anne* (right). Inside, take a moment to admire the long nave with its solid foliate capitals and high altar with a marble Pietà by Coustou. To truly appreciate the masonry, climb up the towers. The route runs up the north tower and down the south. Between the two you get a close-up view of the gallery of chimeras – the fantastic birds and hybrid beasts designed by Viollet-le-Duc along the balustrade. As of 2013, Notre-Dame has eight new bells, forged as part of the cathedral's 850th anniversary year.

★ La Conciergerie

2 bd du Palais, 1st (01.53.40.60.80). M° Cité/RER St-Michel Notre-Dame. **Open** 9.30am-6pm daily. **Admission** €8.50; €5.50 reductions; free under-18s (accompanied by an adult), under-26s (EU citizens). *With Sainte-Chapelle* €12.50; €8.50 reductions. PMP. **Map** p49 B2 ❷

The Conciergerie looks every inch the forbidding medieval fortress. However, much of the façade was added in the 1850s, long after Marie-Antoinette, Danton and Robespierre had been imprisoned here. The 13th-century Bonbec tower, built during the reign of St Louis, the 14th-century twin towers, César and Argent, and the Tour de l'Horloge all survive from the Capetian palace. The visit takes you through the Salle des Gardes, the medieval kitchens

EXPLORE

WALK REVOLUTIONARY ROAD

EXPLORE

If you can manage to keep your head while those around you are losing theirs, get on the blocks for our promenade through the goriest spots of regicidal fever. You'll need stout shoes and a fervent imagination. Start at place de la Concorde.

The key date here is 21 January 1793. Since 8am the gates of Paris have been locked, the shutters barred. A crowd of 20,000 has assembled in place Louis XV, renamed place de la Révolution. At 10am there is a drum roll, Louis XVI is strapped to a plank and pushed towards the guillotine. The device slices through his neck, the crowd roars and clamours to soak their hankies in the monarch's blood. But to see how the nation reached this bloodthirsty state, we have to step back in time.

Walk through the gates from Concorde into the Jardin des Tuileries. The palace that used to stand here was the scene of repeated revolutionary fracas. On 13 July 1789, the eve of Bastille Day, a crowd ransacked the royal *garde-meubles* for weapons. This was only a taster of what was to come, though. On the night of King Louis' arrest in 1792, 600 of his Swiss Guards were murdered, their genitals hacked off and fed to dogs.

Turn right on to rue de Rivoli and walk to the Palais-Royal. The Duc d'Orléans' pleasure palace was a revolutionary hotbed as nobles and plebs mingled among the coffee shops and sideshows.

Walk through the arch in the Louvre's north wing to place du Carrousel, where the guillotine briefly stood. Cross Pont des Arts and head down rue Bonaparte. On your left you'll see the Ecole des Beaux-Arts, where Alexandre Lenoir tried to save France's heritage from the mob – he threw himself on the grave of Richelieu and took a stab in the back for his pains.

Rue de l'Abbaye was the site of one of the revolution's worst atrocities, in September 1792, when 115 priests were trapped in the garden and butchered. The red brick Abbot's Palace is now the Institut Catholique. Take rue Garancière past St-Sulpice to the Palais du Luxembourg. Now the Senate, the palace was commandeered as a prison and housed, among others, activists Danton and Thomas Paine. Take rue Rotrou through place de l'Odéon, where influential pamphleteer Camille Desmoulins lived at no.2, and follow rue de l'Odéon, where Paine, having escaped the guillotine, lived at no.10. Cross boulevard St-Germain to Café Procope at 13 rue de l'Ancienne Comédie. A favourite slugging ground of Voltaire, Rousseau, Danton and Marat, it contains Voltaire's desk.

Head back across boulevard St-Germain and take rue de l'Ecole de Médecine, where the Cordeliers' Club met at no.15 in the former Couvent des Cordeliers. No.18 was the scene of pamphleteer Marat's infamous demise, when Charlotte Corday stabbed him in the bath with a kitchen knife.

Follow the road east and cut up rue St-Jacques and rue Dante until you meet rue Galande. By the time the Terror started, every available space was being used as a prison. At no.52, the Caveau des Oubliettes jazz club gets its name from a gory death sentence whereby prisoners were thrown into cells and 'forgotten'.

At Pont St-Michel, cross on to Ile de la Cité and call in at the Conciergerie. This 'vast antechamber of death' was one of the most appalling prisons of the revolution, where prisoners slept in their own excrement. Not so Marie-Antoinette, who had a room with a bed and wallpaper.

Cross the Seine again and you'll find yourself in front of the Hôtel de Ville. In October 1789, a mob of 3,000 fishwives and others commandeered the guns and cannon from here before marching to Versailles to lynch the King. They returned with the severed heads of two guards.

Take rue du Temple, the road of no return for Louis XVI, turn right into rue St-Croix-de-la-Bretonnerie and left into rue Vieille-du-Temple. Now take rue des Francs-Bourgeois on the right, which will bring you to the Musée Carnavalet with its fine collection of revolutionary history.

Follow rue de Sévigné south to the church of St-Paul-St-Louis on rue St-Antoine, from which the hearts of Louis XIII and XIV were seized and sold to a painter. Take boulevard Henri IV and notice the brown bricks in the road as you approach place de la Bastille. These mark the spot where the Bastille prison stood; similar marks can be seen on rue St-Antoine, where no.5 is the site of the main gate and the famous 'storming' that took place on 14 July 1789. On place de la Bastille, in June 1794, the guillotine claimed 73 victims in three days.

Finally, walk east to place de la Nation (or hop on a bus heading along rue du Faubourg Saint-Antoine). Nation, formerly place du Trône, was the guillotine's last stand before the murderous device moved back to Concorde to give Robespierre the chop.

EXPLORE

with their four huge chimneys, and the Salle des Gens d'Armes, a vaulted Gothic hall built between 1301 and 1315 for Philippe 'le Bel'. After the royals moved to the Louvre, the fortress became a prison under the watch of the Concierge. The wealthy had private cells with their own furniture, which they paid for; others crowded on beds of straw. A list of Revolutionary prisoners, including a hairdresser, shows that not all victims were nobles. In Marie-Antoinette's cell, the Chapelle des Girondins, are her crucifix, some portraits and a guillotine blade.

La Crypte Archéologique

Pl Jean-Paul II, 4th (01.55.42.50.10, www.crypte. paris.fr). M° Cité/RER St-Michel Notre-Dame. **Open** 10am-6pm Tue-Sun. **Admission** €7; €5 reductions; free under-18s. PMP. **Map** p49 C3 ❸
Hidden under the forecourt in front of the cathedral is a large void that contains bits and pieces of Roman quaysides, ramparts and hypocausts, medieval cellars, shops and pavements, the foundations of the Eglise Ste-Geneviève-des-Ardens (the church where Geneviève's remains were stored during the Norman invasions), an 18th-century foundling hospital and a 19th-century sewer, all excavated since the 1960s. It's not always easy to work out exactly which wall, column or staircase is which – but you do get a vivid sense of the layers of history piled one atop another during 16 centuries.

FREE Mémorial des Martyrs de la Déportation

Sq de l'Ile de France, 4th (01.46.33.87.56). M° Cité/ RER St-Michel Notre-Dame. **Open** *Oct-Mar* 10am-5pm Tue-Sun. *Apr-Sept* 10am-7pm Tue-Sun. **Admission** free. **Map** p49 C4 ❹
This sober tribute to the 200,000 Jews, Communists, homosexuals and *résistants* deported to concentration camps from France in World War II stands on the eastern tip of the island. A blind staircase descends to river level, where simple chambers are lined with tiny lights and the walls are inscribed with verse. A barred window looks out at the Seine.

Sainte-Chapelle

4 bd du Palais, 1st (01.53.40.60.80). M° Cité/RER St-Michel Notre-Dame. **Open** *Mar-Oct* 9.30am-6pm daily. *Nov-Feb* 9am-5pm daily. **Admission** €8.50; €5.50 reductions; free under-18s (with an adult), under-26s (EU citizens). *With Conciergerie* €12.50; €8.50 reductions. **Map** p49 B2 ❺
Devout King Louis IX (St Louis, 1226-70) had a hobby of accumulating holy relics. In the 1240s, he bought what was advertised as the Crown of Thorns, and ordered Pierre de Montreuil to design a shrine. The result was Sainte-Chapelle. With 15m (49ft) windows, the upper level appears to consist almost entirely of stained glass. The windows depict hundreds of scenes from the Old and New Testaments.

Shops & Services

L'Occitane en Provence

1 rue d'Arcole, 4th (01.55.42.06.11, www.loccitane. com). M° Cité. **Open** 10.30am-7.30pm daily. **Map** p49 B3 ❻ **Health & beauty**
The many branches of this popular Provençal chain offer natural beauty products in neat packaging.

ILE ST-LOUIS

In the 4th arrondissement.

For hundreds of years, the island was a swampy pasture belonging to Notre-Dame, known as Ile Notre-Dame and used as a retreat for fishermen, swimmers and courting couples. In the 14th century, Charles V built a fortified canal through the middle, thus creating the Ile aux Vaches (Island of Cows). Its real-estate potential wasn't realised until 1614, though, when speculator Christophe Marie persuaded Louis XIII to fill

Sainte-Chapelle.

in the canal (present-day rue Poulletier) and plan streets, bridges and houses. The island was renamed in honour of the king's pious predecessor, and the venture proved a huge success, thanks to architect Louis Le Vau, who from the 1630s built fashionable residences along the quai d'Anjou, quai de Bourbon and quai de Béthune, as well as the **Eglise St-Louis-en-l'Ile**. By the 1660s the island was full; its smart reception rooms were set at the front of courtyards to give residents riverside views.

Rue St-Louis-en-l'Ile runs the length of the island. The grandiose **Hôtel Lambert** at no.2 was built by Le Vau in 1641 for Louis XIII's secretary. At no.51 – **Hôtel Chenizot** – look out for the bearded faun adorning the rocaille doorway, flanked by stern dragons. Across the street, the **Hôtel du Jeu de Paume** at no.54 was once a tennis court; at no.31, famous ice-cream maker **Berthillon** still draws a crowd. At 6 quai d'Orléans, the **Adam Mickiewicz library-museum** (01.55.42.83.88) is dedicated to the poet, journalist and campaigner for Polish freedom.

Sights & Museums

FREE Eglise St-Louis-en-l'Ile

19bis rue St-Louis-en-l'Ile, 4th (01.46.34.11.60, www.saintlouisenlile.catholique.fr). M° Pont Marie. **Open** 9.30am-1pm, 2-7.30pm Mon-Sat; 9am-1pm, 2-7pm Sun. **Admission** free. **Map** p49 C5 **7**
The island's church was built between 1664 and 1765. The Baroque interior boasts Corinthian columns and a sunburst over the altar.

Restaurants

Brasserie de l'Ile St-Louis

55 quai de Bourbon, 4th (01.43.54.02.59, www.labrasserie-isl.fr). M° Pont Marie. **Open** noon-11pm Mon, Tue, Thur-Sun. Closed Aug. **Main courses** €20. **Map** p49 C5 **8 Brasserie**
Happily, this old-fashioned brasserie soldiers on. The terrace has one of the best summer views in Paris and is invariably packed, though nothing here

is gastronomically gripping: a well-dressed *frisée aux lardons* perhaps, or a more successful pan of warming tripes.

Mon Vieil Ami

69 rue St-Louis-en-l'Ile, 4th (01.40.46.01.35, www.mon-vieil-ami.com). M° Pont Marie. **Open** noon-2.30pm, 7-11pm daily. **Main courses** €15.50-€26. **Prix fixe** €47.50. **Map** p49 C4 **9 Bistro**
Antoine Westermann has created a true foodie destination here. Starters such as tartare of finely diced raw vegetables with sautéed baby squid on top impress with their deft seasoning. Typical of the mains is wild boar with celeriac and pears or a cast-iron casserole of roast duck with caramelised turnips and couscous.

Le Sergent Recruteur

41 rue St-Louis-en-l'Ile, 4th (01.43.54.75.42, www.lesergentrecruteur.fr). M° Pont Marie or Sully-Morland. **Open** 7-11pm Tue-Thur; 12.30-2pm, 7-11pm Fri, Sat. **Prix fixe** *Lunch* €48, €100. *Dinner* €100, €145. **Map** p49 C5 **10 Haute cuisine**
Avant-garde Spanish designer Jaime Hayón and Antonin Bonnet turned this former pub into a handsome restaurant. The 'carte blanche' menus, where you're led by the whims of the chef, Noam Gedalof, offer daring versions of classic French dishes: perhaps foie gras with rhubarb confit, wild duck with spelt, and mango and herb ice-cream. Service is adroit and professional.

Cafés & Bars

Berthillon

29-31 rue St-Louis en l'Ile, 4th (01.43.54.31.61, www.berthillon.fr). M° Pont Marie. **Open** 10am-8pm Wed-Sun. **No credit cards**. **Map** p49 C5 **11**
The flavours at this famous ice-cream parlour change throughout the season. In winter Berthillon serves delicious hot chocolate and – even naughtier – a chocolate *affogato* (a ball of vanilla ice-cream served in a white porcelain mug with hot chocolate poured over and topped with praline cream).

Shops & Services

Pylones

57 rue St-Louis-en-l'Ile, 4th (01.40.51.75.33, www.pylones.com). **Open** 10.30am-7pm Mon-Fri; 10.30am-7.30pm Sat, Sun. **Map** p49 C5 **12 Gifts & souvenirs**
This novelty and design shop has everything you could want for your home, but with a twist. That dustpan is actually in the shape of a woman in a ball-gown and those salad tongs bear a striking resemblance to a swimmer – it's all so delightfully kitsch. With several shops all over the city, Pylones is an easy and affordable place to pick up a few novelty items or a new pair of duck-shaped scissors to make cutting paper just that much more exciting. **Other locations** throughout the city.

EXPLORE

Opéra to Les Halles

In centuries gone by, these two districts were the city's commercial and provisioning powerhouses, home to most of the newspapers, banks and major mercantile institutions. Nowadays, though, the focus is firmly on shopping: mass-market stuff in and around Les Halles, shading into more exclusive brands the further one moves west, in particular around rue St-Honoré, where Stella and Olympia Le-Tan rub shoulder pads. Les Halles itself was, famously, the city's wholesale food market until 1969, when the iron-framed buildings that housed it were ripped out. The soulless shopping mall that filled the gap in the 1970s is itself being replaced by a glory of gardens, glass and brighter spaces. Beyond the boutiques, art comes to the fore – Monet's water lilies at the Orangerie, Leonardo et al at the Louvre, and anything you fancy putting your hand up for at the Hôtel Drouot auction house.

Frenchie.

Don't Miss

1 **Musée de l'Orangerie** Monet displayed in all his majesty (p63).

2 **Colette** The original concept store (p69).

3 **Olympia Le-Tan** The designer and A-list fave now has her own boutique (p72).

4 **Musée du Louvre** An evolving masterpiece – inside and out (p63).

5 **Frenchie** Essential eats if you can snag a table (p85).

TUILERIES & PALAIS-ROYAL

In the 1st & 8th arrondissements.

Once the monarchs had moved from the Ile de la Cité to spacious new quarters on the Right Bank, the Louvre and, later, the palaces of the **Tuileries** and **Palais-Royal** became the centres of royal power. **The Louvre** still exerts considerable influence today: first as a grandiose architectural ensemble; and, second, as a symbol of the capital's cultural pre-eminence. What had been simply a fortress along Philippe-Auguste's city wall in 1190 was transformed by Charles V into a royal residence with all the latest Gothic comforts; François I turned it into a sumptuous palace. For centuries, it was a work in progress: everyone wanted to make their mark – including the most monarchical of presidents, François Mitterrand, who added IM Pei's glass pyramid, doubled the exhibition space and added the Carrousel du Louvre shopping mall, auditorium and food halls.

The palace has always attracted crowds: first courtiers and ministers; then artists; and, since 1793, when it was first turned into a museum, art-lovers – though the last department of the Finance Ministry moved out as late as 1991. Around the Louvre, other subsidiary palaces grew up: Catherine de Médicis commissioned Philibert Delorme to begin work on one in the Tuileries; and Richelieu built the Palais Cardinal, which later became the Palais-Royal.

On place du Louvre, opposite Claude Perrault's grandiose eastern façade of the Louvre, is **Eglise St-Germain-l'Auxerrois**, once the French kings' parish church and home to the only original Flamboyant Gothic porch in Paris, built in 1435. Mirroring it to the left of the belfry is the 19th-century first arrondissement *mairie*, with its fanciful rose window and classical porch. Next door is the stylish **Le Fumoir**, with a Mona Lisa of its own: amaretto, orange juice and champagne.

Across rue de Rivoli from the Louvre, past the **Louvre des Antiquaires** antiques emporium, stands the understatedly elegant **Palais-Royal**, once Cardinal Richelieu's private mansion and now the Conseil d'Etat and ministry of culture. After a stroll in its quiet gardens, it's hard to believe that this was once the most debauched corner of Paris.

In the 1780s, the Palais was a boisterous centre of Paris life, where aristocrats and the financially challenged inhabitants of the *faubourgs* rubbed shoulders. The coffee houses in its arcades generated radical debate: here Camille Desmoulins called the city to arms on the eve of the storming of the Bastille; and after the Napoleonic Wars, Wellington and Field Marshal von Blücher lost so much money in the gambling dens that Parisians claimed they had won back their entire dues for war reparations. Only haute cuisine restaurant

Le Grand Véfour, founded as Café de Chartres in the 1780s, survives from this era, albeit with decoration dating from a little later.

The **Comédie Française** theatre ('La Maison de Molière'; *see p289*) stands on the south-west corner. The company, created by Louis XIV in 1680, moved here in 1799. Molière himself is honoured with a fountain on the corner of rue Molière and rue de Richelieu. Brass-fronted Café Nemours on place Colette – Colette used to buy cigars from old-fashioned **A la Civette** nearby (157 rue St-Honoré, 1st, 01.42.96.04.99) – is another thespian favourite. In front of it, the métro entrance by artist Jean-Michel Othoniel, all glass baubles and aluminium struts, is a kitsch take on Guimard's celebrated art nouveau entrances.

Today, the stately arcades of the Palais-Royal house an eclectic succession of antiques dealers, philatelists, specialists in tin soldiers and musical boxes – and fashion showcases. Here you'll find chic vintage clothes specialist **Didier Ludot** and the elegant perfumery **Salons du Palais-Royal Shiseido**. Passing through the arcades to rue de Montpensier, the neo-rococo Théâtre du Palais-Royal and the centuries-old café **L'Entr'acte**, you'll find narrow, stepped passages that run between here and rue de Richelieu. On the other side of the palace towards Les Halles is galerie Véro-Dodat. Built by rich *charcutiers* during the Restoration period, it features wonderfully preserved neoclassical wooden shopfronts.

At the western end of the Louvre, by rue de Rivoli, are the **Musée des Arts Décoratifs**, the **Musée de la Mode et du Textile** and the **Musée de la Publicité**. All of these are administered independently of the Musée du Louvre, but were refreshed as part of the Grand Louvre scheme. Across place du Carrousel from the Louvre pyramid, the **Arc du Carrousel**, a mini-Arc de Triomphe, was built in polychrome marble for Napoleon Bonaparte from 1806 to 1809. The chariot on the top was originally drawn by the antique horses from San Marco in Venice, snapped up by Napoleon but returned in 1815. From the arch, the extraordinary axis along the **Jardin des Tuileries**, the Champs-Elysées up to the Arc de Triomphe and on to the Grande Arche de la Défense is plain to see.

The Jardin des Tuileries stretched as far as the Tuileries palace, until that was destroyed in the 1871 Paris Commune. The garden was laid out in the 17th century by André Le Nôtre and remains a pleasure area, with a funfair in summer; it also serves as an open-air gallery for modern art sculptures. Overlooking focal place de la Concorde is the **Musée de l'Orangerie** and the **Jeu de Paume**, built as a court for real tennis and now a centre for photographic exhibitions.

The stretch of rue de Rivoli running beside the Louvre towards Concorde was laid out by Napoleon's architects Percier and Fontaine from 1802 to 1811, and is notable for its arcaded façades. It runs in a straight line between place de la Concorde and rue St-Antoine, in the Marais; at the western end it's filled with tacky souvenir shops – though old-fashioned hotels remain, and there are also gentlemen's outfitters, bookshop **WH Smith** and tearoom **Angelina**. The area was inhabited by English aristocrats, writers and artists during the 1830s and '40s after the Napoleonic Wars, bedding down at **Le Meurice** (*see p339*) and dining in the fancy restaurants of the Palais-Royal.

Place des Pyramides, at the junction of rue de Rivoli and rue des Pyramides, contains a gleaming gilt equestrian statue of Joan of Arc. One of four statues of her in the city, it's fêted as a proud symbol of French nationalism every May Day by supporters of the Front National.

Ancient rue St-Honoré, running parallel to rue de Rivoli, is one of those streets that changes style as it goes along: smart shops line it near place Vendôme, small cafés and inexpensive bistros predominate towards Les Halles. The Baroque **Eglise St-Roch** is still pitted with bullet holes made by Napoleon's troops when they crushed a royalist revolt in 1795. With its old houses, adjoining rue St-Roch still feels wonderfully authentic; a couple of shops are built into the side of the church. Further up stands **Chapelle Notre-Dame de l'Assomption** (1670-76), now used by the city's Polish community, its dome so disproportionately large that locals have dubbed it *sot dôme* ('stupid dome'; a pun on 'Sodom').

Concept store **Colette** brought some glamour to a once-staid shopping area, drawing a swarm of similar stores along in its wake. All are ideally placed for the fashionistas and film stars who touch down at **Hôtel Costes** (*see p338*). Opposite Colette is rue du Marché-St-Honoré, which once led to the covered Marché St-Honoré, since replaced by offices, in a square lined with trendy restaurants; to the north, rue Danielle-Casanova boasts 18th-century houses.

Further west along rue St-Honoré lies the wonderful, eight-sided **place Vendôme** and a perspective stretching from rue de Rivoli up to Opéra. At the end of the Tuileries, **place de la Concorde**, originally laid out for the glorification of Louis XV, is a masterclass in the use of open space, and spectacular when lit up at night. The winged Marly horses (only reproductions, the originals are in the Louvre) frame the entrance to the Champs-Elysées.

Smart rue Royale has tearoom **Ladurée** and famed restaurant **Maxim's** (3 rue Royale, 8th, 01.42.65.27.94), with a fabulous museum of art nouveau, **La Collection 1900**, attached. Rue Boissy d'Anglas proffers stylish shops and the trendy **Buddha Bar** (no.8, 8th, 01.53.05.90.00); and high-end designs at **Yves Saint Laurent** and others set the plush tone.

Sights & Museums

La Collection 1900

Maxim's, 3 rue Royale, 8th (01.42.65.30.47, www. maxims-musee-artnouveau.com). M° Madeleine. **Open** *Guided tours (reservations essential)* 2pm Wed-Sun (English); 3.15pm (French). **Admission** €15. **No credit cards. Map** p60 B3 ❶

Couturier Pierre Cardin has owned belle époque restaurant Maxim's since 1981, and now he has added a museum of art nouveau, which he has been collecting since the age of 18. There are rooms and rooms of exhibits, arranged so as to evoke a 19th-century courtesan's boudoir. Read Zola's *Nana* before your visit to grasp the full effect of the dreamy lake maidens sculpted in glistening faience, pewter vanity sets in the shape of reclining nudes, and beds inlaid with opium flowers to promote sleep. Dinner settings on display include Gustave Eiffel's own chunky tureens, just crying out for turtle soup.

🆓 Eglise St-Germain-l'Auxerrois

2 pl du Louvre, 1st (01.42.60.13.96, www. saintgermainauxerrois.cef.fr). M° Louvre Rivoli or Pont Neuf. **Open** 9am-7pm Mon-Sat; 9.30am-8.30pm Sun. **Admission** free. **Map** p61 E5 ❷

The architecture of this former royal church spans several eras: the elaborate Flamboyant Gothic porch is the most striking feature. The interior is home to the 13th-century Lady Chapel and a canopied, carved bench by Le Brun, which was made for the royal family in 1682. The church achieved notoriety on 24 August 1572, when its bell signalled the Saint Bartholomew's Day massacre.

★ 🆓 Eglise St-Roch

296 rue St-Honoré, 1st (01.42.44.13.20, www. saintrochparis.cef.fr). M° Pyramides or Tuileries. **Open** 8.30am-7pm daily. **Admission** free. **Map** p60 D4 ❸

Begun in the 1650s in what was then the heart of Paris, this long church was designed chiefly by Jacques Lemercier; work took so long, the church was only finally consecrated in 1740. Famed parishioners and patrons are remembered in funerary monuments: Le Nôtre, Mignard, Corneille and Diderot are all here, as are busts by Coysevox and Coustou, Falconet's statue *Christ on the Mount of Olives* and Anguier's superb *Nativity*. Bullet marks from a 1795 shoot-out between royalists and conventionists still pit the façade.

★ 🆓 Jardin des Tuileries

Rue de Rivoli, 1st. M° Concorde or Tuileries. **Open** *Apr, May, Sept* 7am-9pm daily. *June-Aug* 7am-11pm daily. *Oct-Mar* 7.30am-7.30pm daily. **Admission** free. **Map** p60 B4 ❹

Between the Louvre and place de la Concorde, the gravelled alleyways of these gardens have been a chic promenade ever since they opened to the public in the 16th century; and the popular mood

EXPLORE

My museum in Paris...

persists with the funfair that sets up along the rue de Rivoli side in summer. André Le Nôtre created the prototypical French garden with terraces and central vista running down the *Grand Axe* through circular and hexagonal ponds. When the Tuileries palace was burned down during the Paris Commune in 1871, the park was expanded. As part of Mitterrand's Grand Louvre project, fragile sculptures such as Coysevox's winged horses were transferred to the Louvre and replaced by reproductions, and the Maillol sculptures were returned to the Jardins du Carrousel; a handful of modern sculptures has been added, including bronzes by Laurens, Moore, Ernst and Giacometti, and Dubuffet's *Le Bel Costumé*. Replanting has restored parts of Le Nôtre's design and replaced damaged trees, and there's a gardeners' bookshop by place de la Concorde.

Jeu de Paume

1 pl de la Concorde, 8th (01.47.03.12.50, www. jeudepaume.org). M° Concorde. **Open** 11am-9pm Tue; 11am-7pm Wed-Sun (last entry 30mins before closing). **Admission** €10; €7.50 reductions; free under-26s last Tue of mth. **Map** p60 B3 ❺

The Centre National de la Photographie moved into this site in 2005. The building, which once served as a tennis court, has been divided into two white, almost hangar-like galleries. It is not an intimate space, but it works well for showcase retrospectives. A video art and cinema suite in the basement shows new digital installation work, as well as feature-length films made by artists. There's also a sleek café and a decent bookshop.

★ Musée des Arts Décoratifs

107 rue de Rivoli, 1st (01.44.55.57.50, www. lesartsdecoratifs.fr). M° Palais Royal Musée du Louvre or Pyramides. **Open** 11am-6pm Tue, Wed, Fri-Sun; 11am-9pm Thur (late opening during exhibitions only). **Admission** (with Musée de la Mode & Musée de la Publicité) €11; €8.50 reductions; free under-18s, under-26s (EU citizens). PMP. **Map** p60 D4 ❻

Taken as a whole along with the Musée de la Mode et du Textile (*see right*) and Musée de la Publicité (*see p64*), this is one of the world's major collections of design and the decorative arts. Located in the west wing of the Louvre since its opening a century ago, the venue reopened a few years ago after a decade-long, €35-million restoration of the building and of 6,000 of the 150,000 items donated mainly by private collectors. The major focus here is French furniture and tableware. From extravagant carpets to delicate crystal and porcelain, there is much to admire. Clever spotlighting and black settings show the exquisite treasures – including *châtelaines* made for medieval royalty and Maison Falize enamel work – to their best advantage. Other galleries are categorised by theme: glass, wallpaper, drawings and toys. There are cases devoted to Chinese head jewellery and the Japanese art of seduction with combs. Of

most immediate attraction to the layperson are the reconstructed period rooms, ten in all, showing how the other (French) half lived from the late 1400s to the early 20th century.

Musée du Louvre

Rue de Rivoli, 1st (01.40.20.53.17, www.louvre.fr). M° Palais Royal Musée du Louvre. **Open** 9am-6pm Mon, Thur, Sat, Sun; 9am-9.45pm Wed, Fri. **Admission** *Permanent collections* €12 (incl entry to the Musée Delacroix but not shows at the Salle Napoléon); free under-18s, under-26s (EU citizens), all under-26s 6-9.45pm Fri, all 1st Sun of mth (Oct-Mar). PMP. *Exhibitions* €13. *Combined ticket* €16. **Map** p61 E5 ❼

See p80 **Finishing Touches**.

Musée de la Mode et du Textile

107 rue de Rivoli, 1st (01.44.55.57.50, www. lesartsdecoratifs.fr). M° Palais Royal Musée du Louvre or Pyramides. **Open** 11am-6pm Tue, Wed, Fri-Sun; 11am-9pm Thur (late opening during exhibitions only). **Admission** (with Musée des Arts Décoratifs & Musée de la Publicité) €11; €8.50 reductions; free under-18s, under-26s (EU citizens). PMP. **Map** p60 D4 ❽

This municipal fashion museum holds Elsa Schiaparelli's entire archive and hosts exciting themed exhibitions. Dramatic black-walled rooms make a fine background to the clothes, and video screens and a small cinema space show how the clothes move, as well as interviews with the creators.

★ Musée de l'Orangerie

Jardin des Tuileries, 1st (01.44.77.80.07, www. musee-orangerie.fr). M° Concorde. **Open** 9am-6pm

EXPLORE

Jeu de Paume.

Palais-Royal.

Mon, Wed-Sun. **Admission** €9; €6.50 reductions; free under-18s, under-26s (EU citizens), all 1st Sun of mth. PMP. **Map** p60 B4 ❾

This Monet showcase is a firm fixture on the tourist radar, so you can expect long queues. The look is utilitarian and fuss-free, with the museum's eight tapestry-sized *Nymphéas* (water lilies) paintings housed in two plain oval rooms. They provide a simple backdrop for the astonishing, ethereal romanticism of Monet's works, painted late in his life. Depicting Monet's *'jardin d'eau'* at his house in Giverny, the *tableaux* have an intense, dreamy quality – partly reflecting the artist's absorption in the private world of his garden. Downstairs, the Jean Walter and Paul Guillaume collection of Impressionism and the Ecole de Paris is a mixed bag of sweet-toothed Cézanne and Renoir portraits, along with works by the likes of Modigliani, Rousseau, Matisse, Picasso and Derain.

Musée de la Publicité

107 rue de Rivoli, 1st (01.44.55.57.50, www. lesartsdecoratifs.fr). M° Palais Royal Musée du Louvre or Pyramides. **Open** 11am-6pm Tue, Wed, Fri-Sun; 11am-9pm Thur (late opening during exhibitions only). **Admission** (with Musée des Arts Décoratifs & Musée de la Mode) €11; €8.50 reductions; free under-18s, under-26s (EU citizens). PMP. **Map** p60 D4 ❿

The upstairs element of the trio of museums in the Louvre west wing, the advertising museum has a distressed interior by Jean Nouvel. Only a fraction of the vast collection of posters, promotional objects and packaging can be seen at any one time; vintage posters are accessed in the multimedia space.

★ FREE Palais-Royal

Pl du Palais-Royal, 1st. M° Palais Royal Musée du Louvre. **Open** *Gardens* Apr, May 7am-10.15pm daily. June-Aug 7am-11pm daily. Sept 7am-9.30pm daily. Oct-Mar 7am-8.30pm daily. **Admission** free. **Map** p60 D4 ⓫

Built for Cardinal Richelieu by Jacques Lemercier, this building was once known as the Palais Cardinal. Richelieu left it to Louis XIII, whose widow Anne d'Autriche preferred it to the chilly Louvre and rechristened it when she moved in with her son, the young Louis XIV. In the 1780s, the Duc d'Orléans, Louis XVI's fun-loving brother, enclosed the gardens in a three-storey peristyle and filled it with cafés, shops, theatres, sideshows and accommodation to raise money for rebuilding the burned-down opera. In stark contrast to Versailles, the Palais-Royal was a place where people of all classes could mingle, and its arcades became a trysting venue. Today, Daniel Buren's installation of black-and-white columns graces the main courtyard.

FREE Place de la Concorde

1st, 8th. M° Concorde. **Map** p60 A4 ⓬

This is the city's largest square, its grand east–west perspectives stretching from the Louvre to the Arc de Triomphe, and north–south from the Madeleine to the Assemblée Nationale across the Seine. Royal architect Gabriel designed it in the 1750s, along with the two colonnaded mansions astride rue Royale; the west one houses the chic Hôtel de Crillon (currently closed for renovations) and the Automobile Club de France, the other is the Naval Ministry. In 1792, the centre statue of Louis XV was replaced with the guillotine that would be used on Louis XVI,

Marie-Antoinette and many more. The square was embellished in the 19th century with sturdy lamp-posts, the Luxor obelisk (from the Viceroy of Egypt), and ornate tiered fountains.

FREE Place Vendôme

1st. M° Opéra or Tuileries. **Map** p60 C3 ⑬
Elegant place Vendôme got its name from a *hôtel particulier* built by the Duc de Vendôme that stood on the site. Opened in 1699, the eight-sided square was conceived by Hardouin-Mansart to show off an equestrian statue of the Sun King, torn down in 1792 and replaced in 1806 by the Colonne de la Grande Armée. Modelled on Trajan's Column in Rome and featuring a spiral comic strip illustrating Napoleon's military exploits, it was cast from 1,250 Russian and Austrian cannon captured at the Battle of Austerlitz. During the 1871 Commune this symbol of 'brute force and false glory' was pulled down; the present column is a replica. Hardouin-Mansart designed only the façades, with their ground-floor arcade and giant Corinthian pilasters; the buildings behind were put up by nobles and speculators. Today, the square houses sparkling jewellers, top fashion houses and the justice ministry. At no.12, you can visit the Grand Salon where Chopin died in 1849; its fabulous allegorical decoration dates from 1777 and has been restored as part of the new museum above the jewellers Chaumet (01.44.77.26.26).

Restaurants

★ L'Ardoise

28 rue du Mont-Thabor, 1st (01.42.96.28.18, www.lardoise-paris.com). M° Concorde or Tuileries. **Open** noon-3pm, 6.30-11pm Mon-Sat; 6.30-11pm Sun. **Main courses** €27. **Prix fixe** €38. **Map** p60 B3 ⑭ **Bistro**
This plain-looking bistro attracts a fair number of foreigners given its location near place Vendôme and its early opening hours, but the food proves their judgement to be spot-on. Chef Pierre Jay doesn't skimp on quality ingredients in dishes such as shellfish papillote or chicken in parmesan cream sauce, making his set menu an absolute bargain for the area. A lightly chilled Chinon is a perfect complement. Unusually for Paris, the restaurant is open on Sundays.

Le Grand Véfour

17 rue de Beaujolais, 1st (01.42.96.56.27, www.grand-vefour.com). M° Palais Royal Musée du Louvre. **Open** 12.30-2pm, 8-10pm Mon-Fri. Closed 1st 3wks Aug. **Main courses** €96-€114. **Prix fixe** *Lunch* €98. *Dinner* €298. **Map** p61 E3 ⑮ **Haute cuisine**
Opened in 1784 (as the Café de Chartres), this is one of the oldest and most historic restaurants in the French capital. An à la carte meal here begins with a fantasia suite of delicacies: tiny frogs' legs,

for example, arranged within a circle of sage sauce; a first course of creamed Breton sea urchins served in their spiny shells with a quail's egg and topped with caviar. Fish dishes may be a touch overcooked, and the adventurous desserts are not always entirely successful, but you'll forgive all after a glass or two of vintage armagnac.

€ Higuma

32bis rue Ste-Anne, 1st (01.47.03.38.59, www. higuma.fr). M° Pyramides. **Open** 11.30am-10pm daily. **Main courses** €7.50-€10. **Prix fixe** €11-€13.50. **Map** p60 D3 ⑯ **Japanese**
Higuma's no-nonsense food and service make it one of the area's most popular destinations. On entering, customers are greeted by plumes of aromatic steam emanating from the open kitchen-cum-bar, where a small team of chefs ladle out giant bowls of noodle soup piled with meat, vegetables or seafood. You can slurp at the counter or sit at a plastic-topped table. **Other locations** 163 rue St-Honoré, 1st (01.58.62.49.22); 27 bd des Italiens, 2nd (01.40.07.11.81).

Place de la Concorde.

EXPLORE

★ Le Meurice

Hôtel Meurice, 228 rue de Rivoli, 1st (01.44.58.10.55, www.lemeurice.com). M° Tuileries. **Open** *7-10.30am, 12.30-2pm, 7.30-10pm Mon-Fri; 7-11.30am Sat, Sun. Closed 2wks Feb & Aug.* **Main courses** *€95-€185.* **Prix fixe** *Breakfast €40-€72. Lunch €130, €380. Dinner €380.* **Map** p60 C4 **17 Haute cuisine**

With the departure of Yannick Alléno in 2013, Alain Ducasse has now taken over the reins at Le Meurice's gorgeous dining room, launching a new menu that eschews excess and focuses instead on a simpler approach (to the food, not the prices). Head chef Christophe Saintagne turns out delightfully deconstructed dishes such as 'turbot, olives', 'mallard, grapes' and 'spicy lamb, artichokes'.

Racines 2

39 rue de l'Arbre Sec, 1st (01.42.60.77.34, www.racinesparis.com). M° Louvre Rivoli. **Open** *noon-2.30pm, 7.30-10.30pm Mon-Fri; 7.30-10.30pm Sat.* **Main courses** *€25-€33.* **Prix fixe** *Lunch €28, €32. Dinner €55.* **Map** p61 F5 **18 Bistro**

Racines' little brother is the rebellious one, with its tattooed young chef and Scandinavian-influenced decor from bad-boy designer Philippe Starck (we particularly like the antler lamps). The feel is modern bistro with attitude: starters might include puff pastry *feuilleté* with snails, cream of shallots and fresh herbs or *vitello tonnato*, followed by pork belly with crisp vegetables or beef with herby potato purée and mesclun salad. Prices are on the steep side, but the area's upmarket clientele are unlikely to be too fazed by the bill.

★ Restaurant du Palais-Royal

110 galerie Valois, 1st (01.40.20.00.27, www.restaurantdupalaisroyal.com). M° Bourse or Palais Royal Musée du Louvre. **Map** p61 E3 **19 Bistro**

There can be few more magical places to dine on a summer evening than the terrace of the Restaurant du Palais-Royal. Inside is memorable too: you sit in a red dining room alongside the commissars of arts and letters who work at the ministry of culture a few doors down. The restaurant was undergoing renovations at the time of writing, but was due to reopen in June 2015 with chef Philip Chronopoulos at the helm.

Spring

6 rue Bailleul, 1st (01.45.96.05.72, www.springparis.fr). M° Louvre Rivoli. **Open** *6.30-10.30pm Tue-Sat.* **Prix fixe** *Dinner €84.* **Map** p61 E5 **20 Bistro**

To join the privileged few who dine at Spring, you'll have to book months in advance and arm yourself with plenty of patience. You'll also need to leave any cravings at the door and just let chef Daniel Rose do his thing. Rose's unique menu changes daily, and sometimes at the last moment, depending on the availability of market produce. So in autumn, you

might sample wild mushrooms with a crab emulsion and a slow-cooked egg or duck with celeriac, quince and mustard leaves. Just watch out for the pricey wine list, which can quickly send the bill sky high.

★ Thaïm

46 rue de Richelieu, 1st (01.42.96.54.67). M° Bourse or Palais Royal Musée du Louvre. **Open** *12.15-2.15pm, 7.15-10.30pm Mon-Fri; 7.15-11pm Sat.* **Prix fixe** *Lunch €17.50. Dinner €27.50.* **Map** p60 D3 **21 Thai**

Steering well away from Thai clichés, Thaïm has an elegant decor of dark wood and plum fabrics, and a brief menu that changes often, keeping the regulars coming back. Particularly good value is the three-course lunch menu, which might bring crisp fried parcels filled with spiced vegetables, an aromatic green fish curry (there is a choice of fish, meat or poultry every day), and sweet coconut-pumpkin soup. There is an extensive choice of teas, including a delicious iced ginger-coconut version.

Verjus

52 rue de Richelieu, 1st (01.42.97.54.40, www.hkmenus.com). M° Pyramides. **Open** *7-11pm Mon-Fri.* **Prix fixe** *€68.* **Map** p61 E3 **22 Bistro**

Braden Perkins and Laura Adrian started out in Paris running a well-regarded supper club, 'Hidden Kitchen', so it's little surprise that Verjus – opened after rave reviews paved the way for a full-blown restaurant – hasn't quite lost its word-of-mouth feel. You reach the small, stylish dining room through an unmarked iron gate. There's one eight-course tasting menu at dinner, updated monthly (plus an optional cheese board, and optional matched wines). At €68 a head without the extras, save it for a special occasion – but it will be special. On our visit, a Scandinavian-inspired plate of trout and potatoes brought a vivid citrus-cured curl of fish with slices of smoked potatoes and a salty scoop of bright orange roe, while thick slices of tender pink duck breast with their rich fat and golden skin nestled snugly on a bed of sharp winter sauerkraut.

Zen

8 rue de l'Echelle, 1st (01.42.61.93.99). M° Louvre Rivoli. **Open** *noon-2.30pm, 7-10.30pm Mon-Fri; noon-3pm, 7-10.30pm Sat, Sun. Closed last 3wks Aug.* **Prix fixe** *Lunch €12-€20. Dinner €20-€65.* **Map** p60 D4 **23 Japanese**

There's no shortage of Japanese restaurants in this neighbourhood, but the recently opened Zen is refreshing in a couple of ways. First, there is no pale wood in sight; the colour scheme here is sharp white, green and yellow for a cheerful effect. Second, the menu has a lot to choose from – bowls of ramen, sushi and *chirashi*, hearty dishes such as chicken with egg on rice or *tonkatsu* – yet no detail is neglected. This is a perfect choice if you're planning on spending a day at the Louvre – you can be in and out in 30 minutes.

Cafés & Bars

★ Angelina

226 rue de Rivoli, 1st (01.42.60.82.00, www.angelina-paris.fr). M° Tuileries. **Open** 7.30am-7pm Mon-Thur; 7.30am-7.30pm Fri; 8.30am-7.30pm Sat, Sun. **Map** p60 C4 ㉔

Angelina is home to Paris's most lip-smackingly scrumptious desserts – all served in the faded grandeur of a belle époque salon just steps from the Louvre. The hot chocolate is pure decadence; try the speciality 'African', a velvety potion so thick that you need a spoon to consume it. Epicurean delights include the Mont Blanc dessert, a ball of meringue covered in whipped cream and sweet chestnut, and, for those with a waistline to watch, a sugar- and

Angelina.

butter-free *brioche aux fruits rouges*. The place heaves at weekends, so be prepared to queue.

Le Café des Initiés

3 pl des Deux-Ecus, 1st (01.42.33.78.29, www.lecafedesinities.com). M° Louvre Rivoli or Les Halles. **Open** 7.30am-2am Mon-Fri; 9am-2am Sat, Sun. **Map** p61 E4 ㉕

Friendly staff and a central location have turned this designer hangout into a top spot for a trendy tipple, especially after work – cocktails will set you back just €6.50 between 5pm and 8pm. The main room is lined with aerodynamic red banquettes, a long zinc bar provides character, and sleek, black articulated lamps peer down from the ceiling. When hunger strikes, homely favourites such as shoulder of lamb baked in honey or tartare of salmon never fail to please.

Café Marly

93 rue de Rivoli, cour Napoléon, 1st (01.49.26.06.60, www.cafe-marly.com). M° Palais Royal Musée du Louvre. **Open** 8am-2am daily. **Map** p60 D4 ㉖

In the arcaded terrace overlooking the Louvre's glass pyramid, this classy, Napoleon III-style hangout (reached through the passage Richelieu, the entrance for advance Louvre ticket holders) is in an unrivalled location. One would expect nothing else from the ubiquitous Costes brothers – it's just a shame about the beer prices: it's €7 for a Leffe, so you might as well splash out €18 on a mojito. Most wines are under €15 a glass, and everything is impeccably served by razor-sharp staff. Brasserie fare and sandwiches are on offer too.

Le Dernier Bar Avant la Fin du Monde

19 av Victoria, 1st (01.53.00.98.95, www.dernierbar.com). M° Châtelet. **Open** 10am-1am daily. **Map** p61 F6 ㉗

The cult of the geek in Paris received a well-oiled boost with the opening of this bar. Medieval and steampunk dominate the decor, with plenty of other bonkers sci-fi touches: as you walk in, a replica of the Millennium Falcon overlooks a timer counting down to the apocalypse predicted by the Mayans next to a window full of *Star Wars* memorabilia. Inside, the big, friendly bar is as much about alternative and popular culture as it is about drinking. A library, board games and science fiction books rub shoulders with the holy grail from *Indiana Jones and the Last Crusade* and other philtres, potions and skeletons. The prevailing atmosphere of heroic collaboration keeps prices low.

L'Entr'acte

47 rue de Montpensier, 1st (01.42.97.57.76). M° Pyramides or Palais Royal Musée du Louvre. **Open** 5.30-11pm Mon; 10.30am-4pm, 5.30pm-1.30am Tue-Sat; 2-8.30pm Sun. **Map** p61 E3 ㉘

Take a little detour off avenue de l'Opéra, down an 18th-century staircase, and you'll find an unexpected

EXPLORE

EXPLORE

congregation spread across the pavement: half are here for this little bar near the Comédie Française, half for the adjoining Sicilian pizzeria. There's food to be had at L'Entr'acte too – €12 plates of cheese and charcuterie, standard pastas and so on – but most come to enjoy an early-evening glass of house Bourgueil. The interior is tiny.

Le Fumoir
6 rue de l'Amiral-de-Coligny, 1st (01.42.92.00.24, www.lefumoir.com). M° Louvre Rivoli. **Open** 11am-2am daily. **Map** p61 E5 ㉙
There aren't many places around the Louvre that can compete with this elegant local institution: neo-colonial fans whirr lazily and oil paintings adorn the walls. A sleek crowd sips martinis or reads papers at the long mahogany bar (originally from a Chicago speakeasy), giving way to young professionals in the restaurant and pretty things in the library. It all feels a wee bit try-hard and resolutely well behaved, but the cocktails get tongues wagging soon enough, and food is consistently top notch.

Le Saut du Loup
107 rue de Rivoli, 1st (01.42.25.49.55, www.lesautduloup.fr). M° Palais Royal Musée du Louvre. **Open** noon-midnight daily (until 7pm Sun in winter). **Map** p60 D4 ㉚
Museums are usually daytime destinations, places of discovery that welcome their guests then politely expel them well before dusk. However the Saut du Loup, set inside the Musée des Arts Décoratifs, has made a concerted effort to reel in the Parigots after hours with a dapper restaurant, terrace views to die for over the Tuileries gardens, and a bar that'll knock you up a decent cocktail or two before bedtime. You can always tell a good joint from the quality of its mojitos, and Le Saut du Loup's version of the drink passes the test with flying colours: not too sweet and not too sour; you get an initial slap from the rum and lime, before the fresh mint and sugar settle things down. Perfect.

Télescope Café
5 rue Villedo, 1st (01.42.61.33.14, www.telescope cafe.com). M° Pyramides. **Open** 8.30am-5pm Mon-Fri; 9.30am-6.30pm Sat. **No credit cards.** **Map** p60 D3 ㉛
David Flynn is something of a coffee purist, and his newly opened Télescope Café has a stripped-down look to it; whitewashed walls, a pale blue wooden counter with a plate of cakes, a Marzocco espresso machine and a strange water-heating device that he says is called an 'über-boiler'. Even the coffee menu looks pretty minimalist – no trendy flat whites here – but it turns out that Télescope also doubles as a coffee roaster, only keeping small stocks of beans to ensure freshness.

Shops & Services

★ Alice Cadolle
4 rue Cambon, 1st (01.42.60.94.22, www.cadolle. com). M° Concorde or Madeleine. **Open** 11am-7pm Mon-Sat. Closed Aug. **Map** p60 B3 ㉜ **Fashion**
Five generations of lingerie-makers are behind this boutique, founded by Hermine Cadolle, who claimed to be the original inventor of the bra. Now her great-great-granddaughter, Poupie Cadolle, continues the tradition in a cosy space devoted to a luxury ready-to-wear line of bras, panties and corsets.
▶ *For a special treat, Cadolle Couture (255 rue St-Honoré, 1st, 01.42.60.94.94) will create indulgent bespoke lingerie (by appointment only).*

Alice Cadolle.

American Apparel

29 pl du Marché-St-Honoré, 1st (01.44.50.10.65, www.americanapparel.net). M° Opéra, Pyramides or Tuileries. **Open** 11am-7pm Mon-Fri; 11am-8pm Sat; 1-6pm Sun. **Map** p60 C3 ❸ **Fashion**
Paris has acquired a taste for American Apparel's sweatshop-free, unisex cotton basics.
Other locations throughout the city.

Anne Sémonin

2 rue des Petits Champs, 2nd (01.42.60.94.66, www.annesemonin.com). M° Bourse. **Open** 10am-2pm, 3-7pm Mon; 10am-7pm Tue-Sat. **Map** p61 E3 ❸ **Health & beauty**
Facials involve delicious concoctions of basil, lavender, lemongrass, ginger and plant essences. Also on offer are reflexology and a selection of massage styles, from Thai to ayurvedic. Body treatments cost from €65 to €195. Sémonin's renowned seaweed skincare products and essential oils are also on sale.

Appartement 217

217 rue St-Honoré, 1st (01.42.96.00.96, www.lappartement217.com). M° Tuileries. **Open** 10am-7pm Tue-Sat. **Map** p60 C3 ❸
Health & beauty
A beautiful feng-shuied Haussmannian apartment is the setting for facials using organic beauty guru Dr Hauschka's products and ayurvedic or deep tissue massages. The water has been decalcified, electrical currents are insulated, and the silky-soft kimonos are made from organic wood pulp.

Astier de Villatte

173 rue St-Honoré, 1st (01.42.60.74.13, www. astierdevillatte.com). M° Palais Royal Musée du Louvre. **Open** 11am-7.30pm Mon-Sat. **Map** p60 D4 ❸ **Homewares**
Once home to Napoleon's silversmith, this ancient warren of rooms now houses beautiful ceramics inspired by 17th- and 18th-century designs, handmade by the Astier de Villatte siblings in their Bastille workshop.

Boucheron

26 pl Vendôme, 1st (01.42.61.58.16, www. boucheron.com). M° Opéra. **Open** 10.30am-7pm Mon-Sat. **Map** p60 C3 ❸ **Accessories**
Boucheron was the first *joaillier* to set up shop on place Vendôme. Owned by Gucci, the grand jeweller produces stunning pieces, using traditional motifs with new accents.
Other location 32 rue du Fbg-St-Honoré, 8th (01.44.51.95.20).

By Terry

21 & 36 passage Véro-Dodat, 1st (01.44.76.00.76, www.byterry.com). M° Palais Royal Musée du Louvre. **Open** 10am-7pm Mon-Sat. **Map** p61 E4 ❸ **Health & beauty**

Terry de Gunzburg, who earned her reputation at Yves Saint Laurent, offers made-to-measure 'haute couleur' make-up by skilled chemists and colourists combining high-tech treatments and handmade precision. There's prêt-à-porter too.
Other location 10 av Victor-Hugo, 16th (01.55.73.00.73).

★ Chanel

31 rue Cambon, 1st (01.44.50.66.00, www.chanel. com). M° Concorde or Madeleine. **Open** 10am-7pm Mon-Sat. **Map** p60 B3 ❸ **Fashion**
Fashion legend Chanel has managed to stay relevant, thanks to Karl Lagerfeld. Coco opened her first boutique in this street, at no.21, in 1910, and the tradition continues in this elegant interior. Lagerfeld has been designing for Chanel since 1983, and keeps on revamping the classics – the little black dress and the Chanel suit – with great success.
Other locations 42 av Montaigne, 8th (01.40.70.82.00); 51 av Montaigne, 8th (01.44.50.73.00); 25 rue Royale, 8th (01.44.51.92.93); 21 rue du Fbg-St-Honoré, 8th (01.53.05.98.95).

Chanel Joaillerie

18 pl Vendôme, 1st (01.40.98.55.55, www.chanel. com). M° Opéra. **Open** 10.30am-6.30pm Mon-Fri. **Map** p60 C3 ❹ **Accessories**
Chanel launched its fine jewellery in the 1990s, reissuing the single collection – big on platinum and diamonds – that Coco herself designed some 60 years previously. The current line reinterprets the motifs – camellias, stars and comets – to create a collection of contemporary classics.

Christian Louboutin

19 rue Jean-Jacques-Rousseau, 1st (00.800. 10.19.19.19, www.christianlouboutin.com). M° Palais Royal Musée du Louvre. **Open** 10.30am-7pm Mon-Sat. **Map** p61 E4 ❹ **Accessories**
Every fashionista, WAG and shoe fiend worth her salt owns or hankers after a pair of Christian Louboutin's trademark red-soled creations. Each design is displayed to maximum advantage in an individual frame.
Other locations 38 rue de Grenelle, 7th (00.800.10.19.19.19); 68 rue du Fbg-St-Honoré, 8th (00.800.10.19.19.19).

★ Colette

213 rue St-Honoré, 1st (01.55.35.33.90, www. colette.fr). M° Pyramides or Tuileries. **Open** 11am-7pm Mon-Sat. **Map** p60 C4 ❹ **Fashion**
The renowned one-stop concept and lifestyle store features a highly eclectic selection of must-have accessories, fashion, sneakers, books, media, shiny new gadgets, and hair and beauty brands, all in a swanky space. Expect to find Zippo lighters a few feet away from Smythson diaries, a few feet away from Ladurée macaroons, all one flight of stairs away from Alexander Wang and Valentino.

EXPLORE

EXPLORE

Delfonics

*Carrousel du Louvre, 99 rue de Rivoli, 1st
(01.47.03.14.24, www.delfonics.fr). M° Palais
Royal Musée du Louvre.* **Open** 10am-8pm daily.
Map p60 D4 ⓐ **Books & music**
Concentrating on minimalist designs using durable
materials (linen, rayon, canvas, leather and resin),
Delfonics is a haven for stationery addicts looking
for Japanese and European notebooks, files, pens
and much more. This flagship wood-lined store near
the Louvre is the only one in Europe for the moment,
offering nearly 55sq m of temptingly affordable
things such as Post-it notes in cute designs, vinyl
pencil cases and electronic letter-openers.

Didier Ludot

*24 galerie de Montpensier, 1st (01.42.96.06.56,
www.didierludot.fr). M° Palais Royal Musée
du Louvre.* **Open** 10.30am-7pm Mon-Sat.
Map p60 D4 ⓐ **Fashion**
Didier Ludot's temples to vintage haute couture
appear in Printemps, Harrods and New York's
Barneys. The prices may be on the steep side, but
the pieces are stunning: Dior, Molyneux, Balenciaga,
Pucci, Féraud and, of course, Chanel, from the 1920s
onwards. Ludot also curates exhibitions, using the
exclusive shop windows around the Palais-Royal
as a gallery.
▶ *Didier Ludot stocks his own line of vintage
little black dresses, which are also available at
La Petite Robe Noire (125 galerie de Valois,
1st, 01.40.15.01.04).*

Dior Joaillerie

*8 pl Vendôme, 1st (01.42.96.30.84, www.dior.com).
M° Opéra or Tuileries.* **Open** 10.30am-7pm daily.
Map p60 C3 ⓐ **Accessories**
The unabashed bling of Victoire de Castellane's
designs is responsible for the fad of semi-precious
coloured stones and runaway success of the 'Mimi
Oui', a ring with a tiny diamond on a slim chain.
Other location 28 av Montaigne, 8th
(01.47.23.52.39).

Eglé Bespoke

*26 rue du Mont-Thabor, 1st (01.44.15.98.31,
www.eglebespoke.com). M° Concorde or Tuileries.*
Open 11am-7.30pm Mon-Sat. **Map** p60 C3
ⓐ **Fashion**
Two young entrepreneurs are reviving bespoke for
a new generation in this tiny shop. Custom shirts
start from about €120 and can be delivered in a week
or so; they will also make or copy shirts for women
and produce made-to-order jeans for both sexes.
Laser-printed buttons are perfect for stamping your
beloved's shirt with a saucy message.

★ Fifi Chachnil

*231 rue St-Honoré, 1st (01.42.61.21.83, www.
fifichachnil.com). M° Tuileries.* **Open** 11am-7pm
Mon-Sat. **Map** p60 C3 ⓐ **Fashion**

Chachnil has a new approach to frou-frou underwear
in the pin-up tradition. Her chic mixes – deep red silk
bras with boudoir-pink bows, and pale turquoise
girdles with orange trim – will have ladies and their
male admirers purring in delight. The transparent
black babydoll negligées with an Empire-line bust
are classic saucy retro.
Other locations 68 rue Jean-Jacques-Rousseau,
1st (01.42.21.19.93); 34 rue de Grenelle, 7th
(01.42.22.08.23).

★ Gabrielle Geppert

*31-34 & 41 galerie Montpensier, 1st
(01.42.61.53.52, www.gabriellegeppert.com).
M° Palais Royal Musée du Louvre.* **Open** 10am-
7.30pm Mon-Sat. **Map** p60 D4 ⓐ **Fashion**
Much fun can be had here rummaging in the back
room or trying on the outrageous collection of '70s
sunglasses (about €380 a pop, but they will get you
into any party worth going to). No.31 is dedicated
to luxury vintage with a selection of clothes and
accessories by Hermès, Chanel and Dior, plus shoes
by Chanel and Louboutin. At nos.32-33, Geppert
sells her own-brand jewellery and clothes.

La Galerie du Carrousel du Louvre

*99 rue de Rivoli, 1st (01.43.16.47.10, www.
carrouseldulouvre.com). M° Palais Royal Musée
du Louvre.* **Open** 10am-8pm daily. **Map** p60 D4
ⓐ **Mall**
This massive underground centre – open every day
of the year – is home to more than 35 shops, mostly
big-name chains vying for your attention and cash.
Options include an Apple Store, Swatch Store and
L'Occitane en Provence.

Galignani

*224 rue de Rivoli, 1st (01.42.60.76.07, www.
galignani.com). M° Palais Royal Musée du
Louvre or Tuileries.* **Open** 10am-7pm Mon-Sat.
Map p60 C4 ⓐ **Books & music**
Opened in 1802, this was the first English-language
bookshop in mainland Europe. Today, it stocks
fine art books, French and English literature,
philosophical tomes and magazines.

Hervé Léger

*24 rue Cambon, 1st (01.42.60.02.00, www.
herveleger.com). M° Concorde.* **Open** 10am-7pm
Mon-Sat. **Map** p60 B3 ⓐ **Fashion**
A couple of decades ago, Hervé Léger's silhouette-
cinching bandage dresses were as evocative of
the era as supermodels Linda, Christy, Naomi
and Cindy. But somewhere in the mid-'90s women
lost their love of Lycra, longing for the more
conventional figure-flattering techniques of bias
cut and tailoring. In the past few seasons, however,
updated reinterpretations of Léger's style, by the
likes of Christopher Kane and Marios Schwab,
have been nothing short of a fashion phenomenon.
Less modified versions, sold by the Léger label

or Pyramides. **Open** 11am-7.30pm Mon-Sat. **Map** p61 E3 **63 Fashion**
The London/Paris style collective now has its own boutique, which offers the entire catalogue of music compilations, as well as branded clothing that takes a back-to-basics approach using quality producers. You'll find Scottish cashmere, Japanese jeans and Italian shirts, together with items made in collaboration with Pierre Hardy, Scheisser underwear and James Heeley.

Louvre des Antiquaires

2 pl du Palais-Royal, 1st (01.42.97.27.27, www. louvre-antiquaires.com). M° Palais Royal Musée du Louvre. **Open** 11am-7pm Tue-Sun. Closed Sun in July & Aug. **Map** p60 D4 **64 Homewares**
This upmarket antiques centre is home to more than 250 antiques dealers: the perfect spot for Louis XV furniture, tapestries, porcelain, jewellery, model ships and tin soldiers.

★ Maison Fabre

128 galerie de Valois, 1st (01.42.60.75.88, www.maisonfabre.com). M° Palais Royal Musée du Louvre. **Open** 11am-7pm Mon-Sat. **Map** p61 E4 **65 Accessories**
This Millau glovemaker, which was founded in 1924, has capitalised on its racy designs from the sports-car eras of the 1920s and '60s. Classic gloves made from the softest leather (€115) come in various wild colours. Then there are the variations: crocodile, python, coyote, fur-trimmed, fingerless. But the ultimate lust object is the patent leather 'Auto' glove fastened with a massive button.

Manoush

217 rue St Honoré, 1st (01.40.20.04.44, www. manoush.com). M° Tuileries. **Open** 10.30am-7.30pm Mon-Sat. **Map** p60 C4 **66 Fashion**
Manoush, which means 'gypsy' in French slang, has proved more than just a flash in the pan for the boho craze of 2005 and now has five Paris boutiques touting designer Frédérique Trou-Roy's kooky vision.
Other locations throughout the city.

Marc by Marc Jacobs

19 pl du Marché-St-Honoré, 1st (women's 01.40.20.11.30, men's 01.40.20.12.80, www. marcjacobs.com). M° Tuileries. **Open** 11am-7pm Mon-Sat. **Map** p60 C3 **67 Fashion**
The new store for Jacobs' casual, punky line has fashionistas clustering like bees round a honeypot, not least for the fabulously inexpensive accessories that make great gifts. A skateboard table and giant pedalo in the form of a swan are the centrepieces of the store, which stocks men's and women's prêt-à-porter, shoes and special editions. At no.17, Bookmarc Paris (01.75.77.85.90) sells books, stationery, DVDs, Marc by Marc Jacobs accessories, tech accessories and gifts.

EXPLORE

Gabrielle Geppert.

itself (now owned and designed by Max Azria of BCBG fame), have been less critically acclaimed, but celebrities just adore them.

★ Jay Ahr

2-4 rue du 29 Juillet, 1st (01.42.96.95.23, www. jayahr.com). M° Tuileries. **Open** 10am-7pm Mon-Sat. **Map** p60 C4 **62 Fashion**
Former jewellery designer Jonathan Riss opened this shop as a fashion stylist in 2004, and soon struck gold with simple, 1960s-inspired dresses. Think plunging necklines and Bianca Jagger in her heyday, with Ali MacGraw and Anita Pallenberg in the mix. There are no price tags on the dresses, so you have to ask; they start at around €800 (€400 for skirts).

Kitsuné

52 rue de Richelieu, 1st (01.42.60.34.28, www. kitsune.fr). M° Palais Royal Musée du Louvre

EXPLORE

Martin Margiela

23 & 25bis rue de Montpensier, 1st (womenswear 01.40.15.07.55, menswear 01.40.15.06.44, www. maisonmartinmargiela.com). M° Palais Royal Musée du Louvre. **Open** 11am-7pm Mon-Sat. **Map** p60 D4 ⑤⑨ **Fashion**

The original Paris outlet for the JD Salinger of fashion is a pristine, white, unlabelled space. His collection for women (Line 1) has a blank label but is recognisable by its external white stitching. You'll also find Line 6 (women's basics) and Line 10 (menswear), plus a range of accessories and shoes. **Other location** 13 rue de Grenelle, 7th (01.45.49.06.68).

Nature et Découvertes

Carrousel du Louvre, 99 rue de Rivoli, 1st (01.47.03.47.43, www.natureetdecouvertes.com). M° Palais Royal Musée du Louvre. **Open** 10am-8pm daily. **Map** p60 D4 ⑤⑨ **Gifts & souvenirs**

This store stocks a great range of stuff for junior and grown-up gadgeteers, from infrared parent detectors to high-tech weather stations. Ten per cent of all the group's profits go to support environmental causes. **Other locations** throughout the city.

Nouvelles Frontières

13 av de l'Opéra, 1st (01.42.61.02.62, www. nouvelles-frontieres.fr). M° Pyramides. **Open** 10am-7pm Mon-Sat. **Map** p60 D3 ⑥⓪ **Travel**

Travel agent with several branches in the capital. **Other locations** throughout the city.

Olympia Le-Tan

Passage des Deux Pavillons, 1st (01.42.36.42.92, www.olympialetan.com). M° Pyramides or Bourse. **Open** 11am-7pm Mon-Sat. **Map** p61 E3 ⑥① **Accessories**

Olympia Le-Tan has become one of the city's most sought-after accessory designers. Her limited-edition, 1950s-style purses and clutch bags, all hand-sewn and hand-embroidered, are inspired by Olympia's fetish authors (including Ernest Hemingway and Gustave Flaubert). In fact, at first glance, the bags look like little books; it's only when you examine the detail that you realise there's a clasp and embroidery. There's also ready-to-wear at this new shop, which opened in 2015.

Paule Ka

223 rue St-Honoré, 1st (01.42.97.57.06, www. pauleka.com). M° Tuileries. **Open** 10.30am-7pm daily. **Map** p60 C3 ⑥② **Fashion**

Serge Cajfinger's '60s couture-influenced collections continue to gather a loyal following. With the opening of his rue St-Honoré boutique, he now has a foot in each of the city's fashion districts. **Other locations** 20 rue Malher, 4th (01.40.29.96.03); 192 bd St-Germain, 6th (01.45.44.92.60); 45 rue François 1er, 8th (01.47.20.76.10).

★ Pierre Hardy

156 galerie de Valois, 1st (01.42.60.59.75, www.pierrehardy.com). M° Palais Royal Musée du Louvre. **Open** 11am-7pm Mon-Sat. **Map** p61 E4 ⑥③ **Accessories**

This classy black-and-white shoebox is home to Hardy's range of superbly conceived footwear – with a price tag to match – for men and women. **Other location** 9-11 pl du Palais Bourbon, 7th (01.45.55.00.67).

Rick Owens

Jardins du Palais-Royal, 130-133 galerie de Valois, 1st (01.40.20.42.52, www.owenscorp.com). M° Palais Royal Musée du Louvre. **Open** 10.30am-7pm Mon-Fri; 11am-7pm Sat. **Map** p61 E4 ⑥④ **Fashion**

The LA designer and rock-star favourite brings his glamour-meets-grunge style to the Palais-Royal, with a selection of hoods, zips and asymmetrical wrappings for men and women. It's not the place for animal lovers – the upstairs has a mink section.

★ Salons du Palais-Royal Shiseido

Jardins du Palais-Royal, 142 galerie de Valois, 1st (01.49.27.09.09, www.sergelutens.com). M° Palais Royal Musée du Louvre. **Open** 10am-7pm Mon-Sat. **Map** p61 E4 ⑥⑤ **Health & beauty**

Under the arcades of the Palais-Royal, Shiseido's perfumer Serge Lutens practises his aromatic arts. A former photographer at Paris *Vogue* and artistic director of make-up at Christian Dior, Lutens is a maestro of rare taste. Bottles of his concoctions – Tubéreuse Criminelle, Rahat Loukoum and Ambre Sultan – can be sampled by visitors. Look out for Fleurs d'Oranger, which the great man defines as the smell of happiness. Prices start at €78.

Stella McCartney

Jardins du Palais-Royal, 114-121 galerie du Valois, 1st (01.47.03.03.80, www.stellamccartney.com). M° Palais Royal Musée du Louvre. **Open** 10.30am-7pm Mon-Sat. **Map** p61 E4 ⑥⑥ **Fashion**

McCartney is crazy about the 'clash of history, fashion and contemporary art' at the Palais-Royal, where she opened her sumptuous boutique. Thick carpets, maplewood and metal sculptures create a rarefied setting for women's prêt-à-porter, bags, shoes, sunglasses, lingerie, perfume and skincare.

Torréfacteur Verlet

256 rue St-Honoré, 1st (01.42.60.67.39, www. cafesverlet.com). M° Palais Royal Musée du Louvre. **Open** 9.30am-7pm Mon-Sat. Closed Aug. **Map** p60 D4 ⑥⑦ **Food & drink**

Eric Duchossoy roasts rare coffee beans to perfection – sip a cup here or take some home to savour.

WH Smith

248 rue de Rivoli, 1st (01.44.77.88.99, www. whsmith.fr). M° Concorde. **Open** 9am-7pm Mon-Sat; 12.30-7pm Sun. **Map** p60 B3 ⑥⑧ **Books & music**

With 70,000 English-language titles and extensive magazine shelves, this is a home from home for Brits craving a fix of their native periodicals; the first floor has books, DVDs and audiobooks.

Yohji Yamamoto

25 rue du Louvre, 1st (01.42.21.42.93, www. yohjiyamamoto.co.jp). M° *Les Halles.* **Open** 10.30am-7pm Mon-Sat. **Map** p61 F4 ⑥ **Fashion**
One of the few true pioneers working in fashion today, Yamamoto is a master of cut and finish, both strongly inspired by the kimono and traditional Tibetan costume. His dexterity with form makes for unique shapes and styles, largely in black. But when he does colour, it's a blast of brilliance.
Other location 4 rue Cambon, 1st (01.40.20.00.71).

THE BOURSE

In the 1st & 2nd arrondissements.

Far less frenzied than New York's Wall Street, the city's traditional business district is squeezed between the elegant calm of the Palais-Royal and shopping hub the Grands Boulevards. Along rue du Quatre-Septembre, La Bourse (the stock exchange) is where financiers and stockbrokers beaver away in grandiose buildings. The Banque de France, France's national central bank, has occupied the 17th-century Hôtel de Toulouse since 1811, its long gallery still hung with Old Masters. Nearby, fashion and finance meet at stylish **place des Victoires**, designed by Hardouin-Mansart.

West of the square is shop-lined galerie Vivienne, the smartest of the covered passages in Paris, adjoining galerie Colbert. Also look out for temporary exhibitions at the **Bibliothèque Nationale de France – Richelieu**. You can linger at the luxury food and wine merchant **Legrand**, or head along passage des Petits-Pères to admire the 17th- to 18th-century Eglise Notre-Dame-des-Victoires, the remains of an Augustine convent with a cycle of paintings around the choir by Carle van Loo.

Rue de la Banque leads to the Bourse, set behind a neoclassical colonnade. The area has a relaxed feel – it's dead at weekends – but lively pockets exist at such places as **Le Vaudeville** (29 rue Vivienne, 2nd, 01.40.20. 04.62, www. vaudevilleparis.com) and **Gallopin** (40 rue Notre-Dame-des-Victoires, 2nd, 01.42.36.45.38, www.brasseriegallopin.com), busy brasseries frequented by stockbrokers and journalists. Rue des Colonnes is a quiet street lined with porticoes and acanthus motifs from the 1790s; its design nemesis, the 1970s concrete-and-glass HQ of Agence France-Presse, the nation's biggest news agency, stands on the other side of rue du Quatre-Septembre.

Olympia Le-Tan.

EXPLORE

EXPLORE

Sights & Museums

FREE Bibliothèque Nationale de France – Richelieu & Musée du Cabinet des Médailles

58 rue de Richelieu, 2nd (01.53.79.59.59, www.bnf.fr). M° Bourse. **Open** times vary. **Admission** varies. **Map** p61 E3 **70**

The history of the French National Library began in the 1660s, when Louis XIV moved manuscripts that couldn't be housed in the Louvre to this lavish Louis XIII townhouse. The library was first opened to the public in 1692, and by 1724 it had received so many new acquisitions that the adjoining Hôtel de Nevers had to be added. Some of the original painted decoration by Romanelli and Grimaldi can still be seen in Galeries Mansart and Mazarine. The highlights, however, are the two circular reading rooms: the Salle Ovale, which is full of researchers, note-takers and readers, and the magnificent Salle de Travail, a temple to learning, with its arrangement of nine domes supported on slender columns. On the first floor is the Musée du Cabinet des Médailles, a modest two-room collection of coins and medals, including Greek, Roman and medieval examples. There is also a miscellany of other items, including Merovingian king Dagobert's throne, Charlemagne's chess set and small artefacts from the Classical world and ancient Egypt. The whole site is undergoing major renovations until at least 2017 and some of the collection has had to be transferred to the BNF François Mitterrand (*see p188*).

FREE Place des Victoires

1st, 2nd. M° Bourse. **Map** p61 E3 **71**

This circular square, the first of its kind, was designed by Hardouin-Mansart in 1685 to show off a statue of Louis XIV that marked victories against Holland. The original statue was destroyed after the Revolution (although the massive slaves from its base are now in the Louvre), and replaced in 1822 with an equestrian statue by Bosio. Among the occupants of the grand buildings that encircle the 'square' are boutiques Kenzo and Victoire.

Restaurants

A Noste

6 bis rue du 4 Septembre, 2nd (01.47.03.91.91, www.a-noste.com). M° Bourse. **Open** 8am-2am daily. *Food served* noon-2pm, 7-10.30pm daily (tapas noon-11pm). **Tapas** €6-€19. **Prix fixe** *Lunch* €38. *Dinner* €60. **Map** p61 E2 **72 Bistro**

Why open one restaurant when you can squeeze three into a single venue? Julien Duboué, erstwhile chef at Afaria, doesn't do things by halves: his new venture is essentially three eateries in one, each serving a different variety of Basque cuisine in a different setting. In the bustling downstairs room, diners sit around high communal tables and tuck into platters of succulent tapas. On the ground level, those in a

Place des Victoires.

hurry grab takeaway *taloa* (corn pancakes) from a pop-up stall. Things get serious upstairs, where the more genteel clientele relish the various courses of the set menu. The meat is divine and the products are all sourced from south-west France (including some vegetables from Duboué's father's garden).

★ € Bistrot Victoires

6 rue de la Vrillière, 1st (01.42.61.43.78). M° Bourse. **Open** noon-3pm, 7-11pm daily. **Main courses** €10-€11. **Map** p61 E3 **73 Bistro**

Bistros with vintage decor serving no-nonsense food at generous prices are growing thin on the ground in Paris, so it's no surprise that this gem is packed to the gills with bargain-loving office workers and locals every day. The *steak-frites* are exemplary, featuring a slab of entrecôte topped with a smoking sprig of thyme, but *plats du jour* such as *blanquette de veau* (veal in cream sauce) are equally comforting. The wines by the glass can be rough, but the authentic buzz should make up for any flaws.

★ Chez Miki

5 rue de Louvois, 2nd (01.42.96.04.88). M° Bourse. **Open** noon-2.30pm Mon; noon-2.30pm, 7-10.30pm Tue-Sat; 7-10.30pm Sun. **Main courses** €15-€20. **Prix fixe** *Lunch* €15. **Map** p61 E3 **74 Japanese**

There are plenty of Japanese restaurants to choose from along nearby rue Ste-Anne, but none is as original – nor as friendly – as this tiny bistro run entirely by women, next to the square Louvois. The speciality here is bento boxes, which you compose yourself from a scribbled blackboard list (in Japanese and French). For €15 you can choose two small dishes – marinated sardines and fried chicken wings are especially popular – and a larger dish, such as grilled pork with ginger.

Les Fines Gueules

43 rue Croix-des-Petits-Champs, 1st (01.42.61.35.41, www.lesfinesgueules.fr). Mº Bourse or Sentier. **Open** noon-2.30pm, 7.30-10.30pm Mon-Fri; noon-3pm, 7.30-11pm Sat; noon-3pm, 7.30-10.30pm Sun. **Main courses** €18-€26. **Map** p61 E4 🟥 **Bistro**

At first glance, Les Fines Gueules might seem like an ordinary corner café, but a closer look at the menu reveals unusual attention to ingredients at this mini wine bar/bistro. Even if you've never heard of Hugo (Desnoyer, star butcher and supplier to some of the city's finest restaurants) or Jean-Luc (Poujauran, a celebrity Paris baker), you can taste the difference when the pedigree steak tartare arrives with a salad of baby leaves dressed in truffle oil. There are just a few seats around the bar, but upstairs is a buzzy dining room. There's a good selection of wines.

Hokkaido

14 rue Chabanais, 2nd (01.42.60.50.95). Mº Bourse. **Open** 11.30am-10.30pm Mon, Tue, Thur-Sun. **Main courses** €7-€14. **Prix fixe** €11. **Map** p60 D3 🟥 **Japanese**

A tiny canteen on rue Chabanais, Hokkaido is very basic but always promisingly full of regulars. Generous, well-priced dishes are offered to take away or eat *sur place* – a bowl of ramen noodles will set you back around €8, pork gyoza with white cabbage and ginger around €5.50 for seven.

★ Liza

14 rue de la Banque, 2nd (01.55.35.00.66, www.restaurant-liza.com). Mº Bourse. **Open** noon-2.15pm, 8-10.30pm Mon-Thur; noon-2.15pm, 8-11pm Fri; 8-11pm Sat; noon-3.30pm Sun. **Main courses** €25. **Prix fixe** *Lunch* €16, €21, €22. *Dinner* €42, €49. **Map** p61 E3 🟥 **Lebanese**

Liza Soughayar's restaurant showcases the style and superb food of contemporary Beirut. Lentil, fried onion and orange salad is delicious. Main courses, such as minced lamb with coriander-spiced spinach and rice, are light, flavoursome and well presented. Try one of the excellent Lebanese wines to accompany your meal, and finish with the halva ice-cream with carob molasses.

Michi

58bis rue Sainte-Anne, 2nd (01.40.20.49.93). Mº Quatre-Septembre. **Open** noon-2pm, 7-10pm Tue-Sat. **Main courses** €5-€9. **Prix fixe** *Lunch* €14, €18. *Dinner* €23. **Map** p60 D3 🟥 **Japanese**

Rue Sainte-Anne and its surroundings are full of Japanese treasures, tiny restaurants serving excellent ramen, gyoza, udon and soba – but not sushi. However, at no.58, 'sushi' is spelled out in big letters across a slightly decrepit-looking front window. Don't be put off – this is the real deal. Sit at the bar if you can and watch the chef preparing the dishes with disconcerting speed. At midday, the set sushi menus come with soup, salad, rice and dessert. Salmon, tuna, prawn, bream, eel and scallop sushi will all come out in a long procession, with flavours that put most of Paris's sushi dives to shame.

Saturne

17 rue Notre-Dame des Victoires, 2nd (01.42.60.31.90, www.saturne-paris.fr). Mº Bourse. **Open** noon-2.30pm, 8-10.30pm Mon-Fri. **Prix fixe** *Lunch* €45, €70. *Dinner* €70. **Map** p61 E3 🟥 **Bistro**

All done out in wood, metal and stone, with bouquets of flowers and an open kitchen at the back, Saturne is a calming space. The cooking shows a similar talent for detail and harmony with flashes of inspiration: a refreshing crab dish surrounded by a citrus syllabub and baby leeks; a lovely piece of plaice served with cockles, parsley and fennel. The chef and the sommelier, Sven Chartier and Ewen Lemoigne, work hand in glove to pair fine ingredients and natural wines. All in all, an excellent address.

Cafés & Bars

★ La Conserverie

37bis rue du Sentier, 2nd (01.40.26.14.94, www.laconserveriebar.com). Mº Bonne-Nouvelle. **Open** 12.30pm-midnight Mon, Tue; 12.30pm-2am Wed-Fri; 8pm-2am Sat. **Map** p61 F2 🟢

The gorgeous *nuit bleue* interior will win you over as soon as you step inside, and by the time you sit on the velvet sofas and taste the cocktails you'll want to make this your favourite hangout. The staff are incredibly friendly by Parisian standards. There's a quirky selection of nibbles in tin cans – sardines, anyone? – and regular music nights (live gipsy jazz bands on Mondays; electro on Thursdays and Fridays). Highly recommended.

Dédé la Frite

135 rue Montmartre, 2nd (01.40.41.99.90). Mº Sentier or Bourse. **Open** 8am-2am Mon-Sat; 9am-2am Sun. **Map** p61 F2 🟢

Suits from the nearby Bourse flock here for after-work cocktails and beers, before giving in to the tempting aromas emanating from the kitchen: Dédé's frites at just €3 a tray are legendary and the rest of the American diner food (burgers, fries, ketchup on the bar) is an absolute bargain too. The place looks cool as well, with distressed walls, long bar and bright colours. After hours, when the alcohol flows and the munchies have been satisfied, the music is cranked up and the party really starts.

★ La Garde Robe

41 rue de l'Arbre-Sec, 1st (01.49.26.90.60). Mº Louvre Rivoli. **Open** 12.30-2.30pm, 6.30pm-midnight Mon-Fri; 6.30pm-midnight Sat. **Map** p61 F5 🟢

EXPLORE

EXPLORE

This tiny wine bar, where bottles line the walls like books in a library, is perfect for an end-of-the-day snifter, preferably accompanied by one of the platters of delicious parma ham, cheese or oysters. Organic and bio-dynamic wines stand their ground next to vintages from around the world.

O Château

68 rue Jean-Jacques Rousseau, 1st (01.44.73.97.80, www.o-chateau.com). M° Les Halles. **Open** 4pm-midnight Mon-Thur; 4pm-2am Fri, Sat. **Map** p61 F4 🔞
The food is great and the vibe convivial, but a night here is all about the wine. There are no less than 500 by the bottle and 40 by the glass, including the chance to taste some very rare and expensive bottles in *soupçon*-sized quantities thanks to high-tech wine-saving devices. Tastings take place in the intimate tasting rooms at 12.15pm daily.

Le Truskel

12 rue Feydeau, 2nd (01.40.26.59.97, www.truskel. com). M° Bourse. **Open** 6pm-5am Tue-Sat. Closed Aug. **Map** p61 E2 🔞
The formula is simple at this pub-cum-club: an excellent selection of beers slakes your thirst, while an extensive repertoire of Britpop – sometimes live (ex-Pulp man and Paris resident Jarvis Cocker has been known to splice the night here, as have Pete Doherty and Franz Ferdinand) – assaults your ears.

Zenzoo

13 rue Chabanais, 2nd (01.42.96.27.28, www.zen-zoo.com). M° Quatre-Septembre. **Open** noon-7pm Mon-Sat. **Map** p60 D3 🔞
Between 2.30pm and 7pm, this tiny Taiwanese restaurant doubles as a 'tea bar', one of the few places in Paris that serves China's famous tapioca cocktails – sometimes known as 'bubble tea', they are served with an extra-wide straw to suck up the little tapioca balls at the bottom. The sensation may seem strange at first, but the tastes are great; among the flavours are mango, coconut and kumquat. Up the road at no.2, a spin-off boutique sells excellent oolong flower teas.

Shops & Services

Legrand Filles et Fils

1 rue de la Banque, 2nd (01.42.60.07.12, www. caves-legrand.com). M° Bourse. **Open** 11am-7pm Mon; 10am-7.30pm Tue-Thur; 10.30am-8pm Fri; 10.30am-7.30pm Sat. Closed Mon in Aug. **Map** p61 E3 🔞 **Food & drink**
Fine wines and brandies, teas and *bonbons*, as well as a showroom for regular wine tastings.

Village Joué Club

3-5 bd des Italiens, 2nd (01.53.45.41.41, http://villageparis.joueclubdrive.fr). M° Richelieu Drouot. **Open** 10am-8pm Mon-Sat. **Map** p61 E2 🔞 **Children**

Village Joué Club, the largest toy store in Paris, is spread out in and around passage des Princes. There's even a children's hairdresser and a room for birthday parties.

OPERA & AROUND

In the 2nd, 8th & 9th arrondissements.

Charles Garnier's wedding-cake **Palais Garnier** is all gilt and grandeur, as an opera house should be. Garnier was also responsible for the ritzy **Café de la Paix** and the **InterContinental Paris Le Grand** (*see p341*) overlooking place de l'Opéra. Behind, in the basement of what is now the Hôtel Scribe, the Lumière brothers held the world's first public cinema screening in 1895. The **Olympia** concert hall (*see p275*), the celebrated host of the Beatles, Piaf and anyone in *chanson*, was knocked down, but rose again nearby. Over the road at no.35, pioneering portrait photographer Nadar opened a studio in the 1860s, frequented by the likes of Dumas *père*, Offenbach and Doré. In 1874, it hosted the first Impressionists' exhibition. Pedestrianised rue Edouard VII, laid out in 1911, leads to the octagonal square of the same name with Landowski's equestrian statue of the English monarch. Through an arch, another square contains the handsome belle époque Théâtre de l'Athénée-Louis Jouvet.

The **Eglise de la Madeleine**, a monument to Napoleon's Grand Army, stands guard at the end of the boulevard. At the head of rue Royale, its classical portico mirrors the Assemblée Nationale on the other side of place de la Concorde and over the river, and the interior is a riot of marble and altars. Well worth a quick browse is the wonderfully extravagant delicatessen **Fauchon** (24-26 place de la Madeleine) and other luxury food shops; here, too, is haute cuisine restaurant **Senderens**.

Sights & Museums

FREE Eglise de la Madeleine

Pl de la Madeleine, 8th (01.44.51.69.00, www.eglise-lamadeleine.com). M° Concorde or Madeleine. **Open** 9.30am-7pm daily. **Admission** free. **Map** p60 B2 🔞
The building of a church on this site began in 1764, and in 1806 Napoleon sent instructions from Poland for Barthélémy Vignon to design a 'Temple of Glory' dedicated to his Grand Army. After the emperor's fall, construction slowed and the building, by now a church again, was finally consecrated in 1845. The exterior is ringed by huge, fluted Corinthian columns, with a double row at the front, and a frieze of the Last Judgement just above the portico. Inside are giant domes, an organ and side altars in a sea of multicoloured marble.

FREE **Eglise St-Augustin**

46 bd Malesherbes, 8th (01.45.22.23.12, www.saintaugustin.net). M° St-Augustin. **Open** 8.30am-7pm Mon-Fri; 9am-12.30pm, 2.30-7.30pm Sat; 8.30am-12.30pm, 4-8pm Sun. **Admission** free. **Map** p60 A1 ❻❾

St-Augustin, designed between 1860 and 1871 by Victor Baltard, is not what it seems. The domed, neo-Renaissance stone exterior is merely a shell: inside is an iron vault structure; even the decorative angels are cast in metal. Impressive paintings by Adolphe William Bouguereau hang in the transept.

Musée de la Franc-Maçonnerie

16 rue Cadet, 9th (01.45.23.74.09, www.musee fm.org). M° Cadet. **Open** 10am-12.30pm, 2-6pm Tue-Fri; 10am-1pm, 2-7pm Sat. **Admission** €6; €4 reductions; free under-18s. **No credit cards.** **Map** p61 F1 ❾❶

Tucked away at the back of the French Masonic Great Lodge, the Musée de la Franc-Maçonnerie first opened in 1973. It traces the history of French freemasonry, ranging from detailed information on stonemasons' guilds to prints of masons General Lafayette and the 1848 revolutionary leaders Blanc and Barbès.

Musée de l'Opéra

Palais Garnier, 1 pl de l'Opéra, 9th (01.53.79.37.47, www.bnf.fr). M° Opéra. **Open** 10am-5pm Mon-Sat. **Admission** €7; €5 reductions; free under-18s. **No credit cards.** **Map** p60 C2 ❾❶

The Palais Garnier (*see also p283*) houses temporary exhibitions relating to current opera or ballet productions, along with a permanent collection of paintings, scores and bijou opera sets housed in delightful period cases.

FREE **Musées des Parfumeries-Fragonard**

9 rue Scribe, 9th (01.47.42.04.56, www.fragonard. com) & 39 bd des Capucines, 2nd (01.42.60.37.14, www.fragonard.com). M° Opéra. **Open** 9am-6pm Mon-Sat; 9am-5pm Sun (rue Scribe only). **Admission** free. **Map** p60 C2 ❾❷

The rue Scribe museum showcases the collection of perfume house Fragonard: five rooms range from Ancient Egyptian ointment flasks to Meissen scent bottles; the boulevard des Capucines museum has bottles by Lalique and Schiaparelli.

Restaurants

Drouant

18 pl Gaillon, 2nd (01.42.65.15.16, www.drouant. com). M° Pyramides or Quatre Septembre. **Open** noon-2.30pm, 7pm-midnight daily. **Main courses** €20-€49. **Prix fixe** *Lunch* €45 Mon-Fri. *Brunch* €36 Sat, Sun. *Dinner* (9.30pm-midnight) €47-€59. **Map** p60 D3 ❾❸ **Brasserie**

Chef Antoine Westermann has whisked this 1880 brasserie into the 21st century with bronze-coloured banquettes and butter-yellow fabrics. Westermann has dedicated this restaurant to the art of the hors d'oeuvre, served in themed sets ranging from global (Thai beef salad with brightly coloured vegetables, coriander, and a sweet and spicy sauce) to nostalgic (silky leeks in vinaigrette). The bite-sized surprises continue with the main course accompaniments.

Cafés & Bars

★ Café de la Paix

12 bd des Capucines, 9th (01.40.07.36.36, www. cafedelapaix.fr). M° Opéra. **Open** 8am-midnight daily. **Map** p60 C2 ❾❹

O Château.

EXPLORE

FAUCHON
P A R I S

26-30 place de la Madeleine - Paris 8ᵉ
www.fauchon.com

Lap up every detail – this is once-in-a-holiday stuff. Whether you're out on the historic terrace or looking up at the ornate stucco ceiling, you'll be sipping in the footsteps of the likes of Oscar Wilde, Josephine Baker, Emile Zola, and Bartholdi and the Franco-American Union (as they sketched out the Statue of Liberty). Let the immaculate staff bring you a kir or, for an afternoon treat, the vanilla millefeuille.

★ Harry's New York Bar

5 rue Daunou, 2nd (01.42.61.71.14, www. harrys-bar.fr). M° Opéra. **Open** noon-2am Mon-Thur, Sun; noon-3am Fri, Sat. **Map** p60 C3 ⓽⓹
The city's most stylish American bar is beloved of expats, visitors and hard-drinking Parisians (there are over 300 whiskies). The white-coated bartenders mix some of the most sophisticated cocktails in town, from the trademark bloody mary and white lady (both invented here, so they say) to the Pétrifiant, an aptly named elixir of half a dozen spirits splashed into a beer mug. They can also whip up personalised creations that will have you swooning in the downstairs piano bar, where Gershwin composed *An American in Paris.*

Shops & Services

Apple Store

12 rue Halévy, 9th (01.44.83.42.00, www.apple. com). M° Opéra. **Map** p60 D2 ⓽⓺ **Electronics & photography**
This store is located in a stunning belle époque former bank facing the Opéra Garnier. To fit in with such hallowed surroundings, Apple strayed from its standard store model, retaining the original carved wooden staircase, wrought-iron railings, marble columns and mosaic tile floor.
Other location Carrousel du Louvre, 99 rue de Rivoli, 1st (01.43.16.78.00).

★ Cartier

13 rue de la Paix, 2nd (01.58.18.23.00, www. cartier.com). M° Opéra. **Open** 11am-7pm Mon-Sat. **Map** p60 C2 ⓽⓻ **Accessories**
This iconic French jeweller and watchmaker has impressive landmark headquarters. Downstairs, pearls, panthers and the Trinity ring jostle for attention among historic pieces commissioned by crowned heads; the upper salons house perfumer Mathilde Laurent's bespoke scents.
Other locations throughout the city.

★ Lavinia

3 bd de la Madeleine, 1st (01.42.97.20.20, www. lavinia.fr). M° Madeleine. **Open** 10am-8.30pm Mon-Sat. **Map** p60 C2 ⓽⓽ **Food & drink**
Lavinia stocks a wonderfully broad selection of French vintages alongside many non-French wines; its glassed-in *cave* has everything from a 1961 Hermitage La Chapelle Paul Jaboulet Aîné at €26,872 to trendy and 'fragile' wines for under €10.

★ Repetto

22 rue de la Paix, 2nd (01.44.71.83.12, www. repetto.com). M° Opéra. **Open** 9.30am-7.30pm Mon-Sat. **Map** p60 D2 ⓽⓽ **Accessories**
This ballet shoe-maker struck gold when it decided to reissue its dance shoes with pavement soles. The prowly *ballerines* and showbiz dance boots in black, metallic and spangly finishes are fun, stylish and exceptionally comfortable. They are sold alongside the full range of real balletwear; you can try out your *pointes* on a red carpet with a *barre* if you really want to show off.
Other locations 51 rue des Francs Bourgeois, 4th (01.70.79.89.37); 51 rue du Four, 6th (01.45.44.98.65); 20 rue de Charonne, 11th (01.70.79.89.48); 36 rue de Passy, 16th (01.70.79.89.41).

Talents – Création Contemporaine

1bis rue Scribe, 9th (01.40.17.98.38, www. ateliersdart.com). M° Opéra. **Open** 11am-7pm Mon-Sat. **Map** p60 C2 ⓵⓪⓪ **Homewares**
This contemporary showroom for 70 creators affiliated to the craftworkers' federation Ateliers d'Art de France is a pure white space in which you'll find one-off designs in furniture, lighting, glass, ceramics and jewellery. If you want something made to measure they can put you in touch directly with the designers.
Other location 26 av Niel, 17th (01.44.40.22.80).

THE GRANDS BOULEVARDS

In the 2nd & 9th arrondissements.

Contrary to popular belief, the string of Grands Boulevards between Madeleine and République (des Italiens, Montmartre, Poissonnière, Bonne-Nouvelle, St-Denis, St-Martin) was not built by Baron Haussmann, but by Louis XIV in 1670, replacing the fortifications of King Philippe-Auguste's city wall. Their ramparts have left their traces in the strange changes of levels, with stairways climbing up to side streets at the eastern end. The boulevards burgeoned after the French Revolution, as residences, theatres and covered passages were put up on land taken from aristocrats and monasteries. To this day, they offer a glimpse of the city's divergent personalities – a stroll from Opéra to République runs from luxury shops via St-Denis prostitutes – and the phrase *théâtre des boulevards* is still used for lowbrow theatre. Between boulevard des Italiens and rue de Richelieu is place Boïeldieu and the **Opéra Comique** (*see p285*), where Bizet's *Carmen* had its première in 1875.

The 18th-century Hôtel d'Augny (6 rue Drouot), which is now the town hall of the ninth arrondissement, was once home to the infamous *bals des victimes*, where every guest had to have a relative who had lost his or her head to the guillotine. The **Hôtel Drouot** auction house

EXPLORE

FINISHING TOUCHES

The Louvre continues to improve.

The world's largest museum remains its most visited, with a remarkable 9.3 million visitors in 2014. The **Musée du Louvre** (*see p63*) is a city within the city, a vast, multi-level maze of galleries, passageways, staircases and escalators. It's famous for the artistic glories within, but the very fabric of the museum is a masterpiece in itself – or rather, a collection of masterpieces modified and added to from one century to another. And the additions and modifications continue into the present day, with the opening of a wonderful new two-storey Islamic Arts department beneath the Cour Visconti in late 2012; the 2014 return of the seminal, 2,200-year-old *Winged Victory of Samothrace* statue after a year's brush-up; and the franchising of the Louvre 'brand' via new outposts in Lens in northern France (*see p298*) and Abu Dhabi (scheduled to open in December 2015).

Much like the building itself, the Louvre's collections were built up over the centuries. They encompass a rich visual history of the western world, from Ancient Egypt and Mesopotamia to the 19th century. Indeed, one of the most impressive things about the Louvre is the way it juxtaposes architecture and content. Look up from a case of Greek or Roman antiquities and you might see an 18th-century painted ceiling, or two doves by Braque. In the Egyptian section you'll find Louis XIV's bedchamber, complete with his gilded bed, while Renaissance art is housed in the Grande Galerie, where the Sun King performed the 'scrofula ceremony', blessing the sick. In between exhibits, the Louvre's long windows afford stunning views of the building's façades, gardens and lovely interior courtyards.

Some 35,000 works of art and artefacts are on show, split into eight departments and housed in three wings: Denon, Sully and Richelieu. Under the atrium of the glass pyramid, which is itself undergoing a three-year revamp from 2015 – since IM Pei's creation was completed in 1989, visitor numbers have more than doubled – each wing has its own entrance, though you can pass from one to another. Treasures from the Egyptians, Etruscans, Greeks and Romans each have their own galleries in the Denon and Sully wings, as do Middle Eastern and Islamic art, now accommodated in a new space in the Cour Visconti. The first floor of Richelieu is taken up with European decorative arts from the Middle Ages up to the 19th century, including room after room of Napoleon III's lavish apartments.

Two glass-roofed sculpture courts contain the famous Marly horses on the ground floor of Richelieu, with French sculpture below and Italian Renaissance pieces in the Denon wing. Oh, and lest we forget, there's a painting by Leonardo da Vinci that attracts its fair share of attention – some 80 per cent of those nine million visitors are really only here to catch La Gioconda's eye.

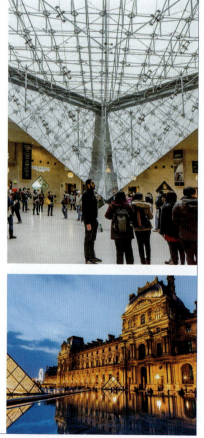

EXPLORE

is ringed by antiques shops, coin- and stamp-dealers and wine bar Les Caves Drouot. There are several grand *hôtels particuliers* on rue de la Grange-Batelière, which leads on one side down the curious passage Verdeau, occupied by a range of antiques dealers, and on the other back to the boulevards via passage Jouffroy. With its grand, barrel-vaulted glass-and-iron roof, this is home to the delightful **Hôtel Chopin** (*see p343*), shop windows of doll's houses, antique walking sticks, art books and film posters, and the colourful entrance of the **Grévin** waxworks (*see p244*).

Over the boulevard, passage des Panoramas is the oldest remaining covered arcade in Paris. When it opened in 1800, panoramas – vast illuminated circular paintings – of Rome, Jerusalem, London and other cities drew large crowds. Today, the passage contains a selection of coin- and stamp-sellers, furniture-makers and old-fashioned printers. It leads into a tangle of other little passages and the stage door of the **Théâtre des Variétés** (7 bd Montmartre, 2nd, 01.42.33.09.92, www.theatre-des-varietes.fr), a pretty neoclassical theatre where Offenbach premièred *La Belle Hélène*.

Rue du Fbg-Montmartre is home to celebrated belle époque *bouillon* **Chartier** (*see p243*), which serves up hundreds of meals a day to the budget-minded. The street is also part of a significant Jewish quarter, less well known than the Marais, that grew up in the 19th century. There are several kosher bakers and restaurants, and France's largest synagogue at 44 rue de la Victoire, an opulent Second Empire affair completed in 1876. Cobbled Cité Bergère, constructed in 1825 with desirable residences, now houses budget hotels, though the pretty iron-and-glass *portes-cochères* remain. On rue Richer stands the art deco **Folies-Bergère** (no.32, 9th, 08.92.68.16.50, www.foliesbergere.com), nowadays used for cabaret revues. To the south of boulevard Bonne-Nouvelle lies the **Sentier** district, and to the north rue du Fbg-Poissonnière is a mixture of rag-trade outlets and *hôtels particuliers*.

Back on the boulevard is evidence of a move north of the Marais by trendsetting hubs, including **Rex** (*see p268*). East of here are Louis XIV's twin triumphal arches, the **Porte St-Denis** and **Porte St-Martin**, which were erected to commemorate his military victories.

Sights & Museums

★ Grand Rex

1 bd Poissonnière, 2nd (www.legrandrex.com). M° Bonne Nouvelle. **Tour** *Les Etoiles du Rex* every 5mins 10am-7pm Wed-Sun; daily during school hols. **Admission** €11; €9 reductions. **Map** p61 G2 ⓛ

Opened in 1932, this huge art deco cinema (*see also p251*) was designed by Auguste Bluysen with fantasy Hispanic interiors by US designer John Eberson. Go behind the scenes in the crazy 50-minute Etoiles du Rex guided tour, which includes a presentation about the construction of the auditorium and a visit to the projection room.

Hôtel Drouot

9 rue Drouot, 9th (01.48.00.20.20, www.drouot.fr). M° Richelieu Drouot. **Open** 11am-6pm Mon-Sat. **Auctions** 2pm Mon-Sat. **Map** p61 E1 ⓛ

A spiky aluminium-and-marble concoction is the unlikely location for France's second largest art market. Inside, escalators take you up to a number of small salerooms, where everything from medieval manuscripts and antique furniture to oriental arts, modern paintings, posters, jewellery and fine wines might be up for sale. Details of forthcoming auctions are published in the weekly *Gazette de l'Hôtel Drouot*, sold at various newsstands around the city. Not as daunting as it might seem, an afternoon at Drouot can be great fun, even if you don't fancy spending. On the day before the auction (and on the morning itself), drool over the objects for sale, then come back for the show (usually 2pm). Anyone can take part; and you don't have to sign up beforehand. **Other location** Drouot-Montmartre, 64 rue Doudeauville, 18th (01.48.00.20.99).

FREE Porte St-Denis & Porte St-Martin

Rue St-Denis/bd St-Denis, 2nd; 33 bd St-Martin, 10th. M° Strasbourg St-Denis. **Map** p61 H2 ⓛ

These twin triumphal gates were erected in 1672 and 1674 at important entry points to the city as part of Colbert's strategy to glorify Paris and celebrate Louis XIV's victories on the Rhine. They are modelled on the triumphal arches of ancient Rome. The Porte St-Denis is based on a perfect square with a single arch, bearing Latin inscriptions and decorated with military trophies and battle scenes. Porte St-Martin bears allegorical reliefs of Louis XIV's campaigns.

Restaurants

Big Fernand

55 rue du Faubourg Poissonnière, 9th (01.73.70.51.52, www.bigfernand.com). M° Cadet or Poissonnière. **Open** noon-2.30pm, 7.30-10.30pm Mon-Sat. **Hamburgers** €11-€13. **Prix fixe** €14-€19. **Map** p61 G1 ⓛ **Burgers**

This trendy takeaway burger joint has been dubbed 'l'atelier du hamburger' – 'the hamburger workshop'. The concept is for customers to build their own burgers, selecting a combination of meat (beef, chicken, lamb or veal), cheese (goat's cheese, saint nectaire, tomme de savoie), grilled vegetables, spices and an array of sauces.

Other locations 40 pl du Marché St-Honoré, 1st (01.81.63.08.63); 32 rue du St-Sauveur, 2nd (09.67.22.40.06).

EXPLORE

Les Fils à Maman

7 bis Rue Geoffroy-Marie, 9th (01.48.24.59.39, www.lesfilsamaman.com). M° Grands Boulevards. **Open** noon-2.30pm, 7.30-11pm Mon-Fri; 7.30-11pm Sat. **Main courses** *Lunch* €13. *Dinner* €16-€21. **Prix fixe** *Lunch* €17-€21. **Map** p61 F1 **105 Bistro**
In the up-and-coming neighbourhood near the Folies Bergère a band of five 'mothers' boys' has created a restaurant evoking their mums' home cooking. Even the mums themselves get into the kitchen on the first Tuesday of the month to turn out *blanquette de veau*, chicken cordon bleu with beaufort cheese and Nutella-flavoured puddings. Whether or not you think Babybel has a place in Gallic cuisine, it's a chance to relive the school French exchange or 1980s après-ski in the company of an ebullient crowd.

Racines

8 passage des Panoramas, 2nd (01.40.13.06.41). M° Bourse or Bonne Nouvelle. **Open** noon-2.30pm, 8-10.30pm Mon-Fri. **Main courses** €21-€35. **Map** p61 F2 **106 Wine bar**
The 19th-century passage des Panoramas contains an eclectic collection of shops and restaurants – among them this wildly popular wine bar opened by the former owners of La Crèmerie in St-Germain-des-Prés. The menu is limited to superb-quality cheese and charcuterie plates, plus a couple of hot dishes, perhaps pork cheeks stewed in red wine or braised lamb, and a few comforting desserts. Many of the intense-tasting wines are biodynamic and, despite the rather hectic atmosphere, lingering over an extra glass or two is cheerfully tolerated.

Cafés & Bars

Le Brébant

32 bd Poissonnière, 9th (01.47.70.01.02, www.cafelebrebantparis.com). M° Grands Boulevards. **Open** 7.30am-6am daily. **Map** p61 F2 **107**
The change that continues to sweep the Grands Boulevards is embodied in this prominent, round-the-clock bar-bistro. There's a permanently busy terrace beneath a colourful, stripy awning, and the cavernous, split-level interior has a cool neo-industrial feel. Prices are steep, so push the boat out and opt for an expertly made fruit daiquiri, or a Bonne Nouvelle of Bombay Sapphire gin and Pisang Ambon. There are rarer bottled beers too – Monaco, Picon and sundry brews from Brabant. A board advertises a decent range of proper eats.

Shops & Services

Galeries Lafayette

40 bd Haussmann, 9th (01.42.82.34.56, Lafayette Gourmet 01.40.23.52.67, www.galerieslafayette. com). M° Chaussée d'Antin/RER Auber. **Open** 9.30am-8pm Mon-Wed, Fri, Sat; 9.30am-9pm Thur. *Lafayette Gourmet* 8.30am-9.30pm Mon-Sat. **Map** p60 D1 **108 Department store**

The store has been undergoing a massive renovation programme of late, with the opening of Espace Luxe on the first floor, featuring luxury prêt-à-porter and accessories, and the unveiling of a vast new shoe department in the basement featuring some 150 brands. The men's fashion space on the third floor, Lafayette Homme, has natty designer corners and a 'Club' area with internet access. On the first floor, Lafayette Gourmet has exotic foods galore, plus a vast wine cellar including its own Bordeauxthèque.
▶ *Lafayette Maison, over the road, has five floors of home furnishings and interior design products.*
Other location Centre Commercial Montparnasse, 22 rue du Départ, 14th (01.45.38.52.87).

★ Printemps

64 bd Haussmann, 9th (01.42.82.50.00, www. printemps.com). M° Havre Caumartin/RER Auber. **Open** 9.35am-8pm Mon-Wed, Fri, Sat; 9.35am-10pm Thur. **Map** p60 C1 **109 Department store**
In the magnificently appointed Printemps you'll find everything you didn't even know you wanted and English-speaking assistants to help you find it. But fashion is where it really excels; an entire floor is devoted to shoes, and the beauty department stocks more than 200 brands. In all, there are six floors of men's and women's fashion. In Printemps de la Mode, French designers sit alongside all the big international designers. The Fashion Loft offers a younger take on current trends. Along with furnishings, Printemps de la Maison stocks everything from tableware to design classics.
▶ *For fast refuelling, Printemps has a tearoom, sushi bar and Café Be, an Alain Ducasse bakery. Or head up to Le Déli-cieux, on the ninth floor of Printemps Maison, for a drink on the terrace.*
Other locations Carrousel du Louvre, 99 rue de Rivoli, 1st (01.76.77.41.00); Centre Commercial Italie 2, 30 av d'Italie, 13th (01.40.78.17.17); 21-25 cours de Vincennes, 20th (01.43.71.12.41).

LES HALLES & SENTIER

In the 1st & 2nd arrondissements.

For centuries, Les Halles was the city's wholesale food market. Covered markets were set up here in 1181 by King Philippe-Auguste; in the 1850s Baltard's spectacular cast-iron and glass pavilions were erected. In 1969, the market was relocated to the suburb of Rungis. Baltard's ten pavilions were knocked down (one was saved and now stands at Nogent-sur-Marne), leaving a giant hole. After a long political dispute, it was filled in the early 1980s by the miserable **Forum des Halles** underground mall and transport hub, and the unloved Jardin des Halles. The Forum is currently undergoing a vast makeover, with a new canopy, revamped park and completion date of 2016. If you want to check out the progress of this *grand projet*, visit www.forumdeshalles.com.

East of the Forum, in the middle of place Joachim-du-Bellay, stands the Renaissance **Fontaine des Innocents**. The canopied fountain has swirling stone reliefs of water nymphs and titans by Jean Goujon (the ones you see today are replicas; the originals are in the Louvre). It was inaugurated for Henri II's arrival in Paris in 1549 on the traditional royal route along rue St-Denis. It was moved and reconstructed here when the nearby Cimetière des Innocents, the city's main burial ground, was demolished in 1786, after flesh-eating rats started gnawing into people's living rooms; the bones were transferred to the catacombs.

Pedestrianised rue des Lombards is a beacon of live jazz, with **Sunset/Sunside** (*see p279*), **Baiser Salé** (*see p278*) and **Au Duc des Lombards** (*see p278*). In 1610, King Henri IV was assassinated by a Catholic fanatic named François Ravaillac on nearby rue de la Ferronnerie. Today, the street has become an extension of the Marais gay circuit.

The ancient, easternmost stretch of rue St-Honoré runs into the southern edge of Les Halles. The Fontaine du Trahoir stands at the corner with rue de l'Arbre-Sec. Opposite, the **Hôtel de Truden** (52 rue de l'Arbre-Sec) was built in 1717 for a rich wine merchant; in the courtyard on rue des Prouvaires, the market-traders' favourite **La Tour de Montlhéry** serves up meaty fare through the night. Fashion chains line the commercial stretch of the rue de Rivoli south of Les Halles. Running towards the Seine, ancient little streets such as rue des Lavandiers-Ste-Opportune and rue Jean-Lantier show a different side of Les Halles. Between rue de Rivoli and the Pont Neuf is former department store La Samaritaine, which is due to reopen in 2016 as luxury hotel Le Cheval Blanc.

Looming over the northern edge of the Jardin des Halles is the massive **Eglise St-Eustache**, with Renaissance motifs inside and chunky flying buttresses outside. At the western end of the gardens is the circular, domed **Bourse de Commerce**. In front of it, an astrological column is all that remains from a grand palace belonging to Marie de Médicis that stood here.

The empire of French designer **Agnès b** stretches along most of rue du Jour, with outlets such as **Kiliwatch** clustered along rue Tiquetonne. On rue Etienne-Marcel, the restored **Tour Jean Sans Peur** is a weird Gothic relic of the fortified medieval townhouse of Jean Sans Peur, duke of Burgundy.

Busy, pedestrianised rue Montorgueil is lined with grocers, delicatessens and cafés. Some historic façades remain from when this was an area in which the well-heeled and the working class mingled: **Pâtisserie Stohrer** (no.51, 2nd, 01.42.33.38.20, www.stohrer.fr), founded in 1730 and credited with the invention of the sugary

IN THE KNOW AND RELAX

Pioneer Swiss urban spa **After the Rain** (www.aftertherain.ch) makes a glorious retreat from the designer shopping stresses of nearby rue du Faubourg-St-Honoré. Signature massages include Honey Release and Aroma Stone Therapy, or enjoy a romantic massage *à deux* – it comes complete with rose petal bath, strawberries and champagne.

puits d'amour; and the golden snail sign in front of **L'Escargot Montorgueil** (no.38, 01.42.36.83.51), a restaurant established in 1832.

Stretching north, bordered by boulevard de Bonne-Nouvelle to the north and boulevard Sébastopol to the east, lies Sentier, the historic garment district, and cocky rue St-Denis, which has long relied on strumpets and strip joints. The grime is unremitting along its northern continuation, rue du Fbg-St-Denis.

Rue Réaumur is lined with striking art nouveau buildings. Between rue des Petits-Carreaux and rue St-Denis is the site of the medieval Cour des Miracles – a refuge where paupers would 'miraculously' regain use of their eyes or limbs. A disused aristocratic estate, it was a sanctuary for the underworld until it was cleared out in 1667.

Printemps.

EXPLORE

SWEET TREATS

The cream of the capital's neo-pâtisseries.

Within a few days of **Aux Merveilleux de Fred** opening its latest branch (2 rue Monge, 5th, www.auxmerveilleux.com), it had a queue of sweet-toothed foodies eager to try its *merveilleux* – a northern French combination of meringue, whipped cream and flakes of chocolate. Across the street, others lined up at **Ciel** (3 rue Monge, 5th, www.patisserie-ciel.com) to sample Japanese chef Aya Tamura's heavenly angel cakes. Both are part of the current craze for specialist pâtisseries and the success of the blogosphere that makes the right cake the latest fashion accessory.

There seem to be two main schools of cake thought. On one side are the inventors, creating new cakes and rethinking old ones. Cyril Lignac, France's equivalent of Jamie Oliver, recently opened his second **Pâtisserie Cyril Lignac** (2 rue de Chaillot, 16th, www.lapatisseriecyrillignac.com) in a boutique opposite the Palais Galliera, where you can try his takes on old classics such as tarte au citron and millefeuille, baked in the 'laboratory' in the cellar.

Then there are the 'monomaniacs', who take a single obsession to the extreme. The craze of the moment is choux-shaped, making macaroons look positively passé. Marais boutique **Popelini** (29 rue Debelleyme, 3rd, 01.44.61.31.44, www.popelini.com; *pictured*) sells round *choux à la crème* (profiteroles) and nothing but; Christophe Adam's **L'Eclair de Génie** (14 rue Pavée, 4th, 01.42.77.85.11, www.leclairdegenie.com) is devoted to the eclair in every colour;

L'Atelier de l'Eclair (16 rue Bauchaumont, 2nd, 01.42.36.40.54, www.latelierdeleclair.fr), serves eclairs topped with everything from salted butter caramel to lemon meringue, plus savoury sandwich eclairs such as curried chicken or smoked salmon; and Christophe Michalak has teamed up with Alain Ducasse and designer Patrick Jouin at **Choux d'Enfer** (Gare du Nord, 10th, 01.47.83.26.67), a kiosk where choux – Ducasse's 'memories of childhood' – are filled on the spot, as the craze for street food meets sweet food.

Sentier's streets buzz with porters shouldering linen bundles, as sweatshops churn out copies of catwalk creations. Streets such as rue du Caire, rue d'Aboukir and rue du Nil reflect the craze that followed Napoleon's Egyptian campaign in 1798 and 1799.

Sights & Museums

FREE Bourse de Commerce

2 rue de Viarmes, 1st (01.55.65.55.65).
M° Louvre Rivoli. **Open** *tour groups* 9am-6pm Mon-Fri. **Admission** free. **Map** p61 F4 ⑩
Housing the Paris chamber of commerce, this trade centre for coffee and sugar was built as a grain market in 1767. The circular building was then covered by a wooden dome, replaced by an avant-garde iron structure in 1809. In his 1831 novel

Notre-Dame de Paris, Victor Hugo summed up the building thus: '*Le dôme de la Halle-au-Blé est une casquette de jockey anglais sur une grande échelle.*'

FREE Eglise St-Eustache

Rue du Jour, 1st (01.42.36.31.05, www.saint-eustache.org). M° *Les Halles.* **Open** 9.30am-7pm Mon-Fri; 10am-7pm Sat; 9am-7pm Sun. **Admission** free. **Map** p61 F4 ⑪
This barn-like church, built between 1532 and 1640, has a Gothic structure but Renaissance decoration in its façade and Corinthian capitals. Among the paintings in the side chapels are a *Descent from the Cross* by Luca Giordano. *Photo p86.*

★ Tour Jean Sans Peur

20 rue Etienne-Marcel, 2nd (01.40.26.20.28, www.tourjeansanspeur.com). M° *Etienne Marcel.*

Open 1.30-6pm Wed-Sun. *Tour* 3pm Sat, Sun. **Admission** €5; €3 reductions; free under-7s. *Tour* €8. **No credit cards. Map** p61 G4 ⓬
This Gothic turret (1409-11) is the remnant of the townhouse of Jean Sans Peur, duke of Burgundy. He was responsible for the assassination of his rival Louis d'Orléans, which sparked the Hundred Years' War and saw Burgundy become allied to the English crown. You can climb the tower.

Restatants

L'Autobus Impérial
14 rue Mondétour, 1st (01.42.36.00.18, www. autobus-imperial.fr). Mº Les Halles. **Open** 11am-2am Mon; 11am-5am Fri, Sat. **Main courses** €18-€25. **Tapas** €8-€12. **Prix fixe** *Lunch* €15.50-€20. **Map** p61 G4 ⓭ **Brasserie**
Tucked away in a corner of Les Halles, L'Autobus Impérial is a hidden gem. The rather unattractive entrance does little justice to the superb art nouveau dining room, built in 1910 and boasting a listed glass ceiling. Food is traditional but inventive, and remains very reasonably priced. The bar has the longest zinc counter in Paris.

Blend
44 rue d'Argout, 2nd (01.40.26.84.57, www. blendhamburger.com). Mº Bourse or Sentier. **Open** noon-11pm daily. **Main courses** €10. **Prix fixe** *Lunch* €15 (noon-4pm Mon-Fri). **Map** p61 F3 ⓮ **Burgers**
Parisians are burger bonkers: after Camion qui Fume (www.lecamionquifume.com), Blend has opened its doors in the bobo quarters of Etienne Marcel. The secret is in the ingredients: made with hand-cut veal and beef mince, provided by star butcher Yves-Marie le Bourdonnec, burgers are succulent and flavoursome, and marry wonderfully with the fresh toppings (think bacon, bleu d'Auvergne cheese, spinach leaves, chorizo, mint and cheddar). The bread and fries (both potato and sweet potato) are also home-made.
Other locations 1 bd des Filles du Calvaire, 3rd (01.44.78.28.93); 3 rue Yves Toudic, 10th (01.42.45.47.26); 19 rue de Ménilmontant, 20th (01.42.52.96.50).

Chez Vong
10 rue de la Grande-Truanderie, 1st (01.40.26.09.36, www.chez-vong.com). Mº Etienne Marcel or Les Halles. **Open** noon-2.15pm, 7-11.15pm Mon-Sat. Closed 3wks Aug. **Main courses** €26-€34. **Prix fixe** *Lunch* €26.50. **Map** p61 G4 ⓯ **Chinese**
The staff at this cosy Chinese restaurant take pride in its excellent cooking. From the greeting at the door to the knowledgeable, trilingual service (Cantonese, Mandarin and French), each part of the experience is thoughtfully orchestrated. Any doubts about authenticity are extinguished with the arrival of the beautifully presented dishes. Expertly cooked spicy shrimp glistens in a smooth, characterful sauce of onions and ginger, and *ma po tofu* melts in the mouth, its spicy and peppery flavours melding with those of the fine pork mince.

★ Frenchie
5 rue du Nil, 2nd (01.40.39.96.19, www.frenchie-restaurant.com). Mº Sentier. **Open** 6.30-10pm Mon-Fri. **Main courses** €35-€40. **Prix fixe** €68. **Map** p61 G3 ⓰ **Bistro**
Grégory Marchand honed his craft with Jamie Oliver in London before opening this loft-style bistro next to the market street rue Montorgueil. It has been a huge hit thanks to the bold flavours of dishes such as crab with cape gooseberry; braised lamb with roasted aubergine and spinach; and wild blackberries with lime and hazelnut. Book several days ahead to secure a table.
▶ *Marchand also has a wine bar, Frenchie Bar à Vins (see p86), on the same street.*

Le Pharamond
24 rue de la Grande Truanderie, 1st (01.40.28.45.18, www.pharamond.fr). Mº Etienne Marcel. **Open** noon-3pm, 7-10.30pm daily. **Main courses** €17.50-€26.50. **Prix fixe** *Lunch* €15.90 (Mon-Fri), €29.90, €39.90. *Dinner* €29.90, €39.90. **Map** p61 G4 ⓱ **Brasserie**
There has been a restaurant on this site for well over a century and the interior is a joy to behold, with its carved wood panelling, elaborate tiling and stunning painted mirrors. The menu runs the gamut from *terrine de lapin* and *escargots* to *tripes à la mode de Caen* and *baba Normand au Calvados*. One thing's for sure – you won't be going home hungry.

Pirouette
5 rue Mondétour, 1st (01.40.26.47.81, www. oenolis.com). Mº Etienne Marcel. **Open** 12.30-2.30pm, 7.30-10.30pm Mon-Sat. **Main courses** €22-€32. **Prix fixe** *Lunch* €20. *Dinner* €42, €62. **Map** p61 G4 ⓲ **Bistro**
A restaurant called Pirouette suggests both deft manoeuvering and a dash of panache. Set in a secluded little courtyard behind Les Halles, the stage set for the meal is immediately promising. Starters might include *alouette sans tête* (headless lark), a fanciful name for a paupiette of pigeon and foie gras enriched with *lardo di Colonnata*. Mains are a triumph – a lovely piece of mullet with salsify and meat gravy, perhaps, or beautifully tender *pigeon royale* with a delicate foie gras sauce. All in all, a round of applause for the chef (Tommy Gousset, trained in some of the city's best kitchens), the excellent wine list, and the elegant, affordable whole.

★ La Tour de Montlhéry (Chez Denise)
5 rue des Prouvaires, 1st (01.42.36.21.82). Mº Les Halles/RER Châtelet Les Halles. **Open** noon-3pm, 7.30pm-5.30am Mon-Fri. Closed mid July-mid Aug. **Main courses** €25. **Map** p61 F5 ⓳ **Bistro**

EXPLORE

Eglise St-Eustache. *See p84*

At the stroke of midnight, this place is packed, jovial and hungry. Savoury traditional dishes, washed down by litres of the house Brouilly, are the order of the day. Les Halles was the city's wholesale food market, and game, beef and offal still rule here. Diners devour towering rib steaks served with marrow and a heaped platter of chips, among the best in town. Brave souls can also try the *tripes au calvados* or grilled *andouillette*, or perhaps go for a stewed venison with celery root and home-made jam.

Cafés & Bars

Le Ballroom du Beefclub
58 rue Jean-Jacques Rousseau, 1st (09.52.52.89.34). Mᵒ Les Halles. **Open** 7pm-2am Mon-Sat. **Map** p61 F4 ⑫⓪
You reach Le Ballroom, another venture from the trio behind the Experimental Cocktail Club, via an unmarked black door and down a spiral staircase beneath the Beefclub restaurant. Waistcoat-wearing bartenders serve up drinks and banter at the *comptoir*, or there are chesterfield sofas at candlelit tables for more intimacy. The drinks menu is on the pricey side, but the mixology delivers. If you get peckish, soak up the drinks with a plate of seafood, cold meats, cheese or even profiteroles. The eclectic playlist might feature rap, funk, soul or jazz.

Le Cochon à l'Oreille
15 rue Montmartre, 1st (01.42.36.07.56). Mᵒ Les Halles. **Open** 11am-2am. **Map** p61 F4 ⑫①
Some old bistros have the setting, others get the food. This place does a good job with both: the antique public telephone, the imposing zinc counter and the cosy wooden booths are charming reminders of Les Halles' heyday as the city's celebrated food market – note the tiles that depict scenes of the market in all its chaotic splendour. Food-wise, expect hearty

dishes like stuffed pork on a bed of lentils and *confit de canard*, best accompanied by one of the many wines on the list.

★ Frenchie Bar à Vins
6 rue du Nil, 2nd (01.40.39.96.19, www.frenchie-restaurant.com). Mᵒ Sentier. **Open** *Kitchen* 7-11pm Mon-Fri. *Bar* 7pm-2am daily. **Map** p61 G3 ⑫②
You'd be forgiven for suspecting that Frenchie Bar à Vins was opened merely as a solution to the near impossible problem of getting a table at Frenchie (*see p85*) across the street. But it has become a destination in its own right. The look is similar to the sister restaurant – exposed stone walls and bare lightbulbs suspended from copper tubing – but here there are no reservations. You simply turn up (early or after 10pm is easiest) and grab one of the stools grouped around the high communal tables. A similarly flexible approach applies to the food, with the choice of tucking into several courses or simply snacking on a starter or two. Wines range in price from a simple €20 Loire to a Mouton Rothschild 1998 that'll set you back more than €1,000. The list itself is curiously uninformative, although on-the-spot sommelier Aurélien Massay can offer guidance.

Le Lockwood
73 rue d'Aboukir, 2nd (01.77.32.97.21). Mᵒ Sentier. **Open** 8am-2am Mon-Sat. **Map** p61 F3 ⑫③
Tucked away on rue d'Aboukir, Lockwood's plain exterior and handwritten sign suggest another trendy New York-inspired bar with appropriately hipster staff. But this time, owners the Lehoux brothers (Silencio, Ten Belles) have added a twist to draw in the crowds: this is a whole new concept for Paris, open all day long and covering everything from coffee shop to cocktails. You can wake up with coffee from a Belleville roastery and one of the pastries sitting under glass domes. For a proper meal, there are

things like a sophisticated salad of beetroot, polenta and goat's cheese (€6.50). In the evenings, there's an Italian-style *aperitivo* with a free buffet, followed by drinks and dancing downstairs. Order a whisky cocktail and let the good times roll.

Le Tambour

*41 rue Montmartre, 2nd (01.42.33.06.90). M°
Sentier.* **Open** 8.30am-6am daily. **Map** p61 F4 **124**
Decked out with vintage transport paraphernalia, slatted wooden banquettes and bus stop-sign bar stools, the Tambour has a split personality: there's the daytime Tambour, frequented by pretty much everybody; and then there's the nighttime Tambour, a well-loved nighthawks' bar where the chatty regulars give the 24-hour clock their best shot.

Shops & Services

Agnès b

2, 3, 4 & 6 rue du Jour, 1st (men 01.42.33.04.13, women 01.45.08.56.56, www.agnesb.com). M° Les Halles. **Open** *Oct-Apr* 10am-7pm Mon-Sat. *May-Sept* 10.30am-7.30pm Mon-Fri; 10am-7.30pm Sat.
Map p61 F4 **125** Fashion
Agnès b rarely wavers from her design vision: pure lines in fine quality cotton, merino wool and silk. Her mini-empire of men's, women's, children's, travel and sportswear shops is compact.
Other locations throughout the city.

★ E Dehillerin

*18 rue Coquillière, 1st (01.42.36.53.13, www.
e-dehillerin.fr). M° Les Halles.* **Open** 9am-12.30pm, 2-6pm Mon; 9am-6pm Tue-Sat.
Map p61 F4 **126** Homewares
This no-nonsense warehouse stocks just about every kitchen utensil ever invented.

Fnac Forum

*Levels -1 to -3, Porte Lescot, Forum des Halles, 1st (08.25.02.00.20, www.fnac.com, ticket office www.
fnacspectacles.com). M° Les Halles.* **Open** 10am-8pm Mon-Sat. **Map** p61 F5 **127** Books & music
Fnac is a supermarket of culture: books, DVDs, CDs, audio kit, computers and photographic equipment. Most branches stock everything; others specialise. All branches operate as a concert box office.
Other locations throughout the city.

Forum des Halles

*Rue Pierre-Lescot & rue Rambuteau, 1st (01.44.76.96.56, www.forumdeshalles.com).
M° Les Halles/RER Châtelet Les Halles.* **Open** 10am-8pm Mon-Sat. **Map** p61 F5 **128** Mall
The Forum des Halles is Paris's least pleasant shopping mall, although a facelift due to be completed in 2016 should help. Extending three levels underground, it incorporates métro stations, multiplex, gym, swimming pool and numerous restaurants. High-street retailers dominate.

Kiliwatch

*64 rue Tiquetonne, 2nd (01.42.21.17.37, www.
espacekiliwatch.fr). M° Etienne Marcel.* **Open** 10.30am-7pm Mon; 10.30am-7.30pm Mon-Sat.
Map p61 F4 **129** Fashion
The trailblazer of the rue Etienne-Marcel revival is filled with hoodies, casual shirts and washed-out jeans. Brands such as Gas, Edwin and Pepe Jeans accompany pricey second-hand garb.

Kokon To Zai

*48 rue Tiquetonne, 2nd (01.42.36.92.41, www.
kokontozai.co.uk). M° Etienne Marcel.* **Open** 11.30am-7.30pm Mon-Sat. **Map** p61 G4 **130** Fashion
Always a spot-on spotter of the latest creations, this tiny style emporium is sister to the Kokon To Zai in London. The neon-lit club feel of the mirrored interior matches the dark glamour of the designs. Unique pieces straight off the catwalk share space with creations by Marjan Peijoski, Noki, Raf Simons, Ziad Ghanem and new Norwegian designers.

Monster Melodies

*9 rue des Déchargeurs, 1st (01.40.28.09.39, www.
monstermelodies.fr). M° Les Halles.* **Open** noon-7pm Mon-Sat. **Map** p61 F5 **131** Books & music
The owners are very willing to help you hunt down your treasured tracks – and with more than 10,000 second-hand CDs of every variety, that's just as well.

Pull-In Underwear

*13 rue de Turbigo, 2nd (01.40.39.93.64, www.
pull-in.com). M° Etienne Marcel.* **Open** 11am-1pm, 2-7.30pm Mon-Fri; 11am-7.30pm Sat.
Map p61 G4 **132** Accessories
Hailing from south-west France, Pull-In is the official underwear supplier to the French rugby team. The ultra-trendy brand makes swimwear, but its boxers in wacko patterns are *the* visible waistband for Gallic hip hoppers.
Other locations throughout the city.

Royal Cheese

22-24 rue Tiquetonne, 2nd (01.42.21.30.65, www.royalcheese.com). M° Etienne Marcel.
Open 11am-1pm, 2-8pm Mon-Fri; 11am-8pm Sat. **Map** p61 G4 **133** Fashion
Clubbers hit Royal Cheese to snaffle up hard-to-find imports: Stüssy, Cheap Monday and Lee for the boys; Insight, Sessun, Edwin and Lazy Oaf for the girls. Prices are hefty: Japanese jeans cost €200.
Other locations throughout the city.

Spa Nuxe

*32 rue Montorgueil, 1st (01.42.36.65.65, www.
nuxe.com). M° Les Halles.* **Open** 10am-9pm Mon-Fri; 9.30am-7.30pm Sat. **Map** p61 F4 **134**
Health & beauty
This day spa housed in stone vaults with wooden cabins and safari-style tents offers massages and skin treatments using Nuxe's plant-based products.

EXPLORE

Champs-Elysées & Western Paris

There seems to be an unwritten law in France that no mention of the capital's most famous thoroughfare can be made without calling it '*la plus belle avenue du monde*'. In truth, it's not that beautiful and it heaves with cars, crowds and overpriced restaurants. The hordes aren't here for beauty, though. They're here for the shops, which the avenue supplies in abundance. Fortunately, in the midst of all this are museums covering such topics as architecture, life on the ocean waves and fashion through the ages (natch), plus a greatly extended Palais de Tokyo and the dramatic new Fondation Louis Vuitton. And come late 2015, two revamped museums – the Musée de l'Homme and the Musée Jean-Jacques Henner – will also be back on the cultural map.

Palais de Tokyo.

Don't Miss

1 Arc de Triomphe Head to the top for one of the best views in the city (p90).

2 Palais de Tokyo Tripled in size and still pushing the boundaries (p96).

3 Fondation Louis Vuitton Come for the building, stay for the art (p107).

4 Lazare This station brasserie is worth missing the train for (p105).

5 Ladurée Indulge in hot chocolate heaven (p99).

CHAMPS-ELYSEES

In the 8th, 16th & 17th arrondissements.

The Champs-Elysées is, and has long been, a symbolic gathering place. Sports victories, New Year's Eve, displays of military might on 14 July – all are celebrated here. Over the past decade, the avenue has undergone a renaissance, thanks initially to a facelift instigated by Jacques Chirac.

Chi-chi shops and chic hotels have set up in the 'golden triangle' (avenues George V, Montaigne and the Champs): **Louis Vuitton**, **Dior** and **Balenciaga**, the **Marriott** (70 av des Champs-Elysées, 8th, 01.53.93.55.00) and **Pershing Hall** (*see p347*). The **Four Seasons George V** (*see p345*) has undergone a revamp, and fashionable restaurants draw affluent and screamingly fashionable diners. Crowds line up for the glitzy **Le Lido** cabaret (*see p270*), the now commercialised **Queen** nightclub (*see p268*) and numerous cinemas, or stroll down the avenue to floodlit place de la Concorde. The famous **Drugstore Publicis** is where locals head to stock up on late-night wines and groceries.

This great spine of western Paris started life as an extension to the Tuileries, laid out by Le Nôtre in the 17th century. By the Revolution, the avenue had reached its full extent, but it was during the Second Empire that it became a focus for fashionable society, military parades and royal processions.

The lower, landscaped reach of the avenue hides two theatres and elegant restaurants **Laurent** (41 av Gabriel, 8th, 01.42.25.00.39, www.le-laurent.com) and **Pavillon Ledoyen** (1 av Dutuit, 8th, 01.53.05.10.01, www.yannick-alleno.com), housed in fancy Napoleon III pavilions. Ledoyen is enjoying a new lease of life after Yannick Alléno took over in 2014, winning a third Michelin star in 2015. At the Rond-Point des Champs-Elysées, no.7 (now the Artcurial gallery bookshop and auction house) and no.9 give visitors some idea of the magnificent mansions that once lined the avenue. From here on, it's platinum cards and lanky women aplenty, as avenue Montaigne rolls out a full deck of fashion houses.

Models and magnates nibble on the terrace at fashionable restaurant **L'Avenue** (no.41, 8th, 01.40.70.14.91, www.avenue-restaurant.com). You can admire the lavish **Hôtel Plaza Athénée** (*see p347*) and Auguste Perret's innovative 1911-13 **Théâtre des Champs-Elysées** concert hall (*see p285*), with an auditorium painted by Maurice Denis.

South of the avenue, the glass-domed **Grand Palais** and Petit Palais, both built for the 1900 Exposition Universelle and still used for major art exhibitions, create a magnificent vista across the Pont Alexandre III to Les Invalides. The rear

wing of the Grand Palais, opening on to avenue Franklin-D-Roosevelt, contains the **Palais de la Découverte** science museum.

To the north lie more smart shops, antiques dealers and bastions of officialdom; on circular place Beauvau, wrought-iron gates herald the Ministry of the Interior. The 18th-century Palais de l'Elysée, the official presidential residence, is at 55-57 rue du Fbg-St-Honoré. Nearby, with gardens extending to avenue Gabriel, are the palatial **British Embassy** and ambassadorial residence, which was once the Hôtel Borghèse.

The western end of the Champs-Elysées is dominated by the **Arc de Triomphe** towering above place Charles-de-Gaulle, also known as L'Etoile. Built by Napoleon, the arch was modified to celebrate the Revolutionary armies. From the top, visitors can gaze over the square (commissioned later by Haussmann), with 12 avenues radiating out in all directions.

South of the arch, avenue Kléber leads to the monumental buildings and terraced gardens of the panoramic Trocadéro, now housing the aquarium and cinema, **Cinéaqua**. The vast 1930s **Palais de Chaillot** dominates the hill and houses four museums, plus the **Théâtre National de Chaillot** (*see p287*).

To the west of Chaillot, along avenue du Président-Wilson, are two of the capital's major museums: the **Musée d'Art Moderne de la Ville de Paris** and the **Palais de Tokyo: Site de Création Contemporaine** are both inside the **Palais de Tokyo** building. Opposite is the newly revamped **Palais Galliera**, and up the hill at place d'Iéna are the Asian and oriental art collections of the **Musée National des Arts Asiatiques – Guimet**.

Towards the Champs-Elysées, the former townhouse of avant-garde patron Marie-Laure de Noailles has been given a cheeky revamp. It now houses the **Galerie-Musée Baccarat**.

Sights & Museums

★ Arc de Triomphe
Pl Charles-de-Gaulle (access via underpass), 8th (01.55.37.73.77). M° Charles de Gaulle Etoile. **Open** *Oct-Mar* 10am-10.30pm daily.

IN THE KNOW
CHAMPS-ELYSEES

Bismarck was so impressed with the Champs-Elysées when he arrived with the conquering Prussian army in 1871 that he had a replica, the Ku'damm, built in Berlin, and Hitler's troops made a point of marching down it in 1940, as did their Allied counterparts four years later.

EXPLORE

Apr-Sept 10am-11pm daily. **Admission** €9.50; €6 reductions; free under-18s, under-26s (EU citizens). PMP. **Map** p92 C3 ❶

The Arc de Triomphe is the city's second most iconic monument after the Eiffel Tower – older, shorter, but far more symbolically important: indeed, the island on which it stands, in the centre of the vast traffic junction of l'Etoile, is the nearest thing to sacred ground in all of secular France, indelibly associated as it is with two of French history's greatest men – Napoleon and Charles de Gaulle. Despite such grand associations, until recently the interior of the Arc was far less impressive, having changed little since the 1930s. But now, after a revamp by architect Christophe Girault and artist Maurice Benayouna, there is an impressive museum with interactive screens allowing visitors to look at other famous arches throughout Europe and the world, as well as displays exploring the Arc's tumultuous 200-year history. But the main reason to head up here is the rooftop view, one of the finest in the city.

★ Chapelle Expiatoire

29 rue Pasquier, 8th (01.44.32.18.00). M° St-Augustin. **Open** times vary; call in advance. **Admission** €5.50; €4 reductions; free under-18s, under-26s (EU citizens). PMP. **Map** p92 C6 ❷

The chapel was commissioned by Louis XVIII in memory of his executed predecessors, his brother Louis XVI and Marie-Antoinette. Their remains, along with those of 3,000 victims of the Revolution, including Camille Desmoulins, Danton, Malesherbes and Lavoisier, were found in 1814 on the spot where the altar stands. The bodies of Louis XVI and Marie-Antoinette were transferred the following year to the Basilique St-Denis; the pair are now represented by marble statues, kneeling at the feet of Religion. Every January, ardent (albeit unfulfilled) royalists gather here for a memorial service.

FREE Cimetière de Passy

2 rue du Commandant-Schloesing, 16th (01.53.70.40.80). M° Trocadéro. **Open** *16 Mar-5 Nov* 8am-6pm Mon-Fri; 8.30am-6pm Sat; 9am-6pm Sun. *6 Nov-15 Mar* 8am-5.30pm Mon-Fri; 8.30am-5.30pm Sat; 9am-5.30pm Sun. **Admission** free. **Map** p93 E2 ❸

Since 1874, this cemetery has been one of the most desirable Paris locations in which to be laid to rest. Here you'll find Debussy and Fauré, Manet and his sister-in-law Berthe Morisot, and writer Giraudoux, along with various generals and politicians.

★ Cinéaqua

2 av des Nations Unies, 16th (01.40.69.23.23, www.cineaqua.com). M° Trocadéro. **Open** 10am-7pm daily. **Admission** €20.50; €13-€16 reductions; free under-3s. **Map** p93 F2 ❹

This aquarium and three-screen cinema is a wonderful attraction and was a key element in the renaissance of the once moribund Trocadéro. Children in particular love the shark tunnel and the petting pool (*bassin de caresses*) where you can stroke the friendly sturgeon. Also interesting (though less theatrical) is the section on the River Seine, showing the sorts of fish that still survive in Paris's river despite the pollution. Some people baulk at the admission fee, but you can easily spend a long afternoon here, watching cartoons in the cinemas and observing the sealife. On Wednesdays and weekends, there are special children's shows too. Perfect for a rainy day in the capital.

EXPLORE

Arc de Triomphe.

EXPLORE

EXPLORE

Cité de l'Architecture et du Patrimoine.

EXPLORE

★ Cité de l'Architecture et du Patrimoine

Palais de Chaillot, 1 pl du Trocadéro, 16th (01.58.51.52.00, www.citechaillot.fr). Mº Trocadéro. **Open** 11am-7pm Mon, Wed, Fri-Sun; 11am-9pm Thur. **Admission** €8; €6 reductions; free under-18s, under-26s (EU citizens). **Map** p93 E2 ❺

This architecture and heritage museum impresses principally by its scale. The expansive ground floor is filled with life-size mock-ups of cathedral façades and heritage buildings, and interactive screens place the models in context. Upstairs, darkened rooms house full-scale copies of medieval and Renaissance murals and stained-glass windows. The highlight of the modern architecture section is the walk-in replica of an apartment from Le Corbusier's Cité Radieuse in Marseille. Temporary exhibitions are housed in the large basement area.

FREE Fondation d'Entreprise Paul Ricard

12 rue Boissy d'Anglas, 8th (01.53.30.88.00, www.fondation-entreprise-ricard.com). Mº Concorde. **Open** 11am-7pm Tue-Sat. **Admission** free. **Map** p92 D6 ❻

The pastis firm promotes modern art with the Prix Paul Ricard – young French artists are shortlisted by an independent curator for an annual prize.

▶ *The Prix Paul Ricard coincides with the FIAC art fair (www.fiac.com) each autumn.*

Fondation Pierre Bergé Yves Saint Laurent

3 rue Léonce-Reynaud, 16th (01.44.31.64.31, www.fondation-pb-ysl.net). Mº Alma Marceau.

Open 11am-6pm Tue-Sun (only during exhibitions). **Admission** €7; €5 reductions; free under-10s. **Map** p93 E3 ❼

When the late Yves Saint Laurent bowed out of designing in 2002, he reopened his fashion house as this foundation, exhibiting Picasso and Warhol paintings with the dresses they closely inspired. Every sketch and every *toile* has been carefully catalogued, and many of Saint Laurent's friends and clients presented the designer with the dresses he created for them. The foundation stages two or three exhibitions every year.

★ Galerie-Musée Baccarat

11 pl des Etats-Unis, 16th (01.40.22.11.00, www. baccarat.fr). Mº Boissière or Iéna. **Open** 10am-6pm Mon, Wed-Sat. **Admission** €7; €5 reductions; free under-18s. **Map** p92 D3 ❽

Philippe Starck has created a neo-rococo wonderland in the former mansion of the Vicomtesse de Noailles. From the red-carpet entrance with a chandelier in a fish tank to the Alchemy room, decorated by Gérard Garouste, there's a play of light and movement that makes Baccarat's work sing. See items by designers Georges Chevalier and Ettore Sottsass, services made for princes and maharajahs, and monumental items made for the great exhibitions of the 1800s.

▶ *If you want to eat at the opulent Le Cristal Room restaurant (01.40.22.11.10), be sure to book.*

Galeries Nationales du Grand Palais

3 av du Général-Eisenhower, 8th (01.44.13.17.17, www.grandpalais.fr). Mº Champs-Elysées Clemenceau. **Open** times vary. **Admission** prices vary. **Map** p92 D5 ❾

Built for the 1900 Exposition Universelle, the Grand Palais was the work of three different architects, each of whom designed a façade. During World War II it accommodated Nazi tanks. In 1994, the magnificent glass-roofed central hall was closed when bits of metal started falling off. After major restoration, the Palais reopened in 2005. The space hosts blockbuster exhibitions, including a major Jean Paul Gaultier retrospective in 2015.

Mona Bismarck American Center for Art & Culture

34 av de New-York, 16th (01.47.23.38.88, www.monabismarck.org). M° Alma Marceau. **Open** 11am-6pm Wed-Sun. Closed Aug. **Admission** prices vary. **Map** p93 E3 ❿

The Mona Bismarck Foundation supports this Paris cultural centre set in Countess Bismarck's former townhouse across the Seine from the Eiffel Tower. The Foundation puts on an eclectic programme – a 2014 exhibition celebrated the work of comic book artist Alex Ross.

FREE Musée d'Art Moderne de la Ville de Paris

11 av du Président-Wilson, 16th (01.53.67.40.00, www.mam.paris.fr). M° Alma Marceau or Iéna. **Open** 10am-6pm Tue-Sun. **Admission** free. *Temporary exhibitions* €5-€12; €2.50-€5.50 reductions; free under-18s. **No credit cards**. **Map** p93 E3 ⓫

This monumental 1930s building, housing the city's modern art collection, features painting, sculpture, installation, photography and video. The museum is particularly strong on the Cubists, Fauves, Delaunays, Rouault and Ecole de Paris artists Soutine and van Dongen.

Musée de la Contrefaçon

16 rue de la Faisanderie, 16th (01.56.26.14.03, www.musee-contrefacon.com). M° Porte Dauphine. **Open** 2-5.30pm Tue-Sun. **Admission** €6; €5 reductions; free under-12s. **No credit cards**. **Map** p92 D1 ⓬

This museum was set up by the French anti-counterfeiting association with the aim of deterring forgers – but playing spot-the-fake with such brands as Reebok, Lacoste and Vuitton is fun for visitors.

Musée Dapper

35bis rue Paul-Valéry, 16th (01.45.00.91.75, www.dapper.com.fr). M° Victor Hugo. **Open** 11am-7pm Mon, Wed, Fri-Sun. **Admission** €6; €4 reductions; free under-26s, all last Wed of mth. **Map** p92 D2 ⓭

Named after the 17th-century Dutch humanist Olfert Dapper, the Fondation Dapper began life as an organisation dedicated to preserving sub-Saharan art. Reopened in 2000, the venue created by architect Alain Moatti houses a performance space, bookshop and café.

★ Musée National des Arts Asiatiques – Guimet

6 pl d'Iéna, 16th (01.56.52.53.00, www.guimet.fr). M° Iéna. **Open** 10am-6pm Mon, Wed-Sun. **Admission** €7.50; €5.50 reductions; free under-18s, under-26s (EU citizens). PMP. **Map** p93 E3 ⓮

Founded by the industrialist Emile Guimet in 1889 to house his collection of Chinese and Japanese religious art, and later incorporating oriental collections from the Louvre, this museum features 45,000 objects from neolithic times onwards. Lower galleries focus on India and South-east Asia, centred on stunning Hindu and Buddhist Khmer sculpture from Cambodia. Don't miss the Giant's Way, part of the entrance to a temple complex at Angkor Wat. Upstairs, Chinese antiquities include a collection of mysterious jade discs. Afghan glassware and Moghul jewellery also feature.

Musée National de la Marine

Palais de Chaillot, 17 pl du Trocadéro, 16th (01.53.65.69.69, www.musee-marine.fr). M° Trocadéro. **Open** 11am-6pm Mon, Wed-Fri; 11am-7pm Sat, Sun. **Admission** *Main collection & temporary exhibitions* €10; €2-€8 reductions. *Main collection* €8.50; €6 reductions; free under-18s, under-26s (EU citizens). PMP. **Map** p93 E2 ⓯

Four centuries of French naval history are outlined in detailed models of battleships and Vernet's series of paintings of French ports (1754-65). There's also an imperial barge, built when Napoleon's delusions of grandeur were reaching their zenith in 1810.

FREE Palais de Chaillot

Pl du Trocadéro, 16th. M° Trocadéro. **Admission** free. **Map** p93 E2 ⓰

This immense pseudo-classical building was constructed by Azéma, Boileau and Carlu for the 1937 international exhibition, with giant sculptures of Apollo by Henri Bouchard, and inscriptions by Paul Valéry. The Palais houses the Musée National de la Marine and the Musée de l'Homme (closed for renovation until October 2015). In the east wing are the Théâtre National de Chaillot (*see p287*) and the Cité de l'Architecture et du Patrimoine (*see p94*).

★ Palais de la Découverte

Av Franklin-D.-Roosevelt, 8th (01.56.43.20.21, www.palais-decouverte.fr). M° Champs-Elysées Clemenceau or Franklin D. Roosevelt. **Open** 9.30am-6pm Tue-Sat; 10am-7pm Sun (last entry 30mins before closing). **Admission** €9; €7 reductions; free under-6s. *Planetarium* €3 supplement. **Map** p93 E5 ⓱

This science museum houses designs dating from Leonardo da Vinci's time to the present. Models, real apparatus and audio-visual material bring displays to life, and permanent exhibits cover astrophysics, astronomy, biology, chemistry, physics and earth sciences. The Planète Terre section highlights meteorology, and one room is dedicated to the sun.

EXPLORE

Palais Galliera – Musée de la Mode

10 av Pierre 1er de Serbie, 16th (01.56.52.86.00, www.palaisgalliera.paris.fr). M° Alma Marceau or Iéna. **Open** 10am-6pm Tue, Wed, Fri-Sun; 10am-9pm Thur. **Admission** varies. **Map** p93 E3 ⑱

Since the reopening of the Palais Galliera, it's been hard to decide whether to be more impressed by the building or the clothes on show inside. This extraordinary mock-Renaissance folly, as only the 19th century knew how to do them, has been brought back to its full glory of Pompeian red walls, black woodwork, mosaic floors and vaulted ceilings painted with grotesqueries and arabesques. As before, the Galliera is dedicated solely to temporary exhibitions – due to the fragility of the fabrics, clothes can only be exhibited for four months at a time under strictly controlled lighting – but the shows manage to provide a decent glimpse of the Palais' incredibly rich collection, which stretches from late 17th-century period costume, via the birth of haute couture, to the creators of today.

Palais de Tokyo: Site de Création Contemporaine

13 av du Président-Wilson, 16th (01.81.97.35.88, www.palaisdetokyo.com). M° Alma Marceau or Iéna. **Open** noon-midnight Mon, Wed-Sun. **Admission** €10; €8 reductions; free under-18s. **Map** p93 E3 ⑲

Paris's most happening major art space since it opened in 2002, the Palais de Tokyo has now virtually tripled in size to become the largest contemporary art centre in Europe. The organisation is known for its highly international approach, and for blurring boundaries between art, music, science and politics – as well as for its artist-designed Tokyo Eat restaurant and Black Block shop. Architects Lacaton & Vassal, who transformed the 1937 building in 2002, employing a deliberately raw, distressed style (as much for budget reasons as aesthetics), have now tackled the vast remaining spaces, many of them unused for over 30 years.

Pinacothèque

28 place de la Madeleine, 8th (01.42.68.02.01, www. pinacotheque.com). M° Madeleine. **Open** 10.30am-6.30pm Mon, Thur, Sat, Sun; 10.30am-8.30pm Wed, Fri. **Admission** prices vary. **Map** p92 D6 ⑳

At place de la Madeleine, every square metre of real estate is so sought after that you'd never think there'd be room for a large museum. So imagine Paris's surprise when Crédit Agricole turned its office block into the Pinacothèque – an art museum dedicated to expression through the ages, displaying a steadily rotating series of exhibitions focusing on everything from archaeological finds to modern art. Roy Lichtenstein, Goya and Jackson Pollock have all had retrospectives.

Restaurants

Alain Ducasse au Plaza Athénée

Hôtel Plaza Athénée, 25 av Montaigne, 8th (01.53.67.65.00, www.alain-ducasse.com). M° Alma Marceau. **Open** 7.30-10.15pm Mon-Wed; 12.45-2.15pm, 7.30-10.15pm Thur, Fri. Closed late July-late Aug & 1wk Dec. **Main courses** €85-€195. **Prix fixe** €380. **Map** p93 E4 ㉑ Haute cuisine

The sheer glamour factor would be enough to recommend this restaurant, Alain Ducasse's most lofty Paris undertaking, whose ceiling drips with 10,000 crystals. The restaurant reopened in 2014 after renovations and now offers a virtually meat-free menu, championing fish, vegetables and cereals. Cheese is predictably delicious, as is the *citron niçois* to finish. All of this luxury indulgence doesn't come cheap, of course, but haute doesn't get more haute.

Le Bistrot Napolitain

18 av Franklin D. Roosevelt, 8th (01.45.62.08.37). M° St-Philippe-du-Roule. **Open** noon-2.30pm, 7-10.30pm Mon-Fri. Closed late July-early Sept & 24 Dec-3 Jan. **Main courses** €20-€45. **Map** p92 D4 ㉒ Italian

Palais de Tokyo.

Alain Ducasse au Plaza Athénée.

This chic Italian bistro is about as far from a tourist joint as it is possible to be. At lunchtimes, it is full of suave Italianate businessmen. Generosity defines the food – not just big plates, but lashings of the ingredients that others skimp on, such as the slices of tangy parmesan piled high over rocket on the tender beef carpaccio. The pizzas are very good: the Enzo comes with milky, almost raw *mozzarella di bufala* and tasty tomatoes. For pasta you can choose between dried and fresh, with variations such as fresh saffron tagliatelle.

★ Granterroirs
30 rue de Miromesnil, 8th (01.47.42.18.18, www. granterroirs.com). M° Miromesnil. **Open** 9am-5pm Mon-Fri (lunch noon-3pm). Closed 2wks Aug. **Main courses** €17-€25. **Map** p92 C5 **㉒ Bistro**
This *épicerie* with a difference is the perfect remedy for anyone for whom the word 'terroir' conjures up visions of grease-soaked peasant food. Here, the walls heave with more than 600 enticing specialities from southern France, including Périgord foie gras, charcuterie from Aubrac and a fine selection of wines. All of them make excellent gift ideas – but why not sample some of the goodies by enjoying the midday *table d'hôte* feast? Come in early to ensure that you can choose from the five *plats du jour* on offer (such as marinated salmon with dill on a bed of warm potatoes).

€ Le Hide
10 rue du Général-Lanrezac, 17th (01.45.74.15.81, www.lehide.fr). M° Charles de Gaulle Etoile. **Open** 6pm-midnight Mon-Sat. **Main courses** €19-€25. **Prix fixe** €27, €35. **Map** p92 C3 **㉔ Bistro**
This snug bistro is packed with a happy crowd of bistro-lovers who appreciate Japanese-born chef Hide Kobayashi's superb cooking and good-value prices. Expect such dishes as duck foie gras terrine with pear-and-thyme compôte to start, followed by tender *faux-filet* steak in a light foie gras sauce or skate wing with a lemon-accented *beurre noisette*. Desserts are excellent: perfect tarte tatin comes with crème fraîche from Normandy. Good, affordable wines explain the merriment.

Lasserre
17 av Franklin-Roosevelt, 8th (01.43.59.02.13, www.restaurant-lasserre.com). M° Franklin D. Roosevelt. **Open** 7-10pm Tue, Wed, Sat; noon-2pm, 7-10pm Thur, Fri. **Main courses** €85-€220. **Prix fixe** *Lunch* €90, €120, €220. *Dinner* €220. **Map** p93 E4 **㉕ Haute cuisine**
Lasserre's rich history is definitely a part of the dining experience: Audrey Hepburn, André Malraux and Salvador Dali were regulars. But its illustrious past is nothing next to the food: chef Christophe Moret (ex-Plaza Athénée) and his pastry chef Claire Heitzler (ex-Ritz) create lip-smacking delicacies

to die for. The upstairs dining room, accessed by a bellboy-operated lift, is a sumptuous affair in taupe and white, with solid silver table decorations and a retractable roof that opens just enough for you to see the stars at night.

Miss Kô

49 av George V, 8th (01.53.67.84.60, www. miss-ko.com). Mº George V. **Open** noon-2am daily. **Main courses** €18-€32. **Prix fixe** *Lunch* €24. **Map** p92 D3 **26 Chinese**

Philippe Starck's latest venture is set up to look like a narrow Chinatown street, bustling and colourful at night with open kitchens at the end where chefs work away beneath an array of suspended woks and neon lights. There are a dozen dishes, of which the star is beef tataki – a sort of carpaccio with teriyaki sauce, shiitake mushrooms and purée perfumed with ginger. The 'black salmon & Kô' burger is equally alluring, the bread coloured black with squid ink and garnished with avocado, mizuna, gravlax and tempura-fried green beans. For lighter meals, the creative sushi (gyoza with foie gras, perhaps) go perfectly with a cocktail or bubble tea. The bar and terrace are suitably hip.

Pierre Gagnaire

6 rue Balzac, 8th (01.58.36.12.50, www.pierre-gagnaire.com). Mº Charles de Gaulle Etoile or George V. **Open** noon-1.30pm, 7.30-9.30pm Mon-Fri. Closed 3wks Aug. **Main courses** €130-€180. **Prix fixe** *Lunch* €150, €295. *Dinner* €295. **Map** p92 C4 **27 Haute cuisine**

At Pierre Gagnaire the prix fixe starts at a staggering €150, which seems to be the price of culinary experimentation these days. This cheaper lunch menu is far from the full-blown experience of the *carte*: the former is presented in three courses, whereas the latter involves four or five plates for each course. Even the amuse-bouches fill the table: an egg 'raviole', ricotta with apple, fish in a cauliflower jelly, and glazed monkfish. The best thing about the lunch menu is that it includes four very indulgent desserts: clementine, raspberry and vanilla, chocolate, and passion fruit.

Rech

62 av des Ternes, 17th (01.45.72.29.47, www. restaurant-rech.fr). Mº Ternes. **Open** noon-2pm, 7.30-10pm Tue-Sat. Closed Aug & 1wk Dec. **Main courses** €39-€68. **Prix fixe** *Lunch* €44, €76. *Dinner* €54, €76. **Map** p92 B3 **28 Bistro**

Alain Ducasse's personal touches are everywhere in this art deco seafood restaurant, from the Japanese fish prints on the walls of the upstairs dining room to the blown-glass candleholders on the main-floor tables. The kitchen turns out the kind of precise, Mediterranean-inspired cooking you would expect from Ducasse: glistening sardine fillets marinated with preserved lemon, silky lobster ravioli, and octopus carpaccio painted with pesto. As the fish

Miss Kô.

dishes are light, you can almost justify indulging in a perfectly aged camembert and the XL éclair, which is an event in itself.

★ Restaurant L'Entredgeu

83 rue Laugier, 17th (01.40.54.97.24). Mº Porte de Champerret. **Open** noon-2pm, 7.30-10pm Tue-Sat. Closed 2wks mid Aug & 1wk Dec. **Prix fixe** *Lunch* €26, €36. *Dinner* €36. **Map** p92 B3 **29 Bistro**

Reading the menu here will make you seriously doubt your capacity for pudding. But have no fear. The heartiness of the dishes belies refined, perfectly gauged cooking, served in civilised portions. The table turnover is fast, but this is not a place to linger smoochily in any case – you'll be too busy marvelling at the sharp *gribiche* sauce cutting through the milky crisp-battered oysters, the depth and aroma of the saffron-infused fish soup, the perfect layered execution of the caramelised pork belly, and the delicate desserts. The wine list is creative and assured.

Roca

31 rue Guillaume Tell, 17th (01.47.64.86.04, www.rocaparis.com). Mº Pereire or Porte de Champerret. **Open** noon-2.30pm, 7.30-10.30pm Mon-Fri. **Main courses** €21-€26. **Prix fixe** *Lunch* €19. **Map** p92 B3 **30 Bistro**

This neo-bistro is a real find. The menu is fairly short (four each of starters, mains and desserts) but varied enough to hold your attention: a ceviche of pollack with beetroot, black sesame mousse and orange caramel to start, perhaps, followed by topside of veal with salsify, ginger, spinach and a curry sauce. The cooking is simple, creative and elegant, executed with real charm. Finish with a pumpkin cake with cream cheese, whisky-flavoured caramel and lemon confit, a delicately sweet final note to a memorable and affordable meal.

La Table Lauriston

129 rue de Lauriston, 16th (01.47.27.00.07, www. restaurantlatablelauriston.com). M° Trocadéro. **Open** noon-2.30pm, 7-10.30pm Mon-Fri; 7- 10.30pm Sat. Closed Aug. **Main courses** €21-€44. **Prix fixe** *Lunch* €28. **Map** p93 E2 ③ **Bistro**

Serge Barbey's dining room has a refreshingly feminine touch. The emphasis here is firmly on good-quality ingredients, skilfully prepared to show off their freshness. In spring, stalks of asparagus from the Landes are expertly trimmed to avoid any trace of stringiness and delightfully served with the simplest *vinaigrette d'herbes.* More extravagant is the *foie gras cuit au torchon,* in which the duck liver is wrapped in a cloth and poached in a bouillon. Skip the crème brûlée, which you could have anywhere, and order a dessert with attitude instead: the giant *baba au rhum.*

Taillevent

15 rue Lamennais, 8th (01.44.95.15.01, www. taillevent.com). M° George V. **Open** 12.15-1.30pm, 7.15-9.30pm Mon-Fri. Closed 25 July-25 Aug. **Main courses** €54-€240. **Prix fixe** *Lunch* €88, €104, €218, €350. *Dinner* €218, €350. **Map** p92 C4 ③ **Haute cuisine**

Prices here are not quite as shocking as in some restaurants at this level; for instance, there's an €88 lunch menu. *Rémoulade de coquilles St-Jacques* is a technical feat, with slices of raw, marinated scallop wrapped in a tube shape around a finely diced apple filling, encircled by a mayonnaise-like rémoulade sauce. An earthier and lip-smacking dish is the signature *épeautre* – an ancient wheat – which is cooked 'like a risotto' with bone marrow, black truffle, whipped cream and parmesan, and topped with sautéed frogs' legs. *Ravioli au chocolat araguani* is a surprising and wonderful dessert. Men must wear a jacket.

Cafés & Bars

Charlie Birdy

124 rue La Boétie, 8th (01.42.25.18.06, www. charliebirdy.com). M° Franklin D. Roosevelt. **Open** noon-2am daily. **Map** p92 D4 ③

Take a New York loft and meld it with a colonial English gentleman's club and you're looking at Charlie Birdy – a large 'pub' with a live music programme of jazz, soul and funk that's worth listening to. If you're in a hurry, stay away – the service can be irritatingly slow. But if you take your time choosing from the 50-strong cocktail menu, sink into a comfy chesterfield and let the evening wash over you, it'll be worth it. Between 4pm and 8pm Monday to Friday, cocktails are half-price.

Le Dada

12 av des Ternes, 17th (01.43.80.60.12). M° Ternes. **Open** 6am-2am Mon-Sat; 6am- 9pm Sun. **Map** p92 C3 ③

Perhaps the hippest café in this stuffy part of town, Le Dada is best known for its well-placed, sunny terrace. Inside, the wood-block carved tables and red walls provide a warm atmosphere for a crowd that tends towards the well-heeled, well-spoken and, well, loaded. That said, the atmosphere is friendly; if terracing is your thing, you could happily spend a summer's day here – just remember to bring along your Prada shades.

★ Ladurée

75 av des Champs-Elysées, 8th (01.40.75.08.75, www.laduree.fr). M° George V or Franklin D. Roosevelt. **Open** 7.30am-11.30pm Mon-Thur; 7.30am-12.30am Fri; 8.30am-12.30am Sat; 8.30am-11.30pm Sun. **Map** p92 D4 ③

Decadence permeates this elegant tearoom, from the 19th century-style interior and service to the labyrinthine corridors that lead to the toilets. While you bask in the warm glow of bygone wealth, indulge in tea, pastries (the pistachio pain au chocolat is heavenly) and, above all, the hot chocolate. It's a rich, bitter, velvety tar that will leave you in the requisite stupor for any lazy afternoon.

▶ *The original branch at 16 rue Royale (8th, 01.42.60.21.79) is famed for its macaroons.* **Other branches** 21 rue Bonaparte, 6th (01.44.07.64.87).

Sir Winston

5 rue de Presbourg, 16th (01.40.67.17.37, www.sirwinston.fr). M° Charles de Gaulle Etoile. **Open** 9am-2am Mon-Sat; noon-2am Sun. **Map** p92 D3 ③

A bit of an anomaly, this. Grand and imperial, with a bit of Baroque thrown in for good measure, and located within sight of high-end glitz, Sir Winston does a nice line in jazz and gospel brunches on a Sunday. Colonial knick-knacks, chesterfields and chandeliers make up the decor, with Winnie himself framed behind a sturdy bar counter. A battalion of whiskies stands guard beside him, and the wine list is equally *recherché.*

Shops & Services

Abercrombie & Fitch

23 av des Champs-Elysées, 8th (08.05.11.15.59, www.abercrombie.com). M° Franklin D. Roosevelt. **Open** 10am-8pm Mon-Sat; 11am-7pm Sun. **Map** p92 D4 ③ **Fashion**

The US brand's store has been causing a stir on the Champs since it opened, with banging tunes and topless male models in the doorway. As at its sister stores in London and New York, the box-hedged garden, dimmed lighting and scent of aftershave make the place feel more like a club than a shop.

EXPLORE

EXPLORE

★ Alléosse
*13 rue Poncelet, 17th (01.46.22.50.45, www.
fromage-alleosse.com). M° Ternes.* **Open**
9am-1.15pm, 3-7.15pm Tue-Fri; 9am-7pm Sat;
9am-1pm Sun. **Map** p92 B3 ❸ **Food & drink**
People cross town for these cheeses – wonderful
farmhouse camemberts, delicate st-marcellins, a
choice of *chèvres* and several rarities.

★ Balenciaga
*10 av George V, 8th (01.47.20.21.11, www.
balenciaga.com). M° Alma Marceau.* **Open**
10am-7pm Mon-Sat. **Map** p93 E4 ❸ **Fashion**
With Alexander Wang now at the helm, the Spanish
fashion house is ahead of Japanese and Belgian
designers in the hip stakes. Floating fabrics contrast
with dramatic cuts, producing a sophisticated urban
style. Bags and shoes are also available.

Balmain
*44 rue François 1er, 8th (01.47.20.57.58, www.
balmain.com). M° George V.* **Open** 10.30am-7pm
Mon-Sat. **Map** p92 D4 ❹ **Fashion**
A large portrait of the late Pierre Balmain surveys
the scene at his eponymous shop. What would he
have made of the clothes around him? Long gone
are the afternoon dresses with perfectly positioned
waists, full skirts and trapezoidal necklines. While
the clothes are still astonishingly expensive and
exquisitely finished, the racks are these days lined
with studded jackets and animal print drainpipes.

Les Caves Augé
*116 bd Haussmann, 8th (01.45.22.16.97,
www.cavesauge.com). M° St-Augustin.* **Open**
10am-7.30pm Mon-Sat. Closed Mon in Aug.
Map p92 C5 ❹ **Food & drink**
Les Caves Augé is the oldest wine shop in Paris –
Marcel Proust was a regular customer – and offers a
serious and professional service.

Les Caves Taillevent
*228 rue du Fbg-St-Honoré, 8th (01.45.61.14.09,
www.taillevent.com). M° Charles de Gaulle Etoile
or Ternes.* **Open** 10am-7.30pm Mon-Sat. Closed
1st 3wks Aug. **Map** p92 C4 ❹ **Food & drink**
Choose from a vast range of wines at this boutique
arm of the smart Taillevent restaurant. Sommeliers
are on hand to help you choose.

Comme des Garçons
*54 rue du Fbg-St-Honoré, 8th (01.53.30.27.27,
www.comme-des-garcons.com). M° Concorde.* **Open**
11am-7pm Mon-Sat. **Map** p92 D5 ❹ **Fashion**
Rei Kawakubo's design ideas and revolutionary
mix of materials have heavily influenced fashions
of the past two decades, and are showcased in this
fibreglass store.
▶ *Comme des Garçons Parfums (23 pl du Marché-
St-Honoré, 1st, 01.47.03.15.03) provides a
futuristic setting for the brand's fragrances.*

Dior
*26-30 av Montaigne, 8th (01.40.73.73.73,
www.dior.com). M° Franklin D. Roosevelt.* **Open**
10am-7pm Mon-Sat. **Map** p92 D4 ❷ **Fashion**
The Dior universe is here on avenue Montaigne,
from the main prêt-à-porter store and jewellery,
menswear and eyewear to Baby Dior.
Other locations throughout the city.

Drugstore Publicis
*133 av des Champs-Elysées, 8th (01.44.43.79.00,
www.publicisdrugstore.com). M° Charles de Gaulle
Etoile.* **Open** 8am-2am Mon-Fri; 10am-2am Sat,
Sun. **Map** p92 D3 ❹ **Department store**
A 1960s legend, Drugstore Publicis was clad with
neon swirls following a renovation a few years ago; a
glass-and-steel café stretches out on to the pavement.
On the ground floor there's a newsagent, pharmacy,
bookshop and upmarket deli full of quality olive
oils and elegant biscuits. The basement is a macho
take on Colette, keeping selected design items and
lifestyle magazines, and replacing high fashion with
fine wines and a cigar cellar.

Erès
*2 rue Tronchet, 8th (01.47.42.28.82, www.
eres.fr). M° Madeleine.* **Open** 10am-7pm
Mon-Sat. **Map** p92 D6 ❹ **Fashion**
Erès's beautifully cut swimwear has embraced a
sexy '60s look complete with buttons on the low-
cut briefs. The top and bottom can be purchased in
different sizes or you can buy one piece of a bikini.
Other locations throughout the city.

Fauchon
*24-26 & 30 pl de la Madeleine, 8th (01.70.39.38.00,
www.fauchon.com). M° Madeleine.* **Open** *Nos.24-
26* 8.30am-8.30pm Mon-Sat. *No.30* 9am-8pm Mon-
Sat. **Map** p92 D6 ❹ **Food & drink**
The city's most famous food shop is worth a visit,
particularly for the beautifully packaged gift items
and the stunning pastries and cakes – or, as Fauchon
likes to call them, *'le snacking chic'.*

Givenchy
*28 rue du Fbg-St-Honoré, 8th (01.42.68.31.00,
www.givenchy.com). M° Madeleine.* **Open**
10.30am-7pm Mon-Sat. **Map** p92 D6 ❹ **Fashion**
A few years ago, Givenchy opened this handsome
flagship store for men's and women's prêt-à-porter
and accessories. It incorporates surreal rooms
within rooms – cut-out boxes lined with white, black
or mahogany panelling – providing an art gallery
setting for Givenchy's cutting-edge, sculptural and
monochrome designs.

Glup's
*84 av des Champs-Elysées, 8th (01.42.89.84.11,
www.glups.fr). M° George V.* **Open** 11am-11.45pm
Mon, Fri; 10am-11.45pm Tue-Thur, Sat, Sun.
Map p92 D4 ❹ **Food & drink**

With 33 stores in France, Glup's is the brash younger sibling to the charming, wood-panelled village *confiserie*. Among the 250 kinds of candy sold in help-yourself dispensers are fizzy Smurfs, sugar-speckled Eiffel Towers, kilos of jelly beans, giant spider gummies, chocolate marshmallows and Magnificat milk caramels wrapped in gold paper.

Guerlain

68 av des Champs-Elysées, 8th (01.45.62.52.57, www.guerlain.com). M° Franklin D. Roosevelt.
Open 10.30am-8pm Mon-Sat; noon-7pm Sun.
Map p92 D4 ⑤ Health & beauty
The golden oldie of luxury beauty products and scents is looking as ravishing as ever. Head to the first floor to get the full measure of the history behind the house that created the mythic Samsara, Mitsouko and L'Heure Bleue.
Other locations 29 rue de Sèvres, 6th (01.42.22.46.60); 66 bd du Montparnasse, 15th (01.43.20.95.40); 93 rue de Passy, 16th (01.42.88.41.62).

★ Hédiard

21 pl de la Madeleine, 8th (01.43.12.88.88, www.hediard.fr). M° Madeleine. **Open** 9am-8pm Mon-Sat. **Map** p92 D6 ㉛ Food & drink
Hédiard's charming shop dates back to 1880, when it introduced exotic foods to Paris, specialising in rare teas and coffees, spices, jams and candied fruits.
Other locations throughout the city.

Hugo Boss

115 av des Champs-Elysées, 8th (01.53.57.35.40, www.hugoboss.com). M° George V. **Open** 10.30am-8pm Mon-Sat; 11am-6.30pm Sun. **Map** p92 D3 ㉜ Fashion

Hugo Boss's flagship store is all straight lines and steely greys – rather like the signature Boss suits worn by the sales assistants. Big screens flash images of Hugo Boss catwalk shows – inspiration for your shopping as you browse the minimalist rows of the brand's smart designer garb. Boss has various other outlets dotted around town, but this is its biggest store.
Other locations throughout the city.

★ Jabugo Ibérico & Co

11 rue Clément-Marot, 8th (01.47.20.03.13, www.bellota-bellota.com). M° Franklin D. Roosevelt. **Open** 10am-9.30pm Mon-Sat.
Map p92 D4 ㉝ Food & drink
Spanish hams here have the Bellota-Bellota label, meaning that the pigs have been allowed to feast on acorns. Manager Philippe Poulachon compares his cured hams to the delicacy of truffles.
► *Restaurant Bellota-Bellota (18 rue Jean-Nicot, 7th, 01.53.59.96.96) also sells hams at its adjoining épicerie.*

Lanvin

22 rue du Fbg St-Honoré, 8th (01.44.71.31.73, www.lanvin.com). M° Concorde or Madeleine. **Open** 10.30am-7pm Mon-Sat. **Map** p92 D6
㉞ Fashion
The couture house that began in the 1920s with Jeanne Lanvin has been reinvented by the talented and indefatigable Albert Elbaz. In October 2007, he unveiled this, the revamped showroom that set new aesthetic standards for luxury fashion retailing, incorporating original furniture from the Lanvin archive that has been restored. All this would be nothing, of course, if the clothes were not exquisite.

EXPLORE

Guerlain.

EXPLORE

LE66

66 av des Champs-Elysées, 8th (01.53.53.33.80, www.le66.fr). M° George V. **Open** *11.30am-8.30pm Mon-Sat; 1-8pm Sun.* **Map** *p92 D4* 🟣 **Fashion**
This fashion concept store is youthful and accessible, with an ever-changing selection of hip brands. Assistants, who are also the buyers and designers, make for a motivated team. The shop takes the form of three transparent modules.

Longchamp

77 av des Champs-Elysées, 8th (01.53.76.27.76, www.longchamp.com). M° George V. **Open** *10am-8pm Mon-Sat; 11am-7pm Sun.* **Map** *p92 D4* 🟣 **Accessories**
French accessories label Longchamp's bags are a staple of leathery luxury. Head to this new flagship store to choose from luggage, hangbags, wallets and other accoutrements in classic designs, all in an atmosphere of utter elegance.
Other locations 404 rue Saint Honoré, 1st (01.43.16.00.16); 21 rue du Vieux Colombier, 6th (01.42.22.74.75).

★ Louis Vuitton

101 av des Champs-Elysées, 8th (01.53.57.52.00, www.louisvuitton.fr). M° George V. **Open** *10am-8pm Mon-Sat; 11am-7pm Sun.* **Map** *p92 D3* 🟣 **Fashion**
The 'Promenade' flagship sets the tone for Vuitton's global image, from the 'bag bar', bookstore and jewellery department to the women's and men's ready-to-wear. Contemporary art, videos by Tim White Sobieski and a pitch-black elevator by Olafur Eliasson complete the picture. Accessed by lift, the Espace Vuitton hosts temporary art exhibits – but the star of the show is the view over Paris.
Other locations throughout the city.

Marché Président-Wilson

Av Président-Wilson, 16th. M° Alma-Marceau or Iéna. **Open** *7am-2.30pm Wed; 7am-3pm Sat.* **Map** *p92 E3* 🟣 **Market**
A classy market attracting the city's top chefs, who snap up ancient vegetable varieties.

Marks & Spencer

100 av des Champs-Elysées & 1 rue de Berri, 8th (01.56.69.19.20, www.marksandspencer.fr). M° George V. **Open** *10am-9pm daily.* **Map** *p92 D4* 🟣 **Department store**
Marks opened its new Paris store in late 2011. While most French people love nothing more than criticising British food, give them an M&S chicken tikka sarnie and the superlatives flow like wine from a barrel. They're also secret admirers of British fashion, and M&S offers cuts, colours and fabrics not readily available in France.

Nauti Store

30 av de la Grande Armée, 17th (01.43.80.28.28, www.nautistore.fr). M° Argentine. **Open** *10am-7pm Mon-Sat.* **Map** *p92 C2* 🟣 **Accessories**
This shop stocks a vast range of sailing clothes and shoes from labels such as Helly Hansen, Musto, Aigle and Sebago.

Paul Smith

3 rue du Fbg-St-Honoré, 8th (01.42.68.27.10, www.paulsmith.co.uk). M° Concorde. **Open** *10.30am-7pm Mon-Sat.* **Map** *p92 D6* 🟣 **Fashion**
A 'so British' atmosphere is cultivated with '40s wallpaper, antiques, old books and bric-a-brac, much of it for sale along with the colourful shirts and knitwear in which Smith excels. Collections for men, women and children, plus eyewear and accessories, are all gathered in this elegant apartment.

Longchamp.

Louis Vuitton.

Other locations 32 rue de Grenelle, 6th (01.44.39.00.40); 22-24 bd Raspail, 7th (01.53.63.08.74).

Prada
10 av Montaigne, 8th (01.53.23.99.40, www.prada.com). M° Alma Marceau. **Open** 10am-7pm Mon-Sat. **Map** p92 E4 ⓬ **Fashion**
Miuccia Prada's elegant stores pull in fashionistas of all ages. Handbags of choice are complemented by the coveted ready-to-wear range.
Other locations 5 rue de Grenelle, 6th (01.45.48.53.14); 6 rue du Fbg-St-Honoré, 8th (01.58.18.63.30).

Roger Vivier
29 rue du Fbg-St-Honoré, 8th (01.53.43.00.85, www.rogervivier.com). M° Madeleine. **Open** 11am-7pm Mon-Sat. **Map** p92 D6 ⓭ **Accessories**
The fashion editors' (late) shoeman of choice, Vivier is credited with inventing the stiletto.

Sephora
70-72 av des Champs-Elysées, 8th (01.53.93.22.50, www.sephora.fr). M° Franklin D. Roosevelt. **Open** 10am-8pm daily. **Map** p92 D4 ⓮ **Health & beauty**
Founded in 1969, the Sephora chain has more than 750 shops around the globe. The Champs-Elysées flagship houses 12,000 brands of scent and slap.
Other locations throughout the city.

MONCEAU & BATIGNOLLES

In the 8th & 17th arrondissements.

Parc Monceau, with its wonderful neo-antique follies and large lily pond, lies at the far end of avenue Hoche (the main entrance, a circular pavilion by Ledoux, is on boulevard de Courcelles). Three museums capture the extravagance of the area when it was newly fashionable in the 19th century: the **Musée Jacquemart-André**, with its Old Masters,

the **Musée Nissim de Camondo** (superb 18th-century decorative arts), and the **Musée Cernuschi** (Chinese art). There are some nice exotic touches too, such as the red lacquer **Galerie Ching Tsai Too** (48 rue de Courcelles, 8th), built in 1926 for a dealer in oriental art near the wrought-iron gates of Parc Monceau, and the onion domes of the Russian Orthodox **Alexander Nevsky Cathedral** on rue Daru. Built in the mid 19th century, when a stay in Paris was essential to the education of every Russian aristocrat, it is still very much at the heart of an émigré little Russia.

The Quartier des Batignolles to the north-east towards place de Clichy was more working-class, housing the rue de Lévis market, tenements lining the deep railway canyon and square des Batignolles park, with the pretty Eglise Ste-Marie-de-Batignolles.

Sights & Museums

★ FREE Alexander Nevsky Cathedral
12 rue Daru, 8th (01.42.27.37.34, www.cathedrale-orthodoxe.com). M° Courcelles. **Open** times vary. **Admission** free. **Map** p92 C4 ⓯
All onion domes, icons and incense, this Russian Orthodox church was completed in 1861 in the neo-Byzantine Novgorod style of the 1600s by the tsar's architect Kouzmin, who was also responsible for the Fine Arts Academy in St Petersburg. *Photo p104.*

FREE Cimetière des Batignolles
8 rue St-Just, 17th (01.53.06.38.68). M° Porte de Clichy. **Open** *16 Mar-6 Nov* 8am-5.45pm Mon-Fri; 8.30am-5.45pm Sat; 9am-5.45pm Sun & public hols. *7 Nov-15 Mar* 8am-5.15pm Mon-Fri; 8.30am-5.15pm Sat; 9am-5.15pm Sun & public hols. **Admission** free. **Map** p92 A5 ⓰
Squeezed inside the Périphérique are the graves of poet Paul Verlaine, Surrealist André Breton, and Léon Bakst, costume designer of the Ballets Russes.

EXPLORE

★ FREE Musée Cernuschi

7 av Vélasquez, 8th (01.53.96.21.50, www. cernuschi.paris.fr). M° Monceau or Villiers. **Open** 10am-6pm Tue-Sun. **Admission** free. *Temporary exhibitions* €4-€11; €2-€8 reductions; free under-18s. **Map** p92 B5 ⑥⑦

Since the banker Henri Cernuschi built a *hôtel particulier* by the Parc Monceau for the treasures he found in the Far East in 1871, this collection of Chinese art has grown steadily. The fabulous displays range from legions of Han and Wei dynasty funeral statues to refined Tang celadon wares.

★ Musée Jacquemart-André

158 bd Haussmann, 8th (01.45.62.11.59, www. musee-jacquemart-andre.com). M° Miromesnil or St-Philippe-du-Roule. **Open** 10am-6pm daily (late opening Mon & Sat until 8.30pm during exhibitions). **Admission** €12; €10 reductions; free under-7s. **Map** p92 C4 ⑥⑧

Long terrace steps and a pair of handsome stone lions usher visitors into this grand 19th-century mansion, home to a collection of *objets d'art* and fine paintings. The collection was assembled by Edouard André and his artist wife Nélie Jacquemart, using money inherited from his rich banking family. The mansion was built to order to house their art hoard, which includes Rembrandts, Tiepolo frescoes and various paintings by Italian masters Uccello, Mantegna and Carpaccio.

▶ *The adjacent tearoom (open 11.45am-5.30pm daily) is a favourite with the smart lunch set.*

★ Musée National Jean-Jacques Henner

43 av de Villiers, 17th (01.47.63.42.73, www. musee-henner.fr). M° Malesherbes. **Map** p92 B4 ⑥⑨

The Musée National Jean-Jacques Henner traces the life of one of France's most respected artists, from his humble beginnings in Alsace in 1829 to his rise as one of the most sought-after painters in Paris. On the first floor, Alsatian landscapes and family portraits are a reminder of the artist's lifelong attachment to his native region. What brought Henner most acclaim (and criticism), however, was his trademark nymph paintings. The museum is closed until November 2015 for renovations.

Musée Nissim de Camondo

63 rue de Monceau, 8th (01.53.89.06.50, www. lesartsdecoratifs.fr). M° Monceau or Villiers. **Open** 10am-5.30pm Wed-Sun. **Admission** €9; €6.50 reductions; free under-18s, under-26s (EU citizens). PMP. **Map** p92 C5 ⑦⓪

Put together by Count Moïse de Camondo, this collection is named after his son Nissim, who was killed in World War I. Moïse replaced the family's two houses near Parc Monceau with this palatial residence and lived here in a style perfectly in keeping with his love of the 18th century. Grand first-floor reception rooms are filled with furniture

Alexander Nevsky Cathedral. *See p103.*

by craftsmen of the Louis XV and XVI eras, Sèvres and Meissen porcelain, Savonnerie carpets and Aubusson tapestries.

FREE Parc Monceau

Bd de Courcelles, av Hoche, rue Monceau, 8th. M° Monceau. **Open** *Nov-Mar* 7am-8pm daily. *Apr-Oct* 7am-10pm daily. **Admission** free. **Map** p92 B4 ⑦①

Surrounded by grand *hôtels particuliers* and elegant Haussmannian apartments, Monceau is a favourite with well-dressed children and their nannies. It was laid out in the 18th century for the Duc de Chartres in the English style, with a lake, lawns and a variety of follies: an Egyptian pyramid, a Corinthian colonnade, a Venetian bridge and sarcophagi.

Restaurants

Atao

86 rue Lemercier, 17th (01.46.27.81.12). M° La Fourche. **Open** noon-2pm, 7-10pm Tue-Sun. **Main courses** €18-€47. **Map** p92 A5 ⑦② **Seafood**

Atao looks like a dream of a fisherman's cabin – marine blue on the outside, then wood, white and colourful touches inside, with an old mariner's portrait, an anchor and a black-and-white flag. At night, soft candlelight enhances the atmosphere even further. This pretty place is owned by the daughter of an oyster farmer from Morbihan, who serves up platters of fine oysters – flat native *plates* and huge Japanese *creuses* (alive and cooked). Main dishes – fish stew, dorado with basil, scallop carpaccio – are pricey but worth every cent.

Bar à Sushi Izimi

55 bd des Batignolles, 8th (01.45.22.43.55, www. lebarasushi.com). M° Villiers. **Open** noon-2.30pm,

7.30-10pm Tue-Sat. **Main courses** €4.50-€30. **Prix fixe** *Lunch* €11-€19.50. *Dinner* €17-€90. **Map** p92 B5 🔞 **Sushi**

Blink and you'll miss it, but this tiny sushi bar punches far above its size. It quickly made a name for itself when it opened in 2011, educating Paris diners about the delights of fatty tuna, eel and wagyu beef. The eel arrives still smoking, perfectly grilled, swiped with a delicious sweet sauce then arranged in a *chirachi* bowl with fish, omelette and prawns on a warm bed of rice and sesame. The wagyu beef, with its remarkable texture and nutty flavour, is served as *tataki* (a sort of half-cooked carpaccio) or sushi. Have it with one of the sakes – a fruity Tatenokawa, a flavourful Muroka, an intense Kenbishi, or a taster of all three.

Gare au Gorille

68 rue des Dames, 17th (01.42.94.24.02). M° Rome or Place de Clichy. **Open** 12.15-2pm, 7.30-10pm Tue-Sat. **Main courses** €39-€41.

Small plates €6-€14. **Prix fixe** *Lunch* €25. **Map** p92 B5 🇫🇷 **Bistro**

This bistro set in a long, white-walled room studded with copper pipes has Scandinavian elegance and an exceptionally welcoming atmosphere. The kitchen has serious pedigree as well – both chef Marc Grébault and sommelier Louis Langevin put in time at the famous Septime. And it shows in dishes such as cod with mussels flanked by slices of Jura sausage or lamb shoulder with Pardailhan turnips and crunchy cauliflower pickle. Then to finish, chocolate creams topped with grilled almonds and verbena ice cream. A good selection of wines is listed by region.

Lazare

Parvis de la Gare St Lazare, 8th (01.44.90.80.80, www.lazare-paris.fr). M° St Lazare. **Open** 7.30am-midnight daily (lunch noon-3pm, dinner 7-11pm). **Main courses** €19-€36. **Prix fixe** *Sun lunch* €39. **Map** p92 C6 🇫🇷 **Brasserie**

See below **First-class Food**.

FIRST-CLASS FOOD

Lazare is no ordinary station buffet.

The biggest buzz on the Paris food scene in early 2014 wasn't caused by an haute cuisine restaurant or a primped-up bistro, but by a railway brasserie. **Lazare** (*see above*), in the eponymous station, is run by star chef Eric Frechon, who won the Hôtel Bristol's restaurant its third Michelin star and opened the Mini Palais in 2010. Gare St Lazare was the station that originally brought Frechon to Paris from his native Normandy, and he calls the restaurant a '*retour aux sources*' – a return to the roots of country cooking from all over France.

When you enter from the recently revamped station, the centrepiece is a magnificent copper bar. A blackboard above the bar lists different 'arrivals' – tea with girlfriends, afterwork drinks, dinner with friends – in the style of a timetable, each claiming to be '*à l'heure*'. To the left are floor-to-ceiling shelves piled high with plates and jugs, while clusters of globe lights make for a modern take on traditional brasserie decor. A glance around the tables shows a real cross-section of Paris life – not just foodies but families, first-daters and after-workers too.

As befits a station brasserie, food arrives swiftly – a starter of salmon 'marinated like a herring' on warm potatoes, perhaps, or a whole cold mackerel in white wine gelée with horseradish sauce; bread is plonked on the table in its paper bag with artful nonchalance.

Then the main courses arrive, and you see what all the fuss is about as you tuck into the likes of grilled pork belly on a bed of turnip choucroute. Prices are no bargain, but daily specials are €19 (think pot-au-feu or beef bourguignon). Cheeses from Claire Griffon include stunning rocamadour and comté.

EXPLORE

Cafés & Bars

Les Caves Populaires
22 rue des Dames, 17th (01.53.04.08.32).
M° Place de Clichy. **Open** 8.30am-1.30am
Mon-Sat. **Map** p92 B6 ⑦
An old soak props up the bar with his *petit rouge*,
while others play chess and groups of bobos
(bourgeois bohemians) revel in the cheap prices –
from €2.40 for a glass of quaffable wine, €2.70 for a
beer and €5.50 for a cheese platter. It's a charming
place and vaguely reminiscent of a wooden chalet,
hence its second name, Les Caves du Châlet.

L'Endroit
67 pl du Dr-Félix-Lobligeois, 17th (01.42.29.50.00).
M° La Fourche or Rome. **Open** daily
(sometimes stays open later). **Map** p92 A5 ⑦
L'Endroit is one of the best spots in old Batignolles
village, with views over neoclassical Ste-Marie-des-
Batignolles church, a cool thirtysomething crowd,
decent wines, cocktails a go-go and excellent food
that won't break the bank.

Shops & Services

French Touche
1 rue Jacquemont, 17th (01.42.63.31.36,
www.frenchtouche.com). M° La Fourche. **Open**
1-8pm Tue-Fri; 11am-8pm Sat. **Map** p92 A6
⑦ **Accessories**
Bags adorn the walls, trinkets sit atop small wooden
shelves, and lamps are dotted around the room –
French Touche is a shop where one could happily
rummage for hours on end. Nestled in the heart
of the 17th for the past decade, this 'gallery of
touching objects' was one of the first concept stores
in the capital. Dreamed up by the lovely Valérie, it's
teeming with original creations, from retro knitted
cat badges to Beatles patches and micro-notebook
keychains. At the back is a fascinating selection
of clothing, boots and crockery unearthed from
various antiques stores.

Fromagerie Dubois et Fils
80 rue de Tocqueville, 17th (01.42.27.11.38). M°
Malesherbes or Villiers. **Open** 8am-1pm, 4-8pm
Tue-Thur; 8am-8pm Fri, Sat; 9am-1pm Sun. Closed
1st 3wks Aug. **Map** p92 A4 ⑦ **Food & drink**
Superchef darling Dubois stocks 80 types of goat's
cheese, plus prized, aged st-félicien.

Marché Batignolles
Rue Lemercier, 17th. M° Brochant. **Open**
8.30am-1pm, 3.30-8pm Tue-Fri; 8.30am-8pm
Sat; 8.30am-2pm Sun. **Map** p92 A5 ⑧ **Market**
Batignolles is more down to earth than the better-
known Raspail organic market, with a quirky
selection of stallholders, many of whom produce
what they sell. Prices are higher here than at
ordinary markets, but the goods are worth it.

Thomas Cook
45 av de Wagram, 17th (01.55.37.72.72,
www.thomascook.fr). M° Opéra. **Open** 10am-
7pm Mon-Sat. **Map** p92 C3 ⑧ **Travel**
More than 30 branches in and around Paris.
Other locations throughout the city.

Le Vin en Tête
30 rue des Batignolles, 17th (01.44.69.04.57,
http://infogen.levinentete.fr). M° Place de Clichy
or Rome. **Open** 10am-2pm, 4-9pm Mon-Thur;
10am-9pm Fri, Sat; 11am-2pm, 5-8pm Sun.
Map p92 A5 ⑧ **Food & drink**
Le Vin en Tête has been supplying wine enthusiasts
for more than a decade now. Not content with
stocking more than 1,200 wines and spirits, it also
seeks to explain the science behind wine-making
to as many people as possible. If you're interested
in learning the subtle differences between natural
and biodynamic wine (80% of the wines here are
produced biodynamically), you can sign up for one
of the numerous courses or go to the weekly tastings.

PASSY & AUTEUIL
In the 16th arrondissement.

West of l'Etoile, the extensive 16th
arrondissement is the epitome of bourgeois
respectability, with grandiose apartments and
exclusive residences lining the private roads. It's
also home to some seminal examples of modernist
architecture, plus several of the city's most
important museums. When Balzac lived at no.47
rue Raynouard in the 1840s, Passy was a country
village (it was absorbed into the city in 1860) where
the rich came to take cures at its mineral springs –
a history alluded to by rue des Eaux. The novelist's
former abode, **Maison de Balzac**, is open to the
public. The **Musée du Vin** is of interest if only
for its setting in the cellars of the wine-producing
Abbaye de Minimes, destroyed in the Revolution.
Rue de Passy, formerly the village high street,
and parallel rue de l'Assomption, are the focus
of local life, with fashion shops and *traiteurs*,
the department store **Franck et Fils** (80 rue de
Passy, 16th, 01.44.14.38.00, www.francketfils.fr)
and a covered market.

West of the former high-society pleasure
gardens of the Jardin du Ranelagh you'll find
the **Musée Marmottan**, with its superb
collection of Monet's late water-lily canvases,
other Impressionists and Empire furniture.

Next to the Pont de Grenelle stands the circular
Maison de Radio France, the giant home of
state broadcasting, which is currently undergoing
a massive six-year renovation. From here, in more
upmarket Auteuil, you can head up rue La
Fontaine, the best place to find art nouveau
architecture by Hector Guimard, of *métro*
entrance fame. He also designed the less

EXPLORE

ambitious nos.19 and 21. At no.96 pay homage to Marcel Proust, who was born here.

Nearby, **Fondation Le Corbusier** occupies two of the architect's avant-garde houses in square du Dr-Blanche. A little further up rue du Dr-Blanche sculptor Henri Bouchard himself commissioned the studio and house that is now the dusty Atelier-Musée Henri Bouchard. Much of the rest of Auteuil is private territory, with exclusive streets of residences off rue Chardon-Lagache; the studio of 19th-century sculptor Jean-Baptiste Carpeaux remains, looking rather lost, at no.39 boulevard Exelmans.

West of the 16th, across the Périphérique, sprawls the parkland of **Bois de Boulogne**. At porte d'Auteuil is the romantic **Jardin des Serres d'Auteuil** and sports venues the **Parc des Princes**, home of football club Paris St-Germain, and **Roland Garros**, host of the French Tennis Open. Another attraction opened its doors in late 2014: the much-delayed **Fondation Louis Vuitton**.

Sights & Museums

★ FREE Bois de Boulogne
16th. M° Les Sablons or Porte Dauphine.
Admission free. **Map** p92 C1 ⑧⑨

Bois de Boulogne.

Covering 865 hectares, the Bois was once the Forêt de Rouvray hunting grounds. It was landscaped in the 1860s, when artificial grottoes and waterfalls were created around the Lac Inférieur. The Jardin de Bagatelle is famous for its roses, daffodils and water lilies, and contains an orangery that rings to the sound of Chopin in summer. The Jardin d'Acclimatation (*see p249*) is a children's amusement park. The Bois also boasts two racecourses (Longchamp and Auteuil), sports clubs and stables, and restaurants, including the seriously smart Le Pré Catelan (01.44.14.41.00, www.precatelanparis.com).

Castel Béranger
14 rue La Fontaine, 16th. M° Jasmin.
Map p93 G1 ⑧⑨
Guimard's masterpiece of 1895-98 epitomises art nouveau in Paris. From outside you can see his love of brick, wrought iron and asymmetry, and his renunciation of harsh angles not found in nature. The faces on the balconies are thought to be self-portraits, inspired by Japanese figures, to ward off evil spirits.

Fondation Le Corbusier
Maison La Roche, 10 square du Dr-Blanche, 16th (01.42.88.75.72, www.fondationlecorbusier.fr). M° Jasmin. **Open** 1.30-6pm Mon; 10am-6pm Tue-Sat. Closed Aug. **Admission** €8; €5 reductions; free under-14s. **No credit cards. Map** p93 G1 ⑧⑤
Designed by Le Corbusier in 1923 for a Swiss art collector, this house shows the architect's ideas in practice, with its stilts, strip windows, roof terraces and balconies, built-in furniture and an unsuspected use of colour inside: sludge green, blue and pinky beige. A sculptural cylindrical staircase and split volumes create a variety of geometrical vistas; inside, Le Corbusier's own neo-Cubist paintings and furniture sit alongside pieces by Perriand. The adjoining Maison Jeanneret houses the foundation's extensive library.

Fondation Louis Vuitton
8 av du Mahatma Gandhi, Bois de Boulogne, 16th (01.40.69.96.00, www.fondationlouis vuitton.fr). M° Sablons or Fondation shuttle bus (€1; every 15mins during opening hours) from Place Charles de Gaulle. **Open** 11am-8pm Mon, Wed, Thur; 11am-11pm Fri; 10am-8pm Sat, Sun. **Admission** €14; €5-€10 reductions; free under-3s. **Map** p92 C1 ⑧⑥
See p108 **Art Ahoy!**.

FREE Le Jardin des Serres d'Auteuil
3 av de la Porte d'Auteuil, 16th. M° Porte d'Auteuil. **Open** *Summer* 8am-8.30pm Mon-Fri; 9am-8.30pm Sat, Sun. *Winter* 8am-7.30pm Mon-Fri; 9am-7.30pm Sat, Sun. **Admission** free. **Map** p93 G1 ⑧⑦
These romantic glasshouses were opened in 1895 to cultivate plants for Paris parks and public spaces.

EXPLORE

ART AHOY!

The Fondation Louis Vuitton has washed up in the Bois de Boulogne.

The **Fondation Louis Vuitton** (*see p107*) is made up of a series of massive curved glass sails, an ambitious statement building by Canadian-American star achitect Frank Gehry that proclaims the arrival of Louis Vuitton and its chairman Bernard Arnault – previously active as a sponsor of exhibitions and heritage restoration – as an artworld force in the French capital. Worth a visit for the architecture as much as what's inside, there's no doubt that the Fondation is a mega ego trip for two powerful men.

Gehry has described a moment of inspiration on his first visit to the site: 'Within the Bois de Boulogne and the Jardin d'Acclimitation, the idea of a glass pavilion was the only possible way forward. It seemed inappropriate to me to create a solid object. I wanted to express a notion of transparency.'

This is not, of course, the first building by Frank Gehry in the capital. Well before the Guggenheim Bilbao put him on the European art map, he designed what was originally the American Center (now the Cinémathèque Française) in Bercy in 1994, giving the city a taste of his deconstructionist style of cascading planes. But the Fondation takes the concept to a new scale and complexity.

Inside the huge, airy foyer, the first thing that strikes you is the sheer size of the building with its vast spaces and high ceilings, and Gehry's desire for transparency in an incredible combination of sails made from thousands of panels of curved glass, white iceberg-like boxes, a wooden roof structure and huge steel beams.

But where is the art? With massive white illuminated escalators that lead to the galleries above and below, it feels rather like entering some futuristic clinic. In the basement are two large galleries for prestige exhibitions, while the second and third floors contain a curious array of nine galleries – some strangely shaped and hard to find, which is no surprise given the sail architecture – and tiers of roof terraces overlooking the Jardin d'Acclimatation.

Apart from a few commissions – Olafur Eliasson's *Inside the Horizon* is made up of 43 triangular columns, clad on two sides in mirror and on the other in illuminated panes of yellow glass – the collection remains something of an enigma. Since opening in October 2014, there have been shows of Gehry, Richter, Tillmans, Giacometti and Eliasson, followed by Keys to a Passion – a sort of greatest hits of modern art (Nolde, Mondrian, Monet, Malevich, Rothko and more). A display of luxury culture from a master of luxury shopping.

EXPLORE

Today, there are seasonal displays of orchids and begonias. Look out for the tropical pavilion, which is home to palms, birds and Japanese ornamental carp.

FREE Maison de Balzac
47 rue Raynouard, 16th (01.55.74.41.80, www. balzac.paris.fr). Mº Passy. **Open** 10am-6pm Tue-Sun. **Admission** free. *Exhibitions* prices vary. **Map** p93 F2 ⑱
Honoré de Balzac rented this apartment in 1840 to escape his creditors. Mementos include first editions and letters, plus portraits of friends and the novelist's mistress Mme Hanska. Along with a 'family tree' of his characters that extends across several walls, you can see Balzac's desk and the monogrammed coffee pot that fuelled all-night work on *La Comédie Humaine*.

★ Musée Marmottan – Claude Monet
2 rue Louis-Boilly, 16th (01.44.96.50.33, www. marmottan.fr). Mº La Muette. **Open** 10am-6pm Tue, Wed, Fri-Sun; 10am-9pm Thur. **Admission** €11; €6.50 reductions; free under-7s. **Map** p93 F1 ⑲
Originally a museum of the Empire period left to the state by collector Paul Marmottan, this old hunting pavilion has become a famed holder of Impressionist art thanks to two bequests: the first by the daughter of the doctor of Manet, Monet, Pissarro, Sisley and Renoir; the second by Monet's son Michel. Its Monet collection, the largest in the world, numbers 165 works, plus sketchbooks, palette and photos. A special circular room was created for the breathtaking late water-lily canvases; upstairs are works by Renoir, Manet, Gauguin, Caillebotte and Berthe Morisot, 15th-century primitives, a Sèvres clock and a collection of First Empire furniture.

Musée du Vin
5 square Charles Dickens, Rue des Eaux, 16th (01.45.25.63.26, www.museeduvinparis.com). Mº Passy. **Open** 10am-6pm Tue-Sun. **Admission** €10; €9 reductions; free under-9s, diners in the restaurant. **Map** p93 F2 ⑳
Here the Confrères Bacchiques defend French wines from imports and advertising laws. In the cellars of an old wine-producing monastery are displays on the history of viticulture, with waxwork peasants, old tools, bottles and corkscrews. Visits finish with a wine tasting and, a paid extra, a meal. The museum is a reminder that, for centuries, Passy was a wine-growing area. Louis XIII used to stop off for a drink here after hunting in the Bois de Boulogne.

Restaurants

Astrance
4 rue Beethoven, 16th (01.40.50.84.40, www. astrancerestaurant.com). Mº Passy. **Open** 12.15-1.15pm, 8.15-9.15pm Tue-Fri. Closed 1wk Dec & late July-late Aug. **Prix fixe** *Lunch* €70, €150, €230. *Dinner* €230. **Map** p93 F2 ㉛ Haute cuisine

La Pâtisserie des Rêves.

When Pascal Barbot opened Astrance, he was praised for creating a new style of Paris restaurant – refined, yet casual and affordable. A few years later, this small, slate-grey dining room feels just like an haute cuisine restaurant. Most customers, having reserved at least a month ahead, give free rein to the chef with the 'Menu Astrance'. Barbot has an original touch, combining foie gras with slices of white mushrooms and a lemon condiment, or sweet lobster with candied grapefruit peel, a grapefruit and rosemary sorbet, and raw baby spinach. Wines are reasonably priced.

Shops & Services

La Maison du Chocolat
120 av Victor-Hugo, 16th (01.40.67.77.83, www. lamaisonduchocolat.com). Mº Victor Hugo. **Open** 10am-7.30pm Mon-Sat; 10am-1pm Sun. Closed Sun in July & Aug. **Map** p92 D1 ㉜ Food & drink
Robert Linxe opened his first Paris shop in 1977, and has been inventing new chocolates ever since, using Asian spices, fresh fruits and herbal infusions. **Other locations** throughout the city.

La Pâtisserie des Rêves
11 rue de Longchamp, 16th (01.47.04.00.24, www.lapatisseriedesreves.com). Mº Victor Hugo. **Open** *Shop* 10am-7pm Tue-Fri; 9am-7pm Sat, Sun. *Salon de thé* noon-7pm Fri-Sun. **Map** p92 E3 ㉝ Food & drink
Looking for your dream pâtisserie? Look no further than cake-maker *extraordinaire* Philippe Conticini's boutique and tearoom. The Saint-Honoré (a puff-pastry delight filled with whipped cream and caramelised sugar) is rectangular so that you can cut it into slices, and the famous Paris-Brest (a praline cream éclair) comes with a runny praline centre.

EXPLORE

Montmartre & Pigalle

Long gone are the days when Montmartre was a tranquil village full of windmills and vineyards, although two *moulins* and a small patch of vines do still survive – and the history of the hill is on display at the newly revamped and expanded Musée de Montmartre. Perched high on the 'Butte' (Paris's highest hill), the area is packed with houses spiralling round the mound below the dominant dome of the Sacré-Coeur. Despite the thronging tourists (chiefly around place du Tertre), it remains the most unabashedly romantic district in Paris. Further north, romance gives way to retail at one of the world's biggest flea markets, the Marché de St-Ouen. South from Montmartre, Pigalle has long had a reputation as Paris's centre for sleaze. But while peep shows still tout for business, a younger, hipper crew line the pavements nowadays, queuing to get into cool gigs and clubs.

Marché de St-Ouen.

Don't Miss

1 **Sacré-Coeur** *Le tout Paris* spread out before your feet (p115).

2 **Le Flamboire** Flame-grilled meat feast (p119).

3 **Cimetière de Montmartre** Resting place of Truffaut, Nijinsky and others (p115).

4 **Marché de St-Ouen** Flea market fantasy (p117).

5 **Musée de Montmartre** New material and a new approach at this revamped history of the hill (p115).

MONTMARTRE

In the 18th arrondissement.

For centuries, Montmartre was a tranquil village. When Haussmann sliced through the capital in the mid 19th century, working-class families started to move out, and migrants poured into an industrialising Paris from across France. The *butte* was absorbed into the city of Paris in 1860, but remained proudly independent. Its key role in the Commune in 1871, fending off government troops, is marked by a plaque on rue du Chevalier-de-la-Barre. Artists started to move into the area from the 1880s. Renoir found plenty of subject matter in the cafés and *guinguettes*, while Toulouse-Lautrec patronised the local bars and immortalised its cabarets in his famous posters. Later, it was frequented by Picasso and artists of the Ecole de Paris.

You can start a wander from Abbesses métro station, one of only two in Paris (along with Porte Dauphine) to retain its original art nouveau metal-and-glass awning designed by Hector Guimard. Across place des Abbesses is art nouveau **St-Jean-de-Montmartre** church, a pioneering reinforced concrete structure with turquoise mosaics around the door. Along rue des Abbesses and rue Lepic, which winds its way up the hill, are food shops, boutiques, wine merchants and cafés, including the ever-popular **Le Sancerre**.

In the other direction from Abbesses, at 11 rue Yvonne-Le-Tac, is the **Chapelle du Martyr**. According to legend, St Denis picked up his head here after his execution during the third century. Rue Orsel, with a cluster of retro design, ethnic and vintage clothes shops, leads to place Charles-Dullin, where a few cafés overlook the respected **Théâtre de l'Atelier** (1 pl Charles-Dullin, 18th, 01.46.06.49.24, www.theatre-atelier.com).

Up the hill, the cafés of rue des Trois-Frères are popular spots for evening drinks. The street leads into place Emile-Goudeau, whose staircases, wrought-iron streetlights and old houses are so evocative of days gone by. The **Bâteau Lavoir**, a piano factory that stood at no.13, witnessed the birth of Cubism. Divided in the 1890s into a warren of studios for impoverished artists, it was here that Picasso painted *Les Demoiselles d'Avignon* in 1906 and 1907, when he, Braque and Juan Gris were all residents. The building burned down in 1970, but has since been reconstructed.

On rue Lepic, which winds up the hill from rue des Abbesses, are the village's two remaining windmills: the **Moulin Radet**, which was moved here in the 17th century from its hillock near the Palais-Royal; and the **Moulin de la Galette**, site of the celebrated dancehall depicted by Renoir (now in the Musée d'Orsay) and today a smart restaurant. Vincent van Gogh and his beloved brother Theo lived at no.54 from 1886 to 1888.

On tourist-swamped **place du Tertre**, at the top of the hill, painters flog lurid views of Paris or offer to draw your portrait; nearby **Espace Dalí** (11 rue Poulbot, 18th, 01.42.64.40.10, www.daliparis.com) has rather more illustrious art. Just off the square is **St-Pierre-de-Montmartre**, the oldest church in the district, its columns bent with age. Founded in 1133, it's an example of early Gothic, in contrast to its extravagant mock Romano-Byzantine neighbour, the Sacré-Coeur.

For all its kitsch and swarms of tourists, **Sacré-Coeur** is well worth the visit for its 19th-century excess. Rather than the main steps, take the staircase down rue Maurice-Utrillo to pause on a café terrace on the small square at the top of rue Muller, or wander down through the adjoining park to the **Halle St-Pierre**. The old covered market is now used for shows of naïve art, but the surrounding square and streets, known as the **Marché St-Pierre**, are packed with fabric shops.

On the north side of place du Tertre in rue Cortot is the quiet 17th-century manor that houses the newly expanded **Musée de Montmartre**, dedicated to the neighbourhood and its famous former inhabitants. Dufy, Renoir and Utrillo all used to have studios in the entrance pavilion. Nearby in rue des Saules is the Montmartre vineyard, planted by local artist Poulbot in 1933 in commemoration of the vines that once covered the area. The grape harvest here every autumn is a local highlight, celebrated with great pomp. Further down the hill, among rustic, shuttered houses, is the cabaret **Au Lapin Agile** (*see p270*). This old artists' meeting point got its name from André Gill, who painted the inn sign of a rabbit (the 'lapin à Gill').

A series of squares leads to rue Caulaincourt, crossing the **Cimetière de Montmartre** (enter on avenue Rachel, reached by stairs from rue Caulaincourt or place de Clichy). A stone's throw south of here is the *chanson* venue **Les Trois Baudets** (*see p277*), which saw the Paris debuts of Brel, Brassens, Vian, Gainsbourg, Gréco and others. Winding down the back of the hill, avenue Junot is lined with exclusive residences, such as the avant-garde house built by Adolf Loos for poet Tristan Tzara at no.15, exemplifying his Modernist maxim: 'Ornament is crime.'

La Goutte d'Or is primarily an African and Arab neighbourhood, and can seem like a slice of the Middle East or a state under perpetual siege owing to the frequent police raids. Down rue Doudeauville, you'll find lively ethnic music shops; rue Polonceau contains African grocers and Senegalese restaurants. Square Léon is the focus for La Goutte d'Or en Fête in June, which brings together local musicians. Some of them, such as Africando and the Orchestre National de Barbès, have become well known across the capital. A market sets up under the métro tracks along boulevard de la Chapelle on Monday,

Wednesday and Saturday mornings, with stalls selling exotic vegetables and African fabrics. Further north, at porte de Clignancourt, is the city's largest flea market, **Marché aux Puces de St-Ouen**, which teems with 3,000 traders and up to 180,000 bargain-hunters each weekend.

Sights & Museums

★ FREE Cimetière de Montmartre
20 av Rachel, access by staircase from rue Caulaincourt, 18th (01.53.42.36.30). M° Blanche or Place de Clichy. **Open** *6 Nov-15 Mar* 8am-5.30pm Mon-Fri; 8.30am-5.30pm Sat; 9am-5.30pm Sun & public hols. *16 Mar-5 Nov* 8am-6pm Mon-Fri; 8.30am-6pm Sat; 9am-6pm Sun & public hols. **Admission** free. **Map** p113 A3 ❶
Truffaut, Nijinsky, Berlioz, Degas, Offenbach and German poet Heine are all buried here. So, too, are La Goulue, the first great cancan star and model for Toulouse-Lautrec, celebrated local beauty Mme Récamier, and the consumptive heroine Alphonsine Plessis, inspiration for Dumas's *La Dame aux Camélias* and Verdi's *La Traviata*, who died at the tender age of 23. Flowers are still left on the grave of pop diva and gay icon Dalida *(see right* **In the Know**).

Musée d'Art Halle St-Pierre
2 rue Ronsard, 18th (01.42.58.72.89, www.hallesaintpierre.org). M° Anvers. **Open** *Jan-July, Sept-Dec* 11am-6pm Mon-Fri; 11am-7pm Sat; noon-6pm Sun; *Aug* noon-6pm Mon-Fri. **Admission** prices vary. **Map** p113 C4 ❷
The former covered market in the shadow of Sacré-Coeur specialises in *art brut, art outsider* and *art singulier* from its own and other collections.

Musée de Montmartre
12 rue Cortot, 18th (01.49.25.89.39, www.museedemontmartre.fr). M° Anvers or Lamarck-Caulaincourt. **Open** 10am-6pm daily. **Admission** €9.50; €5.50-€7.50 reductions; free under-10s. **Map** p113 C3 ❸
See p116 **Montmartre in the Making**.

★ FREE Sacré-Coeur
35 rue du Chevalier-de-la-Barre, 18th (01.53.41.89.00, www.sacre-coeur-montmartre.com). M° Abbesses or Anvers. **Open** *Basilica* 6am-10.30pm daily. *Crypt & dome* Winter 10am-5.45pm daily. Summer 9am-6.45pm daily. **Admission** free. *Crypt & dome* €8. **Map** p113 C3 ❹
Work on this enormous mock Romano-Byzantine edifice began in 1877. It was commissioned after the nation's defeat by Prussia in 1870 and built from public subscription. Completed in 1914, it was consecrated in 1919 – by which time a jumble of architects had succeeded Paul Abadie, winner of the original competition. The interior boasts lavish mosaics, including 'Christ in Majesty' in the apse – one of the world's largest. It sits atop Paris's highest point, and the views are as heavenly as the surroundings.

> **IN THE KNOW**
> **DALIDA'S MONTMARTRE**
>
> During her 30-year career, Egyptian-born icon Dalida recorded more than 1,000 songs, scoring 45 gold records and two platinum albums, before committing suicide in the late 1980s. Much of the Dalida myth is rooted in Montmartre: she lived in the 'Castle of Sleeping Beauty', a four-storey house on rue d'Orchampt; place Dalida is graced by a bronze bust of the idol; and her grave in the Montmartre cemetery is a place of pilgrimage.

Restaurants

Le Coq Rico
98 rue Lepic, 18th (01.42.59.82.89, www.lecoqrico.com). M° Abbesses, Blanche or Lamarck-Caulaincourt. **Open** noon-2.30pm, 7-11pm daily. **Main courses** €22-€39. **Map** p113 B3 ❺ **Bistro**
The Coq Rico is a classy *'bistrotisserie'*, a place where comfort food standards are transformed into gourmet treats – boiled egg comes with crunchy soldiers and truffle-infused butter, and the *planchette de béatilles* features nibble-sized pieces of chicken heart, gizzards and sticky chicken wings, all perfectly seasoned. There's a list of poultry suppliers on the menu, a transparency that appeals to health-conscious locals – even if prices are high (€98 for a chicken serving two to four). Wine choice is excellent.

Ma Cocotte
106 rue des Rosiers, 93400 St-Ouen (01.49.51.70.00, www.macocotte-lespuces.com). M° Garibaldi. **Open** noon-3pm, 7-11pm Mon-Fri; 8am-11pm Sat, Sun. **Main courses** €17-€33. **Prix fixe** €25, €30 (Mon-Fri). **Map** p113 C1 ❻ **Bistro**
Ma Cocotte bustles with families and young couples queuing for a seat. On the menu, conviviality is the order of the day, with litre pitchers of Starck (champagne, passionfruit, cucumber, ginger and mint); sharing plates of radish, foie gras or caviar; and mains such as rôtisserie farm chicken for four (€82) or côte de boeuf for two or three (€92), prepared by head chef Rudy Fradin and a vast army of kitchen staff all decked out in Chairman Mao-style blue cap and overalls. After years in the doldrums, the Puces is starting to show signs of life again, and the weekend crowds are sure to fancy a post-browse brunch at Ma Cocotte.

Le Miroir
94 rue des Martyrs, 18th (01.46.06.50.73, www.restaurantmiroir.com). M° Abbesses. **Open** noon-2pm, 7.30-10.30pm daily. **Main courses** €22. **Prix fixe** *Lunch* €19.50, €27, €34, €44. *Dinner* €27, €34, €44. **Map** p113 C4 ❼ **Bistro**

EXPLORE

MONTMARTRE IN THE MAKING

Explore the history of the hill at this newly expanded museum.

Until now, the **Musée de Montmartre** (see p115) was a bit of a tease: showing no more than an ankle when we wanted the whole can-can. But in 2011, its management was taken over by a private company. Out of the dusty archives came a wealth of fascinating material, a new approach to displaying it (with English translations) and the longed-for opening of painter Suzanne Valadon's rooftop atelier at the end of 2014. A building larger than the main museum itself is now devoted to temporary exhibitions, the gardens have been restored and there's a delightful café.

The main museum knits together the different periods of Montmartre's history.

Moving upwards in chronological order through four floors, it runs from the Romans to what Montmartre is most famous for: the belle époque with its cabarets and artists' colony – a recreation of an absinthe bar and a room lined with scenery from the mysterious shadow theatre at the Chat Noir are two new additions.

Suzanne Valadon's atelier, where she lived with her son, the future artist Maurice Utrillo, is hugely atmospheric, down to the chill in the unheated room. Recreated from photographs, including Utrillo's little bed with its ragged soft toy, it feels as though the artist could walk in at any moment and pick up one of the brushes.

This friendly modern bistro is a welcome addition to the neighbourhood. Big mirrors, red banquettes and a glass ceiling at the back give it character, while the very professional food and service reflect the owners' haute cuisine training. Expect such dishes as a salad of whelks with white beans, crisp-skinned duck and chanterelle mushrooms.

Le Moulin de la Galette

83 rue Lepic, 18th (01.46.06.84.77, www.le moulindelagalette.fr). M° Notre-Dame-de-Lorette. **Open** noon-11pm daily. **Main courses** €19-€29. **Prix fixe** *Lunch* €15, €23, €29. *Dinner* €35. **Map** p113 B3 ❽ **Bistro**

The Butte Montmartre was once dotted with windmills, and this survivor houses a chic restaurant with a few tables in the cobbled courtyard. It's hard to imagine a lovelier setting in Montmartre, but the kitchen makes an effort nonetheless, coming up with dishes such as foie gras with melting beetroot cooked in lemon balm and juniper.

Cafés & Bars

La Fourmi

74 rue des Martyrs, 18th (01.42.64.70.35). M° Pigalle. **Open** 8am-2am Mon-Thur; 8am-4am Fri, Sat; 10am-2am Sun. **Map** p113 C4 ❾

This old bistro has been converted for today's tastes, with picture windows lighting the spacious, roughshod interior, cool staff (and customers) and excellent music. The zinc bar is crowned by industrial lights, which helps you to see what you're reading as you rifle through the piles of flyers.

Le Kremlin

6 rue André Antoine, 18th (no phone). M° Abbesses or Pigalle. **Open** 6pm-2am daily. **Map** p113 C4 ❿

This Russian outpost has been heaving from the word go – it's difficult to navigate a path to the bar to order one of the fantastic imported vodkas or original cocktails. Try the Red Star (mezcal, fresh beetroot and Carpano) or the Red Army (Gin Carpano, green chartreuse and orange bitters). Once you've finally got hold of your drink, pass an eye over the sumptuous communist red decor, punctuated with propaganda posters and Soviet-style furniture.

Marlusse et Lapin

14 rue Germain Pilon, 18th (01.42.59.17.97, www.marlusseetlapin.fr). M° Abbesses or Pigalle. **Open** 4pm-2am daily. **Map** p113 B4 ⓫

Marlusse et Lapin is named after the couple that run this bonkers bar. Here, after-hours drinking is a riot, drenched in absinthe and crazy shots that will bring you back again and again to chat with the locals – and not least because of the great prices. The bar is microscopic, but in the room behind there's a surprising amount of space: this is 'Grandma's Chamber', with its flowered wallpaper, a bed pressed into service as a double banquette, a switchboard-era telephone, a sewing machine and a Normandy chest of drawers.

La Recyclerie

83 bd Ornano, 18th (01.42.57.58.49, www. larecyclerie.com). M° Porte de Clignancourt. **Open** 7am-midnight Mon-Wed; 7am-1am Thur; 7am-2am Fri, Sat; 7am-10pm Sun. **Map** p113 C1 ⓬ *See p119* **Track Star**.

Au Rendez-vous des Amis

23 rue Gabrielle, 18th (01.46.06.01.60). M°
Abbesses. **Open** 10am-2am daily. **Map** p113 C3 ⑬
Considering its proximity to the Sacré-Coeur, Au
Rendez-vous des Amis is still remarkably cheap,
especially during happy hour (6-8pm), making it
popular with locals and foreign students, and the odd
tourist. There are some cosy nooks round the back
with plenty of upholstered spots to choose from.

Le Rosie

3 rue Muller, 18th (09.51.91.32.87). M° Barbès
Rochechouart. **Open** 6pm-2am Tue-Sat. **Map**
p113 D3 ⑭
Decorated with comfortable armchairs, colourful
patterned cushions, coffee tables and low lighting, Le
Rosie looks like a stylish apartment. All the young,
laid-back waiters are friends of Nicolas Ullmann, a
Paris nightlife guru who had the idea of opening a
bar just opposite Maison Muller, where he organises
barbecues, parties, short film screenings, garage
sales and mini-concerts. On weekends, a DJ sets up.

Le Sancerre

35 rue des Abbesses, 18th (01.42.58.08.20). M°
Abbesses. **Open** 7am-2am daily. **Map** p113 B4 ⑮
It's official: Le Sancerre, a rock bar that attracted
everyone from alcohol-fuelled transvestites to
tourists and local bobos, has cleaned up its act. Gone
forever are the cheap beer and trashy music. Instead
you'll find a buzzing 1930s-style café with traditional
fare and bourgeois punters who fight for a spot on
the terrace. If you're in the area, pop by for a glass of
chardonnay and the special triple burgers.

Shops & Services

Arnaud Larher

53 rue Caulaincourt, 18th (01.42.57.68.08, www.
arnaud-larher.com). M° Lamarck Caulaincourt.
Open 10am-7.30pm Tue-Sat; 10am-1pm Sun.
Map p113 B3 ⑯ Food & drink
Look out for the strawberry-and-lychee flavoured
bonheur and the chocolate-and-thyme *récif* from this
master *pâtissier*.

Bières Cultes

40 rue Damrémont, 18th (01.42.23.49.93,
www.bierescultes.fr). M° Lamarck Caulaincourt.
Open 3-8pm Mon-Fri; 11am-2pm, 3-8pm Sat.
Map p113 B3 ⑰ Food & drink
Since 2007, Bières Cultes (Cult Beers) has been developing a particularly fine menu of flavours from a
range of source breweries: make sure to discuss
flavours and brands with the competent, friendly
staff. As well as an impressive stock of specialist,
rare and imported beers, Bières Cultes keeps a few
33cl and 75cl bottles chilled for the impatient, plus
other goodies guaranteed to satisfy anyone's inner
beer fetish. An interesting and affordable spot to lay
down supplies or kick off an evening in style.

★ Marché aux Puces de St-Ouen

Av de la Porte de Clignancourt, 18th. M° Porte de
Clignancourt (www.marcheauxpuces-saintouen.
com). **Open** 11am-5pm Mon; 9am-6pm Sat;
10am-6pm Sun. **Map** p113 C1 ⑱ Market
With 3,000 traders and up to 180,000 visitors each
weekend, this is thought to be the biggest flea market
in the world. The fleas left long ago, and since 1885
what started as a rag-and-bone shantytown outside
the city limits has been organised into a series of
enclosed villages. It's also home to Philippe Starck's
restaurant, Ma Cocotte (*see p115*).

Paperdolls

5 rue Houdon, 18th (01.42.51.29.87, www.
paperdolls.fr). M° Pigalle. **Open** 11am-7.30pm Mon-
Sat; 2.30-7pm Sun. **Map** p113 C4 ⑲ Accessories
Briton Candy Miller's boutique is truly girly, offering
everything from bird-shaped handbags to delicate
shoes. The layout is more akin to an apartment than
a shop (dining room, dressing room, bathroom, living
room). The counter is a gas cooker, jewellery hangs
from hooks and taps, and you try on shoes in a bath
transformed into a sofa. Only work by independent
designers is featured.

Tati

4 bd de Rochechouart, 18th (01.55.29.50.00,
www.tati.fr). M° Barbès Rochechouart. **Open**
10am-7pm Mon-Fri; 9.30am-7pm Sat. **Map**
p113 D4 ⑳ Department store
Expect to find anything from T-shirts to wedding
dresses, as well as bargain children's clothes and
household goods at this discount heaven.
Other locations throughout the city.

Tienda Esquipulas

20 rue Houdon, 18th (01.42.55.64.38, www.
esquipulas.fr). M° Abbesses or Pigalle. **Open**
2-7pm Mon, Sun; 11.30am-8pm Tue-Sat. **Map**
p113 C4 ㉑ Souvenirs
Effigies of Frida Kahlo, wrestling masks, floral
printed fabrics, woollen ponchos, Jesus and Mary
fridge magnets, lucky skeleton charms and hand-
painted ceramics from San Caterina Palopo. No,
you're not living a weird Latino dream, you're in
Tienda Esquipulas, a small boutique in the heart
of Montmartre, dedicated to supporting Mexican
and Guatemalan artisans. Each item has been hand-
picked by the shop's owner, Ana, and represents her
vision of modern popular culture in Latin America.

PIGALLE & LA NOUVELLE ATHENES

In the 9th & 18th arrondissements

In the 1890s, Toulouse-Lautrec's posters of Jane
Avril at the Divan Japonais, Chat Noir and Moulin
Rouge, and of *chanson* star Aristide Bruant,
were landmarks of art and advertising and

EXPLORE

EXPLORE

immortalised Pigalle's cabarets. It's still a happening area: Le Divan Japonais is now **Le Divan du Monde** (*see p265*); a hip crowd packs into **La Fourmi** (*see p263*) opposite; and up the hill, there's a cluster of *atelier*-boutiques where designers have set up their sewing machines.

Along the boulevard, behind its bright red windmill, the **Moulin Rouge** (*see p270*), once the image of naughty 1890s Paris, is now a cheesy tourist draw. Its befeathered dancers still cavort across the stage, but are no substitute for La Goulue and Joseph Pujol – *le pétomane* who could pass wind melodically. In stark contrast is the **Cité Véron** next door, a cobbled alley with a small theatre and cottagey buildings.

Just south of Pigalle and east of rue Blanche lies this often overlooked quarter, dubbed New Athens when it was colonised by a wave of artists, writers and composers in the early 19th century. Long-forgotten actresses and *demi-mondaines* had mansions built here.

Just off rue Taitbout is square d'Orléans, a remarkable housing estate that was built in 1829 by English architect Edward Cresy. These flats and studios attracted the glitterati of the day, including George Sand and her lover Chopin. In the house built for Dutch painter Ary Scheffer in nearby rue Chaptal, the **Musée de la Vie Romantique** displays Sand's mementos.

The **Musée National Gustave Moreau** is reason alone to visit, featuring the artist's apartment and magnificent studio. Fragments of bohemia can still be gleaned in the area, although Café La Roche, where Moreau met Degas for drinks and rows, has been downsized to **Café Matisse** (57 rue Notre-Dame-de-Lorette, 9th, 01.53.16.44.58). Degas painted most of his memorable ballet scenes in rue Frochot, and Renoir hired his first proper studio at 35 rue St-Georges. A few streets away in Cité Pigalle, a collection of studios, is van Gogh's last Paris house (no.5), from where he moved out to Auvers-sur-Oise. There is a plaque here, but nothing marks the building in rue Pigalle where Toulouse-Lautrec slowly drank himself to an early grave.

The area around the neoclassical **Eglise Notre-Dame-de-Lorette** was built up in Louis-Philippe's reign and was famous for its courtesans or *lorettes*, elegant ladies named after their haunt of rue Notre-Dame-de-Lorette. In 1848, Gauguin was born at no.56; from 1844 to 1857, Delacroix had a studio at no.58.

The lower stretch of rue des Martyrs is packed with tempting food shops, and a little further up the hill you should look out for the prosperous residences of the Cité Malesherbes and avenue Trudaine. Circular place St-Georges was home to the true Empress of Napoleon III's Paris: the Russian-born Madame Païva. La Païva shot herself after a passionate affair with the millionaire cousin of Chancellor Bismarck.

**IN THE KNOW
RUE DES ABBESSES**

Rue des Abbesses got its title because it once led to the Women's Abbey of Montmartre, which was nicknamed the 'army's whorehouse on the hill' following the seduction of the abbess in 1590 by the besieging Henri de Navarre.

Sights & Museums

FREE Eglise de la Trinité

Pl Estienne-d'Orves, 9th (01.48.74.12.77, www.latriniteparis.com). M° Trinité. **Open** 7.15am-8pm Mon-Fri; 11am-8pm Sat; 8.30am-8.30pm Sun. **Admission** free. **Map** p113 B5 ㉒

Noted for its tiered bell tower, this neo-Renaissance church was built between 1861 and 1867. Olivier Messiaen (1908-92) was organist here for over 30 years.

Musée de l'Erotisme

72 bd de Clichy, 18th (01.42.58.28.73, www.musee-erotisme.com). M° Blanche. **Open** 10am-2am daily. **Admission** €10; €8 reductions. **Map** p113 B4 ㉓

Seven floors of erotic art and artefacts amassed by collectors Alain Plumey and Joseph Khalif. The first three run from first-century Peruvian phallic pottery through Etruscan fertility symbols to Yoni sculptures from Nepal; the fourth gives a history of Paris brothels; and the refurbished top floors host exhibitions of modern erotic art.

★ Musée National Gustave Moreau

14 rue de La Rochefoucauld, 9th (01.48.74.38.50, www.musee-moreau.fr). M° Trinité. **Open** 10am-12.45pm, 2-5.15pm Mon, Wed, Thur; 10am-5.15pm Fri-Sun. **Admission** €5; €3 reductions; free under-18s, under-26s (EU citizens), all 1st Sun of mth. PMP. **Map** p113 B5 ㉔

This wonderful museum combines the small private apartment of Symbolist painter Gustave Moreau (1825-98) with the vast gallery he built to display his work – set out as a museum by the painter himself, and opened in 1903. Downstairs shows his obsessive collector's nature with family portraits, Grand Tour souvenirs and a boudoir devoted to the object of his unrequited love, Alexandrine Durem. Upstairs is Moreau's fantasy realm, which plunders Greek mythology and biblical scenes for canvases filled with writhing maidens, trance-like visages, mystical beasts and strange plants.

FREE Musée de la Vie Romantique

Hôtel Scheffer-Renan, 16 rue Chaptal, 9th (01.55.31.95.67, www.vie-romantique.paris.fr). M° Blanche or St-Georges. **Open** 10am-6pm Tue-Sun. **Admission** free. *Exhibitions* prices vary. **Map** p113 B4 ㉕

When Dutch artist Ary Scheffer lived in this small villa, the area teemed with composers, writers and artists. Aurore Dupin, Baronne Dudevant (George Sand) was a guest at Scheffer's soirées, along with great names such as Chopin and Liszt. The museum is devoted to Sand, although the watercolours, lockets, jewels and plastercast of her right arm that she left behind reveal little of her ideas or affairs. The museum has a charming café (see p120).

Restaurants

Buvette Gastrothèque

28 rue Henry Monnier, 9th (01.44.63.41.71, www. ilovebuvette.com). M° Pigalle or Saint-Georges. **Open** 8.30am-midnight Mon-Fri; 10am-midnight Sat, Sun. **Main courses** €6-€12. **Map** p113 C5 **26 Bistro**

Jody Williams, a purebred New Yorker, has brought a bit of Greenwich Village to Pigalle. The interior is all rough brick walls and wooden tables that sit well around the huge marble bar. The menu is a selection of small plates and fresh sandwiches, with a decent wine list arranged by region. There are also more substantial dishes such as *coq au vin en cocotte*.

★ Le Flamboire

54 rue Blanche, 9th (06.95.01.77.38, leflamboire. com). M° Blanche, Trinité or Liège. **Open** noon-3pm, 6.30-11.30pm Mon-Sat. **Main courses** €22-€39. **Map** p113 B5 **27 Bistro**

Le Flamboire is a straightforward meat-lover's paradise with kitsch flames painted on the walls and a no-nonsense carnivorous menu that really delivers. The grills are the main thing here – you

TRACK STAR

La Recyclerie has brought life to a disused railway line.

A restaurant, bar, café, farm and vegetable garden featuring daily DIY workshops, ethical values and a relaxed, welcoming vibe... all this and more makes up **La Recyclerie** (see p116), in a former station on the Petite Ceinture, a disused railway that loops around the city.

The Recyclerie project is organised by a handful of local hospitality associations who cut their teeth on, variously, Comptoir Général, Glazart, Divan du Monde and Machine du Moulin Rouge. They're specialists in all things second-hand, passionate about investing clapped-out spaces with new life. And the result certainly works: the high ceiling soars above a wrought-iron framework, with an

enormous glass window offering a sweeping view over the old tracks, now surrounded by a long terrace, a mobile exterior bar and local allotments. Inside, the space is done out in vintage furniture and fresh greenery, with colourful chairs, an enormous bar, an open kitchen, big vats of natural wine (sourced from En Vrac), climbing plants – and in a corner behind a glass screen, L'Atelier de René, the in-house handyman who will repair absolutely anything (and teach you how to do it yourself).

The menu changes each week and you can eat while watching staff working on the urban farm – soon, drinks will be served between a tethered goat and a plot of tomatoes.

EXPLORE

can watch the meat cooking over the flames on the huge open fire. It's a difficult choice: *côte de boeuf* to share, chateaubriand, bavette, lamb steaks and more. Team with perfect potatoes browned in the oven, seasonal baby vegetables and little ramekins of béarnaise or chive sauce. Highly recommended.

Le Garde-Temps
19bis rue Fontaine, 9th (09.81.48.50.55, www. restaurant-legardetemps.fr). M° Blanche or Saint-Georges. **Open** noon-2pm, 7pm-midnight (last orders 10.30pm) Mon-Fri; 7pm-midnight (last orders 10.30pm) Sat. **Main courses** €20-€35. **Prix fixe** €28, €35. **Map** p113 B4 ㉘ **Bistro**
Le Garde-Temps isn't the address for a romantic dinner, with tables lined up closely on either side of the small dining room with its fashionable New York decor. The menu starts with the likes of mullet tartare marinated in espelette pepper with a chorizo and mustard sprout sauce. The mains (scallops, perhaps, or a Black Angus beef onglet with hand-cut chips) are priced extraordinarily well for the amount of care taken on the plate. Desserts are slightly less even.

La Maison Mère
4 rue de Navarin, 9th (01.42.81.11.00, www. lamaisonmere.fr). M° Pigalle or Saint-Georges. **Open** noon-3pm (last orders 2.30pm), 7pm-2am (last orders 11pm Mon-Thur, 11.30pm Fri, Sat) Mon-Sat; noon-4pm Sun. **Main courses** €14-€25. **Prix fixe** *Lunch* €15 (Mon-Fri). **Map** p113 C5 ㉙ **Bistro**
Forget ideas of a traditional French kitchen. Embrace, instead, the New York-style decor, with vintage furniture, enamelled mirrors, lamps disguised as bowler hats and a sign declaring: 'In food we trust'. The menu is what you'd expect given the setting, with a few dashing bourgeois touches. Leek vinaigrette, eggs 'mimosa', bone marrow sandwiches, grilled cockerel and chocolate mousse all appear alongside crab cake, Brooklyn platters, Long Island platters and so on. The five burgers will delight enthusiasts, be it a breaded cod burger or the Black Label with its thick-cut Black Angus steak. Friendly service, decent wine and top cheesecake complete the picture.

★ Pétrelle
34 rue Pétrelle, 9th (01.42.82.11.02, www.petrelle. fr). M° Anvers. **Open** 8-10pm Tue-Sat. Closed 1st 10 days May, 4wks July/Aug & 1wk Dec. **Main courses** €25-€40. **Map** p113 D4 ㉚ **Bistro**
Jean-Luc André is as inspired a decorator as he is a cook, and the quirky charm of his dining room has made it popular with fashion designers and film stars. But behind the style there's some serious substance. André seeks out the best ingredients from local producers, and the quality shines through. The no-choice menu is very good value for money (marinated sardines with tomato relish, rosemary-scented rabbit with roasted vegetables, deep-purple poached figs) – or you can splash out with luxurious à la carte dishes such as tournedos Rossini.

Rose Bakery
46 rue des Martyrs, 9th (01.42.82.12.80). M° Notre-Dame-de-Lorette. **Open** 9am-6pm Tue-Sun. **Main courses** €7.50-€19.50. **Map** p113 C5 ㉛ **British**
This English-themed café stands out for the quality of its ingredients – organic or from small producers – as well as the too-good-to-be-true puddings: carrot cake, sticky toffee pudding and, in winter, chocolate-chestnut tart. The DIY salad plate is crunchily satisfying, but the thin-crusted *pizzettes*, soups and risottos are equally good choices.
Other location 30 rue Debelleyme, 3rd (01.49.96.54.01).

Cafés & Bars

Dirty Dick
10 rue Frochot, 9th (no phone). M° Pigalle. **Open** 6pm-2am daily. **Map** p113 B4 ㉜
SoPi welcomes another hip venue to this once down-at-heel area. A former hostess bar (they've kept the name, evidently), the only phallic elements now are the Polynesian totems scattered throughout the bar, which has a kitsch, exotic 'tiki' vibe and lots of free-flowing rum. The flower-shirted barmen cater to the crowds with a list of 20 or so cocktails served in giant shells or miniature volcanoes.

Jardin du Musée de la Vie Romantique
16 rue Chaptal, 9th (01.55.31.95.67, www.cafe-vie-romantique.com). M° Pigalle or St-Georges. **Open** 10am-6pm Tue-Sun. Closed mid Oct-mid Mar. **Map** p113 B4 ㉝
Buried in the heart of touristy Montmartre, this café adjoins the Musée de la Vie Romantique and feels like it was created with the same theme in mind. The terrace is fringed with roses and fuchsias, and the inside of the café is equally quaint, with floral wallpaper and a greenhouse ceiling. Go up to order, and then sit back and relax in the peaceful garden.

Le Mansart
1 rue Mansart, 9th (01.56.92.05.99). M° Blanche or Pigalle. **Open** 9am-2am daily. **Map** p113 B4 ㉞
With its large terrace occupied by a small army of young moustached men wearing lumberjack shirts, Le Mansart wears its hipster credentials proudly – not surprising given its location in trendy SoPi. Inside it's packed with people elbowing each other to get to the bar, and music so loud it's hard to make yourself heard. It's not particularly cheap, but it does have table football, rare in Parisian bars.

★ Rouge Passion
14 rue Jean-Baptiste Pigalle, 9th (01.42.85.07.62, www.rouge-passion.fr). M° St Georges or Pigalle. **Open** noon-3pm Mon; noon-midnight Tue-Fri; 6pm-midnight Sat. **Map** p113 B5 ㉟
Two bright upstarts (Anne and Sébastien) are behind this venture – and they're going about it the right way. Offering a long list of wines (from just

Causses.

€4), free *assiettes apéros* (peanuts, olives, tapenades on toast) and decor that is perfect vintage chic, the formula is spot on. A small but mouthwatering selection of hot dishes, salads, cheese and *saucisson* platters help to soak up the wine. Look out for the tasting classes, given by a guest sommelier.

Shops & Services

★ Arnaud Delmontel
39 rue des Martyrs, 9th (01.48.78.29.33, www. arnaud-delmontel.com). M° St-Georges. **Open** 7am-8.30pm Mon, Wed-Sun. **Map** p113 C5 ❸⓺
Food & drink
With its crisp crust and chewy crumb shot through with irregular holes, Delmontel's Renaissance bread is one of the finest in Paris.
Other locations throughout the city.

★ Causses
55 rue Notre-Dame de la Lorette, 9th (01.53.16.10.10, www.causses.org). M° Pigalle or St-Georges. **Open** 10am-9pm Mon-Sat.
Map p113 B5 ❸⓻ **Food & drink**
Causses offers a winning formula of quality seasonal produce (fruit 'n' veg, hams and cheeses), gourmet preserves and take-away breads, sandwiches and salads, plus a fill-your-own-bottle area next to the orange squeezing machine. You'll also find an array of interesting seasonings, including smoked salt and *sel fou* (salt mixed with oriental spices and pink peppercorns). For expats, Tyrrell's crisps, Covent Garden soups and HP sauce abound.

Détaille 1905
10 rue St-Lazare, 9th (01.48.78.68.50, www. detaille.com). M° Notre-Dame-de-Lorette. **Open** 11am-2pm, 3-7pm Tue-Sat. **Map** p113 C5 ❸⓼
Health & beauty

Step back in time at this gorgeous perfume shop, opened, as the name suggests, in 1905 by war artist Edouard Détaille. There are six fragrances available (three for men and three for women), all conjured up from century-old recipes.

La Fausse Boutique
32 rue Pierre Fontaine, 9th (06.62.17.59.02, www.lafausseboutique.com). M° Blanche or Pigalle. **Open** noon-7.30pm Mon-Sat. **Map** p113 B4 ❸⓽
Gifts & souvenirs
The False Boutique focuses on so-called 'surrealist products'. You might find offbeat tourist guides such as *Paris à Gratter* (modelled on a scratchcard, where you scratch to reveal monuments) and satirical board games such as Méditations Foireuses (half-assed meditations), produced by a collective of designers who work in the offices at the back of the showroom. A great place to find original gifts.

Marché Anvers
Pl d'Anvers, 9th. M° Anvers. **Open** 3-8.30pm Fri. **Map** p113 C4 ❹⓪ **Market**
An afternoon market that adds to the village atmosphere of a peaceful *quartier* down the hill from Montmartre. Among its highlights are regional vegetables, hams from the Auvergne, lovingly aged cheeses and award-winning honey.

Millimètres
19 rue Milton, 9th (01.71.70.96.99, www. millimetres.fr). M° Notre-Dame-de-Lorette. **Open** 11am-7pm Tue-Sat. **Map** p113 C5 ❹① **Children**
A concept store for people too young to have their own credit card, Millimètres strikes a nice balance between toyshop and kid-friendly interior decoration. It's a very Parisian space that overflows with cool present ideas: ethical wooden toys by Polish company Wooden Story, bath linen made from recycled plastic, and plenty of clothes with cute animal prints. There are some major names in children's design on the shelves, such as April Showers, Donna Wilson, Kiddimoto, and Enfantillages from Quebec.

Première Pression Provence
9 rue des Martyrs, 9th (01.48.78.86.51, www. ppp-olive.com). M° Notre-Dame-de-Lorette. **Open** 10.30am-2.30pm, 3.30-7.30pm Mon-Fri; 10.30am-1.30pm Sun. **Map** p113 C5 ❹②
Food & drink
PPP is L'Occitan creator Olivier Baussan's project, where you're encouraged to taste spoonfuls of single-producer olive oil to educate your palate about the nuances of *vert, mûr* and *noir*. Two dozen small producers send oils direct from their Provençal olive groves to the boutiques, where they're sold in aluminium cans with colour-coded labels.
Other locations 7 rue Sainte-Croix de la Bretonnerie, 4th (01.44.54.93.71); 8 rue du Commerce Saint André, 6th (01.43.26.79.72); 37 rue de Villiers, 17th (09.65.30.88.86).

EXPLORE

Beaubourg & the Marais

For the last two decades the Marais has been one of the hippest parts of the city, packed to the hilt with modish hotels, vintage boutiques, restaurants and bars – in no small part due to its popularity with the gay crowd (this is the only part of Paris where the blokes tend to get winked at more than the ladies). But it's also prime territory for art-lovers. A vast concentration of galleries and museums, more often than not set in aristocratic 18th-century mansions spared by Haussmann, make it a charming place in which to get lost for a few hours. And as an extra bonus, the Musée Picasso has finally reopened its doors with triple the exhibition space after a five-year renovation fraught with controversy. The Marais' neighbour to the west is Beaubourg, the focal point of which is the iconic Centre Pompidou, with the city's all-important Hôtel de Ville a stone's throw to the south.

Gaîté Lyrique.

Don't Miss

1 **Centre Pompidou** A modern must-see – inside and out (p124).

2 **Gaîté Lyrique** Digital design download (p128).

3 **Musée National Picasso** After a five-year wait, the master is back (p131).

4 **Merci** Concept store with class, and a *cantine* to match (p140).

5 **Comme à Lisbonne** *Pasteis de nata* and perfect coffee (p136).

BEAUBOURG & HOTEL DE VILLE

In the 3rd & 4th arrondissements.

Modern architecture in Paris took off with the **Centre Pompidou**, a benchmark of inside-out high tech designed by Richard Rogers and Renzo Piano that's as much an attraction as the **Musée National d'Art Moderne** within. The piazza outside attracts all manner of street performers and artists; the reconstructed **Atelier Brancusi**, left by the sculptor to the state, was moved here from the 15th arrondissement.

On the other side of the piazza, rue Quincampoix houses galleries, bars and cobbled passage Molière. Beside the Centre Pompidou is place Igor-Stravinsky and the Fontaine Stravinsky – full of spraying kinetic fountains, and a colourful snake by the late artists Niki de Saint Phalle and Jean Tinguely – as well as the red-brick **IRCAM** music institute (*see p283*), also designed by Renzo Piano.

South of here stands the spiky Gothic **Tour St-Jacques**. Towards the river, on the site of the Grand Châtelet (a fortress put up in the 12th century to defend Pont au Change), place du Châtelet's Egyptian-themed fountain is framed by twin theatres designed by Davioud as part of Haussmann's urban improvements in the 1860s. They're now major arts venues: the **Théâtre de la Ville** and the **Théâtre du Châtelet** (for both, *see p287*).

Beyond Châtelet, the **Hôtel de Ville** (city hall) has been the symbol of municipal power since 1260. The equestrian statue out front is of 14th-century merchant leader and rebel Etienne Marcel. Revolutionaries made the Hôtel de Ville their base in the 1871 Commune, but it was set on fire by the Communards themselves and wrecked during fighting. It was rebuilt according to the original model, on a larger scale, in fanciful neo-Renaissance style, with knights in armour along the roof and statues of French luminaries dotted all over the walls. The square outside was formerly called place de Grève, after the nearby riverside wharf. During the 16th-century Wars of Religion, Protestant heretics were burned in the square, and the guillotine stood here during the Terror, when Danton, Marat and Robespierre made the Hôtel de Ville their seat of government. Today, the square hosts an ice rink every December, and screenings of major sports events. Across the road stands the BHV (Bazar de l'Hôtel de Ville) department store, newly restyled and retitled **BHV Marais**.

Sights & Museums

FREE Atelier Brancusi

Piazza Beaubourg, 4th (01.44.78.12.33, www.centrepompidou.fr). M° Hôtel de Ville or Rambuteau. **Open** 2-6pm Mon, Wed-Sun. **Admission** free. **Map** p125 B3 ❶

When Constantin Brancusi died in 1957, he left his studio and its contents to the state, and it was later moved and rebuilt by the Centre Pompidou. His fragile works in wood and plaster, the endless columns and streamlined bird forms show how Brancusi revolutionised sculpture.

★ Centre Pompidou (Musée National d'Art Moderne)

Rue St-Martin, 4th (01.44.78.12.33, www.centrepompidou.fr). M° Hôtel de Ville or Rambuteau. **Open** 11am-10pm (last entry 8pm) Mon, Wed-Sun (until 11pm some exhibitions). **Admission** *Museum & exhibitions* €11-€13; €9-€10 reductions; free under-18s, under-26s (EU citizens), all 1st Sun of mth (museum only). PMP. **Map** p125 B3 ❷

The primary colours, exposed pipes and air ducts make this one of the best-known sights in Paris. The then-unknown Italo-British architectural duo of Renzo Piano and Richard Rogers won the competition with their 'inside-out' boilerhouse approach, which put air-conditioning, pipes, lifts and the escalators on the outside, leaving an adaptable space within. The multidisciplinary concept of modern art museum (the most important in Europe), library, exhibition and performance spaces, and repertory cinema was also revolutionary. When the centre opened in 1977, its success exceeded all expectations. After a two-year revamp, the centre reopened in 2000 with an enlarged museum, renewed performance spaces, vista-rich Georges restaurant and a mission to get back to the stimulating interdisciplinary mix of old. Entrance to the forum is free (as is the library, which has a separate entrance), but you now have to pay to go up the escalators (€3).

The Centre Pompidou (or 'Beaubourg') holds the largest collection of modern art in Europe, rivalled only in its breadth and quality by MoMA in New York. Sample the contents of its vaults (50,000 works of art by 5,000 artists) on the website, as only a fraction – about 600 works – can be seen for real at any one time. There is a partial rehang each year. For the main collection, buy tickets on the ground floor and take the escalators to level four for post-1960s art. Level five spans 1905 to 1960. There are four temporary exhibition spaces on each of these two levels (included in the ticket). Main temporary exhibitions take place on the ground floor, in gallery two on level six, in the south gallery, level one and in Espace 315, which is devoted to artists aged under 40.

On level five, the historic section takes a chronological sweep through the history of modern art, via Primitivism, Fauvism, Cubism, Dadaism and Surrealism up to American Color-Field painting and Abstract Expressionism. Masterful ensembles let you see the span of Matisse's career on canvas and in bronze, the variety of Picasso's invention, and the development of cubic orphism by Sonia and Robert Delaunay. Others on the hits list include Braque, Duchamp, Mondrian, Malevich, Kandinsky, Dalí, Giacometti, Ernst, Miró, Calder, Magritte, Rothko

EXPLORE

EXPLORE

Place des Vosges. *See p131.*

and Pollock. Don't miss the reconstruction of a wall of André Breton's studio, combining the tribal art, folk art, flea-market finds and drawings by fellow artists that the Surrealist artist and theorist had amassed. The photography collection also has an impressive roll call, including Brassaï, Kertész, Man Ray, Cartier-Bresson and Doisneau.

Level four houses post-'60s art. Its thematic rooms concentrate on the career of one artist or focus on movements such as Anti-form or *arte povera*. Recent acquisitions line the central corridor, and at the far end you can find architecture and design. Video art and installations by the likes of Mathieu Mercier and Dominique Gonzalez-Foerster are in a room devoted to *nouvelle création*.

▶ *An 80-minute TGV ride from Paris, the Centre Pompidou Metz (see p298) opened in 2010.*

FREE Hôtel de Ville
29 rue de Rivoli, 4th (01.42.76.43.43, www.paris. fr). M° Hôtel de Ville. **Open** 10am-7pm Mon-Sat. **Admission** free. **Map** p125 B4 ❸
Rebuilt by Ballu after the Commune, the palatial, multi-purpose Hôtel de Ville is the very heart of the city administration, and a place in which to entertain visiting dignitaries. Free exhibitions are held in the Salon d'Accueil (open 10am-6pm Mon-Fri). The rest of the building, which is accessible by weekly guided tours (you need to book in advance), has parquet floors, marble statues, crystal chandeliers and painted ceilings.

Tour St-Jacques
Square de La-Tour-St-Jacques, 4th. M° Châtelet. **Map** p125 A3 ❹
Loved by the Surrealists, this solitary Flamboyant Gothic belltower with its leering gargoyles is all

that remains of St-Jacques-La-Boucherie church, which was built for the powerful Butchers' Guild in 1508-22. The statue of Blaise Pascal at the base commemorates his experiments on atmospheric pressure, carried out in the 17th century. A weather station now crowns the 52m (171ft) tower.

▶ *After being closed to the public for the best part of 500 years, the tower now opens for a couple of months during the summer, with access to the roof – and stunning views – via a 300-step spiral staircase. Tours (€3-€6) last 45 minutes and run daily from 10am to 5pm (reservations on site).*

Cafés & Bars

Café Livres
10 rue St-Martin, 4th (01.42.72.18.13). M° Châtelet or Hôtel de Ville. **Open** 8am-midnight Mon-Fri; 9am-1am Sat; 10am-8pm Sun. **Map** p125 A3 ❺
This charming café with a terrace in the shade of the Tour Saint-Jacques has lines and lines of books surrounding patrons inside. Since this is as central as can be, a cappuccino will set you back €6, but the atmosphere is pleasantly relaxing after a shopping marathon on rue de Rivoli. Food is served non-stop from noon to 11pm.

Shops & Services

Les Bains du Marais
31-33 rue des Blancs-Manteaux, 4th (01.44.61.02.02, www.lesbainsdumarais.com). M° St-Paul. **Open** *Men* 10am-11pm Thur; 10am-8pm Fri. *Women* 10am-11pm Tue; 10am-7pm Wed. *Mixed (swimwear required)* 7-11pm Wed; 10am-8pm Sat; 10am-11pm Sun. **Map** p125 B3 ❻ **Health & beauty**

This hammam and spa mixes the modern and traditional (lounging beds and mint tea). Facials, waxing and essential oil massages (€70) are also available. The hammam and standard massage are €35 each.

BHV Marais

52-64 rue de Rivoli, 4th (09.77.40.14.00, www.bhv.fr). M° Hôtel de Ville. **Open** 9.30am-8pm Mon, Tue, Thur-Sat; 9.30am-9pm Wed. **Map** p125 B3 ❼ **Department store**
It's homeware heaven at this department store. The upper floors have a good range of men's outdoor wear, bedlinen, toys, books and household appliances.

★ FR66

25 rue du Renard, 4th (01.44.54.35.36, www. fr66.com). M° Hôtel de Ville. **Open** 10am-7pm Mon-Sat. Closed Aug. **Map** p125 B3 ❽ **Gallery**
Somewhere between a gallery and a shop, this two-level space accommodates artists and designers who produce exciting and original products for the home.

I Love My Blender

36 rue du Temple, 3rd (01.42.77.50.32, www. ilovemyblender.fr). M° Hôtel de Ville. **Open** 10am-7pm Tue-Sat. **Map** p125 B3 ❾ **Books & music**
Christophe Persouyre left a career in advertising to share his passion for literature: all the books he stocks were originally penned in English and here you can find mother-tongue and translated versions.

THE MARAIS

In the 3rd & 4th arrondissements.

The narrow streets of the Marais contain aristocratic *hôtels particuliers*, art galleries, boutiques and stylish cafés, with beautiful carved doorways and early street signs carved into the stone. The Marais, or 'marsh', started life as a piece of swampy ground inhabited by a few monasteries, sheep and market gardens. This was one of the last parts of central Paris to be built up. In the 16th century, the elegant Hôtel Carnavalet and Hôtel Lamoignon sparked the area's phenomenal rise as an aristocratic residential district; Henri IV began building **place des Vosges** in 1605. Nobles and royal officials followed, building smart townhouses where literary ladies such as Mme de Sévigné held court. The area fell from fashion a century later; many of the narrow streets remained unchanged as mansions were transformed into workshops, studios, schools and tenements.

Rue des Francs-Bourgeois, crammed with impressive mansions and original boutiques, runs like a backbone right through the Marais, becoming more aristocratic as it leaves the food shops of rue Rambuteau behind. Two of the most refined early 18th-century residences are

Hôtel d'Albret (no.31), a venue for jazz concerts during the Paris, Quartier d'Eté festival, and the palatial **Hôtel de Soubise** (no.60), the national archives. Begun in 1704 for the Prince and Princesse de Soubise, it has interiors by Boucher and Lemoine and currently hosts the **Musée de l'Histoire de France**, along with the neighbouring Hôtel de Rohan. There's also a surprising series of rose gardens.

Facing the Archives Nationales, the **Crédit Municipal** (no.55) acts as a sort of municipal pawnshop: people exchange goods for cash, and items never reclaimed are sold at auction. On the corner of rue Pavée is the Renaissance Hôtel Lamoignon. Built in 1585, it now contains the **Bibliothèque Historique de la Ville de Paris** (no.24, 01.44.59.29.40). Further up, the **Musée Carnavalet** runs across the Hôtel Carnavalet and Hôtel le Peletier de St-Fargeau.

At its eastern end, rue des Francs-Bourgeois leads into the beautiful brick-and-stone place des Vosges. At one corner is the **Maison de Victor Hugo**, where the writer lived from 1833 to 1848. An archway in the south-west corner leads to the **Hôtel de Sully**, which houses the Centre des Monuments Nationaux headquarters. Designed in 1624, the building belonged to the Duc de Sully.

Several other important museums are also found in sumptuous *hôtels*. The Hôtel Salé on rue de Thorigny, built in 1656, was nicknamed ('salty') after its owner, Fontenay, who collected the salt tax. It is home to the **Musée National Picasso**, which reopened in late 2014 after a lengthy makeover (*see p132* **Pablo's Back**). Nearby, the pretty Hôtel Donon, built in 1598, contains the **Musée Cognacq-Jay** and has remarkable 18th-century panelled interiors, and the Hôtel Guénégaud contains the **Musée de la Chasse et de la Nature**.

The Marais has also long been a focus for the Jewish community. Today, Jewish businesses are clustered along rue des Rosiers, rue des Ecouffes and rue Pavée, where there's a synagogue designed by Guimard. Originally made up mainly of Ashkenazi Jews, who fled the pogroms in eastern Europe at the end of the 19th century (many were later deported during World War II), the community expanded in the 1950s and '60s with a wave of Sephardic Jewish immigration after French withdrawal from North Africa.

The lower ends of rue des Archives and rue Vieille-du-Temple are the centre of café life and

EXPLORE

the hub of the gay scene. Bars such as the **Open Café** (*see p257*) draw gay crowds in the early evening. In their midst, the 15th-century **Cloître des Billettes** at 22-26 rue des Archives is the only surviving Gothic cloister in Paris.

Workaday rue du Temple is full of surprises. Near rue de Rivoli, **Le Noveau Latina** (*see p254*) specialises in Latin American films and holds tango balls in the room above. At no.41, an archway leads into the former Aigle d'Or coaching inn, now the **Café de la Gare** *café-théâtre* (*see p271*). Further north, at no.71, the grandiose Hôtel de St-Aignan, built in 1650, contains the **Musée d'Art et d'Histoire du Judaïsme**. The top end of rue du Temple and adjoining streets, such as rue des Gravilliers, are packed with costume jewellery, handbag and rag-trade wholesalers in what is the city's oldest Chinatown.

The north-west corner of the Marais hinges on the **Musée des Arts et Métiers**, a science museum with early flying machines displayed in the 12th-century chapel of the former priory of St-Martin-des-Champs, and the adjoining Conservatoire des Arts et Métiers. Across rue St-Martin on square Emile-Chautemps, the belle époque **Gaîté Lyrique** theatre reopened in 2011 as a centre for contemporary music and the 'digital arts'.

Despite the Marais' rise to fashion, the less gentrified streets around the northern stretch of rue Vieille-du-Temple towards place de la République are awash with designers on the rise and old craft workshops. Rue Charlot, housing an occasional contemporary art gallery at the passage de Retz at no.9, is typical of the trend. At the top, the **Marché des Enfants-Rouges** (once an orphanage whose inhabitants were attired in red uniforms) is one of the city's oldest markets, founded in 1615.

Sights & Museums

FREE Eglise St-Gervais-St-Protais

Pl St-Gervais, 4th (01.48.87.32.02). M° Hôtel de Ville. **Open** times vary. **Admission** free. **Map** p125 B4 ⑩
Gothic at the rear and classical at the front, this church also has an impressive Flamboyant Gothic interior, most of which dates from the 16th century. The nave gives an impression of enormous height, with tall columns that soar up to the vault. There are plenty of fine funerary monuments.

FREE Eglise St-Paul-St-Louis

99 rue St-Antoine, 4th (01.42.72.30.32, www.spsl.fr). M° St-Paul. **Open** 8am-8pm daily. **Admission** free. **Map** p125 C4 ⑪
This domed Baroque Counter-Reformation church is modelled, like all Jesuit churches, on the Chiesa del Gesù in Rome. Completed in 1641, it features a single nave, side chapels and a three-storey façade featuring statues of Saints Louis, Anne and Catherine – all replacements. The provider of

confessors to the kings of France, the Eglise St-Paul-St-Louis was richly endowed until Revolutionary iconoclasts pinched its treasures, including the hearts of Louis XIII and XIV. Afterwards, in 1802, it was converted back into a church, and today it houses Delacroix's *Christ in the Garden of Olives*.

★ Gaîté Lyrique

3bis rue Papin, 3rd (01.53.01.51.51, www.gaite-lyrique.net). M° Réaumur Sébastapol. **Open** Box office 2-8pm Tue-Sat; noon-6pm Sun. **Map** p125 B2 ⑫
After a huge revamp, the belle époque Gaîté Lyrique theatre, built in 1862, has been turned into Paris's first digital cultural centre; a seven-floor, multi-disciplinary concert hall-cum-gallery that thrusts visitors deep into the realms of digital art, music, graphics, film, fashion, design and video games. After being an haut-lieu of operetta and Russian ballet, it was pillaged by the Nazis, only to become a circus school in the 1970s and a mini-theme park in the 1980s. But this time its multi-million euro interior, which combines the original belle époque

Gaîté Lyrique.

foyer with starkly modern spaces by architect Manuelle Gautrand, is set to become a permanent fixture on the cultural scene. There are no fewer than three electronic music concerts each week and around 120 live multimedia performances a year.

Maison Européenne de la Photographie

5-7 rue de Foucry, 4th (01.44.78.75.00, www. mep-fr.org). M° St-Paul. **Open** 11am-7.45pm Wed-Sun. **Admission** €8; €4.50 reductions; free under-8s, all 5-7.45pm Wed. **Map** p125 C4 ⓭
Probably the capital's best photography exhibition space, hosting major retrospectives alongside work by emerging photographers. The building, an airy mansion with a modern extension, contains a huge permanent collection.

FREE Maison de Victor Hugo

Hôtel de Rohan-Guéménée, 6 pl des Vosges, 4th (01.42.72.10.16, www.musee-hugo.paris.fr). M° Bastille or St-Paul. **Open** 10am-6pm Tue-Sun. **Admission** free. *Exhibitions* prices vary. **Map** p125 D4 ⓮
Victor Hugo lived here from 1833 to 1848, and today the house is a museum devoted to his life and work. On display are his first editions, nearly 500 drawings and, more bizarrely, Hugo's home-made furniture.

★ FREE Le Mémorial de la Shoah

17 rue Geoffroy-l'Asnier, 4th (01.42.77.44.72, www.memorialdelashoah.org). M° Pont Marie or St-Paul. **Open** 10am-6pm Mon-Wed, Fri, Sun; 10am-10pm Thur. *Research centre* 10am-5.30pm Mon-Wed, Fri, Sun; 10am-7.30pm Thur. **Admission** free. **Map** p125 B4 ⓯
Airport-style security checks mean queues, but don't let that put you off: the Mémorial du Martyr Juif Inconnu is an impressively presented and moving memorial to the Holocaust. Enter via the Wall of Names, where limestone slabs are engraved with the first and last names of each of the 76,000 Jews deported from France from 1942 to 1944 with, as an inscription reminds the visitor, the say-so of the Vichy government. The basement-level permanent exhibition documents the plight of French and European Jews through photographs, texts, films and individual stories: 'The French,' reads one label (captioning is given in French and English), 'were not particularly interested in the fate of French Jews at this point.'
▶ *The Shoah Memorial organises free guided tours in English on the second Sunday of the month. Tours start at 3pm and no reservation is needed.*

★ Musée d'Art et d'Histoire du Judaïsme

Hôtel de St-Aignan, 71 rue du Temple, 3rd (01.53.01.86.60, www.mahj.org). M° Rambuteau. **Open** 11am-6pm Mon-Fri; 10am-6pm Sun. Closed Jewish hols. **Admission** €8; €6 reductions; free under-26s (EU citizens). **Map** p125 B3 ⓰

It's fitting that a museum of Judaism should be lodged in one of the grandest mansions of the Marais, for centuries the epicentre of local Jewish life. It sprang from the collection of a private association formed in 1948 to safeguard Jewish heritage after the Holocaust. Pick up a free audio-guide in English to help you navigate through displays illustrating ceremonies, rites and learning, and showing how styles were adapted across the globe through examples of Jewish decorative arts. Photographic portraits of modern French Jews, each of whom tells his or her own story on the audio soundtrack, bring a contemporary edge. There are documents and paintings relating to the emancipation of French Jewry after the Revolution and the infamous Dreyfus case, from Zola's *J'Accuse!* to anti-Semitic cartoons. Paintings by the early 20th-century avant-garde include works by El Lissitsky and Chagall. The Holocaust is marked by Boris Taslitzky's stark sketches from Buchenwald and Christian Boltanski's courtyard memorial to the Jews who lived in the building in 1939, 13 of whom died in the camps.

Musée des Arts et Métiers

60 rue Réaumur, 3rd (01.53.01.82.00, www. arts-et-metiers.net). M° Arts et Métiers. **Open** 10am-6pm Tue, Wed, Fri-Sun; 10am-9.30pm Thur. **Admission** €6.50; €4.50 reductions; free under-18s, under-26s (EU citizens), all 6-9.30pm Thur & 1st Sun of mth. PMP. **Map** p125 B2 ⓱
The 'arts and trades' museum is, in fact, Europe's oldest science museum, founded in 1794 by the constitutional bishop Henri Grégoire, initially as a way to educate France's manufacturing industry in useful scientific techniques. Housed in the former Benedictine priory of St-Martin-des-Champs, it became a museum proper in 1819; it's a fascinating, attractively laid out and vast collection of treasures. Here are beautiful astrolabes, celestial spheres, barometers, clocks, weighing devices, some of Pascal's calculating devices, amazing scale models of buildings and machines that must have demanded at least as much engineering skill as the originals, the Lumière brothers' cinematograph, an enormous 1938 TV set, and still larger exhibits such as Cugnot's 1770 'Fardier' (the first ever powered vehicle) and Clément Ader's bat-like, steam-powered Avion 3. The visit concludes in the chapel, which now contains old cars, a scale model of the Statue of Liberty, the monoplane in which Blériot crossed the Channel in 1909, and a Foucault pendulum.
▶ *Try to time your visit to coincide with one of the spellbinding demonstrations of the museum's old music boxes in the Théâtre des Automates.*

★ FREE Musée Carnavalet

23 rue de Sévigné, 3rd (01.44.59.58.58, www. carnavalet.paris.fr). M° St-Paul. **Open** 10am-6pm Tue-Sun. **Admission** free. *Exhibitions* prices vary. **Map** p125 C3 ⓲

EXPLORE

REVAMPING REPUBLIQUE

Paris's most symbolic square has been given a brush-up.

Nowhere is more symbolic for Parisians than place de la République. Originally an avenue of trees created for Louis XIV, then a pleasure garden just before the Revolution, it was laid out in its current grandiose dimensions by Baron Haussmann in 1865. It became place de la République following the Paris Commune, when it acquired its statue of Marianne to celebrate the centenary of the Revolution in 1889. The tradition of protesters climbing on to the statue began almost immediately, and the square remains a key gathering point for the *manifestations* (marches) that are an intrinsic part of city life.

This key right to protest was one of the central considerations when the Mairie decided to revamp the square at a final cost of more than £20m – the space had to remain symbolically open and even the fountains now disappear into the ground during mass gatherings (though this removes the chance of dancing through them dressed only in a *tricolore*). Doubling the pedestrian area and making it into a huge plaza that runs right up to the military barracks on the north side provides Paris with its largest public square. The architects, TVK, describe it as a 'supersurface' that can be adapted to multiple uses, from a venue for large cultural events to a simple place to cool off in the summer among the raised terraces and fountains.

The existing plane trees have been retained and 18 new honey locust trees planted. The 19th-century lampposts have been moved to the back of the square, where they cast a moody green-blue light into the trees, and there's column lighting to make the area safer and more attractive at night. While the disruption has given Parisians another thing to complain about, the work makes place de la République once again worthy of its illustrious name.

EXPLORE

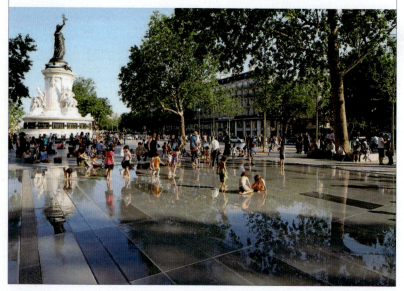

Here, 140 chronological rooms depict the history of Paris, from pre-Roman Gaul to the 20th century. Built in 1548 and transformed by Mansart in 1660, this fine house became a museum in 1866, when Haussmann persuaded the city to preserve its beautiful interiors. Original 16th-century rooms house Renaissance collections, with portraits by Clouet and furniture and pictures relating to the Wars of Religion. The first floor covers the period up to 1789, with furniture and paintings displayed in restored period interiors; neighbouring Hôtel Le Peletier de St-Fargeau covers the period from 1789 onwards. Displays relating to 1789 detail that year's convoluted politics and bloodshed, with prints and memorabilia, including a chunk of the Bastille. There are items belonging to Napoleon, a cradle given by the city to Napoleon III, and a reconstruction of Proust's cork-lined bedroom.

★ Musée de la Chasse et de la Nature

Hôtel Guénégaud, 62 rue des Archives, 3rd (01.53.01.92.40, www.chassenature.org). M° *Rambuteau.* **Open** 11am-6pm Tue, Thur-Sun; 11am-9.30pm Wed. **Admission** €8; €6 reductions; free under-18s, all 1st Sun of mth. **Map** p125 C3 ⓳
A two-year overhaul turned the three-floor hunting museum from a musty old-timer into something really rather special. The history of hunting and man's larger relationship with the natural world are examined in such things as a quirky series of wooden cabinets devoted to the owl, wolf, boar and stag, each equipped with a bleached skull, small drawers you can open to reveal droppings and footprint casts, and a binocular eyepiece you can peer into for footage of the animal in the wild. A cleverly simple mirrored box contains a stuffed hen that is replicated into infinity on every side; and a stuffed fox is set curled up on a Louis XVI chair as though it were a domestic pet. Thought-provoking stuff.

FREE Musée Cognacq-Jay

Hôtel Donon, 8 rue Elzévir, 3rd (01.40.27.07.21, www.cognacq-jay.paris.fr). M° St-Paul. **Open** 10am-6pm Tue-Sun. **Admission** free. **Map** p125 C3 ⓴
This cosy museum houses a collection put together in the early 1900s by La Samaritaine founder Ernest Cognacq and his wife Marie-Louise Jay. They stuck mainly to 18th-century French works, focusing on rococo artists such as Watteau, Fragonard, Boucher, Greuze and pastellist Quentin de la Tour, though some English artists (Reynolds, Romney, Lawrence) and Dutch and Flemish names (an early Rembrandt, Ruysdael, Rubens), plus Canalettos and Guardis, have managed to slip in. Pictures are displayed in panelled rooms with furniture, porcelain, tapestries and sculpture of the same period.

Musée de l'Histoire de France (Musée des Archives Nationales)

Hôtel de Soubise, 60 rue des Francs-Bourgeois, 3rd (01.40.27.60.96, www.archives-nationales. culture.gouv.fr). M° Hôtel de Ville or Rambuteau.

Open 10am-5.30pm Mon, Wed-Fri; 2-5.30pm Sat, Sun. **Admission** €3-€6; €2-€4 reductions; free under-26s. **Map** p125 C3 ㉑
Documents and artefacts covering everything from the founding of the Sorbonne to an ordinance about umbrellas are displayed in the recently renovated Hôtel de Soubise. Its rococo interiors feature paintings by François Boucher and Carle van Loo.

★ Musée National Picasso

5 rue de Thorigny, 3rd (01.85.56.00.36, www. museepicassoparis.fr). M° St-Paul. **Open** 11.30am-6pm Tue-Fri; 9.30am-6pm Sat, Sun. **Admission** €11; free under-18s, under-26s (EU citizens) & all 1st Sun of mth. **Map** p125 C3 ㉒
See p132 **Pablo's Back**.

FREE Pavillon de l'Arsenal

21 bd Morland, 4th (01.42.76.33.97, www.pavillon-arsenal.com). M° Sully Morland. **Open** 10.30am-6.30pm Tue-Sat; 11am-7pm Sun. **Admission** free. **Map** p125 C5 ㉓
The setting is a fantastic 1880s gallery with an iron frame and glass roof; the subject is the built history of Paris. Exhibits were previously limited to a few storyboards, maps and photos, and three city models set into the floor (done far more impressively at the Musée d'Orsay), but a new permanent exhibition, Paris, a City in the Making, boasts a 37sq m Google Earth model of the city with four touchscreens to explore the different *quartiers* in delicious digital detail.

FREE Place des Vosges

4th. M° St-Paul. **Map** p125 D4 ㉔
Paris's first planned square was commissioned in 1605 by Henri IV and inaugurated by his son Louis XIII in 1612. With harmonious red-brick and stone arcaded façades and steeply pitched slate roofs, it differs from the later pomp of the Bourbons. It was called place Royale prior to the Napoleonic Wars, when the Vosges was the first region to pay its war taxes. Mme de Sévigné, salon hostess and letter-writer, was born at no.1bis in 1626. At that time the garden hosted duels and trysts; now it attracts children from the nearby nursery school. *Photo p126.*

Restaurants

★ L'Ambassade d'Auvergne

22 rue du Grenier-St-Lazare, 3rd (01.42.72.31.22, www.ambassade-auvergne.com). M° Arts et Métiers. **Open** noon-2pm, 7.30-10pm Mon-Thur; noon-2pm, 7-10pm Fri-Sun. **Main courses** €18-€27. **Prix fixe** *Lunch* €22.50. *Dinner* €33. **Map** p125 B2 ㉕ **Bistro**
This rustic-style *auberge* is a fitting embassy for the hearty fare of central France. An order of cured ham comes as two hefty, plate-filling slices, and the salad bowl is chock-full of green lentils cooked in goose fat, studded with bacon and shallots. The *rôti d'agneau* arrives as a pot of melting chunks of lamb in a rich, meaty sauce with a helping of tender white

EXPLORE

beans. Dishes arrive with the flagship *aligot*, the creamy, elastic mash-and-cheese concoction.

Le Barav

6 rue Charles François Dupuis, 3rd (01.48.04.57.59, www.lebarav.fr). Mº République or Temple. **Open** noon-3pm, 6pm-12.30am Mon-Fri; 6pm-12.30am Sat. **Main courses** €11.50-€14. **Prix fixe** *Lunch* €10.90. **Map** p125 C2 **㉖ Wine bar**

It might be a little out of the way, but Le Barav has plenty to recommend. Prices are more than reasonable – the €14 *parmentier de canard confit* is the most expensive dish. If you haven't reserved or got there before 6pm, you'll need to hang about for a table to eat, maybe snacking on spicy pork terrine

while you wait. The wine list is drawn from the Barav wine store just next door, and bottles from the *cave* are available for an extra €5 corkage fee. The food doesn't quite match the wine's quality, but the friendly atmosphere and the staff's enthusiasm make Le Barav an excellent all-rounder.

Bofinger

5-7 rue de la Bastille, 4th (01.42.72.87.82, www.bofingerparis.com). Mº Bastille. **Open** noon-3pm, 6.30pm-midnight Mon-Fri; noon-3.30pm, 6.30pm-midnight Sat; noon-11.30pm Sun. **Main courses** €22-€46. **Prix fixe** *Lunch* €33 (Mon-Fri). *Lunch & Dinner* €31, €38, €61. **Map** p125 D4 **㉗ Brasserie**

PABLO'S BACK

The renovated Musée Picasso is a work of art in itself.

After a five-year closure and some last-minute staff changes, the **Musée National Picasso** (*see p131*) has made a fine comeback, almost tripling the display space by moving former offices out of the building, and preserving the dual appeal of the world's largest public collection of works by Picasso and one of the Marais' most beautiful mansions.

The 17th-century golden-hued Hôtel Salé was built in 1656-60 by architect Jean Boullier for Pierre Aubert de Fontenay, collector of the salt tax (the term 'salé' is still used for an undesirably hefty bill). It has been handsomely restored, while keeping some of the alterations by architect Roland Simounet, and the bronze lights and furniture by Diego Giacometti, from when it first opened as a museum in the 1980s. A new ticket office and bookshop in the glazed-over courtyard

of the right wing have enabled the preservation of the magnificent sculpted grand staircase as the centrepiece of the museum.

The majestic main route is given a new fluidity on the ground, first and second floors, from early – *Little Girl in a Red Dress* painted in 1895 by Picasso at the age of 15 – to late works from 1972. Paintings and sculptures are mixed with drawings and prints (the works on paper will be changed frequently because of their fragility) and allowed to speak for themselves: visitors are given a booklet to provide more information.

While most of the display is roughly chronological, showing Picasso's numerous styles and periods – blue and pink periods, cubism, surrealism from the 1920s, Riviera beaches, the Spanish Civil War, '60s pop period, the painter and his model, late paintings after the Old Masters – there are also some fascinating themed rooms dotted through the display, covering the likes of self-portraits, the guitar and bullfighting. Among exceptional works are studies for *Les Demoiselles d'Avignon*, the first modern collages, the extraordinary *Les Femmes à leur toilette* wallpaper collage created in the studio on Quai des Grands-Augustins, and the sculpture *Little Girl with Skipping Rope*.

Two shorter routes intend to spread out the crowds. A quick route round the cellars concentrates on large-scale sculptures, some of them previously seen in the garden, plus photos of Picasso. In the newly restored vaulted attic spaces sits Picasso's own art collection, donated by his widow, which includes some magnificent paintings by Renoir, Cézanne, Rousseau and Matisse.

Bofinger draws big crowds for its authentic art nouveau setting and brasserie atmosphere. Downstairs is the prettiest place in which to eat, but the upstairs room is air-conditioned. An à la carte selection might start with plump, garlicky escargots or a well-made langoustine terrine, followed by an intensely seasoned salmon tartare, a generous (if unremarkable) cod steak, or calf's liver accompanied by cooked melon. Alternatively, you could have the foolproof brasserie meal of oysters and fillet steak, washed down with the fine Gigondas.

€ Breizh Café

109 rue Vieille-du-Temple, 3rd (01.42.72.13.77, www.breizhcafe.com). Mº Filles du Calvaire. **Open** 11.30am-11pm Wed-Sat; 11.30am-10pm Sun. Closed 3wks Aug. **Main courses** €7-€15. **Map** p125 C3 ㉘ Crêperie

With its modern interior of pale wood and its choice of 15 artisanal ciders, this outpost of a restaurant in Cancale, Brittany, is a world away from the average crêperie. For the complete faux-seaside experience, you might start with a plate of *creuse* oysters from Cancale before indulging in an inventive buckwheat *galette* such as the Cancalaise, made with potato, smoked herring from Brittany and herring roe. The choice of fillings is fairly limited, but the ingredients are of high quality – including the use of Valrhona chocolate with 70% cocoa solids in the dessert crêpes.

★ € Cantine Merci

111 bd Beaumarchais, 3rd (01.42.77.79.28, www.merci-merci.com). Mº St-Sébastien Froissart. **Open** noon-3.30pm Mon-Sat (until 6pm for tea). **Main courses** €8-€21. **Map** p125 D3 ㉙ Café

Fairtrade concept store Merci is all about feeling virtuous even as you indulge, and its basement canteen is a perfect example. Fresh and colourful salads, soup and risotto of the day, an organic salmon plate, and the *assiette merci* (perhaps chicken kefta with two salads) make up the brief, Rose Bakery-esque menu, complete with invigorating teas and juices. Rustic desserts add just the right handmade touch.

★ € Chez Hanna

54 rue des Rosiers, 4th (01.42.74.74.99, www.chezhanna-restaurant.fr). Mº St-Paul. **Open** 11.30am-midnight Tue-Sun. **Main courses** €12-€20. **Map** p125 C3 ㉚ Jewish

By noon on a Sunday, there is a queue outside almost every falafel shop along rue des Rosiers. The long-established L'As du Fallafel, a little further up the street, still reigns supreme, whereas Chez Hanna remains something of a locals' secret, quietly serving up falafel and shawarma sandwiches to rival any in the world. A pitta sandwich bursting with crunchy chickpea-and-herb balls, tahini sauce and vegetables costs just €5.50 if you order from the takeaway window, €9.50 if you sit at one of the tables in the buzzy dining room. Either way, you really can't lose.

Chez Jenny

39 bd du Temple, 3rd (01.44.54.39.00, www.chez-jenny.com). Mº République. **Open** noon-midnight Mon-Thur, Sun; noon-1am Fri, Sat. **Main courses** €14.50-€50.10. **Prix fixe** €20.80, €26.90 (Mon-Fri). **Map** p125 C2 ㉛ Brasserie

Chez Jenny is a legendary Alsatian brasserie. As well as the famous *choucroute* (sauerkraut) and traditional oyster bar, the menu features specialities such as *flammekueche*, caramelised pork shank, strudel and *kouglof*. Sitting down to eat at Chez Jenny is like taking a train from Gare de L'Est to the Alsatian foothills. Just be aware that outside of the well-chosen set menus (which don't include any of the local specialities), the bill can mount up alarmingly – for example, allow €20-€30 for sauerkraut. A real regret is that there aren't any speciality Alsatian beers on the menu.

Chez Julien

1 rue du Pont Louis-Philippe, 4th (01.42.78.31.64, www.beaumarly.com). Mº Pont Marie. **Open** noon-2.30pm, 7.30-10.30pm Mon-Fri; 12.30-3pm, 7.30-11pm Sat, Sun. **Main courses** €23-€40. **Prix fixe** *Lunch* €22 (Apr-Sept Mon-Fri), €65, €85, €115. *Dinner* €65, €85, €115. **Map** p125 B4 ㉜ Bistro

Thierry Costes discreetly took over this vintage bistro overlooking the Seine in 2007. The zebra banquette near the loo upstairs is most reminiscent of the Costes style, but the 1920s dining room is also unmistakably chic with plum walls, a big chandelier and red banquettes, and the terrace outside stretches across the pedestrian street. The food is predictable – crab salad, steak with shoestring fries – and pricey, but it's hard not to enjoy this slice of Paris life.

★ € Chez Omar

47 rue de Bretagne, 3rd (01.42.72.36.26). Mº Arts et Métiers or Temple. **Open** noon-2.30pm, 7-11.30pm Mon-Sat; 7-11.30pm Sun. **Main courses** €12-€26. **No credit cards**. **Map** p125 C2 ㉝ North African

The once-fashionable Omar doesn't take any reservations, and the queue can often stretch the length of the zinc bar and through the door. Everyone is waiting for the same thing: couscous. Prices range from €12 (vegetarian) to €26 (*royale*); there are no tagines or other traditional Maghreb mains, only a handful of French classics (duck, fish, steak). Overstretched waiters slip through the crowds with mounds of semolina, vats of vegetable-laden broth and steel platters heaving with meat, including the stellar merguez. Even on packed nights, there's an offer of seconds – gratis – to encourage you to stay.

Cru

7 rue Charlemagne, 4th (01.40.27.81.84, www.restaurantcru.fr). Mº St-Paul. **Open** 12.30-2.30pm, 7.30-11pm Tue-Sat; 12.30-3pm Sun. **Main courses** €9-€28. **Prix fixe** *Lunch* €19 (Mon-Fri). *Brunch* (Sun) €24. **Map** p125 C4 ㉞ Bistro

EXPLORE

Opening a raw-food restaurant is a gamble, so the owners of Cru cheat here and there, offering root vegetable 'chips' and a few *plancha* dishes. Still, the extensive menu has plenty for the crudivore, such as some unusual carpaccios (the veal with preserved lemon is particularly good) and intriguing 'red' and 'green' plates, variations on the tomato and cucumber. The food is perfectly good, but the real reason to come here is the gorgeous courtyard terrace.

★ Derrière

69 rue des Gravilliers, 3rd (01.44.61.91.95, www.derriere-resto.com). M° Arts et Métiers. **Open** noon-2.30pm, 8-11.30pm Mon-Sat; noon-4.30pm, 8-11pm Sun. **Main courses** €14-€38. **Prix fixe** *Lunch* €25, €30 (Mon-Fri). *Brunch* €38 (Sun). **Map** p125 B2 ㉟ **Bistro**

Mourad Mazouz, the man behind Momo and Sketch in London, has hit on another winning formula with this apartment-restaurant in the same street as his North African restaurant 404 and bar Andy Wahloo. The cluttered-chic look mixes contemporary fixtures and antique furniture, such as the beat-up armchairs in the smoking room hidden behind a wardrobe door upstairs. It attracts a young, hip crowd that appreciates the high-calorie comfort food: roast chicken with buttery mashed potatoes, macaroni gratin with taramasalata, and chocolate mousse.

Glou

101 rue Vieille du Temple, 3rd (01.42.74.44.32, www.glou-resto.com). M° St-Sébastien Froissart. **Open** 12.30-2.30pm, 8-11pm Mon-Fri; noon-5pm, 7.30-11.30pm Sat; noon-5pm, 7.30-10.30pm Sun. **Main courses** €16-€27. **Prix fixe** *Lunch* €17, €21 (Mon-Fri). **Map** p125 C3 ㊱ **Bistro**

For a restaurant founded by a man the *New York Times* dubbed the 'wizard of offal', it's initially disappointing that Glou keeps its tongue (and heart, testicles and other offcuts) in cheek and off the menu. Instead this charming bistro plays things straight and pan-continental with Spanish meat boards, subtle pasta dishes and bold French desserts. Smoked duck stuffed with foie gras might be followed by a seasonal cep ravioli. To finish, a crispy chocolate and praline tartlet with a glass of 'Sugar Baby Love', a dessert wine. Glou is a 'food with friends' affair, with friendly staff and a communal table that reverberates with the laughter of Marais hipsters.

Le Hangar

12 impasse Berthaud, 3rd (01.42.74.55.44). M° Rambuteau. **Open** noon-2.30pm, 7.30-11pm Tue-Sat. Closed Aug. **Main courses** €19-€30. **No credit cards. Map** p125 B3 ㊲ **Bistro**

It's worth making the effort to find this bistro by the Centre Pompidou, with its terrace tucked away in a hidden alley and excellent cooking. A bowl of

tapenade and toast is supplied to keep you going while choosing from the extensive *carte*. It yields, for starters, tasty and grease-free *rillettes de lapereau* (rabbit) alongside perfectly balanced pumpkin and chestnut soup. Main courses include pan-fried foie gras on a smooth potato purée.

★ L'Ilot

4 rue de la Corderie, 3rd (06.95.12.86.61, www.lilot-restaurant.com). M° Filles du Calvaire, République or Temple. **Open** 6.30pm-12.30am Tue-Fri; 12.30-2.30pm, 6.30pm-12.30am Sat. **Main courses** €9.50-€24. **Map** p125 C2 ㊳ **Seafood**

At l'Ilot, you don't have to pay Paris prices for the best catch of the day. The venue is tiny but beautiful, with big slate menus, earthenware pots and white parquet, a bay window, a few photos on the walls and a terrace for nice days – it all has a solid charm. Perch yourself on a stool and order a glass of white wine, then browse the menu: €6.50 for a serving of sardines or salmon rillettes, €5 to €9.50 for grey or pink Madagascan prawns, €6.50 for whelks and €8 for a half crab (€14 for the whole). There are also beautiful oysters, while the fish is smoked or marinated. The value of the set lunch menu is unbeatable, at €12.50 for a starter, main and glass of wine. A delight.

MG Road

205 rue Saint-Martin, 3rd (01 42 76 04 32, www.mgroadrestaurant.com). M° Arts et Métiers. **Open** 12.15-2pm, 7.30pm-midnight Tue-Fri; 12.15-2.45pm, 7.30pm-midnight Sat. **Main courses** €17-€21. **Map** p125 B2 ㊴ **Indian**

MG Road is a modern, upmarket take on cafés run by Persian immigrants in Bombay in the 1930s (they were known as 'Irani') – bright colours, huge mirrors and sober floor tiles hint at this aesthetic heritage, though not as much as the delicious smells wafting out of the kitchen, which is run by Manoj Sharma, an alumnus of London's famous Cinnamon Club. Dishes such as Bengali fish tikka made with line-caught salmon marinated in mustard, aniseed, ginger and chilli showcase the kitchen's talent for modern versions of classic dishes. Prices are a little steep, but the quality of the cooking matches up.

Le Potager du Marais

24 rue Rambuteau, 4th (01.57.40.98.57, www.lepotagerdumarais.fr). M° Rambuteau. **Open** noon-3pm, 7-10.30pm Wed-Sun. **Main courses** €16.50-€18. **Map** p125 B3 ㊵ **Vegetarian**

This organic vegetarian restaurant is proof that you can fit an entire restaurant into a shoebox. But what the Potager lacks in space, it makes up for on the plate with luscious dishes brimming with pulses, tofu, crunchy vegetables and beans. The mushroom terrine, served with gherkins and salad, is a real winner, as are mains such as sweet pumpkin *hachis parmentier* (veggie shepherd's pie). If you require gluten-free, the Potager gets brownie points for its multiple choice of dishes – a real rarity in Paris.

EXPLORE

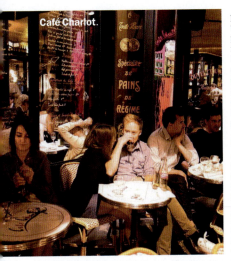

Café Charlot.

price tags to match. After a browse, head through the little door that leads to the in-house café. Inside, pretty wooden tables are arranged around a light-filled room. Coffee comes from a La Marzocco perco-later, and the morning patisserie selection includes sinful blueberry cheesecake. The rest of the day, there's a choice of inventive dishes (€7.50-€17.50), such as aubergine velouté with lemon and almonds or a superb platter of charcuterie garnished with a bunch of grapes. It's all very *soigné*, from the com-position of the dishes to the origin of the produce.

Café Charlot

38 rue de Bretagne, 3rd (01.44.54.03.30, www.cafecharlotparis.com). Mº Filles du Calvaire. **Open** 7am-2am daily. **Map** p125 C2 ④④

Café Charlot is one of the loveliest cafés in the Marais, with a magnificent old-school bakery shop-front and a retro ambience that has seduced local hipsters who come to sun themselves on its lovely terrace on the corner opposite the Enfants Rouges market. Inside, large, round leather benches match the old-fashioned counter. During happy hour, the delicious cocktails start at €6.50, but come early to grab a place on the terrace.

La Caféothèque

52 rue de l'Hôtel de Ville, 4th (01.53.01.83.84, www.lacafeotheque.com). Mº St-Paul. **Open** 10am-7pm Mon-Sat; noon-7pm Sun. **Map** p125 B4 ④⑤

The Caféothèque is where the coffee revolution in Paris kicked off seven years ago. The café is next door to artist's residence La Cité Internationale des Arts, which ensures a cosmopolitan clientele, while its picture-postcard location on the banks of the Seine means tourists are always dropping by as well. *Photo p136.*

Café Suédois

11 rue Payenne, 3rd (01.44.78.80.11). Mº Chemin Vert or St-Paul. **Open** noon-6pm Tue-Sun. **No credit cards.** **Map** p125 C3 ④⑥

The Café Suédois is an integral part of the Swedish Cultural Institute in the Hôtel de Marle, a magnificent mansion in the Marais built between the 15th and 18th centuries. You can while away a sunny afternoon with a good book in its peaceful paved courtyard, or retreat to the pretty café if it's cold and wet. Every morning before opening, a passionate team of Swedish pastry chefs prepare fresh bread, elderflower cordial and a range of seasonal delicacies. The lunch menu consists of a selection of sandwiches, including succulent marinated salmon, as well as carrot cake, cinnamon rolls, cranberry tart and a daily soup special in winter.

Cafés & Bars

★ Andy Wahloo

69 rue des Gravilliers, 3rd (01.42.71.20.38, www.andywahloo-bar.com). Mº Arts et Métiers. **Open** 7pm-1.45am Tue-Sat. **Map** p125 B2 ④①

Andy Wahloo, created by the people behind its neighbour 404 and London's Momo and Sketch, is Arabic for 'I have nothing'. Bijou? This place brings new meaning to the word. The formidably fashionable crowd fights for coveted 'seats' on upturned paint cans; from head to toe, it's a beautifully designed venue, crammed with Moroccan artefacts and a spice rack of colours. It's quiet early on, with a surge around 9pm, and the atmosphere heats up as the night goes on.

Le Baromètre

17 rue Charlot, 3rd (01.48.87.04.54). Mº Arts et Métiers. **Open** 10am-midnight Mon-Sat. Closed 3wks Aug. **Map** p125 C2 ④②

This unpretentious wine bar is popular with artisan types. Lunchtimes are heaving, so unless you're after the sit-down *menu du jour* (€13-€14) served at the back, you're better off coming along for a lazy afternoon. Order a plate of cheese or the house speciality, bacon and andouillette gratin, and choose from a 20-strong list of wines by the glass, most under €5.

Broken Arm

12 rue Perrée, 3rd (01.44.61.53.60, www.the-broken-arm.com). Mº Arts et Métiers or Temple. **Open** *Shop* 11am-7pm Tue-Sat. *Café* 9am-6pm Tue-Sat. **Map** p125 C2 ④③

The Broken Arm concept store, founded by three bright young things from the Des Jeunes Gens Modernes lifestyle collective, is full of handpicked clothes, books, music, furniture and shoes, with

★ Candelaria

52 rue de Saintonge, 3rd (01.42.74.41.28, www.candelariaparis.com). Mº Filles du Calvaire or République. **Open** 12.30-11pm Mon-Wed, Sun; noon-midnight Thur-Sat. **Map** p125 C2 ④⑦

La Caféothèque. See p135.

Has Paris woken up to the temptations of the taco? Apparently so, thanks to this taqueria, where local hipsters come to sip margaritas or house specials such as the *guêpe verte* (tequila, lime, pepper, cucumber, spices and agave syrup). On the food front, you have the choice between tacos and tostadas.

★ Comme à Lisbonne

37 rue du Roi de Sicile, 4th (07.61.23.42.30, www.commealisbonne.com). Mº Hôtel de Ville.
Open 11am-7pm Tue-Sun. **Map** p125 B4 ❹

Opened in 2011 by the cheerful Portuguese barista Victor Silveira, this hole-in-the-wall bar in a chic corner of the Marais may be impossibly small, but it has become a runaway success with its irresistible freshly baked *pasteis de nata* accompanied by traditional Portuguese coffee. The *pasteis*, succulent custard tarts, are baked according to Victor's mother's secret recipe. Although there are no seats and just a small bar at which to sip your coffee and nibble a *pasteis*, there is also a deli section with a host of traditional Portuguese goodies.

L'Estaminet

39 rue de Bretagne, 3rd (01.42.72.28.12, www.lestaminetdesenfantsrouges.com). Mº Temple. **Open** 9am-8pm Tue-Sat; 9am-3pm Sun (9am-11pm Thur-Sat in summer). **Map** p125 C2 ❹

L'Estaminet is tucked away in the Marché des Enfants-Rouges, a charming neighbourhood market and one of the city's oldest. The café has a warm interior, with a grandfather clock in the corner and guests eating €13 *plats du jour* off Limoges porcelain. Wines from €3.90 a glass.

★ L'Etoile Manquante

34 rue Vieille-du-Temple, 4th (01.42.72.48.34, www.cafeine.com). Mº Hôtel de Ville or St-Paul.
Open 9am-2am daily. **Map** p125 B3 ❺

L'Etoile Manquante is the hippest of Xavier Denamur's merry Marais bars. Cocktails are punchy, traditional tipples just as good, and the salads and snacks reasonably priced and tasty – but it's the design and buzz that are the main draws. The decor is trendy but comfortable, embellished with interesting art. As in all Denamur's places, no visit is complete without a trip to the toilets: here, an electric train shuttles between cubicles, starlight beams down from the ceiling, and a hidden camera films you washing your hands. Just watch the small screen on the wall behind you.

Lizard Lounge

18 rue du Bourg-Tibourg, 4th (01.42.72.81.34, www.cheapblonde.com). Mº Hôtel de Ville.
Open noon-2am daily. **Map** p125 B3 ❺

An anglophone favourite located deep in the heart of the Marais, this loud and lively (hetero) pick-up joint provides lager in pints (€6), plus cocktails (€7) and a viewing platform for beer-goggled oglers. Bare brick and polished woodwork are offset by the occasional lizard and a housey soundtrack. Bargain boozing (cocktails €6) kicks off at 4pm (until 8pm Tue-Thur, 10pm Fri, Sat); from 8pm to 10pm, there's another happy hour in the sweaty cellar bar (complete with minuscule dancefloor); on Mondays, it lasts all night. A popular weekend brunch of bacon, sausages and eggs benedict caters to the homesick.

Le Loir dans la Théière

3 rue des Rosiers, 4th (01.42.72.90.61). Mº St-Paul.
Open 9am-7.30pm daily. **Map** p125 C4 ❺

Le Loir is named after the unfortunate dormouse that gets dunked in the pot at the Mad Hatter's tea party in *Alice in Wonderland*. Its squishy sofas are the perfect complement to its comfort food: it specialises in baked goods, and the famed lemon meringue and chocolate fondant are divine. At weekends, it's packed out with tourists in search of brunch; long queues of people looking enviously at your plate, plus occasionally patchy service, can mar the experience. Be prepared to queue.

La Perle

78 rue Vieille-du-Temple, 3rd (01.42.72.69.93, www.cafelaperle.com). M° Chemin Vert or St-Paul. **Open** 6.30am-2am daily. **Map** p125 C3 ❸

The Pearl achieves a rare balance between all-day and late-night venue, and has a good hetero/homo mix. In the morning, it draws early risers; lunchtime is for a business crowd; the afternoon reels in retired locals, and in the evening, screenwriters rub elbows with young dandies, keeping one eye on the mirror and an ear on the electro-rock. The menu runs the gamut from omelettes to *salade marine*. Expect a DJ later on.

Le Petit Fer à Cheval

30 rue Vieille-du-Temple, 4th (01.42.72.47.47, www.cafeine.com). M° St-Paul. **Open** 9am-2am daily. **Map** p125 B3 ❺

Even a miniature Shetland pony would be pushed to squeeze his hoof into this *fer à cheval* (horseshoe) – the adorable little café, which has been in business for more than 100 years, has one of France's smallest bars. Tucked in behind the glassy façade is a friendly dining room lined with reclaimed métro benches; if you want scenery, the tables out front overlook the bustle of rue Vieille-du-Temple. As with its sister bar L'Etoile Manquante (*see p136*), the loos are worth the detour – they look as if they've been pummelled out of a defunct Dalek, with metal panels and strange knobs everywhere.

La Petite Table

27 rue de Saintonge, 3rd (01.74.64.00.36, www. lapetitetableparis.com). M° Filles du Calvaire or St-Sébastien Froissart. **Open** 9am-11pm Mon, Wed-Sun. **Map** p125 C2 ❺

La Petite Table serves up everything you could want from a Paris café-diner. Pastries are piled high in the window, grey banquettes go perfectly with the colourful tiles, a coffee machine rumbles comfortingly, and dozens of little tables hold big bouquets of fresh-cut flowers. In the evenings, a substantial menu offers Italian antipasti: bruschetta with cherry tomatoes, cheese platters, caramelised endives with parmesan, or fresh burratta with persimmon. Finish up with some home-made pastries: honey and pistachio cake, cappuccino tartlet, muffins, macaroons and cookies. With a decent Italian wine list, this funky little hangout is a great one for the address book.

Stolly's

16 rue Cloche-Perce, 4th (01.42.76.06.76, www. cheapblonde.com). M° Hôtel de Ville or St-Paul. **Open** 4.30pm-1.30am daily. **Map** p125 B4 ❺

This seen-it-all drinking den has been serving a mainly anglophone crowd for nights immemorial. The staff make the place what it is, and a summer terrace eases libation, as do the long happy hours; but don't expect anyone at Stolly's to faff about with food. There's football on TV and a plastic shark to compensate.

Le Temps des Cérises

31 rue de la Cerisaie, 4th (01.42.72.08.63). M° Bastille. **Open** 8.30am-2am Mon-Fri; 10am-2am Sat, Sun. **Map** p125 C5 ❺

Not to be confused with several other cafés of the same name, this one-room *bistro à vins* has changed very little over the years. Faded net curtains, Duralex tumblers behind the zinc bar and prices that begin at €4 for a *vin* are reminiscent of a bygone age. The blackboard wine list is limited but the selection is always well chosen, and food is old-fashioned and hearty (think beef stew and *blanquette de veau*). The general banter is football-centred, so get ready to rumble with the natives about the goings-on at PSG.

Shops & Services

AB33

33 rue Charlot, 3rd (01.42.71.02.82, www.ab33.fr). M° Filles du Calvaire. **Open** 10.30am-7.30pm Tue-Sat; 11am-7pm Sun. **Map** p125 C2 ❺ **Fashion**

Delicate in summer, cosy in winter, the pretty, unstructured clothes in AB33 may not make the wish list of any sultry, groomed Parisienne, but would be perfect for her up-from-the-country Bardot-esque cousin. Owner Agathe Buchotte sells Forte, Forte, Kristina Ti and Philip Lim.

Anikalena Skärström

16 rue du Pont aux Choux, 3rd (09.83.82.32.85, www.anikalena.com). M° St-Sébastien Froissart. **Open** 10am-7pm Mon-Fri; noon-7pm Sat. Closed 2wks Aug. **Map** p125 D3 ❺ **Fashion**

Clean lines and streamlining are the guiding aesthetic for Anikalena Skärström's collections

Candelaria. *See p135.*

EXPLORE

of sporty, sexy day and evening dresses and separates, with the occasional wow piece like the grass-green suede coat a few seasons ago.

Anne et Valentin
4 rue Ste-Croix-de-la-Bretonnerie, 4th (01.40.29.93.01, www.anneetvalentin.com). M° Hôtel de Ville or St-Paul. **Open** noon-8pm Mon; 11am-8pm Tue-Sat. Closed 1wk Aug. **Map** p125 B3 ❻⓿ Accessories
This modish eyewear firm occupies a three-floor boutique. A&V design chic unisex frames: light titanium models have names like Tarzan and Truman; coloured acetate frames have inventive details.

April 77
49 rue de Saintonge, 3rd (01.40.29.07.30, www.april77.fr). M° Filles du Calvaire. **Open** 2-7.30pm Mon; 11am-7.30pm Tue-Sat. **Map** p125 C2 ❻❶ Fashion
The cult skinny jeans brand has acquired its own boutique, designed by Steven Thomas, to show off a collection inspired by the mid-'80s music scene.
Other location 7-9 rue Charonne, 11th (01.43.38.39.74).

Au Nom de la Rose
87 rue St-Antoine, 4th (01.42.71.34.24, www.aunomdelarose.fr). M° St-Paul. **Open** Sept-July 9am-9pm Mon-Sat; 9am-2pm, 3-6pm Sun. Aug 10am-9pm Mon-Sat. **Map** p125 C4 ❻❷ Gifts & souvenirs
Specialising in roses, Au Nom can supply a bouquet, as well as rose-based beauty products and candles.
Other locations throughout the city.

Azzedine Alaïa
7 rue de Moussy, 4th (01.42.72.30.69, www.alaia.fr). M° Hôtel de Ville. **Open** 10am-7pm Mon-Sat. **Map** p125 B3 ❻❸ Fashion
Ringing the doorbell gains you entry to the factory-style showroom in the same building as Alaïa's headquarters and apartment, where the Tunisian creator continues to astound with his originality. Stunning haute couture creations are in the back room, and sexy shoes are scattered among the rails.
Other location 5 rue de Marignan, 8th (01.76.72.91.01).

ba&sh
22 rue des Francs-Bourgeois, 3rd (01.42.78.55.10, www.ba-sh.com). M° Jacques Bonsergent. **Open** 11am-7.30pm Mon-Sat; noon-7.30pm Sun. **Map** p125 C3 ❻❹ Fashion
At this fresh, Paris-based label, you'll find dresses, skirts and blouses with ethnic touches on one side and drapey jersey on the other.
Other locations throughout the city.

★ Christophe Lemaire
28 rue de Poitou, 3rd (01.44.78.00.09, www.christophelemaire.com). M° St-Sébastien Froissart.

Open 1-7pm Mon; noon-7.30pm Tue-Fri; 11am-7.30pm Sat. **Map** p125 C3 ❻❺ Fashion
Creative director for Lacoste for seven years, Lemaire opened his own boutique in an old pharmacy. It's decorated like a fantasy apartment: the salon, in '70s gold and glitz, stocks his own-label menswear and womenswear in high-tech Japanese textiles, and leads into a soundproofed music room with a wall of old speakers where you can buy collectable Lacoste and Lemaire's own fave CDs. Next door the seductive 'Japanese salon' holds the jeans range. You can also buy the vintage lighting on display here.

COS
4 rue des Rosiers, 4th (01.44.54.37.70, www.cosstores.com). M° St-Paul. **Open** 10am-7.30pm Mon-Sat. **Map** p125 C4 ❻❻ Fashion
H&M's upmarket brand Collection of Style (COS) now has a Paris outpost, designed by William Russell, in rue des Rosiers, causing some consternation among those who'd rather have kept this a chain-free zone.

Dammann Frères
15 pl des Vosges, 4th (01.44.54.04.88, www.dammann.fr). M° St-Paul. **Open** 11am-7pm Mon-Fri; 10am-8pm Sat, Sun. **Map** p125 C4 ❻❼ Food & drink
Dammann Frères, fine tea importers since 1825, have finally opened their own boutique, a wonderful den of a place with a beamed roof and mahogany shelves displaying hundreds of their exquisite black boxes. The *orgue à thés* allows you to sniff the aromas of 160 blends. A small tin of loose tea or 24 tea bags costs around €10-€12 and they also sell traditional oriental iron teapots. Everything is attractively gift-wrapped.

★ L'Eclaireur
40 rue de Sévigné, 4th (01.48.87.10.22, www.leclaireur.com). M° St-Paul. **Open** 11am-7pm Mon-Sat; 2-7pm Sun. **Map** p125 C3 ❻❽ Fashion
Housed in a dandified warehouse, L'Eclaireur stocks designs by the likes of Comme des Garçons, Martin Margiela, Dries van Noten, Carpe Diem and Junya Watanabe. Among its exclusive finds, check out smocks by Finnish designer Jasmin Santanen. At the secretive rue Hérold branch you have to ring the doorbell to enter.
Other locations 10 rue Hérold, 1st (01.40.41.09.89); 26 av des Champs-Elysées, 8th (01.45.62.12.32); 10 rue Boissy d'Anglas, 8th (01.53.43.03.70); 39-41 av Hoche, 8th (01.56.68.10.47).

★ Finger in the Nose
60 rue Saintonge, 3rd (01.42.71.43.40, www.fingerinthenose.com). M° St-Sébastien Froissart. **Open** 11am-7pm Tue-Sat. **Map** p125 C2 ❻❾ Children
As the name suggests, there is nothing remotely twee about the kidswear from this cool Norwegian

EXPLORE

Galerie Fatiha Selam.

Tatiana Trouvé and Bernard Frize, he also features radical Austrian collective Gelatin.

Galerie Fatiha Selam
58 rue Chapon, 3rd (09.83.33.65.69, www. fatihaselam.com). M° Arts et Métiers. **Open** 11am-7pm Tue-Sat. **Map** p125 B2 **73 Gallery**
This new addition to a burgeoning gallery street opened in late 2012 with an exhibition of US artist Stephen Schultz's dreamlike canvases. Fatiha Selam brings a fresh eye to the NoMa art scene and promises to explore figurative and abstract contemporary artists both known and emerging.

★ Iro
53 rue Vieille-du-Temple, 4th (01.42.77.25.09, www.iro.fr). M° St-Paul. **Open** 10.30am-7.30pm Mon-Sat; noon-7.30pm Sun. **Map** p125 B3
74 Fashion
Fashion editors have tipped designers Laurent and Arik Bitton for stardom with what they call 'basic deluxe': skinny knits, skinny jeans, babydoll dresses and the 'perfecto' mini leather jacket. With a background in music, the brothers know how to hit just the right note for a French silhouette.
Other locations throughout the city.

Izraël
30 rue François-Miron, 4th (01.42.72.66.23). M° Hôtel de Ville. **Open** 11am-1pm, 2-7pm Tue-Fri; 11am-7pm Sat. Closed Aug. **Map** p125 B4
75 Food & drink
A Marais fixture, this narrow shop stocks spices and other delights from Mexico, Turkey and India.

Jacenko
38 rue de Poitou, 3rd (01.42.71.80.38). M° St-Sébastien Froissart. **Open** 12.30-7.30pm Tue-Sat. **Map** p125 C3 **76 Fashion**
The owner of this tasteful little boutique has a faultless eye for shirts, jackets, woollens and accessories that are dandy but not downright gay. McQ, Viktor & Rolf, Givenchy and John Smedley all appear.

Jacques Génin
133 rue de Turenne, 3rd (01.45.77.29.01, www.jacquesgenin.fr). M° Filles du Calvaire. **Open** 11am-7pm Mon-Fri, Sun; 11am-8pm Sat. **Map** p125 C2 **77 Food & drink**
Jacques Génin was voted the 'best *chocolatier* in the world' by critic Mort Rosenblum, but his creations could previously be tasted only in top restaurants. But now his impressive Marais boutique allows you to taste *sur place* or take a bag home. The signature éclairs and tarts glisten in glass cases, and the millefeuilles are made to order for perfect freshness. The chocolate ganaches include Menthe Amante, a two-phase taste sensation. One part of the space is given over to a tearoom, and a spiral staircase leads to the *ateliers*.
Other location 27 rue de Varenne, 7th (01.53.71.72.21).

designer. In this Marais boutique blackboard walls with chalk slogans and drawings set off tough rebel urban wear for six- to 16-year-olds.
Other location 11 rue de l'Echaudé, 6th (09.83.01.76.75).

Finkelsztajn
27 rue des Rosiers, 4th (01.42.72.78.91, www. laboutiquejaune.com). M° St-Paul. **Open** 10am-7pm Mon, Wed-Sun. Closed mid July-mid Aug. **Map** p125 C3 **70 Food & drink**
This motherly, yellow-fronted shop, in business since 1946, stocks dense Jewish cakes filled with poppy seeds, apples or cream cheese.

Free 'P' Star
52 rue de la Verrerie, 4th (www.freepstar.com). M° St-Paul. **Open** 11am-9pm Mon-Fri; noon-9pm Sat, Sun. **Map** p125 B3 **71 Fashion**
Late-night shopping is fun at this Aladdin's cave of retro glitz, ex-army wear and glad rags that has provided fancy dress for many a Paris party.
Other locations 61 rue de la Verrerie, 4th (01.42.78.00.76); 20 rue de Rivoli, 4th (01.42.77.63.43).

★ Galerie Emmanuel Perrotin
76 rue de Turenne, 3rd (01.42.16.79.79, www. galerieperrotin.com). M° St-Sébastien Froissart. **Open** 11am-7pm Tue-Sat. **Map** p125 D3 **72 Gallery**
Perrotin is one of the sharpest figures in town: not content with owning a gallery in Miami and a glossy magazine, he has recently jumped on the design bandwagon with shows by Robert Stadler and Eric Benqué. As well as the quirky Japanese set of Takashi Murakami, Mariko Mori et al, and big French names such as Sophie Calle, Xavier Veilhan,

EXPLORE

Jimmy Fairly
*64 rue Vieille du Temple, 4th (01.79.72.60.20,
www.jimmyfairly.com). M° St-Paul.* **Open** 11am-
7.30pm daily. **Map** p125 C3 **78 Accessories**
Probably the city's largest supplier of eyewear
to bearded hipsters, Jimmy Fairly launched as a
website before opening a store in 2012. There are
around 30 retro-style designs: pick up a Monroe,
Hamilton or Watson for just €95, lenses included (if
you don't need a prescription or to have them fitted
with anti-reflective glass). What's more, the 'Buy
one give one' model means that for every pair of
glasses sold, Jimmy Fairly gives a brand new pair to
someone in need.
Other location 45 rue Montorgueil, 2nd
(01.79.72.60.20).

★ K Jacques
*16 rue Pavée, 4th (01.40.27.03.57, www.kjacques.
fr). M° St-Paul.* **Open** 10am-7.30pm Mon-Sat;
11am-7.30pm Sun. **Map** p125 C4 **79 Accessories**
Set up in Saint-Tropez in 1933 by Jacques Keklikian
and his wife, the K Jacques workshop started life
stitching together basic leather sandals for visitors
to the Med resort. The Homère (or Homer) was, and
still is, the signature piece – Picasso loved them.

Martin Grant
*10 rue Charlot, 3rd (01.42.71.39.49, www.
martingrantparis.com). M° Temple.* **Open**
10am-1pm, 2-6pm Mon-Fri. Closed 3wks Aug.
Map p125 C3 **80 Fashion**
This high-end shop is tucked away in a second-floor
Marais apartment. If you're a stickler for steady
cuts, pure textiles and unfussy designs, Australian
Martin Grant's interpretation of couture is for you.

Merci.

★ Merci
*111 bd Beaumarchais, 3rd (01.42.77.00.33, www.
merci-merci.com). M° St-Sébastien Froissart.* **Open**
10am-7pm Mon-Sat. **Map** p125 D3 **81 Homewares**
Merci is housed in a 19th-century fabric factory.
Inside, three loft-like floors heave with furniture,
jewellery, stationery, fashion, household products,
childrenswear and a haberdashery. That's not all. In
a move that takes the trend for retailer responsibility
to a new level, this most generous of general stores
gives all its profits to charity.

Nodus
*22 rue Vieille-du-Temple, 4th (01.42.77.07.96,
www.nodus.fr). M° Hôtel de Ville or St-Paul.*
Open 10.45am-2pm, 3-7.30pm Mon-Sat;
1-7.30pm Sun. **Map** p125 B4 **82 Fashion**
Under the wooden beams of this men's shirt specialist
are neat rows of striped, checked and plain dress
shirts, silk ties and silver-plated crystal cufflinks.
Other locations throughout the city.

Nomade Shop
*37 bd Bourdon, 4th (01.44.54.07.44, www.nomade
shop.com). M° Bastille.* **Open** 11am-1.30pm, 2.30-
7.30pm Tue-Fri; 10am-7pm Sat; noon-6pm Sun.
Map p125 D5 **83 Skateboarding**
For some years now, this has been the go-to place for
skaters in Paris. Though considerably more expensive than its online rivals, Nomade Shop has main-
tained its edge for two reasons: it allows you to try
skateboards and rollerskates before purchasing, and
it houses a repair shop that doubles up as a custo-
misation service. The shop also offers a bewildering
array of gadgets and accessories that range from the
life-saving (helmets) to the outlandish (Poweriser
jumping stilts, anyone?).

Ofr.
*20 rue Dupetit-Thouars, 3rd (01.42.45.72.88,
www.ofrsystem.com). M° Temple.* **Open** 10am-
8pm Mon-Sat; 2pm-7pm Sun. **Map** p125 C2
84 Books & magazines
Adored by fans of fashion and contemporary arts
magazines, Ofr. bookshop stocks fanzines, arty
postcards, boutique publications and fashion accessories. You can find everything from the latest issue
of *Love* to the best street-style shots of Facehunter,
but Ofr. is also an independent publishing house
that creates works in collaboration with a wide
range of artists, like the photographer Ami Sioux.
Just moments from République, Ofr. regularly holds
exhibitions on anything from children's art to modernist graphics, surfing to Basque dance – nothing
scares this ultra-specialist avant-garde space. Also
check out the boutique at the rear, where you'll find
up-and-coming fashion labels and more exhibitions.

Polka Galerie
*Cour de Venise, 12 rue Saint-Gilles, 3rd
(01.76.21.41.30, www.polkagalerie.com).*

EXPLORE

M° Bréguet-Sabin or Chemin Vert. **Open**
11am-7.30pm Tue-Sat. **Map** p125 D3 **⑤ Gallery**
'Every photo has a tale to tell': such is the leitmotif
at Polka Galerie, where Adélie de Ipanema and
Edouard Genestar have devoted their art space
to photojournalism. Works on display are signed
by photographers such as Ethan Levitas, Marc
Riboud, Reza and Daido Morayima. While
you're there, pick up a copy of *Polka Magazine*, a
fortnightly spread brimming with picture-rich
articles, many of which tie in with the exhibitions
in the gallery.

Pozzetto

*39 rue du Roi de Sicile, 4th (01.42.77.08.64,
www.pozzetto.biz). M° Hôtel de Ville or St-Paul.*
Open noon-11.30pm Mon-Thur; noon-12.45am
Fri, Sat; noon-midnight Sun. **Map** p125 B4
⑥ Food & drink
Pozzetto might not be the most famous *gelateria*
in Paris, but it's one of the best, serving classic
Italian flavours such as *gianduia torinese* (a Turin
speciality of chocolate and hazelnuts), *fior di latte*
(made from milk, cream and sugar) and *pistacchio*
(a creamy Sicilian pistachio blend). Fruit-lovers
are in for a treat, too, with peach, berry, pear and
orange sorbets all made from real fruit. Order your
scoop through the little window overlooking rue
du Roi de Sicile.
Other location 16 rue Vieille-du-Temple, 3rd
(01.42.71.49.18).

★ Les Prairies de Paris

*23 rue Debelleyme, 3rd (01.48.04.91.16, www.
lesprairiesdeparis.com). M° St-Sébastien Froissart.*
Open 11.30am-2pm, 3-7.30pm Tue-Sat; 2-7pm Sun.
Map p125 C2 **⑦ Fashion**
The ground floor of Laeticia Ivanez's boutique
is given over to art shows, gigs and happenings.
Downstairs the 1960s theme continues, with a
cocoon-like setting in which to commune with the
disco-glam separates and cute children's collection.
Other location 6 rue du Pré aux Clercs, 7th
(01.40.20.44.12).

Surface 2 Air

*108 rue Vieille-du-Temple, 3rd (01.44.61.76.27,
www.surface2airparis.com). M° St-Sébastien
Froissart.* **Open** 11.30am-7.30pm Mon-Sat;
1.30-7.30pm Sun. **Map** p125 C3 **⑧ Fashion**
This non-concept concept store also acts as an art
gallery. The cult clothing selection takes in Alice
McCall's sassy frocks, Fifth Avenue Shoe Repair
jeans and printed dresses by Wood Wood. For men,
labels include Marios, Wendy & Jim and F-Troupe.

Les Vignoles

*7 rue Commines, 3rd (09.51.62.93.63, www.
atelierdesvignoles.com). M° Filles du Calvaire
or St-Sébastien Froissart.* **Open** 2-7pm Mon;
11am-7.30pm Tue-Sat. **Map** p125 D2 **⑨ Fashion**

This Marais concept store plays elegantly with
Parisian and French identity – the owners Yann
and Yannick bring together stylists, designers and
other contemporary artists inspired by the City of
Light. But there are no tacky souvenirs for tourists
– everything is Paris chic, with a knowing wink.
Macaroons show up in bracelets, space invaders
(usually found decorating the walls of the capital's
buildings) adorn T-shirts. Also on show are Kobja's
taxidermy handbags and jewellery made from
toads, snakes and other amphibians. Anyone for a
genuine frog wallet?

Le Village St-Paul

*Rue St-Paul, rue Charlemagne & quai des
Célestins, 4th (www.levillagesaintpaul.com).
M° St-Paul.* **Open** 11am-7pm Mon, Thur-Sun.
Map p125 C4 **⑩ Homewares**
This colony of antiques sellers is a source of retro
furniture, kitchenware and wine gadgets.

Vintage Bar

*16 rue de la Verrerie, 4th (06.72.11.13.58).
M° Hôtel de Ville or St-Paul.* **Open** noon-8pm
Mon-Sat; 1-8pm Sun. **Map** p125 B3 **⑪ Fashion**
Vintage Bar is pretty luxurious, in an area where
clothes can usually be found at bargain prices. Once
inside, though, it's hard to imagine that the clothes
have three-figure labels; it couldn't feel further from
a high-end hangout. Trinkets clutter up the floor, and
fur coats hanging from the ceiling casually brush
your face as you walk by. The boutique also acts as
a *dépôt-vente* – if you have designer threads lying
about you want to get rid of, they'll sell them on, with
a percentage of the price returning to you.

WAIT

*9 rue Notre-Dame de Nazareth, 3rd (09.82.52.84.34,
www.wait-paris.com). M° République.* **Open** 11am-
7pm Mon; 10am-7pm Tue-Fri; 2-7pm Sat. **Map**
p125 C1 **⑫ Accessories**
Imagine a man's ultimate fantasy living room and
you have WAIT, a shop filled with everything from
retro video game consoles, surfboards, skateboards
and shades to a reconditioned racing bike, vintage
furniture, cool shirts, T-shirts and baseball caps.
Plus the crucial accessory for the modern man –
scented candles.

Zadig & Voltaire

*42 rue des Francs-Bourgeois, 3rd (01.44.54.00.60,
www.zadig-et-voltaire.com). M° Hôtel de Ville or
St-Paul.* **Open** 10.30am-7.30pm Mon-Sat; noon-
7.30pm Sun. **Map** p125 C3 **⑬ Fashion**
Zadig &Voltaire's relaxed, urban collection is a
winner. Popular separates include cotton tops,
shirts and faded jeans; its winter range of cashmere
jumpers is superb.
▶ *The more upmarket Zadig & Voltaire De Luxe
is at 18 rue François 1er, 8th (01.40.70.97.89).*
Other locations throughout the city.

EXPLORE

Bastille & Eastern Paris

Place de la Bastille has remained a symbol of popular revolt ever since the storming of the grim fortress-prison that kicked off the Revolution in 1789. The square is still a gathering point for demonstrations and Bastille Day festivities, but the only remnants of the prison are found in the métro station underneath. In fact, with its opera house, lively market along boulevard Richard-Lenoir, and bobo bars and restaurants, Bastille is positively hip these days – especially at night when rue Amelot, rue de la Roquette and rue de Charonne serve party-crazed Parisians enough drinks to sink the canal boats in the nearby Port de l'Arsenal. The Bercy district has seen its star rise, too, thanks to Frank Gehry's striking Cinémathèque Française, and the shops and cafés housed in old wine warehouses at Bercy Village.

Bois de Vincennes.

Don't Miss

1 **Cimetière du Père-Lachaise** Home to some of France's most creative corpses (p144).

2 **Chambelland** Baking brilliance (p154).

3 **Bois de Vincennes** Paris's biggest park is buzzing with activity (p156).

4 **Cité Nationale de l'Histoire de l'Immigration** Immigration laid bare (p156).

5 **DPAM** Cool kids' clothes (p154).

BASTILLE & FURTHER EAST

In the 11th, 12th & 20th arrondissements.

The area around place de la Bastille was transformed in the 1980s with the arrival of the **Opéra Bastille** (*see p283*), along with a slew of fashionable cafés, restaurants and bars. The present-day square occupies the site of the long-vanished prison ramparts, and is dominated by the Opéra's curved façade. Opened in 1989 on the bicentenary of Bastille Day, the venue remains controversial, criticised for its poor acoustics and design. South of the square is the Port de l'Arsenal marina. The canal continues underground north of the square, running beneath boulevard Richard-Lenoir.

Rue du Fbg-St-Antoine has been the heart of the furniture-makers' district for centuries. Showrooms still line the street, though they've been joined by clothes shops and bars. Cobbled rue de Lappe typifies the shift, as the last remaining furniture workshops hold out against theme bars overrun at weekends by suburban youths. Pockets of bohemian resistance remain on rue de Charonne, however, with the **Pause Café** and its busy terrace, bistro **Chez Paul** (no.13, 11th, 01.47.00.34.57, www.chezpaul.com) and dealers in colourful 1960s furniture. Rue des Taillandiers and rue Keller are a focus for record stores, streetwear shops and fashion designers.

Narrow street frontages hide cobbled alleys, lined with craftsmen's workshops or quirky bistros dating from the 18th century. Note the cours de l'Ours, du Cheval Blanc, du Bel Air (and hidden garden) and de la Maison Brûlée, the passage du Chantier on rue du Fbg-St-Antoine, the rustic-looking passage de l'Etoile d'Or and the passage de l'Homme, with wooden shopfronts on rue de Charonne. This area was originally located outside the city walls on the lands of the Convent of St-Antoine (parts of which survive as the Hôpital St-Antoine). In the Middle Ages, skilled furniture-makers not belonging to the city's restrictive guilds earned the neighbourhood a reputation for free thinking that was cemented a few hundred years later during the Revolution.

Further down rue du Fbg-St-Antoine is place d'Aligre, home to a rowdy, cheap produce market, a more sedate covered food hall and the only flea market within the city walls. The road ends in the major intersection of place de la Nation, another grand square. It was originally called place du Trône, after a throne that was positioned here when Louis XIV and his bride Marie-Thérèse entered the city in 1660. After the Revolution, between 13 June and 28 July 1794, thousands were guillotined on the site, their bodies carted to the nearby **Cimetière de Picpus** (*see p156*). The square still has two of Ledoux's toll houses and tall Doric columns from the 1787 Mur des Fermiers-Généraux. In the centre stands Jules Dalou's sculpture *Le Triomphe de la République*, erected for the centenary of the Revolution in 1889. East of place de la Nation, broad cours de Vincennes has a market on Wednesday and Saturday mornings.

North of place de la Bastille, boulevard Beaumarchais divides Bastille from the Marais. East of place Voltaire, on rue de la Roquette, which heads east towards the Ménilmontant area and **Père-Lachaise** cemetery, a small park and playground marks the site of the prison of La Roquette, where a plaque remembers the 4,000 Resistance members imprisoned here in World War II. East of Père-Lachaise on rue de Bagnolet, **La Flèche d'Or** (*see p273*), a converted station on the defunct Petite Ceinture railway line, is a landmark music venue. Beyond, the medieval Eglise St-Germain-de-Charonne (currently closed for renovations) is at the heart of what is left of the village of Charonne. Set at the top of steps next to its presbytery, below a hill once covered with vines, it is one of only two churches in Paris still to have its own graveyard. Below, centred on the old high street of rue St-Blaise, is a prettified backwater of quiet tearooms and bistros, where old shops have been taken over by art classes.

Towards porte de Bagnolet, where rue de Bagnolet and rue des Balkans meet on the edge of a small park, the **Pavillon de l'Hermitage** is a small aristocratic relic built in the 1720s for Françoise-Marie de Bourbon, the daughter of Louis XIV, when it was in the grounds of the Château de Bagnolet. A little further south at porte de Montreuil, cross the Périphérique for the Puces de Montreuil market (7am-7pm Mon, Sat, Sun).

Sights & Museums

★ **FREE Cimetière du Père-Lachaise**
Bd de Ménilmontant, 20th (01.55.25.82.10). M° Père-Lachaise. **Open** *6 Nov-15 Mar* 8am-5.30pm Mon-Fri; 8.30am-5.30pm Sat; 9am-5.30pm Sun. *16 Mar-5 Nov* 8am-6pm Mon-Fri; 8.30am-6pm Sat; 9am-6pm Sun. **Admission** free. **Map** p146 B6 ❶ *See p148* **Walk**.

Bones.

This heart-warming bistro gets it right almost down to the last crumb. A starter salad of *ris de veau* illustrates the point, with lightly browned veal sweetbreads perched on a bed of green beans and baby carrots with a sauce of sherry vinegar. A roast shoulder of suckling pig and a thick steak with a raft of golden, thick-cut *frites* look inviting indeed. Desserts are superb too.

Bones
43 rue Godefroy Cavaignac, 11th (09.80.75.32.08, www.bonesparis.com). Mº Voltaire. **Open** 7pm-1.30am Tue-Sat (food served until 11pm). **Prix fixe** €55, €63. **Map** p146 C4 **⑤ Bistro**
Youthful, self-taught Aussie chef James Henry flexes his muscles, tattoos and chutzpah at this new venture where the ingredients are the stars. Book several weeks in advance for the no-choice four-course tasting menu, served in the 25-seater dining room, or try the bar for craft beers, oysters and home-made charcuterie. *See also p153* **Foodie Eldorado**.

La Maison Rouge – Fondation Antoine de Galbert
10 bd de la Bastille, 12th (01.40.01.08.81, www.lamaisonrouge.org). Mº Quai de la Rapée. **Open** 11am-7pm Wed, Fri-Sun; 11am-9pm Thur. **Admission** €9; €6 reductions; free under-13s. **Map** p147 E2 **②**
Created by art collector Antoine de Galbert and set in a former printworks, the Red House is an independently run space focusing on contemporary works. Solo shows alternate with themed exhibitions featuring pieces from international collections. The bright on-site café is run by the Rose Bakery team.

Restaurants

Le 6 Paul Bert
6 rue Paul Bert, 11th (01.43.79.14.32). Mº Charonne. **Open** 7.30-11pm Tue; noon-2.30pm, 7.30-11pm Wed-Fri. **Main courses** €10-€18. **Prix fixe** *Lunch* €19. *Dinner* €38, €44. **Map** p146 D4 **③ Bistro**
Charming, efficient staff welcome you into the light-filled room dominated by an enormous zinc bar, surrounded by Formica tables and studded with lamps made from forks and bottles of wine. The menu revisits bistro jazz standards (tartare, herring, seasonal vegetables), but they're adapted according to the produce available in the market and the whims of the chef. You might enjoy roasted scallops with parsley and lemon, or a little quail with beetroot purée and a bouquet of pickled carrots. A short but well-chosen wine list offers bottles from all over France.

★ Le Bistrot Paul Bert
18 rue Paul-Bert, 11th (01.43.72.24.01). Mº Charonne or Faidherbe Chaligny. **Open** noon-2pm, 7.30-11pm Tue-Sat. Closed Aug. **Main courses** €14-€27. **Prix fixe** *Lunch* €19, €38. *Dinner* €38. **Map** p146 D4 **④ Bistro**

La Crêperie Bretonne Fleurie de l'Epouse du Marin
67 rue de Charonne, 11th (01.43.55.62.29, www.creperiebretonnefleurie.fr). Mº Charonne, Ledru-Rollin or Voltaire. **Open** noon-2.30pm, 7-11pm Mon-Sat; 7-10pm Sun. **Main courses** €6.40-€10.40. **Prix fixe** *Lunch* €9.90. **No credit cards. Map** p146 D3 **⑥ Crêperie**
The spectacularly named 'flower-filled Breton crêperie run by a sailor's wife' feels like the haunt of old sea-dogs, all wood, old posters, antiques and postcards from all over the world. The menu offers a wide choice of crêpes and galettes – the origin of the ingredients is carefully marked, as if to reassure those traumatised by the indigestible crêpes sold along rue Oberkampf. Prices range between €2.90 for a buckwheat pancake with butter to €10.90 for a version with goat's cheese, bacon and eggs. The picture is completed with a good bottle of cider at €11 and a fantastic classic sweet crêpe, the 'Gwenn ha Du' with own-made chocolate sauce and a scoop of vanilla ice-cream (€6.40).

€ L'Encrier
55 rue Traversière, 12th (01.44.68.08.16). Mº Gare de Lyon or Ledru-Rollin. **Open** noon-2.15pm, 7.30-11pm Mon-Fri; 7-11pm Sat. **Main courses** €10.50-€25.90. **Prix fixe** *Lunch* €15.50-€25.90. *Dinner* €17, €20.90, €25.90. **Map** p147 E3 **⑦ Bistro**
Through the door and past the velvet curtain, you find yourself face to face with the kitchen – and a crowd of locals, many of whom seem to know the charming boss personally. Start with fried rabbit kidneys on a bed of salad dressed with raspberry vinegar, perhaps, an original and wholly successful combination, and follow with goose *magret* with honey – served with crunchy, thinly sliced sautéed potatoes. To end, share a chocolate cake, or try the popular profiteroles. The Chinon is a classy red.

EXPLORE

EXPLORE

EXPLORE

WALK DEAD FAMOUS

Take a stroll round Père-Lachaise.

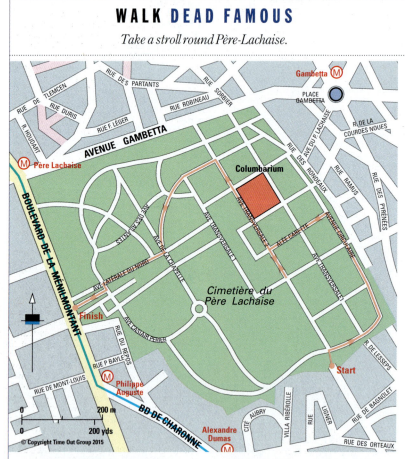

The **Cimetière du Père-Lachaise** (*see p144*), Paris's largest cemetery, is probably still best known to foreign visitors as the final resting place of one **James Douglas Morrison**, lead singer of the Doors. But ask a local what this 48-hectare site in the 20th arrondissement means to them, and they're more likely to mention the Mur des Fédérés or **Molière** than the Lizard King. On this walk, therefore, you'll pay tribute to the heroes and victims of French political history, and visit the tombs of some of France's greatest writers.

Rather than entering Père-Lachaise by the main entrance located on boulevard Ménilmontant, start at the much more discreet gate set into the southern wall of the cemetery on rue de la Réunion, just off rue de Bagnolet. You join avenue Circulaire, which hugs the cemetery wall. Turn right and then follow the path round until you reach the **Mur des Fédérés** in the south-east corner.

It was here, during the last week of May 1871, that the few remaining partisans of the **Paris Commune** (known as *fédérés* or communards) were lined up against a wall and summarily executed by troops loyal to the National Assembly at Versailles. A memorial procession to the wall, the Montée au Mur des Fédérés, takes place every year in May.

Across the path, in plot or '*division*' No.97, stand a number of memorials to the victims of Nazism and Fascism. Next to an urn containing ashes from the crematorium at the Flossenburg concentration camp is a striking ziggurat commemorating people who were 'tortured, gassed, shot or hanged' at Mauthausen. And just behind this loom two enormous manacled hands hewn from stone, a deeply unsettling monument to the women who died at Ravensbrück. A little further along avenue Circulaire, on the same side, is the tomb of people who perished in 1962 at the hands of the police at Charonne métro station, after a demonstration in favour of Algerian independence.

Follow avenue Circulaire along the northern wall until you reach the Jardin du Souvenir. Turn left up avenue Carette, keeping an eye out on your right for the monumental sarcophagus housing the remains of **Oscar Wilde**, who died in Paris in 1900 aged just 46.

When you reach avenue Transversale no.2, turn left and walk down the hill until you reach a bronze effigy of **Victor Noir**, a journalist who was shot by a cousin of Napoleon III in 1870. You'll notice that the effigy depicts Noir with a distinct enlargement in the region of the groin, and also that the area in question appears to have been rubbed down rather energetically: many *parisiennes* have believed that a little *frottage* with Victor would make them fertile.

Now retrace your steps in the direction of the crematorium and columbarium. On your left hand side, in division 86, is the rough-hewn headstone of early 20th-century poet **Guillaume Appolinaire**. Across the path, **Marcel Proust** lies in an austere tomb with various other family members.

Continue along avenue Transversale No.2, until you reach avenue des Thuryas. Turn left and walk down the hill into gently curving chemin Casimir Delavigne. About halfway down on the right is a bronze bust of **Honoré de Balzac**. The bust is accompanied by a bronze book and quill, upon which, on a recent visit, an admirer had left an apple with a heart carved in it.

Walk straight on, down chemin Mont-Louis. Through the trees you'll catch a few tantalising glimpses of the Paris skyline as you head towards avenue Principale, and beyond that the main gate of the cemetery, and the din and traffic of boulevard Ménilmontant.

La Gazzetta
29 rue de Cotte, 12th (01.43.47.47.05, www. lagazzetta.fr). M° Ledru-Rollin. **Open** noon-3pm, 7.30-10.30pm Tue-Sat; noon-4pm Sun. Closed Aug. **Main courses** €26. **Prix fixe** *Lunch* €19, €24. *Dinner* €39, €59. **Map** p146 D3 **8** **Bistro**
Opened by the team behind Le Fumoir, La Gazzetta has a similarly moody feel, with dim lighting, a long zinc bar and retro decor. Chef Petter Nilssen is Swedish, but he made his name in the south of France, and his food shows a strong Scandinavian influence in dishes such as bonito in a sweet-salty marinade with caraway, borage leaves, radish and pomelo, or new potatoes from the Ile de Noirmoutier off the Atlantic coast with seaweed butter and dill.

Au Passage
1bis passage Saint-Sébastien, 11th (01.73.20.23.23, www.restaurant-aupassage.fr). M° St Sébastien Froissart. **Open** 7pm-1.30am Mon-Sat. **Tapas** €4-€15. **Map** p146 B2 **9** **Tapas**
See p153 **Foodie Eldorado**.

La Pulpéria
1 rue Richard Lenoir, 11th (01.40.09.03.70, www. lapulperiaparis.fr). M° Charonne or Voltaire. **Open** 7.30-11pm Mon; noon-2.30pm, 8-11pm Tue-Fri; 7-11pm Sat. **Main courses** €25-€30. **Prix fixe** *Lunch* €18, €22. **Map** p146 C4 **10** **South American**
The Meat at La Pulpéria comes with a capital M, served in a noisy, welcoming little dining room and whipped up in the white-tiled kitchen by talented Argentinian chef Fernando Di Tomaso and his South American team. The menu changes daily, but dishes might include a pretty cod ceviche surrounded with fine slices of sweet potato, avocado purée and a splash of lemon juice, or a bloody, magnificent *churrasco* cut of beef served with rissole potatoes and garlicky chimichurri sauce. Prices might seem a bit high, but for the quality of the products and cooking, it's really very reasonable.

Restaurant Boucherie les Provinces
20 rue d'Aligre, 12th (01.43.43.91.64, www. boucherie-lesprovinces.fr). M° Faidherbe-Chaligny or Ledru-Rollin. **Open** noon-2pm Tue, Wed, Sun; noon-2pm, 7-9.30pm Thur, Fri. **Main courses** €13.80-€24. **Map** p146 D3 **11** **Bistro**
The Marché d'Aligre is already one of Paris's favourite foodie markets, and now there's a new reason to visit. Young artisan butcher Christophe Dru began to make a name for himself hosting events in his shop during the annual Le Fooding festival. The success of these tastings gave him the idea to transform his butcher's shop into a no-reservations restaurant as well, and the place has been packed out since the day it opened. As you walk in, all the meat is displayed on the left as usual, with Aligre locals lining up to do their shopping, while the rest of the space is a jumble of tables and counters, heaving with hungry meat-eaters tucking into a

EXPLORE

giant entrecôte, sweet lamb chops or juicy pork ribs. Prices are very reasonable, basically the same 'per kilo' rate as at the meat counter plus €9 for the cooking. There's a small but excellent wine list.

Septime

80 rue de Charonne, 11th (01.43.67.38.29, www. septime-charonne.fr). M° Charonne, Faidherbe-Chaligny or Ledru-Rollin. **Open** 7.30-10pm Mon; 12.15-2pm, 7.30-10pm Tue-Fri. **Prix fixe** *Lunch* €30, €60. *Dinner* €65. **Map** p146 D4 ⑫ **Bistro**
This area has been making waves on the food scene for a while, so it's no surprise to find Bertrand Grébaut's latest restaurant venture here. Grébaut is a former pupil at Penninghen design school and the decor reflects his background: huge mirrors, industrial installations, antique furniture, reinforced concrete and bare wood. The cooking is direct, pure and serious: raw horse mackerel with yoghurt and red cabbage was superb; Iberico ham and pumpkin was tender and delicious. Dessert was a lovely mixture of apples, fromage blanc, honey and thyme. It's all topped off with charming service. *See also p153* **Foodie Eldorado.**

★ Le Souk

1 rue Keller, 11th (01.49.29.05.08, www.le-souk-paris.com). M° Bastille or Ledru-Rollin. **Open** noon-2.30pm, 7pm-midnight Tue-Sun. **Main courses** €13-€16. **Prix fixe** €16.50, €22.50. **Map** p146 D3 ⑬ **North African**
Potted olive trees mark the entrance to this lively den of Moroccan cuisine. Start with savoury *b'stilla*, a pastry stuffed with duck, raisins and nuts, flavoured with orange-blossom water and sprinkled with cinnamon and powdered sugar. Don't fill up, though, as the first-rate tagines and couscous are enormous. The *tagine canette* (duckling stewed with honey, onions, apricots, figs and cinnamon, then showered with toasted almonds) is terrific. For dessert, try the excellent millefeuille with fresh figs, while sweet mint tea is poured in a long stream by a *djellaba*-clad waiter.

Unico

15 rue Paul-Bert, 11th (01.43.67.68.08, www. resto-unico.com). M° Faidherbe-Chaligny. **Open** 8-10.45pm Mon; noon-3pm, 8-10.30pm Tue-Sat. **Main courses** €27-€39. **Prix fixe** *Lunch* €17. **Map** p146 D4 ⑭ **South American**
Architect Marcelo Joulia and photographer Enrique Zanoni were wise enough to retain the vintage 1970s decor of this former butcher's shop when they opened their temple to Argentinian beef. Orange tiles and matching light fixtures provide the backdrop for the fashionable, black-dressed crowd that comes here for thick slabs of meat grilled over charcoal and served with a selection of sauces. If you find yourself hesitating, opt for the *lomo* (fillet) with *chimichurri*, a mild salsa – and don't forget to wash it down with Argentinian wine, a rarity in Paris.

★ Au Vieux Chêne

7 rue du Dahomey, 11th (01.43.71.67.69, www. vieuxchene.fr). M° Faidherbe-Chaligny. **Open** noon-2pm, 8-10.30pm Mon-Fri. Closed 1wk July & 2wks Aug. **Main courses** €20-€25. **Prix fixe** *Lunch* €16, €20. *Dinner* €28, €33. **Map** p146 D4 ⑮ **Bistro**
Although everyone loves the zinc-capped bar by the entrance, and the tiled floor, what makes this bistro so special is its desire to please. A starter of langoustines encased in fine crunchy angel hair and garnished with slices of fresh mango is delicious and refreshing, and chilled tomato soup is garnished with mint, a ball of tomato sorbet and a drizzle of olive oil. Stéphane Chevassus is a gifted game cook, too, as proved by the tender roast pigeon sautéed with Chinese cabbage.

Cafés & Bars

Le 114

114 rue Oberkampf, 11th (09.82.33.62.39, www.le-114.fr). M° Ménilmontant or Parmentier. **Open** 8pm-4.30am Tue-Sat. **Map** p146 A3 ⑯
Opened in partnership with Puma Social and in association with the new magazine *Plugged*, Le 114 proudly parades its motto on its front window: 'C'est comme chez toi, mais en mieux' (It's just like home, but better). Squishy armchairs and huge sofas back up this assertion, even if the atmosphere isn't quite as warm as the sign might suggest. However,

Le Calbar.

the bar's creators hit on a great concept when they decided to invite groups to play for free on the small stage. The schedule displays decent taste in rock and pop, and the door policy is run according to time-honoured principles: first come, first served.

★ Ave Maria

1 rue Jacquard, 11th (01.47.00.61.73). M°
Parmentier. **Open** 7pm-2am daily. **Map** p146 A3 ⑰
Unlike some places that eschew good food for alcohol and a funky interior, colourful Ave Maria scores highly for all three. The kitsch interior is decked out in a canopy of chinoiserie parasols and a vast collection of Hindu gods. Music, a combination of reggae, funk, soul and dub, is cool but unobtrusive. Strangers sharing wooden benches devour exotic dishes from the Brazilian-inspired menu, which combines meat, spices, lentils, rice and fruit. Cocktails are equally quirky – try the Aguas Borobora (with mango, rose, vodka and champagne).

Le Baron Rouge

1 rue Théophile-Roussel, 12th (01.43.43.14.32).
M° Ledru-Rollin. **Open** 5-10pm Mon; 10am-2pm, 5-10pm Tue-Fri; 10am-10pm Sat; 10am-4pm Sun.
Map p147 E3 ⑱
It sells wine, certainly – great barrels of the stuff are piled high and sold by the glass at very reasonable prices. But the Red Baron is not just a wine bar; it's more like a local chat room, where regulars congregate to yak over their *vin*, or perhaps one of the few draught beers, and maybe a snack of sausages or oysters. Despite its lack of seating (there are only four tables), it's a popular pre-dinner spot, so arrive early and don't expect too much elbow room.

Café Aouba

30 rue d'Aligre, 12th (01.43.43.22.24). M° Ledru-Rollin. **Open** 8am-7pm Tue-Sat; 8am-5pm Sun.
No credit cards. Map p146 D3 ⑲
Opened in 1938 by a Portuguese butcher, this is the ultimate market bar, tiny and packed with boisterous stallholders, shoppers and curious tourists. Aouba has had a new lease of life since it was bought a few years ago by Emmie Bolatoglu, a dynamic young Turkish woman who has always lived in the neighbourhood. Don't expect any designer deco here, just a basic red Formica counter with elbow room for half-a-dozen customers, and a shining Faema espresso machine.

Café de la Presse

36 bd de la Bastille, 12th (01.43.43.79.79, www. cafedelapresse.fr). M° Ledru-Rollin. **Open** 8am-2am Mon-Thur; 8am-5am Fri; 9am-5am Sat; 10am-6pm Sun. **Map** p146 D2 ⑳
'Having historically hosted printing presses and an energy factory, today the site of Café de la Presse is looking to rediscover its role as a motivating force in the neighbourhood.' Thus reads the Facebook page of this venue, opened in spring 2014. Everything on

the menu comes with wordplay: *bloc de foie gras en rubrique, fusilli paparazzi champignons* or *salade HuffPost*. Portions are generous, ideal for mopping up the alcohol, lining the stomach for a DJ set or refuelling during a tattoo exhibition. There's a lively programme of club nights, DJ brunches, cinema screenings and more.

Café Titon

34 rue Titon, 11th (09.53.17.94.10, www.cafetiton. com). M° Faidherbe-Chaligny or Rue des Boulets. **Open** 8am-2am Mon-Sat; 10am-7pm Sun. **Map** p147 E3 ㉑
The funky Titon is Paris's only Franco-German café – and certainly the only place in town to flog *currywurst* (German sausage in curry sauce) and chips for a bargain €6.20. It even transforms into a giant *biergarten* during Oktoberfest. Its Parisian side doesn't get forgotten, though, with *croques, tartines*, an unbeatable lunch menu and scrumptious cocktails.

Le Calbar

82 rue de Charenton, 12th (01.84.06.18.90, www.lecalbarcocktail.com). M° Ledru-Rollin. **Open** 5pm-2am Mon-Sat. **Map** p147 E3 ㉒
The look of this former wine bar recalls a New York loft, with bare bricks, street art, wooden furniture – and waiters decked out in underwear, aprons, braces and bow ties. You have to climb a caged stairway to find the lounge, furnished with comfortable chesterfields and post-industrial coffee tables, and hip hop and electro playing in the background. Cocktails feature premium spirits such as Monkey 47 (a German liqueur with 47 ingredients), Nikka Japanese whisky or even Tanqueray Ten (gin made from fresh fruit). There's no happy hour, but instead a monthly *apéro* where underwear as outerwear is a prerequisite for both sexes (free dressing room available) to get hold of the special cocktail, the Dagobear.

Les Caves de Prague

8 rue de Prague, 12th (01.72.68.07.36). M° Ledru-Rollin. **Open** 10am-1pm, 4-11.30pm Tue; 4-11.30pm Wed-Sat. **Map** p147 E3 ㉓
Travel guides routinely point tourists to Le Baron Rouge (*see left*), declaiming it to be the best wine bar around the Marché d'Aligre. If only they'd thought to look around the corner. Les Caves de Prague has equally fine wines, fewer crowds and no corkage fee (buy one of their bottles and you can drink it on site for free). Food is the usual wine-inspired affair: patrons chow down on pâtés, meat platters and rye bread on the pretty outdoor terrace, or around a large wooden table in winter.

★ Chez Prosper

7 av du Trône, 11th (01.43.73.08.51). M° Nation. **Open** 7.30am-1.30am daily. **Map** p147 E6 ㉔
Chez Prosper welcomes punters all day long with that simplest of gestures: a smile. Yes, even when squeezing past people queuing for a spot on the

EXPLORE

EXPLORE

sun terrace, the waiters are positively beaming. The dining/drinks area – tiled floor, large mirrors, wooden furniture – is run with military precision, and orders arrive promptly. The *steak-frites* and *croques* (served on Poîlane bread) are hearty, and the naughty Nutella tiramisu is worth crossing town for.

China

50 rue de Charenton, 12th (01.43.46.08.09, www.lechina.eu). M° Bastille or Ledru Rollin. **Open** 10am-2am Mon-Thur; 10am-4am Fri-Sun. Closed Aug. **Map** p146 D3 ㉕

This sexy take on a 1930s Shanghai gentleman's club, with red walls, leather chesterfields and the longest bar in Paris, serves some of the finest cocktails in town (including its signature singapore sling). The Cantonese cuisine is pricey, so skip dinner and head upstairs to the cigar bar (if you're romantically inclined) or downstairs to the cellar for weekly jazz, pop and world music concerts.

L'Entrée des Artistes

8 rue de Crussol, 11th (09.50.99.67.11). M° Filles du Calvaire or Oberkampf. **Open** 7pm-2am Tue-Sat. **Map** p146 B2 ㉖

Having mixed drinks at Murano and the Experimental Cocktail Club, two friends decided to open Entrée des Artistes. The relaxed venue offers sophisticated cocktails and a more straightforward wine list, plus smart snacks such as foie gras, Italian cheeses and a classy *plat du jour*. Warm and intimate, the small space has an old-world feel cluttered with beautiful vintage objects, from soda siphons to an old metal cash register. Dandified city slickers and Marais hipsters have quickly appropriated the handful of tables, and the place is packed out from cocktail hour onwards, fuelled by a mix of hip hop, jazz, funk, disco and soul.

★ Les Furieux

74 rue de la Roquette, 11th (01.47.00.78.44). M° Bastille or Voltaire. **Open** 4pm-2am Tue-Thur; 4pm-5am Fri, Sat. **Map** p146 C3 ㉗

Just when it looked as if 'lounge attitude' would contaminate every bar on rue de la Roquette, Les Furieux fought back with a healthy dose of rock and metal, padded red walls, faux-leather banquettes, black paint, and photography exhibitions. Locals flock here for the happy hour (6pm to 8pm), when cocktails with rockin' names like Grunge, Scud, and, er, Boris are half price. Diehards can pay tribute to Paris's hedonistic heyday with 12 different absinthes.

Moonshiner

5 rue Sedaine, 11th (09.50.73.12.99). M° Bastille or Bréguet-Sabin. **Open** 6pm-2am daily. **Map** p146 C2 ㉘

Moonshiner is a 'speakeasy' bar inspired by the clandestine drinking spots of Prohibition-era America. To get in, you have to make your way through the restaurant Pizza da Vito, then push your way through the metal door of the walk-in fridge. Once inside, the temperature drops ten degrees so you start drinking pretty quickly. It's all cocktails and whiskies, at a large range of prices – from €6 for the delicious seasonal punch to €14 for a more complex cocktail such as Smokey Island. There are 83 whiskies listed, showing a love for the peaty stuff, while the house beer is very affordable, at €5 a pint. With its hushed atmosphere, dim lighting, retro jazz on the gramophone and a strongbox in the elegant *fumoir* (if you manage to open it, you win what's in there), the clandestine vibe is respected throughout.

Le Motel

8 passage Josset, 11th (01.58.30.84.68, www.lemotel.fr). M° Ledru-Rollin. **Open** 6pm-1.45am Tue-Sun. **Map** p146 D3 ㉙

Le Motel has a simple formula: cheap drinks and excellent music. During happy hour (6pm to 9pm) a pint of *blonde* costs €3.50 and cocktails €5. With DJs almost every night, music ranges from cutting-edge indie to contemporary neo-folk and rock classics, with the odd Motown hit thrown in. Friendly twentysomethings cluster around faux Louis XVI armchairs or try their luck in the Sunday pop quiz.

Pause Café

41 rue de Charonne, 11th (01.48.06.80.33). M° Ledru-Rollin. **Open** 9am-2am Mon-Sat; 9am-8pm Sun. **Map** p146 D3 ㉚

Featured in Cedric Klapisch's 1996 film *Chacun Cherche son Chat*, which was shot on location in the neighbourhood, the Pause Café has managed to prolong its moment of glory thanks to its large terrace on the corner of rues Charonne and Keller. Inside, the modern salons benefit from a smattering of primary colours with ornately plastered ceilings and plenty of light. The food – traditional French café fare with an Asian twist – is not bad, but you might be waiting for a while.

Les Pères Populaires

46 rue de Buzenval, 20th (01.43.48.49.22). M° Buzenval. **Open** 8am-2am Mon-Fri; 10am-2am Sat, Sun. **Map** p146 D6 ㉛

Could this funky number be the cheapest bar in Paris? Wine is a mere €2.30 a glass, beer is €2.80 (€5.30 for a pint) and flavoured rums cost €5. To get an idea of the look of the place, think 1970s canteen-cum-retro classroom and you'll come close. During the day, the freelance media crowd and a handful of musicians squat tables for free Wi-Fi; at night DJs spin electro sounds and a party atmosphere reigns.

Le P'tit Bar

7 rue Richard Lenoir, 11th (no phone). M° Charonne. **Open** 5pm-2am daily. **No credit cards.** **Map** p146 C4 ㉜

You couldn't invent this place if you tried: local soaks, immigrant South Americans, twentysomething students, Brits and retired war veterans all pop in

FOODIE ELDORADO

Cooking up a storm in the 11th.

When it's dinner time in Paris, pull up a chair in the 11th, where a plethora of young chefs have been opening some of the capital's most exciting new restaurants. Some launched their careers on TV cooking shows; others perfected their techniques in Michelin-starred kitchens; one even taught himself. All are helping to revolutionise Paris's culinary landscape and turning the north-east into the place to dine.

Kickstarting the trend north of République was self-taught Basque chef Iñaki Aizpitarte with **Châteaubriand** (*see p168*), which opened almost a decade ago. Times may have changed, but his neo-bistro is still one of the best places in town for gutsy dishes that evolve according to the chef's mood and the market's offerings (think squid with sea asparagus, and steak tartare with a quail's egg).

If fusion's your forte, head to Oberkampf to sample *Top Chef* finalist Pierre Sang's second restaurant, **Pierre Sang on Gambey** (6 rue Gambey, www.pierresangboyer.com), where unique Franco-Korean inspired creations such as mandoo poultry dumplings (filled with anchovy cream and lemon caviar)

or lobster with sweet potato noodles roll out on daring no-choice menus.

Just around the corner is gluten-free **Chambelland** (*see p154; pictured*), the only Paris bakery to have opened its own mill in Provence to ensure a consistently excellent supply of rice flour and buckwheat. The cakes are superlative, and the bread so good that Alain Ducasse orders it for the Plaza Athenée.

You'll have to book two months in advance for a table at **Septime** (*see p150*), but the wait will be worth it: this is where chef Bertrand Grébaut (disciple of the great Alain Passard) serves mind-blowing dishes such as raw venison with kalamata olives and tarragon, and pear and verbena crumble. Fish-lovers (and those who can't get a table) pile into Clamato, his seafood tapas bar next door, for delicacies such as scallops with butternut squash, and fresh oysters with shallot vinegar.

And don't leave the arrondissement without trying the following: **Bones** (*see p145*) for pedigree *côte de boeuf* and a fine choice of natural wines and craft beers; and **Au Passage** (*see p149*) for excellent wines and creative tapas served by a funky team.

EXPLORE

EXPLORE

for a taste of the most surreal experience in town, courtesy of the elderly Madame Polo, her fluffy cat and her canaries. A word of warning, though: don't drink out of the glasses – Madame Polo isn't too keen on cleaning. Opt instead for a €3 bottle of beer.

Le Red House
1bis rue de la Forge Royale, 12th (01.43.67.06.43). Mº Bastille, Faidherbe-Chaligny or Ledru-Rollin. **Open** 5pm-2am daily. **Map** p146 D4 ㉝
Le Red House, dominated by a majestic bull's skull hanging over the bar, has the air of a Texan saloon in the middle of Bastille, and the crowd is colourful, young, lively and loud. DJs spin rock, punk, funk and electro, and the place never seems to be empty – luckily it's huge, with two connected rooms with exposed beams, each equipped with its own bar. Try a Wild West Side (tequila, chilli, cucumber and lime) or Red House Flambeau (bourbon, apricot brandy, spicy syrup, lemon and ginger).

Tape Bar
21 rue de la Roquette, 11th (01.43.38.69.28). Mº Bastille or Bréguet-Sabin. **Open** 11am-2am daily. **Map** p146 C3 ㉞
To get away from rue de Lappe, frequented by students and tourists, follow rue de la Roquette to a little bar that's close by but a world away. Tape Bar recalls New York's underground dive scene with its mix-tape and street-art feel, and is owned by friendly, dynamic young people who leave graffiti artists to express themselves on the walls and the DJs to mix mostly hip hop and funk sets, with some dubstep, drum'n'bass and rock as well. The ambience is relaxed, the drinks are affordable, the hipster crowd is young, and it all stays humming until late.

Shops & Services

★ Caravane Chambre 19
19 rue St-Nicolas, 12th (01.53.02.96.96, www.caravane.fr). Mº Ledru-Rollin. **Open** 11am-7pm Tue-Sat. Closed 2wks Aug. **Map** p146 D3 ㉟ **Homewares**
This offshoot of Françoise Dorget's original Marais shop has goodies such as exquisite hand-sewn quilts from west Bengal, crisp cotton and organdie tunics, Berber scarves, lounging sofas and daybeds.
Other locations 6 rue Pavée, 4th (01.44.61.04.20); 22 rue St-Nicolas, 12th (01.53.17.18.55).

Chambelland
14 rue Ternaux, 11th (01.43.55.07.30, www.chambelland.com). Mº Parmentier. **Open** 9am-8pm Tue-Sun. **Map** p146 A3 ㊳ **Food & drink**
See *p153* **Foodie Eldorado**.

La Cocotte
5 rue Paul Bert, 11th (09.54.73.17.77, www.la cocotte.net). Mº Faidherbe-Chaligny. **Open** 12.30-7pm Tue-Sat. **Map** p146 D4 ㊲ **Homewares**

Previously a bookshop, this cute boutique now focuses on homeware, with its chick logo appearing on mugs, aprons and tote bags. Graphic artists Laetitia Bertrand and Andrea Wainer created their feathered friend in 2007, and now have a whole range of branded textiles and accessories for the kitchen, including dishcloths, oven gloves and even lollipop moulds. A world of bright colours and joyful prints that will cheer up the most dispiriting kitchen task.

★ DPAM
120-122 rue du Fbg-St-Antoine, 12th (01.43.44.67.46, www.dpam.com). Mº Ledru-Rollin. **Open** 10am-7pm Mon-Sat. **Map** p146 D3 ㊳ **Children**
Bright, cleverly designed and well made basics for children aged three months to 14 years, at refreshingly low prices. The Bébé branch, for kids up to two years, is a good source of gifts.
Other locations throughout the city.

Fargo
42 rue de la Folie-Méricourt, 11th (01.48.05.49.52, www.fargostore.com). Mº Parmentier or St-Ambroise. **Open** 11am-7.30pm Mon-Sat. **Map** p146 B3 ㊳ **Books & music**
With its handsome wooden façade and neon lights, Fargo wouldn't look out of place in San Francisco. It's got a Far West feel inside, too, with collections that cover country music in all its forms (rock, pop, folk and new wave). The shop has only been around since 2010, but it's got good connections: Moriarty and Steve Smyth have both played here.

Les Fleurs
6 passage Josset, 11th (01.43.55.12.94, www.boutiquelesfleurs.com). Mº Ledru-Rollin. **Open** noon-7.30pm Mon-Sat. **Map** p146 D3 ㊵ **Accessories**
There are two reasons to walk down passage Josset: it's quaint and off the beaten track; and it's home to Les Fleurs, a girly boutique that drips with funky jewellery, bags, rococo mirrors and all sorts of gizmos and gadgets for little and grown-up girls alike. Lucie Deniset has hand-picked designers such as Nat&Nin, Adeline Affre and Titlee to create a range of desirables quite unlike any other in Paris.

Galerie Patrick Seguin
5 rue des Taillandiers, 11th (01.47.00.32.35, www.patrickseguin.com). Mº Bastille. **Open** 10am-7pm Mon-Sat. **Map** p146 D3 ㊶ **Homewares**
Seguin specialises in French design from the 1950s: items by Jean Prouvé and Charlotte Perriand are on display in this handsome showroom designed by Jean Nouvel. Seguin has also collaborated on some ground-breaking exhibitions around the world.

★ Isabel Marant
16 rue de Charonne, 11th (01.49.29.71.55, www.isabelmarant.tm.fr). Mº Ledru-Rollin. **Open** 11am-7pm Mon; 10.30am-7.30pm Tue-Sat. **Map** p146 D3 ㊷ **Fashion**

Loulou Addict.

Isabel Marant's style is easily recognisable in her ethno-babe brocades, blanket-like coats and decorated sweaters. It's a firm favourite among Paris's young trendies.

Other locations 47 rue Saintonge, 3rd (01.42.78.19.24); 1 rue Jacob, 6th (01.43.26.04.12); 151 av Victor Hugo, 16th (01.47.04.99.95).

Loulou Addict

25 rue Keller, 11th (01.49.29.00.61, www.loulou addict.com). Mº Bastille, Ledru-Rollin or Voltaire. **Open** 11.30am-2pm, 3-7pm Tue-Fri; 11am-7pm Sat. **Map** p146 C3 ❸ **Accessories**

Retro motifs, English flourishes, Japanese ornaments and bright colours abound in this boutique, which specialises in home decor and accessories for children (especially girls) and their mothers. This is the place to invest in a mini 2CV in lacquered wood by Vilac or a crocheted doll by Anne-Claire Petit. For *madame*, perhaps a 1970s maroon purse with orange flowers by Blafre or an arty cushion by La Cerise.

★ Marché Bastille

Bd Richard-Lenoir, 11th. Mº Richard-Lenoir. **Open** 7am-2.30pm Thur; 7am-3pm Sun. **Map** p146 C2 ❹ **Market**

One of the biggest markets in Paris. A favourite of political campaigners, it's also a great source of local cheeses, farmers' chicken and excellent fish.

Marché Beauvau

Pl d'Aligre, 12th. Mº Ledru-Rollin. **Open** 9am-1pm, 4-7.30pm Tue-Fri; 9am-1pm, 3.30-7.30pm Sat; 9am-1.30pm Sun. **Map** p147 E3 ❺ **Market**

This lively market remains proudly working class. Stall-holders do their very best to out-shout each other, and price-conscious shoppers don't compromise on quality.

Marché aux Puces d'Aligre

Pl d'Aligre, rue d'Aligre, 12th. Mº Ledru-Rollin. **Open** 7am-2pm Tue-Sun. **Map** p147 E3 ❻ **Market**

The only flea market in central Paris, Aligre stays true to its junk tradition with a handful of *brocanteurs* peddling books, phone cards, kitchenware and oddities at what seem to be optimistic prices.

Moisan

5 pl d'Aligre, 12th (09.50.27.67.04, www.pain moisan.fr). Mº Ledru-Rollin. **Open** 6.30am-8.30pm Tue-Sat; 6.30am-2pm Sun. **Map** p147 E3 ❼ **Food & drink**

Moisan's organic bread, *viennoiseries* and rustic tarts are outstanding. At this branch, situated by the market, there's always a healthy queue.

Other locations throughout the city.

★ A La Providence (Quincaillerie Leclercq)

151 rue du Fbg-St-Antoine, 11th (01.43.43.06.41, www.alaprovidence.fr). Mº Ledru-Rollin. **Open** 10am-1pm, 2.30-6pm Tue-Sat. **Map** p146 D3 ❽ **Homewares**

Step into the past at this museum-piece *quincaillerie* in which 170-year-old wooden cabinets are filled with knobs, locks and other brass accoutrements for dolling up or restoring old furniture and doors.

Silvera

41 rue du Fbg-St-Antoine, 11th (01.43.43.06.75, www.silvera.fr). Mº Bastille or Ledru-Rollin. **Open** 10am-7pm Mon-Sat. Closed 2wks Aug. **Map** p146 D2 ❾ **Homewares**

The former Le Bihan was taken over by Silvera in 2005 and is now a three-floor showcase for modern design. Look out for furniture and lighting from Perriand, Pesce, Pillet, Morrison, Arad and others. **Other locations** throughout the city.

Souffle Continu

22 rue Gerbier, 11th (01.40.24.17.21, www.souffle continu.com). Mº Philippe Auguste. **Open** noon-8pm Mon-Sat. **Map** p146 C4 ❺⓪ **Books & music**

Souffle Continu is one of the musical stars of the neighbourhood thanks to its owners, Bernard and Théo, a pair passionate about vinyl. From jazz improv to harsh noise, from indie rock to black metal, the stands groan with rare treasures.

BERCY & DAUMESNIL

In the 12th arrondissement.

The **Viaduc des Arts** is a former railway viaduct along avenue Daumesnil; its row of glass-fronted arches enclose craft boutiques and workshops. Above sprout the blooms and bamboo of the **Promenade Plantée**. In 1969, the steam engines on avenue Daumesnil's viaduct whistled their last and the train line between

EXPLORE

Bastille and Vincennes closed forever. While the Bastille station was replaced by today's opera house, the old lines became a 5km-long trail (the Promenade Plantée), made up of elevated gardens, the Jardin de Reuilly and tree-lined cycling paths.

Eglise du Saint-Esprit is a copy of Istanbul's Hagia Sofia; the nearby **Cimetière de Picpus** contains the graves of many of the victims of the Terror, as well as American War of Independence hero General La Fayette.

Just before the Périphérique, the **Palais de la Porte Dorée** was built in 1931 for the Exposition Coloniale. Originally the Musée des Colonies, then the Musée des Arts d'Afrique et d'Océanie, it's home to the **Cité Nationale de l'Histoire de l'Immigration**.

As recently as the 1980s, wine was unloaded from barges at Bercy, but this stretch of the Seine is now home to the vast Ministère de l'Economie et du Budget. To the east is the Bercy Expo centre. In between lie the **Parc de Bercy** and the former American Center, built in the 1990s by Frank Gehry. It now houses the Cinémathèque Française. At the eastern edge of the park is **Bercy Village**, where warehouses have been sympathetically restored and opened as shops and cafés.

Sights & Museums

★ FREE Bois de Vincennes

12th. M° Château de Vincennes or Porte Dorée.
Map p147 G6 ❺❶
This is Paris's biggest park, created when the former royal hunting forest was landscaped by Alphand. There are boating lakes, a Buddhist temple, a racecourse, restaurants, a baseball field and a farm. The park also contains the Cartoucherie theatre complex (*see p289*). The Parc Floral is a cross between a botanical garden and an amusement park, including crazy golf and an adventure playground. Next to the park stands the Château de Vincennes, where England's Henry V died in 1422 (*see p237*).

Cimetière de Picpus

35 rue de Picpus, 12th (01.43.44.18.54). M° Daumesnil, Nation or Picpus. **Open** *15 Apr-14 Oct* 2-6pm Tue-Sun. *15 Oct-14 Apr* 2-4pm Tue-Sun.
Admission €3. **No credit cards. Map** p147 F6 ❺❷
This cemetery in a working convent is the resting place for the thousands of victims of the Revolution's aftermath, guillotined at place du Trône (now place de la Nation) between 13 June and 28 July 1794. At the end of a walled garden is a graveyard of aristocratic French families. In one corner is the tomb of General La Fayette, who fought in the American War of Independence and was married to the aristocratic Marie Adrienne Françoise de Noailles. In the chapel, two tablets list the names and occupations of the executed: 'domestic servant' and 'farmer' figure alongside 'lawyer' and 'prince and priest'.

Cité Nationale de l'Histoire de l'Immigration.

★ Cité Nationale de l'Histoire de l'Immigration

293 av Daumesnil, 12th (01.53.59.58.60, www. histoire-immigration.fr). M° Porte Dorée. **Open** 10am-5.30pm Tue-Fri; 10am-7pm Sat, Sun.
Admission €4.50-€6; free under-26s & all 1st Sun of mth. *Aquarium* €5-€7; €3.50-€5 reductions. PMP. **No credit cards. Map** p147 H6 ❺❸
The collections here trace more than 200 years of immigration history. There are thought-provoking images (film and photography), everyday objects (suitcases, accordions, sewing machines and so on) and artworks that symbolise the struggles immigrants had to face when integrating into French society. Don't miss the permanent Repères (bearings) exhibition that looks at why many immigrants chose France, the problems they faced upon arrival, and the way sport, work, language, religion and culture can ease integration. One of the most moving areas is the Galerie des Dons – memorabilia donated by individuals whose families came from foreign countries. There's also an aquarium in the basement.

FREE Eglise du Saint-Esprit

186 av Daumesnil, 12th (01.44.75.77.50, www. st-esprit.org). M° Daumesnil. **Open** 9.30am-noon, 3-7pm Mon-Fri; 9.30am-noon, 4-6pm Sat; from 9am Sun. **Admission** free. **Map** p147 G6 ❺❹
This unusual 1920s concrete church follows a square plan around a central dome, lit by a scalloped ring of windows. Architect Paul Tournon was inspired by the Hagia Sofia cathedral in Istanbul, though the inside is decorated with frescoes rather than mosaics.

EXPLORE

Musée des Arts Forains

53 av des Terroirs-de-France, 12th (01.43.40.16.15, www.pavillons-de-bercy.com). M° Cour St-Emilion. **Open** groups only, min 15 people, by appointment. **Admission** €16; €8 reductions. **No credit cards. Map** p147 H5 ⑮

Housed in a collection of Eiffel-era wine warehouses is a fantastical collection of 19th- and early 20th-century fairground attractions. The venue is hired out most evenings, and staff may well be setting the tables when you visit. Of the three halls, the most wonderful is the Salon de la Musique, where a musical sculpture by Jacques Rémus chimes and flashes in time with the 1934 Mortier organ and a modern-day digital grand piano playing *Murder on the Orient Express*.

FREE Parc de Bercy

Rue de Bercy, 12th. M° Bercy or Cour St-Emilion. **Open** *Winter* 8am-5.30pm Mon-Fri; 9am-5.30pm Sat, Sun. *Summer* 8am-9pm Mon-Fri; 9am-9pm Sat, Sun. **Map** p147 G4 ⑯

Bercy park features a large lawn, a grid with square rose, herb and vegetable plots, an orchard, and gardens laid out to represent the four seasons.

FREE Le Viaduc des Arts

15-121 av Daumesnil, 12th (www.leviaducdesarts. com). M° Gare de Lyon. **Map** p147 E4 ⑰

Glass-fronted workshops in the arches beneath the Promenade Plantée provide showrooms for furniture and fashion designers, picture-frame gilders, tapestry restorers, porcelain decorators, and chandelier, violin and flute makers.

IN THE KNOW
GRAFFITI WORKSHOPS

If you've always secretly envied those who dare to make their mark on the urban landscape but were too law-abiding to try, Paris has the answer. A skate park near Bercy has been given over to 'legal graffiti', and it's here that **Underground Paris** (www.undergroundparis.org) has extended its on-the-pulse street art tours to actually showing you how it's done – if you've never handled a spray can before, it's not as easy as it sounds. Three-hour sessions might start with sweeping last night's beer cans from the bench in front of the wall. First you work on paper to stylise your writing, then paint over part of an existing mural to make a white base. After practising techniques using a safe paint brand manufactured for street artists, the team works together to colour the letters, outline them then set them into relief, finally adding some highlights. Bar a few splodges and wavy lines, the results look almost authentic.

Restaurants

★ € A la Biche au Bois

45 av Ledru-Rollin, 12th (01.43.43.34.38). M° Gare de Lyon. **Open** 7-11pm Mon; 12.30-2pm, 7-11pm Tue-Fri. Closed 4wks July-Aug & Christmas wk. **Main courses** €17. **Prix fixe** €30.40. **Map** p147 E2 ⑱ **Bistro**

However crowded it gets here, it doesn't matter because everyone always seems so happy with the food and the convivial atmosphere. It's impossible not to be enthusiastic about the more than generous portions offered with the prix fixe menu. Mains might include wild duck in blackcurrant sauce, partridge with cabbage or wild venison stew. If you can still do dessert, go for one of the home-made tarts laden with seasonal fruits. The wine list has a reputation as one of the best-value selections in town.

Le Réparate

128 rue de Charenton, 12th (01.40.19.15.68). M° Gare de Lyon. **Open** 11.30am-4pm Mon-Thur; 11.30am-4pm, 6-9pm Fri. **Main courses** €11.50. **Map** p147 E4 ⑲ **Bistro**

Réparate's blue walls and affordable cooking bring a shot of Nice sunshine to the neighbourhood with an above-average range of salads, sandwiches and traditional dishes, including a '*socca*' chickpea crêpe. Sit at a wooden table with a view of the chalkboard menu and the glass-topped bar, and enjoy a hot *pan bagnat* sandwich overflowing with fresh vegetables, potatoes and succulent chicken or stuffed vegetables drenched in fruity olive oil. Finish with a lemon meringue tart, both sweet and citrus sour.

Le Train Bleu

Gare de Lyon, pl Louis-Armand, 12th (01.43.43.09.06, www.le-train-bleu.com). M° Gare de Lyon. **Open** 11.30am-2.45pm, 7-10.45pm daily. **Main courses** €27-€48. **Prix fixe** *Lunch* €48, €62, €105. *Dinner* €62, €105. **Map** p147 F3 ⑳ **Brasserie**

This listed dining room with vintage frescoes exudes a pleasant air of expectation. Don't expect cutting-edge cooking, but rather fine renderings of French classics. Lobster served on walnut oil-dressed salad leaves is a beautifully prepared starter, as is pistachio-studded *saucisson de Lyon* with a warm salad of small ratte potatoes.

Shops & Services

Bercy Village 2

Cour St Emilion, 12th (08.25.16.60.75, www. bercyvillage.com). M° Cour St-Emilion. **Open** 11am-9pm daily. **Map** p147 H4 ㉑ **Mall**

This retail and leisure development housed in old wine warehouses is a relaxed place in which to shop. The shops include Agnès b, Nature et Découvertes, Pacific Adventure, L'Occitane, Oliviers & Co and Sephora. There are also several cafés and restaurants, a park and a multiplex cinema.

EXPLORE

North-east Paris

The Canal St-Martin's iron footbridges and tree-shaded quays formed the backdrop for some of *Amélie*'s most atmospheric scenes, and nowadays this 19th-century waterway draws a hipster crowd to its shabby-chic bars and bistros. Heading north along the Canal, the must-visit den of artistic creation is Point Ephemère. From here the Canal widens into the Bassin de la Villette and Canal de l'Ourcq, famed for its twin MK2 cinemas, retro-futurist 1970s tower blocks and watersports during Paris-Plages. Once you've crossed the quirky 1885 hydraulic lift bridge, Pont de Crimée, you're in Parc de la Villette territory. Futuristic and cutting-edge, this is where you can visit major science and music museums, picnic on the lawns, and take in concerts at venues such as Trabendo, Zénith – and, since early 2015, Jean Nouvel's newly opened (and desperately delayed) 2,400-seat Philharmonie.

Cité des Sciences
et de l'Industrie.

Don't Miss

1 **Cité des Sciences et de l'Industrie** Edutainment galore at this science museum (p161).

2 **104** Accessible art – and pizzas too (p161).

3 **Parc des Buttes-Chaumont** Great park, glorious views (p168).

4 **Porte 12** Open the door to cool design and culinary wizardry (p165).

5 **Chez Prune** Lounge by the canal with bobos and beer (p165).

PORTE ST-DENIS TO LA VILLETTE

In the 10th & 19th arrondissements.

North of Porte St-Denis and Porte St-Martin, two of the oldest thoroughfares leading out of the city, rue du Fbg-St-Denis and rue du Fbg-St-Martin, traverse an area that was transformed in the 19th century by the railways, when it became the site of the Gare du Nord and Gare de l'Est. The grubby rue du Fbg-St-Denis is almost souk-like with its food shops, narrow passages and sinister courtyards. Garishly lit passage Brady is a little piece of India in Paris, full of restaurants, hairdressers and costume shops, whereas the art deco passage du Prado is more a continuation of the Sentier rag trade. Rue du Fbg-St-Martin follows the trace of the Roman road out of the city, and is home to clothes wholesalers, atmospheric courtyards and the ornate Mairie for the tenth.

Rue de Paradis is known for its porcelain and glass outlets, and rue d'Hauteville shows traces of the area's grander days (notably the **Petit Hôtel Bourrienne**, at no.58). Opposite, Cité Paradis is an alley of early industrial buildings. At the top of the street are the twin towers and terraced gardens of the **Eglise St-Vincent-de-Paul**. On boulevard Magenta, **Marché St-Quentin**, built in the 1860s, is one of the city's last remaining cast-iron, covered market halls.

Boulevard de Strasbourg was cut through in the 19th century to create a vista up to the Gare de l'Est. At no.2, a neo-Renaissance creation houses the last fan-maker in Paris and the **Musée de l'Eventail**. Towards the station, **Eglise St-Laurent** (69 bd de Magenta, 119 rue du Fbg-St-Martin, 10th) is one of the city's oldest churches, an eclectic composition with a 12th-century tower, Gothic nave, Baroque lady chapel, 19th-century façade and 1930s stained glass. Between the Gare de l'Est and **Canal St-Martin** are the restored **Couvent des Récollets** and Square Villemin park.

Canal St-Martin, built between 1805 and 1825, begins at the Seine at Pont Morland, disappears underground at Bastille, hides under boulevard Richard-Lenoir, then emerges after crossing rue du Fbg-du-Temple, east of place de la République. Rue du Fbg-du-Temple itself is scruffy and cosmopolitan, lined with cheap grocers and discount stores, hidden courtyards and stalwarts of Paris nightlife: **Le Gibus** (*see p266*), bar-restaurant **Favela Chic** (*see p265*) and vintage dancehall **La Java** (*see p266*).

The first stretch of the canal, lined with shady trees and crossed by iron footbridges and locks, has the most appeal. The quays are traffic-free on Sundays. Many canalside warehouses have been snapped up by artists and designers or turned into loft apartments.

IN THE KNOW CANAL CRUISE

For a cruise with a difference, take a trip along the city's second waterway, the pretty tree-lined Canal St-Martin, with **Canauxrama** (www.canauxrama.com). The cruise takes in four double locks and two swing bridges, and even heads underground, where the tunnel walls are enlivened by a light show.

East from here, the Hôpital St-Louis was commissioned in 1607 by Henri IV to house plague victims, and was built as a series of isolated pavilions in the same brick-and-stone style as place des Vosges, far enough from the town to prevent risk of infection. Behind the hospital, the rue de la Grange-aux-Belles housed the Montfaucon gibbet, put up in 1233, where victims were hanged and left to the elements. East of the hospital, the lovely cobbled rue Ste-Marthe and place Ste-Marthe have a provincial air, busy at night with multi-ethnic eateries.

North, on place du Colonel-Fabien, is the headquarters of the **Parti Communiste Français**, a modernist masterpiece built between 1968 and 1971 by Oscar Niemeyer with Paul Chemetov and Jean Deroche. The canal disappears briefly again under place de Stalingrad, a locale that's best avoided after dark. The square was landscaped in 1989 to showcase the Rotonde de la Villette, one of Ledoux's grandiose 1780s toll houses that once marked the boundary of Paris; it now displays exhibitions and archaeological finds.

Here the canal widens into the Bassin de la Villette, and the new developments along the quai de Loire and further quai de la Marne, as well as some of the worst 1960s and '70s housing in the blocks that stretch along rue de Flandres. At 104 rue d'Aubervilliers, the old municipal undertaker's today houses art space **104**.

At the eastern end of the basin is an unusual 1885 hydraulic lifting bridge, Pont de Crimée. Thursday and Sunday mornings add vitality with a market at place de Joinville. East of here, the Canal de l'Ourcq (created in 1813 to provide drinking water, as well as for freight haulage) divides: Canal St-Denis runs north towards the Seine, and Canal de l'Ourcq continues east through La Villette and the suburbs. Long the city's main abattoir district (still reflected in the Grande Halle de la Villette and in some of the old meaty brasseries along boulevard de la Villette), the area has been revitalised since the late 1980s by the postmodern **Parc de la Villette** complex, with the **Cité des Sciences et de l'Industrie** science museum – and as of 2015, the spectacular **Philharmonie** concert hall (*see p284*).

Sights & Museums

★ FREE 104

5 rue Curial, 19th (01.53.35.50.00, www.104.fr).
M° Riquet. **Open** noon-7pm Tue-Fri; 11am-7pm
Sat, Sun. **Admission** free. *Exhibitions* prices
vary. **Map** p162 C4 ❶

104, described as a 'space for artistic creation',
occupies a vast 19th-century building that used to
house Paris's municipal undertakers. The site was
saved from developers by Roger Madec, the mayor
of the 19th, who made its renovation the centrepiece
of a massive project of cultural and urban renewal.
There aren't any constraints on the kind of work
the resident artists do – 104 is open to 'all the arts'
– but they're expected to show finished pieces in
one of four annual 'festivals'. And they're also
required to get involved in projects with the public,
the fruits of which are shown in a space next door.
The community vibe continues via the onsite café,
bookshop, kids' play area and Emmaüs bric-a-brac
store, a great address where you can mix with hip
hop dancers and cultural performers to bargain-hunt
in a boutique done out like someone's apartment.
Another treat is the Pizza 104 van (think marinated
aubergines, smoked salmon, rocket and parma ham).

★ La Cité des Sciences et de l'Industrie

La Villette, 30 av Corentin-Cariou, 19th
(01.40.05.70.00, www.cite-sciences.fr). M° Porte
de la Villette. **Open** 10am-6pm Tue-Sat; 10am-
7pm Sun. **Admission** €9; €7 reductions; free
under-6s. PMP. **Map** p162 B5 ❷

104.

This ultra-modern science museum pulls in several
million visitors a year. Explora, the permanent show,
occupies the upper two floors, whisking visitors
through 30,000sq m (320,000sq ft) of space, life,
matter and communication: scale models of satellites
including the Ariane space shuttle, planes and
robots, plus the chance to experience weightlessness,
make for an exciting journey. In the Espace Images,
try the delayed camera and other optical illusions,
draw 3D images on a computer or lend your voice to
the *Mona Lisa*. The hothouse garden investigates
developments in agriculture and biotechnology.
Once everyone's IQ has been bolstered, the grassy
expanses of Parc de la Villette are ideal for a stroll
or a picnic. You can also combine your ticket with
the Géode IMAX cinema, which shows fun, science-
related 3D films (*see p252*).
▶ *The brilliant, newly expanded Cité des Enfants,*
which spreads across several themed zones and is
aimed at under-12s, runs loads of workshops for
younger children. See the website for details.

FREE Couvent des Récollets

148 rue du Fbg-St-Martin, 10th. M° Gare de l'Est.
Admission free. **Map** p163 E2 ❸

Founded as a monastery in the 17th century when
still outside the city walls, this barracks, spinning
factory and hospice was a military hospital from
1860 to 1968. Left empty, the convent was squatted
by artists, Les Anges des Récollets, in the early
1990s. The buildings were renovated and reopened
in 2004. One half, the Maison de l'Architecture (www.
maisonarchitecture-idf.org), hosts a garden café
and architectural debates. The other is the Centre
International d'Accueil et d'Echanges des Récollets:
studios and duplexes for foreign 'creators' – artists
and researchers (from painters to neurobiologists).

★ FREE Eglise St-Vincent-de-Paul

5 rue de Belzunce, 10th (01.48.78.47.47, www.
paroissesvp.fr). M° Gare du Nord. **Open** 2-7pm
Mon; 8am-noon, 2-7pm Tue-Fri; 8am-noon,
2-7.30pm Sat; 9.30am-noon, 4.30-7.30pm Sun.
Admission free. **Map** p163 E1 ❹

Set at the top of terraced gardens, this church
was begun in 1824 by Jean-Baptiste Lepère and
completed in 1844 by his son-in-law, Jacques Hittorff,
who also designed the Gare du Nord (*see below*)
and the Cirque d'Hiver (*see p248*). The twin towers,
pedimented Greek temple portico and sculptures of
the four evangelists along the parapet are in high
classical mode. The interior has a splendid double-
storey arcade of columns, murals by Jean-Hippolyte
Flandrin and church furniture by François Rude.

Gare du Nord

Rue de Dunkerque, 10th. M° Gare du Nord.
Map p162 D2 ❺

The grandest of the great 19th-century train stations
(and Eurostar terminal since 1994) was designed by
Jacques Hittorff in the 1860s. A conventional stone

EXPLORE

façade, with Ionic capitals and statues representing towns served by the station, hides a vast iron-and-glass vault. The Gare du Nord is one of the busiest stations in Europe.

Musée de la Musique

Cité de la Musique, 221 av Jean-Jaurès, 19th (01.44.84.44.84, www.cite-musique.fr). M° Porte de Pantin. **Open** noon-6pm Tue-Sat; 10am-6pm Sun. **Admission** €7; €5.60 reductions; free under-26s. PMP. **Map** p162 C6 ❻

Alongside the concert hall, this innovative music museum houses a gleamingly restored collection of instruments from the old Conservatoire, interactive computers and scale models of opera houses and concert halls. Visitors are supplied with an audio-guide in a choice of languages, and the musical commentary is a joy, playing the appropriate instrument as you approach each exhibit. Alongside the trumpeting brass, curly woodwind instruments and precious strings (highlights include a Stradivarius violin and Django Reinhardt's guitar) are more unusual items, such as the Indonesian gamelan orchestra, whose sounds influenced the work of Debussy and Ravel. Concerts in the amphitheatre use instruments from the collection.

★ FREE Parc de la Villette

Av Corentin-Cariou, 19th (01.40.03.75.75, www.villette.com). M° Porte de la Villette. Av Jean-Jaurès, 19th. M° Porte de Pantin. **Map** p162 B6 ❼

Dotted with red pavilions, or *folies*, the park was designed by Bernard Tschumi and is a postmodern feast. The *folies* serve as glorious giant climbing frames, as well as a first-aid post, burger bar, children's art centre and gig venue. As well as the lawns, which are used for an open-air film festival in summer, there are ten themed gardens bearing evocative names, such as the Garden of Mirrors, of Mists, of Acrobatics and of Childhood Frights. South of the canal are the Zénith concert venue (*see p276*), and the Grande Halle de la Villette – now used for trade fairs, exhibitions and September's jazz festival. It is flanked by the Conservatoire de la Musique and the Cité de la Musique, with rehearsal rooms, concert halls and the Musée de la Musique (*see above*). The whole is now overshadowed by Jean Nouvel's dramatic 2,400-seat Philharmonie.

Petit Hôtel Bourrienne

58 rue d'Hauteville, 10th (01.47.70.51.14). M° Bonne Nouvelle or Poissonnière. **Open** *Guided visits 1-15 July, Sept* noon-6pm daily. Rest of year by appointment Sat. **Admission** €7. **No credit cards. Map** p163 F1 ❽

A rare example of the Consulaire style, this small *hôtel particulier* was built between 1789 and 1798. It was occupied by Fortunée Hamelin, born (like her friend the Empress Josephine) on the French Caribbean island of Martinique, and notorious for parading topless down the Champs-Elysées.

Le Verre Volé.

A bedroom boudoir painted with tropical birds was her only decoration before the site was taken over by Louis Fauvelet de Bourrienne, Napoleon's private secretary. He had it decorated according to the latest fashion, making sure to keep his political options open (the dining room ceiling is painted with motifs favourable to monarchy and empire).

Restaurants

52 Faubourg Saint-Denis

52 rue du Faubourg Saint-Denis, 10th (no phone). M° Château d'Eau. **Open** 8am-midnight daily. **Main courses** €16-€18. **Map** p163 F2 ❾ **Bistro**

With a location in a former butcher's shop, concrete-chic decor, a no-reservations policy, good-looking staff and an all-day menu, the third venue from Charles Compagnon (after Le Richer and L'Office) is as hip as can be. There's plenty of imagination on the plate: a starter of marinated swordfish with black olives, pears, radishes, almonds and a spicy crisp-bread, perhaps. Mains play safer with the flavours, such as rich pink squares of roasted duck with a beetroot purée and a tangle of slow-roasted endives.

Abri

92 rue du Fbg-Poissonnière, 10th (01.83.97.00.00). M° Poissonnière. **Open** noon-3pm Mon; 12.30-3pm, 8-10pm Tue-Sat. **Prix fixe** *Lunch* €25 (Tue-Fri). *Dinner* €40. **Map** p163 E1 ❿ **Bistro**

A pocket-sized restaurant next to the Poissonière métro, Abri ('shelter') serves everything from multi-layered sandwiches (Mondays and Saturdays) to sophisticated French cuisine enhanced with Far Eastern touches: marinated mackerel, for example, with almost transparent sliced vegetables, or a winter squash soup with pumpkin seeds and coffee. You'll need to reserve far in advance to secure a table in the postage stamp-sized room, but it's definitely worth the effort. Service is charming.

Les Bancs Publics

2 rue de Nantes, 19th (09.80.76.36.71). M° Crimée. **Open** 12.30-2.30pm, 7.30-10.30pm Mon-Sat. **Main courses** €13-€18. **Prix fixe** *Lunch* €12.90, €15.90 (Mon-Fri). **Map** p162 C5 ⓫ **Bistro**

This smart bistro with its inventive menu opened in September 2014. There are tables outside overlooking the canal on sunny days and an agreeable sense of people enjoying themselves – the extremely conservative pricing and good selection of draught beers may help. It's a classic affair where the chalkboard menu is propped on a chair at your table while you choose, but the execution of the dishes shows a taste for adventure: a starter of pickled beetroot and trout roe, followed by pork belly and razor clams.

Floyd's Bar & Grill

11 rue d'Enghien, 10th (01.44.79.05.52, www. floyds.fr). M° Château d'Eau. **Open** noon-3pm, 6-11.30pm Tue-Fri; 6-11.30pm Sat; noon-4pm Sun. **Main courses** €17-€42.50. **Prix fixe** *Lunch* €19 (Tue-Fri), €18 (Sun). **Map** p163 F1 ⑫ **Grill**
Don't be fooled by the discreet façade – this new darling of the St-Denis foodie scene is all about deceptive sizes. The first surprise is the main room, its improbably vast dimensions harbouring a modern, tastefully furnished dining area that opens on to an inner courtyard. The second is the Sunday roast, a feast of meat, veg and succulent Yorkshire pudding. Sundays aside, Floyd's serves up no less detectable meat and seafood dishes, such as coddled oysters and T-bone steaks, all prepared on the charcoal grill.

★ Porte 12

12 rue des Messageries, 10th (01.42.46.22.64, www.porte12.com). M° Poissonnière. **Open** noon-2.30pm, 7-10pm Tue-Fri; 7-10pm Sat. **Prix fixe** *Lunch* €35. *Dinner* €65. **Map** p163 E1 ⑬ **Bistro** *See p166* **In Good Taste**.

Le Verre Volé

67 rue de Lancry, 10th (01.48.03.17.34, www. leverrevole.fr). M° Jacques Bonsergent. **Open** *Cave à vins* 9am-1am daily. *Restaurant* 12.30-2pm, 7.30-10.30pm daily. **Main courses** €16-€26. **Map** p163 F3 ⑭ **Bistro**
This organic-only *cave à vins* doubles up as a restaurant. Although wine (around €6 per glass) is the focus, you're obliged to eat; a hearty sausage and mash will set you back around €16. It's good to know that staff will sell you a bottle of wine (and open it) for you to drink by the canal.

▶ *For lunch on the hoof, head for the Verre Volé's deli offshoot (54 rue de la Folie-Méricourt, 11th), which serves up gourmet sandwiches such as calf's head pâté, gribiche sauce and watercress.*

Cafés & Bars

Bar Ourcq

68 quai de la Loire, 19th (01.42.40.12.26, http://barourcq.free.fr). M° Laumière. **Open** 3pm-midnight Tue-Thur; 3pm-2am Fri, Sat; 3-10pm Sun. **No credit cards**. **Map** p162 C4 ⑮
This was one of the first hip joints to hit the Canal de l'Ourcq, with an embankment broad enough to accommodate *pétanque* games (ask at the bar) and a cluster of deckchairs. It's a completely different scene from the crowded bustle along Canal St-Martin – more discerning and less self-satisfied. The cabin-like interior is cosy, and drinks are listed in a hit parade of prices. Exhibitions and a regular DJ spot keep the cool clientele sated.

★ Chez Jeannette

47 rue du Fbg-St-Denis, 10th (01.47.70.30.89, www.chezjeannette.com). M° Château d'Eau or Strasbourg St-Denis. **Open** 8am-1.45am Mon-Sat; 9am-1.45am Sun. **Map** p163 F2 ⑯
When she sold her café a few years ago, Jeannette handed over to the young team from Chez Justine because they promised not to change a thing. The monstrous 1940s dust-coated lights, leaky loos, tobacco-stained wallpaper depicting the Moulin Rouge and PVC-covered banquettes have been cleaned up, and the café is now one of Paris's hippest spots for an aperitif. There's a *plat du jour* at lunch and plates of cheese and charcuterie at night.

★ Chez Prune

36 rue Beaurepaire, 10th (01.42.41.30.47). M° Jacques Bonsergent. **Open** 8am-2am Mon-Sat; 10am-2am Sun. **Map** p163 ⑰
Chez Prune is still one of the best places in which to spend an evening on the Canal St-Martin. The local bobo HQ, this traditional café, with high ceilings and low lighting, sticks to a simple formula: groups of friends crowd around the cosily ordered banquettes, picking at moderately priced cheese or meat platters. Mostly, though, they come for a few leisurely drinks or an *apéro* before heading off to one of the late-night venues in the area.

Le Cinquante

50 rue de Lancry, 10th (01.42.02.36.83). M° Jacques Bonsergent. **Open** 5.30pm-2am daily. Closed Aug. **Map** p163 F3 ⑱
The bare brick, Formica and framed '50s ads of this funky venue attract an inner circle of regulars. Reasonable prices – half-litre pitchers of sauvignon, Brouilly and Chablis in the €10 range – attract a mixed bag of tastes and generations. The two rooms behind the main bar are set aside for dining (affordable classics) and music (generally acoustic).

Le CopperBay

5 rue Bouchardon, 10th (www.copperbay.fr). M° Jacques Bonsergent. **Open** 6pm-2am Tue-Sat. **Map** p163 F2 ⑲
Nautical-themed drinking hole CopperBay is a sophisticated cocktail bar. Against a backdrop of wood panelling and ropes, experienced cocktail crafters Elfi, Julien and Aurélie serve up a sailor-friendly rum on the rocks or something a little more adventurous from the ambitious drinks menu. It's classy, yet not extortionate by Paris standards: cocktails cost around €10 each.

EXPLORE

Delaville Café
34 bd de Bonne-Nouvelle, 10th (01.48.24.48.09, www.delavillecafe.com). M° Bonne Nouvelle. **Open** 8.30am-2am daily. **Map** p163 F1 ⓴
The Delaville is an unmissable stop on the Grands Boulevards, with a vast terrace open from spring onwards. The vibe is a little precious, but the decor of the huge venue is a delight, a mixture of ancient gilt rococo and post-industrial baroque (it used to be a *maison dose*). The high glass ceiling between the bar and the terrace is stunning, full of light even in winter, and the back room surprises with all the decadence of an upmarket London club: think red leather banquettes, stuffed animals and plasma screens. DJs mix electro lounge sets at weekends.

★ Le Fantôme
36 rue de Paradis, 10th (09.66.87.11.20, www. lefanto.me). M° Poissonnière. **Open** 11am-2am Mon-Fri; 6pm-2am Sat. **Map** p163 E1 ㉑
Only the black lacquered tiles give away the location of Le Fantôme, the new venue from the crew behind Le Baron. The enormous space is a fantasy venue for fans of retrogaming: as well as a huge bar, Formica chairs and faux leather banquettes, the Fantôme offers a fistful of arcade games, a Pacman table (often reserved) and table football. Drinks-wise, the resident mixologist is an inspired Californian called David West who refuses to churn out mojitos, but has instead produced a list of five inventive cocktails to go with the menu of hefty pizzas.

Shops & Services

Antoine et Lili
95 quai de Valmy, 10th (01.40.37.41.55, www. antoineetlili.com). M° Jacques Bonsergent. **Open** 11am-8pm Mon-Fri; 10am-8pm Sat; 11am-7pm Sun. **Map** p163 F3 ㉒ Fashion
Antoine et Lili's fuchsia-pink, custard-yellow and apple-green shopfronts are a new raver's dream. The bobo designer's clothes, often in wraparound styles, adapt to all sizes and shapes. The Canal St-Martin 'village' comprises womenswear, a kitsch home decoration boutique and childrenswear.
Other locations throughout the city.

IN GOOD TASTE
Open the door to divine dishes at Porte 12.

Opened in September 2014 on a fairly nondescript street in the 10th, **Porte 12**'s (*see p165*) burnished bronze door leads to an intimate split-level room where chef Vincent Crépel is busy creating small masterpieces on the plate. Appropriately enough, as the building used to be a lingerie workshop. But there the resemblance ends, as this outfit is neither racy nor frou-frou.

The space, crowned by a flowing iron staircase, is an exercise in the best kind of understated good taste – all taupe walls, warm wood, blue banquettes and airy cages of dangling bronze lamps, with a scattering of spotlights. A lot of thought has clearly gone into the design, which must have struggled to accommodate the kitchen behind its glass screen – the cooks look a little cramped.

No matter for the diners, though, who can rejoice in the precise and complex flavours issuing from within. At lunch, try the extremely good-value set menus. A bowl of rich, dark, tender duck hearts in a multi-layered onion bouillon comes cosseted under buttery whipped potatoes planted with sprigs of salty glasswort. Silky raw petals of sea bream are laid on small, rich squares of slow-cooked vegetables and dotted with an intense basil vinaigrette, which has none of the dominating tang that the name suggests.

Main dishes might include a tender round of veal with whipped parsnips, roasted spring onions and fresh raspberries, or a toothsome tranche of chicken on a bed of Sardinian fregola, flanked by a lively drift of crisped corn shoots. Flavours and textures across the board are complex without being overwhelming, leaving room to share a perfect plate of slow-roasted figs with meringue and beurre noisette. Service is top-notch, sending diners on their way with that happy glow that comes from being spoiled at a place with both originality and savoir faire, and which doesn't feel the need to make your credit card go up in flames. Like all the best small luxuries, Porte 12 is one you'll want to return to, and soon.

★ Culture(s)

*46 rue de Lancry, 10th (09.81.74.58.71, www.
jeanmariepatois.com). M° Jacques Bonsergent.*
Open 10.30am-7.30pm Tue-Sat. **Map** p163 F2
㉓ Gifts & souvenirs
In a loft-style studio, this unusual florist combines
exotic flowers, trees and garden-themed items, such
as floral printed rain hats. Truly original.

★ Du Pain et des Idées

*34 rue Yves Toudic, 10th (01.42.40.44.52, www.
dupainetdesidees.com). M° Jacques Bonsergent.*
Open 6.45am-8pm Mon-Fri. **Map** p163 F3 ㉔
Food & drink
Christophe Vasseur is a former winner of the Gault-
Millau prize for Best Bakery. Among his specialities
are Le Pagnol aux Pommes, bread studded with
apple (skin on), raisins and orange flower water.

L'Eau et les Rêves

*Quai de l'Oise, 19th (01.42.05.99.70, www.
penichelibrairie.com).* **Open** 1-7pm
Wed-Sun. **Map** p162 C5 ㉕ **Books & music**
What do you get when you marry a sailor and a
book buyer? A book barge, naturally. Unlike British
narrowboats, a Parisian *péniche* glories in space, and
the team behind this floating library, café and activity
centre have embraced the nautical theme with fabulous results. There's a kids' area, theatre workshops,
talks and signings, and a set of *bouquiniste*-style
stalls for second-hand books on the upper deck.

L'Epicerie Musicale

*55 bis quai de Valmy, 10th (07.51.65.38.02,
www.epiceriemusicale.com). M° Goncourt.* **Open**
noon-3.30pm, 5-9pm Tue-Fri; 12.30-4pm Sat, Sun.
Map p163 F3 ㉖ **Food & drink**
Ideally situated on the Canal St-Martin, L'Epicerie
Musicale is a delightful hybrid of café-bar, restaurant, deli and music store. The retro furniture gives
the interior all the charm of an old Sicilian café, offset
by graffiti art on the walls, a deli section with fish,
wine, oils, hams, cheeses and more imported from
Italy, and a jazz, soul, funk, tropical and retro-latino
vinyl soundtrack. Highly recommended.

Maison DoDuDinDon

*3 rue Alexandre Parodi, 10th (01.42.09.99.47,
www.dodudindon.com). M° Louis Blanc.* **Open**
11am-7pm Tue-Sat; 11am-5.30pm Sun. **Map**
p163 E3 ㉗ **Children**
This bright new emporium draws kids and adults
alike with its welcoming vibe and stacks of toys,
teddies and clothes. It's enough to keep the little ones
busy for hours.

Potemkine

*30 rue Beaurepaire, 11th (01.40.18.01.81,
www.potemkine.fr). M° République* **Open**
11am-7pm Mon; 11am-8pm Tue-Sat; 2-7pm
Sun. **Map** p163 F3 ㉘ **Films**

If you know what the name 'Potemkine' refers to
(Eisenstein's 1925 silent movie *Battleship Potemkin*),
chances are this boutique off the Canal St-Martin is
for you. Its orderly walls are lined with shelves laden
with DVDs covering everything from Fellini classics
to rare experimental films by Stan Brakhage and
docu-dramas by Peter Watkins.

BELLEVILLE & MENILMONTANT

In the 11th, 19th & 20th arrondissements.

When the city boundaries were expanded in
1860, Ménilmontant and Belleville, once villages
that provided Paris with fruit, wine and weekend
escapes, were absorbed. They were built up with
housing for migrants, first from rural France and
later from former colonies in North Africa and
South-east Asia. The area encompasses one of the
city's most beautiful parks, **Buttes-Chaumont**.

On boulevard de Belleville, Chinese and
Vietnamese shops rub shoulders with Muslim
and kosher groceries, and couscous and falafel
eateries; a street market takes place here on
Tuesday and Friday mornings. North of here,
along avenue Simon-Bolivar, is the **Parc des
Buttes-Chaumont**. This is the most desirable
part of north-east Paris, with Haussmannian
apartments overlooking the park: to the east,
near place de Rhin-et-Danube, is a small area
of tiny, hilly streets lined with small houses and
gardens, known by locals as Quartier Mouzaïa.

Up on the slopes of the Hauts de Belleville,
there are views over the city from rue Piat and
rue des Envierges, which lead to the modern but
charming **Parc de Belleville** with its Maison
des Vents devoted to birds and kites. Below the
park, rue Ramponneau mixes new housing and
relics of old Belleville. At no.23 an old smithy has
been turned into La Forge, an artists' squat.

'Mesnil-Montant' used to be a few houses on a
hill with vines and fruit trees – then came the
bistros, bordellos and workers' housing. It became
part of Paris in 1860. These days it's a thriving
centre of alternative Paris, as artists and young
professionals have moved in, and rue Oberkampf
is home to some of the city's most humming bars.

The area mixes 1960s and '70s housing projects
with older dwellings. Just below rue des Pyrénées,
which cuts through the 20th, you can rummage
around the rustic Cité Leroy or Villa l'Ermitage,
cobbled cul-de-sacs of little houses and gardens,
and old craft workshops. Rue de l'Ermitage has a
curious neo-Gothic house at no.19 – and a bird's-eye
view from the junction with rue de Ménilmontant
down to the Centre Pompidou. On rue Boyer, **La
Maroquinerie** (*see p275*) puts on an eclectic mix
of literary events, political debate and live music,
and at 88 rue de Ménilmontant, graffiti-covered art
squat **La Miroiterie** opens house for art shows
and the *magasin gratuit*, a free swap shop.

EXPLORE

IN THE KNOW PINK PIZZA

Pink Flamingo (67 rue Bichat, 10th, www. pinkflamingopizza.com) is one of the least traditional pizza joints in Paris, but the quirky toppings (think eight cheeses or aubergine and houmous) never fail to hit the spot. If you fancy eating canalside on warmer evenings, they'll hand you a helium balloon when you order, and the delivery boy will come and find your picnic spot on the Canal St-Martin. How's that for service?

Sights & Museums

FREE Musée Edith Piaf

5 rue Crespin-du-Gast, 11th (01.43.55.52.72). M° Ménilmontant. **Open** *By appointment only* 1-6pm Mon-Wed; 10am-noon Thur. **Admission** free (donations welcome). **Map** p163 G5 ㉙

Set in an apartment where Piaf lived at the age of 18, when she sang on the streets of Ménilmontant, this tiny museum consists of two red-painted rooms crammed with letters, pictures, framed discs and objects belonging to the singer. The museum's real treasures are two letters, one a chatty number written on her 28th birthday, and another more passionate pen to actor Robert Dalban. She died at the age of 47 and is buried in Père-Lachaise *(see p144)*.

★ FREE Parc des Buttes-Chaumont

Rue Botzaris, rue Manin, rue de Crimée, 19th. M° Buttes Chaumont. **Open** *Oct-Apr* 7am-8pm daily. *May-Sept* 7am-10pm daily. **Map** p162 D5 ㉚

When the city's boundaries were expanded in 1860, the Buttes-Chaumont was created on the site of a former quarry. The park, with its meandering paths, waterfalls, temples and vertical cliffs, was designed by Adolphe Alphand, and was opened as part of the celebrations for the Universal Exhibition in 1867. After lounging with the locals, head for the park's Rosa Bonheur *guinguette* (www.rosabonheur.fr). Open till midnight, it makes the perfect place to sip an *apéro* and take in the stunning views of the city below. Also worth a look is the Pavillon du Lac (www. lepavillondulac.fr), one of five pavilions opened in 1868. Restored in 2010 after lying abandoned for ten years, it has been transformed into a high-class restaurant with chef Fabien Borgel in the kitchen. The park is undergoing major renovations until 2016, but will remain open throughout.

Restaurants

★ Le Baratin

3 rue Jouye-Rouve, 20th (01.43.49.39.70). M° Pyrénées. **Open** noon-2pm, 7.30-11pm Tue-Fri; 7.30-11pm Sat. **Main courses** €20-€30. **Prix fixe** *Lunch* €19. **Map** p163 F5 ㉛ **Bistro**

Star pastry chef Pierre Hermé visits this cheerful little bistro and wine bar high up in Belleville to fill up on Raquel Carena's homely cooking with the occasional exotic twist. Typical of her style, which draws on her native Argentina, are tuna carpaccio with cherries, roast Basque lamb with new potatoes and spinach, and hazelnut pudding.

€ Le Cambodge

10 av Richerand, 10th (01.44.84.37.70, www. lecambodge.fr). M° Goncourt or République. **Open** noon-2.30pm, 7-11pm Mon-Thur; noon-2.30pm, 7-11.30pm Fri; noon-11.30pm Sat; noon-11pm Sun. Closed last 2wks Dec. **Main courses** €10-€16. **Map** p163 F3 ㉜ **Cambodian**

The system at Le Cambodge is simple: you write your order on a piece of paper, including any preferences such as 'no coriander', 'no peanuts' or 'extra rice', and after a short wait the dishes appear. Two favourites are the *bobun spécial*, a hot and cold mix of sautéed beef, noodles, salad, bean sprouts and imperial rolls, and *banhoy*, a selection of the same ingredients to be wrapped in lettuce and mint leaves and dipped in a sauce.

★ Le Chateaubriand

129 av Parmentier, 11th (01.43.57.45.95, www.lechateaubriand.net). M° Goncourt. **Open** 7.30-11pm Tue-Sat. **Prix fixe** €70, €135. **Map** p163 G4 ㉝ **Bistro**

Self-taught Basque chef Iñaki Aizpitarte runs this stylish bistro. Dishes have been deconstructed down to their very essence and put back together again. You'll understand if you try starters like chunky steak tartare with a quail's egg, or asparagus with tahini foam and little splinters of sesame-seed brittle. The cooking's not always so cerebral – Aizpitarte's Spanish goat's cheese with stewed apple jam is brilliant. Be sure to book ahead.

Le Dauphin

131 av Parmentier, 11th (01.55.28.78.88, www.restaurantledauphin.net). M° Goncourt. **Open** 5.30pm-2am Tue-Sat. **Tapas** €5-€18. **Map** p163 F3 ㉞ **Wine bar**

Iñaki Aizpitarte's Le Dauphin, a Rem Koolhaus-designed tapas-style place, offers sub-€15 dishes such as *magret séché, tempura de gambas* and *tarte au citron meringuée*. As at Le Chateaubriand, sourcing is all-important – bread comes from award-winning Du Pain et des Idées.

★ € Dong Huong

14 rue Louis-Bonnet, 11th (01.43.57.42.81, www.dong-huong.com). M° Belleville. **Open** noon-10.30pm Mon, Wed-Sun. Closed 3wks summer. **Main courses** €7-€10. **Map** p163 F4 ㉟ **Vietnamese**

The excellent food at this Vietnamese noodle joint attracts a buzzy crowd. The delicious *bành cuôn*, steamed Vietnamese ravioli stuffed with minced meat, mushrooms, bean sprouts, spring onions and deep-fried onion, are served piping hot. *Com ga lui*, chicken kebabs with lemongrass, though not as delicate, come with tasty rice. For dessert, the mandarin, lychee and mango sorbets are superb.

Le Galopin

34 rue Ste-Marthe, 10th (01.42.06.05.03, www. le-galopin.com). M° Belleville or Colonel Fabien. **Open** 7.30-11pm Mon-Fri. Closed 2wks Aug & 1wk Dec. **Prix fixe** €54. **Map** p163 F4 **36 Bistro**
Award-winning chef Romain Tischenko serves up a creative, daily-changing menu at this little restaurant on pretty place Ste-Marthe. Tischenko's USP is taking unfashionable vegetables and turning them into fusion cuisine 2.0 – think parsnips, artichokes, pumpkins and celery combined with cocoa, scallops and caramel. Staff are attentive and full of good advice on the wines, all of which are produced by independent winemakers.

Haï Kaï

104 quai de Jemmapes, 10th (09.81.99.98.88, www.haikai.fr). M° Goncourt. **Open** noon-3pm, 7-11pm Tue-Sat; noon-5pm Sun. **Main courses** €18-€100. **Prix fixe** *Lunch* €22, €27. *Dinner* €50. Closed last 3wks Aug. **Map** p163 F3 **37 Bistro**
Amélie Darvas has a distinguished chef's CV. Her new 2014 venture is all pale walls and wood, brought to life with lots of plants and bright flashes of colour. Haikai is a satirical Japanese verse form, a nod to the Far Eastern influences in the decor and cooking. Everything looks as good as it tastes, such as beef with oysters and winter radishes or Norwegian smoked salmon, candied eggs and beetroot.

€ La Madonnina

10 rue Marie-et-Louise, 10th (01.42.01.25.26). M° Goncourt or Jacques Bonsergent. **Open** 12.15-2.30pm, 8-11pm Mon-Thur; 8-11.30pm Fri, Sat. **Main courses** €13-€18. **Prix fixe** *Lunch* €15. **Map** p163 F3 **38 Italian**
The newly refurbished Madonnina describes itself as a *trattoria napoletana*, but most of the dishes are pan-southern Italian. The short menu changes monthly; don't miss the home-made pastas, such as artichoke and ricotta ravioli. The cassata, an extremely sweet Sicilian version of cheesecake, is authentic and unusual to see on menus outside Italy.

Le Rouleau de Printemps

42 rue de Tourtille, 20th (01.46.36.98.95). M° Belleville or Pyrénées. **Open** 11.30am-3.30pm, 7.30-11pm Mon, Tue, Thur-Sun. **Main courses** €7. **Map** p163 F5 **39 Vietnamese**
The secret's been out about Rouleau de Printemps for some time, but it never disappoints. You can't reserve a place in the two postcard-sized rooms, so arrive early. A coriander-scented *bo bun*, some plump crunchy egg rolls, a vegetarian spring roll and some steamed prawn ravioli washed down with jasmine tea or Tsingtao beer won't cost you much more than €20, so go easy on the sometimes chaotic service.

Cafés & Bars

Le 9b

68 bd de la Villette, 19th (01.40.18.08.10, www. le9b.com). M° Colonel Fabien. **Open** 10am-2am Mon-Sat. **Map** p163 E4 **40**
Does the name remind you of anything? It's our old favourite, Le 9 Billards. This bar – which preceded Les Disquaires on rue Jean-Pierre Timbaud – has been reborn on boulevard de la Villette. It's full to bursting each night with a grand blend of electro, hip hop, funk and rock on the crammed dancefloor, and cocktails and couscous on the menu.

L'Alimentation Générale

64 rue Jean-Pierre-Timbaud, 11th (01.43.55.42.50, www.alimentation-generale.net). M° Parmentier. **Open** 7pm-2am Wed, Thur, Sun; 7pm-5am Fri, Sat. **Map** p163 G4 **41**

EXPLORE

Parc des Buttes-Chaumont.

The 'Grocery Store' is a big old space filled with junk. Cupboards of kitsch china and lampshades made from kitchen sponges are an inspired touch. The beer is well chosen – Flag, Sagres, Picon and Orval – and the unusual house cocktail involves basil and figs. DJs rock the joint: expect a €10 cover price (including a drink) for big names or live bands.

La Bellevilloise

19-21 rue Boyer, 20th (01.46.36.07.07, www. labellevilloise.com). M° Gambetta. **Open** 7pm-1am Wed, Thur; 7pm-2am Fri; times vary Sat, Sun. **Map** p163 G6 ㊷

The Bellevilloise multitasks as a bar, restaurant, club and exhibition space, hosting regular film and music festivals on the top level (where there's a fake lawn with deckchairs and a massage area). Enjoy brunch in the Halle aux Oliviers or decent views of the *quartier* from the charming terrace; downstairs the club-cum-concert venue has launched some of Paris's most exciting new bands, and on '80s nights you can hardly move for the fortysomethings living it up like they were teens again.

Café Charbon

109 rue Oberkampf, 11th (01.43.57.55.13, www.nouveaucasino.net). M° Parmentier or Ménilmontant. **Open** 9am-2am Mon-Wed, Sun; 9am-4am Thur-Sat. **Map** p163 G4 ㊸

The bar in this beautifully restored belle époque building sparked the Oberkampf nightlife boom. Its booths, mirrors and adventurous music policy put trendy locals at ease, capturing the essence of café culture spanning each end of the 20th century. After more than 15 years, the formula still works – and is copied by nearby bars. Avoid coming on weekend evenings, as the bar is rammed and the waiters are overwhelmed. The terrace is a good bet in summer.

★ Café Chéri(e)

44 bd de la Villette, 19th (01.42.02.02.05, www. cafecherie.blogspot.fr). M° Belleville. **Open** 11am-2am Mon-Fri; 10.30am-2am Sat; noon-2am Sun. **Map** p163 F4 ㊹

This splendid DJ bar is also an all-day café – but it doesn't compromise any of the cool that keeps it well ahead of the pack after dark. Music comes from all over, and runs from electro, rock, funk, hip hop, indie, dance and jazz to golden oldies and ghetto-inspired grooves. The interior sparkles with wit – note the marvellous mural alluding to the personal sacrifices made for a life of coupledom. There's a front terrace if you need respite from the BPM.

▶ *There's music from Thursdays to Saturdays after 9pm.*

Le Café des Sports

94 rue de Ménilmontant, 20th (01.46.36.48.18, www.lecafedessportsmenilmontant.com). M° Gambetta. **Open** 10am-2am daily. Closed Aug. **Map** p163 G6 ㊺

Le Café des Sports' eclectic music programme ranges from electro (Saturdays), to pop or *chanson* (Tuesdays and Thursdays) to world dub. Beer and wine are fabulously cheap and there's sometimes free couscous or tapas with your drink on a Monday evening. Unlike its sprawling neighbours, Le Café des Sports has just one room to call home. DJs play in the space at the back.

La Cale Sèche

18 rue des Panoyaux, 20th (no phone). M° Ménilmontant. **Open** 5pm-2am Tue-Sat; 3pm-2am Sun. **Map** p163 G5 ㊻

This bar is easy to miss, thanks to its unpretentious façade. But once inside, you'll find a long bar with a surprise at the back – a pretty, leafy terrace flanked by public tennis courts. Inside, the decor is a jumble of storm lamps, old shoes suspended from the ceiling and posters for punk, rock and French *chanson* artists (who make up the soundtrack). The well-chosen range of beers includes Maes, Chimay, Chouffe and Cuvée des Trolls.

La Cave à Michel

36 rue Ste-Marthe, 10th (01.42.45.94.47). M° Colonel Fabien or Goncourt. **Open** *Cave à vins* 3-11pm Wed-Sun. *Food served* 7pm-midnight Wed-Sun. **Main courses** €5-€12. **Map** p163 F4 ㊼

Formerly wine cellar Contre-Etiquette, the Cave à Michel has been spruced up to be able to welcome customers in for a drink. Simple and rustic, the *cave à vins* oozes charm. Portuguese *azulejos* brighten up the wooden countertop and tables, and outside is a little courtyard. Welcoming and chatty, the manager Fabrice is a crucial part of the package. Platters of meat cuts bought from the Spanish shop just over the road are served alongside the wine from a high-quality, organically produced selection.

La Gouttière

96 av Parmentier, 11th (01.43.55.46.42). M° Parmentier. **Open** 10am-3pm, 5pm-2am Mon-Sat. **Map** p163 G4 ㊽

The Gutter is not out-and-out libertine, but you're on the right lines. Certainly, a come-what-may approach to music, drinking and eye contact abounds in the crowded venue. Decor consists of a few LP covers and the kind of colour scheme often put to good use in adventure playgrounds. Reasonably priced lunches (a mix of French and North African), the occasional live band, chess and card games complete the picture.

La Maroquinerie

23 rue Boyer, 20th (01.40.33.35.05, www. lamaroquinerie.fr). M° Gambetta. **Open** 6.30-11.30pm daily. *Concerts* times vary. Closed Aug. **Map** p163 G6 ㊾

La Maroquinerie's former life as a leather factory is little in evidence these days. It's now a bright café and bar in competition with La Bellevilloise (*see left*), with a coveted downstairs music venue that hosts

EXPLORE

the odd literary debate and a wealth of cool acts. The food is excellent – you can eat your way through the menu for around €30 – and wine sourced from across France starts at €3 a glass. The interior is cosy, and in summer chirpy locals invade the shaded terrace.

La Sardine
32 rue Ste-Marthe, 10th (01.42.49.19.46, www.bar lasardine.com). M° Belleville. **Open** *9am-2am daily.* **Map** p163 F4 ⑤⓪
Never was a bar more aptly named: this quaint *café-resto* gets extremely packed. La Sardine's popularity has something to do with its location on place Ste-Marthe, with a tree-shaded terrace and hardly any passing traffic. It's also got a decent wine list, with a choice of organic varieties, best accompanied by tapas (serrano ham, caviar of aubergine, chorizo).

★ Les Trois Arts
21 rue des Rigoles, 20th (01.43.49.36.27, www.les3arts.free.fr). M° Jourdain. **Open** *5pm-2am Tue-Sun.* **Map** p163 F6 ⑤①
This Breton tavern offers a mix of live arts and lessons on the art of living. You can hear folk, jazz, klemer or classical concerts, or take part in French, Irish, Mediterranean and Eastern European storytelling evenings. Occasionally, you'll happen upon plays, improv and comedy. All that goes on in the basement, but the bar upstairs also lays on activities. You can borrow board games to pore over in the library, and they'll even lend you works of art on show as part of the *De l'art chez toi* initiative. Every Friday, food offerings include *kig ha farz*, a traditional Breton dish. Enjoy with a barley ale, glass of cider or *chouchen*, a honey-based Breton aperitif.

Le Troquet des Glaces
46 rue du Fbg-du-Temple, 11th (01.48.05.98.39). M° Goncourt. **Open** *4pm-2am Mon-Fri, Sun; noon-2am Sat.* **Map** p163 F3 ⑤②
Le Troquet des Glaces hasn't been here long – it opened in 2013 – yet it has all the charm of an established neighbourhood bar. Fine wines and gourmet sandwiches are the order of the day, though it's worth shelling out for one of the divine cheese and meat platters. But what elevates Le Troquet above its neighbours is Yassin, the charming owner.

Shops & Services

GoldyMama
14 rue du Surmelin, 20th (01.40.30.08.00, www.goldymama.com). M° Pelleport. **Open** *11am-7.30pm Tue-Sat.* **Map** p163 G6 ⑥③ **Fashion**
Finding well-presented vintage clothes is possible – GoldyMama is the proof. This small boutique in the heights of the 20th has retro treasures aplenty and makes an original spot for gift hunting. Once you've tried on half the shop, free your inner child at GoldyMama's 'Bar à Bonbons' filled with boiled sweets, caramels and all sorts of naughty treats.

★ Hammam Medina Center
43-45 rue Petit, 19th (01.42.02.31.05, www.hammam-medina.com). M° Ourcq. **Open** *Women* 11am-10pm Mon-Fri; 9am-7pm Sun. *Mixed (swimwear required)* 10am-9pm Sat. **Map** p162 D5 ⑤④ **Health & beauty**
This hammam is hard to beat – spotless mosaic-tiled surroundings, flowered sarongs and a relaxing pool. The exotic 'Forfait floral' option (€125) will have you enveloped in rose petals and massaged with *huile d'Argan* from Morocco, and the more simple hammam and *gommage* followed by mint tea and pastries is €44. Plan to spend a few hours here.

Le Monte-en-l'air
71 rue de Ménilmontant, 20th (01.40.33.04.54). M° Ménilmontant. **Open** *1-8pm Mon-Fri, Sun; 10am-8pm Sat.* **Map** p163 G5 ⑤⑤ **Books & music**
This glorious shop is a triple-purpose space with a 'curiosity shop' for atypical and disturbing novels, a 'gallery' where different paintings and photos are hung every three weeks, and the main *'librairie'*, where you'll find everything from graphic novels to classic literature and modern poetry. Hang around long enough and you might even catch some live music or meet an author on a book signing.

La Tête dans les Olives
2 rue Sainte-Marthe, 10th (09.51.31.33.34, www.latetedanslesolives.com). M° Colonel Fabien or Goncourt. **Open** *2-7pm Tue-Fri; 10am-1pm, 2-7pm Sat.* **Map** p163 F4 ⑤⑥ **Food & drink**
La Tête dans les Olives entices foodies with the promise of fruity olive oil fit for the finest kitchens. Sicilian owner Cédric knows his oils like a sommelier knows their wines and can recommend types to match what you're cooking. You'll also find delicacies such as sundried patataro tomatoes, top-grade pasta, herbs and deliciously tangy capers.

Viveka Bergström
23 rue de la Grange aux Belles, 10th (01.40.03.04.92, www.viveka-bergstrom.com). M° Colonel Fabien. **Open** *noon-7pm Tue-Sat.* **Map** p163 E3 ⑤⑦ **Accessories**
The daughter of Saab's aeroplane designer in the 1950s, Viveka Bergström makes slinky tassel necklaces, oversized beaten gold rings and brooches, and conversation starters like the angel-wing bracelet and a necklace featuring a map of Paris.

Un Zèbre O Grenier
16 rue Villiers de l'Isle Adam, 20th (09.52.62.88.70, www.unzebreaugrenier.fr). M° Gambetta. **Open** *10.30am-1.30pm, 3-7pm Tue-Fri; 10.30am-7pm Sat.* **Map** p163 G6 ⑤⑧ **Children**
This charming children's toy shop is hidden away near Gambetta. Catering for 0-8s, it has thought of everything – you can find things for tots to wear, play with, read and rest on. Another little plus is that the shop welcomes pre-loved toys through its ingenious system of reselling used items.

EXPLORE

The Latin Quarter & the 13th

The Latin Quarter holds considerable mystique, thanks to the historical presence of Hemingway, Orwell and Miller, and to it being the seedbed of the 1968 revolt. Many of the narrow, crooked streets are charming, and there are some real architectural glories, especially ecclesiastical ones. To the southeast of the Latin Quarter, the Docks en Seine is transforming the 13th into an essential Left Bank hangout, while the much-delayed Fondation Pathé, which finally opened in 2014, makes a stunning home for Pathé's heritage. The former village of Butte-aux-Cailles may be surrounded by malls and tower blocks now, but an old-world vibe still prevails. During the Paris Commune, its residents were some of the feistiest fighters. Now the only battles being fought are over a table in one of its student bars.

Shakespeare & Co

Don't Miss

1 Diptyque Pomander perfection – the finest candles around (p179).

2 Institut du Monde Arabe One of the city's most innovative museums (p184).

3 Fondation Pathé Star billing, inside and out (p174).

4 Docks en Seine Left Bank party HQ (p188).

5 Shakespeare & Co Literary legend (p179).

ST-SEVERIN & ST-JULIEN-LE-PAUVRE

In the 5th arrondissement.

Boulevard St-Michel used to be synonymous with student rebellion; now it's a ribbon of fast-food joints and clothing shops, though Gibert Joseph continues to furnish books and stationery to students. East of here, the semi-pedestrianised patch by the Seine has retained much of its medieval street plan. Rue de la Huchette and rue de la Harpe are now best known for their kebabs and pizzas, though there are 18th-century wrought-iron balconies and carved masks in the latter street. At the tiny **Théâtre de la Huchette** (*see p292*), Ionesco's absurdist drama *La Cantatrice Chauve* (The Bald Soprano) has been playing continuously since 1957. Also of interest are rue du Chat-qui-Pêche, supposedly the city's narrowest street, and rue de la Parcheminerie, named after the parchment sellers and copyists who once lived here. Among the tourist shops stands the city's most charming medieval church, the **Eglise St-Séverin**, complete with leering gargoyles, spiky gabled side chapels and an exuberantly vaulted Flamboyant Gothic interior.

STAR QUALITY

The new Fondation Pathé building is a wonder inside and out.

Don't be fooled by the classic 1869 Rodin-sculpted façade of the new **Fondation Jérôme Seydoux-Pathé** HQ (73 av des Gobelins, 13th, 01.83.79.18.96, www.fondation-jeromeseydoux-pathe.com): beyond lies one of Paris's most daring contemporary architectural works – a sinuous, metallic 'vessel' (reminiscent of the body of a swimming whale) designed by Renzo Piano and devoted to Pathé's cinematographic heritage, and most notably its silent movies.

Some 5,000 protective shutters cover the structure like a futuristic armadillo shell, allowing natural light to flood the interior. Inside, five floors display some of France's most important film memorabilia – from document archives (open by appointment only) to a camera and projector collection on the first floor that includes hitherto unseen models dating from as far back as 1896. There's also a 70-seat projection room with regular silent movie retrospectives, many projected to live music.

Film buffs will be in heaven, of course, but the building itself deserves star billing. Entering from the street, below Rodin's masterpiece, one encounters a transparent, greenhouse-like area. From here, the 'whale' looks like some retro-futurist, space-age pod, seemingly floating in the middle of the courtyard. The unusual form, aside from its aesthetic qualities, was actually designed with the neighbours in mind: by not making contact with the surrounding buildings, air and light can circulate more freely.

Perhaps most intriguing, though, is the view from the street at night. The upper part of the structure is made of glass so that the centre's offices can soak up the daylight; but when the sun sets, it shines from the inside out like a giant glow worm – an unusual sight on this classical Haussmannian avenue.

Across ancient rue St-Jacques is the **Eglise St-Julien-le-Pauvre**, built as a resting place for 12th-century pilgrims. Nearby rue Galande has old houses and the **Trois Mailletz** cabaret (5th, 01.43.54.42.94, www.lestroismailletz.fr). The medieval cellars of the **Caveau des Oubliettes** jazz club (*see p279*) were used as a prison after the French Revolution (*oubliette* is the French word for a pit into which prisoners were thrown, then forgotten). At no.42 is arts cinema **Studio Galande** (*see p254*). Nearby, in place Viviani, stands what is perhaps the city's oldest tree, a false acacia that was planted in 1602; it's now half-swamped by ivy and propped up by concrete buttresses.

The little streets between here and the eastern stretch of boulevard St-Germain are among the city's oldest: streets such as rue de Bièvre, which follows the course of the Bièvre river that flowed into the Seine in the Middle Ages; rue du Maître-Albert; and rue des Grands-Degrès, with traces of old shop signs painted on its buildings' façades. Remnants of the **Collège des Bernardins**, built for the Cistercian order, can be seen in rue de Poissy, where the 13th- to 14th-century Gothic monks' refectory has been restored after use as firemen's barracks. Nearby are the **Eglise St-Nicolas du Chardonnet** (23 rue des Bernardins, 5th, 01.44.27.07.90, www.saintnicolasduchardonnet. fr), associated with the schismatic Society of St Pius X and one of a small number of churches where you can hear the Tridentine Mass in Paris, and the art deco **Maison de la Mutualité** (24 rue St-Victor, 5th, 01.83.92.24.00, www.maisondela mutualite.com), home to everything from trade unions meetings to rock concerts.

Place Maubert, now a breezy morning marketplace (Tue, Thur, Sat), witnessed the hanging of Protestants during the 16th-century Wars of Religion. Just behind the square, the modern police station is home to an array of grisly criminal evidence in the **Musée de la Préfecture de Police**.

On the corner of boulevard St-Germain and boulevard St-Michel stand the striking ruins of the late second-century **Thermes de Cluny**, the Romans' main baths complex; the adjoining Gothic Hôtel de Cluny provides a suitable setting for the **Musée National du Moyen Age**, the national collection of medieval art. Adjoining boulevard St-Germain, its garden has been replanted with species portrayed in medieval tapestries, paintings and treatises.

Sights & Museums

FREE Eglise St-Julien-le-Pauvre
Rue St-Julien-le-Pauvre, 5th (01.43.54.52.16, www.sjlpmelkites.fr). M° Cluny La Sorbonne. **Open** 9.30am-1pm, 3-6.30pm daily. **Admission** free. **Map** p176 B2 ❶

A former sanctuary for pilgrims on their way to Compostela, this much-mauled church dates from the late 12th century, on the cusp of Romanesque and Gothic, and has capitals richly decorated with vines, acanthus leaves and winged harpies. Once part of a priory, it became the university church when colleges migrated to the Left Bank. Since 1889, it has been used by the Greek Orthodox Church.

★ FREE Eglise St-Séverin
3 rue des Prêtres-St-Séverin, 5th (01.42.34.93.50, www.saint-severin.com). M° Cluny La Sorbonne or St-Michel. **Open** 11am-7.30pm Mon-Sat; 9am-8.30pm Sun. **Admission** free. **Map** p176 B2 ❷

Built on the site of the chapel of the hermit Séverin, itself set on a much earlier Merovingian burial ground, this lovely Flamboyant Gothic edifice was long the parish church of the Left Bank. It was rebuilt on various occasions to repair damage after ransacking by Normans and to meet the needs of the growing population. The church dates from the 15th century, though the doorway, carved with foliage, was added in 1837 from the demolished Eglise St-Pierre-aux-Boeufs on Ile de la Cité. The double ambulatory is famed for its forest of 'palm tree' vaulting, which meets at the end in a unique spiral column that inspired a series of paintings by Robert Delaunay. The bell tower, a survivor from one of the earlier churches on the site, has the oldest bell in Paris (1412). Around the nave are stained-glass windows dating from the 14th and 15th centuries, and the choir apse has stained glass designed by Jean René Bazaine in the 1960s. Next door, around the former cemetery, is the only remaining charnel house in Paris.

★ Musée National du Moyen Age – Thermes de Cluny
6 pl Paul-Painlevé, 5th (01.53.73.78.00, www.musee-moyenage.fr). M° Cluny La Sorbonne. **Open** 9.15am-5.45pm Mon, Wed-Sun. **Admission** €8; €6 reductions; free under-18s, under-26s (EU citizens), all 1st Sun of mth. PMP. **Map** p176 B1 ❸

The national museum of medieval art is best known for the beautiful, allegorical *Lady and the Unicorn* tapestry cycle, which is gleaming after a two-year restoration project, but it also has important collections of medieval sculpture and enamels. The building itself, commonly known as Cluny, is also a rare example of 15th-century secular Gothic architecture, with its foliate Gothic doorways, hexagonal staircase jutting out of the façade and vaulted chapel. It was built from 1485 to 1498 – on top of a Gallo-Roman baths complex. The baths, built in characteristic Roman bands of stone and brick masonry, are the finest Roman remains in Paris. The vaulted *frigidarium* (cold bath), *tepidarium* (warm bath), *caldarium* (hot bath) and part of the hypocaust heating system are all still visible. A themed garden fronts the whole complex. Recent acquisitions include the illuminated manuscript

EXPLORE

EXPLORE

EXPLORE

Diptyque.

L'Ascension du Christ from the Abbey of Cluny, dating back to the 12th century, and the 16th-century triptych Assomption de la Vierge.

FREE Musée de la Préfecture de Police
4 rue de la Montagne-Ste-Geneviève, 5th (01.44.41.52.50, www.prefecturedepolice.interieur. gouv.fr). M° Maubert Mutualité. **Open** *9.30am-5pm Mon-Fri.* **Admission** *free.* **Map** p176 C2 ❹

The police museum is housed in a working *commissariat*, which makes for a slightly intimidating entry procedure. You need to walk boldly past the police officer on guard outside and up the steps to the lobby, where you have to ask at the reception booth to be let in – queuing, if necessary, with locals there on other, but usually police-related, errands. The museum is on the second floor; start from the Accueil and work your way clockwise. None of the displays is labelled in English (though there is a bilingual booklet), and a handful are not labelled at all; but if you have basic French and any sort of interest in criminology, this extensive collection is well worth seeing. It starts in the early 17th century and runs to the Occupation, via the founding of the Préfecture de Police by Napoleon in 1800. Exhibits include a prison register open at the entry for Ravaillac, assassin of Henri IV; a section on the Anarchist bombings of the 1890s; the automatic pistol used to assassinate President Doumer in 1932; a blood-chilling collection of murder weapons – hammers, ice picks and knives; sections on serial killers Landru and Petiot; and less dangerous items, such as a gadget used to snag banknotes from the apron pockets of market sellers.

Restaurants

Atelier Maître Albert
1 rue Maître-Albert, 5th (01.56.81.30.01, www. ateliermaitrealbert.com). M° Maubert Mutualité or St-Michel. **Open** *noon-2.30pm, 6.30-11.30pm Mon-Wed; noon-2.30pm, 6.30pm-1am Thur, Fri; 6.30pm-1am Sat; 6.30-11.30pm Sun.* **Main courses** *€22-€34.* **Prix fixe** *Lunch €26, €31. Dinner €36, €70.* **Map** p176 B2 ❺ **Bistro**

This Guy Savoy outpost in the fifth arrondissement has slick decor designed by Jean-Michel Wilmotte. The indigo-painted, grey marble-floored dining room with open kitchen and rôtisseries on view is attractive, but it does mean that the place can get very noisy. The short menu lets you have a Savoy classic or two to start with, including oysters in seawater *gelée*, perhaps, or more inventive dishes such as the *ballotine* of chicken, foie gras and celeriac in a chicken-liver sauce. Next up could be tuna served with tiny iron casseroles of dauphinois potatoes, accompanied by cauliflower in béchamel sauce.

Le Pré Verre
8 rue Thénard, 5th (01.43.54.59.47, www. lepreverre.com). M° Maubert Mutualité. **Open** *noon-2pm, 7.30-10.30pm Tue-Sat.* **Main courses** *€20.* **Prix fixe** *Lunch €14.50, €32. Dinner €32.* **Map** p176 B2 ❻ **Bistro**

Philippe Delacourcelle knows how to handle spices like few other French chefs. He also trained with the late Bernard Loiseau, and learned the art of French pastry at Fauchon. Salt cod with cassia bark and smoked potato purée is a classic: what the fish lacks in size it makes up for in rich, cinnamon-like flavour and crunchy texture, and smooth potato cooked in a smoker makes a startling accompaniment. Spices have a way of making desserts seem esoteric, but the roast figs with olives are an exception to the rule.

★ Ribouldingue
10 rue St-Julien-le-Pauvre, 5th (01.46.33.98.80, www.ribouldingue-restaurant.fr). M° St-Michel. **Open** *noon-2pm, 7-11pm Tue-Sat.* **Main courses** *Lunch €16.* **Prix fixe** *€28, €34.* **Map** p176 B2 ❼ **Bistro**

This bistro facing St-Julien-le-Pauvre church is the creation of Nadège Varigny, who spent ten years working with Yves Camdeborde before opening a restaurant inspired by the food of her childhood in Grenoble. It's usually full of people, including critics and chefs, who love simple, honest bistro fare, such as *daube de boeuf* or seared tuna on a bed of melting aubergine. And if you have an appetite for offal,

EXPLORE

go for the gently sautéed brains with new potatoes, or the veal kidneys with a perfectly prepared potato gratin. For dessert, try the fresh ewe's cheese with bitter honey.

Cafés & Bars

Da Zavola
24 rue des Bernadins, 5th (01.46.34.66.97, www.dazavola.com). M° Maubert-Mutualité. **Open** 11am-10pm Tue-Sat. **Map** p176 B2 ❽
Da Zavola is a contemporary café of the sort the Italians term a *gastronomia*, where you can taste gourmet treats from across Italy and get an outstanding espresso. The bar is open all day serving everything from prosciutto crudo and mozzarella to grilled aubergines and toasted foccacia, pasta at lunch and dinner, and *aperitivi* in the early evening. And for the perfect treat after *cannoli*, a traditional Sicilian dessert, order a *marocchino*, a lethal glass of syrupy liquid chocolate topped off with an espresso and a drop of frothy milk.

Shops & Services

Abbey Bookshop
29 rue de la Parcheminerie, 5th (01.46.33.16.24, www.abbeybookshop.fr). M° St-Michel or Cluny La Sorbonne. **Open** 10am-7pm Mon-Sat. **Map** p176 B1 ❾ Books & music
The tiny Abbey Bookshop is the domain of Canadian renaissance man Brian Spence, who organises weekend hikes as well as dressing up in doublet and hose for a game of 17th-century dancing. The tiny, narrow shop stocks old and new works, a specialised Canadian section, and highbrow subjects down the rickety staircase. Several thousand more books are tucked away in storage, and he can normally order titles for collection within two days.

Album
67 bd Saint-Germain, 5th (01.53.10.00.60, www.album.fr). M° Cluny La Sorbonne. **Open** 10am-8pm Mon-Sat; noon-7pm Sun. **Map** p176 B2 ❿ Books & music
Proud denizens of boulevard Saint-Germain for more than 20 years, the three 'Album' shops reign supreme over the Paris comic scene. Under the watchful eye of the owners who dispense both advice and anecdotes, this is a comic-lover's paradise, with titles for children and adults (Marvel, DC comics, TPB Vertigo), and whole shelves dedicated to merchandising. From classic posters signed by Hugo Pratt to umbrellas and Star Wars-branded USB sticks, there's something here to make every geek and figurine collector happy. Imported limited-edition mangas and book signings are the specialities of this address, open seven days a week.
Other locations 84 bd St-Germain, 5th (01.43.25.25.68, French and Belgian comics); 8 rue Dante, 5th (01.43.25.85.19, action figures).

★ Diptyque
34 bd St-Germain, 5th (01.43.26.77.44, www.diptyqueparis.com). M° Maubert Mutualité. **Open** 10am-7pm Mon-Sat. **Map** p176 B2 ⓫ Gifts & souvenirs
Diptyque's divinely scented candles are the quintessential gift from Paris. They come in 48 different varieties, from wild fennel to pomander. Prices are not cheap, but with 50 to 60 hours' burn time, they're worth every euro.

★ Shakespeare & Company
37 rue de la Bûcherie, 5th (01.43.25.40.93, www.shakespeareandcompany.com). M° St-Michel. **Open** 10am-11pm daily. **Map** p176 B2 ⓬ Books & music
Unequivocably the best bookshop in Paris, the ramshackle Shakespeare & Company is always packed with expat and tourist book-lovers. There's a large second-hand section, antiquarian books next door, and just about anything you could ask for new.

THE SORBONNE, MONTAGNE STE-GENEVIEVE & MOUFFETARD

In the 5th arrondissement.

An influx of well-heeled residents in the 1980s put paid to the days of horn-rims, pipes and turtlenecks: accommodation here is now beyond the reach of most students. The intellectual tradition persists, however, in the concentration of academic institutions around Montagne Ste-Geneviève, and students throng the specialist bookstores and art cinemas on rue Champollion and rue des Ecoles.

The district's long-running association with learning began in about 1100, when a number of renowned scholars, including Pierre Abélard, began to live and teach on the Montagne, independent of the established cathedral school of Notre-Dame. This loose association of scholars came to be referred to as a 'university'. The Paris schools attracted students from all over Europe, and the 'colleges' – in reality student residences dotted round the area (some still survive) – multiplied, until the University of Paris was given official recognition with a charter from Pope Innocent III in 1215.

By the 16th century, the university – named the **Sorbonne** after the most famous of its colleges – had been co-opted by the Catholic Church. A century later, Cardinal Richelieu rebuilt it. Following the Revolution, when it was forced to close, Napoleon revived the Sorbonne as the cornerstone of his new, centralised education system. The university participated enthusiastically in the uprisings of the 19th century; it was also a seedbed of the 1968 revolt, when it was occupied by protesting students.

EXPLORE

Also on rue des Ecoles, the independent **Collège de France** was founded in 1530 by a group of humanists led by Guillaume Budé under the patronage of François I. The neighbouring **Brasserie Balzar** (no.49, 5th, 01.43.54.13.67, www.brasseriebalzar.com) has been fuelling amateur philosophy for years.

From here, climb rue St-Jacques to rue Soufflot for the most impressive introduction to place du Panthéon. Otherwise, follow rue des Carmes – with its Baroque chapel, now used by the Syrian Church – and continue on rue Valette past the brick and stone entrance of the Collège Ste-Barbe, where Ignatius Loyola, Montgolfier and Eiffel studied. Alternatively, follow the serpentine rue de la Montagne-Ste-Geneviève; at the junction of rue Descartes, cafés and eccentric wine bistros overlook the sculpted 19th-century entrance to what was once the elite Ecole Polytechnique (since moved to the suburbs) and is now the research ministry. There's a small park here, and popular bistro **L'Ecurie** (2 rue Laplace, 5th, 01.46.33.68.49) – an old stable burrowed into medieval cellars.

Louis XV commissioned the huge, domed **Panthéon** to honour Geneviève, the city's patron saint, but it was converted during the Revolution into a secular temple for France's *grands hommes*. The surrounding place du Panthéon, which was also conceived by Panthéon architect Jacques-Germain Soufflot, is one of the city's great set pieces: looking on to it are the elegant fifth arrondissement town hall and, opposite, the law faculty. On the north side, the Ste-Geneviève university library, built by Labrouste with an iron-framed reading room, contains medieval manuscripts. On the other side you'll find the historic **Hôtel des Grands Hommes** (no.17, 5th, 01.46.34.19.60, www.hoteldesgrandshommes. com), where Surrealist mandarin André Breton invented 'automatic writing' in the 1920s.

Pascal, Racine and the remains of Sainte Geneviève are all interred in **Eglise St-Etienne-du-Mont**, on the north-east corner of the square. Just behind it, within the illustrious Lycée Henri IV, is the Gothic-Romanesque **Tour de Clovis**, part of the former Abbaye Ste-Geneviève. Take a look through the entrance (open during termtime) and you'll also catch glimpses of the cloister and other monastic structures.

Further from place du Panthéon, along rue Clovis, is a chunk of Philippe-Auguste's 12th-century city wall. The exiled monarch James II once resided at 65 rue du Cardinal-Lemoine, in the severe buildings of the former Collège des Ecossais (now a school), founded in 1372 to house Scottish students; the king's brain was preserved here until carried off and lost during the French Revolution. Other well known ex-residents include Ernest Hemingway, who lived at 79 rue du Cardinal-Lemoine (note the plaque) and 39 rue

Descartes in the 1920s, and James Joyce; the latter completed *Ulysses* while staying at 71 rue du Cardinal-Lemoine. Rimbaud lived in rue Descartes, and Descartes himself lived on nearby rue Rollin.

This area is still a mix of tourist picturesque and gentle village, where some of the buildings hide courtyards and gardens. Pretty place de la Contrescarpe has been a famous rendezvous since the 1530s, when writers as renowned as Rabelais, Ronsard and Du Bellay frequented the Cabaret de la Pomme de Pin at no.1; it still has some lively cafés. When George Orwell stayed at 6 rue du Pot-de-Fer in 1928 and 1929 (he described his time here and his work as a dishwasher in *Down and Out in Paris and London*), it was a place of astounding poverty; today, the street is lined with bargain bars and restaurants, and the restored houses along rue Tournefort bear little relation to the garrets of Balzac's *Le Père Goriot*.

Rue Mouffetard, originally the road to Rome and one of the oldest streets in the city, winds south as a suite of cheap bistros, tavernas and knick-knack shops thronged with tourists; the vibe described by Hemingway – 'that wonderful narrow crowded market street, beloved of bohemians' – has faded. The street market (Tue-Sat, Sun morn) on the lower half seethes at weekends, when it spills on to the square and around the cafés in front of **Eglise St-Médard**. There's another busy market, more frequented by locals, at place Monge (Wed, Fri, Sun morning).

Back to the west of the Panthéon, head south beyond rue Soufflot and you'll notice that rue St-Jacques becomes prettier. Here you'll find several ancient buildings, including the *hôtel* at no.151, good food shops and vintage bistro **Perraudin** (no.157, 5th, 01.46.33.15.75, www. restaurant-perraudin.com). Rue d'Ulm contains the elite **Ecole Normale Supérieure** (no.45, 5th, 01.44.32.30.00, www.ens.fr), occupied in protest by the unemployed in January 1998; in an echo of 1968, students also joined in.

Turn off up hilly rue des Fossés-St-Jacques to discover place de l'Estrapade; in the 17th century the *estrapade* was a tall wooden tower from which deserters were dropped repeatedly until they died. Nearby, in rue des Irlandais, the Centre Culturel Irlandais hosts concerts, exhibitions, films, plays and spoken-word events promoting Irish culture. Back to the west of rue St-Jacques, rue Soufflot and broad rue Gay-Lussac (a hotspot of the May 1968 revolt), with their Haussmannian apartment buildings, lead to boulevard St-Michel and the Jardin du Luxembourg.

Further south on rue St-Jacques, in the potters' quarter of Roman Lutetia, is the most ornate of the city's Baroque churches, the **Eglise du Val-de-Grâce**. Round the corner, at 6 rue du Val-de-Grâce, is the former home of Alfons Maria Mucha, the influential Moravian art nouveau artist, best known for his posters of Sarah Bernhardt.

Sights & Museums

FREE Collège de France

11 pl Marcelin-Berthelot, 5th (01.44.27.12.11, 01.44.27.11.47, www.college-de-france.fr). M° Cluny La Sorbonne or Maubert Mutualité/ RER Luxembourg. **Open** 9am-5pm Mon-Fri. **Admission** free. **Map** p176 C2 ⑬

Founded in 1530 with the patronage of François I, the college is a place of learning and a research institute. The present building dates from the 16th and 17th centuries; there's also a later annexe. All lectures are free and open to the public; some have been given by such eminent figures as anthropologist Claude Lévi-Strauss, philosopher Maurice Merleau-Ponty and mathematician Jacques Tits.

★ FREE Eglise St-Etienne-du-Mont

Pl Ste-Geneviève, 5th (01.43.54.11.79, www.saint etiennedumont.fr). M° Cardinal Lemoine/RER Luxembourg. **Open** 8.45am-7.45pm Tue-Fri; 8.45am-noon, 2-7.45pm Sat; 8.45am-12.15pm, 2-7.45pm Sun (*July, Aug* 10am-noon, 4-7.45pm Tue-Sat; 10am-12.45pm, 4-6.45pm Sun). **Admission** free. **Map** p176 C2 ⑭

Geneviève, patron saint of Paris, is credited with having miraculously saved the city from the ravages of Attila the Hun in 451, and her shrine has been a site of pilgrimage ever since. The present church was built in an amalgam of Gothic and Renaissance styles between 1492 and 1626, and once adjoined the abbey church of Ste-Geneviève. The façade mixes Gothic rose windows with rusticated roman columns and reliefs of classically draped figures. The interior is wonderfully tall and light, with soaring columns and

Eglise St-Etienne-du-Mont.

a classical balustrade. The stunning Renaissance rood screen, with its double spiral staircase and ornate stone strapwork, is the only surviving one in Paris, and was possibly designed by Philibert Delorme. The decorative canopied wooden pulpit by Germaine Pillon dates from 1651, and is adorned with figures of the Graces and supported by a muscular Samson sitting on the defeated lion. Sainte Geneviève's elaborate neo-Gothic brass-and-glass shrine (shielding the ancient tombstone) is located to the right of the choir, surrounded by an assortment of reliquaries and dozens of marble plaques bearing messages of thanks. At the back of the church (and reached through the sacristy), the catechism chapel constructed by Baltard in the 1860s contains a cycle of paintings relating the saint's life story.

FREE Eglise St-Médard

141 rue Mouffetard, 5th (01.44.08.87.00, www. saintmedard.org). M° Censier Daubenton. **Open** 8am-12.30pm, 2.30-7.30pm Tue-Sat; 8.30am-12.30pm, 4-8.30pm Sun. **Admission** free. **Map** p176 D2 ⑮

The original chapel here was a dependency of the Abbaye Ste-Geneviève. The rebuilding towards the end of the 15th century created a somewhat larger, late Gothic structure best known for its elaborate vaulted ambulatory.

FREE Eglise du Val-de-Grâce

Pl Alphonse-Laveran, 5th (www.valdegrace.org). RER Luxembourg or Port-Royal. **Open** 2-6pm Mon-Sat; 9am-noon, 2-6pm Sun. **Admission** free. **Map** p176 D1 ⑯

Anne of Austria, the wife of Louis XIII, vowed to erect 'a magnificent temple' if God blessed her with a son. She got two. The resulting church and surrounding Benedictine monastery – these days a military hospital and the Musée du Service de Santé des Armées (*see below*) – were built by François Mansart and Jacques Lemercier. This is the most luxuriously Baroque of the city's 17th-century domed churches, its ornate altar decorated with twisted barley-sugar columns. The swirling colours of the dome frescoes painted by Pierre Mignard in 1669 (which Molière himself once eulogised) are designed to give a foretaste of heaven. In contrast, the surrounding monastery offers the perfect example of François Mansart's classical restraint.

Musée du Service de Santé des Armées

Val de Grâce, pl Alphonse-Laveran, 5th (01.40.51.51.92). RER Luxembourg or Port Royal. **Open** noon-6pm Tue, Wed, Sat, Sun. Closed Aug. **Admission** €5; €2.50 reductions; free under-6s. **No credit cards. Map** p176 D1 ⑰

Housed in the royal convent designed by Mansart, this museum traces the history of military medicine via replicas of field hospitals and ambulance trains, as well as displays of antique medical instruments. The section on World War I demonstrates how much the conflict propelled medical progress.

EXPLORE

★ Le Panthéon

Pl du Panthéon, 5th (01.44.32.18.00). M° Cardinal Lemoine/RER Luxembourg. **Open** 10am-6pm (until 6.30pm summer) daily. **Admission** €7.50; €4.50 reductions; free under-18s, under-26s (EU citizens). PMP. **Map** p176 C2 ⑱

Soufflot's neoclassical megastructure was the architectural *grand projet* of its day, commissioned by a grateful Louis XV to thank Sainte Geneviève for his recovery from illness. But by the time it was ready in 1790, a lot had changed; during the Revolution, the Panthéon was rededicated as a 'temple of reason' and the resting place of the nation's great men. The austere barrel-vaulted crypt now houses such illustrious figures as Voltaire, Rousseau, Hugo and Zola. New heroes are installed but rarely: Pierre and Marie Curie's remains were transferred here in 1995; Alexandre Dumas in 2002. Inside are Greek columns and domes, along with 19th-century murals of Geneviève's life by Symbolist painter Puvis de Chavannes, a formative influence on Picasso during the latter's blue period.

Mount the steep spiral stairs to the colonnade encircling the dome for superb views. A replica of Foucault's Pendulum hangs here; the original proved that the earth does indeed spin on its axis, via a universal joint that lets the direction of the pendulum's swing rotate as the earth revolves.

La Sorbonne

17 rue de la Sorbonne, 5th (01.40.46.22.11, www.sorbonne.fr). M° Cluny La Sorbonne. **Open** 9am-5pm Mon-Fri. *Tours* by appointment. Closed July & Aug. **Map** p176 C1 ⑲

Founded in 1253, the University of the Sorbonne was at the centre of the Latin Quarter's intellectual activity from the Middle Ages until 1968, when it was occupied by students and stormed by the riot police. The authorities then split the University of Paris into safer outposts, but the Sorbonne still houses the Faculté des Lettres. Rebuilt by Richelieu and reorganised by Napoleon, the present buildings date from the late 1800s, and have a labyrinth of classrooms and lecture theatres, as well as an observatory tower. The elegant dome of the 17th-century chapel dominates place de la Sorbonne; Cardinal Richelieu is buried inside. It's open to the public only for exhibitions or concerts.

Restaurants

Les Papilles

30 rue Gay-Lussac, 5th (01.43.25.20.79, www. lespapillesparis.fr). M° Luxembourg. **Open** noon-2pm, 7-10.30pm Tue-Sat. **Main courses** €20. **Prix fixe** €35. **Map** p176 C1 ⑳ **Bistro**

This quaint little bistro, which doubles as a wine shop and *épicerie*, is a safe bet in an otherwise touristy neighbourhood. Waiters rattle off the menu, then invite you to choose your bottle of wine from the wall. Wine aficionados will have a field day; wine

amateurs, ask for help. A €7 corkage fee is applied to each bottle. On the plate, expect seasonal tastes such as carrot soup poured over crispy bacon and sour cream, cod with capers in a sizzling hot copper dish, and salted caramel and poached pear panna cotta. It gets crowded and the noise level picks up later on.

Cafés & Bars

Ciel

3 rue Monge, 5th (01.43.29.40.78, www.patisserie-ciel.com). M° Maubert Mutualité. **Open** 11am-8pm Mon-Fri, Sun; 11am-9pm Sat. **Map** p176 B2 ㉑

Macaroons, cupcakes and choux buns have all had their food fashion moments in Paris, and now it's the turn of the angel cake – light, fluffy American treats, here adapted by a Japanese kitchen. There are six flavours on offer at Ciel, a *salon de thé* entirely devoted to angel cake: from the classic (rose, chocolate and vanilla-caramel) to the more unusual (lemon *yuzu* or green tea *matcha*).

★ Le Crocodile

6 rue Royer-Collard, 5th (01.71.93.49.68). RER Luxembourg. **Open** 6pm-2am Mon-Sat. **No credit cards. Map** p176 C1 ㉒

Ignore the apparently boarded-up windows at Le Crocodile; if you're here late, then it's open. Friendly young regulars line the sides of this small, narrow bar and try to decide what to drink – not easy, given the length of the cocktail list: at last count there were 363 varieties. The generous €7-per-cocktail happy hour (6-11pm Mon-Thur, 6-10pm Fri, Sat) will allow you to start with a champagne *accroche-coeur*, followed up with a Goldschläger (served with gold leaf) before moving on to the rest of the list.

Le Pantalon

7 rue Royer-Collard, 5th (no phone). RER Luxembourg. **Open** 5.30pm-1.45am daily. **No credit cards. Map** p176 C1 ㉓

A local café that seems familiar yet is utterly surreal. It has the standard fixtures, including the old soaks at the bar – but the regulars and staff are enough to tip the balance firmly into eccentricity. Friendly and funny French grown-ups and foreign students chat in a variety of languages; drinks are cheap enough to make you tipsy without the worry of a cash hangover.

Le Requin Chagrin

10 rue Mouffetard, 5th (06.68.44.05.48). M° Place Monge. **Open** 4pm-2am Mon-Thur, Sun; 4pm-4am Fri, Sat. **Map** p176 C2 ㉔

The 'depressed shark' hasn't lost its bite. Students and beer guzzlers of all ages still cram in for the ten *bières* on tap and extended happy hour (4-9.30pm), when the cheapest pints are a steal at just €4. You'll find the usual Left Bank suspects: groups of friends, blokes trying to get laid and *intellos* from the nearby universities playing chess and quoits.

Ciel.

Hidden among the hotels of rue Monge is the entrance to the **Arènes de Lutèce**, a Roman amphitheatre. The remains of a circular arena and its tiers of stone seating were discovered in 1869. Excavation started in 1883, thanks to lobbying by Victor Hugo. Nearby rise the white minaret and green pantiled roof of the **Mosquée de Paris**, built in 1922. Its beautiful Moorish tearoom is a student haunt.

The mosque looks over the **Jardin des Plantes** botanical garden. Opened in 1626 as a garden for medicinal plants, it features an 18th-century maze and a winter garden bristling with rare species. It also houses the Muséum National d'Histoire Naturelle, with its brilliant **Grande Galerie de l'Evolution**, and a zoo, La Ménagerie, an unlikely by-product of the Revolution, when royal and noble collections of wild animals were impounded. Street names and the lovely animal-themed fountain on the corner of rue Cuvier pay homage to the many naturalists and other scientists who worked here. A short way away, at 11-13bis rue Geoffroy-St-Hilaire, the words 'Chevaux', 'Poneys' and 'Anes' are still visible on the façade of the old horse market.

Sights & Museums

FREE Arènes de Lutèce
Rue Monge, rue de Navarre or rue des Arènes, 5th. M° Cardinal Lemoine or Place Monge. **Open** *Summer* 9am-9.30pm daily. *Winter* 8am-5.30pm daily. **Admission** free. **Map** p176 C2 ㉖
This Roman arena, where wild beasts and gladiators once fought, could seat 10,000 people. It was still visible during the reign of Philippe-Auguste in the 12th century, then disappeared under rubble. The site was only rediscovered in 1869 and now incorporates a romantically planted garden. These days, it attracts an assortment of skateboarders, footballers and boules players.

★ Grande Galerie de l'Evolution
36 rue Geoffroy-St-Hilaire, 2 rue Bouffon or pl Valhubert, 5th (01.40.79.56.01, www.mnhn.fr). M° Gare d'Austerlitz or Jussieu. **Open** *Grande Galerie* 10am-6pm Mon, Wed-Sun. *Galerie de Paléontologie et d'Anatomie Comparée* 10am-5pm daily. **Admission** *Grande Galerie* €7; €5 reductions. *Galerie de Paléontologie et d'Anatomie Comparée* €7; €5 reductions; free under-26s. **No credit cards**. **Map** p176 D3 ㉗
One of the city's most child-friendly attractions (*see also p246*), this is guaranteed to bowl adults over too. Located within the Jardin des Plantes (*see p184*), this beauty of a 19th-century iron-framed, glass-roofed structure has been modernised with lifts, galleries and false floors, and filled with life-size models of tentacle-waving squids, open-mawed sharks, tigers hanging off elephants and monkeys swarming down from the ceiling. The centrepiece

Shops & Services

Crocodisc
40-42 rue des Ecoles, 5th (01.43.54.47.95, www.crocodisc.com). M° Maubert Mutualité. **Open** 11am-7pm Tue-Sat. Closed last wk July, 1st 2wks Aug. **Map** p176 B2 ㉕ **Books & music**
The excellent albeit expensive range includes rock, funk, African, country and classical, in the form of new and second-hand vinyl and CDs. For jazz and blues, try sister shop Crocojazz.
Other location Crocojazz, 64 rue de la Montagne-Ste-Geneviève, 5th (01.46.34.78.38).

AROUND THE JARDIN DES PLANTES

In the 5th arrondissement.

The quiet, easternmost part of the fifth arrondissement is home to yet more academic institutions, the Paris mosque and another Roman relic. Old-fashioned bistros on rue des Fossés-St-Bernard contrast with the forbidding 1960s architecture of the massive university campus of Paris VI and VII, the science faculty (known as Jussieu) built on what had been the site of the important Abbaye St-Victor. Between the Seine and Jussieu is the newly revamped, glass-faced **Institut du Monde Arabe**. The **Jardin Tino Rossi**, by the river, contains the **Musée de la Sculpture en Plein Air**; in summer this is a spot for dancing and picnicking.

EXPLORE

EXPLORE

is a procession of African wildlife across the first floor that resembles the procession into Noah's Ark. Glass-sided lifts take you up through suspended birds to the second floor, which deals with man's impact on nature (crocodile into handbag). The third floor focuses on endangered and extinct species. The separate Galerie de Paléontologie et d'Anatomie Comparée contains more than a million skeletons, as well as a world-class fossil collection.

Institut du Monde Arabe

1 rue des Fossés-St-Bernard, 5th (01.40.51.38.38, www.imarabe.org). M° Jussieu. **Open** *Museum* 10am-6pm Tue-Thur; 10am-9.30pm Fri; 10am-7pm Sat, Sun. Library Closed during 2015. Tours 3pm Tue-Fri; 3pm & 4.30pm Sat, Sun.* **Admission** *Museum* €8; €4-€6 reductions; free under-18s, under-26s (EU citizens). PMP. *Exhibitions varies.* **Map** p176 C3 **28**
One of Paris's most innovative museums reopened to the public in 2012 after a three-year revamp. The beautiful museum of the Institut du Monde Arabe, dedicated to the development of Islamic art and the history and culture of the Arab world, has been transformed, and reopened in time to mark its 25th anniversary. Collections from the 22 Arab countries that co-founded the museum can now be enjoyed once again, in an exciting and dynamic new interior. Some 600 items are on display, from places as diverse as Damascus, Aleppo, Latakia, Amman, Kairouan and Manama, as well as the Musée du Louvre, the Musée du Quai Branly and the Bibliothèque Nationale de France. And where before the collection was limited to art, the new museum has widened its scope (as well as its physical space), showcasing the Arab world in thematic ways, covering its ethno-linguistic, historical, cultural, anthropological and geographical diversity. What's more, there's a lively programme of events (exhibitions, film screenings, music and dance) and an excellent Middle East bookshop on the ground floor, and the views from the roof terrace (to which access is free) are fabulous.

★ FREE Jardin des Plantes

36 rue Geoffroy-St-Hilaire, 2 rue Buffon, pl Valhubert or 57 rue Cuvier, 5th (01.40.79.56.01, www.jardindesplantes.net). M° Gare d'Austerlitz or Place Monge. **Open** *Main garden* Winter 8am-5.30pm daily. Summer 7.30am-8pm daily. *Alpine garden* Apr-Oct 8am-4pm Mon-Fri; 1.30-6pm Sat, Sun. Closed Nov-Mar. *Ménagerie* times vary. **Admission** *Alpine Garden* free Mon-Fri; €2 Sat, Sun. *Jardin des Plantes* free. *Ménagerie* €13; €9 reductions; free under-4s. **Map** p176 C3 **29**
The Paris botanical garden – which contains more than 10,000 species and includes tropical greenhouses and rose, winter and Alpine gardens – is an enchanting place. Begun by Louis XIII's doctor as the royal medicinal plant garden in 1626, it opened to the public in 1640. The formal garden, which runs between two dead-straight avenues of trees parallel to rue Buffon, is like something out of *Alice in Wonderland*. There's also the Ménagerie (www.mnhn.fr) and the terrific Grande Galerie de l'Evolution (*see p183*). Ancient trees on view include a false acacia planted in 1636 and a cedar from 1734.

FREE Jardin Tino Rossi (Musée de la Sculpture en Plein Air)

Quai St-Bernard, 5th. M° Gare d'Austerlitz. **Admission** free. **Map** p176 C3 **30**
This open-air sculpture museum by the Seine fights a constant battle against graffiti. Still, it's a pleasant place for a stroll. Most of the works are second-rate, aside from Etienne Martin's bronze *Demeure I* and the Carrara marble *Fenêtre* by Cuban artist Careras.
▶ *From May to September, the gardens turn into an open-air dance studio.*

La Mosquée de Paris

2bis pl du Puits-de-l'Ermite, 5th (01.45.35.97.33, www.mosquee-de-paris.net). M° Monge. **Open** *Tours* 9am-noon, 2-6pm Mon-Thur, Sat, Sun (closed Muslim hols). *Tearoom* 9am-midnight daily. *Restaurant*

Jardin des Plantes.

noon-midnight Mon-Thur, Sat, Sun; 2-11.30pm Fri. *Baths* (women) 10am-9pm Mon-Thur, Sat, Sun. **Admission** €3; €2 reductions; free under-7s. *Tearoom* free. *Baths* €18-€63. **Map** p176 D3 **31**
Some distance removed from the Arabic-speaking inner-city enclaves of Barbès and Belleville, this vast Hispano-Moorish construct is nevertheless the spiritual heart of France's Algerian-dominated Muslim population. Built from 1922 to 1926 with elements inspired by the Alhambra and the Bou Inania Medersa in Fès, the Paris mosque is dominated by a stunning green-and-white tiled square minaret. In plan and function it divides into three sections: religious (grand patio, prayer room and minaret, all for worshippers and not curious tourists); scholarly (Islamic school and library); and, via rue Geoffroy-St-Hilaire, commercial (café and domed hammam). La Mosquée café is delightful – a modest courtyard with blue-and-white mosaic-topped tables shaded beneath green foliage and scented with the sweet smell of sheesha smoke (€10).

Restaurants

Le Buisson Ardent
25 rue Jussieu, 5th (01.43.54.93.02, www. lebuissonardent.fr). M° Jussieu. **Open** noon-2pm, 7.30-10pm Mon-Thur; noon-2pm, 7.30-10.30pm Fri, Sat; noon-2.30pm, 7.30-10pm Sun. **Main courses** €26. **Prix fixe** *Lunch* €25, €28. *Dinner* €39.90. **Map** p176 C3 **32** Bistro
This bistro's square front dining room with its red banquettes and painted glass panels dating from 1923 has a quintessentially Paris charm. There is plenty for adventurous eaters on the menu, such as pan-fried squid with chorizo and quinoa or white bean and pig's ear salad with pan-fried foie gras, but it also does conventional dishes (chestnut velouté with spice bread croûtons) very well.

La Tour d'Argent
15 quai de la Tournelle, 5th (01.43.54.23.31, www. latourdargent.com). M° Maubert Mutualité. **Open** noon-2pm, 7.30-10pm Tue-Sat. Closed Aug. **Main courses** €70-€140. **Prix fixe** *Lunch* €85. *Dinner* €200. **Map** p176 B2 **33** Haute cuisine
This Paris institution is regaining its lustre following the death of aged owner Claude Terrail in 2006. Start with snails in a mustard sauce, perhaps, followed by Tour d'Argent duck (the house speciality). If you still have any space left, desserts include the likes of chocolate mousse or carrot cheesecake. Following in his father's footsteps, Terrail's soft-spoken son André now does the rounds.

Shops & Services

Le Boulanger de Monge
123 rue Monge, 5th (01.43.37.54.20). M° Censier Daubenton. **Open** 7am-8.30pm Tue-Sun. **Map** p176 D2 **34** Food & drink

Dominique Saibron uses spices to give inimitable flavour to his organic sourdough *boule*. Every day about 2,000 bread-lovers visit this boutique, which also produces one of the city's best baguettes. **Other location** 48 rue de la Clef, 5th (01.47.07.28.19).

★ Hammam de la Grande Mosquée
39 rue Geoffrey St-Hilaire, 5th (01.43.31.38.20, www.la-mosquee.com). M° Censier Daubenton. **Open** 10am-9pm Mon, Wed-Sun. **Map** p176 D3 **35** Health & beauty
The authentic, women-only hammam experience in this beautiful 1920s mosque has become popular with locals, so avoid the weekends when the volume of traffic makes it less relaxing. Follow a steam session with a *gommage* (exfoliation with a rough mitt), then a massage. Swimwear is compulsory.

★ Marché Monge
Pl Monge, 5th. M° Place Monge. **Open** 7am-2.30pm Wed, Fri; 7am-3pm Sun. **Map** p176 D2 **36** Market
This pretty, compact market is set on a leafy square. It has a high proportion of producers and is much less touristy than nearby rue Mouffetard.

LES GOBELINS & LA SALPETRIERE
In the 13th arrondissement.

Its defining features might be 1960s tower blocks, but the 13th arrondissement is also historic, especially in the area bordering the fifth. The **Manufacture Nationale des Gobelins**, home to the state weaving companies, continues a tradition founded in the 15th century, when tanneries, dyers and weaving workshops lined the Bièvre river. This putrid waterway became notorious, and the slums that grew up around it were depicted in Victor Hugo's *Les Misérables*.
The area was tidied up in the 1930s, when a small park, square René-Le-Gall, was laid out on the allotments used by tapestry workers. The river was built over, but local enthusiasts have since opened up a small stretch in the park. Nearby, through a gateway at 17 rue des Gobelins, you can spot the turret and first floor of a medieval house. The so-called Château de la Reine Blanche on rue Gustave-Geffroy is named after Queen Blanche of Provence, who had a château here; it was probably rebuilt in the 1520s for the Gobelin family.
In the northern corner of the 13th, next to Gare d'Austerlitz, sprawls the huge Hôpital de la Pitié-Salpêtrière founded in 1656, with its striking **Chapelle St-Louis**.

FREE Chapelle St-Louis-de-la-Salpêtrière
47 bd de l'Hôpital, 13th (01.42.16.04.24). M° Gare d'Austerlitz. **Open** 8.30am-6pm Mon-Fri, Sun; 11am-6pm Sat. **Admission** free. **Map** p176 D4 **37**

Chapelle St-Louis-de-la-Salpêtrière
See p185.

This austerely beautiful chapel, designed by Libéral Bruand and completed in 1677, features an octagonal dome in the centre and eight naves in which the sick were separated from the insane, the destitute from the debauched. Around the chapel sprawls the vast Hôpital de la Pitié-Salpêtrière, founded on the site of a gunpowder factory (hence the name, derived from saltpetre) by Louis XIV to house rounded-up vagrant women. It became a centre for research into insanity in the 1790s, when renowned doctor Philippe Pinel began to treat some of the inmates as sick rather than criminal; Jean-Martin Charcot later pioneered neuropsychology here. Salpêtrière is today one of the city's main teaching hospitals, but the chapel is also used for contemporary art installations.

Manufacture Nationale des Gobelins

42 av des Gobelins, 13th (01.44.08.53.59). M° Les Gobelins. **Open** 11am-6pm Tue-Sun. **Admission** €6; €4 reductions; free last Sun of mth. *Tours* call for details. **No credit cards. Map** p177 E3 ⑱
The royal tapestry factory was founded by Colbert when he set up the Manufacture Royale des Meubles de la Couronne in 1662; it's named after Jean Gobelin, a dyer who owned the site. It reached the summit of its renown during the Ancien Régime, when Gobelins tapestries were produced for royal residences under artists such as Le Brun. Tapestries are still made here and visitors can watch weavers at work. Tours (in French; €7.50-€11) through the 1912 factory take in the 18th-century chapel and the Beauvais workshops.

CHINATOWN & THE BUTTE-AUX-CAILLES

In the 13th arrondissement.

South of rue de Tolbiac, the shop signs turn Chinese or Vietnamese. The city's main Chinatown runs along avenue d'Ivry, avenue de Choisy and

into the 1960s tower blocks between. Whereas much of the public housing in and around Paris is pretty bleak, here a distinctly eastern vibe reigns, with restaurants, Vietnamese *pho* noodle bars and Chinese pâtisseries, hairdressers and purveyors of exotic groceries; not to mention the expansive **Tang Frères** supermarket (48 av d'Ivry, 13th, 01.45.70.80.00). There's even a Buddhist temple hidden in a car park beneath the tallest tower (av d'Ivry, opposite rue Frères d'Astier-de-la-Vigerie, 13th). Lion and dragon dances, and martial arts demonstrations, take place on the streets at Chinese New Year.

In contrast to Chinatown, the villagey Butte-aux-Cailles, occupying the wedge between boulevard Auguste-Blanqui and rue Bobillot, is a neighbourhood of old houses, winding streets, funky bars and restaurants. This area, which was home in the 19th century to many small factories, was one of the first to fight during the 1848 Revolution and the Paris Commune.

The Butte has kept its rebellious character, with residents standing up to commercial developers. This predominantly *soixante-huitard* resistance is concentrated in the cobbled rue de la Butte-aux-Cailles and rue des Cinq-Diamants. Here you'll find inexpensive bistros such as **Le Temps des Cerises** (18 rue Butte-aux-Cailles, 13th, 01.45.89.69.48, www.letempsdescerisescoop. com), run as a co-operative, and **Chez Gladines**. The cottages built in 1912 in a mock-Alsatian style around a central green at 10 rue Daviel were among the earliest public-housing schemes in Paris. Just across rue Bobillot, the **Piscine Butte-aux-Cailles** (*see p249*) is a charming Arts and Crafts-style swimming pool.

Further south, you can explore passage Vandrezanne, the little houses and gardens of square des Peupliers, rue des Peupliers and rue Dieulafoy, and the flower-named streets of the

Cité Florale. By the Périphérique, the **Stade Charléty** (17 av Pierre-de-Coubertin, 13th) is a superb piece of stadium architecture.

Restaurants

L'Auberge du 15
15 rue de la Santé, 13th (01.47.07.07.45, www. laubergedu15.com). M° Les Gobelins. **Open** noon-2.30pm, 7.30-11pm Tue-Thur; noon-2.30pm, 7-11pm Fri, Sat. **Prix fixe** *Lunch* €39, €68. *Dinner* €68, €85, €98, €125. **Map** p177 E1 ㊴ **Brasserie**
L'Auberge du 15 cultivates the air of a country brasserie, with Moroccan tiles lining the open kitchen and a hunting motif on the curtains. No more than ten tables fill the long room, waited on by hip young things. The seasonal menu echoes a farmhouse kitchen – soup from a tureen, cake sliced on its stand. You might get a silky *potage* of chestnuts and ceps poured over a scoop of crème fraîche. Then a hearty dish of tender veal with sweet vegetables and a cream and white wine sauce: pure indulgence.

€ Le Bambou
70 rue Baudricourt, 13th (01.45.70.91.75). M° Olympiades or Tolbiac. **Open** 11.30am-3.30pm, 6.30-10.30pm Tue-Sun. **Main courses** €7-€14.50. **Map** p177 G4 ㊵ **Vietnamese**
The Vietnamese fare here is a notch above what is normally served in Paris. Seating is elbow to elbow and, should you come on your own, the waiter will draw a line down the middle of the paper tablecloth and seat a stranger on the other side. That stranger might offer pointers on how to eat certain dishes, such as the no.42: grilled marinated pork to be wrapped in lettuce with beansprouts and herbs and eaten by hand, dipped into the accompanying sauce.

€ Chez Gladines
30 rue des Cinq Diamants, 13th (01.45.80.70.10, www.gladines.com). M° Place d'Italie. **Open** noon-3pm, 7pm-midnight Mon, Tue; noon-3pm, 7pm-1am Wed-Fri; noon-4pm, 7pm-1am Sat; noon-4pm, 7pm-midnight Sun. **Main courses** €4-€14.50. **Map** p177 F2 ㊶ **Bistro**
This Basque canteen is renowned for cheap nosh, large portions and tables packed so tightly that befriending your neighbour (or at least his elbows) becomes part of the experience. The gargantuan bowls of salads are the stars, all served with lashings of fried potatoes, cheese, eggs and meat (usually ham or lardons), and Basque specialities such as *poulet basquaise* (chicken in a spicy tomato sauce). Needless to say Chez Gladines is a popular spot so get there early or be prepared to queue.

€ Pho 14
129 av de Choisy, 13th (01.45.83.61.15). M° Olympiades or Tolbiac. **Open** 9am-11pm daily. **Main courses** €7.60-€9.50. **No credit cards.** **Map** p177 F3 ㊷ **Vietnamese**

Vietnamese canteen Pho 14 is the place to come for delicious *pho* soups, filled with noodles, meatballs, beef or chicken, all served with fresh mint and basil. Other highlights include crispy pork spring rolls and dumplings. There's takeaway, too, if you don't want to wait for a table (there's usually a queue).

Cafés & Bars

Le Merle Moqueur
11 rue de la Butte aux Cailles, 13th (no phone). M° Place d'Italie. **Open** 5pm-2am daily. **No credit cards.** **Map** p177 F2 ㊸
Amid semi-faded pseudo-tropical decor and '80s music, the Teasing Blackbird – a Butte-aux-Cailles institution – tantalises students and nostalgists with its splendid selection of rums (over 20) and a long list of cocktails. The atmosphere gets pretty raucous after 10pm – make sure you get in early to grab one of the three tables.

Sputnik
14 rue de la Butte aux Cailles, 13th (01.45.65.19.82, www.sputnik.fr). M° Place d'Italie. **Open** 2pm-2am Mon-Sat (from 5pm Mon-Thur in winter); 4pm-midnight Sun. **Map** p177 F2 ㊹
A hip young crowd gathers in this rock-oriented bar, which doubles as a sports bar during important fixtures, and trebles as an internet café at other times. Changing art exhibitions add interest to the walls, and live music once a month draws an indie crowd. Fancy falling in love? Try the €8 love potion cocktail Philtre d'Amour, which is made from a fruity concoction of gin, Malibu, pineapple and strawberries.

Shops & Services

Les Abeilles
21 rue de la Butte-aux-Cailles, 13th (01.45.81.43.48, www.lesabeilles.biz). M° Corvisart or Place d'Italie. **Open** 11am-7pm Tue-Sat. **Map** p177 F2 ㊺
Gifts & souvenirs
This tiny boutique sells everything bee-related, from candles to honey vinegar, honey mustard and speciality 'Miel de Paris', gathered by owner Jean-Jacques from his hives in Parc Kellerman. There's also a wonderful selection of honey pots and soaps.

EXPLORE

IN THE KNOW BOARDING PARTY

El Alamein (www.bateauelalamein.com), a charming purple *péniche* moored next to the Bibliothèque Nationale de France, is a breath of fresh air. On the terrace, a café springs up in summer amid the plants. But this boat also has a lot going on inside, with an eclectic programme that ranges from jazz to French *chanson* via rock and theatrical performance.

Le Trac.

FURTHER EAST

The arrival in the 1990s of the **Bibliothèque Nationale de France** breathed new life into the desolate area, now known as the **ZAC Rive Gauche**, between Gare d'Austerlitz and the Périphérique. The ambitious, long-term ZAC project includes a new university quarter, new housing projects and a tramway linking to the suburbs. The pedestrian **Passerelle Simone-de-Beauvoir** spans the Seine between the BNF and the Cinémathèque Française; the floating **Piscine Josephine-Baker** (*see p249*) is a focus for the Paris-Plages entertainments; and the much-delayed **Cité de la Mode et du Design** (Docks en Seine), originally due to open in 2009, is finally up and running.

Sights & Museums

Bibliothèque Nationale de France François Mitterrand

10 quai François-Mauriac, 13th (01.53.79.59.59, www.bnf.fr). M° Bibliothèque François Mitterrand. **Open** 2-7pm Mon; 9am-7pm Tue-Sat; 1-7pm Sun. **Admission** *1 day* €3.50. *1 year* €38; €20 reductions. **Map** p177 E5 ㊻

Opened in 1996, the new national library was the last and costliest of Mitterrand's *grands projets*. Its

architect, Dominique Perrault, was criticised for his dated design, which hides readers underground and stores the books in four L-shaped glass towers. He also forgot to specify blinds to protect books from sunlight; they had to be added later. The library houses over ten million volumes and can accommodate 3,000 readers. Much of the library is open to the public: books, newspapers and periodicals are accessible to anyone over 18, and you can browse through photographic, film and sound archives.

Docks en Seine

28-36 quai d'Austerlitz, 13th (www.paris-docks-en-seine.fr). M° Chevaleret or Gare d'Austerlitz. **Map** p176 D4 ㊼

The apple-green caterpillar of Docks en Seine finally, belatedly opened its doors in 2012, transforming an industrial wasteland into a futuristic vision of culture and entertainment. A grassy terrace runs down to the water, there's a spanking new restaurant on the roof (the Moon Roof) and a bar/club (Wanderlust, by the team behind Silencio) on the first floor, and there are open-air screenings and exhibitions at the Cité de la Mode et du Design. The resurrection was completed with the opening of another club, Nüba, in late 2012.

Musée Art Ludique

34 quai d'Austerlitz, 13th (01.45.70.09.49, www.artludique.com). M° Chevaleret or Gare d'Austerlitz. **Open** 11am-7pm Mon, Thur; 11am-10pm Wed; 10am-10pm Fri; 10am-8pm Sat, Sun. **Admission** €15.50; €10-€12.50 reductions; free under-4s. **Map** p176 D4 ㊽

See p189 **Art of Entertainment**.

Cafés & Bars

L'Arobase

101 rue du Chevaleret, 13th (01.45.86.64.09, www.arobasecafe.com). M° Bibliothèque François Mitterrand. **Open** 8.30am-9pm Mon-Fri; noon-9pm Sat; 11am-5pm Sun. **Map** p177 F5 ㊾

Ideally located for students from the nearby BNF who've emerged to refuel, L'Arobase knows how to pander to its customer base. Very reasonable set lunches and a great selection of cakes and pâtisseries make this a useful pit stop. The spacious seating area has ample table space and comfy banquettes at the back to commandeer for an afternoon, though if you're keen to get your nose back in the books you can also ask to take away. The long opening hours and internet café downstairs for those without their own laptop are useful extras.

★ Petit Bain

7 port de la Gare, 13th (01.80.48.49.81, www.petitbain.org). M° Bibliothèque François Mitterrand or Quai de la Gare. **Open** 6pm-midnight Tue, Wed; 6pm-2am Thur-Sat (occasional Sundays). **Map** p177 E5 ㊿

Not so much a terrace here as an upper deck, this arts centre has been afloat at the foot of the BNF since 2010. And it's been giving the Batofar (Paris's stalwart floating nightclub) a run for its money, with an excellent line-up of concerts and art exhibitions. The coveted terrace doubles as a bar, restaurant and octopus gardener's paradise, decked out with myriad aquatic plants. The venue regularly hosts live music in a range of genres, from minimalist Norwegian pop and indie folk to rock and jazz. It's eclectic enough to match Le Petit Bain's architecture: designed by the Encore Heureux collective, it looks like a fluorescent green barge topped by a cubist wooden tree house.

Le Trac

72 av de France, 13th (01.45.85.37.17). M° Bibliothèque François Mitterrand. **Open** 7.30am-1am Mon-Wed; 7.30am-2am Thur, Fri; 9am-2am Sat. **Map** p177 F5 🔂

Opened in late 2014, Trac is a must-see Parisian bar: doubling as a culture hub, the venue has a weekly schedule of live music sets, jam sessions, masterclasses, open mic, theatre improv, DJ sets and even stand-up comedy. During Happy Hour, Trac Punch will only set you back a fiver, so go ahead and indulge. In summer, the large terrace is a gorgeous place to sit out; the rest of the year, take a seat under the heaters – Trac even provides blankets. What could be nicer?

Shops & Services

Air de Paris

32 rue Louise-Weiss, 13th (01.44.23.02.77, www.airdeparis.com). M° Chevaleret. **Open** 11am-7pm Tue-Sat. **Map** p177 E4 🔂 **Gallery**
This gallery shows experimental, neo-conceptual and chaotic material. A hip stable of artists includes Liam Gillick, Carsten Höller and Sarah Morris.

ART OF ENTERTAINMENT

Classic comic creations at the Musée Art Ludique.

EXPLORE

Paris takes pride in its world-class museums, which display works from a vast range of artistic movements: impressionism is the focus at the Musée d'Orsay, 20th-century 'isms' (fauvism, surrealism, cubism) make up the Musée d'Art Moderne's collections, and modern and postmodern take centre stage at the Centre Pompidou. Even the 21st-century digital art movement got its own showcase in 2010 when the Gaîté Lyrique opened in the Marais. And it's thanks to this ongoing thirst for cultural contextualisation that Paris is now home to the world's first museum dedicated solely to entertainment art, the **Musée Art Ludique** (see p188), which opened in late 2013 inside the fluorescent green Docks en Seine building.

The entertainment industry imbues all areas of popular culture with works that break down the boundaries between comic books, live action films, video games, manga and

animated movies. Yet the artists and the animation, film and games studios involved often remain as unknown to the general public as the technologies they use for their creations. For the first time ever, the Musée Art Ludique shines light on the creative processes behind it all, through a rolling series of exhibitions.

Kicking things off in November 2013 was Pixar, 25 Years of Animation, complete with blueprints and models from hit films such as *Ratatouille* and *Monsters Inc*. Next up was Art of the Marvel Superheroes, and 2015 is all about Wallace and Gromit in Aardman – Art That Takes Shape.

If you can't get enough of it all, fear not: the museum's passionate director Jean-Jacques Launier also runs the Arludik art gallery (12-14 rue St-Louis en l'Ile, 4th, www.arludik.com), packed to the gunnels with original drawings and prints from comics and films.

St-Germain-des-Prés & Odéon

St-Germain may be more Louis Vuitton than Boris Vian these days, but there are still enough small galleries and bookshops to ensure that it retains a whiff of its bohemian past. In the middle third of the 20th century, the area was the haunt of Picasso, Giacometti, Camus, Prévert and, *bien sûr*, Jean-Paul Sartre and Simone de Beauvoir; the hotspot of the Paris jazz boom after World War II; and the heart of the Paris book trade. This is where the cliché of café terrace intellectualising was coined, but nowadays most of the local patrons of the Flore and the Deux Magots are in the fashion business. Never mind: it's a smart and attractive part of the city, and also has some very good bars and restaurants, intimate museums such as the Zadkine and Delacroix, and green space aplenty in the Jardin du Luxembourg.

Hermès.

Don't Miss

1 Semilla All things market-led and locally grown (p196).

2 Hermès Stunning shop, spiffing scarves (p198).

3 Jardin du Luxembourg The quintessential Paris park (p200).

4 Musée Zadkine Modern art in a magical Left Bank setting (p200).

5 Monnaie de Paris The revamped Mint, now with Guy Savoy in place (p195).

BOULEVARD ST-GERMAIN TO THE SEINE

In the 6th arrondissement.

Hit by shortages of coal during World War II, Sartre shunned his cold apartment on rue Bonaparte. 'The principal interest of the Café de Flore,' he noted at the time, 'was that it had a stove, a nearby métro and no Germans.' Although you can spend more on a few coffees here than on a week's heating these days, the **Café de Flore** remains an arty favourite, and hosts *café-philo* evenings in English. Rival **Les Deux Magots**, facing historic **Eglise St-Germain-des-Prés**, is frequented largely by tourists. Nearby is the celebrity favourite **Brasserie Lipp** (151 bd St-Germain, 6th, 01.45.48.53.91); art nouveau fans tend to prefer **Brasserie Vagenende** (142 bd St-Germain, 6th, 01.43.26.68.18, www.vagenende. com). Swish bookshop **La Hune** provides sustenance of a more intellectual kind.

St-Germain-des-Prés grew up around the medieval abbey, the oldest church in Paris. There are traces of its cloister and part of the abbot's palace behind the church on rue de l'Abbaye. Constructed in 1586 in red brick with stone facing, the palace prefigured the architecture of place des Vosges. Charming place de Furstemberg (once the palace stables) is home to the house and studio where the elderly Delacroix lived when painting the murals in St-Sulpice; it now houses the **Musée National Delacroix**. Wagner, Ingres and Colette lived on nearby rue Jacob; its elegant 17th-century *hôtels particuliers* now contain specialist book, design and antiques shops and a few pleasant hotels.

Further east, rue de Buci hosts a street market and upmarket food shops, and is also home to legendary local **Bar du Marché** (no.16, 6th, 01.43.26.55.15). **Hôtel La Louisiane** (60 rue de Seine, 6th, 01.44.32.17.17, www.hotel-lalouisiane. com) has hosted jazz stars Chet Baker and Miles Davis, and Existentialist lovers Sartre and de Beauvoir. Rue de Seine, rue des Beaux-Arts and rue Bonaparte (Manet was born in the latter, at no.5, in 1832) are still packed with art galleries. It was in rue des Beaux-Arts, at the Hôtel d'Alsace, that Oscar Wilde complained about the wallpaper and then checked out for good. Now fashionably renovated, it houses the hip **L'Hôtel** (*see p358*). **La Palette** is a great pit stop with an enviable terrace; rue Mazarine, with shops selling lighting, vintage toys and jewellery, is also home to Terence Conran's bright, buzzing and wonderfully stylish **L'Alcazar** brasserie (no.62, 6th, 01.53.10.19.99, www.alcazar.fr). Set in the confines of a 17th-century real tennis court, and once a notorious transvestite bar, the space has been transformed with a glass roof, cool lighting and a changing series of photographic exhibits.

Eglise St-Germain-des-Prés.

On quai de Conti stands the neoclassical Hôtel des Monnaies, built for Louis XV by architect Jacques-Denis Antoine: the **Monnaie de Paris** traces the history of French coinage. Next door stands the domed **Institut de France**, cleaned to within an inch of its classical life. Opposite, the iron Pont des Arts footbridge leads directly to the Louvre. Further along, the city's main fine arts school, the **Ecole Nationale Supérieure des Beaux-Arts**, occupies an old monastery.

Sights & Museums

Ecole Nationale Supérieure des Beaux-Arts (Ensb-a)

14 rue Bonaparte, 6th (01.47.03.50.00, www. ensba.fr). M° St-Germain-des-Prés. **Open** 1-7pm Tue-Sun. **Admission** €7.50; free under-18s. *Exhibitions* prices vary. **Map** p193 C2 ❶

The city's most prestigious fine arts school resides in what remains of the 17th-century Couvent des Petits-Augustins, the 18th-century Hôtel de Chimay, some 19th-century additions and some chunks of assorted French châteaux that were moved here after the Revolution (when the buildings briefly served as a museum of French monuments, before becoming the art school in 1816).

★ FREE Eglise St-Germain-des-Prés

3 pl St-Germain-des-Prés, 6th (01.55.42.81.10, www.eglise-sgp.org). M° St-Germain-des-Prés. **Open** 8am-7.45pm Mon-Sat; 9am-8pm Sun. **Admission** free. **Map** p193 C3 ❷

This is the oldest church in Paris. On the advice of Germain (later Bishop of Paris), Childebert, son of Clovis, had a basilica and monastery built here around 543. It was first dedicated to St Vincent,

EXPLORE

and came to be known as St-Germain-le-Doré ('the gilded') because of its copper roof, then later as St-Germain-des-Prés ('of the fields'). During the Revolution the abbey was burned and a saltpetre refinery installed; the spire was added in a clumsy 19th-century restoration. Still, most of the present structure is 12th century, and ornate carved capitals and the tower remain from the 11th. Tombs include those of Jean-Casimir, the deposed King of Poland who became Abbot of St-Germain in 1669, and of Scots nobleman William Douglas. Under the window in the second chapel is the funeral stone of philosopher-mathematician Descartes.

Institut de France

23 quai de Conti, 6th (01.44.41.44.41, www. institut-de-france.fr). M° Louvre Rivoli or Pont Neuf. **Open** *Guided tours only* (call 01.44.41.43.32 for times). **Admission** prices vary. **No credit cards. Map** p193 C2 ❸

This elegant domed building with sweeping curved wings was designed as a school by Louis Le Vau and opened in 1684. The five academies of the Institut (Académie Française, Académie des Inscriptions et Belles-Lettres, Académie des Beaux-Arts, Académie des Sciences, Académie des Sciences Morales et Politiques) moved here in 1805. Inside is Mazarin's ornate tomb, and the Bibliothèque Mazarine (open to over-18s with ID and two photos; €15/year). The Académie Française was founded by Cardinal Richelieu in 1635 with the aim of preserving the purity of the French language from corrupting outside influences (such as English).

Monnaie de Paris

11 quai de Conti, 6th (01.40.46.56.66, www. monnaiedeparis.fr). M° Odéon. **Open** 11am-7pm Mon-Wed, Fri-Sun; 11am-10pm Thur. **Admission** varies. **Map** p193 D2 ❹

Housed in the handsome Palais Conti, a neoclassical mint built in the 1770s, this high-tech museum tells the tale of global and local coinage from its pre-Roman origins, using sophisticated displays and audiovisual presentations. The history of the franc, from its wartime debut in 1360, is outlined in detail. Alongside its historical heritage, the Monnaie embraces modernity: the stunning Palais is mainly used as an exhibition space for contemporary artists and a culture hub for Parisians. By 2016, the larger museum grounds (spanning an impressive 12,000sq m at the heart of the 6th arrondissement) should be fully renovated. On the cards are five interior pedestrian streets, art and foundry workshops, gardens, shops and a gourmet restaurant by renowned chef Guy Savoy (www.guysavoy.com) that opened in May 2015.

Musée National Delacroix

6 rue de Furstenberg, 6th (01.44.41.86.50, www.musee-delacroix.fr). M° St-Germain-des-Prés. **Open** 9.30am-5pm Mon, Wed-Sun.

Admission €6; free under-18s, under-26s (EU citizens), all 1st Sun of mth. PMP. **Map** p193 C2 ❺

Eugène Delacroix moved into this apartment and studio in 1857 in order to be near the Eglise St-Sulpice, where he was painting murals. This collection includes small oil paintings, free pastel studies of skies, sketches and lithographs, as well as his palette.

Restaurants

Le 21

21 rue Mazarine, 6th (01.46.33.76.90). M° Odéon. **Open** 12.30-2pm, 8-11pm Tue-Sat. **Main courses** €80-€110. **Map** p193 D2 ❻ **Bistro**

This clubby restaurant in St-Germain-des-Prés is a big hit with a *beau monde* crowd of antiques dealers, book editors and politicians. Chef Paul Minchelli's original minimalist style has evolved towards more homely preparations, as seen in a delicious sauté of flaked cod, potatoes, onions and green peppers, or squid in a squid ink sauce with black rice. To keep the waistline-watching regulars happy, a few of his old classics, including grilled red mullet, are still offered. Don't miss the chocolate fondant cake for dessert, and don't be shy about asking for help with the pricey wine list.

★ L'Epigramme

9 rue de l'Eperon, 6th (01.44.41.00.09). M° Odéon. **Open** noon-2.30pm, 7-10.30pm Tue-Sat. **Prix fixe** *Lunch* €24, €28. *Dinner* €38. **Map** p193 D3 ❼ **Bistro**

Monnaie de Paris

L'Epigramme is a pleasantly bourgeois dining room with terracotta floor tiles, wood beams, a glassed-in kitchen and comfortable chairs. Like the decor, the food doesn't aim to innovate but instead sticks to tried and true classics with the occasional twist. Marinated mackerel in a mustardy dressing on toasted country bread gets things off to a promising start, but the chef's skill really comes through in the main courses, such as perfectly seared lamb with glazed root vegetables and intense jus.

Germain

25-27 rue de Buci, 6th (01.43.26.02.93, www. beaumarly.com). M° Mabillon or Odéon. **Open** noon-midnight daily. **Main courses** €20-€25. **Map** p193 C3 ❺ **Brasserie**

Quaint rue de Buci has been shaken up by the extravagance of Germain, a versatile brasserie halfway between *Alice in Wonderland* and London's Sketch. The heated terrace is great for people watching, and the main ground-floor room, which features the lower part of a vast yellow statue piercing through the ceiling above, is perfect for a quick lunch. There's also a cosy salon for cocktails, a more conservative dining room at the back, and a private room on the first floor with a snooker table and the top half of the yellow statue. The food is almost childishly classic, but always with a twist.

Lapérouse

51 quai des Grands-Augustins, 6th (01.43.26. 68.04, www.laperouse.com). M° St-Michel. **Open** noon-2.30pm, 7.30-11pm Mon-Fri; 7.30-11pm Sat. **Main courses** from €35. **Prix fixe** *Lunch* €45, €55. *Dinner* €125, €145. **Map** p193 D2 ❾ **Brasserie**

One of the most romantic spots in Paris, Lapérouse was formerly a clandestine rendezvous for French politicians and their mistresses; the tiny private dining rooms upstairs used to lock from the inside. Chef Christophe Guibert does a wonderful take on classic French cooking: chateaubriand is glazed with port in a hazelnut crust; tender saddle of rabbit is cooked in a clay crust, flavoured with lavender and rosemary and served with ravioli of onions.

Little Breizh

11 rue Grégoire de Tours, 6th (01.43.54.60.74). M° Mabillon or Odéon. **Open** noon-2.30pm, 7-10.30pm Tue-Sat. **Main courses** €9.90-€13.90. **Map** p193 C3 ❿ **Crêperie**

Among the many crêperies in Paris, few really stand out. Despite its location, in the middle of a very touristy street, Little Breizh promises something a little different with its creatively named crêpes and quality ingredients. If none of the nine house specialities tempt you, you can also create your own. In the Saint-Jacques de la Coquine Saint-Jacques, toasted nuts are laid on a pear fondue coated with an onion and cream sauce. The Say Cheese, garnished with goat's cheese, cooked apples, nuts and honey, has the perfect balance between sweet and sour and

a light touch of rosemary. On the sweet side, it's hard to imagine a more gourmand dessert that the Teddy Breizh (€11.50): two crêpes buried under a mountain of chocolate sauce with caramel, powdered biscuits, marshmallow bears, Chantilly and vanilla ice cream.

★ Le Restaurant

L'Hôtel, 13 rue des Beaux-Arts, 6th (01.44.41. 99.01, www.l-hotel.com). M° St-Germain-des-Prés. **Open** 7-10.30am, 12.30-2.30pm, 7.30-10pm Tue-Sat. **Main courses** €50. **Prix fixe** *Breakfast* €20. *Lunch* €45, €55. *Degustation* €110, €135. **Map** p193 C2 ⓫ **Haute cuisine**

L'Hôtel's restaurant is a wonderfully atmospheric spot for lunch or dinner, with a charming terrace during the summer months. You can choose from a short seasonal menu with such dishes as pan-fried tuna, John Dory or suckling pig. But for the same price you can also enjoy the marvellous four-course *menu dégustation* or, even better, the *menu surprise*. Highlights of the autumn menu were the wild Breton crab stuffed with fennel, avocado and *huile d'Argan*, and a main course of pigeon on a bed of beetroot.

Semilla

54 rue de Seine, 6th (01.43.54.34.50). M° Odéon. **Open** noon-11pm daily. **Main courses** €25-€40. **Map** p193 C3 ⓬ **Bistro**

Run by an American and a New Zealander (Juan Sanchez and Drew Harré), and with an extremely distinguished chef in the kitchen (Eric Trochon, a 'Meilleur Ouvrier de France') this distinctive bistro serves bright, bold dishes. Many are available in 'entier' or 'demi', so you can snack or mix and match as you please. Starters might include crispy fried *barbajuan* – a type of ravioli originally from Monaco – rich with ricotta and spinach and prettily arranged on a bed of dark green spinach and cauliflower. Mains are equally successful. Crispy, creamy veal sweetbreads come perched on a tumble of salsify, slicked with a sweet honey-based sauce. Reservations are highly recommended, but it's not the most formal venue – just an exciting place doing interesting things with great ingredients.

Shu

8 rue Suger, 6th (01.46.34.25.88, www.restaurant-shu.com). M° St-Michel or Odéon. **Open** 6.30-11.30pm Mon-Sat. **Prix fixe** €38, €48, €63. **Map** p193 D3 ⓭ **Japanese**

IN THE KNOW BOUQUINISTES

The green, open-air boxes along the Seine *quais* are one of the city's institutions. Most sell second-hand books – rummage through boxes packed with ancient paperbacks for something existential to peruse over a *chocolat chaud* at La Palette.

EXPLORE

Prescription Cocktail Club. See p198.

Shu specialises in *kushi-agué* – a sort of Japanese kebab, with different ingredients breaded and fired on sticks. But where it really excels is in the starters, often more refined than at the purest *kaïseki* bar. Despite the price, you should opt for the more expensive menu, which represents better value for money: €63 for an amuse-bouche, a delicious assortment of incredibly fresh sashimi, three seasonal dishes, nine *kushi-agué* and a choice of *ochazuké* (rice with green tea and condiments) or *inaniwa* (fine udon noodles) served cold with their own cooking liquor. There are some very good sakes on the wine list and the service is impeccable.

Cafés & Bars

★ Le Bar du Marché
75 rue de Seine, 6th (01.43.26.55.15). M° Mabillon or Odéon. **Open** 8am-2am daily. **Map** p193 C3 ⑭
The market in question is the Cours des Halles, the bar a convivial corner café opening on to the pleasing bustle of St-Germain-des-Prés. Simple dishes like a ham omelette or a plate of herrings are in the €7 range, and Brouilly or muscadet is €4-€5 a glass – all proffered by waiters dressed in matching dungarees. It couldn't be anywhere else in the world.

Café de Flore
172 bd St-Germain, 6th (01.45.48.55.26, www.cafedeflore.fr). M° St-Germain-des-Prés. **Open** 7am-2am daily. **Map** p193 C2 ⑮
Bourgeois locals crowd the terrace tables at lunch, eating club sandwiches with knives and forks as anxious waiters frown at couples with pushchairs or single diners occupying tables for four. This historic café, former HQ of the Lost Generation intelligentsia, attracts tourists and, yes, celebrities from time to time. But a *café crème* is €5.70, and the omelettes and croque-monsieurs are eschewed in favour of the better dishes on the menu (€12-€19). There are philosophy debates on the first Wednesday of the month, at 8pm, in English.

Les Deux Magots
6 pl St-Germain-des-Prés, 6th (01.45.48.55.25, www.lesdeuxmagots.com). M° St-Germain-des-Prés. **Open** 7.30am-1am daily. **Map** p193 C3 ⑯
If you stand outside Les Deux Magots, you have to be prepared to photograph tourists wanting proof of their encounter with French philosophy. The former haunt of Sartre and de Beauvoir now attracts a less pensive crowd that can be all too *m'as-tu vu*, particularly at weekends. The hot chocolate is still good, though, and served in generous portions. Visit on a weekday afternoon when the editors return, manuscripts in hand, to the inside tables, leaving enough elbow room for some serious discussion.

Un Dimanche à Paris
4-8 cour du Commerce Saint-André, 6th (01.56.81.18.18, www.un-dimanche-a-paris.com). M° Odéon. **Open** noon-2.30pm, 7-10pm Tue-Sat; 11am-7pm Sun. **Map** p193 D3 ⑰
Chocoholics will be in paradise at this concept store dedicated to cocoa, where an upscale brunch is served on Sundays. There are no muffins, but rather a madeleine, a mini-éclair and a slice of cake – all of which go perfectly with one of the best hot chocolates in Paris, made with real melted chocolate, milk, a little cream and a touch of cinnamon and vanilla. Naturally, it's not cheap, but the level of refinement justifies the price. And you can always dial up the decadence to the max while you're there with a cheeky visit to the chocolate shop next door.

★ La Palette
43 rue de Seine, 6th (01.43.26.68.15, www. cafelapaletteparis.com). M° Odéon. **Open** 8am-2am Mon-Sat; 10am-2pm Sun. **Map** p193 C2 ⑱
La Palette is the café-bar of choice for the very *beaux* Beaux-Arts students who study at the venerable institution around the corner, and young couples who steal kisses in the wonderfully preserved art deco back room decorated with illustrations. It ain't cheap – a glass of Chablis sets you back around €7,

a demi €5 – but you're paying for the prime location once frequented by such luminaries as Jim Morrison, Picasso and Ernest Hemingway.

Prescription Cocktail Club

23 rue Mazarine, 6th (09.50.35.72.87, www. prescriptioncocktailclub.com). M° Odéon. **Open** 7pm-2am Mon-Thur; 7pm-4am Fri, Sat; 8pm-2am Sun. **Map** p193 C2 ⑲

This stylish 1930s-style speakeasy has a retro Prohibition feel but remains severely Left Bank, with crowds of well-dressed people sipping cocktails by candlelight. It's always busy and almost impossible to navigate at weekends. *Photo p197.*

Shops & Services

Arty Dandy

1 rue de Furstemberg, 6th (01.43.54.00.36, www.artydandy.com). M° Mabillon. **Open** 10.30am-7.30pm Mon-Sat. **Map** p193 C2 ⑳ **Gifts & souvenirs**

'Dandyism is the last spark of heroism amid decadence,' said Baudelaire. Taking this as its motto, Arty Dandy is a concept shop that embraces the surreal, the tongue-in-cheek and the poetic – an R.MUTT sticker to create your own Duchampian loo, and the 'Karl who?' bag (which KL himself has carried) are instant pleasers. More sublime offerings include Jaime Hayon's 'Lover' figurines.

Hermès

17 rue de Sèvres, 6th (01.42.22.80.83, www. hermes.com). M° Sèvres Babylone. **Open** 10.30am-7pm Mon-Sat. **Map** p193 B3 ㉑ **Fashion**

If you thought that Hermès was about horsey scarves and little else, a visit to the rue de Sèvres shop should dispel the equestrian rumours forever. Designed by Denis Montel, the concept store is set in the Hôtel Lutetia's former indoor pool. It's one of the best-looking retail spaces on the Left Bank. While the trademark scarves and ties are all present, the three-floor store also focuses on homewares, from wallpaper and carpets to sumptuous reproductions of 1930s-era furniture by Jean-Michel Frank.

Huilerie Artisanale Leblanc

12 rue Jacob, 6th (01.44.07.36.58, www.huile-leblanc.com). M° St-Germain-des-Prés. **Open** 11am-1.30pm, 2.30-7pm Tue-Sat. **Map** p193 C2 ㉒ **Food & drink**

The Leblanc family from Burgundy started making walnut oil before branching out to press pure oils from hazelnuts, almonds, pine nuts, grilled peanuts and olives. There are vinegars and mustards too.

★ La Hune

18 rue de l'Abbaye, 6th (01.45.48.35.85). M° St-Germain-des-Prés. **Open** 11am-8pm Mon-Thur, Sun; 11am-10pm Fri, Sat. **Map** p193 C2 ㉓ **Books & music**

This Left Bank institution boasts a global selection of art and design books, and a magnificent collection of French literature and theory. As a sign of the times, the shop has recently moved from its illustrious boulevard St-Germain location, to be replaced by a new Louis Vuitton.

Joseph

147 bd St-Germain, 6th (01.55.42.77.56, www. joseph.co.uk). M° St-Germain-des-Prés. **Open** 10am-7pm Mon-Sat. **Map** p193 C2 ㉔ **Fashion**

Taking a cue from its London store, Joseph's multi-brand shop stocks pieces by the likes of Balmain and Lanvin, as well as accessories by Bijoux de Sophie and handbags by Jérôme Dreyfuss.

Other locations throughout the city.

Lefranc.ferrant

22 rue de l'Echaudé, 6th (01.40.21.03.29, www. lefranc-ferrant.fr). M° St-Germain-des-Prés. **Open** 11am-7pm Tue-Sat. **Map** p193 C3 ㉕ **Fashion**

The opening of this boutique was eagerly awaited by keen followers of the talented Paris duo Béatrice Ferrant and Mario Lefranc. Their trademark is a surreal approach to tailoring, as in a strapless yellow evening gown made like a pair of men's trousers – complete with flies. Prices are in the €1,000 range.

Patrick Roger

108 bd St-Germain, 6th (01.43.29.38.42, www. patrickroger.com). M° Odéon. **Open** 10.30am-7.30pm daily. **Map** p193 B2 ㉖ **Food & drink**

Roger is shaking up the art of chocolate-making. Whereas other *chocolatiers* aim for gloss, Roger may create a brushed effect on hens so realistic you almost expect them to lay (chocolate) eggs.

Other locations throughout the city.

★ Sonia Rykiel

175 bd St-Germain, 6th (01.49.54.60.60, www. soniarykiel.com). M° St-Germain-des-Prés or Sèvres Babylone. **Open** 10.30am-7pm Mon-Sat. **Map** p193 C3 ㉗ **Fashion**

The queen of St-Germain celebrated the 40th birthday of her flagship store with a glamorous black and smoked glass refit perfect for narcissists: tons of mirrors reflect the gorgeous flowing gowns. Two newer boutiques stock the younger, more affordable Sonia by Sonia Rykiel range (6 rue de Grenelle, 6th, 01.49.54.61.00) and kids' togs (4 rue de Grenelle, 6th, 01.49.54.61.10).

Other locations throughout the city.

ST-SULPICE & THE LUXEMBOURG

In the 6th arrondissement.

Crammed with historic buildings and inviting shops, the quarter south of boulevard St-Germain between Odéon and Luxembourg epitomises

EXPLORE

civilised Paris. Just off the boulevard lies the covered market of St-Germain, now the site of a shopping arcade, auditorium, food hall and underground swimming pool. There are bars and bistros along rue Guisarde, nicknamed rue de la Soif ('thirst street') thanks to its carousers; it contains the late-night **Birdland** bar (no.8, 6th, 01.43.26.97.59) and a couple of notable bistros, including **Mâchon d'Henri** (no.8, 6th, 01.43.29.08.70, www.lemachondhenri.fr). Rue Princesse and rue des Canettes are a mix of budget restaurants and nocturnal haunts.

Pass the fashion boutiques, pâtisseries and antiquarian book and print shops and you come to **Eglise St-Sulpice**, a surprising 18th-century exercise in classical form with two unmatching turrets and a colonnaded façade. The square in front was designed in the 19th century by Visconti; it contains his lion-flanked Fontaine des Quatre Points Cardinaux (a pun on cardinal points and the statues of Bishops Bossuet, Fénelon, Massilon and Flechier, none of whom was actually a cardinal).

Among shops of religious artefacts, the chic boutiques on place and rue St-Sulpice include **Yves Saint Laurent**, **Vanessa Bruno** and milliner **Marie Mercié**. Prime shopping continues further west: clothes on rue Bonaparte and rue du Four, and accessory and fashion shops on rue du Dragon, rue de Grenelle and rue du Cherche-Midi. If you spot a lengthy queue in the latter, it's most likely for bread at **Poilâne**. Across the street, at the junction of rue de Sèvres and rue du Cherche-Midi, César's bronze *Centaur* is the sculptor's tribute to Picasso.

The early 17th-century chapel of St-Joseph-des-Carmes – once a Carmelite convent, now hidden within the **Institut Catholique**

(21 rue d'Assas, 6th, 01.44.39.52.00, www.icp.fr) – was the scene of the murder of 115 priests during the Terror in 1792. To the east lies wide rue de Tournon, lined by such grand 18th-century residences as the elegant Hôtel de Brancas (no.6), with figures of Justice and Prudence over the door. This street opens up to the **Palais du Luxembourg**, which now serves as the Senate, and the adjoining **Jardin du Luxembourg**.

Towards boulevard St-Germain is the neoclassical **Odéon, Théâtre de l'Europe** (*see p292*), built in 1779. A house in the square in front was home to Revolutionary hero Camille Desmoulins, who incited the mob to attack the Bastille in 1789. It's now occupied by **La Méditerranée** (2 pl de l'Odéon, 6th, 01.43.26.02.30, www.la-mediterranee.com); the restaurant's menus and plates were designed by Jean Cocteau. Joyce's *Ulysses* was published in 1922 by Sylvia Beach at the celebrated **Shakespeare & Company** (*see p179*).

Further along the street, at 12 rue de l'Ecole-de-Médecine, is the neoclassical Université René Descartes (Paris V) medical school, and the Musée d'Histoire de la Médecine. The Club des Cordeliers, set up by Danton in 1790, devised revolutionary plots across the street at the **Couvent des Cordeliers** (no.15); the 14th-century refectory, all that remains of the monastery founded by St Louis, houses modern art exhibitions. Marat, one of the club's leading lights, was stabbed to death in the bathtub at his home in the same street; David depicted the moment after the crime in his iconic painting, the *Death of Marat*. This was the surgeons' district: observe the building at no.5, once the barbers' and surgeons' guild. Climb rue André-Dubois to

EXPLORE

Jardin du Luxembourg. *See p200.*

rue Monsieur-le-Prince to budget restaurant **Polidor** (no.41, 6th, 01.43.26.95.34, www. polidor.com), open since 1845.

Sights & Museums

FREE Eglise St-Sulpice

Pl St-Sulpice, 6th (01.42.34.59.98, www.paroisse-saint-sulpice-paris.org). M° St-Sulpice. **Open** 8am-7.30pm daily. **Admission** free. **Map** p193 C3 ❷

It took 120 years and six architects to finish St-Sulpice. The grandiose façade, with its two-tier colonnade, was designed by Jean-Baptiste Servandoni. He died in 1766 before the second tower was finished, leaving one tower a good five metres shorter than the other. The trio of murals by Delacroix in the first chapel – *Jacob's Fight with the Angel, Heliodorus Chased from the Temple* and *St Michael Killing the Dragon* – create a sombre atmosphere.

Fondation Dubuffet

137 rue de Sèvres, 6th (01.47.34.12.63, www. dubuffetfondation.com). M° Duroc. **Open** 2-6pm Mon-Fri. Closed Aug. **Admission** €6; €4 reductions; free under-10s. **No credit cards. Map** p193 A4 ❷

You walk up a winding garden path to get to this museum, founded by Jean Dubuffet, wine merchant and master of *art brut*. There's a changing display of Dubuffet's lively drawings, paintings and sculptures, as well as models of the architectural sculptures from the *Hourloupe* cycle.

▶ *The foundation also looks after the Closerie Falbala, the 3D masterpiece of the Hourloupe cycle, housed at Périgny-sur-Yerres, east of Paris.*

★ FREE Jardin & Palais du Luxembourg

Pl André Honnorat, pl Edmond-Rostand or rue de Vaugirard, 6th (01.44.54.19.49, www.senat.fr/ visite). M° Odéon/RER Luxembourg. **Open** *Jardin* summer 7.30am-dusk daily; winter 8am-dusk daily. **Map** p193 C4 ❸

The palace itself was built in the 1620s for Marie de Médicis, widow of Henri IV, by Salomon de Brosse. Its Italianate style was intended to remind her of the Pitti Palace in her native Florence. The palace now houses the French parliament's upper house, the Sénat (open only to guided visits). The mansion next door (Le Petit Luxembourg) is the residence of the Sénat's president. The gardens, though, are the real draw: part formal (terraces and gravel paths), part 'English garden' (lawns and mature trees). The garden is crowded with sculptures: a looming Cyclops (on the 1624 Fontaine de Médicis), queens of France, a mini Statue of Liberty, wild animals, busts of Flaubert and Baudelaire, and a monument to Delacroix. The Musée du Luxembourg (*see right*) hosts prestigious exhibitions. Most interesting, though, are the people: a mixture of *flâneurs* and *dragueurs*, chess players and martial-arts practitioners, as well as children on ponies, in sandpits and playing with boats on the pond. *Photo p199.*

Eglise St-Sulpice.

★ Musée des Lettres et Manuscrits

222 bd St-Germain, 7th (01.42.22.48.48, www. museedeslettres.fr). M° Rue du Bac. **Open** 10am-7pm Tue, Wed, Fri-Sun; 10am-9.30pm Thur. **Admission** €7; €5 reductions; free under-12s. **Map** p193 B2 ❸

More than 2,000 documents and letters give an insight into the lives of the great and the good, from Magritte to Mozart. Einstein arrives at the theory of relativity on notes scattered in authentic disorder, Baudelaire complains about his money problems in a letter to his mother, and HMS *Northumberland*'s logbook records the day Napoleon boarded the ship to be exiled to St Helena.

Musée du Luxembourg

19 rue de Vaugirard, 6th (01.40.13.62.00, www. museeduluxembourg.fr). M° Cluny La Sorbonne or Odéon/RER Luxembourg. **Open** 10am-10pm Mon, Fri; 10am-7.30pm Tue-Thur, Sat, Sun. **Admission** Prices vary. **Map** p193 C4 ❸

When it opened in 1750, this small museum was the first public gallery in France. After closing for more than a year, the museum reopened in early 2011 with a Cranach exhibition, followed by a major Chagall retrospective in 2013. Book ahead to avoid queues.

★ FREE Musée Zadkine

100bis rue d'Assas, 6th (01.55.42.77.20, www. zadkine.paris.fr). M° Notre-Dame-des-Champs/ RER Port-Royal. **Open** 10am-6pm Tue-Sun. **Admission** free. *Exhibitions* €4; €2-€3 reductions; free under-13s. **Map** p193 C5 ❸

This is one of the most intimate museums in Paris, a peaceful hideaway where you can also get a good dose of modern art. The former studio of

Russian-born cubist sculptor Ossip Zadkine was converted into a museum in 1932, and has always had a particular charm, conserving the spirit of the place where the sculptor and his wife, painter Valentine Prax, lived for more than 40 years. There's barely a wink to Valentine, just a solitary canvas hung at the head of a staircase: Zadkine is the master of this place, dominated by his angular portraits and women's bodies carved out of tree trunks in African-inspired elliptical forms. Don't miss the garden planted with stylised bronze statues (including the famous *Monument à la Ville Détruite de Rotterdam*). The museum reopened in late 2012 after undergoing an extensive revamp.

Restaurants

Blueberry

6 rue du Sabot, 6th (01.42.22.21.56, www.blueberrymakibar.com). M° Mabillon. **Open** noon-2.30pm, 7-10.30pm Tue-Fri; 12.30-3pm, 7.30-11pm Sat. **Makis** €10-€15. **Map** p193 C3 ❸❹ **Sushi**

A creative, unconventional sushi restaurant, with bright pop colours on the walls and on your plate. The mood is set by the house cocktails – such as 'Dawn over Tokyo' – that mix well-known flavours (Martini, saké) with less familiar tastes (purple-leaved shisho). The results are fresh, light and fruity. *Makis* (rolled sushi) are Blueberry's great speciality. They're served in sixes, each more weirdly named than the last (Les Trublions, Rackam le Rouge, Iroquois, Transsibérien). They're elaborate, well thought through and unusual – not for sushi purists.

★ Bouillon Racine

3 rue Racine, 6th (01.44.32.15.60, www.bouillon-racine.com). M° Odéon. **Open** noon-11pm daily. **Main courses** €17-€23. **Prix fixe** *Lunch* €15.95, €31.90, €41.90. *Dinner* €31.90, €41.90. **Map** p193 D3 ❸❺ **Brasserie**

Originally opened as a *bouillon* (soup kitchen) in the early 20th century to feed hungry city workers, this beautifully renovated two-storey brasserie lives on as an art nouveau gem. Food is suitably traditional, with classic dishes such as foie gras, *escargots de Bourgogne* and *confit de canard* dominating the reasonably priced menu. Dishes are served non-stop from noon to 11pm.

Bread & Roses

62 rue Madame, 6th (01.42.22.06.06, www.breadandroses.fr). M° St-Placide. **Open** 8am-7.30pm Mon-Sat. **Main courses** €18. **Map** p193 C4 ❸❻ **Bakery/café**

Come for a morning croissant and you might find yourself staying on for lunch, so tempting are the wares at this Anglo-influenced *boulangerie/épicerie/* café. Giant wedges of cheesecake sit alongside French pastries, and huge savoury puff-pastry tarts are perched on the counter. Attention to detail shows even in the authentically pale taramasalata,

which is matched with buckwheat-and-seaweed bread. Prices reflect the quality of the often organic ingredients, but that doesn't seem to deter any of the moneyed locals, who order towering birthday cakes here for their snappily dressed offspring.

Caméléon

6 rue de Chevreuse, 6th (01.43.27.43.27). M° Vavin. **Open** noon-2.15pm, 7-10.45pm Tue-Sat. **Main courses** €36-€49. **Prix fixe** *Lunch* €33, €39, €49. **Map** p193 C5 ❸❼ **Bistro**

Young chef David Frémondière is in charge in the kitchen (previously of Le Bristol), and his cooking is precise and inspired. The menu offers sophisticated traditional dishes cooked with regional ingredients, which never fail to be inventive. For example, the legendary veal liver from Corrèze that's glazed with wine vinegar before being served in a thick slice with a hearty macaroni cheese. Service is impeccable, and prices match the Left Bank location.

Coffee Parisien

4 rue Princesse, 6th (01.43.54.18.18, www.coffee-parisien.fr). M° Mabillon. **Open** noon-11.30pm daily. **Main courses** €12-€17.50. **Map** p193 C3 ❸❽ **Burgers**

When the grand old dames and moody wannabe writers tire of Café de Flore, they head to Coffee Parisien. Behind the bar, crowded with hurried diners, you can see the chefs at work – coleslaw virtuosos, hash brown geniuses. On the walls, there are portraits of Kennedy and Obama, Stars and Stripes, frescoes of dollars and clippings from the *New York Times*, all overlooking battered old red leather banquettes. Food-wise, the New York feel continues. Divine cheeseburgers, fluffy pancakes, crisp bagels and eggs benedict.

Le Comptoir

Hôtel Le Relais Saint-Germain, 9 carrefour de l'Odéon, 6th (01.43.29.12.05). M° Odéon. **Open** 12.30-5.30pm, 8.30-11pm (last orders 9pm) Mon-Fri; noon-11pm Sat, Sun (no booking on weekends). **Main courses** €15. **Prix fixe** *Dinner* (Mon-Fri) €60. **Map** p193 C3 ❸❾ **Brasserie**

Yves Camdeborde runs the bijou Hôtel Le Relais Saint-Germain (*see p359*), whose art deco dining room, Le Comptoir, serves brasserie fare from 12.30pm to 5.30pm and on weekend nights, and a five-course prix fixe feast on weekday evenings. The single dinner sitting lets the chef take real pleasure in his work. On the daily menu, you might find dishes like rolled saddle of lamb with vegetable-stuffed 'Basque ravioli'. The catch? The prix fixe dinner is booked up as much as six months in advance.

Ecole Ferrandi

28 rue de l'Abbé Grégoire, 6th (01.49.54.17.31, www.ferrandi-paris.fr). M° Saint-Placide. **Open** *Lunch* 12.30pm Wed-Fri. *Dinner* 7.30pm Mon, Tue. Closed school hols. **Prix fixe** *Lunch* €25, €30. *Dinner* €45. **Map** p193 B4 ❹⓪ **Cookery school**

EXPLORE

Ferrandi is one of the most important cookery schools in France, with over 1,300 students learning how to be bakers, barstaff, waiters and chefs. Of course they have to practise their skills on the general public, so the Ecole has set up two restaurants that are favourites with foodies-in-the-know (the waiting list can stretch for months). Le Premier is a showcase for students learning a basic cooking apprenticeship. Restaurant 28, though, is reserved for high-level students. The standard is hugely impressive and the bill comes to €25 or €30 for a five-course lunch.

La Ferrandaise

8 rue de Vaugirard, 6th (01.43.26.36.36, www. laferrandaise.com). M° Odéon/RER Luxembourg. **Open** 7-10.30pm Mon, Sat; noon-2.30pm, 7-10.30pm Tue-Fri. **Prix fixe** *Lunch* €16, €37. *Dinner* €37, €50. **Map** p193 D3 **㊶ Bistro**
This bistro has established a following for its solid, classic food with a twist. A platter of excellent ham, sausage and terrine arrives as you study the blackboard menu, and the bread is crisp-crusted, thickly sliced sourdough. Two specialities are the potato stuffed with escargots in a camembert sauce, and a wonderfully flavoured, slightly rosé slice of veal. Desserts might include intense chocolate with rum-soaked bananas. Wines start at €22.

Huîtrerie Régis

3 rue de Montfaucon, 6th (01.44.41.10.07, www. huitrerieregis.com). M° Mabillon. **Open** noon-2.30pm, 6.30-10.30pm Tue-Sun. Closed mid July-mid Sept. **Main courses** €32. **Prix fixe** €24-€59. **Map** p193 C3 **㊷ Oyster bar**
Paris oyster fans are often obliged to use one of the city's big brasseries to get their fix of shellfish, but what if you just want to eat a reasonably priced platter of oysters? Enter Régis and his cosy 14-seat oyster bar. The tiny room feels pristine and the tables are properly laid. Here you can enjoy the freshest oysters from Marennes for around €30 a dozen. Hungry souls can supplement their feast with a slice of home-made apple tart or the cheese of the day.

Joséphine Chez Dumonet

117 rue du Cherche-Midi, 6th (01.45.48.52.40). M° Duroc. **Open** 12.30-2pm, 7.30-10.30pm Mon-Fri. **Main courses** €30-€35. **Map** p193 A4 **㊸ Bistro**
This bastion of classic bistro cooking, where the use of luxury ingredients brings a splash of glamour, is guaranteed to please the faithful, well-heeled clientele. The good news is that several dishes are available as half portions, opening up the possibility of exploring some classy numbers without your credit card melting. A half portion of salad of lamb's lettuce, warm potatoes and truffle shavings is a sexy dish, with the perfume of black truffles gloriously present. Tournedos Rossini, with fresh truffles and a slice of foie gras on the tender fillet, comes with sautéed potatoes, rich in goose fat and a touch of garlic. Puddings make for a sumptuous finish.

Pizza Chic

13 rue de Mézières, 6th (01.45.48.30.38, www. pizzachic.fr). M° Rennes, Sèvres-Babylone or St-Sulpice. **Open** 12.30-2.30pm, 7.30-11pm Mon-Thur; 12.30-2.30pm, 7.30-11.30pm Fri, Sat; noon-3pm, 7.30-10pm Sun. **Main courses** €14-€22. **Map** p193 B3 **㊹ Pizza**
An address that could only exist on the Left Bank, where 'chic' is a religion in itself. But this contemporary, polished pizzeria isn't the least bit ostentatious and the pizzas are among the best in Paris. White (with no tomato base) or red, the pizzas are beautiful as well as delicious: tuck into the luxurious spiciness of the carciofi (artichoke cream, raw artichokes, rocket, 24-month aged parmesan) or the simplicity of the aurora (tomato, mozzarella, fresh basil). You'll leave delighted at having found a Parisian version of Italian chic for around €20.

Cafés & Bars

★ Le Bar Dix

10 rue de l'Odéon, 6th (01.43.26.66.83, www. lebar10.com). M° Odéon. **Open** 6pm-2am daily. **No credit cards. Map** p193 D3 **㊺**
Generations of students have glugged back jugs of the celebrated home-made sangria (€3 a glass during happy hour) while squeezed into the cramped upper bar, tattily authentic with its Jacques Brel record sleeves, Yves Montand handbills and pre-war light fittings. Spelunkers and hopeless romantics negotiate the hazardous stone staircase to drink in the cellar bar, with its candlelight and century-old advertising murals. Can someone please come and slap a preservation order on the place?

★ Chez Georges

11 rue des Canettes, 6th (01.43.26.79.15). M° Mabillon. **Open** 3pm-2am Mon-Fri; noon-2am Sat; 7pm-2am Sun. Closed Aug. **Map** p193 C3 **㊻**
One of a dying breed of *cave-bars*, Chez Georges is beloved of students, professionals and local eccentrics. Regulars pop in during the day to sip wine over a game of chess, and at night the *cave* fills up with people dancing to *chanson*, pop and even the odd bar mitzvah tune. The heat is mascara-melting and it's not for the claustrophobic.

La Compagnie des Vins Surnaturels

7 rue Lobineau, 6th (09.54.90.20.20, www. compagniedesvinssurnaturels.com). M° Mabillon or Odéon. **Open** 6pm-2am daily. **Map** p193 C3 **㊼**
Forget cheap plonk – both drinks and food here are nothing but the best. The wine list has more than 3,000 bottles listed, and to go with the booze there are some first-class treats such as *burrata, prosciutto al tartufo*, truffles and fine cheeses. The menu performs leaps and bounds from €6 to €65 a glass, and from €30 to €3,500 a bottle. But even if you don't have four months' rent to spare, the lower end of the selection is worth a look.

EXPLORE

Les Editeurs

4 carrefour de l'Odéon, 6th (01.43.26.67.76, www.lesediteurs.fr). M° Odéon. **Open** 8am-2am daily. **Map** p193 C3 ➍➑

It's no surprise to see row upon row of books in the bright, modern interior of Les Editeurs. A café with literary leanings, it sits on the lovely carrefour de l'Odéon. Bask in the glory of literary greats as portraits of authors and their editors look down on you. The weekend brunch is good value at €26.

Moose

16 rue des Quatre Vents, 6th (01.46.33.77.00, www.mooseparis.com). M° Odeon. **Open** 11am-2am daily. **Map** p193 C3 ➍➒

This Canadian sports bar serves a vast selection of beers and even some organic Australian wines. A friendly atmosphere and delicious burgers make the Moose a great place to kick off the evening.

Le Rostand

6 pl Edmond-Rostand, 6th (01.43.54.61.58). RER Luxembourg. **Open** 8am-1am daily. **Map** p193 D4 ➎➊

Le Rostand has a truly wonderful view of the Jardin du Luxembourg from its classy interior, decked out with oriental paintings, a mahogany bar and wall-length mirrors. Whiskies and cocktails are pricey, as is the brasserie menu, but the snack menu serves delicious omelettes and *croques* for around €9.

Le Select

99 bd du Montparnasse, 6th (01.45.48.38.24). M° Vavin. **Open** 7am-3am Mon-Fri; 7am-5am Sat, Sun. **Map** p193 B5 ➎➊

For a decade between the wars, the junction of boulevards Raspail and du Montparnasse was where Man Ray, Cocteau and Lost Generation Americans hung out in the vast, glass-fronted cafés. Eight decades on, Le Select is the best of what have inevitably become tourist haunts. Its pricey menu is big on historical detail and short on authenticity, but it manages to hold on to its heyday with dignity.

Shops & Services

Adrenaline

30 rue Racine, 6th (01.44.27.09.05, www.adrenaline-vintage.com). M° Odéon. **Open** 11am-7pm Mon-Sat. **Map** p193 D3 ➎➋ **Accessories**

This *dépot-vente* specialises in vintage luggage and handbags. Iconic Vuitton suitcases and Kelly and Birkin bags command enormous prices, but there are some slightly more affordable pieces and a small collection of '60s couture.

APC

38 rue Madame, 6th (01.42.22.12.77, www.apc.fr). M° St-Placide. **Open** 11am-7.30pm Mon-Sat. **Map** p193 C3 ➎➌ **Fashion**

The look is simple but stylish: perfectly cut basics in muted tones. Hip without trying too hard, its jeans are a big hit with denim aficionados – the skinny version nearly caused a stampede when it came out. **Other locations** throughout the city.

Chantelivre

13 rue de Sèvres, 6th (01.45.48.87.90, www.chantelivre.com). M° St-Sulpice or Sèvres-Babylone. **Open** 1-7.30pm Mon; 10.30am-7.30pm Tue-Sat. **Map** p193 B3 ➎➍ **Children**

Chantelivre was the first – and remains the best – children's bookshop in Paris, housing a vast catalogue of children's literature. It also has activities for children (talks, concerts, special guests, book signings) all year round, and occasionally for adults too – such as a recent visit from Apollonia Poilâne.

Christian Constant

37 rue d'Assas, 6th (01.53.63.15.15, www.christianconstant.fr). M° Rennes or St-Placide. **Open** 9.30am-8.30pm Mon-Fri; 8am-8pm Sat, Sun. **Map** p193 B4 ➎➎ **Food & drink**

A master chocolate-maker and *traiteur*, Constant scours the globe for new ideas. His ganaches are subtly flavoured with verbena, jasmine or cardamom.

EXPLORE

Les Editeurs.

Fnac Junior

*19 rue Vavin, 6th (08.92.35.06.66, www.
eveiletjeux.com). M° Vavin.* **Open** 10am-
7.30pm Mon-Sat. **Map** p193 B4 **56** Children
Fnac Junior stocks a wide range of books, toys,
DVDs, CDs and CD-Roms for under-12s. Storytelling
and other activities take place for over-twos.
Other locations throughout the city.

Gérard Mulot

*76 rue de Seine, 6th (01.43.26.85.77, www.
gerard-mulot.com). M° Odéon.* **Open** 6.45am-
8pm Mon, Tue, Thur-Sun. Closed Easter & Aug.
Map p193 C3 **57** Food & drink
Gérard Mulot rustles up stunning pastries. Try the
mabillon: caramel mousse with apricot marmalade.
Other locations 6 rue du Pas de la Mule, 3rd
(01.42.78.52.17); 93 rue de la Glacière, 13th
(01.45.81.39.09).

Gibert Joseph

*26 bd St-Michel, 6th (01.44.41.88.88, www.
gibertjoseph.com). M° St-Michel.* **Open** 10am-8pm
Mon-Sat. **Map** p193 D3 **58** Books & music
Formed back in 1929, this string of bookshops is
normally packed out with students.
▶ *Further up bd St-Michel (nos. 30, 32 & 34)
are branches specialising in stationery, CDs,
DVDs and art materials.*

★ Hervé Chapelier

*1bis rue du Vieux-Colombier, 6th (01.44.07.06.50,
www.hervechapelier.fr). M° St-Germain-des-Prés.*
Open 10.15am-7pm Mon-Sat. **Map** p193 C3
59 Accessories
Bag yourself a classic, chic, bicoloured tote at Hervé
Chapelier. Sizes and prices range from a small
handbag at €30 to a canvas travel bag at €500.
Other location 390 rue Saint-Honoré, 1st
(01.42.96.38.04).

Jean-Charles Rochoux

*16 rue d'Assas, 6th (01.42.84.29.45, www.
jcrochoux.com). M° Rennes or St-Sulpice.*
Open 1-7.30pm Mon; 10.30am-7.30pm
Tue-Sat. **Map** p193 B3 **60** Food & drink
After learning the ropes with chocolate wizz Michel
Chaudun, this young *chocolatier* has become something of a star. The first things you notice in the boutique are the perfectly shaped figurines and animals
(often made from moulds created by Jean-Charles in
the shop basement). You can even buy a man's chocolate torso (a nod to the term '*plaquette de chocolat*',
used in French to describe a six-pack). If you're passing by on a Saturday, try one of the chocolate bars
made from fresh fruit.

★ Jean-Paul Hévin

*3 rue Vavin, 6th (01.43.54.09.85, www.jphevin.
com). M° Vavin.* **Open** 10am-7pm Tue-Sat.
Closed Aug. **Map** p193 C4 **61** Food & drink

Poilâne

Hévin specialises in the beguiling combination of
chocolate with potent cheese fillings, which loyal
customers serve with wine as an aperitif.
Other locations 231 rue St-Honoré, 1st
(01.55.35.35.96); 23bis av de La Motte-Picquet,
7th (01.45.51.77.48).

Kenzo

*60-62 rue de Rennes, 6th (01.45.44.27.88,
www.kenzo.com). M° St-Sulpice.* **Open** 10.30am-
7.30pm Mon-Sat. **Map** p193 C3 **62** Fashion
Kenzo has long been a friend of Paris, having
dressed the city itself in its various extravagant pub-
licity campaigns. This flagship store has three floors
of men's and women's fashion.
Other locations throughout the city.

LMDW

*6 carrefour de l'Odéon, 6th (01.46.34.70.20,
www.finespirits.fr). M° Odéon.* **Open** 10am-
8pm Mon-Sat. **Map** p193 D3 **63** Food & drink
Three whole floors of this sleek, modern booze shop
are filled with wine, whisky, rum, cognac, calvados, armagnac, tequila, vodka, gin, fruit liqueurs,
grappa, vermouth, saké and almost anything else
that takes on a liquid form, including tea and coffee.
It's worth visiting the boutique even if you don't plan
to buy as some of the bottles (and their packaging)
are veritable works of art.

★ Marie-Hélène de Taillac

*8 rue de Tournon, 6th (01.44.27.07.07,
www.mariehelenedetaillac.com). M° Mabillon.*
Open 11am-7pm Mon-Sat. **Map** p193 C3
64 Accessories
Marie-Hélène de Taillac is a very fine jeweller. But
unlike some of her more famous colleagues across
the Seine, her diamonds and emeralds in simple,

EXPLORE

unpretentious settings work just as well with a pair of jeans and don't make her customers look like ancestral portraits.

★ Marie Mercié

23 rue St-Sulpice, 6th (01.43.26.45.83, www. mariemercie.com). M° Odéon. **Open** 11am-7pm Mon-Sat. **Map** p193 C3 ➏➎ **Accessories**
Mercié's creations make you wish you lived in an era when hats were de rigueur. Step out in one shaped like curved fingers (complete with shocking-pink nail varnish and pink diamond ring).

Missiessy

87 rue de Seine, 6th (01.83.64.57.57, www.missiessy. com). M° Odéon or Mabillon. **Open** 10am-7pm Mon-Sat. **Map** p193 C3 ➏➏ **Accessories**
This tiny, shiny boutique delivers an offbeat, urban yet cooly stylish feel with its handcrafted leather bags and accessories. Bracelets and purses can be customised with different types of leather and colours, and each belt, buckle, wallet or keychain feels distinctive. Prices are what you'd expect for a quality young designer outfit in St-Germain – upwards of €100 for a stylish wrist cuff, bags from around €370 – but if you want to invest in a colourful, contemporary piece with enough class to go the distance, Missiessy might be just the ticket.

Mouton à Cinq Pattes

8 & 18 rue St-Placide, 6th (01.45.48.86.26, www.moutonacinqpattesparis.com). M° Sèvres Babylone. **Open** 10am-7pm Mon-Sat. **Map** p193 B3 ➌➐ **Vintage**
Fashionistas in the know head to the 'five-legged sheep' (named after Henri Verneuil's 1954 film) for designer vintage and last season's collections in mint condition: Vittadini, Buscat, Donn Adriana, Chanel, Jean Paul Gaultier, Moschino and numerous other labels. Turnover is fast, so this is no place for an indecision crisis. Labels are sometimes cut out, too, so make sure you know what you're buying.
Other location 138 bd St-Germain, 6th (01.43.26.49.25).

Peggy Kingg

9-11 rue Coëtlogon, 6th (01.42.84.83.84, www.phk.fr). M° St-Sulpice. **Open** 11am-7pm Tue-Sat. **Map** p193 B3 ➏➒ **Accessories**
Once the creative director at Cartier, Peggy Kingg now makes bags of boar skin and python, as well as silver jewellery.

Petit Bateau

26 rue Vavin, 6th (01.55.42.02.53, www.petit-bateau.com). M° Vavin. **Open** 10am-7pm Mon-Sat. **Map** p193 C4 ➏➒ **Fashion**
Widely renowned for its comfortable, well-made cotton T-shirts, vests and other separates, Petit Bateau carries an equally coveted teen range.
Other locations throughout the city.

★ Pierre Hermé

72 rue Bonaparte, 6th (01.43.54.47.77, www. pierreherme.com). M° St-Germain-des-Prés or St-Sulpice. **Open** 10am-7pm Mon-Wed, Sun; 10am-7.30pm Thur, Fri; 10am-9pm Sat. Closed Sun in Aug. **Map** p193 C3 ➐➊ **Food & drink**
Pastry superstar Pierre Hermé attracts connoisseurs from St-Germain and further afield with his wonderful seasonal collections.
Other locations throughout the city.

★ Poilâne

8 rue du Cherche-Midi, 6th (01.45.48.42.59, www. poilane.com). M° Sèvres Babylone. **Open** 7.15am-8.15pm Mon-Sat. **Map** p193 B3 ➐➊ **Food & drink**
Apollonia Poilâne runs the family shop, where locals queue for fresh country *miches*, flaky-crusted apple tarts and buttery shortbread biscuits.
Other locations 38 rue Debelleyme, 3rd 01.44.61.83.39; 49 bd de Grenelle, 15th (01.45.79.11.49).

Princesse Tam-Tam

52 bd St-Michel, 6th (01.40.51.72.99, www. princessetamtam.com). M° Cluny La Sorbonne. **Open** 1.30-7pm Mon; 10am-7.30pm Tue-Sat (closed 3-4pm Wed, Thur). **Map** p193 D4 ➐➋ **Fashion**
This inexpensive underwear and swimwear brand has traffic-stopping promotions. Bright colours and sexily transparent and sporty gear rule.
Other locations throughout the city.

Sabbia Rosa

73 rue des Sts-Pères, 6th (01.45.48.88.37). M° St-Germain-des-Prés. **Open** 10am-7pm Mon-Sat. **Map** p193 B3 ➐➌ **Fashion**
Let Moana Moatti tempt you with feather-trimmed satin mules, or satin, silk and chiffon negligées in fine shades of tangerine, lemon, mocha or pistachio. All sizes are medium, others are made *sur mesure*; prices are just the right side of stratospheric.

Vanessa Bruno

25 rue St-Sulpice, 6th (01.43.54.41.04, www. vanessabruno.com). M° Odéon. **Open** 10am-7pm Mon-Sat. **Map** p193 C3 ➐➍ **Fashion**
Mercerised cotton tanks, flattering trousers and feminine tops have a Zen-like quality that stems from Bruno's stay in Japan, and they manage to flatter every figure type. She also makes great bags.
Other locations 12 rue de Castiglione, 1st (01.42.61.44.60); 100 rue Vieille-du-Temple, 3rd (01.42.77.19.41).

Yves Saint Laurent

6 pl St-Sulpice, 6th (01.43.29.43.00, www.ysl.com). M° St-Sulpice. **Open** 11am-7pm Mon; 10.30am-7pm Tue-Sat. **Map** p193 C3 ➐➎ **Fashion**
The memory of the founding designer, who died in 2008, lives on in this elegant boutique, which was splendidly refitted in red in the same year.
Other locations throughout the city.

EXPLORE

Montparnasse & Beyond

Montparnasse's heyday was short, but for a few years between the two world wars it was the emblematic 'gay Paree' district of after-dark merriment and fruitful artistic exchange. A great number of its most prominent figures were expats, and the late-night bars and artists' studios formed a bubble of cordial international relations that was irreparably popped in 1939. The local atmosphere soured further with the completion in the early 1970s of the much-loathed Tour Montparnasse. Fortunately, though, this monolith offers magical views from the 56th floor. Back at ground level, fruitful artistic exchange is still ripe, thanks to the Fondation Cartier, plus museums dedicated to Henri Cartier-Bresson, Roy Adzak and Antoine Bourdelle. It's also rich territory for galettes, with the city's finest crêperies cooking up some Breton brilliance along rue du Montparnasse.

EXPLORE

Les Catacombes.

Don't Miss

1 Les Catacombes
Bones galore in the 'empire of death' (p216).

2 Fondation Cartier
A work of art, inside and out (p209).

3 Tour Montparnasse
Views to savour (p213).

4 La Cantine du Troquet
Christian Etchebest's nose-to-tail dining (p213).

5 Cimetière du Montparnasse Literary legends, from Maupassant to Sartre (p209).

MONTPARNASSE

In the 14th & 15th arrondissements.

Artists Picasso, Léger and Soutine fled to 'Mount Parnassus' in the early 1900s to escape the rising rents of Montmartre. They were soon joined by Chagall, Zadkine and other refugees from the Russian Revolution, along with Americans such as Man Ray, Henry Miller, Ezra Pound and Gertrude Stein. Between the wars the neighbourhood was the epitome of modernity: studios with large windows were built by avant-garde architects; artists, writers and intellectuals drank and debated in the quarter's showy bars; and naughty pastimes – including the then risqué tango – flourished.

Sadly, the Montparnasse of today has lost much of its former soul, dominated as it is by the lofty **Tour Montparnasse** – the first skyscraper to be built in central Paris. At its foot are a shopping centre, the **Mix Club** (www.mixclub.fr), and in winter an open-air ice rink. There are fabulous panoramic views from the newly renovated terrace on the 56th floor, reaching up to 40km (25 miles) on a clear day.

Gare Montparnasse was rebuilt in the 1970s, a grey affair above which can be found the surprisingly oasis-like Jardin Atlantique, the **Mémorial du Maréchal Leclerc** and the **Musée Jean Moulin**. Rue du Montparnasse, appropriately for a street near the station that sends trains to Brittany, is dotted with crêperies. Nearby, strip joints have replaced most of the theatres on ever-saucy rue de la Gaîté, but boulevard Edgar-Quinet has pleasant cafés and a street market (Wed, Sat), plus the entrance to the **Cimetière du Montparnasse**. Boulevard du Montparnasse still buzzes at night, thanks to its many cinemas and dining spots: giant art deco brasserie **La Coupole**; **Le Dôme** (no.108, 14th, 01.43.35.25.81), now a top fish restaurant; and restaurant **La Rotonde** (no.105, 6th, 01.43.26.48.26, www.rotondemontparnasse.com). All were popularised by the literati between the wars, and now use this heritage to their advantage. Nearby, on boulevard Raspail, stands Rodin's statue of Balzac, whose rugged appearance caused such a scandal that it was put in place only after the sculptor's death.

For a whiff of Montparnasse's artistic history, wander down rue de la Grande-Chaumière. Bourdelle and Friesz taught at the venerable **Académie de la Grande-Chaumière** (no.14, 01.43.26.13.72, www.grande-chaumiere.fr), frequented by Calder, Giacometti and Pompon among others (it still offers drawing lessons); Modigliani died at no.8 in 1920, ruined by tuberculosis, drugs and alcohol. Rue Vavin and rue Bréa, leading to the Jardin du Luxembourg, have become an enclave of children's shops.

IN THE KNOW
HANGING GARDENS

The **Jardin Atlantique**, an oasis of green set high above Gare Montparnasse, has been offering Parisians a welcome breath of fresh air for two decades. The garden can be accessed by lift via rue du Commandant Mouchotte and boulevard de Vaugirard.

Look out for no.6, the 1912 white-tiled apartment building where art nouveau architect Henri Sauvage lived.

Further east on boulevard du Montparnasse, literary café **La Closerie des Lilas** (no.171, 01.40.51.34.50, www.closeriedeslilas.fr) was a pre-war favourite with everyone from Lenin and Trotsky to Picasso and Hemingway; brass plaques on the tables indicate where each historic figure used to sit. Next to it is the lovely 19th-century **Fontaine de l'Observatoire**, featuring bronze turtles and thrashing sea horses by Frémiet, and figures of the four continents by Carpeaux.

From here, the Jardins de l'Observatoire form part of the green axis that stretches between the Palais du Luxembourg and the royal observatory, the **Observatoire de Paris**. A curiosity next door is the Maison des Fontainiers, which is built over an expansive (now dry-ish) underground reservoir that was originally commissioned by Marie de Médicis to supply water to fountains around the city.

A relatively recent addition to boulevard Raspail is the glass-and-steel **Fondation Cartier pour l'Art Contemporain**. Designed by architect Jean Nouvel, it houses the jewellers' head offices and an exhibition space dedicated to contemporary art and photography.

West of the train station, the redevelopment of Montparnasse is also evident in the circular place de Catalogne, a piece of 1980s postmodern neoclassicism by Mitterrand's favourite architect, Spaniard Ricardo Bofill, and the housing estates of rue Vercingétorix.

There are still some traces of the old, arty Montparnasse for those willing to look for it: in impasse Lebouis, an avant-garde studio building houses the **Fondation Henri Cartier-Bresson**; at 21 avenue du Maine, an ivy-clad alleyway of old studios contains the artist-run exhibition space Immanence; on rue Antoine-Bourdelle, the newly revamped **Musée Bourdelle** includes another old cluster of studios, where sculptor Antoine Bourdelle, Symbolist painter Eugène Carrière and, briefly, Marc Chagall all worked. Towards Les Invalides, on rue Mayet, craft and restoration workshops are still tucked away in the old courtyards.

Sights & Museums

FREE **Cimetière du Montparnasse**
*3 bd Edgar-Quinet, 14th (01.44.10.86.50).
M° Edgar Quinet or Raspail.* **Open** *16 Mar-
5 Nov* 8am-6pm Mon-Fri; 8.30am-6pm Sat;
9am-6pm Sun. *6 Nov-15 Mar* 8am-5.30pm
Mon-Fri; 8.30am-5.30pm Sat; 9am-5.30pm
Sun. **Admission** free. **Map** p211 F5 ❶
See below **Dead Poets Society**.

★ **Fondation Cartier pour
l'Art Contemporain**
*261 bd Raspail, 14th (01.42.18.56.50, www.
fondation.cartier.fr). M° Denfert-Rochereau or
Raspail.* **Open** 11am-10pm Tue; 11am-8pm
Wed-Sun. **Admission** €10.50; €7 reductions; free
under-13s & under-18s Wed. **Map** p211 G5 ❷
Jean Nouvel's glass and steel building, an exhibition
centre with Cartier's offices above, is as much a
work of art as the installations on display inside.
Shows by artists and photographers often have
wide-ranging themes, such as 'Birds' or 'Desert'.
Live events around the shows are called Soirées
Nomades and feature concerts, screenings, lectures
and performances.

★ **Fondation Henri Cartier-Bresson**
*2 impasse Lebouis, 14th (01.56.80.27.00, www.
henricartierbresson.org). M° Gaîté.* **Open** 1-6.30pm
Tue, Thur, Fri, Sun; 1-8.30pm Wed; 11am-6.45pm
Sat. Closed Aug & between exhibitions.

DEAD POETS SOCIETY
The most literary of all Paris cemeteries.

Opposite the boulevard Edgar Quinet
entrance to Montparnasse cemetery,
a policeman long stood permanent guard
in front of the Albin Michel publishing house.
Why, you may ask, would the publisher of
the latest Stephen King blockbuster need
such security? The reason is this century-old
publisher has a history of supporting freedom
of expression. It also stuck its neck out
to try and free author Irène Némirovsky after
she was deported by the Nazis. Her *Suite
Française* was recently published from a
manuscript and made into a major film.
Némirovsky, tragically, didn't survive to
return to France, but many of Albin Michel's
pioneering writers are buried just opposite in
the **Cimetière du Montparnasse** (*see above*),
the most literary and intellectual of all Paris
cemeteries. And the tradition continues.
One of the newest graves, covered in flowers,
messages and pens, is that of *Charlie Hebdo*
cartoonist Georges Wolinski.

Montparnasse still receives 1,000 new
occupants a year and you don't have to be
distinguished to lie here – it's open to all
Paris residents. How do they find the space?
The secret is in the small notices posted
on neglected graves warning of a '*reprise
administrative*'. If no relative comes forward
after several years, the bones are transferred
to the catacombs. So much for those who
had 'in perpetuity' engraved on their tombs.
Someone actually lives in the cemetery –
in the caretaker's house among the graves
near the main gate. And a team of gardeners
spend their days here, planting, polishing
and keeping the moss at bay.

The laminated map available at the
entrance will direct you to the famous graves
– Baudelaire, buried between his mother and
his hated *beau-père*; Sartre and De Beauvoir,
Maupassant and Gainsbourg (something of
a poet too). Dreyfus of 'Dreyfus affair' fame
is among the many Jewish graves. There are
also several works of art, including Brancusi's
The Kiss and two sparkly sculptures by Niki
de Saint Phalle. But better still is to wander
unaided: many mysteries and curiosities are
revealed by a quiet walk among these graves.

EXPLORE

EXPLORE

Musée Bourdelle.

EXPLORE

Admission €7; €4 reductions; free 6.30-8.30pm Wed. **No credit cards**. **Map** p211 F5 ❸
This two-floor gallery is dedicated to the work of acclaimed photographer Henri Cartier-Bresson. It consists of a tall, narrow *atelier* in a 1913 building, with a minutely catalogued archive, open to researchers, and a lounge on the fourth floor screening films. In the spirit of Cartier-Bresson, who assisted on three Jean Renoir films and drew and painted all his life, the Fondation opens its doors to other disciplines with three annual shows.

FREE Mémorial du Maréchal Leclerc de Hauteclocque et de la Libération de Paris & Musée Jean Moulin

Jardin Atlantique, 23 allée de la 2e DB (above Gare Montparnasse), 15th (01.40.64.39.44, www.ml-leclerc-moulin.paris.fr). Mº Montparnasse Bienvenüe. **Open** 10am-6pm Tue-Sun. **Admission** free. *Exhibitions* €4; €2-€3 reductions; free under-13s. **Map** p211 E5 ❹
This double museum retraces World War II and the Resistance through Free French commander Maréchal Leclerc and left-wing hero Jean Moulin. Documentary material and film archives complement an impressive 270° slide show, complete with sound effects, which tells the story of the Liberation of Paris.

FREE Musée-Atelier Adzak

3 rue Jonquoy, 14th (01.45.43.06.98). Mº Plaisance. **Open** usually 3-7pm Sat, Sun (call in advance). **Admission** free. **Map** p211 E6 ❺
The eccentric house, studio and garden built by the late Roy Adzak, a British-born painter and sculptor who died in 1987, harbour traces of the conceptual

artist's plaster body columns and dehydrations. Now a registered British-run charity, it gives mostly foreign artists a chance to exhibit in Paris.

FREE Musée Bourdelle

16-18 rue Antoine-Bourdelle, 15th (01.49.54.73.73, www.bourdelle.paris.fr). Mº Falguière or Montparnasse Bienvenüe. **Open** 10am-6pm Tue-Sun. **Admission** free. *Exhibitions* €9; €6 reductions; free under-14s. **Map** p211 E4 ❻
Sculptor Antoine Bourdelle (1861-1929), who was a pupil of Rodin, produced a number of monumental works including the modernist relief friezes at the Théâtre des Champs-Elysées, which were inspired by Isadora Duncan and Nijinsky. The museum includes the artist's apartment and studios, which were also used by Eugène Carrière, Dalou and Chagall. A 1950s extension tracks the evolution of Bourdelle's equestrian monument to General Alvear in Buenos Aires, and his masterful *Hercules the Archer*. A modern wing by Christian de Portzamparc houses bronzes, including various studies of Beethoven in different guises. After being closed for renovations for eight months, the museum reopened in 2015 with an exhibition tracing the history of the mannequin from the Renaissance to the 20th century.

Musée Pasteur

Institut Pasteur, 25 rue du Dr-Roux, 15th (01.45.68.82.83, www.pasteur.fr). Mº Pasteur. **Open** 2-5.30pm Mon-Fri. Closed Aug. **Admission** €7; €3 reductions. **Map** p210 D5 ❼
The flat where the famous chemist and his wife lived at the end of his life (1888-95) has not been touched; you can see their furniture and possessions, photos

and instruments. An extravagant mausoleum on the ground floor houses Pasteur's tomb, decorated with mosaics depicting his scientific achievements.

Musée de la Poste
34 bd de Vaugirard, 15th (01.42.79.24.24, www.ladressemuseedelaposte.com). Mº Montparnasse Bienvenüe. **Open** 10am-6pm Mon-Sat. **Admission** €5; €3.50 reductions; free under-26s. PMP. *Temporary exhibitions* €6.50; €5 reductions; free under-13s. **No credit cards. Map** p211 E5 ❽
From among the uniforms, pistols, carriages, official decrees and fumigation tongs emerge snippets of history: during the 1871 Siege of Paris, hot-air balloons and carrier pigeons were used to get post out of the city, and *boules de Moulins*, balls crammed with hundreds of letters, were floated down the Seine in return, mostly never to arrive. The second section covers French and international philately. The museum is currently closed for renovations and is scheduled to reopen in mid 2015. A temporary exhibition is running nearby, at 21 avenue du Maine.

FREE Observatoire de Paris
61 av de l'Observatoire, 14th (01.40.51.22.41, www.obspm.fr). Entry for visitors at 77 av Denfert-Rochereau, 14th. Mº St-Jacques/RER Port-Royal. **Tours** Email visite.paris@obspm.fr or write to Observatoire de Paris, 61 av de l'Observatoire, 75014 Paris. **Map** p211 G5 ❾
The Paris observatory was founded by Louis XIV's finance minister, Colbert, in 1667; it was designed by Claude Perrault (who also worked on the Louvre), with labs and an observation tower. The French meridian line drawn by François Arago in 1806 (which was used here before the Greenwich meridian was adopted as an international standard) runs north–south through the centre of the building. The dome on the tower was added in the 1840s.
▶ *The Observatoire is currently closed but should reopen at some point in late 2015. Check the website for further details.*

★ Tour Montparnasse
33 av du Maine, 15th (01.45.38.52.56, www.tourmontparnasse56.com). Mº Montparnasse Bienvenüe. **Open** Oct-Mar 9.30am-10.30pm Mon-Thur, Sun; 9.30am-11pm Fri, Sat. *Apr-Sept* 9.30am-11.30pm daily. **Admission** €15; €9.20-€11.70 reductions; free under-7s. **Map** p211 F5 ❿
Built in 1974 on the site of the old station, this 209m (686ft) steel-and-glass monolith is actually shorter than the Eiffel Tower, but better placed for fabulous views of the city – including, of course, the Eiffel Tower itself. A lift whisks you up in 38 seconds to the 56th floor, where you'll find a display of aerial scenes of Paris, an upgraded café-lounge, a souvenir shop – and lots and lots of sky. On a clear day you can see up to 40km (25 miles). Another lift takes you all the way up to the roof. Classical concerts are held on the terrace.

Restaurants

La Cantine du Troquet
101 rue de l'Ouest, 14th (01.45.40.04.98). Mº Pernety. **Open** 11.45am-2.15pm, 7-10.45pm Tue-Sat. **Main courses** €16.50-€20. **Map** p211 E6 ⓫ **Bistro**
Christian Etchebest opened Le Troquet, a popular Basque bistro, several years ago, now followed by its 'canteen'. There's no set menu. Instead, you choose dishes from a big blackboard. A bit of a 'nose to tail' exercise, the Cantine du Troquet lets no part of the pig go to waste, and the meats often come with house fries with sea salt and herbs. The chef also turns out masterful fish dishes, and the desserts are the classics of French cuisine. The dishes never go above €20, and the wine list is full of discoveries.

★ La Cerisaie
70 bd Edgar Quinet, 14th (01.43.20.98.98, www.restaurantlacerisaie.com). Mº Edgar Quinet or Montparnasse. **Open** noon-2pm, 7-10pm Mon-Fri. Closed mid July-mid Aug & 1wk Dec. **Main courses** €15-€20. **Map** p211 F5 ⓬ **Bistro**
Nothing about La Cerisaie's unprepossessing red façade hints at the talent that lurks inside. Chef Cyril Lalanne proves his ability to select and prepare the finest produce. On the daily-changing blackboard menu you might find *bourride de maquereau*, a thrifty take on the garlicky southern French fish stew, or *cochon noir de Bigorre*, an ancient breed of pig that puts ordinary pork to shame. *Baba à l'armagnac* comes with stunningly good chantilly.

Cobéa
11 rue Raymond Losserand, 14th (01.43.20.21.39, www.cobea.fr). Mº Gaîté or Pernety. **Open** 12.15-1.45pm (last orders 1.15pm), 7.15-9.45pm (last orders 9.15pm) Tue-Sat. **Prix fixe** *Lunch* €49, €69. *Lunch & Dinner* €79, €99, €119. **Map** p211 F5 ⓭ **Haute cuisine**
Cobéa is a slick new restaurant launched by friends Jerome Cobou and Philippe Bellissent, who won a Michelin star when he was head chef at L'Hôtel. The ethos here is gastronomy without the snobbery. Set in a renovated 1920s house with big windows overlooking a green space, it feels wonderfully peaceful and cosy, while touches such as silverware and Bernardaud porcelain add a luxury feel. The set menus are a treasure chest of reworked classics, plus a daily-changing 'chef's surprise'.

EXPLORE

La Coupole

102 bd du Montparnasse, 14th (01.43.20.14.20, www.lacoupole-paris.com). Mº Vavin. **Open** 8.30am-2.30am, 6.30pm-midnight Mon; 8am-2pm, 6.30pm-midnight Tue-Fri; 8am-midnight Sat; 8.30am-11pm Sun. **Main courses** €22-€42. **Prix fixe** *Lunch* €33 (Mon-Fri), €38, €61. *Dinner* €31 (Mon-Fri, Sun), €38, €61. **Map** p211 F5 **⑭ Brasserie**

La Coupole still glows with some of the old glamour. The people-watching potential remains superb, inside and out, and the long ranks of linen-covered tables, professional waiters, 32 art deco columns painted by different artists of the epoch, mosaic floor and sheer scale of the operation still make coming here an event. The set menu offers unremarkable steaks, foie gras, fish and game stews, but the real treat is the shellfish. Take your pick from the *claires*, *spéciales* and *belons*, or go for a platter brimming with crabs, oysters, prawns, periwinkles and clams.

Le Grand Pan

20 rue Rosenwald, 15th (01.42.50.02.50, www.legrandpan.fr). Mº Convention. **Open** noon-2pm, 7.30-11pm Mon-Fri. **Main courses** €21-€28. **Prix fixe** *Lunch* €30. **Map** p210 D6 **⑮ Bistro**

Young chef Benoît Gauthier trained with Christian Etchebest, and he's come up with a clever formula that surfs the current Paris preference for great produce simply cooked. At dinner, a complimentary starter of soup is served – maybe courgette or white bean – and then you choose from the selection of grilled meats and lobster. Everything comes with a delicious mountain of home-made chips and green salad. Desserts run to homely choices like strawberry crumble or rice pudding with caramel sauce.

Josselin.

€ Josselin

67 rue du Montparnasse, 14th (01.43.20.93.50). Mº Edgar Quinet. **Open** 11am-3pm, 5.30-11.30pm Wed-Fri; 11am-midnight Sat, Sun. Closed 3wks Jan & 2wks Aug. **Main courses** €15-€20. **Prix fixe** *Lunch* €12. **No credit cards.** **Map** p211 F5 **⑯ Crêperie**

Josselin is the star crêperie of the area, and the one with the longest queues. The speciality is the Couple – two layers of galette with the filling in the middle. Wash it all down with bowls of cider, of which the brut is best.

L'Opportun

64 bd Edgar Quinet, 14th (01.43.20.26.89). Mº Edgar Quinet. **Open** noon-3pm, 7-11.30pm Mon-Sat. **Main courses** €20. **Prix fixe** *Lunch & Dinner* €25. **Map** p211 F5 **⑰ Bistro**

Owner-chef Serge Alzérat is passionate about Beaujolais, dubbing his convivial cream and yellow restaurant a centre of 'beaujolaistherapy' and a place for 'the prevention of thirst'. He's also an advocate for good, honest Lyonnais food. Thus his menu is littered with the likes of *sabodet* (thick pork sausage) with a purée of split peas, duck skin salad, *tête de veau* (a favourite of ex-president Chirac) and meat – lots of it. *Fromage* fans should try the st-marcellin by master cheesemaker Hervé Mons.

Le Plomb du Cantal

3 rue de la Gaîté, 14th (01.43.35.16.92). Mº Gaîté. **Open** noon-midnight daily. **Main courses** €18. **Map** p211 F5 **⑱ Bistro**

This homage to the Auvergne may suffer from its 1980s decor, but with food like this, who cares? *Aligot* (potato puréed with fresh tomme cheese) and *truffade* (potatoes sautéed with tomme) are scraped out of copper pots on to plates at the table, the shoestring fries arrive by the saucepan-load, and the omelettes are made with three eggs, 300g of potatoes, and, if you're really hungry, a supplement of tomme. Wines are excellent and the service is friendly.

★ Severo

8 rue des Plantes, 14th (01.45.40.40.91). Mº Alésia, Mouton-Duvernet or Pernety. **Open** noon-2pm, 7.30-10pm Mon-Fri. **Main courses** €15-€40. **Map** p211 F6 **⑲ Bistro**

Severo is all about well-bred meat selected by former butcher William Bernet and partner Hugo Desnoyer. On the menu, all sorts of piggy things to begin with, then mostly beef, from a modest *steak haché* with chips or green beans to a bloody entrecôte. The meat also deserves to be tried raw in a steak tartare – here, the naturally fatty meat is minimally seasoned: no egg, no spice, just an edge of capers and shallots. The chips – often neglected elsewhere – also stand out, set to one side in their own bowl. Among the nursery-style desserts, go for the crème caramel or a lovely plum tart.

Cafés & Bars

Café Milou
10 rue du Maine, 14th (01.43.22.46.09, www. cafe-milou.fr). Mº Montparnasse Bienvenüe or Edgar Quinet. **Open** 9.30am-2am Mon-Sat. **Map** p211 F5 ⑳
Café Milou is a sweet bar and bistro on rue du Maine that for some reason lacks the reputation of trendier hangouts nearby. And happily for its clients – if there aren't as many hipsters propping up the bar, then the smiling staff can take the time to chat. Red wine stains and hearty classic dishes are in vogue here – tartares, gratins, charcuterie boards and cheeses. Locals in the know come here year round to enjoy Corsican cocktails and the recently enlarged terrace.

L'Entrepôt
7-9 rue Francis de Pressensé, 14th (01.45.40.07.50, www.lentrepot.fr). Mº Pernéty. **Open** noon-2.30pm, 7-11pm Mon-Sat; 11.45am-2.45pm, 7-11pm Sun. **Map** p211 E6 ㉑
L'Entrepôt, housed in a former warehouse, is a wonderful multitasker and has enough to keep you keen all week. There's a café where literary readings are held, a restaurant with a terrace (a godsend during the summer), and a bar on the ground floor with live music most Mondays, Thursdays, Fridays and Saturdays – mainly jazz, rap and *chanson*. There's also an arthouse cinema and exhibition space upstairs.

Au Général Beuret
9 place du Général Beuret, 15th (01.42.50.28.62). Mº Vaugirard. **Open** 8am-2am daily. **Map** p210 C5 ㉒
Tucked away on a lovely square in the 15th, Au Général Beuret shines with all the proud distinction of the 19th-century brigadier it's named after. Upon entering, your eyes will be dazzled by the gleaming neon-lined bar. Once they've adjusted, you'll discern a bustling brasserie decked out in superhero decor and abuzz with friendly locals. The food is classic bar fare: cheeseburgers, sirloin steak, chips (which come with a pint for €5.50 during happy hour). Rock music on the stereo and an attractive terrace complete the picture. Unpretentious, unexceptional, but great fun.

KriZa Bar
9 rue Vandamme, 14th (01.43.21.57.58, www. krizabar.com). Mº Edgar Quinet or Gaîté. **Open** noon-2pm, 7pm-2am Tue-Fri; 7pm-2am Sat. **Map** p211 F5 ㉓
KriZa has been a neighbourhood favourite for years. Aperitifs based around Suze gentian bitters or port, decent draught beers and lethal cocktails make up a drinks list that's broad and well priced for the area. The food is classic tapas: manchego, tortilla, olives or foie gras. With big, cosy sofas inside and an interior patio for sunny days, it's a reliable bet.

Le Lock Groove
15 rue Roger, 14th (01.43.22.77.52). Mº Denfert-Rochereau. **Open** 6pm-1am Mon-Sat. **Map** p211 F6 ㉔
The Lock Groove, which opened in late 2013, is a rock bar through and through – the kind of place where only vinyl is played and the bartender will happily engage you in a half-hour chat about the relative merits of Captain Beefheart's late albums. Situated just off lively rue Daguerre, it makes for a pleasant alternative to the self-conscious bars that dot Montparnasse. Pints are affordable, the diner-style food is passable and decor is genuinely antique.

Shops & Services

★ Bogato
7 rue Liancourt, 14th (01.40.47.03.51, www.chez bogato.fr). Mº Denfert-Rochereau. **Open** 10am-7pm Tue-Sat. **Map** p211 F6 ㉕ **Food & drink**
If Hansel and Gretel had a cake shop in Paris it might look like Bogato (a name that sounds like '*beau gateau*'). Everything here is about temptation, from the quaint wooden furniture to pastry chef Anaïs Olmer's brightly coloured cupcakes, towering under glass bells on the counter like sugary art installations. Eat in or take out; and if you like what you've scoffed, sign up for a baking class.

La Cave des Papilles
35 rue Daguerre, 14th (01.43.20.05.74, www. lacavedespapilles.com). Mº Denfert-Rochereau. **Open** 3.30-8.30pm Mon; 10am-1.30pm, 3.30-8.30pm Tue-Fri; 10am-8.30pm Sat; 10am-1.30pm Sun. **Map** p211 F6 ㉖ **Food & drink**
You can't miss the lemon-yellow frontage of La Cave des Papilles. The owner is a lover of 'natural' wine and 80% of the 1,200 wines on offer are produced organically. La Cave des Papilles itself has a hand in certain vintages, producing bottles under the Cave des Papilles brand. It's not outrageously priced either, with a wide choice of bottles for under €20.

Haili
56 rue Daguerre, 14th (01.40.47.54.86). Mº Denfert-Rochereau. **Open** 11am-7.30pm Tue-Sat. **Map** p211 F6 ㉗ **Fashion**
Former stylist Patricia Wang creates looks from the practical to the chic to the unexpected in her boutique, stocked with the creations of European designers. Every season, new names appear: elegant Danes, offbeat Spaniards, dreamy Brits, all creating beautiful clothes. Patricia offers plenty of advice and has built a roster of regulars who are happy to take her recommendations (and their husbands often come seeking gift suggestions).

Hazar & Co
126 rue du Château, 14th (06.19.01.14.99, www. hazar-creations.com). Mº Pernety. **Open** 11.30am-7.30pm Tue-Sat. **Map** p211 E6 ㉘ **Fashion**

EXPLORE

EXPLORE

Anne-Cécile Zitter and her cohorts cleverly mix leather, textiles and paper to create Japanese-influenced rings, necklaces, bracelets, headbands and more. Japan also comes through in the clothing fabrics, with skirts and blouses studded with bits of origami-style colour. They also turn out classic basics, with 1920s-style jackets and coats, sportswear (sweatshirts with lace trims), fancy knitwear and bags. The biggest pieces don't exceed €200, and you can pick some items up for as little as one or two euros.

Jacadi

19bis av du Général Leclerc, 14th (01.43.21.46.03, www.jacadi.fr). M° Mouton-Duvernet. **Open** 10am-7pm Mon-Sat. **Map** p211 G6 ㉙ **Children**
Jacadi's well-made clothes for babies and children – pleated skirts, smocked dresses, dungarees and Fair Isle knits – are a hit with well-to-do parents.
Other locations throughout the city.

★ Madame de

65 rue Daguerre, 14th (01.77. 10.59.46, www. madamede.net). M° Denfert-Rochereau. **Open** 11am-7.30pm Tue-Sat. **Map** p211 F6 ㉚ **Fashion**
This delightful second-hand shop only stocks pieces 'that are like new' – even better, the prices wouldn't look out of place in the sales: a suede Vanessa Bruno bag for €154, perhaps, or a checked Zara dress for €33. For retro decor fans, Madame de also stocks homeware treasures – an art deco carafe with smoked glass goblets, a vintage sewing machine, a Kodak Senior no.1 projector.

La Maison des Bonbons

14 rue Mouton-Duvernet, 14th (01.45.41.25.55). M° Mouton-Duvernet. **Open** 11am-7pm Tue-Sat. **Map** p211 F6 ㉛ **Food & drink**
Those with a sweet tooth or a taste for cutesy bibelots will be in heaven here – start with the rows and rows of sugary treats ranged in glass jars, from liquorice to salted butter caramels. Then check out the miniature peacocks, rabbit-shaped lamps, classic games and pretty lunchboxes.

Marché aux Puces de Vanves

Av Georges-Lafenestre & av Marc-Sangnier, 14th. M° Porte de Vanves. **Open** 7am-2pm Sat, Sun. **Map** p211 E6 ㉜ **Market**
Vanves is the smallest of the Paris flea markets, and the atmosphere is infinitely more tranquil than at Clignancourt. It's a favourite with serious collectors, so arrive early for the best pick of decent vintage clothes, dolls, costume jewellery and silverware.

Storie

20 rue Delambre, 14th (01.83.56.01.98, www.storie blog.com). M° Vavin. **Open** 3-8pm Mon; 11am-2pm, 3-8pm Tue-Sat. **Map** p211 F5 ㉝ **Homewares**
Storie is a tiny, open space a few steps from the Tour Montparnasse. It's stocked with lightbulb-shaped vases, patterned cushions, pewter picture frames:

everything needed to add a touch of luxury to a home. At the back of the shop you'll also find a fine selection of jewellery. A new online shop launched in 2015 at www.storieshop.com.

DENFERT-ROCHEREAU & MONTSOURIS

In the 14th & 15th arrondissements.

In the run-up to the 1789 Revolution, the bones of six million Parisians were wheelbarrowed from the handful of overcrowded city cemeteries to the **Catacombes**, a vast network of tunnels that stretches under much of Paris. The sections under the 13th and 14th arrondissements are open to the public; the gloomy Denfert-Rochereau entrance is next to one of the toll gates of the Mur des Fermiers-Généraux, built by Ledoux in the 1780s.

The bronze *Lion de Belfort* dominates place Denfert-Rochereau, a favourite starting point for countless political demonstrations. The regal beast was sculpted by Bartholdi, of Statue of Liberty fame, and is a scaled-down replica of one in Belfort that commemorates the brave defence by Colonel Denfert-Rochereau of the town in 1870. Nearby, the southern half of rue Daguerre is a pedestrianised market street.

One of the biggest draws of the area is **Parc Montsouris**, with lovely lakes, cascades and an unusual history. Surrounding the western edge of the park are a number of modest, quiet streets – including rue du Parc Montsouris and rue Georges-Braque – that used to be lined during the 1920s and '30s with charming villas and artists' studios by avant-garde architects Le Corbusier and André Lurçat. On the southern edge of the park sprawls the **Cité Universitaire** complex.

Sights & Museums

★ Les Catacombes

1 av du Colonel-Henri-Rol-Tanguy, 14th (01.43.22.47.63, www.catacombes.paris.fr). M°/RER Denfert Rochereau. **Open** 10am-8pm Tue-Sun (last entry 4pm). **Admission** €10; €8 reductions; free under-18s. **Map** p211 G6 ㉞
This is the official entrance to the 3,000km (1,864-mile) tunnel network that runs under much of the city. With public burial pits overflowing in the late 18th century, the bones of six million people were transferred to the *catacombes*. The bones of Marat, Robespierre and their cronies are packed in with wall upon wall of their fellow citizens. A damp tunnel takes you through a series of galleries before you reach the ossuary, the entrance to which is announced by a sign engraved in the stone: 'Stop! This is the empire of death.'

FREE Cité Universitaire

17 bd Jourdan, 14th (01.44.16.64.00, www.ciup.fr). RER Cité Universitaire. **Map** p211 G6 ㉟

Parc Montsouris.

The Cité Universitaire is an odd mix. Created between the wars and inspired by Oxbridge colleges, its 37 halls of residence were designed in a variety of supposedly authentic national styles. Some are by architects of the appropriate nationality (Dutchman Willem Dudok, for instance, designed the De Stijl-style Collège Néerlandais); others, such as the Khmer sculptures and bird-beak roof of the Asie du Sud-Est building, are merely pastiches. You can visit the sculptural white Pavillon Suisse (01.44.16.10.16, www.fondationsuisse.fr), which has a Le Corbusier mural on the ground floor. The spacious landscaped gardens are open to the public.

FREE Parc Montsouris

Bd Jourdan, 14th. RER Cité Universitaire. **Open** 8am-dusk Mon-Fri; 9am-dusk Sat, Sun. **Map** p211 G6 **36**
The most colourful of the capital's parks, Montsouris was laid out for Baron Haussmann by Jean-Charles Adolphe Alphand. It includes a series of gently sloping lawns, an artificial lake and cascades. On the opening day in 1878, the lake inexplicably emptied, and the engineer responsible committed suicide.

FURTHER WEST

In the 15th arrondissement.

The expansive 15th arrondissement has little to offer tourists, though as a largely residential district it has plenty of good restaurants and street markets, and some good small shops. It's worth making a detour to visit **La Ruche** ('beehive'), designed by Eiffel as a wine pavilion for the 1900 Exposition Universelle and moved

here to serve as artists' studios. Nearby is **Parc Georges Brassens**, opened in 1983, and at the porte de Versailles the sprawling Paris-Expo exhibition centre was created in 1923.

Sights & Museums

FREE Parc Georges Brassens

Rue des Morillons, 15th. M° Porte de Vanves or Porte de Versailles. **Open** 8am-dusk Mon-Fri; 9am-dusk Sat, Sun. **Map** p210 C6 **37**
Built on the site of the old Abattoirs de Vaugirard, Parc Georges Brassens prefigured the industrial regeneration of Parc André Citroën and La Villette. The gateways, crowned by bronze bulls, have been kept, as have a series of iron meat-market pavilions, which house a second-hand book market at weekends. The Jardin des Senteurs is planted with aromatic species, and a small vineyard yields 200 bottles of Clos des Morillons every year.

La Ruche

Passage de Dantzig, 15th (www.la-ruche.fr). M° Convention or Porte de Versailles. **Map** p210 C6 **38**
Have a peep through the fence to see the iron-framed former wine pavilion built by Gustave Eiffel for the 1900 Exposition Universelle, and later rebuilt by philanthropic sculptor Alfred Boucher to be let as studios for struggling artists. Chagall, Soutine, Brancusi, Modigliani, Lipchitz and Archipenko all spent periods here, and the 140 studios are still sought after by today's artists and designers.

Restaurants

Afaria

15 rue Desnouettes, 15th (01.48.42.95.90, www. restaurant-afaria.fr). M° Convention. **Open** noon-2pm, 7-11pm Tue-Sat. **Main courses** €19-€28. **Prix fixe** *Lunch* €23, €27 (Mon-Fri). *Lunch & Dinner* €45. **Map** p210 B6 **39** **Bistro**
Basque-born chef Julien Duboué may have handed over the reins at Afaria to his talented young deputy, Ludivine Merlin, but the southern French-inspired menu remains intact. Several dishes are for sharing, in particular a caveman-sized duck *magret* with balsamic fig vinegar, served on a terracotta roof tile with potato gratin perched on a bed of twigs.

★ Jadis

208 rue de la Croix-Nivert, 15th (01.45.57.73.20, www.bistrotjadisparis.com). M° Convention or Porte de Versailles. **Open** 12.15-2pm, 7.15-11pm Mon-Fri. **Main courses** €25. **Prix fixe** *Lunch* €26, €38. *Dinner* €38, €46, €57. **Map** p210 B5 **40** **Bistro**
The 15th has more than its fair share of great bistros, and Jadis confirms the trend. Young chef Guillaume Delage serves a gently updated take on classic French cuisine. The pared-down presentation of such dishes as snails in puff pastry with oyster mushrooms and romaine lettuce lets each element speak for itself.

EXPLORE

The 7th & Western Paris

The seventh arrondissement has long played host to the machinery of state and diplomacy: this is the home of France's parliament, several ministries and a gaggle of foreign embassies, as well as the UNESCO HQ. Fortunately, where politicians go, fine food often follows, so tuck into sublime sweetbrads at Jean-François Piège's new Clover or sweet treats at Michel Chaudun's eponymous chocolate shop. Indulgence over, look up from your plate and you'll spy three of Paris's greatest attractions – an A-shaped assembly of 19th-century iron lattice, a gallery in an old Beaux Arts train station and the river itself, its *berges* now packed with strollers rather than cars.

Rosa Bonheur sur Seine

Don't Miss

1 Eiffel Tower Reach for the skies and check out the new glass floor (p229).

2 Musée d'Orsay The Nouvel Orsay has had a dynamic revamp (p224).

3 David Toutain Treat your taste buds (p232).

4 Rosa Bonheur sur Seine Sip Pernod and drink in the views (p226).

5 Musée National Rodin Greatest hits, from *The Thinker* to *The Gates of Hell* (p224).

THE FAUBOURG ST-GERMAIN

In the 7th arrondissement.

In the early 18th century, when the Marais went out of fashion, aristocrats built palatial new residences on the Faubourg St-Germain, the district developing around the site of the former city wall. It is still a well-bred part of the city, government ministries and foreign embassies colouring the area with flags and diplomatic plates. Many fine *hôtels particuliers* survive; glimpse their elegant entrance courtyards on rue de Grenelle, rue St-Dominique, rue de l'Université and rue de Varenne.

Just west of St-Germain, the 'Carré Rive Gauche' – the quadrangle enclosed by quai Voltaire, rue des Sts-Pères, rue du Bac and rue de l'Université – is filled with antiques shops. On rue des Sts-Pères, *chocolatier* **Debauve & Gallais** (no.30, 7th, 01.45.48.54.67, www.debauve-et-gallais.fr) has been making chocolates since 1800. Rue du Pré-aux-Clercs, named after a field where students used to duel, is now a favourite with fashion insiders. There are still students to be found on rue St-Guillaume, home of the prestigious **Fondation Nationale des Sciences-Politiques** (no.27), more commonly known as 'Sciences-Po'.

Rue de Montalembert is home to two of the Left Bank's most fashionable hotels: the **Hôtel Montalembert** (*see p362*) and the Hôtel Pont Royal, a gastronomic magnet ever since the addition of the trendy **Atelier de Joël Robuchon** (www.joel-robuchon.com). By the river, a Beaux-Arts train station – the towns once served still listed on the façade – houses the unmissable art collections of the **Musée d'Orsay**; outside on the esplanade are 19th-century bronze animal sculptures.

Next door is the lovely 1780s Hôtel de Salm, once the Swedish embassy and now home to the **Musée National de la Légion d'Honneur et des Ordres de Chevalerie** (2 rue de la Légion d'Honneur, 7th, 01.40.62.84.25, www.musee-legiondhonneur.fr), devoted to France's honours system since Louis XI. The Legion of Honour was established by Napoleon in 1802. Across the street, a modern footbridge, the Passerelle Solférino, crosses the Seine to the Tuileries. The fancy Hôtel Bouchardon today houses the **Musée Maillol**. Right beside its curved entrance, the Fontaine des Quatre Saisons by Edmé Bouchardon features statues of the seasons surrounding allegorical figures of Paris above the rivers Seine and Marne.

You'll have to wait for the open-house **Journées du Patrimoine** (*see p38*) to see the decorative interiors and private gardens of other *hôtels*, such as the **Hôtel de Villeroy** (Ministry of Agriculture; 78 rue de Varenne, 7th),

Hôtel **Boisgelin** (Italian Embassy; 51 rue de Varenne, 7th), **Hôtel d'Avaray** (Dutch ambassador's residence; 85 rue de Grenelle, 7th), **Hôtel d'Estrées** (Russian ambassador's residence; 79 rue de Grenelle, 7th) or **Hôtel de Monaco** (Polish Embassy; 57 rue St-Dominique, 7th). Among the most beautiful is the **Hôtel Matignon** (57 rue de Varenne, 7th), residence of the prime minister. It contains the biggest private garden in Paris. The Cité Varenne at no.51 is a lane of exclusive houses with private gardens.

Rue du Bac is home to the city's oldest and most elegant department store, **Le Bon Marché** ('the good bargain'), and to an unlikely pilgrimage spot, the **Chapelle de la Médaille Miraculeuse**. On nearby rue de Babylone, budget bistro **Au Babylone** (no.13, 7th, 01.45.48.72.13) has been serving up cheap lunches for decades, but the Théâtre de Babylone, where Beckett's *Waiting for Godot* was premiered in 1953, is long gone.

At the foot of boulevard St-Germain, facing place de la Concorde across the Seine, is the **Assemblée Nationale**, the lower house of the French parliament. Behind, elegant place du Palais-Bourbon leads into rue de Bourgogne, a rare commercial thoroughfare amid the official buildings, with some delectable pâtisseries.

Beside the Assemblée is the Foreign Ministry, often referred to by its address, 'quai d'Orsay'. Beyond it, a long, grassy esplanade leads up to golden-domed **Les Invalides**. The vast military hospital complex, with its Eglise du Dôme and St-Louis-des-Invalides churches, all built by Louis XIV, epitomises the official grandeur of the Sun King as expression of royal and military power. It now houses the **Musée de l'Armée**, as well as Napoleon's tomb inside the Eglise du Dôme. Stand with your back to the dome to survey the cherubim-laden Pont Alexandre III and the Grand and Petit Palais over the river, all put up for the 1900 Exposition Universelle.

Just beside Les Invalides is the **Musée National Rodin**, occupying the charming 18th-century Hôtel Biron and its romantic gardens. Many of Rodin's great sculptures, including the *Thinker*, the *Burghers of Calais* and the swarming *Gates of Hell*, are displayed in the building and around the gardens – as are those of his mistress, Camille Claudel.

Sights & Museums

FREE **Assemblée Nationale**
33 quai d'Orsay, 7th (www.assemblee-nationale.fr). M° Assemblée Nationale. **Map** p223 F1 ➊
Like the Sénat, the Assemblée Nationale (also known as the Palais Bourbon) is a royal building adapted for republicanism. It was built between 1722 and 1728 for the Duchesse de Bourbon, daughter of Louis XIV and Madame de Montespan, who also put up the neighbouring Hôtel de Lassay for her lover, the

Assemblée Nationale.

Marquis de Lassay. The *palais* was modelled on the Grand Trianon at Versailles, with a colonnaded *cour d'honneur* opening on to rue de l'Université and gardens running down to the Seine. The Prince de Condé extended the palace, linked the two *hôtels* and laid out place du Palais-Bourbon. The Greek temple-style façade facing Pont de la Concorde (the rear of the building) was added in 1806. Flanking this riverside façade are statues of four great statesmen: L'Hôpital, Sully, Colbert and Aguesseau. The Napoleonic frieze on the pediment was replaced by a monarchist one after the restoration: between 1838 and 1841, Cortot sculpted the figures of France, Power and Justice. After the Revolution, the palace became the meeting place for the Conseil des Cinq-Cents. It was the forerunner of the parliament's lower house, which set up here for good in 1827. Visits are by arrangement through a serving *député* (if you're French) or during the Journées du Patrimoine (*see p38*).

★ FREE Chapelle de la Médaille Miraculeuse

Couvent des Soeurs de St-Vincent-de-Paul, 140 rue du Bac, 7th (www.chapellenotredamedelamedaille miraculeuse.com). M° Sèvres Babylone. **Open** 7.45am-1pm, 2.30-7pm Mon, Wed-Sun; 7.45am-7pm Tue. **Admission** free. **Map** p223 G3 ❷

In 1830, saintly Catherine Labouré was said to have seen a vision of the Virgin, who told her to cast a medal that copied her appearance – standing on a globe with rays of light appearing from her outstretched hands. This kitsch chapel – murals, mosaics, statues and the embalmed bodies of Catherine and her mother superior – attracts two million pilgrims every year.

FREE Espace Fondation EDF

6 rue Récamier, 7th (http://fondation.edf.com). M° Sèvres Babylone. **Open** noon-7pm Tue-Sun. **Admission** free. **Map** p223 G3 ❸

This former electricity substation was constructed in 1910 under the guidance of architect Paul Friesé, known for his industrial-style buildings around Paris. Reconverted by EDF, the building has been used for exhibitions since 1990. Themes often deal with the environment or sustainable development.

★ Les Invalides & Musée de l'Armée

Esplanade des Invalides, 7th (08.10.11.33.99, www.invalides.org). M° La Tour Maubourg or Les Invalides. **Open** *Apr-Oct* 10am-6pm Mon, Wed-Sun (Dôme until 7pm July, Aug); 10am-9pm Tue. *Nov-Mar* 10am-5pm daily. **Admission** *Courtyard* free. *Musée de l'Armée & Eglise du Dôme* €9.50; €7.50 reductions; free under-18s, under-26s (EU citizens). PMP. **Map** p223 F2 ❹

Topped by its gilded dome, the Hôtel des Invalides was (and in part still is) a hospital. Commissioned by Louis XIV for wounded soldiers, it once housed as many as 6,000 invalids. Designed by Libéral Bruand (the foundations were laid in 1671) and completed by Jules Hardouin-Mansart, it's a magnificent monument to Louis XIV and Napoleon. Behind lines of cannon and bullet-shaped yews, the main (northern) façade has a relief of Louis XIV (Ludovicus Magnus) and the Sun King's sunburst. Wander through the main courtyard and you'll see grandiose arcades and a statue of Napoleon glaring down from the end; the dormer windows around the courtyards are sculpted to resemble suits of armour.

The complex contains two churches – or, rather, a sort of double church: the Eglise St-Louis was for the soldiers, the Eglise du Dôme for the king. An opening behind the altar connects the two. The long, barrel-vaulted nave of the church of St-Louis is hung with flags captured from enemy troops. Since 1840 the Baroque Eglise du Dôme has been dedicated to the worship of Napoleon, whose body was brought here from St Helena. On the ground floor, under a

EXPLORE

EXPLORE

dome painted by de la Fosse, Jouvenet and Coypel, are chapels featuring monuments to Vauban, Foch and Joseph Napoleon (Napoleon's older brother and King of Naples, Sicily and Spain). Napoleon II (King of Rome) is buried in the crypt opposite his father the emperor. Two dramatic black figures holding up the entrance to the crypt, the red porphyry tomb, the ring of giant figures, and the friezes and texts eulogising the emperor's heroic deeds give the measure of the cult of Napoleon, cherished in France for ruling large swaths of Europe and for creating an administrative and educational system that endures to this day.

The Invalides complex also houses the enormous Musée de l'Armée, in effect several museums in one. Even if militaria are not your thing, the building is splendid, and there's some fine portraiture, such as Ingres' *Emperor Napoleon on his Throne*. The Antique Armour wing is packed full of armour and weapons that look as good as new, from the 16th-century suit made for François I to cabinets full of swords, maces, crossbows and muskets and arquebuses. The Plans-Reliefs section is a collection of gorgeous 18th- and 19th-century scale models of French cities, used for military strategy; also here is a 17th-century model of Mont St-Michel, made by a monk from playing cards.

The World War I rooms bring the conflict into focus with uniforms, paintings, a scale model of a trench and, most sobering of all, white plastercasts of the hideously mutilated faces of two soldiers. The World War II wing covers the Resistance, the Battle of Britain and the war in the Pacific (there's a replica of Little Boy, the bomb dropped on Hiroshima), alternating artefacts with film footage. Also included in the entry price is the Historial Charles de Gaulle (closed Mon), an interactive multimedia space dedicated to the work of the founding President of the Fifth Republic.

Musée Maillol

59-61 rue de Grenelle, 7th (01.42.22.59.58, www.museemaillol.com). Mº Rue du Bac. **Open** 10.30am-7pm (last admission 6.15pm) Mon-Thur, Sat, Sun; 10.30am-9.30pm (last admission 8.45pm) Fri. **Admission** €13; €11 reductions; free under-11s. **Map** p223 G2 ❺

Dina Vierny was 15 when she met Aristide Maillol and became his principal model for the next decade, idealised in such sculptures as *Spring*, *Air* and *Harmony*. In 1995 she opened this delightful museum, exhibiting Maillol's drawings, engravings, pastels, tapestry panels, ceramics and early Nabis-related paintings, as well as the sculptures and terracottas that epitomise his calm, modern classicism. Vierny also set up a Maillol Museum in the Pyrenean village of Banyuls-sur-Mer. This Paris venue also has works by Picasso, Rodin, Gauguin, Degas and Cézanne, a whole room of Matisse drawings, rare Surrealist documents and works by naïve artists. Vierny has also championed

Kandinsky and Ilya Kabakov, whose *Communal Kitchen* installation recreates the atmosphere of Soviet domesticity. Monographic exhibitions are devoted to modern and contemporary artists. In early 2015, there was a fascinating exhibition, Les Borgias et leur Temps.

Musée National Rodin

Hôtel Biron, 79 rue de Varenne, 7th (01.44.18.61.10, www.musee-rodin.fr). Mº Varenne. **Open** 10am-5.45pm Tue, Thur-Sun; 10am-8.45pm Wed. **Admission** €9; €5-€7 reductions; free under-18s, under-26s (EU citizens), all 1st Sun of mth. PMP. *Gardens* €1-€2; free under-18s, under-26s (EU citizens). **Map** p223 F2 ❻

The Rodin museum occupies the *hôtel particulier* where the sculptor lived in the final years of his life. *The Kiss*, the *Cathedral*, the *Walking Man*, portrait busts and early terracottas are exhibited indoors, as are many of the individual figures or small groups that also appear on the *Gates of Hell*. Rodin's works are accompanied by several pieces by his mistress and pupil, Camille Claudel. The walls are hung with paintings by Van Gogh, Monet, Renoir, Carrière and Rodin himself. Most visitors have greatest affection for the gardens: look out for the *Burghers of Calais*, the *Gates of Hell* and the *Thinker*.

★ Musée d'Orsay

1 rue de la Légion-d'Honneur, 7th (01.40.49.48.14, www.musee-orsay.fr). Mº Solférino/RER Musée d'Orsay. **Open** 9.30am-6pm Tue, Wed, Fri-Sun; 9.30am-9.45pm Thur. **Admission** €11; €8.50 reductions; free under-18s, under-26s (EU citizens), all 1st Sun of mth. PMP. **Map** p223 G1 ❼

After partially closing for 18 months, the Musée d'Orsay reopened fully in 2012 to gasps of admiration. On arriving at the fifth-floor Impressionist galleries one is confronted with a huge, wide space where the giant clockface window, previously hidden by corridors, floods the dark room with light. The Impressionist galleries, previously a series of bland, skylit rooms that suffered from bottlenecks and overcrowding, have been utterly transformed with dark, moody colours such as anthracite, purple, vermillion and bottle-green. But it's not just the walls that make the paintings of Monet, Manet, Renoir and Cézanne sing out as if they had been painted yesterday. It is also the Solux lighting, which reveals every colour in the spectrum. The effect is extra-sensory: you can smell the surf of Monet's *Rough Sea at Etretat*, feel the heat of Renoir's surprising *Mosque in Algiers*, and taste the crispness of Pissarro's *White Freeze*, which hangs on a wall of winter paintings directly facing hot, southern scenes. This is part of a dynamic approach to hanging that throws out the traditional chronological or artist-by-artist approach to juxtapose different visions of the same theme. The seating is a work of art, too, with Tokujin Yoshioka's glass benches rippling in the centre of each room.

Restaurants

★ L'Arpège

84 rue de Varenne, 7th (01.47.05.09.06, www.alain-passard.com). M° Varenne. **Open** noon-2.30pm, 7-10.30pm Mon-Fri. **Main courses** €92-€185. **Prix fixe** *Lunch* €140. *Dinner* €320. **Map** p223 F2 ❽ **Haute cuisine**

Assuming you can swallow an exceptionally high bill, chances are you'll have a spectacular time at chef Alain Passard's establishment. His attempt to plane down and simplify the haute experience – the chrome-armed chairs look like something from the former GDR – seems a misstep; but then something edible comes to the table, such as tiny smoked potatoes served with a horseradish mousseline. A main course of sautéed free-range chicken with a roasted shallot, an onion, potato *mousseline* and pan juices is the apotheosis of comfort food.

Clover

5 rue Perronet, 7th (01.75.50.00.05, www.jeanfrancoispiege.com/fr). M° Rue du Bac. **Open** noon-2.30pm, 7.30-10.30pm Tue-Sat. **Prix fixe** *Lunch* €28, €42. *Dinner* €58, €73. **Map** p223 H2 ❾ **Bistro** *See p226* **In Clover**.

Garance

34 rue St-Dominique, 7th (01.45.55.27.56, www.garance-saintdominique.fr). M° Invalides. **Open** noon-2pm, 7.30-10pm Mon-Fri. **Main courses** €36-€50. **Prix fixe** *Lunch* €39, €68. *Dinner* €78. **Map** p223 F1 ❿ **Bistro**

Guillaume Muller (former sommelier at l'Arpège) chose a very upmarket area in which to open the red-hued Garance. There's an elegant, light-filled dining room on the first floor, and downstairs a classic bar where you can eat if you're alone or just want to watch the world go by, and a tiny open kitchen. At lunchtime, the restaurant manages to please both busy workers and relaxed bons vivants with a solid €34 menu. The dishes are enormously generous, and the excellent ingredients preserve their best flavours – strong and punchy (duck confit rubbed with salt, beef tartare with smoked egg yolk), or more adventurous (scallops and monkfish finished with bone marrow). The desserts play with sweet and savoury flavours (chocolate, butternut and vanilla tart, pear sorbet). Wines by the glass and bottle are well chosen. The service fits the venue, careful without overdoing it, relaxed without being over-familiar.

Gaya Rive Gauche

44 rue du Bac, 7th (01.45.44.73.73, www.pierre-gagnaire.com). M° Rue du Bac. **Open** 7-11pm Mon; noon-2.30pm, 7-11pm Tue-Fri; noon-3pm, 7-11pm Sat. **Main courses** €30-€49. **Prix fixe** *Lunch* €65. **Map** p223 G2 ⓫ **Seafood**

Superchef Pierre Gagnaire runs this comparatively affordable fish restaurant. The menu enumerates ingredients without much clue as to how they are put together, though the helpful waiters will explain if you don't like a surprise. The Fats Waller, for instance, turns out to be a soup of grilled red peppers with a bloody mary sorbet in the centre and daubs of quinoa, basmati rice and Chinese spinach.

EXPLORE

Musée d'Orsay.

Cafés & Bars

Le Coutume Café

47 rue de Babylone, 7th (01.45.51.50.47, www.coutumecafe.com). M° Saint-François-Xavier or Sèvres-Babylone. **Open** 8am-7pm Tue-Fri; 10am-7pm Sat, Sun. **Map** p223 F3 ⑫

Coutume is part café, part *torréfacteur*, supplying roasted beans to more than 60 bars, restaurants and hotels across the city. Coutume serves breakfast and lunch, with the emphasis very much on healthy organic products and plenty of vegetarian options. It's also one of the rare coffee bars to sell artisan beers and a small selection of wines. In fact, the vibe here is similar to a wine bar with the barista playing sommelier, explaining the plantations where different beans come from and proposing offbeat mixes.

Rosa Bonheur sur Seine

37 quai d'Orsay, 7th (01.47.53.66.92, www.rosabonheur.fr). M° Invalides. **Open** noon-10pm Wed-Sun. **Map** p223 F1 ⑬

Following Rosa Bonheur in the heart of the Parc Buttes-Chaumont and En Attendant Rosa on the banks of the Seine, we now have Rosa Bonheur sur Seine: a *péniche* moored hard by Pont Alexandre

IN CLOVER

Jean-François Piège's tiny new restaurant is a taste sensation.

Clover (*see p225*), which opened in December 2014, carries a heavy load of expectation on its very narrow shoulders. Not only does it have the thrill of being the love child of highly sought-after chef and restaurateur Jean-François Piège (whose eponymous restaurant at the Hôtel Thoumieux was awarded two Michelin stars in 2011) and his wife Elodie, it has received almost universal raves in the press – and has a long waiting list for a table.

What it offers is an intimate exploration of Piège's highly accomplished contemporary European cooking. Wonderfully, it manages to be sustaining, adventurous, healthy and even fun, all at the same time. The menus are €28 or €42 at lunch, and €58 or €73 at dinner. And though the great man might not be at the stove himself, the food won't disappoint. Intense, smoky green aubergine and black sesame purée comes with a tangle of herbs and crispy quinoa; a single scallop on its shell perches on a blistering hot chunk of granite;

chicken bouillon with toasted Jerusalem artichokes is the perfect gourmet version of a fragrant, comforting winter soup. Main courses are equally rewarding: pollack comes under a trompe l'oeil potato shell shaped like the hull of a boat, and veal sweetbreads are beautifully crisp, nestled around handmade pasta with fine green olives and pecorino. The hay-flavoured ice-cream with sweet baked butternut squash makes a sublime finish.

So far, so lovely. What doesn't quite work is the space's incredibly tight dimensions. Much has been made of the expensive understated decor. And it's perfectly charming for the kitchen to be not so much open as integrated into the dining area, with chefs plating up next to your left ear. But if you need to get up during your meal, you have to shuffle your table away from the single line of banquettes. And you'd better like your neighbours, as you're basically sitting on top of each other in the crush to get one of the sought-after 18 places.

EXPLORE

III. The boat, all wood and glass, offers the calming swell of the water and an unbeatable view of the Bateaux Mouches sailing by. Sip Pernod (€3 a glass) and tuck into fresh sandwiches with interesting fillings (sea urchin taramasalata, €4.50), perfect for a picnic among the barrels on deck while watching the sunset.

Shops & Services

★ Alain Mikli
74 rue des Sts-Pères, 7th (01.45.49.40.00, www. mikli.fr). M° Sèvres Babylone. **Open** 10am-7pm Mon-Sat. **Map** p223 G2 ㉔ **Accessories**
Cult French eyewear designer Mikli uses cellulose acetate, a blend of wood and cotton sliced from blocks. At his flagship Starck-designed boutique, the frames are neatly laid out in a glass counter like designer sweeties.
Other locations throughout the city.

★ L'Artisan Parfumeur
24 bd Raspail, 7th (01.42.22.23.32, www. artisanparfumeur.com). M° Rue du Bac. **Open** 10.30am-7.30pm Mon-Sat. **Map** p223 G2 ㉕ **Health & beauty**
Among the scented candles, potpourri and charms, you'll find some of the finest perfume Paris can offer – Mûres et Musc has been a bestseller for more than two decades.
Other locations throughout the city.

★ Le Bon Marché
24 rue de Sèvres, 7th (01.44.39.80.00, www. bonmarche.fr). M° Sèvres Babylone. **Open** 10am-8pm Mon-Wed, Sat; 10am-9pm Thur, Fri. **Map** p223 G3 ㉙ **Department store**
The city's oldest department store, which opened in 1848, is also its most swish and user-friendly, thanks to an extensive redesign by LVMH. Luxury boutiques, Dior and Chanel among them, take pride of place on the ground floor; escalators designed by Andrée Putman take you up to the fashion floor, which has an excellent selection of global designer labels, from Lanvin to Claudie Pierlot. Designer names also abound in Balthazar, the prestigious menswear section.
▶ *For top-notch nibbles, try the adjoining Grande Epicerie food hall (01.44.39.81.00, www.lagrandeepicerie.fr, 8.30am-9pm Mon-Sat).*

Bonton
82 rue de Grenelle, 7th (01.44.39.09.20, www. bonton.fr). M° Rue du Bac. **Open** 10am-7pm Mon-Sat. **Map** p223 G2 ㉗ **Children**
At this concept store for kids and trendy parents, T-shirts and trousers come in rainbow colours, and at pretty steep prices too. Furniture and accessories are also available, as is a children's hairdresser.
Other location 5 bd des Filles du Calvaire, 3rd (01.42.72.34.69).

▶ *The Bonton Bazar store (84bis rue de Grenelle, 7th, 01.42.22.77.69, www.bonton.fr) offers a range of cute kids' homeware for bedroom, bathroom, kitchen and 'library'.*

Christian Liaigre
42 rue du Bac, 7th (01.53.63.33.66, www. christian-liaigre.fr). M° Rue du Bac. **Open** 10am-7pm Mon-Sat. Closed 3wks Aug. **Map** p223 G2 ㉙ **Homewares**
This French interior decorator fitted out Marc Jacobs's boutiques. His showroom displays his elegant lighting and furniture designs.
Other locations 61 rue de Varenne, 7th (01.47.53.78.76); 33 rue de Verneuil, 7th (01.40.15.55.90).

Deyrolle
46 rue du Bac, 7th (01.42.22.30.07, www. deyrolle.com). M° Rue du Bac. **Open** 10am-1pm, 2-7pm Mon; 10am-7pm Tue-Sat. **Map** p223 G2 ㉙ **Gifts & souvenirs**
Opened in 1831 by Jean-Baptiste Deyrolle, a taxidermist and avid traveller, this shop has always been a curiosity, with its bizarre menagerie of lions, giraffes, polar bears, butterflies and bugs. After a fire swept through the shop in 2008, Parisians came together to save the place. It remains a great place to escape the city, buy a tiger for the living room or crank up your kids' imagination.

Editions de Parfums Frédéric Malle
37 rue de Grenelle, 7th (01.42.22.76.40, www. fredericmalle.com). M° Rue du Bac or St-Sulpice. **Open** noon-7pm Mon; 11am-7pm Tue-Sat. **Map** p223 G2 ㉚ **Health & beauty**
Choose from a range of eight perfumes by Frédéric Malle, former consultant to Hermès and Lacroix. Carnal Flower is seduction in a bottle.
Other locations 21 rue du Mont-Thabor, 1st (01.42.22.16.89); 140 av Victor-Hugo, 16th (01.45.05.39.02).

Epicerie Générale
43 rue de Verneuil, 7th (01.42.60.51.78, www. epiceriegenerale.fr). M° Solférino or Rue du Bac. **Open** 11am-8pm Mon-Fri; 10.30am-7pm Sat. **Map** p223 G1 ㉛ **Food & drink**
Maud, Claude and Lucio opened Epicerie Générale in 2011. Here, the capital's gourmands can pick up their cheese, charcuterie, fruit and vegetables, along with local products such as Miel Béton ('concrete honey'), made on the roofs of Saint-Denis. L'Epicerie Générale is also developing its own range of branded products, such as La Strix, the first organic French vodka.

★ Fromagerie Quatrehomme
62 rue de Sèvres, 7th (01.47.34.33.45, www. quatrehomme.fr). M° Duroc or Vaneau. **Open** 9am-7.45pm Tue-Sat. **Map** p223 F3 ㉜ **Food & drink**

Gâteaux Thoumieux.

Marie Quatrehomme runs this *fromagerie*. Justly famous for her beaufort and st-marcellin, she also sells such specialities as goat's cheese with pesto.

Gâteaux Thoumieux
58 rue St-Dominique, 7th (01.45.51.12.12, www.thoumieux.fr). M° Latour Maubourg. **Open** 10am-8pm Mon, Wed-Sat; 8.30am-5pm Sun. **Map** p223 E1 ㉓ **Food & drink** *See p230* **Seventh Heaven.**

EXPLORE

Iris
28 rue de Grenelle, 7th (01.42.22.89.81, www.iris shoes.com). M° Rue du Bac or St-Sulpice. **Open** 10.30am-7pm Mon-Sat. **Map** p223 G2 ㉔ **Fashion** This white boutique stocks shoes by the likes of Marc Jacobs, John Galliano and Viktor & Rolf.

★ Paul & Joe
64 rue des Sts-Pères, 7th (01.42.22.47.01, www.paulandjoe.com). M° Rue du Bac or St-Germain-des-Prés. **Open** 10am-7pm Mon-Sat. **Map** p223 H2 ㉕ **Fashion** Fashionistas simply adore Sophie Albou's retro-styled creations, dressing Paris's leggy young things in a range of winter shorts, colourful minidresses and voluminous trousers, and their intellectual paramours in slouchy woollens, tailored jackets and chunky boots.
Other locations throughout the city.

Richart
258 bd St-Germain, 7th (01.45.55.66.00, www.chocolats-richart.com). M° Solférino. **Open** 10am-2.30pm, 3-7pm Mon; 10am-7pm Tue-Sat. **Map** p223 G1 ㉖ **Food & drink** Each of Richart's stunning chocolate *ganaches* has an intricate design, packages look like jewel boxes, and every purchase comes with a tract on how best to savour the stuff.

Ryst Dupeyron
79 rue du Bac, 7th (01.45.48.80.93, www. vintageandco.com). M° Rue du Bac. **Open**

12.30-7.30pm Mon; 10.30am-7.30pm Tue-Sat. Closed 2wks Aug. **Map** p223 G2 ㉗ **Food & drink** The Dupeyrons have been selling armagnac for four generations. Treasures include 200 fine Bordeaux wines and an extensive range of vintage port.

★ Sennelier
3 quai Voltaire, 7th (01.42.60.72.15, www. magasinsennelier.fr). M° St-Germain-des-Prés. **Open** 2-6.30pm Mon; 10am-12.45pm, 2-6.30pm Tue-Sat. **Map** p223 H2 ㉘ **Gifts & souvenirs** Old-fashioned colour merchant Sennelier sells oil paints, watercolours and pastels, rare pigments, primed canvases, varnishes and paper.
Other location 4bis rue de la Grande-Chaumière, 6th (01.46.33.72.39).

Sentou Galerie
26 bd Raspail, 7th (01.45.49.00.05, www.sentou. fr). M° Rue du Bac. **Open** 11am-7pm Tue-Sat. **Map** p223 G2 ㉙ **Homewares** A trend-setting shop for colourful tableware and furniture: painted Chinese flasks, vases and so on.
Other location 29 rue François-Miron, 4th (01.42.78.50.60).

WEST & SOUTH OF LES INVALIDES

In the 7th & 15th arrondissements.

South-west of the Invalides is the enormous **Ecole Militaire** (av de La Motte-Picquet, 7th), the military academy built by Louis XV to educate the children of penniless officers; it would later train Napoleon. The severe neoclassical building, designed by Jacques Ange Gabriel, is still used by the army and closed to the public.

From the north-western side of the Ecole Militaire begins the vast Champ de Mars, a market garden converted into a military drilling ground in the 18th century. It has long been home to the most celebrated Paris monument of all, the **Eiffel Tower**. At the south-eastern end of the

Champ de Mars stands the Mur pour la Paix ('wall for peace'), erected in 2000 to articulate hopes for global peace. South-east of the Ecole are the Y-shaped **UNESCO** building, built in 1958, and the modernist Ministry of Labour. Fashionable apartments line broad avenue Bosquet and avenue Suffren, though there's much architectural eclecticism in the area: look at the pseudo-Gothic and pseudo-Renaissance houses on avenue de Villars; Lavirotte's fabulous art nouveau doorway at 27 avenue Rapp; and the striking **Notre Dame de l'Arche de l'Alliance** church (81 rue d'Alleray, 01.56.56.62.56, www.ndarche. org), completed in 1998. For signs of life, visit the Saxe-Breteuil street market. The upper reaches of rue Cler contain classy food shops.

Downstream from the Eiffel Tower is the **Musée du Quai Branly**, which opened in 2006. A short way further on, the high-tech **Maison de la Culture du Japon** stands near Pont Bir-Hakeim on quai Branly. Beyond, the 15th-arrondissement Fronts de Seine riverfront, with its tower-block developments, had some of the worst architecture of the 1970s inflicted upon it. The adjacent Beaugrenelle shopping centre has always been rather dingy, but the mall reopened in late 2013 with a spectacularly modern redesign and 120 shops to browse. Further west, things look up: the sophisticated former headquarters of the Canal+ TV channel (2 rue des Cévennes, 15th), designed by architect Richard Meier, is surrounded by fine modern housing; and the pleasant **Parc André Citroën**, created in the 1990s on the site of the former Citroën car works, runs down to the Seine.

Sights & Museums

★ Eiffel Tower

Champ de Mars, 7th (08.92.70.12.39, www.tour-eiffel.fr). Mº Bir-Hakeim/RER Champ de Mars Tour Eiffel. **Open** *By lift* Mid June-Aug 9am-12.45am daily (last ascent 11pm). Sept-mid June 9.30am-11.45pm daily (last ascent 10.30pm). *By stairs* (1st & 2nd levels) Mid June-Aug 9am-12.45am (last ascent midnight). Sept-mid June 9.30am-6.30pm (last ascent 6pm). **Admission** *By stairs* €5; €3.50-€4 reductions; free under-4s. *By lift* (1st & 2nd level) €9; €4.50-€7 reductions; (3rd level) €15.50; €11-€13.50 reductions; free under-4s. **Map** p222 C2 ❸⓪

No building better symbolises Paris than the Eiffel Tower. Maupassant claimed he left Paris because of it, William Morris visited daily to avoid having to see it from afar – and it was originally meant to be a temporary structure. The cast-iron tower was built for the 1889 World Fair and the centenary of the 1789 Revolution by engineer Gustave Eiffel, who made use of new technology that was already popular in iron-framed buildings. Construction took more than two years and used some 18,000 pieces of metal and

2,500,000 rivets. And not much has changed since – until now. In an attempt to brighten up the rather dingy first floor and make it as much of an attraction as the summit itself, the Eiffel Tower has undergone its third facelift since opening 125 years ago – and what a facelift: the €25m revamp is radical, to say the least, with the central void being filled in with a solid glass floor surrounded by inclined safety barriers, so visitors are able to peer over and eyeball the queues of tourists 57m below. The project features other future-proofing ideas too, including environmentally friendly lighting and power, new teaching areas and the introduction of full disabled access to the first floor. Having welcomed more than 200 million people, the Dame de Fer is finally shedding a few rivets in favour of a more 21st-century style.

FREE Maison de la Culture du Japon

101bis quai Branly, 15th (01.44.37.95.01, www.mcjp.asso.fr). Mº Bir-Hakeim/RER Champ de Mars Tour Eiffel. **Open** noon-7pm Tue, Wed, Fri, Sat; noon-8pm Thur. Closed Aug. **Admission** free. **Map** p222 C2 ❸❶

Constructed in 1996 by the architectural partnership of Kenneth Armstrong and Masayuki Yamanaka, this glass-fronted Japanese cultural centre screens films and puts on a wide selection of exhibitions and plays. It also contains a library, an authentic Japanese tea pavilion on the roof and a well-stocked bookshop and gift shop.

Musée des Egouts

Entrance opposite 93 quai d'Orsay, by Pont de l'Alma, 7th (01.53.68.27.81). Mº Alma Marceau/RER Pont de l'Alma. **Open** 11am-4pm Mon-Wed, Sat, Sun (until 5pm May-Sept). Closed 2wks Jan. **Admission** €4.40; €3.60 reductions; free under-6s. **No credit cards. Map** p222 D1 ❸❷

For centuries, the main source of drinking water in Paris was the Seine, which was also the main sewer. Construction of an underground sewerage system began at the time of Napoleon. Today, the Egouts de Paris constitutes a smelly museum; each sewer in the 2,100km (1,305-mile) system is marked with a replica of the street sign above.

★ Musée du Quai Branly

37 quai Branly, 7th (01.56.61.70.00, www.quaibranly.fr). RER Pont de l'Alma. **Open** 11am-7pm Tue, Wed, Sun; 11am-9pm Thur-Sat. **Admission** €9; €7 reductions; free under-18s, under-26s (EU citizens), all 1st Sun of mth. *With admission to temporary exhibition* €11; €9 reductions; free under-18s, all 1st Sun of mth. **Map** p222 D1 ❸❸

Surrounded by trees on the banks of the Seine, this museum, which is housed in an extraordinary building by Jean Nouvel, is a vast showcase for non-European cultures. Dedicated to the ethnic art of Africa, Oceania, Asia and the Americas, it joins together the collections of the Musée des

EXPLORE

EXPLORE

SEVENTH HEAVEN

Dip your toes in the revamped Berges de Seine.

Parisians have always loved their city's quays: over the centuries they've built iconic monuments along them, stretched bridges between them and written songs about them (check out Lucienne Delyle's 1939 rendition of 'Sur les Quais du Vieux Paris'). But in the 1960s, certain stretches were turned into roads that distanced locals and visitors from the banks and some of the best views in town.

Now the city council has given the quayside between Quai Anatole France and Quai Branly in the 7th back to the people by converting the roads into year-round, car-free promenades known as Les Berges (www.lesberges.fr), with floating gardens, a dramatic *emmarchement* (an apparently airborne flight of stairs connecting the upper and lower quays), activities for families, outdoor stages, restaurants, bars and cycle routes.

Outdoors is the name of the game for families with activities including 100m sprinting lanes, hopscotch zones, teepees, climbing walls, summer terraces filled with board games and renovated cargo crates called 'Zzz' that double as private chill-out cabins (available for hire). During spring and summer, a stream of free open-air concerts are performed on a stage called the Mikado, and throughout the year you can enrol for free yoga, tai chi, fitness and zumba classes organised for hundreds of people at a time.

A mix of seasonal and permanent eateries pepper the banks, too, including food truck Mozza & Co (www.mozzaandco.it) selling some of the finest mozzarella-based dishes in town; Rosa Bonheur sur Seine, a spin-off of Rosa Bonheur (*see p226*); and neighbouring Le Flow (www.flow-paris.com), a café with a coveted summer 'beach' terrace overlooking the river. And if it's a river dance you're after, one all-year-rounder to look out for is über-trendy Le Faust (www.faustparis.fr). Iranian businessman Addy Bakhtiar's latest project beneath Pont Alexandre III gives the Showcase a run for its money, with chic surroundings and champagne aplenty.

Les Berges are near a seventh heaven of another kind: Jean-François Piège's stunning new pastry shop, Gâteaux Thoumieux (*see p228*). Tuck into the likes of *kouign amann* (a buttery, sugary Breton cake) and indulgent chocolate éclairs, before heading back to the sprinting lanes to work it all off.

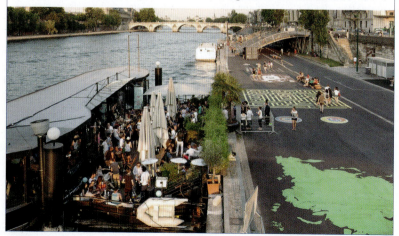

Arts d'Afrique et d'Océanie and the Laboratoire d'Ethnologie du Musée de l'Homme, as well as contemporary indigenous art. Treasures include a tenth-century anthropomorphic Dogon statue from Mali, a 19th-century Hawaiian chief's helmet, a Vietnamese bronze funeral drum, Gabonese masks, Aztec statues, Peruvian feather tunics and rare frescoes from Ethiopia.

FREE Musée Valentin Haüy

5 rue Duroc, 7th (01.44.49.27.27, www.avh. asso.fr). M° Duroc. **Open** 2.30-5pm Tue, Wed (closed July-mid Sept). **Admission** free. **Map** p223 F3 ❸

This tiny museum is devoted to the history of braille. You can explore on your own with the aid of French, English or braille explanatory texts, or allow the curator, Noêle Roy, to show you round. She will give a tour in English if preferred. The first exhibit is a shocking print, depicting the fairground freak show that inspired Valentin Haüy to devote his life to educating not only the blind, but also the public who came to laugh at the likes of this blind orchestra forced to perform in dunce's hats.

FREE Parc André Citroën

Rue Balard, rue St-Charles or quai Citroën, 15th. M° Balard or Javel. **Open** 8am-dusk Mon-Fri; 9am-dusk Sat, Sun, public hols. **Map** p222 A5 ❸

This park is a fun, postmodern version of a French formal garden. It comprises glasshouses, computerised fountains, waterfalls, a wilderness and themed gardens, and is currently being extended. A tethered helium balloon takes visitors up for panoramic views. If the weather looks unreliable, call 01.44.26.20.00 or visit www.ballondeparis.com to check the programme.

FREE UNESCO

7 pl de Fontenoy, 7th (01.45.68.10.00, tours (book in advance) visits@unesco.org, www.unesco.org). M° Ecole Militaire. **Admission** free. **Map** p223 E3 ❸

The Y-shaped UNESCO headquarters, built in 1958, is home to a swarm of international diplomats. It's worth visiting for the sculptures and paintings – by Picasso, Arp, Giacometti, Moore, Calder and Miró – and for the Japanese garden. Tours need to be reserved months in advance.

FREE Village Suisse

78 av de Suffren or 54 av de La Motte-Picquet, 15th (www.villagesuisse.com). M° La Motte Picquet Grenelle. **Open** 10.30am-7pm Mon, Thur-Sun. **Map** p222 D3 ❸

The mountains and waterfalls that were created for the Swiss Village at the 1900 Exposition Universelle are long gone, but the village still lives on. The street level has now been colonised by some 150 boutiques offering various high-quality, pricey antiques and collectibles.

Restaurants

Le 144 Petrossian

144 rue de l'Université, 7th (01.44.11.32.32, www. petrossian.fr). M° La Tour Maubourg. **Open** 12.15-2.30pm, 7.30-10.30pm Tue-Sat. **Main courses** €35. **Prix fixe** *Lunch* €35. *Dinner* €66, €84, €98. **Map** p223 E1 ❸ **Russian**

At this famed caviar house you'll find Russian specialities such as blinis, salmon and caviar from the Petrossian boutique downstairs, plus preparations and spices from all over the world. You might start with a divine risotto made with carnaroli rice, codfish caviar and parmesan. In similar Med-meets-Russia vein are such main courses as roast sea bream with a lemon-vodka sauce.

★ L'Ami Jean

27 rue Malar, 7th (01.47.05.86.89, www.ami jean.eu). M° Ecole Militaire. **Open** noon-2.30pm, 7pm-midnight Tue-Sat. Closed Aug. **Main courses** *Dinner* €40. **Prix fixe** *Lunch* €35, €42, €55. *Dinner* €78. **Map** p223 E1 ❸ **Bistro**

This long-running Basque address is an ongoing hit thanks to chef Stéphane Jégo. Excellent bread from baker Jean-Luc Poujauran is a perfect nibble when slathered with a tangy, herby *fromage blanc* – as is a starter of sautéed baby squid on a bed of ratatouille. Tender veal shank comes de-boned with a lovely side of baby onions and broad beans with tiny cubes of ham, and house-salted cod is soaked, sautéed and doused with an elegant vinaigrette. There's a great wine list, and some lovely Brana eau de vie should you decide to linger.

€ Le Bistro

17 rue Pérignon, 15th (01.45.66.84.03). M° Ségur. **Open** 8am-7pm Mon-Fri; Sat by reservation only. **Main courses** €12-€15. **Prix fixe** €17. **Map** p223 E3 ❹ **Bistro**

At first glance there is nothing to distinguish this corner bistro from hundreds of other cafés in Paris. In the front room, with its wood-panelled ceiling, are a plastic-topped bar and a few bare tables with black banquettes, and in the back is a larger room with red-and-white checked tablecloths. Then you see the plates going by, each one – from the goat's cheese salad to the *pavé de rumsteak* – loaded with golden fried potato rounds or hand-cut chips. This is the kind of neighbourhood bistro you had almost given up hope of finding in Paris.

★ Au Bon Accueil

14 rue de Monttessuy, 7th (01.47.05.46.11, www. aubonaccueilparis.com). M° Alma Marceau. **Open** noon-2.30pm, 7-10.30pm Mon-Fri. Closed 3wks Aug. **Main courses** €36-€48. **Prix fixe** €35, €55. **Map** p222 D1 ❹ **Bistro**

Keita Kitamura turns out the beautiful food here. Perhaps most impressive is his elegant use of little-known fish, such as grey mullet and meagre

EXPLORE

EXPLORE

(*maigre*), rather than the usual endangered species. The €35 lunch menu might highlight such posh ingredients as *suprême de poulet noir du Cros de la Géline*, free-range chicken raised on a farm run by two former cabaret singers. But the biggest surprise comes with desserts, worthy of the finest pastry shops. In summer, book a table on the pavement terrace with its view of the Eiffel Tower.

D'Chez Eux

2 av de Lowendal, 7th (01.47.05.52.55, www. chezeux.com). M° Ecole Militaire. **Open** noon-2pm, 7-11pm daily. Closed Aug. **Main courses** €29-€58. **Prix fixe** *Lunch* €29, €34 Mon-Fri; €44 Sat, Sun. **Map** p223 E2 ❷ **Bistro**

Arm yourself with serious stamina for a meal at this jovial south-western *auberge*, which looks touristy with its red-and-white checked tablecloths but attracts *bons vivants* from the neighbourhood. First come the help-yourself lyonnais-style 'salads' (cooked beetroot, lentils, celeriac rémoulade, ratatouille, etc), before hearty main dishes such as cassoulet or calf's liver with sherry vinegar. The heaving dessert cart will ensure that you waddle out overfed but happy.

Les Cocottes

135 rue St-Dominique, 7th (01.45.55.15.05, www.maisonconstant.com). M° Ecole Militaire/ RER Pont de l'Alma. **Open** noon-11pm daily. **Main courses** €16-€29. **Map** p222 D2 ❸ **Bistro**

Christian Constant has found the perfect recipe for pleasing Parisians at this no-reservations bistro: a flexible menu of salads, soups, *verrines* (light dishes served in jars) and *cocottes* (served in cast-iron pots), all at bargain prices – for this neighbourhood. Service is swift and the food satisfying, though the *vraie salade César Ritz*, which contains hard-boiled egg, shouldn't be confused with US-style Caesar salad. Soups such as an iced pea *velouté* are spot-on, and *cocottes* range from sea bream with ratatouille to potatoes stuffed with pig's trotter.

★ David Toutain

29 rue Surcouf, 7th (01.45.50.11.10, www. davidtoutain.com). M° Invalides or La Tour Maubourg. **Open** noon-2.30pm, 8-10pm Mon-Fri. **Prix fixe** *Lunch* from €45. *Dinner* €72, €105, €165. **Map** p223 E1 ❹ **Bistro**

Eager journalists have already spilled a lot of ink over chef David Toutain's eponymous restaurant since it opened in December 2013. Toutain knows how to cook up a storm out of anything from Granny Smith apples to lemon, parmesan and asparagus, and accompanies each dish with a lively description of the recipe. At times, his cuisine is surprising – salsify in a white chocolate sauce, anybody? – yet the combinations always make sense, and at their best treat your taste buds to an entirely novel experience. The atmosphere never suffers from the stuffiness that mars some restaurants of this calibre. Somehow, everyone seems happy and laid-back. The casual vibe is infectious, and even the steep bill isn't enough to dissipate it. If you need convincing that class and fun aren't mutually exclusive, this is the place to come.

La Gauloise

59 av de la Motte-Picquet, 15th (01.47.34.11.64). M° La Motte-Picquet Grenelle. **Open** noon-2.30pm, 7-11pm daily. **Main courses** €22-€33. **Prix fixe** €24.50, €29.50. **Map** p222 D3 ❹ **Bistro**

This restaurant is chic, calm and welcoming, long regulated by the etiquette of the Parisian bourgeoisie (Mitterand was a longstanding customer). It's done out in immaculate taste (long dark wood bar, plaster mouldings, red velvet banquettes), with an eye to discretion (well-spaced tables throughout multiple rooms). The cooking has kept up with the times, but never goes too far: soft-boiled eggs, a legendary *pot-au-feu*, Aubrac beef, sole meunière, corn-fed poultry with ceps, soufflés and profiteroles.

★ Jules Verne

Pilier Sud, Eiffel Tower, 7th (01.45.55.61.44, www.lejulesverne-paris.com). M° Bir Hakeim or RER Tour Eiffel. **Open** noon-1.30pm, 7-9.30pm daily. **Main courses** €74-€92. **Prix fixe** *Lunch* €105, €190, €230. *Dinner* €190, €230. **Map** p223 C2 ❹ **Haute cuisine**

You have to have courage to take on the Eiffel Tower, but Alain Ducasse has done just that. He has transformed the cuisine and brought in designer Patrick Jouin. Meanwhile, Ducasse protégé Pascal Féraud updates French classics, combining all the grand ingredients you'd expect with light, modern textures. Try dishes like lamb with artichokes or turbot with champagne zabaglione. Book ahead.

Les Ombres

27 quai Branly, 7th (01.47.53.68.00, www. lesombres-restaurant.com). M° Alma-Marceau. **Open** noon-2.30pm, 7-11pm daily. **Main courses** €25-€42. **Prix fixe** *Lunch* €32, €42. *Dinner* €68, €95. **Map** p222 D1 ❹ **Bistro**

The view of the Eiffel Tower at night would be reason enough to come to this glass-and-iron restaurant on the top floor of the Musée du Quai Branly, but the food also demands that you sit up and take notice. In keeping with its location, the menu is themed by continent, providing the chance to sample everything from tabouleh to NY strip steak.

Il Vino

13 bd de La Tour-Maubourg, 7th (01.44.11.72.00, www.ilvinobyenricobernardo.com). M° La Tour-Maubourg. **Open** 12.30-2pm, 7pm-midnight Mon-Fri; 7pm-midnight Sat. **Main courses** €12. **Prix fixe** *Lunch* €29, €38. *Dinner* €75, €95. **Map** p222 E1 **48 Italian**

Enrico Bernardo, youngest winner of the World's Best Sommelier award, runs this restaurant where food plays second fiddle to wine. You are presented with nothing more than a wine list. Each of 15 wines by the glass is matched with a surprise dish, or the chef can build a meal around a bottle of your choice.

Cafés & Bars

Le Café du Marché

38 rue Cler, 7th (01.47.05.51.27). M° Ecole Militaire. **Open** 7am-midnight Mon-Sat; 7am-8pm Sun. **Map** p223 E2 **49**

This well-loved address is frequented by trendy locals, shoppers hunting down a particular type of cheese and tourists who've managed to make it this far from the Eiffel Tower. Its *pichets* of decent house plonk always go down a treat.

Shops & Services

Les Délices d'Orient

52 av Emile-Zola, 15th (01.45.79.10.00). M° Charles Michels. **Open** 7am-8pm Tue-Sun. **Map** p222 B4 **50 Food & drink**

The shelves here groan beneath the weight of stuffed aubergines, halva, falafel and all manner of Middle Eastern delicacies.

Other location 14 rue des Quatre-Frères-Peignot, 15th (01.45.77.82.93).

L'Epicerie du Père Claude

4 rue du Général de Castelnau, 15th (01.47.34.04.04, www.epicerieduperedaude.com). M° La Motte-Picquet Grenelle. **Open** 10am-9.30pm Tue-Sat; 10am-3pm Sun. **Map** p222 D3 **51 Food & drink**

Père Claude's three businesses are just a few steps from one another: the historic restaurant run by Père Claude himself since 1988, a deli opened in 2009, and a new gourmet burger place. The deli is top quality, its shelves loaded with carefully sourced ingredients (rock salt, fine spices), gourmet conserves, sauces and home-made products: brie with truffles, terrines, sausages, merguez, plus tarts, pâtés and foie gras.

Marie-Anne Cantin

12 rue du Champ-de-Mars, 7th (01.45.50.43.94, www.cantin.fr). M° Ecole Militaire. **Open** 2-7.30pm Mon; 8.30am-7.30pm Tue-Sat; 8.30am-1.30pm Sun. **Map** p223 E2 **52 Food & drink**

Cantin, a defender of unpasteurised cheese and supplier to many posh Paris restaurants, offers aged *chèvres* and amazing morbier, mont d'or and comté.

Michel Chaudun

149 rue de l'Université, 7th (01.47.53.74.40). M° La Tour-Maubourg or RER Pont de l'Alma. **Open** 9.30am-12.30pm, 1-6pm Mon; 9.15am-7pm Tue-Sat. **Map** p223 E1 **53 Food & drink**

Chocoholics from the nearby Assemblée Nationale pop into Michel Chaudun's shop throughout the day. But whether you're a famous politician or not, everyone gets the same treatment – a welcome smile and an enthusiasm for chocolate so communicative that you can't help but want to try a square truffle, a Fidgi (a dark chocolate filled with passion fruit ganache) or a Veragua (a heavenly chocolate, praline and caramel layered bonbon). Then there's the setting: Chaudun's chocolate shop has to be the most atmospheric of them all; a wood-panelled affair, covered from floor to ceiling with hand-made chocolate sculptures.

EXPLORE

L'Epicerie du Père Claude.

Beyond the Périphérique

Ten years ago, visitors might not have looked much further than a quick dash round the Louvre and a twilight cruise on the Seine to tick the boxes for their perfect Paris weekend. But now the capital's pleasures are spreading well beyond the cramped confines of the Grands Boulevards, even crossing the Périphérique and into the formerly forbidden lands of the *banlieue*. From art complexes to anatomy museums, Paris no longer stops at the 20th arrondissement, with big-hitters Thaddaeus Ropac and Larry Gagosian both opening landmark galleries in the suburbs, and the gritty suburb of Pantin now dubbed the 'Brooklyn of Paris' by those in the know. Of course, convincing inner-city Parisians to make the same leap of faith is no easy task. But new mayor Anne Hidalgo is committed to 'rubbing out this boundary' for good during the next decade. Prepare for a new chapter for Paris (and a new title for this chapter, perhaps).

Basilique St-Denis.

Don't Miss

1 **La Défense** Soaring skyscrapers and stunning views (p236).

2 **Basilique St-Denis** Gothic grandeur (p236).

3 **Musée de l'Air et de l'Espace** Classic cockpit action (p236).

4 **Centre National de la Danse** Foot-tapping frenzy (p236).

5 **MAC/VAL** Modern art, 1950s to now (p237).

EXPLORE

LA DEFENSE

The skyscrapers and walkways of La Défense – named after a stand against the Prussians in 1870 – create a whole new world. The area has been a showcase for French business since the mid 1950s, when the CNIT hall was built to host trade shows, but it was the arrival of the **Grande Arche** that gave the district its most dramatic monument. On the central esplanade are fountains and sculptures by Miró and Serra.

Grande Arche de La Défense

92044 Paris La Défense (01.49.07.27.27, www.grandearche.com). M° La Défense.
Completed in 1989, the Grande Arche was designed by Danish architect Johan Otto von Spreckelsen. Though it lines up neatly on the Grand Axe – from the Louvre, up the Champs-Elysées to the Arc de Triomphe – the building itself is skewed. Access to the roof has been closed for years amid safety concerns, but the government has now pledged €200m to renovate the arch.

ST-DENIS & THE NORTH

North of Paris, the *département* of Seine St-Denis (and part of adjoining Val d'Oise) best fulfils the negative stereotype of the *banlieue*. It's a victim of its 19th-century industrial boom and the 20th-century housing shortage, when colossal estates went up in La Corneuve, Aulnay-sous-Bois and Sarcelles. It includes some of the poorest *communes* in all of France. Yet the *département* boasts a buzzing theatre scene, with the **MC93** in Bobigny (*see p293*), the **Théâtre Gérard-Philipe** (*see p293*) in St-Denis, and the Théâtre de la Commune in Aubervilliers. Amid the sprawl stands one of the treasures of Gothic architecture: the **Basilique St-Denis**, final resting place for the majority of France's former monarchs.

Le Bourget, home to the city's first airport and still used for private jets and an air fair, contains the **Musée de l'Air et de l'Espace** in its original passenger terminals and hangars. In late 2012, the airport also became home to a bold new **Gagosian** gallery (800 avenue de l'Europe, 93350 Le Bourget, 01.48.16.16.47, www.gagosian.com), housed in a 1950s concrete hangar and designed by none other than Jean Nouvel. North-east of Paris, Pantin arrived on the cultural scene with the opening in 2004 of the **Centre National de la Danse** (*see p287*) in a cleverly revamped office block, and 2012 saw the opening of **Thaddaeus Ropac**'s new art gallery space (69 avenue du Général Leclerc, 93500 Pantin, 01.55.89.01.10, www.ropac.net), which occupies a red-brick factory complex. Now the whole area is on the up, with major multinationals moving in (*see p238* **Peripheral Vision**).

North-west of St-Denis, Ecouen, noted for its Renaissance château, now the **Musée National de la Renaissance**, allows for a glimpse of a more rural past.

★ Basilique St-Denis

1 rue de la Légion-d'Honneur, 93200 St-Denis (01.48.09.83.54). M° St-Denis Basilique. **Open** *Apr-Sept* 10am-6.15pm Mon-Sat; noon-6.15pm Sun. *Oct-Mar* 10am-5pm Mon-Sat; noon-5.15pm Sun. *Tours* 10.30am, 3pm Mon-Sat; 12.15pm, 3pm Sun. **Admission** €7.50; €4.50 reductions; free under-18s, under-26s (EU citizens). PMP.
Legend has it that when St Denis was beheaded, he picked up his noggin and walked with it to Vicus Catulliacus (now St-Denis) to be buried. The first church, parts of which can be seen in the crypt, was built over his tomb in around 475. The present edifice was begun in the 1130s by Abbot Suger. It is considered to be the first example of Gothic architecture, uniting the elements of pointed arches, ogival vaulting and flying buttresses. In the 13th century, master mason Pierre de Montreuil erected the spire and rebuilt the choir nave and transept. St-Denis was the burial place for all but three French monarchs between 996 and the end of the *Ancien Régime*, so the ambulatory is a museum of French funerary sculpture. It includes a fanciful Gothic tomb for Dagobert, the austere effigy of Charles V, and the Renaissance tomb of Louis XII and his wife Anne de Bretagne. In 1792, these tombs were desecrated, and the royal remains thrown into a pit.

★ FREE Musée de l'Air et de l'Espace

Aéroport de Paris-Le Bourget, 93352 Le Bourget Cedex (01.49.92.70.00, www.mae.org). M° Gare du Nord, then bus 350/RER Le Bourget, then bus 152. **Open** *Apr-Sept* 10am-6pm Tue-Sun. *Oct-Mar* 10am-5pm Tue-Sun. **Admission** free. *With 1-3 animations* €8-€16; €6-€12 under-26s; free under-4s. PMP.
Set in the former passenger terminal at Le Bourget airport, the collection begins with the pioneers, including a command cabin of a Zeppelin airship. On the runway are Mirage fighters, a US Thunderchief, a Boeing 747 and Ariane launchers 1 and 5. Hangars house the prototype Concorde 001 and a Dakota. Entry to the main collection is free, but there's a charge for each *animation* (Forfait Avions, Planète Pilote, Planétarium, Simulateurs, Cockpits Secrets).

Musée National de la Renaissance

Château d'Ecouen, 95440 Ecouen (01.34.38.38.50, www.musee-renaissance.fr). Train Gare du Nord to Ecouen-Ezanville then bus 269 or walk. **Open** *Mid Apr-Sept* 9.30am-12.45pm, 2-5.45pm Mon, Wed-Sun. *Oct-mid Apr* 9.30am-12.45pm, 2-5.15pm Mon, Wed-Sun. **Admission** €5; €3.50 reductions; free under-26s, all 1st Sun of mth.
The Renaissance château completed in 1555 for Royal Constable Anne de Montmorency and wife Margaret de Savoie is the setting for a collection

of 16th-century decorative arts (some sections are open only at certain times so it's a good idea to phone ahead). Best are the painted chimney pieces, decorated with biblical and mythological scenes.

Stade de France

For listings, see p247.

The 80,000-capacity Stade de France is the national stadium. It was built for the 1998 football World Cup and staged the final, when France beat Brazil 3-0 to claim the title for the first time. As well as hosting top football matches, it hosts home legs for rugby's Six Nations, athletics meetings and major league concerts. For details of stadium tours, *see p247.*

VINCENNES & THE EAST

The more upmarket residential districts in the east surround the **Bois de Vincennes**, such as Vincennes, with its royal château, St-Mandé and Charenton-le-Pont. **Joinville-le-Pont** and **Champigny-sur-Marne** draw weekenders for the riverside *guinguette* dancehalls.

Château de Vincennes

Av de Paris, 94300 Vincennes (01.48.08.31.20, www.chateau-vincennes.fr). M° Château de Vincennes. **Open** *Mid May-mid Sept* 10am-6pm daily. *Mid Sept-mid May* 10am-5pm daily. **Admission** €8.50; €5.50 reductions; free under-18s, under-26s (EU citizens).

An imposing curtain wall punctuated by towers encloses this 52m-high fortress, which is the tallest medieval fortified structure in Europe. Originally the site of a hunting lodge built for Louis VII in the 12th century, the square keep was begun by Philippe VI and completed in the 14th century by Charles V, who added the curtain wall. English king Henry V died here in 1422, and Louis XIII used the château for hunting expeditions.

Musée de l'Air et de l'Espace.

Pl de la Libération, 94404 Vitry-sur-Seine (01.43.91.64.20, www.macval.fr). M° Porte de Choisy then bus 183/RER Gare de Vitry-sur-Seine then bus 180. **Open** 10am-6pm Tue-Fri; noon-7pm Sat, Sun. **Admission** €5; €2.50 reductions; free under-26s, students, all 1st Sun of mth.

This contemporary art museum's collection offers a stunning snapshot of French art from 1950 to the present, with installations by Gilles Barbier, Jesús Rafael Soto and Christian Boltanski.

Musée Fragonard

7 av du Général de Gaulle, 94704 Maisons-Alfort (01.43.96.71.72, http://musee.vet-alfort.fr). M° Ecole Vétérinaire de Maisons-Alfort. **Open** 2-6pm Wed, Thur, Sat, Sun. Closed Aug. **Admission** €7; free under-26s. **No credit cards**.

In 18th-century French medical schools, study aids were produced in one of two ways. They were either sculpted in coloured wax or made from the real things – organs, limbs, tangled vascular systems – dried or preserved in formaldehyde. Veterinary surgeon Honoré Fragonard was a master of the second method, and many of his most striking works are now on display here. Most grandiose of all, *Cavalier de l'apocalypse* is a flayed man on the back of a flayed galloping horse, inspired by a painting by Dürer.

BOULOGNE & THE WEST

The capital's most desirable suburbs lie to the west. La Défense, Neuilly-sur-Seine, Boulogne-Billancourt, Levallois-Perret and, over the river, Issy-les-Moulineaux have become accepted business addresses for Parisians.

Boulogne-Billancourt is the main town and a lively centre in its own right. In 1320, the Gothic Eglise Notre-Dame was begun in tribute to a miraculous statue of the Virgin that washed up at Boulogne-sur-Mer. By the 18th century, Boulogne was known for its wines and laundries, then, early in the 20th century, for its artist residents (Landowski, Lipchitz, Chagall, Gris), whereas Billancourt was known for car manufacturing, aviation and its film studios.

In the 1920s and '30s, Boulogne-Billancourt was proud of its modernity: Tony Garnier built the elegant new town hall on avenue André-Morizet; a new post office, apartments and schools all went up in the modern style; and private houses were built by the leading avant-garde architects of the day – Le Corbusier, Mallet-Stevens, Perret, Lurçat, Pingusson and Fischer. The **Musée des Années 30** focuses on artists and architects who lived or worked in the town at the time. The glass-fronted apartment block by Le Corbusier – including the flat where he lived from 1933 to 1965 – can be visited each Saturday at 24 rue Nungesser et Coli (reserve on 01.42.88.75.72, www.fondationlecorbusier.asso.fr).

EXPLORE

PERIPHERAL VISION

Pantin's industrial chic is pulling in everyone from galleries to multinationals.

Tell a Parisian that you're going to Pantin and they'll probably look at you blankly and ask why. Like many of Paris's north-eastern suburbs, the town – on the *banlieue* side of the traffic-clogged Périphérique – conjures up images of grotty post-war housing projects, dilapidated factories and delinquency. But as Paris struggles to squeeze any more new-builds into its ancient street plan, Pantin looks set to become a suburban star.

The reasons behind its fast track to fame are simple: it's located on the doorstep of Paris next to the Parc de la Villette cultural hub and borders the Canal de l'Ourcq that links the capital to north-east France. It's also home to an unrivalled supply of large, derelict industrial buildings, several of which have already managed to attract multinationals on the lookout for larger premises.

In 2009, banking giant BNP Paribas kitted out offices for more than 3,000 employees in the Grands Moulins, a former flour mill; in 2012, Chanel took over a vast canalside building for use as research laboratories; in 2013, Hermès opened the gargantuan Cité des Metiers on rue Hoche – a 'mini-city' of industrial conversions and new-builds with offices, gardens and workshops; and in 2016, advertising giant BETC will move into its new canalside headquarters in one of Pantin's most emblematic industrial-era constructions – the graffiti- smothered Magasins Généraux de la Chambre de Commerce.

The area has also attracted plenty of pioneering figures from the art world in the last few years: in 2004, the Centre National de la Danse (*see p236*) first opened its doors in a brutalist-style warehouse; and in 2012, after 30 years in Paris and Salzburg, art dealer Thaddaeus Ropac opened an enormous contemporary art gallery, Galerie Thaddaeus Ropac Pantin, tucked inside a former boiler factory (*see p236*). The opening exhibition featured paintings by Anselm Kiefer, displayed in four long, light-filled galleries, plus a recreation of Joseph Beuys's last exhibition in a separate glass-fronted building. The launch, which pulled in the likes of Lord Norman Foster, Christian Louboutin and Kiefer himself, caused such a stir that fashionistas proclaimed Pantin the new 'Brooklyn' of Paris.

In truth, the area feels more like Berlin than Brooklyn, with its crude urban landscape, deserted spaces and graffiti-clad buildings. But it's certainly getting sexier: a new tram line and a fleet of Vélib bikes now link the area to central Paris (adding to the pre-existing métro stations and RER stop); the number of inhabitants has grown by ten per cent in a decade; and property prices have increased by almost 19 per cent during the past five years. Some parts are still grimy enough to spoil a serendipitous stroll, but you can almost smell the gentrification as more and more buildings go under the hammer.

In the 19th century, riverside towns such as **Chatou**, **Asnières** and **Argenteuil** became places of entertainment – for promenades, *guinguettes* and rowing on the Seine – as depicted in many Impressionist paintings.

At Rueil-Malmaison, the romantic **Château de Malmaison** was loved by Napoleon and Josephine. Josephine had a second château, **La Petite Malmaison** (229bis av Napoléon-Bonaparte), built nearby. The empress is buried in the Eglise St-Pierre St-Paul in the old centre, as is her daughter Hortense de Beauharnais, Queen of Holland and mother of Napoleon III.

Suresnes, across the Seine from the Bois de Boulogne, has been a wine-producing village since Roman times. The 162m (532ft) Mont Valérien was a place of pilgrimage. In 1841, a huge fortress was built here to defend Paris. It was occupied by the German army in World War II; French *résistants* were brought here at night to be shot. The fortress still belongs to the French army, and is the centre of its eavesdropping network. On the surrounding hill is the **American Cemetery** (190 bd de Washington), which contains the graves of American soldiers from World Wars I and II.

St-Germain-en-Laye is a smart suburb with a historic centre and a château. Henri II lived here with his wife Catherine de Médicis and his mistress Diane de Poitiers; it was here also that Mary Queen of Scots grew up, Louis XIV was born and the deposed James II lived for 12 years. Napoléon III turned the château into the **Musée d'Archéologie Nationale**.

Château de Malmaison

Av du Château, 92500 Rueil-Malmaison (01.41.29.05.55, www.chateau-malmaison.fr). M°/RER La Défense then bus 258. **Open** times vary. **Admission** €6.50; €5 reductions; free under-18s, under-26s (EU citizens), all 1st Sun of mth. PMP.
Napoleon and Josephine's love nest, bought by Josephine in 1799, was the emperor's favourite retreat during the Consulate (1800-03). After their divorce, Napoleon gave the château to his ex, who died here in 1814. You can see Napoleon's office, the billiard room and Josephine's tented bedroom.

★ FREE Mémorial de la France Combattante

Av du Professeur-Léon-Bernard, 92150 Suresnes (01.47.28.46.35, www.mont-valerien.fr). Train to Suresnes-Mont-Valérien, or RER La Défense then bus 160, 360 or tram 2. **Open** tour times vary (see website for details). **Admission** free.
Sixteen bronze sculptures by 16 artists represent France's struggle for liberation from Nazi Germany. Behind an eternal flame, the crypt contains tombs of 16 heroes from 16 French battles in World War II. The memorial was built on the site where Resistance members were brought from prisons in Paris. A staircase from within the crypt leads visitors inside the curtain wall, then up to the chapel where prisoners were locked before execution, and down to the Clairière des Fusillés, the clearing where they were shot. The chapel walls were covered in the prisoners' last graffiti; it also contains five of the wooden firing posts. More than 1,000 men were shot here (women were deported). A monument lists the names of victims.

Musée Albert Kahn

10-14 rue du Port, 92100 Boulogne-Billancourt (01.55.19.28.00, www.albert-kahn.hauts-de-seine.net). M° Boulogne – Pont de Saint-Cloud. **Open** 11am-6pm Tue-Sun (until 7pm May-Sept). **Admission** €4; €2.50 reductions; free under-12s & all 1st Sun of mth.
The spectacular ten-acre *jardin* alone makes a visit here worthwhile: each section is modelled on a garden from around the world. Albert Kahn was an early 20th-century banker and philanthropist who financed 'discovery' missions across the world. His main legacy is 'Les Archives de la Planète' on show here – a fascinating collection of film and snapshots brought back from missions in over 60 countries.

Musée des Années 30

Espace Landowski, 28 av André-Morizet, 92100 Boulogne-Billancourt (01.55.18.53.00, www.annees30.com). M° Marcel Sembat. **Open** 11am-6pm Tue-Sun. Closed 2wks Aug. **Admission** (incl Musée-Jardin Paul Landowski) €6; €4 reductions; free under-16s.
The Musée des Années 30 highlights just how much second-rate art was produced in the 1930s, though there are decent modernist sculptures by the Martel brothers, graphic designs, and Juan Gris still lifes and drawings. The star exhibits are the designs by avant-garde architects Auguste Perret, Le Corbusier and Louis-Raymond Fischer.

Musée d'Archéologie Nationale

Château St-Germain, pl Charles-de-Gaulle, 78105 St-Germain-en-Laye (01.39.10.13.00, www.musee-archeologienationale.fr). RER St-Germain-en-Laye. **Open** 10am-5pm Mon, Wed-Sun. **Admission** €7; €5.50 reductions; free under-18s, all 1st Sun of mth.
This awe-inspiring museum traces France's rich archaeological heritage. The redesigned Neolithic galleries feature statue-menhirs, female figures and an ornate tombstone from Cys-la-Commune.

Musée Belmondo

14 rue de L'Abreuvoir, 92100 Boulogne-Billancourt (01.55.18.54.40). M° Boulogne Jean Jaurès. **Open** 2-6pm Tue-Fri; 11am-6pm Sat, Sun. **Admission** €6; €4 reductions; free under-16s & all 1st Sun of mth.
Jean-Paul Belmondo's father, Paul, was one of France's most important 20th-century sculptors. The space is an interior designer's dream – the mix of stark white, black and timber materials lends a different mood to each section.

EXPLORE

Arts & Entertainment

Children

For all its commotion and traffic-clogged boulevards, the capital is actually a very child-friendly place to visit. Disney's out-of-town pleasure park may dominate the thoughts of many junior visitors, but there are plenty of home-grown attractions to divert young minds away from Mickey and friends for a few hours, from the Centre Pompidou's brilliant Galerie des Enfants to the revamped Parc Zoologique and a trip up Gustave Eiffel's glorious lattice confection. The Louvre and Musée d'Orsay are crucial culture stops, of course, but be sure to temper the galleries with playtime in one of the city's excellent parks such as the Jardin du Luxembourg or Buttes-Chaumont. And now a section of the Left Bank has been pedestrianised and transformed into Les Berges (www.lesberges.paris.fr), kids can sample everything from climbing walls and running tracks to tepees and hopscotch along the banks of the Seine.

WHAT'S ON WHEN

Paris's museums and other attractions cater to children as well as adults, and also offer blissful opportunities to offload your kids on to someone else with children's workshops. If your children don't speak French, you can usually request an English speaker in advance. To find out what's coming up, contact the individual museums or check out www.paris.fr. Listings magazines *Pariscope*, *L'Officiel des Spectacles*, *Figaroscope* (with Wednesday's *Le Figaro*) and *Télérama*'s *Sortir* all have kids' sections; and free bi-monthly magazine *Paris-Mômes* is distributed with daily paper *Libération* in toy shops and public libraries.

Sightseeing with children can be made easier with planning. Queues at prime spots such as the **Eiffel Tower** (*see p229*), **Louvre** (*see p63*) and the towers at **Notre-Dame** (*see p51*) are less disheartening in the morning.

GETTING AROUND

One word of advice: walk whenever possible. The métro is difficult to negotiate with babies and toddlers. Two of you might just manage a pushchair, but lone travellers won't and passers-by are notoriously selfish about helping out. If your babe is small enough for a baby carrier, it will save you a lot of hassle when navigating the tight turnstiles and never-ending staircases. Also try to travel between 10.30am and 5pm to avoid the rush-hour crowds. The driverless line 14 (St-Lazare to Olympiades) is a big hit with kids, who can sit at the front and peer down the tunnel as the train advances; the mostly overground lines six (Nation to Charles de Gaulle Étoile) and two (Nation to Porte Dauphine) offer attractive city views; a number of RER stations have lifts, although they are frequently broken.

Buses, on the other hand, are easier thanks to priority seats near the front for passengers with young children; many, such as nos.24, 63 and 95 (www.ratp.fr), pass numerous sights. Three-to 11-year-olds qualify for a half-price *carnet* (a book of ten tickets) for all transport, including the Montmartrobus minibus and Montmartre funicular. Taxi drivers will usually take a family of four (charging €1 to carry a pushchair and a little extra for the fourth person). If you're stuck, try **G7 taxis** (36.07, www.taxisg7.fr), which has an English-speaking booking line.

For older kids, the addition of extra cycle paths across the centre (especially along the Seine, up the Canal St-Martin and along the Canal de l'Ourcq) makes a spin *en famille* an enjoyable way to get around the city while seeing the sights. Short distances are easily covered using the city's **Vélib** self-service scheme (www.velib.fr; *see p368*), and a book, *Paris à Vélib* (also available in English), maps out seven scenic cycle routes around the city. For day-long fun try **Paris à Vélo c'est Sympa** (22 rue Alphonse Baudin, 11th, 01.48.87.60.01, www.parisvelosympa.com). For a day out in beautiful surroundings, the Bois de Vincennes in the east and the Bois de Boulogne in the west provide woodlands, picnic areas, boating lakes and lawns.

EATING OUT

Affordable **Chartier** (7 rue du Fbg-Montmartre, 9th, 01.47.70.86.29, www.restaurant-chartier.com) is always a fun place to take the kids, with its belle époque dining room and waiters clad in black and white. Picky eaters can't help but love the timeless *steak-frites* at mini-chain **Relais d'Entrecote** (www.relaisentrecote.fr) where the only option is, well, steak and chips covered in the restaurant's secret sauce. **Tokyo Eat** at the Palais de Tokyo (13 av du Président-Wilson, 16th, 01.47.20.00.29, www.palaisdetokyo.com) is good too, with wacky decor and round, family-sized tables. Everything at **Bogato** (7 rue Liancourt, 14th, 01.40.47.03.51, www.chezbogato.fr) is designed for temptation. Kids will be in sweet heaven as they sample smooth Nutella tarts, cherry cheesecakes, chocolate-coated marshmallows and Cheshire Cat shortbreads with an edible rice paper smile.

BABIES & TODDLERS

Always pack a portable changing mat. A facility worth remembering is the WC chalet located in the Jardin du Luxembourg, where €0.60 gives

---

IN THE KNOW HOT CHOC

Angelina's (*see p67*) hot chocolate is a crowd-pleaser for kids of all ages. Call it touristy, but there's a solid reason for that – plus it's a great pick-me-up after a long afternoon at the Louvre. The iconic tearoom is an old-world setting for some serious hot beverages. And what kid will complain when the pot of thick, sweet chocolate drink comes served with a generous helping of fluffy whipped chantilly cream?

---

you access to loos with a padded changing table; the **Galeries Lafayette** and **Printemps** (for both, *see p82*) department stores have clean, well-equipped nappy-changing facilities. Breastfeeding in public is more common than ever, but still often frowned upon, so take a scarf for places where modesty is essential, or choose a quiet corner.

A city break with tots in tow doesn't have to mean missing out on the city's galleries and museums. Almost all of the main attractions have child-friendly activities or green spaces nearby – always handy as a reward for good behaviour. There's a carefully tended garden by Notre-Dame, and the dignified **Musée Rodin** (*see p224*) has outdoor distractions such as a sandpit to dig in, a sculpture-filled garden to explore (free entry to parents with a pushchair) and a tempting ice-cream stand. And if the heady heights of the Eiffel Tower prove too daunting, more down-to-earth amusements can be found at the adjacent Champ de Mars, with its play areas and seasonal donkey rides; or there are old-style merry-go-rounds by the river.

BABYSITTING

Many hotels can organise babysitting (ask when you reserve). The **American Church in Paris** (65 quai d'Orsay, 7th, 01.40.62.05.00, www.acparis.org) has a noticeboard displaying ads from English-speaking babysitters and au pairs; **Baby Sitting Services** (01.46.21.33.16, www.babysittingservices.fr) can organise babysitting at short notice.

MUSEUMS & SIGHTSEEING

Most museums offer children's workshops (in French) on Wednesday afternoons, at weekends and in the holidays. At the **Louvre** (*see p63*) the programme for kids varies from learning about facial expressions in paintings to Egyptian sculpture. Next door, the **Musée des Arts Décoratifs** (*see p63*) offers hands-on art workshops for ages four to 14 and special tours (tailored to different age groups). The **Palais de Tokyo** (*see p96*) has inventive 'Tok Tok' story-reading for three- to six-year-olds, workshops for five- to ten-year-olds and family visits (1pm Sun), often led by notable contemporary artists. The **Musée Rodin** (*see p224*) runs children's clay workshops.

★ Centre Pompidou – Galerie des Enfants
Rue St-Martin, 4th (01.44.78.12.33, www. centrepompidou.fr). M° Hôtel de Ville or Rambuteau/RER Châtelet Les Halles. **Open** *Museum* 11am-7pm Mon, Wed-Sun. *Workshops* most Wed, Sat & Sun afternoons & school holidays.

ARTS & ENTERTAINMENT

ARTS & ENTERTAINMENT

Admission *Museum* €13; €10 reductions; free under-18s, under-26s (EU citizens). *Workshops* €10 (1 child & 1 adult). **Map** p402 K5.

In this ground-floor gallery, wonderfully thought-out exhibitions introduce children to interesting aspects of modern art, design and architecture. Kids are kept enthralled with interactive elements and the opportunity to touch. There are also hands-on workshops for three- to 12-year-olds, family workshops and a 13/16 studio for teens. Audio guides for six- to 12-year-olds can also be hired for €4. If you just fancy a gawp over the rooftops from the sixth floor, it's €3 (free under-13s). Outside, look for the colourful Stravinsky fountain on the south side.

Cité de l'Architecture
Palais de Chaillot, 1 pl du Trocadéro, 16th (01.58.51.52.00, www.citechaillot.fr). Mº Trocadéro. **Open** 11am-7pm Mon, Wed, Fri-Sun; 11am-9pm Thur. **Admission** €8; €6 reductions; free under-18s, under-26s (EU citizens). **Map** p400 B5.

More than 850 life-size copies of France's architectural treasures (including portions of great cathedrals such as Chartres) make for a fascinating visit for children of all ages. To help them understand the exhibits, colourful interactive games are dotted around the permanent displays, so they can try their hand at architecture and learn the concepts of Romanesque and Gothic as they create fantastical animal heads, design stained-glass windows or build a Romanesque arch. On Saturday afternoons, three- to seven-year-olds can have a go at doing some building themselves with wooden blocks. Entry is €8 and you don't need to reserve (just turn up about 30 minutes beforehand).

Etoiles du Rex
1 bd Poissonnière, 2nd (www.legrandrex.com, reservations 08.25.05.44.05, www.cultival.fr). Mº Bonne Nouvelle. **Open** times vary; see website for details. **Admission** €11; €9 under-18s. **Map** p402 J4.

The slick but cheesy 50-minute backstage tour of the glorious art deco Grand Rex cinema is a treat for any kids with acting aspirations. Be prepared to ham your heart out when, propelled by automatic doors, lifts and mystery voices, you visit the projection room, climb behind the giant screen and are thrust into a whirlwind of sound dubbing, special effects and an audition for *King Kong*.

Grévin
10 bd Montmartre, 9th (01.47.70.85.05, www.grevin-paris.com). Mº Grands Boulevards. **Open** times vary; see website for details. **Admission** prices vary. **Map** p402 H4.

This wonderfully kitsch version of Madame Tussauds is a hit with kids, who can have their photo taken alongside waxworks of showbiz stars and personalities such as Zinédine Zidane, Brigitte

Bardot, the Queen and Barack Obama, plus new arrivals such as Lady Gaga, Pénélope Cruz and Angelina Jolie. Landmark historical moments, such as Neil Armstrong walking on the moon, are re-enacted in the 'snapshots of the 20th century' area; a small gallery at the top of a spiral staircase near the end shows how waxworks are made; and an impressive hall of mirrors (designed by France's fetish illusionist Arturo Brachetti and with music by Manu Katché) plunges you into scenes such as an Aztec temple.

▶ *On Saturday and Sunday afternoons during termtime there are special children's guided tours (French only) for seven- to 12-year-olds (€20.50).*

Musée des Arts et Métiers
60 rue Réaumur, 3rd (01.53.01.82.00, www.arts-et-metiers.net). Mº Arts et Métiers. **Open** 10am-6pm Tue, Wed, Fri-Sun; 10am-9.30pm Thur. **Admission** €6.50; €4.50 reductions; free under-18s, under-26s (EU citizens), all 1st Sun of mth & after 6pm Thur. *Audio guides* €5. **Map** p402 K5.

Abbot Grégoire founded the fascinating 'arts and trades' museum in the late 18th century as 'a store for useful, new inventions'. Today, it thrills budding scientists, mechanics, astronomers, pilots or kids simply curious about the world around them with highlights that include Foucault's original pendulum, used by physician Léon Foucault in 1851 to make the rotation of the earth visible to the human eye; Clément Ader's steam-powered Avion III, officially the world's first working plane (1897); and Henry Ford's Model T car.

Musée des Egouts
Entrance opposite 93 quai d'Orsay, by Pont de l'Alma, 7th (01.53.68.27.81). Mº Alma-Marceau/ RER Pont de l'Alma. **Open** *May-Sept* 11am-6pm (last entry 5pm) Mon-Wed, Sat, Sun. *Oct-Apr* 11am-5pm (last entry 4pm) Mon-Wed, Sat, Sun. **Admission** €4.40; €3.60 reductions; free under-6s. **Map** p400 D5.

The sewer museum retraces the pungent history of all 2,100km (1,305 miles) of Paris's underworld through a genuinely fascinating series of films, exhibits and a trip through the tunnels. Go early, before all of Paris's homes and restaurants are functioning at full capacity, to avoid the worst of the odours. During bad weather, visiting times may change or the museum may close as sudden surges in water can make the sewers dangerous.

Musée Gourmand du Chocolat
28 bd de Bonne Nouvelle, 10th (01.42.29.68.60, www.museeduchocolat.fr). Mº Bonne Nouvelle. **Open** 10am-6pm (last entry 5pm) daily. **Admission** €9.50; €6.50-€8.50 reductions; free under-6s. **Map** p402 J4.

The chocolate museum – need we say any more? Choco-Story traces the sweet history of every child's

IN THE FRAME

THATLou's treasure hunts turn the Louvre into more than just a museum.

Of the Louvre's 15,000 visitors a day, 80 per cent are only there to see the *Mona Lisa*. And that, says THATLou's Daisy de Plume, is 'a crime that needed to be solved'. So this softly-spoken New Yorker set about devising a way to make visiting the world's largest museum a fun – and affordable – learning experience, inspired by the games her art historian mother devised for her during rainy-day visits to New York's Metropolitan Museum of Art.

Daisy's treasure hunts (THATLou stands for 'Treasure Hunt at the Louvre') are a high- and low-tech mix. Participants use mobile phones or digital cameras to capture the 'treasure', but the clues are scribbled on paper in packs distributed by Daisy herself, who meets the players before they start. Families split into two teams of two to four people, or arrange to play against another family signed up on the same day – which definitely adds to the excitement. It's then a race to get as many points as you can before an agreed finish time (90 minutes to two hours is about right), when the teams meet up to open the sealed envelope revealing where all the treasure was situated, plus answers to the bonus questions. The pack comes with Louvre trinkets for prizes, or you can choose your own incentives.

There are ten themed hunts to choose from, but the best for children are Beauty & the Beast(iary) and Animals in Richelieu. The first takes in everything from the *Mona Lisa* to obscure imaginary creatures in forgotten wings of the museum. The second is good for small children as it confines itself to one wing, avoiding the *Mona Lisa* crowds, and hunts for monkeys, griffins, dancing bears and more. Each of the 'clues' has a picture of the work of art with a lively text explaining its context and offering bonus points – getting down on all-fours and being photographed as the two dogs in *The Wedding Feast at Cana*, for instance – which may bring a smile even to the most stony-faced Louvre custodian.

THATLou

www.thatlou.com. **Treasure hunt** €25 per person (not incl Louvre entry; THATLou can arrange pre-booked queue-jump entry for €18/adult, free under-18s).

ARTS & ENTERTAINMENT

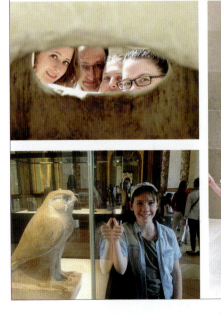

passion. The first part explores its Mayan and Aztec origins, before moving on to its introduction to Europe. The third part delves into chocolate today, including a demonstration of how it's made, a mere hurdle before getting to every kid's favourite part – the gift shop. Finish the visit off with a tasty hot chocolate (€3).

Musée de la Magie

11 rue St-Paul, 4th (01.42.72.13.26, www.musee delamagie.com). M° St-Paul or Sully-Morland. **Open** 2-7pm Wed, Sat, Sun (open extra hours & days during school holidays, check website for details). **Admission** €9; €7 reductions. **No credit cards. Map** p409 L7.

Small kids love the distorting mirrors and putting their hands in the lion's mouth at this museum of magic and curiosities, which is housed in vaulted cellars. A short magic show is included in the visit – it's in French, but rabbits out of hats translate well into any language. There's a great automated museum too (extra charge), where 100 mechanical toys move into action before your kids' eyes.

Musée de la Musique

Parc de la Villette, 221 av Jean-Jaurès, 19th (01.44.84.44.84, www.philharmoniedeparis.fr). M° Porte de Pantin. **Open** noon-6pm Tue-Fri; 10am-6pm Sat, Sun. **Admission** €7; free under-26s. **Map** p403 inset.

This innovative music museum houses a gleamingly restored collection of instruments from the old Conservatoire, interactive computers and scale models of opera houses and concert halls. Visitors are supplied with an audio guide in a choice of languages, and the musical commentary is a joy, playing the appropriate instrument as you approach each exhibit. There are also regular free interactive workshops and concerts for children over seven.

★ Musée National de la Marine

Palais de Chaillot, 17 pl du Trocadéro, 16th (01.53.65.69.69, www.musee-marine.fr). M° Trocadéro. **Open** 11am-6pm Mon, Wed-Fri; 11am-7pm Sat, Sun. **Admission** €8.50; €6 reductions; free under-18s, under-26s (EU citizens). **Map** p400 B5.

Sail your family back in time through 400 years of French naval history. Highlights include the *Océan*, a 19th-century sailing vessel equipped with an impressive 120 cannon; a gilded barge built for Napoleon; and some extravagant, larger-than-life figureheads, from serene-faced angels to leaping seahorses. There are also dozens of model boats, dating from the 18th to the 20th century, and several old-fashioned divers' suits. Guided tours for children run during the school holidays.

Musée de la Poupée

Impasse Berthaud, 3rd (01.42.72.73.11, www. museedelapoupeeparis.com). M° Rambuteau.

Open 1-6pm Tue-Sat. **Admission** €8; €4-€6 reductions; free under-3s. **No credit cards. Map** p406 L7.

This small, private museum and doll hospital enchants little girls with its collection of some 500 dolls (mostly of French origin) and their accompanying accessories and pets, which are arranged in thematic tableaux. A few teddies and quacking ducks are thrown in for young boys, and storytelling sessions and workshops (along the lines of making doll's clothes or miniature food for dolls' houses) are held on Wednesday afternoons (in French, reserve in advance; €14). There's even a *clinique pour poupées* if your doll is starting to fall apart at the seams.

★ Muséum National d'Histoire Naturelle

36 rue Geoffroy-St-Hilaire, 2 rue Bouffon, 57 rue Cuvier, 5th (01.40.79.56.01, www.mnhn.fr). M° Gare d'Austerlitz or Jussieu. **Open** 10am-6pm Mon, Wed-Sun. **Admission** *Grande Galerie de l'Evolution* €9; €7 reductions; free under-26s. *Galeries d'Anatomie Comparée et de Paléontologie* €7; €5 reductions; free under-26s. *Galerie des Enfants* €11; €9 reductions; free under-4s. *Combined tickets available.* **Map** p406 K9.

At the Natural History Museum's impressive Grande Galerie de l'Evolution in the Jardin des Plantes, stuffed creatures parade majestically through their various habitats. Animals of all kinds teach children about the diversity of nature and, in the endangered and vanished section (where a dodo takes pride of place), about the importance of protecting them. Also in the Jardin des Plantes complex are the small Ménagerie zoo (*see p247*); the bony remains of fish, birds, monkeys, dinosaurs and humans in the Galeries d'Anatomie Comparée et de Paléontologie; and the excellent Galerie des Enfants. This 600sq m space is specially designed to help children increase their awareness of the planet's future through three different environments – the city (Paris), the river (La Bassée), and the tropical forest (Kayapo native land in Brazil). Finally, scaling things up to planetary level, they can get to grips with a brief history of life and major ecological issues such as global warming, before finding out what action they can take now and in the future.

IN THE KNOW MASTER CHEF

Elsa and Emmanuelle Condet run **Atelier Cake** (www.cakeletraiteur.fr), a bread-baking workshop for ages six and up. The 90-minute class is held in a purpose-built studio and kitchen, where kids learn about different kinds of grains and flours, before getting up to their elbows in pastry dust. Children leave with a recipe and the loaf of bread they've baked.

Parc Zoologique de Paris. *See p248.*

★ Stade de France

Guided visits via entrance Porte G, Stade de France, Seine St-Denis (01.55.93.00.00, tours 08.92.70.09.00, www.stadefrance.com). M° St-Denis Porte de Paris/RER Stade de France St-Denis. **Tours** 11am-4pm Tue-Sun (daily during school hols). **Admission** €15; €10-€12 reductions; free under-5s.

Football- and rugby-crazy kids will absolutely love the behind-the-scenes tours of France's handsome national sports stadium. After a quick scan of the newly renovated museum (featuring photos, football shirts and electric guitars from the rock stars who also play here), the tour begins by sitting in the stands and ends with a runout through the tunnel to the sound of applause. On the way, you can visit the changing and shower rooms and learn about the on-site hospital and prison cells. On match or concert days, tours are not available.

AQUARIUMS & ZOOS

Cinéaqua

2 av des Nations Unies, 16th (01.40.69.23.23, www.cineaqua.com). M° Trocadéro. **Open** 10am-7pm daily. **Admission** €20.50; €13-€16 reductions; free under-3s. **Map** p400 B5.

Paris's first 'ocean entertainment centre' is a hybrid aquarium-cinema complex containing more than 500 species of fish, invertebrates, sharks and coral, along with several film screens. There are kids' clubs, with face-painting and games, from 2pm to 5pm daily, plus a touch pool offering the chance to stroke carp and sturgeon. The section on the Seine is fascinating.

Ménagerie du Jardin des Plantes

57 rue Cuvier, 5th (01.40.79.56.01, www.mnhn.fr). M° Gare d'Austerlitz, Jussieu or Place Monge. **Open** 9am-5pm daily (until 6pm Mon-Sat, 6.30pm Sun mid Mar-mid Oct). **Admission** €13; €9 reductions; free under-3s. **Map** p406 K8.

Heads rolled during the Terror, leaving many an aristocratic collection of exotic animals without a home. This *ménagerie* became the solution in 1794. Nowadays, its inhabitants include vultures, monkeys, orang-utans, ostriches, flamingos, a century-old turtle plus another one rescued from the sewers, a lovely red panda and lots of satisfyingly scary spiders and snakes. There's a petting zoo with farm animals for small kids, and older ones can zoom in on microscopic species in the Microzoo.

Palais de la Porte Dorée
Aquarium Tropical

293 av Daumesnil, 12th (01.53.59.58.60, www.aquarium-portedoree.fr). M° Porte Dorée. **Open** 10am-5.30pm Tue-Fri; 10am-7pm Sat, Sun. **Admission** €5-€7; €3.50-€5 reductions; free under-4s. **No credit cards.**

The basement of this art deco palace, built for the Colonial Exhibition in 1931, contains the small but much-loved city aquarium. Four alligators were introduced recently when the last of the aquarium's original crocodiles, brought from Senegal in 1948, died; other watery residents include cuttlefish, sharks and luminous deep-water species.

► *Palais de la Porte Dorée is also home to the Cité Nationale de l'Histoire de l'Immigration (see p156).*

Parc de Thoiry

78770 Thoiry-en-Yvelines (01.34.87.53.76, www.thoiry.net). 45km (28 miles) west of Paris; by car A13, A12, then N12 towards Dreux until Thoiry. **Open** times vary, see website for details. **Admission** *Safari park, park & château* €30; €23.70-€27.80 reductions; free under-3s.

As well as a beautiful château, the Parc de Thoiry is also home to one of Europe's first animal reserves. Follow the long safari park trail, accessible only by car, and see zebras rub their noses over your windscreen and bears amble down tracks. In the adjoining zoo, rarities include Siberian lynx and Tonkean macaques.

★ Parc Zoologique de Paris
Rte de la Ceinture du Lac, 12th (08.11.22.41.22,
www.parczoologiquedeparis.fr). Mº Porte Dorée.
Open *Mar-Oct* 10am-6pm Mon-Fri; 9.30am-7.30pm
Sat, Sun. *Oct-Mar* 10am-5pm daily. **Admission**
€22, €14-€16.50 reductions.

After five years of renovation, the Parc Zoologique is
back in business. Regular patrons of the old zoo are
in for a shock: the venue's been subjected to a radical
redesign in which nothing, bar the 65-metre Grand
Rocher centrepiece and of course the beasts themselves, has been spared. Visitors are now greeted by
spots of woodland, a greenhouse, an aviary and five
'biozones'. Efforts have been made to grant the animals more living space and promote the protection of
endangered species, and the experience is framed by
a new pedagogical mission that occasionally borders
on the twee (will kids learn anything from a picture of
a manatee wearing a bib?). *Photo p247.*

PERFORMING ARTS

When school's out on Wednesday afternoons,
at weekends and during holidays, fairytales,
fables and folk stories keep children entertained
at the city's theatres and *café-théâtres*. The
varied programme at the **Théâtre Dunois**
(7 rue Louise-Weiss, 13th, 01.45.84.72.00, www.
theatredunois.org) is almost entirely geared
towards children. For children's theatre in an
unusual setting, the **Abricadabra Péniche
Antipode** (opposite 55 quai de Seine, 19th,
01.42.03.39.07, www.penicheantipode.fr)
is a riverboat on the Canal de l'Ourcq.

In general, children's films are dubbed into
French, but you can see VO (*version originale*)
screenings of the latest Hollywood hits at most
venues across town. Keep a lookout for kids'
showings on Wednesdays and Saturday
afternoons at the Cinémathèque Française and
L'Ecran des Enfants at the **Centre Pompidou**
(*see p124*). The IMAX in La Villette's **Géode**
(*see p251*) will keep kids enthralled too.

Circus

★ Cirque d'Hiver Bouglione
*110 rue Amelot, 11th (01.47.00.28.81, www.
cirquedhiver.com). Mº Filles du Calvaire.* **Shows**
Late Oct-mid Mar days vary. **Admission**
€15-€62. **Map** p409 L5.

This famous circus has been in the same family for
decades. Crowds flock for its twice-yearly seasons,
which include elephants, horses, trapeze artists and
very silly clowns.

Cirque Pinder
*Pelouse de Reuilly, Bois de Vincennes, 12th
(01.45.90.21.25, www.cirquepinder.com).
Mº Porte de Charenton or Porte Dorée.* **Shows**
Mid Nov-mid Jan. **Admission** €7-€45.

Big cats are the stars of the show, but horses,
elephants and monkeys also make Pinder the most
traditional travelling circus in France.

Espace Chapiteaux
*Parc de La Villette, 19th (01.40.03.75.75, www.
villette.com). Mº Porte de la Villette.* **Shows** vary.
Admission varies. **Map** p403 inset.

This big top hosts high-flying companies such as
Cirque Plume, Centre National des Arts du Cirque
and aerialists Les Arts Saut.

SWIMMING & SKATING

Aquaboulevard
*4 rue Louis-Armand, 15th (01.40.60.10.00,
www.aquaboulevard.com). Mº Balard.* **Open**
9am-11pm Mon-Thur; 9am-midnight Fri;
8am-midnight Sat; 8am-11pm Sun. **Admission**
6hrs €23-€29; €15 reductions. **Map** p404 A10.

With year-round summer temperatures, this water
park under a giant atrium is great fun for kids.

Patinoire Sonja Henie
*Palais Omnisports de Paris-Bercy (01.40.02.60.67,
www.bercy.fr). Mº Bercy.* **Open** *Sept-mid June*
3-6pm Wed; 9.30pm-12.30am Fri; 3-6pm,
9.30pm-12.30am Sat; 10am-noon, 3-6pm Sun.
Admission €4-€6; €3-€5 reductions. **No credit
cards. Map** p407 N9.

Bercy's Omnisports arena contains an ice rink, open
on Wednesdays and weekends for skaters of all
levels. Teenagers can also skate until late on Fridays
and Saturdays, when disco lights colour the ice.

Jardin du Luxembourg.

Piscine Butte-aux-Cailles
5 pl Paul-Verlaine, 13th (01.45.89.60.05).
M° Place d'Italie. **Open** times vary; see website
for details. **Admission** €3; €1.70 reductions.
This listed complex, built in the 1920s, has one
main indoor pool and two outdoor pools (open in
the summer). The water is a temptingly warm 28°C,
thanks to the natural sulphurous spring.

★ Piscine Josephine-Baker
Quai François-Mauriac, 13th (01.56.61.96.50).
M° Quai de la Gare. **Open** 7-8.30am, 1-9pm Mon,
Wed, Fri; 7-8.30am, 1-11pm Tue, Thur; 11am-8pm
Sat; 10am-8pm Sun. **Admission** €3; €1.70
reductions. **Map** p407 M10.
Moored on the Seine by the Bibliothèque Nationale,
the pool boasts a 25m main pool (with sliding glass
roof), a paddling pool and café, and a busy schedule
of exercise classes.

PARKS & THEME PARKS

Disneyland Paris/Walt Disney Studios Park
Marne-la-Vallée (www.disneylandparis.com).
32km E of Paris. RER A or TGV Marne-la-Vallée-
Chessy. By car, A4 exit 14. **Open** Times vary,
see website for details. **Admission** Prices vary,
see website for details.
Young ones will get a real kick out of Fantasyland,
with its Alice maze, Sleeping Beauty's castle and
teacup rides. Walt Disney Studios focuses on special
effects and the tricks of the animation trade. The
Twilight Zone Tower of Terror sends daredevils
plummeting down a 13-storey lift shaft and the Rock
'n' Roller Coaster in the Back Lot takes off at mega
speed, before hurtling round hairpin turns and loops
to the funky rhythm of Aerosmith. New in 2014
was Ratatouille the Adventure, a 3D trackless ride
(spectacles provided) following the renowned rat
through the kitchens of Gusteau's restaurant, plus
the 370-seat Bistrot Chez Rémy. Consider a Fastpass
to avoid some of the frustrating queues.

Jardin d'Acclimatation
Bois de Boulogne, 16th (01.40.67.90.85,
www.jardindacclimatation.fr). M° Les Sablons.
Open *Apr-Sept* 10am-7pm Mon-Thur, Sat, Sun;
10am-10pm Fri. *Oct-Mar* 10am-6pm Mon-Thur;
10am-10pm Fri; 10am-7pm Sat, Sun. **Admission**
€3; €1.50 reductions; free under-3s.
Founded in 1860, this amusement park and garden
has animals, a Normandy-style farm and an aviary,
plus boat rides, a funfair with mini rollercoasters,
flying chairs, the Enchanted House for children aged
two to four and two playgrounds. There's also a place
to steer radio-controlled boats and mini golf. Many
of the attractions cost €2.90 a go; others are free. A
miniature train runs from Porte Maillot to the park
entrance, and has space for pushchairs (€2.90; €4.40-
€5.90 with entry included).

Jardin du Luxembourg
Main access 2 rue Auguste Compte, 6th.
M° Odéon/RER Luxembourg. **Open** dawn-
dusk daily. **Map** p408 H8.
The 25-hectare park is a prized family attraction.
Kids come from across the city for its pony rides,
ice-cream stands, puppet shows, pedal karts,
sandpits, metal swingboats and merry-go-round.
The playground has an entrance fee.

★ Parc Astérix
60128 Plailly (08.26.46.66.26, www.parcasterix.
fr). 36km N of Paris. By coach from the Louvre
or RER Roissy-Charles de Gaulle 1 (check website
for departure times). By car, A1 exit Parc Astérix.
Open Times vary, see website for details.
Admission €46; €38 reductions; free under-3s.
Parking €10.
The park is split into Ancient Greece, the Roman
Empire, the Land of the Vikings, the indomitable
Gaulish Village and the Egypt zone. Thrill-seekers
can defy gravity on Goudurix, Europe's largest
rollercoaster, while younger kids get wet on the
Grand Splatch log flume. For a real rush of blood
to the head, though, climb aboard the brand-new
Oziris inverted rollercoaster. For some serious
handshaking, Astérix, Obélix and friends wander
around and a jamboree of live acts pumps up
the pace. In 2014, to coincide with the park's 25th
anniversary, the Forêt d'Idéfix opened with five
tamer rides for the youngest Gauls.

Parc des Buttes-Chaumont
Rue Botzaris, rue Manin, rue de Crimée, 19th.
M° Buttes Chaumont. **Open** *Winter* 7am-9pm
daily. *Summer* 7am-10pm daily. **Map** p403 N2.
This area, which was formerly mined for gypsum,
was turned into a sumptuous park under Napoleon
III. Spectacular in every way (including the views
over Paris), it is a family magnet with Punch and
Judy stands, pony rides, sandpits, waterfalls, picnic
and games areas and drinks stands. The hilly park
makes for some treacherous hikes upwards, but that
just means there's fantastic tumbling potential down
the grassy slopes.

★ Parc de la Villette
Av Corentin-Cariou, 19th (01.40.03.75.75,
www.villette.com). M° Porte de la Villette. Av Jean-
Jaurès, 19th. M° Porte de Pantin. **Map** p403 inset.
Aside from being home to Europe's largest science
museum (which also contains the brilliant Cité
des Enfants, *see p161*), a music museum, an IMAX
cinema, theatres, and the brand new Philharmonie
concert hall, the city's former abattoir district is
now made up of a succession of gardens and playgrounds. Jardin des Voltiges has climbing ropes and
balancing games, and the modern Jardin des Dunes
et Vents has pedal windmills, waves of bouncy tubes
and giant hamster wheels. The whole place makes
for a wonderful family day out.

ARTS & ENTERTAINMENT

Film

During the last few years, French films have set tongues wagging across the globe. Michel Hazanavicius's silent, black-and-white romcom *The Artist* became the most successful French film in history, winning three Golden Globes, seven BAFTAs, six Césars and five Oscars, including best actor for Jean Dujardin. Then Olivier Nakache and Eric Toledano's *Intouchables*, a moving comedy about a quadriplegic millionaire and his petty-criminal carer, raked in $391 million worldwide. And most recently, *La Vie d'Adèle* (*Blue is the Warmest Colour*), an explicit portrait of two young women falling in love, picked up the Palme d'Or and controversy galore in 2013. There has been plenty of small-screen success, too, including zombie thriller *Les Revenants* (*The Returned*) and *policier Engrenages* (*Spiral*). Behind the cameras, Luc Besson's Hollywood-sur-Seine finally opened for business in St-Denis in 2014.

MOVIEGOING IN PARIS

Happily, the rapid rise of the multiplex hasn't meant a reduction in the variety of films on offer in Paris. Multiplexes regularly show films from Eastern Europe, Asia and South America, and countless independent cinemas continue to screen a hugely eclectic assortment of cult, classic and just plain obscure films. As well as retrospectives and cut-price promotions, there are often visits from directors and stars.

IN THE KNOW
HOLLYWOOD-SUR-SEINE

The curtain has finally gone up on the **Cité du Cinéma** (www.citeducinema.org) in the northern suburb of St-Denis. Backed by maverick French film director Luc Besson and nicknamed Hollywood-sur-Seine, the enormous complex houses eight studios and promises to give the national film industry a massive boost.

Local interest is strong enough to sustain several monthly movie magazines and there's a decent selection of specialist film bookshops. Finally, French DVD labels produce some of the most expertly curated discs in the world. At **Fnac** (www.fnac.com), you're more than likely to find American and British titles otherwise unavailable in the US or UK.

INFORMATION AND TICKETS

New releases hit the screens on Wednesdays. Hollywood is well represented, of course, but Paris audiences have a balanced cinematic diet that satisfies their appetite for international films as well as shorts and documentaries. On top of this there are the 150-plus annual releases funded or part-funded with French money (the French film industry is still the world's third largest, after the US and India).

For venues, times and prices, consult one of the city's two main weekly listings magazines: *L'Officiel des Spectacles* and *Pariscope*. *Films nouveaux* are new releases, *Exclusivités* are the also-showing titles, and *Reprises* means rep.

For non-francophone flicks, look out for two letters somewhere near the title: VO (*version originale*) means a screening in the original language with French subtitles; VF (*version française*) means it has been dubbed into French.

Buy tickets in the usual way at the cinema – for new blockbusters, it pays to buy in advance. Online booking may entail a fee. Seats are often discounted by 20 to 30 per cent at Monday or Wednesday screenings, and the Mairie sponsors cut-price promotions throughout the year. If you're in town for a while, it might be a good idea to pick up a *carte illimitée*, a season ticket that allows unlimited viewing: every multiplex chain offers a version.

CINEMAS
Giant screens & multiplexes

Etoile Lilas
Place Maquis du Vercors, 20th (www.etoile-cinemas.com). M° Porte de Lilas. **Admission** €10.50; €4-€7.50 reductions.
This striking new multiplex is housed in a black cube and mixes arty and mainstream across its seven screens. The cinema is topped by a 300sq m terrace, perfect for pre- or post-film drinks.

La Géode
26 av Corentin-Cariou, 19th (01.40.05.79.99, www.lageode.fr). M° Porte de la Villette. **Admission** €12; €9 reductions. **Map** p403 inset.
The IMAX cinema at the Cité des Sciences occupies a shiny dome. The vast screen lets you experience 3D plunges through natural scenery, and adventures in which figures zoom out to grab you.

★ Le Grand Rex
1 bd Poissonnière, 2nd (08.92.68.05.96, www.legrandrex.com). M° Bonne Nouvelle. **Admission** €7.50-€13; €6-€11 reductions. *Les Etoiles du Rex tour* €11; €9 reductions. **Map** p402 J4.
With its wedding-cake exterior and the largest auditorium in Europe (2,650 seats), this listed historical monument is one of the few cinemas to upstage whatever it screens. Its blockbuster programming (usually in French) is suited to its vast screen. There are six smaller screens too.
▶ *The Etoiles du Rex tour is a 50-minute, SFX-laden taste of movie magic.*

Max Linder Panorama
24 bd Poissonnière, 9th (01.48.24.00.47). M° Grands Boulevards. **Admission** €9.50; €7.50 reductions. **Map** p402 J4.
This state-of-the-art cinema, with THX surround sound and an 18m (60ft) screen, is named after the dapper French silent comedian who owned it between 1914 and 1925. The walls and 700 seats are all black to prevent even the tiniest twinkle of reflected light distracting the audience from what's happening on the screen. Look for all-nighters and one-off showings of rare vintage films.

MK2 Bibliothèque
128-162 av de France, 13th (08.92.69.84.84, www.mk2.com). M° Bibliothèque François Mitterrand or Quai de la Gare. **Admission** €10.90; €4.90-€7.90 reductions; €20.08 monthly pass. **Map** p407 M10.
The MK2 chain's flagship offers an all-in-one night out: 14 screens, four restaurants, a bar open until 5am at weekends and two-person 'love seats'. A paragon of imaginative programming, MK2 is growing all the time.

UGC Ciné Cité Bercy
2 cour St-Emilion, 12th (08.92.70.00.00, www.ugc.fr). M° Cour St-Emilion. **Admission** €11.10; €4-€7.90 reductions; €20.08 monthly pass. **Map** p407 P10.
This ambitious 18-screen development screens art movies as well as mainstream fodder, and hosts regular meet-the-director events. The 19-screen UGC Ciné Cité Les Halles branch (7 place de la Rotonde, Nouveau Forum des Halles, 1st, 08.92.70.00.00) serves the same mix of cinema and events.

Showcases

Auditorium du Louvre
Musée du Louvre, 99 rue de Rivoli, 1st (01.40.20.55.00, www.louvre.fr). M° Palais

Le Grand Rex.

Film

Royal Musée du Louvre. **Admission** prices vary. **Map** p402 H5.
The 420-seat Auditorium du Louvre was designed by IM Pei, as part of the Mitterrand-inspired renovation of the Louvre. Film screenings are often related to current exhibitions at the museum; silent movies with accompanying live music are regulars.

Centre Pompidou
Rue St-Martin, 4th (01.44.78.12.33, www.centre pompidou.fr). Mº Hôtel de Ville or Rambuteau. **Admission** €6; €4 reductions. **Map** p406 K6.
The varied programme at the Centre Pompidou features themed series, experimental and artists' films, and a weekly documentary session. This is also the venue for the Cinéma du Réel festival in March (www.cinereel.org).

Le Cinéma des Cinéastes
7 av de Clichy, 17th (08.92.68.97.17, www. cinema-des-cineastes.fr). Mº Place de Clichy. **Admission** €9; €7 reductions. **Map** p401 G2.
Done out to evoke the studios of old, this three-screen showcase of world cinema holds meet-the-director sessions and festivals of classic, foreign, gay and documentary films. The cinema is also big on film for kids, and is one of the hosts of the Mon Premier Festival (www.monpremierfestival.org).

★ Cinémathèque Française
51 rue de Bercy, 12th (01.71.19.33.33, www. cinematheque.fr). Mº Bercy. **Admission** *Films* €6.50; €3-€5.50 reductions. *Museum* €5; €2.50-€4 reductions; free under-6s & all 10am-1pm Sun. **Map** p407 N9.
Relocated to Frank Gehry's striking, spacious cubist building, the Cinémathèque Française boasts four screens, a bookshop, a restaurant, exhibition space and the Musée du Cinéma, where it displays a fraction of its huge collection of memorabilia. The Cinémathèque hosts retrospectives, cult movies, classics, experimental cinema and Q&A sessions.

Forum des Images
2 rue du Cinéma, Forum des Halles, 1st (01.44.76.63.00, www.forumdesimages.fr). Mº Les Halles. **Admission** €6; €4-€5 reductions. **Map** p402 J5.
Partly a screening venue for old and little-known movies, and partly an archive for every kind of film featuring Paris. The Forum's collection numbers over 6,500 documentaries, adverts, newsreels and films, from the Lumière brothers to 21st-century reportage.

Arthouses

Accattone
20 rue Cujas, 5th (01.46.33.86.86). Mº Cluny La Sorbonne/RER Luxembourg. **Admission** €7; €6 reductions & all Wed. **No credit cards.** **Map** p408 J8.

This tiny Latin Quarter cinema, which is located on a narrow street on the site of a former cabaret, has a clear preference for old Italian arthouse. That said, there's still plenty of room on the rolling weekly programme for the likes of Buñuel, Oshima, Roeg and Ken Russell. With around 30 screenings a week, Accatone is an excellent place to improve your cinematic knowledge.

Action
Action Christine *4 rue Christine, 6th (01.43.25.85.78, www.actioncinemas.com). Mº Odéon or St-Michel.* **Admission** €8; €6 reductions. **No credit cards.** **Map** p408 J7.
Grand Action *5 rue des Ecoles, 5th (01.43.54.47.62, www.legrandaction.com). Mº Cardinal Lemoine.* **Admission** €9; €6.50 reductions. **No credit cards.** **Map** p406 K8.
A Left Bank stalwart, the Action group is renowned for screening new prints of old movies. It's heaven for anyone who's nostalgic for Tinseltown classics and quality US independents.

Le Balzac
1 rue Balzac, 8th (01.45.61.10.60, www.cinema balzac.com). Mº George V. **Admission** €10.50; €8.50 reductions. **No credit cards.** **Map** p400 D4.
Built in 1935 and boasting a mock ocean-liner foyer, Le Balzac scores highly for design and programming. Jean-Jacques Schpoliansky, whose grandfather opened the cinema in 1935, has been the manager for the last 40 years and is often found welcoming punters in person.

Le Champo
51 rue des Ecoles, 5th (01.43.54.51.60, www. lechampo.com). Mº Cluny La Sorbonne or Odéon. **Admission** €9; €7 reductions. **No credit cards.** **Map** p408 J7.
The two-screen Champo has been in operation for seven decades. Novel programming includes the occasional Nuits du Champo, a trio of films beginning at midnight and ending with breakfast (€15).

Le Chaplin Denfert
24 pl Denfert-Rochereau, 14th (www.cinema denfert.fr). Mº Denfert Rochereau/RER Denfert Rochereau. **Admission** €9.90; €7.50-€8 reductions. **No credit cards.** **Map** p405 H10.
This charming little cinema offers a nicely eclectic repertory selection that ranges from François Ozon and Hayao Miyazaki to shorts and animation, as well as new-release foreign films.

Le Cinéma du Panthéon
13 rue Victor-Cousin, 5th (01.40.46.01.21, www. whynotproductions.fr/pantheon). RER Luxembourg. **Admission** prices vary. **Map** p408 J8.
The Cinéma du Panthéon continues to screen new, often obscure international films, and hosts meet-the-director nights and discussions.

ARTS & ENTERTAINMENT

ESSENTIAL PARIS FILMS

You're in film-set Paris the second you get off the train.

Subway.

HOTEL DU NORD
MARCEL CARNE (1938)
The Hôtel du Nord is, thanks to Carné's film, a national monument: it, and the adjacent iron footbridge and chunk of Canal St-Martin, were recreated in the studio by Alexandre Trauner. On the bridge, Arletty gives suitor Louis Jouvet the brush-off with the immortal 'Atmosphère! Est-ce que j'ai une gueule d'atmosphère?'

LES 400 COUPS
FRANCOIS TRUFFAUT (1959)
Tearaway 13-year-old kid Antoine Doisnel (Jean-Pierre Léaud in his first role) gets around large parts of Paris, helping to launch the *nouvelle vague* on the way. His troubles start when he catches his mum in an adulterous clinch on place de Clichy. Still one of the cinema's most perceptive forays into childhood.

THE BEAT THAT MY HEART SKIPPED
JACQUES AUDIARD (2005)
Jacques Audiard (*A Self-Made Hero*, *Read My Lips*) translates to modern-day Paris the dilemmas of James Toback's 1978, New York-set *Fingers* – the story of a young man caught between art and crime, between his own ambitions and those of his father.

SUBWAY
LUC BESSON (1985)
Safecracker Christophe Lambert hides out with a bunch of eccentric social misfits in the netherworld of the Paris métro as he attempts to escape from a wealthy businessman's wife (Isabelle Adjani) with whom he has fallen in love, from her husband's thugs and from the métro police in this electrically charged 1980s punk-chic fantasy.

LA HAINE
MATHIEU KASSOVITZ (1995)
Twenty-four hours in the Paris projects: an Arab boy is critically wounded in hospital, gut-shot, and a police revolver has found its way into the hands of a young Jewish skinhead, Vinz (Cassel), who vows to even the score if his pal dies. A vital, scalding piece of work.

LE FABULEUX DESTIN D'AMELIE POULAIN
JEAN-PIERRE JEUNET (2001)
Jean-Pierre Jeunet's rose-tinted Parisian romance stars the wonderful Audrey Tautou as Amélie, who works in a Montmartre café (Café des Deux Moulins, 15 rue Lépic) and has a revelation that her life's work should be to bring good to others. A thoroughly charming love poem to *la vie Parisienne*.

L'Entrepôt

7-9 rue Francis-de-Pressensé, 14th (01.45.40. 07.50, www.lentrepot.fr). M° Pernety or Plaisance. **Admission** €8; €4-€6.50 reductions. **No credit cards. Map** p405 F10.

This multidisciplinary arts centre and cinema is known for its leftfield documentaries, shorts, gay repertoire and productions from developing nations. Regular debates, poetry nights and concerts complete the programme.

★ Le Louxor

170 bd de Magenta, 10th (01.44.63.96.96, www.cinemalouxor.fr). M° Barbès-Rochechouart. **Admission** €9; €4-€7.50 reductions. **No credit cards. Map** p402 J2.

Opened in 1921 and once a temple of silent cinema, the Egyptian art deco Louxor fell on hard times after World War II and became a drug den, 1980s club and gay disco before being left abandoned for 25 years. It reopened triumphantly as a cinema in April 2013, with a new brief to promote cultural, artistic and educational projects. Enjoy a pre-show glass of red in the lovely upstairs bar.

Le Mac Mahon

5 av Mac-Mahon, 17th (01.43.80.24.81, www. cinemamacmahon.com). M° Charles de Gaulle Etoile. **Admission** €7; €5 reductions. **No credit cards. Map** p400 C3.

This single-screen, 1930s-era cinema has changed little since its 1960s heyday (tickets are still of the tear-off variety), when its all-American programming fostered the label '*mac-mahonisme*' among the buffs who haunted the place. Americana still makes up the bulk of what's on the screen.

Le Nouveau Latina

20 rue du Temple, 4th (01.42.78.47.86, www.lenouveaulatina.com). M° Hôtel de Ville. **Admission** €8.50; €7 reductions. **No credit cards. Map** p406 K6.

The exciting programming at this flag-bearer for Latin cultures runs the gamut from Argentinian to Romanian films.

IN THE KNOW
SIP WITH THE STARS

Walk past the ticket office of **Studio 28** (*see right*) and a long corridor brings you out into a magical interior courtyard that opens up every afternoon as a bar, salon de thé and restaurant. Part of it has been left open as a summer terrace, lined with a vast fresco of French cinema's legendary stars – Delon and Bardot, Signoret and Montand, Fernandel and Jean Gabin, Belmondo and Jean Marais.

★ La Pagode

57bis rue de Babylone, 7th (01.45.55.48.48, www.etoile-cinemas.com). M° St-François-Xavier. **Admission** €9.80; €8 reductions. **No credit cards. Map** p405 F7.

This glorious edifice is not, as local legend might have it, a block-by-block import, but a 19th-century replica of a pagoda. Renovated in the 1990s, this is one of the loveliest cinemas in the world.

Studio 28

10 rue Tholozé, 18th (01.46.06.36.07, www. cinemastudio28.com). M° Abbesses or Blanche. **Admission** €8.50; €7 reductions. **No credit cards. Map** p401 H1.

Studio 28 was the venue for the first screening of Buñuel's scandalous *L'Age d'Or*. It offers a decent mixture of classics and recent movies, plus Dolby sound and a civilised bar (*see left* **In the Know**).

Studio Galande

42 rue Galande, 5th (01.43.54.72.71, www.studio galande.fr). M° Cluny La Sorbonne or St-Michel. **Admission** €8.50; €4-€6.50 reductions. **No credit cards. Map** p408 J7.

Some 20 different films are screened in subtitled versions at this venerable Latin Quarter venue every week: it's mostly international arthouse fare.

Festivals & events

Festival International de Films de Femmes

Maison des Arts, pl Salvador-Allende, 94040 Créteil (01.49.80.38.98, www.filmsdefemmes.com). M° Créteil-Préfecture. **Date** Mar.

Now in its 37th year, this highly regarded festival features a selection of retrospectives and new international films by female directors.

Côté Court

Ciné 104, 104 av Jean-Lolive, 93500 Pantin (01.48.91.24.91, www.cotecourt.org). M° Eglise de Pantin. **Date** June.

Côté Court puts on a great selection of new and old short films, shown at Ciné 104 and a handful of neighbouring venues.

Cinéma au Clair de Lune

Various venues (01.44.76.63.00, www.forum desimages.net). **Date** Aug.

Night-time films on giant open-air screens in squares and public gardens around town.

L'Etrange Festival

Forum des Images, for listing see p252 (01.44.76.63.00, www.etrangefestival.com). **Date** Sept. **Map** p404 J5.

Explicit sex, gore and weirdness in the screenings and 'happenings' at this annual feast of all things unconventional draw large crowds.

Gay & Lesbian

Paris is a European capital for all things gay and fabulous, from extravagant local personalities to a neighbourhood teeming with addresses for a night of cavorting. The Marais is the epicentre for nightlife catering to boys and men of all walks, but it's just the beginning. Starting an evening in or around the Marais is the best way to find out from the locals what's going on in other gay bars around town. Whether you're looking to share casual drinks, dance until dawn or have a brush with a local, there's fun to be had any night of the week. Local gays and lesbians say that they encounter very little, if any, discrimination during their day-to-day lives, and feel integrated into mainstream society. However, the annual Marche des Fiertés (Gay Pride), held in June, is a powerful reminder of how much the gay rights movement has accomplished over the last 30 years.

GETTING OUT AND ABOUT

Beaubourg and the '**gay Marais**' are particularly gay-friendly. Most of the dedicated venues are to be found in the area bounded by rue des Archives, rue Vieille-du-Temple and rue Ste-Croix-de-la-Bretonnerie. A light lunch, coffee or cocktail at a neighbourhood café will provide ample opportunity to check out the talent, and a casual stroll through the nearby streets will introduce you to a seductive selection of shops. Fetishists, funky fashionistas, bohemians and bibliophiles will each find a boutique to suit their fancy. A good place to start is **Les Mots à la Bouche**, where you can peruse the gay and lesbian press or pick up a few of the free monthly magazines listing the hottest events.

In the evening, kick off the action at a café or a restaurant before moving on to the bars and clubs, which don't really get going until after midnight. Start by mixing it up at the **Open Café** or the nearby red-hot **Raidd Bar**. The **Queen** on the Champs-Elysées remains a clubbing institution, as does the smaller and more intimate **Le Tango**. The oldest gay club in Paris, **Le Club 18**, is always fun. Lesbians can find a few nice bars of their own on rue du Roi de Sicile.

Information and resources

Magazine *Têtu* (www.tetu.com) reports on goings-on in gay life and has text in English. There are also several free bi-weekly publications, distributed in gay bookshops, bars and clubs, including *Tribumove* (www.tribumove.com). And for the girls, there's *Barbi(e)turix* (www.barbieturix.com). Excellent website www.gayvox.com provides regularly updated listings (in English) of all things gay and lesbian in the city.

Centre Gai et Lesbien
63 rue Beaubourg, 3rd (01.43.57.21.47, www.centrelgbtparis.org). M° Arts et Métiers. **Open** 3.30-8pm Mon-Fri; 1-7pm Sat. *Library* 6-8pm Mon-Wed; 5-7pm Fri, Sat. **Map** p402 K6.

IN THE KNOW TAKE PRIDE

Don't miss out on the action in June as a stream of outrageous floats and flamboyant costumes parade towards Bastille for **Gay Pride** (www.gaypride.fr); then there's an official fête and various club events.

Open Café.

As well as providing information on topics ranging from the sociopolitical (if you don't know what rights gays and lesbians have or don't have in France, you can find out all you need to know here) to the biomedical (the latest developments in the treatment of HIV, where to get tested for free), this multifunctional centre and library also hosts meetings for a variety of support groups and associations.

Inter-LGBT
c/o Maison des Associations du 3ème, boîte 8, 5 rue Perrée, 75003 Paris (01.72.70.39.22, www.inter-lgbt.org). Map p409 L5.
The Interassociative Lesbienne, Gaie, Bi & Trans is an umbrella group of some 50 LGBT associations. It organises the Printemps des Assoces every April and the annual Gay Pride March in June.

SOS Homophobie
01.48.06.42.41, www.sos-homophobie.org. **Open** 6-10pm Mon-Fri; 2-4pm Sat; 6-8pm Sun.
Victims of and witnesses to homophobic crimes and discrimination can report them to this confidential service, which offers support and publishes an annual report on homophobia.

GAY PARIS
Bars & cafés

Banana Café
13 rue de la Ferronnerie, 1st (01.42.33.35.31, www.bananacafeparis.com). M° Châtelet. **Open** 6pm-6am daily. Map p402 J5.
With themed soirées, drag shows and go-go boys that could have taught Joséphine Baker a few moves,

Banana Café is a solid choice for a night on the town. The ground-floor bar and adjacent terrace serve up happy hour drinks (6-11pm). Afterwards, patrons are ushered inside from the terrace and, eventually, downstairs for some dancing and go-go boy antics.

Le Bears' Den
6 rue des Lombards, 4th (01.42.71.08.20, www.bearsden.fr). M° Châtelet. **Open** 4pm-2am Mon-Thur, Sun; 4pm-5am Fri, Sat. Map p406 J6.
The Bears' Den is a friendly local for bears, muscle bears, chubbies and their admirers. Visit the website for details on theme nights such as 'Charcuterie'.

★ Le Café Arena
29 rue St-Denis, 1st (01.45.08.15.16). M° Châtelet. **Open** 11am-5am Mon-Sat; noon-10pm Sun. Map p406 J5.
This bar-restaurant has a great terrace for people-watching and friendly staff; it's still one of the hottest rendezvous in Les Halles.

Café Cox
15 rue des Archives, 4th (01.42.72.08.00, www.cox.fr). M° Hôtel de Ville. **Open** 5.30pm-2am daily. **No credit cards.** Map p409 K6.
Beefy, hairy, shaven-headed men congregate on the pavement in front of Café Cox for post-work drinks. DJs spin on Thursday nights and a lengthy happy hour on Sunday keeps the beer flowing until 2am.

Le Duplex
25 rue Michel-le-Comte, 3rd (01.42.72.80.86, www.duplex-bar.com). M° Hôtel de Ville or Rambuteau. **Open** 8pm-2am Mon-Thur, Sun; 8pm-4am Fri, Sat. Map p409 K5.

This small bar just round the corner from the Centre Pompidou caters to a thirtysomething crowd. It's a popular meeting place for various gay associations, with friendly staff and local art on the walls.

Etamine Café

13 rue des Ecouffes, 4th (01.44.78.09.62, www.etamine-cafe.com). M° St-Paul. **Open** noon-midnight Tue-Sun. **Map** p409 K6.
This simple café is located very close to the lesbian bars of the Marais, and offers a contemporary and inventive twist on old classics. Excellent food, affordable prices, good atmosphere.

Le Feeling Bar

43 rue Sainte-Croix de la Bretonnerie, 4th (01.48.04.70.03). M° Hôtel de Ville. **Open** 5pm-2am daily. **Map** p409 K6.
Le Feeling is a low-key gay and lesbian hangout. It won't be to everyone's taste, but the rainbow decor, Dalida soundtrack and easy-going staff are the perfect antidote to the tumult at Spyce just over the road. The mixed clientele includes a lot of regulars, and the general atmosphere is chatty and welcoming. On the other hand, there's no wasting time – it's an enthusiastic pick-up joint for people of all tastes.

★ Open Café

17 rue des Archives, 4th (01.42.72.26.18, www. opencafe.fr). M° Hôtel de Ville or Rambuteau. **Open** 11am-2am Mon-Thur, Sun; 11am-3am Fri, Sat. **Map** p409 K6.
Cruise and be cruised in the café everybody visits at some point in the evening. Pop out on to the terrace and enjoy the people-watching potential.

★ Le Quetzal

10 rue de la Verrerie, 4th (01.48.87.99.07). M° Hôtel de Ville. **Open** 5pm-2am Mon, Tue, Sun; 5pm-4am Wed-Sat. **Map** p409 K6.
This bar is considered to be one of the 'essential stops' on the Marais circuit, as it's often filled with hot men and a few drag queens to keep things lively. You might be able to find some action in the small, dark space upstairs.

Raidd Bar

23 rue du Temple, 4th (01.42.77.04.88, www. raiddbar.com). M° Hôtel de Ville. **Open** 6pm-4am Mon-Thur, Sun; 6pm-5am Fri, Sat, Sun. **Map** p406 K6.
The Raidd is a Marais LGBT venue to be reckoned with. Famous for its bare-chested barmen straight out of a modelling agency, the major draw is surely the soap sud-covered, brief-sporting, body-building go-go dancers who flaunt their wares under the front window's built-in showers (summer only). The red velvet rooms downstairs are cosier and more relaxed. With free entry, a warm welcome and reasonably priced drinks, this humming club is always busy, and it closes late all week. Tuesday night is nostalgia night, Wednesdays are Latino, and weekends electro.

Les Souffleurs

7 rue de la Verrerie, 4th (01.44.78.04.92, www.les-souffleurs.com). M° Hôtel de Ville or Saint-Paul. **Open** 6pm-2am daily. **Map** p409 K6.
Les Souffleurs is a hip little gay bar in the centre of the gay Marais. In the daytime, it's a quiet place to escape. But the temperature goes up quickly at night, with some out-there DJ mixes and crowds aplenty. Some nights feature concerts and shows.

Le Quetzal.

IN THE KNOW PILLOW TALK

The mixed but very gay-friendly **Hôtel Duo** (www.duoparis.com) is a stylish place to rest your head. What's more, it has helpful staff at the reception – something of a rarity in the trendy Marais.

Le Spyce Bar
23 rue Sainte-Croix de la Bretonnerie, 4th (no phone, www.spycebar.com). M° Hôtel de Ville. **Open** 5pm-3am Mon-Thur, Sun; 5pm-4am Fri, Sat. **Map** p409 K6.
More than an essential gay bar-club in the Marais, Le Spyce is a rallying cry. It heaves at weekends with a young, happy, sweaty, undressed, excitable crowd, ready to dance and take people home on a whim. There's an informal (read: barely there) dress code on the dancefloor, with bold guys welcome to take a place on a podium and dance until 4am. Entry is free and the drinks are reasonably priced, served with a smile by topless staff.

Restaurants

Le Bar à Manger (BAM)
13 rue des Lavandières-Ste-Opportune, 1st (01.42.21.01.72, www.bar-a-manger.fr). M° Les Halles. **Open** noon-3pm, 7-11pm Mon-Sat. **Map** p408 J6.
Excellent, creative cuisine served in a very relaxed setting. There's a *prix fixe* menu available at lunch (€18.80, €21.80).

Le Gai Moulin
10 rue St-Merri, 4th (01.48.87.06.00, www.le-gai-moulin.com). M° Hôtel de Ville. **Open** noon-midnight daily. **Map** p406 K6.
One of the oldest gay-run restaurants in Paris. The owner is famously convivial, creating a lovely, friendly atmosphere. On Tuesdays, a pianist belts out French songs, and it's not uncommon for the whole room to sing along.

Ze Restoo
41 rue des Blancs-Manteaux, 3rd (01.42.74.10.29). M° Rambuteau. **Open** 7.30pm-midnight Mon-Thur; 7.30pm-1am Fri, Sat. **Map** p409 K6.
This restaurant has become a popular place in which to eat with friends before heading out for a fun-filled evening in the Marais. There's a very relaxed atmosphere and decent food.

Clubs

As well as the venues listed here, a mixed but increasingly gay crowd mingles at **Nouveau Casino** (*see p267*). Most gay clubs are very hetero-friendly.

★ Le Club 18
18 rue de Beaujolais, 1st (01.42.97.52.13, www.club18.fr). M° Palais-Royal or Pyramides. **Open** midnight-dawn Fri, Sat. **Admission** (incl 1 drink) €10. **Map** p402 H5.
The oldest gay club in Paris attracts a young and beautiful clientele. It is not very big, and the decor isn't all that great, but the music is fun and there's a very laid-back vibe. Everyone is here to dance and have a good time.

Le CUD Bar
12 rue des Haudriettes, 3rd (01.42.77.44.12). M° Rambuteau. **Open** 11.30pm-6am Mon-Thur, Sun; 11.30pm-7am Fri, Sat. **Map** p409 K5.
Upstairs is a laid-back bar, but downstairs in the old cellar is a dancefloor that can get very crowded, especially after 2am. The crowd is a mixed bunch, and it's popular with the bears.

Les Follivores & les Crazyvores
Bataclan, 50 bd Voltaire, 11th (www.follivores.com). M° Oberkampf. **Open** times vary. **Admission** (incl 1 drink) €19. **Map** p407 M5.
Twice a month, the Bataclan concert hall transforms itself into a club to play host to these two parties. Crazyvores features music from the 1970s and '80s, and at Follivores the DJs spin gay classics from all eras mixed up with cutting-edge techno. These are big events with exuberant crowds; the drag queens put on their best ballgowns and biggest wigs, and the men sport their tightest tops. Great fun.

Queen
102 av des Champs-Elysées, 8th (01.53.89.08.90, www.queen.fr). M° George V. **Open** 11.30pm-6.30am daily. **Admission** varies. **Map** p400 D4.
One of the oldest and largest clubs, Queen's main gay night is Overkitsch on Sundays, but every night is a little gay. Big-name DJs often spin here to a crowd peppered with VIPs.

Scream
18 rue du Fbg-du-Temple, 11th (01.82.09.95.32, www.scream-paris.com). M° République. **Open** midnight-7am Sat. **Admission** €10 before 1am incl 1 drink; €15 after 1am. **Map** p402 L4.
If you're attractive, well-built and not afraid of getting lost, the cavernous Scream club is your ideal party. Between the covered terrace and the two underground dancefloors, there's something for everyone. If you're feeling frisky, there's a designated cruise section too. Drinks are pricey, but at least the eye candy is free – after you've paid the €15 admission, of course.

★ Le Tango (La Boîte à Frissons)
13 rue au Maire, 3rd (01.42.72.17.78, www.boite-a-frissons.fr). M° Arts et Métiers. **Open** 10.30pm-5am Fri, Sat; 6-11pm Sun. **Admission** €9. **Map** p409 K5.

Wacky crowd, Madonna songs and accordion tunes. At the Friday and Saturday Bal de la Boîte à Frissons, couples dance the foxtrot, tango, madison or *guinguette* in the early part of the evening, followed after midnight by music of every variety except techno.

Sex clubs & saunas

Le Bunker
150 rue St-Maur, 11th (01.53.36.01.16, www.bunker-cruising.com). M° Goncourt. **Open** 4pm-2am Mon-Sat; 4pm-midnight Sun. **Admission** €8-€10; €7 reductions. **Map** p403 M4.
This cruising club is the hottest in Paris. It features all-naked and underwear-only nights during the week, and hardcore themes at the weekend. Friday is a very popular night, as is the first Saturday of the month, when Le Bunker hosts its S&M 'Red and Black Night' – not for the faint-hearted.

Le Dépot
10 rue aux Ours, 3rd (01.44.54.96.96, www.ledepot.com). M° Etienne Marcel. **Open** 2pm-8am daily. **Admission** €10-€15. **Map** p402 K5.
A very busy dance club upstairs with a labyrinthine maze of cubicles, glory holes and darkrooms downstairs. The Dépot's glory days are gone now, but it still draws a crowd, particularly at weekends. Pickpockets work the darkrooms, so be careful.

Full Metal
40 rue des Blancs Manteaux, 4th (www.fullmetal.fr). M° Rambuteau. **Open** 5pm-4am Mon-Thur, Sun; 5pm-6am Fri, Sat. **Admission** free. **Map** p409 K6.

The trendier of the two gay fetish clubs in the same street: don't even try to get into Full Metal unless you adhere to the night's dress code. Two backrooms host all sorts of fetish and fantasy escapades, depending on the night, and a harness is also available.

★ IDM
4 rue du Fbg-Montmartre, 9th (01.45.23.10.03, www.idm-sauna.com). M° Grands Boulevards. **Open** noon-1am daily. **Admission** €21; €15 before 9.30pm & under-35s. **Map** p402 J4.
The city's best gay sauna has three levels and plenty of cabins and corridors to prowl. The wet sauna is on two levels, and the small relaxation pool and showers are always at the perfect temperature. A few times a month, there are performances by drag queens.

Impact
18 rue Grenata, 2nd (01.42.21.94.24, www.impact-bar.com). M° Etienne Marcel. **Open** 8pm-3am Mon-Thur; 10pm-6am Fri, Sat; 3pm-3am Sun. **Admission** €16 (incl 1 drink); €10 (incl 1 drink) under-30s. **Map** p406 J5.
Two floors of antics await you at Paris's premier gay nudist bar. Upstairs, drinking and flatscreen porn. Downstairs, well, any variety of impacting, depending on who's there. If sex isn't your thing, there's a buffet on Sunday starting at 9pm.

Next
87 rue St-Honoré, 1st (no phone). M° Les Halles. **Open** noon-3am Mon-Thur; 24hrs Fri-Sun. **Admission** €7 before 7pm; €10-€13 (incl 1 drink) after 7pm; €6 (incl 1 drink) under-26s. **Map** p402 J5.

Le Tango.

ARTS & ENTERTAINMENT

This hot sex club is located in one of the chicest parts of the capital. It doesn't really get going until after many clubs have closed, and at 6am on a Sunday morning it's probably the hottest, hardest place in town. The bar upstairs is a nice place in which to mingle before heading down to the sexy labyrinth.

Secteur X
49 rue des Blancs Manteaux, 4th (www.secteurx.fr). M° Rambuteau. **Open** 3pm-4am Mon-Thur, Sun; 3pm-6am Fri, Sat. **Admission** varies. **Map** p409 K6.
Once a quaint gay dive bar, Secteur X has transformed into one of Paris's most hardcore gay cruise clubs. At Friday Hard Night parties, participants are invited to dress in leather, latex or nothing at all, and Saturday's Leather and Slave Afternoon is only for the truly motivated. For tight budgets, there's no cover charge and a generous happy hour until 9pm. The two lower levels are where the fun takes place with backrooms and corridors galore.

Sun City
62 bd de Sébastopol, 3rd (01.40.09.25.37, www. suncity-paris.fr). M° Etienne Marcel. **Open** noon-6am daily. **Admission** €20 Mon-Thur (€15 after 3am, €12 under-26s); €21 Fri-Sun (€17 after 3am, €14 under-26s). **Map** p402 J5.
Owned and operated by the Dépôt team (*see p259*), this Bollywood-themed venue is the largest gay sauna in Europe, with a pool, large steam room, gym and bar. The clientele is good-looking and knows it.

Shops & services

Les Dessous d'Apollon
15 rue du Bourg-Tibourg, 4th (01.42.71.87.37, www.lesdessousdapollon.com). M° Hôtel de Ville or St-Paul. **Open** 11am-8pm Mon-Sat; 2-8pm Sun. **Map** p409 K6.
Probably the most extensive selection of underwear – from the functional to the downright eccentric – that you'll ever see, plus T-shirts and accessories.

IEM
16 rue Ste-Croix-de-la-Bretonnerie, 4th (01.42.74.01.61, www.iem.fr). M° Hôtel de Ville. **Open** noon-8pm Mon-Thur; noon-9pm Fri, Sat; 2-8pm Sun. **Map** p403 M4.
This sex hypermarket caters for those keen on the harder side of gay life. Videos, clothes and gadgets can all be found; leather and rubber are upstairs.

★ Legay Choc
45 rue Ste-Croix-de-la-Bretonnerie, 4th (01.48.87. 56.88, www.legaychoc.fr). M° Hôtel de Ville. **Open** 7.30am-8pm Mon, Wed-Sun. **Map** p409 K6.
Run by two brothers (one gay, one straight) whose surname just happens to be Legay, this *boulangerie* and pâtisserie is very popular. The pastries are delightful, and the lunch-hour sandwiches are generous, so expect queues.

★ Les Mots à la Bouche
6 rue Ste-Croix-de-la-Bretonnerie, 4th (01.42.78.88.30, www.motsbouche.com). M° Hôtel de Ville or St-Paul. **Open** 11am-11pm Mon-Sat; 1-9pm Sun. **Map** p409 K6.
An institution in the Marais, this bookshop has a large selection of gay fiction, non-fiction, magazines, and English-language books.

Plus Que Parfait
23 rue des Blancs-Manteaux, 4th (01.42.71.09.05). M° Hôtel de Ville or St-Paul. **Open** 3-8pm Mon; 12.30-8pm Tue-Sat; 3-7pm Sun. *Clothes deposit* Mon-Fri. **Map** p409 K6.
This *dépôt vente*, where pristine second-hand designer clothing is sold on commission, is a great place for men's fashion finds.

Space Hair
10 rue Rambuteau, 3rd (01.48.87.28.51, www.space-hair.com). M° Rambuteau. **Open** 11am-10pm Mon; 10am-10pm Tue-Sat; noon-8pm Sun (summer only). **Map** p409 K6.

Legay Choc.

Rosa Bonheur.

Space Hair is divided into two salons, Cosmic and Classic, with a 1980s kitsch feel, late opening hours and cute stylists; it's best to book ahead.

LESBIAN PARIS

The girlie scene continues to flourish, especially near the corner of rue du Roi de Sicile and rue des Ecouffes. Some girl-only parties are staged at clubs such as **Le Tango** (*see p258*); see the free monthly magazine *Barbi(e)turix* for listings.

Le 3W Kafé
8 rue des Ecouffes, 4th (01.48.87.39.26). Mº St-Paul. **Open** 7pm-3am Wed, Thur; 7pm-5am Fri, Sat; 8pm-2am Sun. **Map** p409 K6.
A convivial place where beautiful women go to have a drink, meet other women and listen to good music. There's a small dance space in the basement, and a number of theme nights every month.

★ La Champmeslé
4 rue Chabanais, 2nd (01.42.96.85.20, www. lachampmesle.fr). Mº Bourse or Pyramides. **Open** 4pm-4am Mon-Sat. **Map** p402 H4.
This veteran girlie bar remains a popular venue for lesbian locals and visitors. Beer is the drink of choice; pull up a seat and enjoy the cabaret nights.

Dollhouse
24 rue du Roi de Sicile, 4th (01.40.27.09.21, www.dollhouse.fr). Mº St-Paul. **Open** 1-8pm Mon-Sat; 2-8pm Sun. **Map** p409 L6.
This store specialises in lingerie and gadgets for the girls. Upstairs you'll find a selection of sophisticated underwear; head downstairs for the sexcessories.

Les Jacasses
5 rue des Ecouffes, 4th (01.42.71.15.51). Mº St-Paul. **Open** noon-3pm, 5.30pm-midnight Tue, Wed; noon-2am Fri-Sun. **Map** p409 K6.
This relaxed bar for women is located just around the corner from all the girlie bars on rue du Roi de Sicile in the Marais.

★ Le Rive Gauche
1 rue du Sabot, 6th (01.40.20.43.23). Mº St-Germain-des-Prés. **Open** 11pm-5am Sat. **Admission** €15 (incl 1 drink). **No credit cards**. **Map** p405 G7.
This weekend women-only nightclub is one of the hottest places on the lesbian scene. The decor is '70s and the music eclectic.

Rosa Bonheur
Parc des Buttes Chaumont, 2 av de la Cascade, 19th (01.42.00.00.45, www.rosabonheur.fr). Mº Buttes Chaumont. **Open** noon-midnight Wed-Fri; 10am-midnight Sat, Sun. **Map** p403 N2.
Bucolic delights reign at Rosa Bonheur. Its name loosely translates as 'pink happiness' but refers in particular to 19th-century painter and sculptor Rosa Bonheur, famous for her depictions of animals and her role in the early feminist movement. The bar is managed by Michelle Cassaro, aka Mimi, who used to run lesbian club Pulp – and it's a popular hangout with the lesbian crowd, especially on Sunday evenings.

Le So What!
30 rue du Roi de Sicile, 4th (01.42.71.24.59). Mº St-Paul. **Open** 7pm-2am Wed, Thur; 11pm-5am Fri, Sat. **Map** p409 L6.
Primarily a girlie bar, but everyone's welcome. Recent theme nights have included live rock and drag queens.

Nightlife

Paris has rediscovered its party pzazz with a string of supremely funky new venues. At the moment, the Right Bank's in poll position again (for the last couple of years the Left Bank ruled with its Seine-side clubs in the 13th), with a crop of new addresses around the Champs-Elysées and in SoPi (south Pigalle). Many of these new nightlife stars double up as gig spaces too. Parisians still tend to go out clubbing late and most venues will be empty if you turn up before midnight.

Paris's traditional cabarets cater to the throngs of tourists and businessmen who drop in for an eyeful of boob-bouncing, posh nosh and champers. But if the get-your-glitz-out-for-the-boys genre isn't your cup of tea, then a Gallic giggle can still be had at old-fashioned *café-théâtres*, where songs and sketches accompany dinner.

Clubs

Seine-side clubs in the 13th arrondissement, such as **Batofar**, **Wanderlust** and **Nüba**, are still the major draws on the Left Bank, but a string of new Right Bank venues – such as the **Cartel Club** and **Hobo Club** in the smart 8th arrondissement – are drawing fashionistas back to the Champs-Elysées for some late-night fun. Refreshingly, though, the emphasis is more about having fun than posing. For listings, check out www.parisbouge.com, www.novaplanet.com and www.radiofg.com.

RIGHT BANK
Club bars

L'Alimentation Générale
64 rue Jean-Pierre Timbaud, 11th (01.43.55.42.50, www.alimentation-generale.net). M° Parmentier or Couronnes. **Open** 7pm-2am Wed-Thur, Sun; 7pm-5am Fri, Sat. **Admission** varies (€10 Fri, Sat). **Map** p403 M4.
Doubling as a concert hall, restaurant and club, this funky bar doles out large portions of fun, live music and affordable booze. By midnight the place is absolutely heaving, so arrive early if you want to get a table and some food. The dancefloor splices anything from electro to samba and hip hop late into the night.

★ Andy Wahloo
69 rue des Gravilliers, 3rd (01.42.71.20.38, www.andywahloo-bar.com). M° Arts et Métiers. **Open** 7pm-1.45am Tue-Sat. **Admission** free. **Map** p409 K5.
Owned by the people behind Momo and Sketch in London, Andy Wahloo serves sumptuous snack food and is decorated with Moroccan artefacts and a spice rack of colours. The seating is made from upturned paint cans, and the DJs play an eclectic mix, featuring everything from hip hop to techno and stepping up the volume as the night progresses.

★ Chacha Club
47 rue Berger, 1st (01.40.13.12.12, www.chachadub.fr). M° Châtelet. **Open** 8pm-6am Wed-Sat. **Admission** varies. **Map** p402 J5.
The Chacha Club's *fumoir* is just one of the sexy attributes of this hot haunt that attracts a good-looking clientele through its doors. In the style of a private club, but with no membership requirement (only exacting 'physionomists' stand at the door), it combines restaurant, bar and club in a suite of intimate rooms with subdued lighting and seductive, 1930s-inspired decor.

★ La Fourmi

74 rue des Martyrs, 18th (01.42.64.70.35).
M° Pigalle. **Open** 8am-2am Mon-Thur; 8am-
4am Fri, Sat; 10am-2am Sun. **Admission** free.
Map p402 H2.
La Fourmi was a precursor to all the industrial-
design, informal, music-led bars that have sprung
up around Paris in recent years – and it's still
very much a style leader, attracting everyone from
in-the-know tourists to fashionable Parisians. Great
throughout the day for coffees or a beer, it has a small
seating area outside and an always busy bar with
DJ decks. You can stay into the early hours at weekends, but it's also a handy pre-club rendezvous and
flyer supplier.

★ Panic Room

*101 rue Amelot, 11th (01.58.30.93.43, www.
panicroomparis.com). M° Filles du Calvaire
or St-Sébastien Froissart.* **Open** 6.30pm-2am
Tue-Sat. Closed 2wks Aug. **Admission** free.
Map p409 L5.
This pulsing electro bar has quickly carved out a
niche on the rock scene, and it's not nearly as daunting as its name suggests. Live acts and DJs blast
the sound system in the basement, while upstairs
friendly barmen serve affordable cocktails behind a
concrete counter.

Le Truskel

*12 rue Feydeau, 2nd (01.40.26.59.97, www.
truskel.com). M° Bourse, Grands Boulevards
or Richelieu Drouot.* **Open** 6pm-5am Tue-Sat.
Admission free. **Map** p402 H4.

A popular spot with the indiepop and punk-rock
crowds, this pub-cum-club hits the spot with great
beer and an eclectic repertoire served up by top DJs.
Pete Doherty, Franz Ferdinand and ex-Pulp man
Jarvis Cocker have all played here.

Clubs

Badaboum

*2bis rue des Taillandiers, 11th (01.48.06.50.70,
www.badaboum-paris.com). M° Bastille.* **Open**
7pm-2am Wed; 7pm-4am Thur; 7pm-6.15am Fri,
Sat. **Admission** varies. **Map** p407 M7.
La Scène Bastille has been done up and relaunched
by the same group behind the Panic Room, and is
now the Badaboum. Inside, there's a simple retro-
industrial look, a sound system that makes the light-
strewn ceiling shake, a restaurant and cocktail/tapas
bar open to all from 7pm, and a secret room upstairs
with bachelor pad allure. Nights kick off with gigs
from emerging pop-rock artists, then comes clubbing with a good range of techno DJs.

Le Baron

*6 av Marceau, 8th (01.47.20.04.01, www.club
lebaron.com). M° Alma Marceau.* **Open** 11pm-
6am daily. **Admission** free. **Map** p400 D5.
This small, supremely exclusive hangout for the jet
set used to be home to an upmarket brothel, and it
has the decor to prove it. It only holds 150 people,
most of whom are regulars you'll need to befriend
in order to get past the door. If you do manage to get
in, you'll be rubbing shoulders with celebrities and
super-glossy people.

La Bellevilloise. See p265.

ARTS & ENTERTAINMENT

BANLIEUE BEATS

Electro is the sound of the suburbs at 1936.

The *banlieue* of Seine St-Denis has always had something of an image problem: when there's social unrest, the cameras tend to flock here to film burning cars. But beyond the dingy post-war housing sprawl, things are changing. The Plaine St-Denis district is a triangle of exciting urban renewal between the Stade de France, the *périphérique* (by Porte de la Chapelle) and the Carrefour de Pleyel métro. It's home to Luc Besson's Cité du Cinéma studios ('Hollywood-sur-Seine'), and is also where hipsters are flocking for one of the city's edgiest new club nights: **1936** (146 av des Magasins Généraux, 93210 Seine St-Denis, www.1936paris.com).

The concept is simple: every few weeks, electro collective Lakomune brings a handful of DJs to a warehouse for hedonistic all-nighters that out-shake anything in town. Expect a rave atmosphere (big screens, dry ice) and thumping electro from the likes of Erol Alkan (of Phantasy Sound fame); German dance maestro Michael Mayer; Life and Death label founder DJ Tennis; and French duo the Welderz, known for their dark techno and underground vibes. If you're wondering where the name comes from, the nearest metro to the warehouse is Front Populaire, named after the alliance of left-wing movements whose revolt came to a head in 1936.

Should you catch the *banlieue* bug, check out **Glaz'Art** (*see p266*), on the edge of Seine St-Denis at Porte de la Villette. Set in a converted coach station, it's a club magnet for drum 'n' bass and dubstep fans, and has a funky summer beach with a stage for bands.

La Bellevilloise

19-21 rue Boyer, 20th (01.46.36.07.07, www. labellevilloise.com). M° Gambetta or Ménilmontant. **Open** 7pm-1am Wed, Thur; 7pm-2am Fri; varies Sat, Sun. **Admission** free; concerts vary. **Map** p403 P4.

Set in Paris's first workers' co-operative, this funky venue takes the multidisciplinary concept to new heights, offering food, concerts and regular club nights, as well as art exhibitions. An outside staircase leads to a rooftop bar, plus a loft space used as a club/art space. But the real action happens in the basement, where DJs play everything from '80s pop to reggae and indie-rock. *Photo p263.*

Le Cabaret Sauvage

59 bd Macdonald, 19th (01.42.09.03.09, www. cabaretsauvage.com). M° Porte de la Villette. **Open** 9pm-dawn, days vary. **Admission** €10-€35. **Map** p403 inset.

Dressed up like a circus, this funky, red-velvet venue offers one of the most eclectic clubbing and live music programmes in town: expect anything from world music to pulse-altering electronic and drum 'n' bass nights, as well as techno. Check the website for full details.

Cartel Club

4 rue Arsène Houssaye, 8th (06.43.74.53.39, 06.29.66.83.08, www.carteldubparis.com). M°/RER Charles de Gaulle-Etoile. **Open** 11pm-5am Thur-Sat. **Admission** free. **Map** p400 D3.

This spanking new Mexican-themed club is the city's new fashionista hangout, with 30 tequilas on the menu and shabby-chic decor that wouldn't look out of place on a Latino gangster movie film set. Expect deep house and hip hop, as well as a tough door policy. Book a table if you want guaranteed entry.

La Chapelle des Lombards

19 rue de Lappe, 11th (01.43.57.24.24, www. la-chapelle-des-lombards.com). M° Bastille. **Open** 11pm-6am Wed-Sun. **Admission** free Wed, Thur, Sun; €20 Fri, Sat (incl 1 drink). Ladies free before midnight. **Map** p407 M7.

The management is new, but not much else has changed at this popular world music venue: Afrojazz, ragga and Latino bands and DJs still provide the music, and the dancefloor's as hot and steamy as ever. Smart dress only.

Chez Moune

54 rue Jean-Baptiste Pigalle, 9th (09.67.50.28.44, www.facebook.com/chezmouneofficiel). M° St-Georges. **Open** 11pm-late Wed-Sat. **Admission** free-€8. **Map** p401 H2.

With mirrored walls and ceilings so low you can almost touch them, this basement hipster hangout is the place to come for underground label nights, aftershow parties and splice sessions by cool electro-rock DJs. It's often free, so expect a queue to get in.

★ Chez Régine

49 rue de Ponthieu, 8th (06.20.25.85.11). M° St-Philippe-du-Roule. **Open** 11.30pm-5am Wed; 7pm-4am Thur; 11.30pm-7am Fri, Sat. **Admission** varies. **Map** p401 D4.

Régine was once a key figure on the Paris nightlife scene, and her portrait still sits by the entrance for a touch of '70s nostalgia, but the revamped venue has shifted from disco to sophisticated electro, inviting the cream of international DJs to the decks. The afterwork La French is a safe bet for a wild Thursday.

Le Divan du Monde

75 rue des Martyrs, 18th (01.40.05.06.99, www. divandumonde.com). M° Abbesses or Pigalle. **Open** times vary. **Admission** €6-€33. **Map** p402 H2.

After a drink in the cool Fourmi opposite (*see p263*), pop over to the Divan du Monde for one-off parties and regular events. The upstairs specialises in VJ events, and downstairs holds dub, electro, funk and world music nights.

EKO

14 rue Saint Fiacre, 2nd (www.ekoclub.fr). M° Bonne Nouvelle or Grands Boulevards. **Open** 9pm-6am Fri, Sat. **Admission** €10. **Map** p402 J4.

This ex-synagogue, ex-data centre looks more like a clandestine Tokyo bar than a Paris nightclub – and that's the fun of it all: get your saké fix at the bar, soak it up with Japanese street food, then sing your heart out in the karaoke booths. If dancing's more your forte, the futuristic dancefloor (minimalist with neon lights and screen-covered pillars) pumps soul-warming house and techno.

Etoile Paris

61 rue du Château d'Eau, 10th (01.42.47.16.56, www.etoiles-paris.com). M° Strasbourg Saint-Denis. **Open** 11pm-6am Fri, Sat. **Admission** varies. **Map** p402 K4.

Following a three-year makeover, this former 19th-century theatre looks like a futuristic cabaret, with an intimate stage and a funky ceiling of woven metal ribbons. Expect live music from emerging bands (organised by Live Nation), artistic happenings galore and regular club nights, including the weekly La Cirkus – where cabaret and disco take on a burlesque quality.

★ Favela Chic

18 rue du Fbg-du-Temple, 11th (01.40.21.38.14, www.favelachic.com). M° République. **Open** 7.30pm-2am Tue, Wed; 7.30pm-3am Thur; 7.30pm-4am Fri, Sat. **Admission** free Tue-Thur; €15 Fri, Sat (incl 1 drink). **Map** p402 L4.

Past the usually steely-faced door attendants, amid decor reminiscent of 1930s Brazil, the Favela Chic attracts an up-for-it, international crowd for some serious Latin, rock and electro dancing. There are decent DJs, live acts aplenty, and Brazilian food and drinks. *Photos p266.*

ARTS & ENTERTAINMENT

Favela Chic. See p265.

Le Gibus
18 rue du Fbg-du-Temple, 11th (01.82.09.95.32, www.gibus.fr). M° République. **Open** midnight-7am Thur-Sat. *Concerts* 6-11pm (days vary). **Admission** varies. **Map** p402 L4.
A famous punk venue during the 1980s, Le Gibus has gone through a wide variety of style changes during its life. These days, under new management, it takes in rock, folk, electro, trance and funk, plus the occasional band.

Le Glaz'art
7-15 av de la Porte de la Villette, 19th (01.40.36.55.65, www.glazart.com). M° Porte de la Villette. **Open** varies (check website for details). **Admission** free-€20. **Map** p403 inset.
This converted coach station is just beyond Parc de la Villette, but its strong DJ nights and live acts pull punters in from central Paris. Dub step, break-beat, electro and drum 'n' bass nights have made the venue a magnet for breaks fans. In the summer, the outdoor area is transformed into a sandy beach with pastis, pétanque and merguez: a winning combination. *See also p264* **Banlieue Beats**.

Hobo Club
67 rue Pierre Charron, 8th (01.45.61.18.86, 06.34.11.24.65, www.lehoboclub.com). M° Georges V or Franklin D Roosevelt. **Open** varies (check website). **Admission** free. **Map** p400 D4.
With brick walls and angular mirrors, this funky Manhattan-style club reels in twentysomething fashionistas from the surrounding Golden Triangle. The music's resolutely R'n'B and house, and best washed down with an excellently prepared G&T – especially on Thursday's after-work nights.

La Java
105 rue du Fbg-du-Temple, 10th (01.42.02.20.52, www.la-java.fr). M° Belleville or Goncourt. **Open** midnight-dawn Thur-Sat. *Concerts* vary (see website for details). **Admission** €5-€15. **No credit cards**. **Map** p403 M4.
Tucked inside the crumbling, disused Belleville market, La Java has been a venue for Paris night owls since the 1930s – Django Reinhardt, Edith Piaf and Jean Gabin all played here. In the decades that followed, the rebellious youth came to let their hair down to a rock soundtrack. Then, in the 1980s, the nocturnal fauna of the Parisian 'trash underground' came here to listen to punk rock. There followed a fallow period of low-quality salsa, but La Java has recently rediscovered its original vocation as an anti-establishment club, with a programme featuring garage rock, punk dub and electro-techno nights.

La Machine du Moulin Rouge
90 bd de Clichy, 18th (01.53.41.88.89, www.lamachinedumoulinrouge.com). M° Blanche. **Open** 11pm-6am Fri, Sat (weekdays vary). **Admission** varies. **Map** p401 G2.

This three-floor bar/club/live venue has something for everyone: the main dancefloor, Le Central, holds 1,000 gyrating clubbers; the intimate La Chaufferie, the Moulin Rouge's old boiler room, showcases new and established electro acts; and the upstairs bar adds some bohemian chic, with a coveted terrace and brunch menus.

★ Le Magnifique

25 rue de Richelieu, 1st (01.42.60.70.80, www. lemagnifique.fr). M° Palais Royal-Musée du Louvre. **Open** 7pm-4am daily. **Admission** free. **Map** p401 H5.
Named after a 1970s film starring Jean-Paul Belmondo, this snazzy cocktail bar is a real retro treat. The decor, dominated by wood, dark leather and animal furs, is elegant, with a hint of porno chic that leaves you picturing Warhol and his posse partying away in a corner. The place really comes to life after midnight, when the bar turns into a club with a soundtrack of dancefloor-fillers from the past three decades. The fantastic cocktail menu, a selection of sushi (€10-€30) and the separate *fumoir* add to the overall appeal.

Monseigneur

94 rue d'Amsterdam, 9th (www.monseigneurparis. com). M°/RER Place de Clichy. **Open** 11pm-6am Fri, Sat; weekdays varies (check website). **Admission** free-€14. **Map** p401 G2.
Set in a converted Russian cabaret, this cosy joint has a slamming sound system and hosts a packed programme of hip hop, house, techno and disco. Drinks are cheapish, and the dancefloor's dark.

★ New Morning

7-9 rue des Petites-Ecuries, 10th (01.45.23.51.41, www.newmorning.com). M° Bonne Nouvelle or Château d'Eau. **Open** varies. **Admission** varies. **Map** p402 K3.
Jazz fans crowd into this hip, no-frills joint to natter, drink and boogie to the excellent live music. Low-key it may be, but it's still worth looking out for the occasional A-lister.

Nouveau Casino

109 rue Oberkampf, 11th (01.43.57.57.40, www.nouveaucasino.net). M° Ménilmontant or Parmentier. **Open** varies. **Admission** varies. **Map** p403 M5.
Conveniently surrounded by the numerous bars of rue Oberkampf and tucked behind the legendary Café Charbon, Nouveau Casino is a concert venue that also hosts some of the city's liveliest club nights. Local collectives, international names and record labels host nights here; it's worth checking the website for one-offs and after-parties.

★ Point Ephémère

200 quai de Valmy, 10th (01.40.34.02.48, www. pointephemere.org). M° Jaurès or Louis Blanc. **Open** noon-2am Mon-Sat; noon-midnight Sun. **Admission** varies. **Map** 402 L2.
This hunk of Berlin in Paris was only ever meant to be temporary, but thankfully it's still around. An uncompromising programming policy delivers some of the best electronic music in town; there's also a restaurant and bar with decks and a gallery, and terrace space by the canal in summer.

Hobo Club.

ARTS & ENTERTAINMENT

Wanderlust.

ARTS & ENTERTAINMENT

Queen

102 av des Champs-Elysées, 8th (01.53.89.08.90, www.queen.fr). M° George V or St-Philippe-du-Roule. **Open** 11.30pm-6.30am daily. **Admission** varies. **Map** p400 D4.

Once the city's most fêted gay club and the only venue that could hold a torch to the Rex, with a roster of top local DJs holding court, Queen's star faded a little during the early noughties but is now starting to shine more brightly again. Located along the club-laden Champs-Elysées, this is one of the few places you can party seven nights a week. For more on Queen's gay nights, *see p258*.

★ Rex

5 bd Poissonnière, 2nd (01.42.36.10.96, www. rexclub.com). M° Bonne Nouvelle or Grands Boulevards. **Open** 11.30pm-7am Thur-Sat. **Admission** €5-€15. **Map** p402 J4.

The Rex's sound system puts over 40 different sound configurations at the DJ's fingertips, and is a magnet for top turntable stars. Once associated with iconic techno pioneer Laurent Garnier, the Rex has stayed at the top of the Paris techno scene, and occupies an unassailable position as the city's serious club music venue.

Showcase

Below Pont Alexandre III, 8th (01.45.61.25.43, www.showcase.fr). M° Champs-Elysées Clemenceau or Invalides. **Open** 11.30pm-6am Thur-Sat. **Admission** free-€15. **Map** p401 E5.

This vast venue located below Pont Alexandre III is where techno-, house- and bass-crazed insomniacs come at weekends to dance until daybreak. The club had lost some hype in recent times, but a handful of high-profile guest DJs have been setting the bar higher lately: Carl Cox, will.i.am and Calvin Harris have all made appearances.

Silencio

142 rue de Montmartre, 2nd (www.silencio-club.com). M° Bourse or Grands Boulevards. **Open** 6pm-4am Tue-Thur; 6pm-6am Fri, Sat. **Admission** varies. **Map** p402 J4.

David Lynch's joint, named after the cult venue in his 2001 movie *Mulholland Drive*, is a private, arty networking club that opens its door to the public at midnight. The director designed every aspect of the decor, from the gold-leaf walls to the 1950s-style furniture. There are concerts by up-and-coming bands, film premieres, eclectic club nights and a stream of prestigious guests. Dress right if you want to get in.

★ Le Social Club

142 rue Montmartre, 2nd (01.40.28.05.55, www.parissocialclub.com). M° Bourse or Grands Boulevards. **Open** 11pm-3am Tue, Wed; 11pm-6am Thur-Sat. **Admission** free-€20. **Map** p402 J4.

This retro-futurist electro venue has some of the hippest acts from the French and international scene. Thursday nights are devoted to avant-garde label CUFF and its G-House crews. Fridays are gay-friendly, and Saturdays are open to any music collectives and labels that charm the management's ears.

LEFT BANK
Clubs

★ Batofar

Opposite 11 quai François-Mauriac, 13th (09.71.25.50.61, www.batofar.org). M° Quai de la Gare. **Open** *Concerts* 7-11pm Mon-Sat. *Club* 11.30pm-6am Mon-Sat; 6am-noon 1st Sun of mth. **Admission** free-€18. **Map** p407 N10.

Set on a former fire brigade boat, this quirky venue is still cutting-edge, largely thanks to a top-notch music programme, including electro, dub step, techno and dancehall nights from home-grown and international acts. From June to September (noon-midnight), the bar sets up a temporary beach; come and admire the sunset while sprawling in a sun lounger.

La Dame de Canton
Port de la Gare, 13th (01.53.61.08.49, www. damedecanton.com). M° Quai de la Gare. **Open** 7pm-2am Tue-Thur; 7pm-5am Fri, Sat. **Admission** free-€15. **Map** p407 N10.
The Dame de Canton, which is housed in a superb Chinese junk, features a gig space, striking wooden dancefloor, romantic restaurant in the hold and sun-drenched bridge for *apéros*. The music is eclectic: breakbeats, electro-swing gypsy jazz, electro-tropical candomblé DJs, Thai-funk electro disco, ragga, kompa and plenty more alternative world music you've never heard of.

Le Djoon
22 bd Vincent Auriol, 13th (01.45.70.83.49, www. djoon.com). M° Quai de la Gare. **Open** 6.30pm-1am Thur; 11.30pm-5am Fri, Sat. **Admission** free-€10. **Map** p407 M9.
With its loft-style lounge, large bay windows and a vast curved bar, Le Djoon wouldn't look out of place in NYC. Trendy thirtysomethings pile in for house, deep house, soul and motown nights, spliced by a string of international DJs fresh off the plane from Detroit, Chicago, Berlin, New York and London. Djoon's restaurant won't win any Michelin stars, but it's handy if you want to make a night of it.

Nüba
36 quai d'Austerlitz, 13th (www.nuba-paris.fr). M° Gare d'Austerlitz. **Open** 6pm-5am Tue-Sat; noon-2am Sun. **Admission** free (charge for special events). **Map** p407 M9.
Located on the roof of the Cité de la Mode et du Design, this panoramic, no dress code club adds another layer of excitement to the site that already houses Wanderlust (*see below*). There's a beach hut-style wooden DJ booth playing chillout world music, plus live concerts and clubby electro sets.

Wanderlust
32 quai d'Austerlitz, 13th (www.wanderlust paris.com). M° Quai de la Gare. **Open** varies. **Admission** varies. **Map** p407 M9.
At quay level in the Cité de la Mode et du Design, this club includes a huge wooden terrace, perfect for watching the sunset with a cocktail in hand. Music is minimal techno and house on a decent sound system. The door policy and prices can get a little tiresome (entry is free, but drinks and food come at a premium), but the top-notch programming usually makes it worthwhile. Expect new-generation 'French touch' electronic dance music by the likes of I:Cube or Etienne de Crécy, plus fashion-themed nights, documentary screenings, catwalk shows and performances.

Cabaret, comedy & café-théâtre

More than 120 years since the **Moulin Rouge** introduced the risqué *quadrille réaliste* (which was later dubbed the cancan), busty babes are still shaking their bodies with sequinned panache all across the capital. Cabaret is an all-evening affair, traditionally served up with champagne and a meal. Male dancers and magicians complement the foxy foxtrots, the dancing is perfectly synchronised and the whole caboodle is perfectly respectable. Comedy-wise, there are numerous places for a Gallic giggle, with stand-up comics taking centre stage in most venues. If French (or indeed the French sense of humour) isn't your forte, a handful of diehard expats are keeping English-speaking comedy alive: check out **Sebastian Marx**'s website (www.sebmarx. com) for details on his stand-up and open-mic nights; or try funny gal **Phyllis Wang** (www.comedyrivegauche.com).

RIGHT BANK
Cabaret

Crazy Horse Saloon
12 av George V, 8th (01.47.23.32.32, www. lecrazyhorseparis.com). M° Alma Marceau

Moulin Rouge. *See p270.*

or George V. **Shows** 8.15pm, 10.45pm Mon-Fri, Sun; 7pm, 9.30pm, 11.45pm Sat. **Admission** *Show only* €105. *Show (incl champagne)* €125. **Map** p400 D4.

Somewhat more risqué than the other cabarets, the Horse, whose *art du nu* was invented in 1951 by Alain Bernadin, is an ode to feminine beauty: lookalike dancers with provocative names such as Gloria di Parma and Zula Zazou, and identical body statistics (when standing, the women's nipples and hips are all at the same height), slink around the stage, clad only in rainbow light and strategic strips of black tape. In their latest show, Désirs, the girls put on some tantalising numbers, with titles such as 'God Save Our Bare Skin' (a sexy take on the British Changing the Guard) and 'Red Shoes' – a sensual homage to ballerinas.

Le Lido

116bis av des Champs-Elysées, 8th (01.40.76.56.10, www.lido.fr). M° Franklin D. Roosevelt or George V. **Lunch** 1pm. **Matinée** 3pm Tue, Sun (dates vary). **Dinner** 7pm. **Shows** 9pm, 11pm daily. **Admission** *Lunch & matinée show* €165 (incl champagne). *9pm & 11pm shows* €115-€165 (incl champagne). *Dinner & show* €165-€400. **Map** p400 D4.

In 2015, the largest and chicest of the capital's cabarets opened its spanking new Paris Merveilles show – a collection of sparkling, perfectly synchronised numbers involving fire, water and often avant-garde tableaux mixing movement and silhouettes. Providing these sensual, feathers-in-your-face performances are the resident Bluebell Girls, joined by the hunky Lido Boys. For a special treat, opt for a classic French meal (think foie gras, lobster, etc) by chef Philippe Lacroix and make an evening of it.

Moulin Rouge

82 bd de Clichy, 18th (01.53.09.82.82, www.moulin-rouge.com). M° Blanche. **Dinner** 7pm. **Shows** 9pm, 11pm daily. **Admission** *Show* €87-€210 (incl champagne). *Dinner & show* €190-€420. **Map** p401 G2.

Toulouse-Lautrec posters, glittery lamp-posts and fake trees lend a degree of tacky charm to this revue. On stage, 60 Doriss dancers cavort with faultless synchronisation. Costumes are flamboyant and the *entr'acte* acts funny. The downer is the space, with tables packed in like sardines. There are occasional matinée performances. *Photo p269.*

Café-théâtre

Les Blancs Manteaux

15 rue des Blancs-Manteaux, 4th (01.48.87.15.84, www.blancsmanteaux.fr). M° Hôtel de Ville. **Shows** 7.30pm, 9pm Mon-Wed; 5.30pm, 7.30pm, 9pm Thur-Sat; 5.30pm, 7.30pm Sun. **Admission** *Show* €20; €17 reductions; *2 shows* €34 (except Sat). *Dinner & show* €40. **Map** p409 K6.

For the past 40 years, this Marais institution has been launching new talent with weekly comedy platforms. With a dinner-and-show ticket, you can dine on Thai cuisine at nearby Suan Thai.

Chez Michou

80 rue des Martyrs, 18th (01.46.06.16.04, www.michou.com). M° Pigalle. **Dinner** 8.30pm daily. **Shows** 10.30pm approx. **Admission** *Show* €32-€65. *Dinner & show* €110-€140. **Map** p402 H2.

Drag, sparkling costumes, good food and wine: Michou's show is not quite as 'blue' as his azure attire suggests. Book ahead if you want to dine.

Le Grenier

3 rue Rennequin, 17th (01.43.80.68.01, www.legrenier-dinerspectacle.com). M° Ternes. **Shows** from 9.15pm daily. **Admission** *Show* €18 (Mon-Fri); €20 (Sat, Sun). *Dinner & show* €30-€60. **Map** p400 D2.

If you fancy being entertained while you eat, consider a night at the Grenier, which still retains the allure of an old *café-théâtre* with an eclectic line-up of stand-up, *chansonniers* and magic acts all on the same bill.

★ Au Lapin Agile

22 rue des Saules, 18th (01.46.06.85.87, www.au-lapin-agile.com). M° Lamarck Caulaincourt. **Shows** 9pm-1am Tue-Sun. **Admission** *Show* (incl 1 drink) €28; €20 reductions. **No credit cards.** **Map** p402 H1.

The prices have gone up and they sell their own compilation CDs, but that's all that seems to have changed since this quaint, pink bar first opened in 1860. Tourists now outnumber the locals, but the Lapin harbours an echo of old Montmartre.

Comedy

Café de la Gare

41 rue du Temple, 4th (01.42.78.52.51, www. cdlg.org). Mº Hôtel de Ville. **Shows** varies. **Admission** €10-€24. **Map** p406 K6.
Running since 1968, the most famous fringe theatre in Paris has 300 stage-hugging seats and hosts quality French stand-up and raucous comedies, as well as plays for kids.

Le Comedy Club

42 bd de Bonne Nouvelle, 10th (01.73.54.17.00, www.lecomedyclub.fr). Mº Bonne Nouvelle. **Shows** days vary. **Admission** €10-€30. **Map** p402 J4.
Jamel Debbouze, the comic known for his one-man shows and his roles in films such as *Amélie*, gives the comedy trade a helping hand with this eclectic theatre, which adds club nights, live music and film screenings to the stand-up soirées.

★ Le Point Virgule

7 rue Ste-Croix-de-la-Bretonnerie, 4th (01.42.78.67.03, www.lepointvirgule.com). Mº Hôtel de Ville. **Shows** times vary; see website for details. **Admission** €10-€20. **Map** p409 K6.
This small Marais theatre has become the ultimate launch pad for comedians, with shows, a *café-théâtre* school and an annual comedy festival in September. The theatre launched a new venue in Montparnasse

in late 2012, the Grand Point Virgule (8bis rue de l'Arrivée, 15th, 01.42.78.67.03, www.legrandpoint-virgule.com), to provide some Left Bank laughs.

Le République

23 pl de la République, 3rd (01.47.70.97.96, www.lerepubliqueparis.fr). Mº République. **Shows** vary. **Admission** €24-€37; €19-€24 reductions. **Map** p402 L4.
In 2014, the Caveau de la République closed and became this place: a stand-up comedy venue modelled on London's Comedy Store. Expect the pick of French comics, a handful of on-the-up funsters, and the usual crop of satirical *chansonniers*.

LEFT BANK
Cabaret

★ Paradis Latin

28 rue Cardinal Lemoine, 5th (01.43.25.28.28, www.paradislatin.com). Mº Cardinal Lemoine. **Lunch** noon. **Dinner** 8pm. **Shows** 1.30pm, 9.30pm daily. **Admission** *Show* (incl champagne) €75-€90. *Lunch & show* €120. *Dinner & show* €130-€190. *Show only* €65. **Map** p406 K8.
This is the most authentic of the cabarets, not only because it's family-run but also because the clientele is mostly French, something that has a direct effect on the prices (this is the cheapest revue) and the cuisine, which tends to be high quality. Show-wise you can expect the usual fare: generous doses of glitter, live singing and cheesy *entr'acte* acts performed in a room designed by Eiffel.

Paradis Latin.

ARTS & ENTERTAINMENT

Le Bataclan.

Music

Paris's music scene is bubbling with talent, and the recent emergence of some great new bands speaks volumes about the creativity of today's up-and-coming artists. The capital is overflowing with authentic concert venues, from monster stadiums to intimate bars and jazz clubs, and venues like **Nouveau Casino** (*see p267*) and **L'International** give precious stage space to those on the way up the musical ladder.

Chanson française is still going strong, helped by the success of **Les Trois Baudets**, a government-subsidised *chanson* hall in the heart of Pigalle – French law dictates that 40 per cent of music broadcast in France must be in the French language.

Jazz is having a mini revival too: after the disappearance of old flames like Le Slow Club (once one of the most famous jazz joints in Europe), Le Bilboquet and Les 7 Lézards, a handful of new joints have opened up, while flagship clubs **Au Duc des Lombards**, **New Morning** and **Le Sunset/Le Sunside** continue to book a range of top-notch acts from around the globe. Paris is also a European leader for world music, particularly African and Arab acts. And don't forget that every 21 June, the whole city turns into one giant music venue for the **Fête de la Musique** (*see p34*), when a party in the street is guaranteed.

INFORMATION AND RESOURCES

The weekly magazine *Les Inrockuptibles* is a valuable resource. Alternatively, try bi-monthly gig bible *Lylo*, free in bars and branches of Fnac. The **Fnac** ticket office (www.fnac.com) also displays details of up-and-coming concerts. For reduced-price tickets try www.billetreduc.com. Depending on your tastes (and your French) radio can be useful for tip-offs: Nova (101.5FM) does electro, lounge and world; TSF (89.9FM) and FIP (105.1FM) cover jazz; and Le Mouv' (92.1FM) and OuiFM (102.3FM) are for rock fans.

Box offices are usually closed in the daytime, and most venues take a break in August. Several excellent venues, such as **La Bellevilloise**, host regular free nights – ideal if you're on a budget. For concerts, it's best to turn up at the time stated on the ticket: strict noise curfews mean that start times are adhered to pretty closely.

RIGHT BANK
Rock & pop

Le Bataclan
50 bd Voltaire, 11th (01.43.14.00.30, www. le-batadan.com). M° Oberkampf. **Open** times vary. **Map** p403 M5.

La Cigale.

This distinctive venue, fashioned to look like a Chinese pagoda with a multicoloured façade, first opened in 1864 and remains admirably discerning in its booking of rock, world, jazz and hip hop acts.

Le Bus Palladium
6 rue Fontaine, 9th (01.45.26.80.35, www.lebus palladium.com). M° St-Georges, Pigalle or Blanche. **Open** *Concerts* 9pm-12.30am Thur-Sat. *Club* midnight-5am Fri, Sat. **Map** p401 H2.
This legendary rock venue, graced by the likes of Mick Jagger and The Beatles in its heyday, is back on the map after a 20-year spell out of the limelight with a vintage house vibe somewhere between retro rockabilly and punk psychedelia. While the new generation gets wild in the pit, former regulars are trying to catch their breath at the restaurant upstairs. Check the programme for concerts.

★ La Cigale/La Boule Noire
120 bd de Rochechouart, 18th (01.49.25.89.99, www.lacigale.fr; 01.49.25.81.75, www.laboule-noire.fr). M° Anvers or Pigalle. **Open** varies. **Map** p402 J2.
This is easily one of Paris's finest concert venues. The lovely, horseshoe-shaped theatre La Cigale is linked to more cosy venue La Boule Noire, which is a reliable choice for catching cult-ish visiting indie and rock acts.

Les Disquaires
4-6 rue des Taillandiers, 11th (01.40.21.94.60, www.lesdisquaires.com). M° Bastille. **Open** 6pm-2am Tue-Sat. **Map** p407 M6.

Les Disquaires' little stage directly faces the dancefloor and the decks, and exhibitions by local artists decorate the walls around the bar. The venue is a good bet for enjoying a quality gig over a cocktail or beer during happy hour, and there's plenty to choose from in the packed programme of jazz, funk, hip hop and soul.

Espace B
16 rue Barbanègre, 19th (www.espaceb.net). M° Corentin Cariou. **Open** 9am-1.30am Mon-Fri; 4pm-1.30am Sat, Sun. *Concerts* vary. **No credit cards. Map** p403 inset.
Situated on a quiet street near Parc de la Villette, Espace B is a funny little place somewhere between a neighbourhood bar, an Italian restaurant and a concert hall. The bill is pretty varied, including synth-pop, electro-rock, hip hop, indie, shoegaze, grunge, folktronica, noise, chillwave and more. On some evenings, you can even find burlesque or avant-garde theatre.

La Flèche d'Or
102bis rue de Bagnolet, 20th (01.44.64.01.02, www.flechedor.fr). M° Alexandre Dumas. **Open** varies. *Concerts* vary.
This much-loved indie and electro venue is a great place to check out the capital's live music scene, with three or four bands playing a night. It also gives monthly residencies to local groups and DJs.

★ L'International
5-7 rue Moret, 11th (01.49.29.76.45, www. linternational.fr). M° Ménilmontant. **Open**

ARTS & ENTERTAINMENT

ESSENTIAL PARIS ALBUMS

Sounds of the city.

AUX ARMES ET CÆTERA
SERGE GAINSBOURG
(1979) Recorded in Jamaica, and featuring vocals from the I-Threes, this era-defining classic shifted more than a million copies. The title track (a variation of 'La Marseillaise') was one of the first reggae songs to hit France and so polemical that the Parisian megastar received death threats.

SUPREME NTM
NTM (1998)
Essential listening from *banlieue* tough boys Nique Ta Mère (Mother Fuckers), made up of rappers Joey Starr (Didier Morville) and Kool Shen (Bruno Lopès). This controversial hip hop album influenced a generation with songs such as 'Seine Saint Denis Style' and 'Back dans les Bacs'.

HYMNE A LA MOME
EDITH PIAF (2012)
Edith Piaf, who was born in Belleville, is still hailed by many as the greatest singer France has ever known. This digitally remastered box set of 45 of her most famous songs, including 'La Vie en Rose', 'L'Hymne à l'Amour' and 'Non, Je ne Regrette Rien', serves as a wonderful reminder of her raw talent.

THE NO COMPRENDO
LES RITA MITSOUKO (1986)
Les Rita Mitsouko (guitarist Fred Chichin and singer Catherine Ringer) produced wacky electro pop with real musical substance and quirky text. Three tracks from the *No Comprendo* album – 'Andy', 'C'est Comme Ca' and 'Les Histoires d'a' – are still dancefloor staples today.

MY GOD IS BLUE
SEBASTIEN TELLIER (2012)
Tellier's fourth album plies his trademark brand of cool, transgressive, electro-sexy pop. The bearded guru (who, bizarrely, sang for France in the 2008 Eurovision Song Contest), is the only Parisian who doles out serious electro music without taking himself too seriously.

MIDNIGHT IN PARIS
VARIOUS ARTISTS (2011)
Woody Allen's *Midnight in Paris* is a love letter to a city and, like *Manhattan*, opens with an adoring montage, set to jazz, of the city by day and night. Cue this soundtrack, featuring the likes of Sidney Bechet and Josephine Baker, that added real soul to Allen's romantic ode to the capital.

7pm-2am Mon-Sat. *Concerts* 9pm. *DJ set* 11pm.
Map p403 N4.
This concert-bar is a breath of fresh air, with free entry and a string of on-the-up bands playing to hip indie crowds every night of the week. Once a month there's an after-party until 4am.

Mains d'Oeuvres

1 rue Charles-Garnier, 93400 St-Ouen (01.40.11.25.25, www.mainsdoeuvres.org). M° Garibaldi or Porte de Clignancourt. **Open** 9.30am-midnight Mon-Fri; 11am-8pm Sat; noon-8pm Sun. *Concerts* times vary.
This lively hub for fringe musical and performance activity is located just outside Paris in the suburb of St-Ouen. The Mains d'Oeuvres is an enormous former leisure centre for car factory workers that specialises in leftfield electro, rock mavericks and multimedia artists. It frequently plays hosts to the annual Festival des Attitudes Indé (Sept-Oct) for up-and-coming bands.

La Maroquinerie

23 rue Boyer, 20th (01.40.33.35.05, www. lamaroquinerie.fr). M° Gambetta. **Open** *Box office* (in person only) 2.30-7pm Mon-Fri. Bar 6pm-2am daily; *Concerts* 7.30-11pm (days vary). Closed Aug. **Map** p403 P4.
Literary discussion and rock 'n' roll coexist happily at this happening locale. It's home to the Inrocks Indie Club nights, featuring up-and-coming rock acts, but there are still plenty of traces of its world music roots on show.

★ La Mécanique Ondulatoire

8 passage Thiéré, 11th (01.43.55.69.14). M° Bastille or Ledru Rollin. **Open** 6pm-2am Mon-Sat. **Concerts** times vary. **Map** p407 M7.
Cementing Bastille's status as the capital's prime hangout for rockers, this exciting venue is spread over three levels and alternates eclectic DJ sets with live acts in the cellar, plus there are jazz sessions on Tuesday nights.

Le Motel

8 passage Josset, 11th (01.58.30.84.68, www. lemotel.fr). M° Ledru Rollin. **Open** 6pm-1.45am Tue-Sun. **Map** p407 M7.
This most Anglophile of Paris bars, with Stone Roses and Smiths posters adorning the walls, manages to squeeze plenty of live bands, including some of the best new local talent, on to its tiny stage. On Tuesdays, Wednesdays and alternate Sundays there's a pop quiz that attracts plenty of music-savvy regulars.

Olympia

28 bd des Capucines, 9th (08.92.68.33.68, www.olympiahall.com). M° Opéra. **Open** *Box office* noon-2pm, 5-9.30pm Mon-Sat & 2hrs before shows. By phone 10am-6pm Mon-Fri; 2-6pm Sat, Sun. *Concerts* times vary. **Map** p401 G4.
The Beatles, Frank Sinatra, Jimi Hendrix and Edith Piaf all performed at the historic Olympia. Now it mainly plays host to nostalgia and *variété*, although big names do still drop by – Olly Murs played here in 2015.

ARTS & ENTERTAINMENT

Olympia

O'Sullivans by the Mill

*92 bd de Clichy, 18th (01.53.09.08.49, www.
osullivans-pubs.com). M° Blanche or Place de
Clichy.* **Open** 1pm-5am Mon-Thur; 1pm-6am
Fri; noon-6pm Sat, Sun. *Concerts* times vary.
Map p401 G2.

This Irish chain bar is all about late, late nights, with
grizzly weekend rock gigs that last until sunrise,
DJs and open mic nights the first Wednesday of
the month. Thursday nights are almost guaranteed
to be wild.

Palais des Congrès

*2 pl de la Porte Maillot, 17th (08.92.05.00.50,
www.viparis.com). M° Porte Maillot.* **Open**
times vary. **Map** p400 B2.

The sound and the views are good wherever you sit
in this state-of-the-art amphitheatre. Caetano Veloso
and Gilberto Gil graced the stage in 2015.

Palais Omnisports de Paris-Bercy

*8 bd de Bercy, 12th (08.92.39.04.90, www.bercy
arena.paris). M° Bercy.* **Box office** 11am-6pm
Mon-Sat. **Map** p407 N9.

The traditional venue for rock and pop behemoths:
it's currently being revamped but should reopen
in late 2015.

★ Point Ephémère

*200 quai de Valmy, 10th (01.40.34.02.48, www.
pointephemere.org). M° Jaurès or Louis Blanc.*
Open noon-2am Mon-Sat; noon-midnight Sun.
Concerts times vary. **Map** p402 L2.

This converted warehouse is a classy affair, bringing
together up-and-coming local rock, jazz and world
gigs with a decent restaurant, dance and recording
studios and exhibitions.

Le Reservoir

*16 rue de la Forge-Royale, 11th (01.43.56.39.60,
www.reservoirclub.com). M° Faidherbe Chaligny
or Ledru-Rollin.* **Open** 8pm-2am Mon-Thur;
8pm-4am Fri; 11.30am-5pm, 8pm-4am Sat;
11.30am-5pm Sun. *Concerts* times vary.
Map p407 N7.

This classy, Anglo-inspired venue hosts regular club
nights and indie gigs.

Zénith

*211 av Jean-Jaurès, 19th (www.zenith-paris.
com). M° Porte de Pantin.* **Open** times vary.
Map p403 inset.

State-of-the-art sound and credible bands make this
the large venue of choice. The Prodigy and Blur
both played here in 2015.

Chanson

Chez Adel

*10 rue de la Grange-aux-Belles, 10th
(01.42.08.24.61). M° Jacques Bonsergent.*
Open noon-2am daily. *Concerts* 6pm daily.
Map p402 L3.

Patron Adel is probably the most renowned *chanson*
café owner in Paris, and this fine den of kitsch
attracts countless devotees with its repertoire of

Point Ephémère.

Open *Concerts* 8pm-2am Tue, Thur-Sat.
Closed mid Aug. **Map** p403 N4.
If you're looking for an authentic Belleville
rendezvous, there's no better location than this
old-style café with terrace, where the traditions of
accordion music and croaky-voiced *chanson* endure.

World & traditional

Le Kibélé
*12 rue de l'Echiquier, 10th (01.48.24.57.74,
www.kibele.fr). M° Bonne Nouvelle.* **Open**
noon-2.30pm, 7pm-midnight Mon-Sat.
Concerts times vary. **Map** p402 K4.
Stashed away below a Turkish restaurant, this little
basement is a landmark for new talent and small
groups from far-flung places as they pass through
Paris. Order a drink at the restaurant bar and head
down into the cosy, softly lit vaulted room to enjoy
acoustic concerts of Latin music, klezmer, jazz or
chanson française. Early each night, actors and
comedians try their luck on the little stage (check
listings online).

Musée Guimet
*6 pl d'Iéna, 16th (01.56.52.53.00, auditorium
01.40.73.88.18, www.guimet.fr). M° Iéna.*
Open 10am-6pm Mon, Wed-Sun. *Concerts*
times vary. **Map** p404 C5.
Indian and Asian music by visiting troupes, as well
as dance and theatre, takes pride of place in the
auditorium of the Musée Guimet.

★ Théâtre de la Ville
*2 pl du Châtelet, 4th (01.42.74.22.77, www.theatre
delaville-paris.com). M° Châtelet.* **Open** *Box office*
11am-7pm Mon; 11am-8pm Tue-Sat. *By phone*
11am-7pm Mon-Sat. *Concerts* times vary.
Map p408 J6.
Music and dance of the highest order can be found
here, with jazz and music from just about anywhere
you can think of (Iraq, Japan, Thailand, Brittany)
amid the classical recitals.

Jazz & blues

Ateliers de Charonne
*21 rue de Charonne, 11th (01.40.21.83.35,
www.ateliercharonne.com). M° Charonne or
Ledru-Rollin.* **Open** 8pm-12.30am Mon-Sat;
7pm-midnight Sun. *Concerts* 9pm Mon-Sat;
7.30pm Sun. **Map** p407 M7.
This jazz club is the place in which to see the rising
stars of gypsy jazz (*jazz manouche*). If you want to
grab a good spot, reserve for dinner and the show.

Autour de Midi-Minuit
*11 rue Lepic, 18th (01.55.79.16.48, www.
autourdemidi.fr). M° Blanche.* **Open** noon-
2.30pm, 7pm-late Tue-Sat. *Concerts* 9.30pm
Tue-Thur; 10pm Fri, Sat. **Map** p401 H2.

chanson and Eastern European sounds. The crowd,
fuelled by rum and ginger cocktails (the house
speciality), is always enthusiastic.

Le Limonaire
*18 Cité Bergère, 9th (01.45.23.33.33, http://
limonaire.free.fr). M° Grands Boulevards.*
Open 6pm-2am daily. *Concerts* 8pm Mon;
10pm Tue-Sat; 7pm Sun. **Map** p402 J4.
Serious *chanson* takes the limelight, and performances
vary from piano-led *chansonniers* to cabaret.

Sentier des Halles
*50 rue d'Aboukir, 2nd (01.42.61.89.95, www.
lesentierdeshalles.fr). M° Sentier.* **Open** times
vary. *Concerts* times vary. Closed Aug. **Map** p402 J4.
Le Sentier has developed beyond its traditional
chanson base to embrace a variety of modern styles
plus the occasional stand-up act.

Les Trois Baudets
*64 bd de Clichy, 18th (01.42.62.33.33, www.
lestroisbaudets.com). M° Pigalle.* **Open** times
vary. **Map** p401 H2.
All dolled up in black and red, with a 250-seater
theatre, an enviable sound system, two bars and a
restaurant, this concert hall encourages *chanson
française* and other musical genres (rock, electro, folk
and slam) – as long as they're in French. *Photos p278.*

★ Le Vieux Belleville
*12 rue des Envierges, 20th (01.44.62.92.66,
www.le-vieux-belleville.com). M° Pyrénées.*

Les Trios Baudets. See p277.

The Tuesday night *boeuf* (jam session) is always free, as are many other concerts – some by big names such as Laurent Epstein and Bruno Casties.

Le Baiser Salé
58 rue des Lombards, 1st (01.42.33.37.71, www. lebaisersale.com). M° Châtelet. **Open** 5pm-6am daily. *Concerts* daily (times vary). **Map** p406 J6.
The 'Salty Kiss' divides its time between passing *chanson* merchants, world artists and jazzmen of every stripe, from trad to fusion.

★ Au Duc des Lombards
42 rue des Lombards, 1st (01.42.33.22.88, www.ducdeslombards.com). M° Châtelet. **Open** 7pm-12.30am Mon-Thur; 7pm-4am Fri, Sat. *Concerts* 7.30pm, 9.30pm Mon-Sat. **Map** p406 J6.
This venerable jazz spot attracts a high class of performer and a suitably savvy crowd. Check out the '*bons plans*' section of the website for reduced-price tickets.

Jazz Club Etoile
Hôtel Méridien Etoile, 81 bd Gouvion-St-Cyr, 17th (01.40.68.30.42, www.jazzclub-paris. com). M° Porte Maillot. **Open** 7am-1am Mon, Tue, Sun; 7am-1.30am Wed-Sat. *Concerts*

9.30pm-1am Thur-Sat; 12.30-3pm Sun (musical brunch). **Map** p400 B2.
Created in 1975 by French jazz drummer and actor Moustache, this club continues to be a hotspot for US jazz, plus soul and funk. Connoisseurs can peruse a whisky list as long as the Mississippi.

★ New Morning
7-9 rue des Petites-Ecuries, 10th (01.45.23.51.41, www.newmorning.com). **Open** 7pm-1am daily. *Concerts* times vary. **Map** p402 K3.
One of the best places in which to see the latest jazz exponents, with a policy that also embraces *chanson*, blues, world music and sophisticated pop.

Le Onze
83 rue Jean-Pierre Timbaud, 11th (01.48.06.11.97, www.onzebar.com). M° Couronnes. **Open** 5pm-2am daily. *Concerts* times vary. **Map** p403 N4.
This little boho bar seethes with people day and night. Very hip right now, it's been done up in shabby chic style – the stuffing of the big sofas is oozing out, witness to many wild parties. Daily concerts range from Balkan folk to rock'n'roll, via jazz, blues, funk or afrobeat, with people getting up to dance wherever they can find room to move between the tables and chairs.

Le Sunset/Le Sunside
60 rue des Lombards, 1st (01.40.26.46.60,
www.sunset-sunside.com). M° Châtelet. **Open**
5pm-2am daily. *Concerts* times vary. **Map** p406 J6.
A split-personality venue, with Sunset dealing
in electric groups and Sunside hosting acoustic
performances. Their renown pulls in big jazz names.

Théâtre du Châtelet
1 pl du Châtelet, 4th (01.40.28.28.40, www.
chatelet-theatre.com). M° Châtelet. **Open** times
vary. **Map** p406 J6.
This venerable theatre and classical music hall
has another life as a jazz and *chanson* venue, with
performances by top-notch international musicians.

LEFT BANK
Rock & pop

Batofar
Opposite 11 quai François-Mauriac, 13th
(01.53.60.17.00, www.batofar.org). M° Bibliothèque
François-Mitterrand or Quai de la Gare. **Open**
12.30pm-midnight Tue; 12.30pm-6am Wed-Fri;
6pm-6am Sat. *Concerts* 7-11pm (days vary).
Club 11.30pm-6am (days vary). **Map** p407 N10.
This enduringly hip party boat lays on DJs, rappers
and assorted underground noise-merchants for the
benefit of an up-for-it crowd. It comes into its own in
the summer, when the terrace opens at 7pm.
▶ *For more on Batofar's club nights, see p268.*

Chanson

Au Magique
42 rue de Gergovie, 14th (01.45.42.26.10, www.
aumagique.com). M° Pernety. **Open** 8pm-2am
Wed-Sun. *Concerts* 9pm. **No credit cards**.
Map p405 F10.
Artiste-in-residence Marc Havet serenades punters
with politically incorrect *chanson* at weekends; you
can also expect poetry events and exhibitions.

World & traditional

Institut du Monde Arabe
(Auditorium Rafik Hariri)
1 rue des Fossés-St-Bernard, 5th (01.40.51.38.38,
www.imarabe.org). M° Jussieu. **Open** 10am-6pm
Tue-Thur; 10am-9.30pm Fri; 10am-7pm Sat, Sun.
Tickets 10am-5pm Tue-Sun; 90mins before show.
Concerts usually 8.30pm Fri, Sat. **Map** p409 K7.
This huge, plush auditorium attracts some of the
biggest names in the world of Arab music.

Jazz & blues

Caveau de la Huchette
5 rue de la Huchette, 5th (01.43.26.65.05,
www.caveaudelahuchette.fr). M° St-Michel.

Open 9.30pm-2.30am Mon-Wed, Sun; 9.30pm-6am
Thur-Sat. *Concerts* 10pm. **Map** p408 J7.
This medieval cellar has been a music mainstay
for more than 60 years. Jazz shows are followed
by early-hours performances in a swing, rock, soul
or disco vein.

Caveau des Oubliettes
52 rue Galande, 5th (01.46.34.23.09, www.
caveaudesoubliettes.fr). M° St-Michel. **Open**
5pm-2am Mon, Tue, Sun; 5pm-4am Wed-Sat.
Concerts usually 9pm Tue; 10pm Wed-Fri;
10.30pm Sun. **Map** p408 J7.
A foot-tapping frenzy echoes in the Caveau des
Oubliettes, a medieval dungeon. Mondays are Pop
Rock Jam nights, Tuesdays are Jazz Jam Boogaloo
nights, and there are various other jam sessions
during the rest of the week.

Le Petit Journal Montparnasse
113 rue du Commandant René-Mouchotte, 14th
(01.43.21.56.70, www.petitjournalmontparnasse.
com). M° Gaîté. **Open** 7am-2am Mon-Sat. *Concerts*
9.30pm Mon-Sat. **Map** p405 F9.
An institution for jazz amateurs, this dining/concert
hall is inspired by the jazz of New Orleans and the
soul of Detroit, but also gospel, blues, rock'n'roll,
Latin jazz and bossa nova.

Le Swan Bar
165 bd de Montparnasse, 6th (01.44.27.05.84,
www.swanbar.fr). M° Raspail or Vavin. **Open**
7pm-1am Tue-Sat. *Concerts* 7.30pm & 9.30pm
Tue-Sat. **Map** p405 H9.
The Swan Bar is a modern, American-style jazz bar
for traditional jazz, torch songs and jamming.

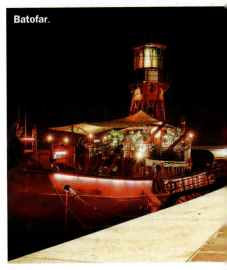
Batofar.

Performing Arts

The biggest news in the world of classical music is the arrival of Jean Nouvel's dramatic 2,400-seat Philharmonie de Paris, which opened its doors in early 2015. Nouvel skipped the first night, complaining that the building was still unfinished, but the response of concertgoers has been resoundingly positive. The Philharmonie takes over from the Salle Pleyel as the capital's main symphony venue, with ticket prices designed to attract more than just the *haut monde*.

Accessibility issues of a different sort come into play with Paris's theatre scene. French-speaking drama buffs can choose from hundreds of shows every week, from offbeat indie to highbrow classic, but Anglophones have to make do with a handful of international companies. Paris is home to a thriving dance scene. There's no shortage of ballet at the Théâtre du Châtelet and Palais Garnier, and the Festival d'Automne has an impressive line-up.

Classical Music & Opera

The Théâtre des Champs-Elysées celebrated 100 years in the limelight with a host of big-name soloists and conductors appearing in 2013. The Opéra de Paris, meanwhile, splits its major productions between the bunker-like Bastille and the glorious Palais Garnier. The main musical provider in summer is **Paris Quartier d'Eté** (01.44.94.98.00, www.quartierdete.com), with concerts in gardens across the capital. The

Festival de Saint-Denis (01.48.13.06.07, www.festival-saint-denis.com) offers top names in a spectacular setting, while the candlelit **Chopin Piano Festival** takes place in the Jardin de Bagatelle (www.frederic-chopin.com).

INFORMATION AND TICKETS

For comprehensive listings, see *L'Officiel des Spectacles* or *Pariscope*. Monthly *Diapason* also lists classical concerts, while *Opéra* magazine provides decent coverage of all things vocal. Look out too for *Cadences* and *La Terrasse*, two free monthlies distributed outside concerts. Also check the Time Out Paris website (www.timeout.fr) for comprehensive cultural listings throughout the year.

ORCHESTRAS & ENSEMBLES

★ Les Arts Florissants

01.43.87.98.88, www.arts-florissants.com.
William Christie's 'Arts Flo' remains France's leading Early Music group, and his conducting has become a true benchmark of authentic performance. The group has not neglected passing on the secrets

---

IN THE KNOW CLASSICAL CUTS

Many venues and orchestras offer cut-rate tickets to students under 26 an hour before curtain-up. For the Fête de la Musique (21 June) all events are free, and year-round freebies crop up at the Maison de Radio France and the Conservatoire de Paris, as well as in certain churches.

of Baroque ornamentation to the next generation, with the Jardin des Voix busy cultivating exciting young talent.

Ensemble Intercontemporain

01.44.84.44.50, www.ensembleinter.com.
German composer-conductor Matthias Pintscher has taken over from Finnish conductor Susanna Mälkki as musical director of this bastion of contemporary music founded by Pierre Boulez. The exacting standard of the 31 soloists is beyond reproach, and the ensemble has an enviable international reputation, making it one of the most popular on the Paris scene.

Orchestre de Chambre de Paris

08.00.42.67.57, www.orchestredechambre deparis.com.
The orchestra has struggled in recent years to find its specificity in a competitive field, but that is all set to improve after a change of name (from Ensemble Orchestral de Paris) and leadership, which has seen the wonderfully talented Thomas Zehetmair take up the baton as principal conductor.

Orchestre Colonne

01.42.33.72.89, www.orchestrecolonne.fr.
Sometimes to be found at the Salle Gaveau (*see p284*), this orchestra – led by composer Laurent Petitgirard – has intelligent programming, with every concert teaming a contemporary work with more popular repertoire. The excellent series of *concerts éveil* continues to provide bargain tickets for

parents and children, making an ideal introduction to classical music.

Orchestre Lamoureux

01.58.39.30.30, www.orchestrelamoureux.com.
This reliable orchestra, which made the first recording of Ravel's *Boléro*, is currently under the leadership of musical director Fayçal Karoui.

Orchestre National de France

01.56.40.15.16, www.radiofrance.fr.
Daniele Gatti is now firmly in charge of France's leading orchestra, bringing along his own brand of warm Italianate theatricality, in sharp contrast to his predecessor, veteran Kurt Masur, and his more structured Germanic approach.

★ Orchestre de Paris

01.42.56.13.13, www.orchestredeparis.com.
Many consider this orchestra to be the finest in France, and the arrival of Estonian-born Paavo Järvi as musical director a few years ago has done even more to boost its lofty reputation. Recent highlights have included a performance of Berlioz's *Symphonie Fantastique* by Lang Lang, and Hélène Grimaud playing Ravel. The orchestra is now resident at the new 2,400-seat Philharmonie (*see p284*).

Orchestre Pasdeloup

01.42.78.10.00, www.concertspasdeloup.com.
The Pasdeloup is the oldest orchestra in Paris, and the calendar always features a great collection of

Orchestre de Paris.

ARTS & ENTERTAINMENT

concerts under the watchful eye of artistic director Patrice Fontanarosa.

Orchestre Philharmonique de Radio France

01.56.40.15.16, www.radiofrance.fr.
Finnish conductor Mikko Franck will take over the baton in September 2015 from Myung-Whun Chung, who has been the musical director here for 15 years. The standard of the orchestra is traditionally considered to lag behind that of the Orchestre National de France, but it puts together a dynamic programme and does plenty to try to attract younger audiences.

VENUES
Right Bank

Auditorium du Louvre

Entrance through Pyramid, Cour Napoléon, Musée du Louvre, rue de Rivoli, 1st (01.40.20.55.55, reservations 01.40.20.55.00, www.louvre.fr). M° *Palais Royal Musée du Louvre.* **Box office** 9am-5.30pm Mon, Wed-Fri. Closed July, Aug. **Admission** €5-€32. **Map** p401 H5.
The Auditorium du Louvre packs in a full season with chamber music, lunchtime concerts and music on film. The season is divided into themed groups with artists performing a wide range of music.

Châtelet – Théâtre Musical de Paris

1 pl du Châtelet, 4th (01.40.28.28.40, www. chatelet-theatre.com). M° *Châtelet.* **Box office** (17 av Victoria) 11am-7pm Mon-Sat; 1hr before performance Sun. *By phone* 11am-7pm Mon-Sat. Closed July, Aug. **Admission** €10-€118. **Map** p408 J6.
Jean-Luc Choplin has radically changed the programming of this bastion of Paris music-making. An attempt to rediscover the theatre's popular roots has seemingly been achieved at the expense of traditional fine music subscribers. There's plenty to appeal in the diverse line-up, though, including an acclaimed recent production of *An American in Paris*.

★ Cité de la Musique

221 av Jean-Jaurès, 19th (01.44.84.44.84, www.cite-musique.fr). M° *Porte de Pantin.* **Box office** noon-6pm Tue-Sat; 10am-6pm Sun. *By phone* 11am-7pm Mon-Sat; 11am-6pm Sun. **Admission** €8-€41. **Map** p403 inset.
The energetic programming here features a vast non-classical repertoire that includes world music and jazz. Concerts are frequently grouped into series with a pedagogic aim, tending to concentrate on the Baroque and the contemporary.
▶ *The Conservatoire de Paris (209 av Jean-Jaurès, 19th, 01.40.40.45.45) hosts world-class performers, and features many free concerts.*

IN THE KNOW PIPE DREAMS

The regular free recitals by guest organists at **Notre-Dame Cathedral** (*see p51*) take advantage of the building's unique acoustics and the awesome sound of the great organ, which was restored in 2012 for the cathedral's 850th anniversary. Programming is eclectic, with the nave echoing to Gothic suites, carillons, fanfares, preludes and symphonies played by visiting organists from around the world.

IRCAM

1 pl Igor-Stravinsky, 4th (01.44.78.48.43, www.ircam.fr). M° *Hôtel de Ville.* **Map** p406 K6.
The underground bunker next to the Centre Pompidou, set up in 1969 by avant-garde composer Pierre Boulez to create electronic microtonal music, is looking less redundant nowadays with a full programme of courses and conferences. Not many concerts take place in the building itself, but IRCAM sponsors concerts with a modernist theme across the city. See the website for details.

Maison de Radio France

116 av du Président-Kennedy, 16th (01.56.40. 15.16, www.radiofrance.fr). M° *Passy/RER Avenue du Pdt Kennedy.* **Box office** 10am-6pm Mon-Sat (July 11am-6pm Mon-Sat). Closed Aug. **Admission** €10- €85. **Map** p404 A7.
The state-owned radio station France Musique broadcasts a broad range of classical concerts from its newly renovated home. The quality of music-making on offer from the Orchestre National de France and the Orchestre Philharmonique de Radio France is impressive.

Opéra National de Paris, Bastille

Pl de la Bastille, 12th (08.92.89.90.90, from abroad 01.71.25.24.23, www.operadeparis.fr). M° *Bastille.* **Box office** (130 rue de Lyon, 12th) 2.30-6.30pm Mon-Sat & 1hr before performance. *By phone* 9am-6pm Mon-Fri; 9am-1pm Sat. **Admission** €5-€214. **Map** p409 M7.
The Bastille is never going to be a beautiful building, and the unflattering acoustics and miles of corridors combine to create an atmosphere more akin to an airport than an opera house. But the standard of performance is what matters, and the Bastille has plenty of exciting evenings under director Nicolas Joel. The 2014/15 season brought to the stage classics such as *La Bohème*, *Don Giovanni* and *Faust*.

★ Opéra National de Paris, Palais Garnier

Pl de l'Opéra, 9th (08.92.89.90.90, from abroad 01.71.25.24.23, www.operadeparis.fr). M° *Opéra.* **Box office** 11.30am-6.30pm Mon-Sat & 1hr

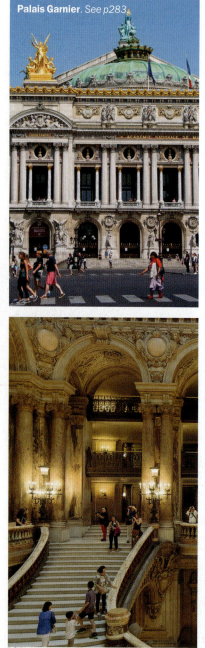

Palais Garnier. See p283.

before performance. *By phone* 9am-6pm
Mon-Fri; 9am-1pm Sat. **Admission** €25-€231.
Map p401 G4.

The Palais Garnier, with its extravagant decor and
ceiling by Marc Chagall, is the jewel in the crown
of Paris music-making, as well as a glistening focal
point for the Right Bank. The Opéra National often
favours the high-tech Bastille (*see p283*) for new
productions, but the matchless acoustics of the
Palais Garnier are superior to the newer Bastille's,
and they were shaken by a stunning production of
Mozart's *The Abduction from the Seraglio* in 2014.

Péniche Opéra

*Facing 46 quai de la Loire, 19th (01.53.35.07.77,
www.penicheopera.com). M° Jaurès or Laumière.*
Box office *By phone* 10am-6pm Mon-Fri; 2-6pm
Sat. **Admission** €15-€20. **Map** p401 M1.

The Péniche Opéra is an enterprising, barge-based
company that produces chamber-scale shows and
concerts, directed by the indefatigable Mireille
Larroche. Programming ranges from Baroque
rarities to contemporary creations via charming
revue-style shows.

★ Philharmonie de Paris

*221 av Jean-Jaurès, 19th (01.44.84.44.84, www.
philharmoniedeparis.fr). M° Porte de Pantin.*
Box office 11am-7pm Mon-Sat; 11am-6pm
Sun. **Admission** €10-€70. **Map** p403 inset.

Paris's new Philharmonie opened its doors in
January 2015. Situated in a working-class corner
of north-east Paris by Porte de Pantin, the extravagant new venue aims to democratise classical
music, drawing in newbies as well as concert hall
veterans. At a time when cultural activities are
getting ever pricier, the Philharmonie hopes to
counter the trend, much as the Opéra Bastille did for
opera. Hopes are running high for the venue, with
construction overseen by French super-composer
Pierre Boulez. As well as the handsome 2,400-seat
concert hall (laid out so no audience member is sat
more than 38 metres from the conductor), it includes
a cavernous exhibition space and a vast educational
centre. *See also p333.*

Salle Cortot

*78 rue Cardinet, 17th (01.47.63.47.48, www.
sallecortot.com). M° Malesherbes.* **No box
office. Admission** varies (phone for details).
Map p401 E2.

This intimate concert hall located inside the Ecole
Normale de Musique has excellent acoustics for
chamber music and master classes, which are often
free of charge.

Salle Gaveau

*45-47 rue de la Boétie, 8th (01.49.53.05.07, www.
sallegaveau.com). M° Miromesnil.* **Box office**
10am-6pm Mon-Fri & 30mins before performance.
Admission €15-€75. **Map** p401 E3.

The Salle Gaveau was built at the start of the 20th century as a chamber music venue. Today, its ever-growing programme includes classical concerts, musicals, a light sprinkling of comedy productions and Les Marmots à Gaveau, aimed at kids with performances followed by a practical workshop called 'Osez la musique'.

Salle Pleyel

252 rue du Fbg-St-Honoré, 8th (01.42.56.13.13, www.sallepleyel.fr). M° Ternes. **Map** p400 D3.
The future of the Salle Pleyel as a classical music venue is now uncertain following the completion of the 2,400-seat Philharmonie in the Parc de la Villette (*see p284*).

★ Théâtre des Bouffes du Nord

37bis bd de la Chapelle, 10th (01.46.07.34.50, www.bouffesdunord.com). M° La Chapelle. **Box office** 5-8pm Mon-Fri; 2-7pm Sat. **Admission** €12-€25. **Map** p402 K1.
This elegant theatre boasts one of the most imaginative programmes of chamber music in the capital. Adventurous programming includes the excellent Beyond My Piano series.

Théâtre des Champs-Elysées

15 av Montaigne, 8th (01.49.52.50.50, www. theatrechampselysees.fr). M° Alma Marceau. **Box office** noon-7pm Mon-Sat; 2hrs before show Sun. *By phone* 11am-6pm Mon-Fri; 2-6pm Sat. **Admission** €5-€160. **Map** p400 D5.

This beautiful art nouveau theatre, with bas-reliefs by Bourdelle, celebrated its centenary in 2013, having hosted the scandalous première of Stravinsky's *Le Sacre du Printemps* in 1913. It remains the favourite venue for visiting foreign orchestras, and the prestigious line-up of visiting maestros has included Vladimir Jurowsky and Andris Nelsons, as well as performances by the likes of Angela Gheorghiou.

Théâtre National de l'Opéra Comique

Pl Boieldieu, 2nd (01.42.44.45.40, tickets 08.25.01.01.23, www.opera-comique.com). M° Richelieu Drouot. **Box office** 11am-7pm Mon-Sat; 11am-5pm Sun. **Admission** €6-€120. **Map** p402 H4.
The Opéra Comique was founded in the early 18th century under the reign of Louis XIV and it is celebrating its 300-year anniversary in style in 2015. Its promotion to national theatre status in 2005 has brought this jewel box of a theatre back to life under the skilful direction of Jérôme Deschamps.

Théâtre de la Ville

2 pl du Châtelet, 4th (01.42.74.22.77, www. theatredelaville-paris.com). M° Châtelet. **Box office** 11am-7pm Mon; 11am-8pm Tue-Sat. *By phone* 11am-7pm Mon-Sat. **Admission** €9-€35. **Map** p408 J6.
The programming in this concrete amphitheatre, which is hidden behind a classical façade, features hip chamber music outfits such as the Kronos and

Philharmonie de Paris.

FESTIVALS **DANCE**

What to see, when.

Faits d'Hiver (Jan-Feb, www.faitsdhiver. com) and hip hop festival **Suresnes Cités Danse** (Jan, www.theatre-suresnes.fr) start the year off with a high kick, followed by **Rencontres Chorégraphiques de Seine-St-Denis** (May-June, www.rencontres choregraphiques.com) and **Onze Bouge** (June, www.festivalonze.org). Founded in 2005, **Les Etés de la Danse** (July, www.lesetesdeladanse.com) puts the spotlight on one or two companies or choreographers, with three weeks of performances. Shows are accompanied by workshops. The ever-popular **Paris Quartier d'Eté** festival (July-Aug, www. quartierdete.com) features eclectic programmes and plenty of free outdoor performances in Paris and around the suburbs. For more than 40 years, the **Festival d'Automne** (Sept-Dec, www. festival-automne.com) has shown the way forward in the performing arts. With a focus on leading French experimental companies, the festival also invites big-name choreographers from around the world to perform.

Takács Quartets, as well as Early Music pioneer Fabio Biondi. World music is also well represented here, with visiting performers from as far afield as Madagascar and China.

▶ *The season here spills over to performances at Les Abbesses (31 rue des Abbesses, 18th), which shares the same phone number and box office hours, but is closed on Mondays.*

Left Bank

Musée National du Moyen Age

6 pl Paul-Painlevé, 5th (01.53.73.78.16, www. musee-moyenage.fr). M° Cluny La Sorbonne. **Admission** varies. **Map** p408 J7.

The museum presents a worthy programme of medieval concerts in which troubadours reflect the museum's collection. There are also occasional 45-minute *heures musicales* in a similar style.

Musée d'Orsay

62 rue de Lille, 7th (01.40.49.47.57, www.musee-orsay.fr). M° Solférino/RER Musée d'Orsay. **Admission** €8-€35. **Map** p405 G6.

The Musée d'Orsay runs a full series of lunchtime and evening concerts. The lunchtime concerts at 12.30pm concentrate on promising young artists. Evening concerts are more prestigious, with recent performances by the likes of Dame Felicity Lott and Susan Graham.

Dance

The Théâtre de la Ville and Théâtre National de Chaillot attract plenty of big names, such as Anne Teresa de Keersmaeker's Rosas company and Ballets de Monte Carlo. There's no shortage of ballet productions at the Théâtre du Châtelet and Palais Garnier either, and the Festival d'Automne will again feature an impressive line-up of innovative dance. As the HQ for over 600 regional companies, the Centre National de la Danse in Pantin reaches out to its audience with well-devised performances, and smaller dance 'laboratories' such as Ménagerie de Verre and Regard du Cygne showcase new work by smaller companies.

INFORMATION AND RESOURCES

For listings, *see Pariscope* and *L'Officiel des Spectacles*. For events coverage, look out for two monthlies: *La Terrasse* (distributed free at major dance venues) and the glossy *Danser*. For shoes and equipment, **Sansha** (52 rue de Clichy, 9th, 01.45.26.01.38, www.sansha.com) has a good reputation, and **Repetto** (22 rue de la Paix, 2nd, 01.44.71.83.12, www.repetto.com) supplies the Opéra with pointes and slippers; **Menkes** (12 rue Rambuteau, 3rd, 01.40.27.91.81, www.menkes.es) sells serious flamenco gear.

Théâtre National de Chaillot.

MAJOR VENUES

Centre National de la Danse

1 rue Victor-Hugo, 93507 Pantin (01.41.83.27.27, box office 01.41.83.98.98, www.cnd.fr). Mº Hoche/ RER Pantin. **Open** *Box office* 10am-7pm Mon-Fri & performance days. **Admission** €10-€18.
This centre first opened its doors in 2004, with the express mission to bridge the divide between stage and spectator. It invites audiences to its quarterly *'Grandes leçons de danse'*, contemporary dance master classes. It also offers an expertly curated selection of performances presented in the studios, exhibitions, and a phenomenal archive of films and choreographic material. *Photo p288.*

Maison des Arts de Créteil

Pl Salvador-Allende, 94000 Créteil (01.45.13.19.19, www.maccreteil.com). Mº Créteil-Préfecture. **Open** *Box office* 10am-7pm Tue-Fri; noon-7pm Sat & show days. Closed mid July-Aug. **Admission** €23-€35.
This suburban arts centre is a vibrant hub, featuring an eclectic programme of theatre, dance, music and digital art. Don't miss the International Exit Festival of contemporary dance in the spring.

★ Palais Garnier

Pl de l'Opéra, 9th (08.92.89.90.90, from abroad 01.71.25.24.23, www.operadeparis.fr). Mº Opéra. **Open** *Box office* 11.30am-6.30pm Mon-Sat. *Phone bookings* 9am-6pm Mon-Fri; 9am-1pm Sat. Closed 15 July-end Aug. **Admission** €12-€121 (ballet). **Map** p401 G4.
The Ballet de l'Opéra National de Paris manages to tread successfully between the classics and new productions, at the Bastille and Palais Garnier. Recent highlights have included Anne Teresa de Keersmaeker's *Rain* and Jean-Guillaume Bart's revival of *La Source*.

Théâtre du Châtelet

1 pl du Châtelet, 4th (01.40.28.28.40, www.chatelet-theatre.com). Mº Châtelet. **Open** *Box office* 11am-7pm Mon-Sat & 1hr before show Sun. **Admission** €16.50-€80.50. **Map** p408 J6.
This classical music institution is strengthening its reputation in other live artistic disciplines – Benjamin Millepied's LA Dance Project are regular visitors. The theatre also plays host to the esteemed Etés de la Danse festival, with the Alvin Ailey American Dance Theater the headline attraction for the 11th edition in July 2015.

Théâtre National de Chaillot

1 pl du Trocadéro, 16th (01.53.65.30.00, www.theatre-chaillot.fr). Mº Trocadéro. **Open** *Box office* 11am-7pm Mon-Sat. *Phone bookings* 11am-7pm Mon-Sat. Closed 2wks Aug. **Admission** €15-€39. **Map** p400 C5.
The Théâtre National de Chaillot's three auditoriums range from cosy and experimental to a vast 2,800-seater amphitheatre. Recent highlights have included performances from the Forsythe Company.

★ Théâtre de la Ville

2 pl du Châtelet, 4th (01.42.74.22.77, www.theatredelaville-paris.com). Mº Châtelet. **Box office** 11am-7pm Mon; 11am-8pm Tue-Sat. *By phone* 11am-7pm Mon-Sat. **Admission** €20-€35. **Map** p408 J6.

This leading venue has nurtured collaborations with major international choreographers. The 2014 programme included Akram Khan and Israel Galván's new work, *Torobaka*.

▶ *Some performances take place at sister venue Théâtre des Abbesses (31 rue des Abbesses, 18th; see p292 for details).*

FRINGE VENUES

L'Etoile du Nord
16 rue Georgette-Agutte, 18th (01.42.26.47.47, www.etoiledunord-theatre.com). M° Guy Môquet. **Open** *Box office* 1hr before performance. Closed July, Aug. **Admission** €10-€15.

This smaller venue splits its programme between theatre and contemporary multimedia dance. The Avis de Turbulences festival (Sept-Oct) features a decent selection of mixed bills.

La Loge
77 rue de Charonne, 11th (01.40.09.70.40, www. lalogeparis.fr). M° Charonne. **Open** *Shows* 7pm, 9pm Tue-Thur. **Admission** €5-€16. **No credit cards.** **Map** p407 N7.

In a hidden courtyard off rue de Charonne, the 100-seater La Loge offers performances that merge theatre, dance and music. Every summer, the Summer of Loge festival invites eight theatre companies to perform, followed by post-show

festivities that have previously included pyjama parties and concerts. The rest of the year, from Tuesday to Thursday, there are two shows a night.

Ménagerie de Verre
12-14 rue Léchevin, 11th (01.43.38.33.44, www.menagerie-de-verre.org). M° Parmentier. **Open** *Box office* 1hr before performance. *Phone bookings* 10am-6pm Mon-Fri. Closed July, Aug. **Admission** €13-€15. **No credit cards.** **Map** p403 N5.

This multidisciplinary hothouse is rooted in the avant-garde, with contemporary dance and classes given by a succession of guest teachers.

★ Le Regard du Cygne
210 rue de Belleville, 20th (01.43.58.55.93, bookings 09.67.32.55.93, www.leregarducygne. com). M° Télégraphe. **Open** *Box office* 1hr before show. Closed Aug. **Admission** €10-€15. **No credit cards.** **Map** p403 Q3.

This pared-down studio located in the north-east of the capital is a great place to get a taste of the alternative dance scene.

▶ *The Spectacles Sauvages nights allow relative unknowns to show a ten-minute piece to the public, while the Rencontres focus on the work of a particular artist and are open to all.*

Théâtre de la Bastille
76 rue de la Roquette, 11th (01.43.57.42.14, www.theatre-bastille.com). M° Bastille or Voltaire. **Open** *Box office* 10am-1pm, 2-6pm Mon-Fri; 2-6pm Sat (Sun on day of performance). Closed July, Aug. **Admission** €14-€26. **Map** p407 M6.

This small theatre showcases a range of innovative contemporary dance and drama pieces.

DANCE CLASSES

Centre de Danse du Marais
41 rue du Temple, 4th (01.42.77.58.19, www. parisdanse.com). M° Hôtel de Ville or Rambuteau. **Open** 9am-9pm Mon-Fri; 9am-8pm Sat; 9am-7pm Sun. **Classes** €18. **Map** p402 K5.

There's a huge choice of classes here, with big-name teachers such as belly dance star Leila Haddad and ballet's Casati-Lazzarelli team.

▶ *The five-class 'sampler' pass is a good deal at €74.*

★ Studio Harmonic
5 passage des Taillandiers, 11th (01.48.07.13.39, www.studioharmonic.fr). M° Bastille. **Open** *Office* 10am-5pm Mon-Fri. *Classes* 9.30am-10pm Mon-Fri; 9am-7.30pm Sat. Closed 3wks Aug. **Classes** €17. **Map** p407 M7.

Studio Harmonic's claim to fame is the trademark Ragga Jam class – created by Laure Courtellemont – which brings together ragga, dancehall, African dance and hip hop. There are lots of children's courses too, from flamenco to street jazz.

Centre National de la Danse. *See p287.*

Théâtre des Bouffes du Nord.

Theatre

The last few years have been tumultuous for some of Paris's most prestigious theatres, with strikes over pay and the temporary closure of the main auditorium at the Comédie Française. Fortunately, though, the Comédie has now been restored to glory, with a schedule marked by trusty old regulars such as Molière and Feydeau.

TICKETS AND INFORMATION

For weekly listings check out *L'Officiel des Spectacles* and *Pariscope* (both available from news kiosks). Tickets can be bought at the theatres, from **Fnac** (www.fnac.com) or online at www.theatreonline.com.

VENUES

Right Bank

Cartoucherie de Vincennes

Route du Champ de Manoeuvre, Bois de Vincennes, 12th. M° Château de Vincennes, then shuttle bus.
Atelier de Paris – Carolyn Carlson
(01.41.74.17.07, www.atelierdeparis.org).
Théâtre de l'Aquarium *(01.43.74.72.74, www.theatredelaquarium.com).*
Théâtre de l'Epée de Bois *(01.48.08.39.74, www.epeedebois.com).*
Théâtre du Soleil *(01.43.74.24.08, www.theatre-du-soleil.fr).*
Théâtre de la Tempête *(01.43.28.36.36, www.la-tempete.fr).*
Past the Château de Vincennes in the middle of the forest, five independent theatres offer up a first-class selection of politically committed fare. The most

famous outfit is Ariane Mnouchkine's avant-garde Théâtre du Soleil, which first transformed these ex-army munitions warehouses into perfomance spaces back in 1970.

★ Comédie Française

All *www.comedie-francaise.fr.*
Salle Richelieu *2 rue Richelieu, 1st (08.25.10.16.80). M° Palais Royal Musée du Louvre.* **Box office** 11am-6pm daily. **Admission** €13-€41; €6-€26 reductions. **Map** p401 H5.
Studio-Théâtre *Galerie du Carrousel du Louvre, 99 rue de Rivoli, 1st (01.44.58.98.58). M° Palais Royal Musée du Louvre.* **Box office** 2-5pm Wed-Sun. **Admission** €20; €11-€15 reductions. **Map** p401 H5.
Théâtre du Vieux Colombier *21 rue du Vieux Colombier, 6th (01.44.39.87.00). M° St-Sulpice.* **Box office** 11am-6pm Mon-Sat. **Admission** €31; €12-€18 reductions. **Map** p405 G7.
The gilded mother of French theatres, the Comédie Française turns out season after season of classics, as well as lofty new productions. The red velvet and gold-flecked Salle Richelieu is located right by the Palais-Royal. Under the same management are the Studio-Théâtre, a black box inside the Carrousel du Louvre, and the Théâtre du Vieux Colombier. The line-up generally includes lashings of Molière.

★ Théâtre des Bouffes du Nord

37bis bd de la Chapelle, 10th (01.46.07.34.50, www.bouffesdunord.com). M° La Chapelle. **Box office** 5-7pm Mon-Fri; 2-7pm Sat. **Admission** €18-€30; €14-€26 reductions. **Map** p402 K2.
Peter Brook's former playground, the Théâtre des Bouffes du Nord treated Parisians to a production of Samuel Beckett's *Fragments* – five short plays – in early 2015.

CURTAIN UP

The Théâtre Paris Villette is back in the limelight.

The place to be for culture right now has to be La Villette in the 19th. In less than 30 years it's gone from abandoned abattoir district to lush modern park dotted with high-profile entertainment venues (including Zénith, Trabendo, La Grande Halle, Cité de la Musique and the new Philharmonie), festivals galore, a contemporary circus (Espace Chapiteaux) and two major museums (Cité des Sciences and Musée de la Musique). And in December 2013, it became home – for the second time – to one of the city's most avant-garde theatres, the **Théâtre Paris Villette** (*see p291*), set amid the elegant arches of Villette's former abattoir sales hall, a neoclassical 19th-century beauty.

The previous Théâtre Paris Villette opened in the 1980s to promote contemporary theatre. The careers of several major modern playwrights were launched here, including Tony Award-winning Yasmina Reza (best

known for *Art* and *God of Carnage*). However, after a stream of financial concerns and poor ticket sales, the theatre closed in 2012.

So imagine the joy when it reopened with everything new bar the name: a new look (a 70-seater all-white room and a 200-seater auditorium), two new directors (Valérie Dassonville and Adrien de Van), and a new charter to bring avant-garde, contemporary theatre to '*la jeunesse*' – youngsters in the broadest sense of the word, from schoolkids to grown-up theatre virgins.

The new theatre has an exciting line-up, mixing traditional and cutting-edge shows that use multimedia technology to enhance stage design and special effects. Tickets range from €10 to €20, and even if you don't fancy a show, come along for the bar – all vintage neo-pop with bold wallpaper and leather sofas. It's a fabulous spot to rub shoulders with the artists after the show.

Théâtre du Châtelet.

▶ *The Bouffes du Nord also has one of the best chamber music programmes in the capital.*

Théâtre du Châtelet

1 pl du Châtelet, 4th (01.40.28.28.40, www.chatelet-theatre.com). M° Châtelet. **Box office** 11am-7pm Mon-Sat; 1hr before show Sun. **Admission** €25-€99. **Map** p408 J6.

The Châtelet is Paris's main venue for musicals hailing from Broadway and the West End – such as *Singin' in the Rain* and *An American in Paris* – which are usually performed in the original language by visiting companies. It's the only venue in Paris to offer such quality musical theatre.

Théâtre de la Madeleine

19 rue de Surène, 8th (01.42.65.07.09, www. theatremadeleine.com). M° Madeleine. **Box office** 11am-7pm Mon-Sat. **Admission** €17-€54. **Map** p401 F4.

The theatre where Sacha Guitry composed 24 of his plays, between 1932 and 1940, continues to contribute to France's repertoire with top-notch creations by emerging and established artists.

Théâtre Marigny

Av de Marigny, 8th (08.92.22.23.33, www.theatre marigny.fr). M° Champs-Elysées Clemenceau or Franklin D. Roosevelt. **Box office** 11am-6.30pm Mon-Sat. **Admission** €25-€79. **Map** p401 E4.

Théâtre Marigny is one of the most expensive nights out for theatregoers in Paris. But then not many other theatres can boast so much: a location off the Champs-Elysées; a deluxe interior conceived by Charles Garnier (of Opéra fame); high-profile casts and an illustrious pedigree stretching back more than 150 years. The theatre is currently closed for renovations but is scheduled to reopen in 2015.

Théâtre National de Chaillot

1 pl du Trocadéro, 16th (01.53.65.30.00, www. theatre-chaillot.fr). M° Trocadéro. **Box office** 11am-6pm Mon-Sat. **Admission** €20-€39; €8-€32 reductions. **Map** p400 B4.

Get here early, grab a cocktail and gaze in awe at the Eiffel Tower through the lobby window. Chaillot's three auditoriums range from cosy and experimental to a 2,800-seater amphitheatre. Recent highlights have included David Bobee's exciting adaptation of *Romeo and Juliet*, complete with acrobats.

Théâtre Paris Villette

211 av Jean-Jaurès, 19th (01.40.03.72.23, www.theatre-paris-villette.fr). M° Porte de Pantin. **Box office** 2-6pm Tue; 11.30am-1pm, 2-6pm Wed-Fri; 3-6pm Sat (and performance days). **Admission** €10-€20; €8-€15 reductions. **Map** p403 inset.

See p290 **Curtain Up**.

Théâtre du Rond Point

2bis av Franklin D. Roosevelt, 8th (01.44.95.98.21, www.theatredurondpoint.fr). M° Champs-Elysées Clemenceau. **Box office** noon-7pm Tue-Sat; noon-4pm Sun (performance days). **Admission** €28-€36; €15-€26 reductions. **Map** p401 E4.

More than just a theatre, this historic venue multitasks as a bookshop, tearoom and restaurant.

Odéon, Théâtre de l'Europe.

So once you've fed your mind on contemporary, avant-garde and sometimes politically slanted theatre, make a night of it and opt for dinner as well.

★ Théâtre de la Ville & Théâtre des Abbesses

01.42.74.22.77, www.theatredelaville-paris. com. **Admission** €19-€35; €9-€26 reductions. **Théâtre de la Ville** *2 pl du Châtelet, 4th. M° Châtelet.* **Box office** 11am-7pm Mon; 11am-8pm Tue-Sat. **Map** p408 J6. **Théâtre des Abbesses** *31 rue des Abbesses, 18th. M° Abbesses.* **Box office** 5-8pm Tue-Sat. **Map** p402 H1.

At its two sites, the 'City Theatre' turns out the most consistently innovative programming in Paris. Instead of running a standard rep company, the house imports music, dance and theatre productions.

Left Bank

Le Lucernaire

53 rue Notre-Dame-des-Champs, 6th (01.45.44. 57.34, www.lucernaire.fr). M° Notre-Dame-des-Champs or Vavin. **Box office** 10.30am-12.30pm, 1.30-10pm Mon-Fri; 1.30-10pm Sat, Sun. **Admission** €25; €10-€20 reductions. **Map** p401 F4.

Three theatres, three cinemas, a restaurant and a bar make up this versatile cultural centre. Theatre-wise, Molière and other classic playwrights get a good thrashing, but so do up-and-coming authors.

★ Odéon, Théâtre de L'Europe

Pl de l'Odéon, 6th (01.44.85.40.00, bookings 01.44.85.40.40, www.theatre-odeon.fr). M° Odéon. **Box office** 11am-6.30pm Mon-Sat. **Admission** €12-€38; €6-€20 reductions. **Map** p408 H7. Highlights in early 2015 included Chekhov's *Ivanov* and Shakespeare's *Henry VI*. The theatre also plays host to the Impatience festival.

Théâtre de la Cité Internationale

17 bd Jourdan, 14th (01.43.13.50.50, www.theatre delacite.com). RER Cité Universitaire. **Box office** 1hr before show. *By phone* 1-6.30pm Mon-Fri; 2-6.30pm Sat. **Admission** €22; €7-€16 reductions. A polished, professional theatre based on the campus of the Cité Universitaire, the Théâtre de la Cité Internationale displays a global flair worthy of its setting. In addition to the main theatre and dance season, the prestigious Ecole du Théâtre National de Strasbourg occupies the stage for a stint each summer.

Théâtre de la Huchette

23 rue de la Huchette, 5th (01.43.26.38.99, www. theatre-huchette.com). M° Cluny La Sorbonne or St-Michel. **Box office** 1.30-7pm Mon; 3.30-9pm Tue-Sat. **Admission** €24; €17 reductions. *Double bill ticket* €36; €26 reductions. **Map** p408 J7.

Théâtre de la Huchette

promoting global cross-cultural exchange with visiting companies from across France and abroad. The theatre is currently undergoing renovations and will reopen towards the end of 2016. The **Théâtre Gérard-Philipe** (59 bd Jules-Guesde, 93200 St-Denis, 01.48.13.70.00, www.theatregerardphilipe.com), recently taken over by Jean Bellorini, offers consistently good fare of an experimental nature. Just beyond La Défense's towers, the **Théâtre Nanterre Amandiers** (7 av Pablo Picasso, 92022 Nanterre, 01.46.14.70.00, www.nanterre-amandiers.com, shuttle bus from RER Nanterre-Préfécture 1hr before show) provides an eclectic mix of probing modern theatre, as well as the great classics and occasional opera. And the **Théâtre d'Ivry Antoine Vitez** (1 rue Simon Dereure, 94200 Ivry, 01.43.90.11.11, www.theatre-quartiers-ivry.com) has a theatre, dance studio and auditorium.

Ionesco's absurdist classic *La Cantatrice Chauve* (The Bald Soprano) has been playing here since 1957, running on a double bill with his *La Leçon*.

Beyond the Périphérique

Culture doesn't come to an end at the city ring road. A combination of measures designed to bring theatre to the masses and extortionate rental rates for productions inside Paris has led to the creation of several excellent out-of-town venues.

In the north-east, **MC93 Bobigny** (1 bd Lénine, 93000 Bobigny, 01.41.60.72.72, www. mc93.com) is a slick institution dedicated to

ALTERNATIVE THEATRE

Point Ephémère (*see p276*) and its older brother **Mains d'Oeuvres** (*see p275*) are cool urban arts centres. **Confluences** (190 bd de Charonne, 20th, 01.40.24.16.46, http://confluences.jimdo.com) is an all-in-one cultural centre equipped with an art gallery, a theatre and a projection room; and **Les Laboratoires d'Aubervilliers** (41 rue Lécuyer, 93300 Aubervilliers, 01.53.56.15.90, www. leslaboratoires.org) churns out some wonderful, conceptualist productions. **Le Tarmac** theatre (159 av Gambetta, 20th, 01.43.64.80.80, http://le tarmac.fr) houses the TILF (Théâtre International de Langue Française), the only theatre in France dedicated to the Francophone world.

Point Ephémère.

Escapes & Excursions

Escapes & Excursions

The forests surrounding Paris were once the playground of royalty and aristocracy, and their extravagant legacy is plain to see in sumptuous châteaux such as Chantilly, Fontainebleau, Versailles and Vaux-le-Vicomte. Artistic legacy is also in plentiful supply near the capital, from Van Gogh's tiny garret to Monet's lily-strewn garden and Cocteau's flamboyant country house. Further afield, the famous cellars of Champagne are less than an hour from Paris by train (perfect if you want to try a glass or two of fizz while you're there). And if the sand of Paris-Plages doesn't quite cut the mustard, even the Med is only a few hours away by TGV if you fancy sampling some bouillabaisse and beach action around Marseille.

Towns & Cities

TOURS

Novelist Honoré de Balzac (1799-1850) once described his beloved birthplace as being 'more fresh, flowery and perfumed than any other town in the world', and Tours has a lot going for it today. In fact, it's a positively pleasant city, bursting with history, medieval quarters, a lively student population, colourful flower markets and enticing bars and restaurants. Only an hour from Paris Gare Montparnasse by TGV, the city is the official gateway to the Loire Valley, and a choice place in which to refuel before overdosing on sumptuous Renaissance castles.

Sandwiched between the Loire (north) and the Cher (south) rivers, it began life as a fertile floodplain, prized by the Turones – a Celtic tribe that gave modern Tours its name. In 57 BC, Julius Caesar conquered the city, modestly changing its name to Caesarodunum (Caesar's hill). Traces of the third-century Gallo-Roman city wall and amphitheatre can still be seen in the Musée des Beaux-Arts gardens.

When Christianity arrived, St Martin, the founder of France's first monastery, became bishop of Tours. After his death in 397, his relics, laid to rest in the Basilique St-Martin, were believed to have healing powers, drawing in thousands of pilgrims en route to Santiago de Compostela in Spain, and prompting the construction of Tours' medieval quarters.

IN THE KNOW AMBOISE

A leisurely 20-minute drive east from Tours (*see left*), Amboise is a small town of narrow streets and quaint residences overlooking the Loire river. It is also home to two star sites: the imposing **Château Royal d'Amboise** (www.chateau-amboise.com), set on a rocky spur and one of the most historically important buildings in the region; and Leonardo da Vinci's former home, the **Clos Lucé** (www.vinci-closluce.com), an exquisitely restored manor house with landscaped gardens and a museum of da Vinci's inventions.

Throughout the 15th and 16th centuries, the city vied with Paris as the seat of power: Charles VII, Louis XI (who established Tours' silk industry), Charles VIII and François I all cherished Tours; Henry IV preferred Paris.

The city was bombarded by the Prussians in 1870 and suffered widespread damage during World War II, especially in the historic centre, which by the 1960s was a no-go zone of crumbling masonry. Nowadays, after 40 years of regeneration, the medieval quarter contains some of Tours' most charming streets. Pedestrianised place Plumereau, with its half-timbered façades housing cafés, galleries and boutiques, is the hub of the town. Wander down lanes such as rue Briçonnet to find concealed courtyards, more half-timbered houses and the occasional crooked tower. In place de Châteauneuf, a lone tower is the only intact segment of the original Basilique St-Martin, sacked by the Huguenots in 1562. The neo-Byzantine **Basilique St-Martin** (www.basiliquesaintmartin.com) houses St Martin's shrine up the road, opposite the ruined vestiges.

The east of Tours is dominated by the **Cathédrale St-Gatien** (02.47.70.21.00, www.paroisse-cathedrale-tours.catholique.fr).

Work began on this splendid building in the 13th century and ended in the 16th century, demonstrating the French Gothic style in its entirety. The stained-glass windows inside are often compared to those of Sainte-Chapelle in Paris. Next door, the archbishop's palace and **Musée des Beaux-Arts** (18 pl François-Sicard, 02.47.05.68.82, www.mba.tours.fr) has a rich collection of paintings by Degas, Rembrandt and Delacroix, plus sculptures by Rodin and Bourdelle. Check out the enormous 200-year-old cedar of Lebanon in the garden.

North of here, Tours' **Château Royal** (25 av André Malraux) looks over the Loire with dishevelled majesty. You can best take in its assorted architecture by following the river: the Tour de Guise (look out for machicolations and a pepper-pot roof) was a 13th-century fortress, and the 15th-century Logis des Gouverneurs on the quay has gable dormers and a chunk of Gallo-Roman wall at its base. Further west, the **Musée du Compagnonnage** (8 rue Nationale, 02.47.21.62.20, www.museecompagnonnage.fr) showcases the handiwork of master craftsmen of the guilds.

For dreamy regional dishes such as *crépine de dinde* (a giant turkey meatball cooked in red wine)

MOVING MASTERPIECES

The capital's most visited museums make for the provinces.

Paris's twin cultural giants, the Louvre and the Centre Pompidou, are the capital's two most visited museums, bringing in more than 12 million visitors each year to gawp at the artistic treasures within.

But while the galleries are stacked full of masterpieces ancient and modern, the problem has always been that their vaults are heaving with acres of unseen treasures. So the Pompidou decided to follow in the footsteps of Tate Liverpool and Guggenheim Bilbao, and open an outpost in the eastern city of Metz in 2010 with the same *raison d'être* as the original – namely to 'present and help discover all forms of artistic expression, raise public awareness of the major works of the 20th and 21st centuries, and take part in Europe's cultural landscape'. And, presumably, to help shift some of that excess stock sitting in the basement. The **Centre Pompidou Metz** (www.centre pompidou-metz.fr) has been a success so far, with visitors flocking to check out the Shigeru Ban-designed multidisciplinary space.

Not to be outdone, the Louvre is now playing its own regeneration game with an outpost in the gritty northern industrial town of Lens. Far from the grandiose surroundings of the 1st arrondissement, the **Musée du Louvre-Lens** (www.louvre lens.fr) sprawls across the site of an old

Musée du Louvre-Lens.

mine works and opened in December 2012. Metz lies just 80 minutes from Paris by TGV and Lens is even closer (70 minutes), which puts it firmly in day-trip distance, as well as tapping into the Lille catchment area.

At the Musée du Louvre-Lens, the main display space, the 2,000sq m Galerie du Temps, displays some 300 artworks taken from every department in the Louvre. There's also a 300-seat auditorium, La Scène, which aims to bring the Louvre's collection to life through live performance.

Centre Pompidou Metz.

and *poire tappée* (poached pear), head to **Le Petit Patrimoine** (58 rue Colbert, 02.47.66.05.81). For a few sneaky glasses of Touraine wine before you head back, **Au Chien Jaune** (74 rue Bernard Palissy, 02.47.05.10.17), a former brothel, is located in a handy spot by the **tourist office** (78 rue Bernard Palissy, 02.47.70.37.37, www.tours-tourisme.fr).

Cathedrals & Châteaux

CHANTILLY

From the 14th century until 1897, the town of Chantilly was the domain of the Princes of Condé, the cousins of the French kings. As well as its impressive château, Chantilly, with its hunting forests and prestigious horse-racing centres, has a rich equestrian history. The town is a half-hour train ride north of the capital (trains leave from Paris Gare du Nord).

Much of the cream-coloured **Château de Chantilly** was destroyed during the Revolution, leaving the main wing to be reconstructed in the 19th century by Henri d'Orléans, Duc d'Aumale. When the duke died in 1897, he bequeathed the entire Domaine de Chantilly – including the Grandes Ecuries, the Hippodrome and the 61 sq km forest – to the Institut de France on the condition that the château be opened to the public as the Musée Condé, and that none of the artworks would be moved or loaned to other museums. The remarkable collection includes three paintings by Raphael, and the *Très Riches Heures du Duc de Berry*, a medieval book of hours, containing the most exquisite colours imaginable. If you thought that the Middle Ages were dull, you can think again.

The main section of the château's sprawling park, designed by royal landscape architect Le Nôtre, features traditional French formal parterres and an extensive canal system, which allows visitors to see the park from electric-powered boats. Head off the beaten path to explore the English Garden, the Island of Love, the kangaroo zoo and the original hamlet that inspired Marie-Antoinette to build her own version at Versailles.

The Grandes Ecuries ('great stables') at the château were commissioned in 1719 by Prince Louis-Henri de Bourbon (who believed he would be reincarnated as a horse). Later, they became one of Napoleon's equestrian training grounds, having suffered only light damage during the Revolution. In 1982, the great horseman Yves Bienaimé restored the stables and turned them into the Musée Vivant du Cheval. The Forêt de Chantilly is full of hiking and cycling trails.

A pleasant walk of around seven kilometres circles four small lakes, the Etangs de Commelles, and passes the Château de la Reine Blanche, a mill that was converted in the 1820s into a pseudo-medieval hunting lodge. For trail details, ask at the **tourist office** (73 rue du Connétable, 03.44.67.37.37, www.chantilly-tourisme.com).

For a post-hike lunch, tuck into the *plat du jour* at **La Capitainerie** (03.44.57.15.89, www.chateaudechantilly.com), which is situated in the original château kitchens. For a taste of Chantilly whipped cream, stop for tea at the **Restaurant du Hameau** (03.44.57.46.21, www.chateaudechantilly.com) in the *hameau* at the château.

Château de Chantilly
Chantilly (03.44.27.31.80, www.chateaudechantilly. com). **Open** *Apr-Oct* 10am-6pm daily. *Nov-Mar* 10.30am-5pm Mon, Wed-Sun. **Admission** *Château & park* €16; €9.50 reductions; free under-4s.

CHARTRES

Seen from a distance, the mismatched spires and dazzling silhouette of the **Cathédrale de Chartres** burst out of the Beauce cornfields and dominate the skyline of this modest town some 90km south-west of Paris (an hour by train from Gare Montparnasse). Chartres was a pilgrimage site long before the cathedral was built, ever since the Sacra Camisia (said to be the Virgin Mary's birthing garment) was donated in 876 by the king.

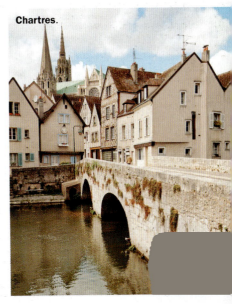

Chartres.

The cathedral is one of the finest examples of Gothic architecture in the world. The west front, or 'Royal Portal' – which was modelled in part on St-Denis – features three sculpted doorways. Inside, there's another era of sculpture, represented in the 16th-century scenes of the life of Christ that surround the choir. In particular, note the circular labyrinth of black and white stones in the floor. The cathedral is famed, above all, for its stained-glass windows depicting biblical scenes, saints and medieval trades in brilliant 'Chartres blue', punctuated by rich reds. During World War II, the windows were removed and stored nearby for safety, only being reinstalled once the war was over. Climb the tower for a great view over the surrounding town and country. English-language tours by lecturer Malcolm Miller – one of the world's most knowledgeable and entertaining experts on the cathedral – take place all year round (02.37.28.15.58, noon & 2.45pm Mon-Sat Apr-Oct, noon Nov-Mar, €10, €5 reductions). Audio guides can also be hired.

The town of Chartres is an attractive tangle of narrow, medieval streets on the banks of the Eure. The **tourist office** can be found at place de la Cathédrale (02.37.18.26.26, www.chartres-tourisme.com). Two sights merit a special mention: the **Musée des Beaux-Arts** (29 cloître Notre-Dame, 02.37.90.45.80), which houses a collection of 18th-century French paintings by Watteau and others; and the memorial to **Jean Moulin**, the legendary figure of the Resistance. A wartime prefect of Chartres until he was dismissed by the Vichy government after his refusal to co-operate with the Nazis, Moulin became de Gaulle's man in France, and died under torture in Lyon in 1943. His memorial is a ten-minute walk west of the cathedral, at the corner of rue Collin d'Arleville and boulevard de la Résistance.

Hungry tourists congregate at **Café Serpente** (2 cloître Notre-Dame, 02.37.21.68.81, www.leserpente.com), in the shadow of the cathedral. But if it's full, there are plenty of easy and worthwhile options nearby. For restaurant cuisine with a riverside view, try **L'Estocade** (1 rue de la Porte Guillaume, 02.37.34.27.17, www.estocade.net). For fireside treats, **La Vieille Maison** (5 rue au Lait, 02.37.34.10.67, www.lavieillemaison.fr) has a cosy 14th-century dining room. For a local speciality, order some Chartres pâté at **Le Saint-Hilaire** (11 rue Pont St-Hilaire, 02.37.30.97.57, www.restaurant-saint-hilaire.fr).

Cathédrale de Chartres
Pl de la Cathédrale (Cathedral 02.37.21.75.02, Tower 02.37.21.22.07, www.cathedrale-chartres. org). **Open** *Cathedral* 8.30am-7.30pm daily (until 10pm Sat, Sun July & Aug). *Tower* May-Aug 9.30am-12.30pm, 2-6pm Mon-Sat; 2-6pm Sun. Sept-Apr 9.30am-12.30pm, 2-5pm Mon-Sat; 2-5pm Sun. **Admission** *Cathedral* free. *Tower* €5.50; €4.50 reductions; free under-18s, under-26s (EU citizens). **No credit cards**.

FONTAINEBLEAU

Home to 14 French kings since François I, the **Château de Fontainebleau** was once a sort of aristocratic club where gentlemen of the day came to hunt and learn the art of chivalry. The town, which lies 60km south of the capital (half an hour by train from Paris Gare de Lyon), grew up around the château in the 19th century.

The château is bite-sized compared to Versailles. A former hunting lodge, it is a real mix of styles. In 1528, François I brought in Italian artists and craftsmen to help architect Gilles le Breton to transform the neglected lodge into the finest Italian Mannerist palace in France. This style, noted for grotesqueries, contorted figures and crazy fireplaces, is still visible in the ballroom and Long Gallery. Henri IV added a tennis court, Louis XIII built a double-horseshoe staircase, and Louis XIV and XV added classical trimmings. Napoleon and Louis-Philippe also spent a fortune on redecoration. The château gardens include Le Nôtre's Grand Parterre. There is also a park.

The 170sq km **Forêt de Fontainebleau** features bizarre geological formations and diverse wildlife. It's the wildest slice of nature near Paris. There are a number of well-marked trails, such as the GR1 from Bois-le-Roi station, but more serious yompers would be better off with an official map such as the TOP25 IGN series 2417-OT, which covers the entire forest. Trail maps are on sale at the **tourist office** (4 rue Royale, 01.60.74.99.99, www.fontainebleau-tourisme.com), which hires out bicycles. Bikes can also be hired from **A la Petite Reine** (14 rue de la Paroisse, 01.60.74.57.57, www.alapetitereine.com).

IN THE KNOW HEAD SOUTH

Thanks to the TGV, you can now reach the Med city of Marseille from Paris in just three hours. France's second city was European Capital of Culture in 2013 and boasts steep streets, tranquil squares and bustling 19th-century thoroughfares that provide a patchwork of backdrops for souk-like markets, chic shops and the colourful Vieux Port, where fishmongers sell their wares along the boat-lined quayside. For some breathtaking views, climb up to the Notre-Dame de la Garde basilica, or stay grounded over a plate of bouillabaisse and go shopping around the vintage boutiques on Cours Julien.

Château de Vaux-le-Vicomte.

Rue Grande is lined with restaurants such as **Au Délice Impérial** (no.1, 01.64.22.20.70). At no.92, picnickers can pick up a wonderful array of cheeses at **Fromagerie Barthélémy** (01.64.22.21.64). The elegant **Hôtel Napoléon** (9 rue Grande, 01.60.39.50.50, www.hotelnapoleon-fontainebleau.com) provides appropriately grand meals at its restaurant.

Château de Fontainebleau

Pl du Général-de-Gaulle (01.60.71.50.70, www. musee-chateau-fontainebleau.fr). **Open** *Château* Apr-Sept 9.30am-6pm Mon, Wed-Sun. Oct-Mar 9.30am-5pm Mon, Wed-Sun. *Park & gardens* Mar, Apr, Oct 9am-6pm daily. May-Sept 9am-7pm daily. Nov-Feb 9am-5pm daily. **Admission** *Château* €11; €9 reductions; free under-18s, under-26s (EU citizens). *Park & gardens* free. PMP.

VAUX-LE-VICOMTE

The lavish **Château de Vaux-le-Vicomte**, 55km south-east of Paris (half an hour by train to Melun from Gare de Lyon then 6km taxi ride), has a valuable lesson to teach: never, ever out-do your king. When Nicolas Fouquet (1615-80), Louis XIV's finance minister (and protégé of Cardinal Mazarin), decided to build an abode fit for his position, he had several hamlets moved away, called on three of France's most talented men (architect Louis Le Vau, painter Charles Lebrun and landscape gardener André Le Nôtre), and hired sculptors such as Giradon, Lespagnandel and Nicolas Poussin to chip in with the decor.

Its completion was celebrated in 1661 with a huge party for which Molière wrote a play. All would have gone swimmingly had it not been for one minor detail: Fouquet invited the king. Louis was disgusted at his minister's display of grandeur; soon after, Fouquet was given a show trial for the embezzlement of state funds. His personal effects were seized by the crown and he was sent into exile, dying 19 years later in prison. But Fouquet's legacy did live on, as Louis later hired Le Vau, Lebrun and Le Nôtre to work some of their magic on Versailles.

A self-guided tour of the interior includes Fouquet's personal suite, the servants' dining room, the huge basement and wine cellar, and the copper-filled kitchen. The dome, with its unfinished ceiling – Lebrun only had time to paint the sky and one eagle before Fouquet was arrested – and the roof are optional extras.

On the south side, a staircase descends to the gardens, where boxed hedges and flowerbeds sweep into a vast expanse of lawns, grottoes, canals, lakes and fountains. Electric cars can be hired to help you cover the site.

Château de Vaux-le-Vicomte

77950 Maincy (01.64.14.41.90, www.vaux-le-vicomte.com). **Open** *Château* Early Mar-early Nov 10am-6pm daily. *Candlelight evenings* Early May-early Oct 7pm-midnight Sat. **Admission** €16.50; €10-€13.50 reductions; free under-6s. *Candlelight evenings* €19.50; €15-€17.50 reductions; free under-6s.

VERSAILLES

The **Château de Versailles**, 20km west of Paris (train from Gare St-Lazare to Versailles Rive Droite then 10min walk) is a masterpiece – and usually packed with visitors as a result. Allow yourself a whole day to appreciate the sumptuous State Apartments and the Hall of Mirrors, the highlights of any visit. The Grand Appartement, where Louis XIV held court, consists of six gilded salons, all opulent examples of Baroque craftsmanship. No less luxurious, the Queen's Apartment includes her bedroom, where royal births took place in view of the court. The Hall of Mirrors, where a united Germany was proclaimed in 1871 and the Treaty of Versailles signed in 1919, is flooded with natural light from its 17 vast windows. Designed to catch the last of the day's rays, it was here that the Sun King would hold extravagant receptions.

Architect Louis Le Vau first embellished the original building – a hunting lodge built during Louis XIII's reign – after Louis XIV saw Vaux-le-Vicomte, the impressive residence of his finance minister, Nicolas Fouquet. André Le Nôtre turned the boggy marshland into terraces, parterres, fountains and lush groves.

After Le Vau's death in 1670, Jules Hardouin-Mansart took over as principal architect, transforming Versailles into the château we know today. He dedicated the last 30 years of his life to adding the two main wings, the Cour des Ministres and the Chapelle Royale. In 1682, Louis moved in, accompanied by his court; thereafter, he rarely set foot in Paris. In the 1770s, Louis XV commissioned Jacques-Ange Gabriel to add the sumptuous Opéra Royal, now used for concerts by the **Centre de Musique Baroque** (01.39.20.78.10, www.cmbv.fr). The expense of building and running Versailles cost France dear. With the fall of the monarchy in 1792, most of

the furniture was lost – but the château was saved by Louis-Philippe.

The gardens of Versailles are really works of art in themselves, their ponds and statues once again embellished by a fully working fountain system. On summer weekends, the spectacular jets of water are set to music, a prelude to the occasional fireworks displays of the Fêtes de Nuit. Beyond the gardens are the Grand Canal and the wooded land and sheep-filled pastures of the estate's park.

In 1687, Hardouin-Mansart built the pink marble Grand Trianon in the north of the park, set away from the protocol of the court. Here Louis XIV and his children's governess and secret second wife, Madame de Maintenon, were able to admire the intimate gardens from the colonnaded portico. It retains the Empire decor of Napoleon, who stayed here with his second Empress, Marie-Louise.

The Petit Trianon, built for Louis XV's mistress Madame de Pompadour, is a wonderful example of neoclassicism. It later became part of the Domaine de Marie-Antoinette, an exclusive hideaway in the wooded parkland. Given to Marie-Antoinette as a wedding gift by her husband Louis XVI in 1774, the *domaine* also includes the chapel adjoining the Petit Trianon, plus a theatre, a neoclassical 'Temple d'Amour', and Marie-Antoinette's fairy-tale farm and dairy, the Hameau de la Reine. Here, the queen escaped from the discontent of her subjects and the revolutionary fervour of Paris.

Outside the château gates are the **Potager du Roi** (the Sun King's vegetable garden,

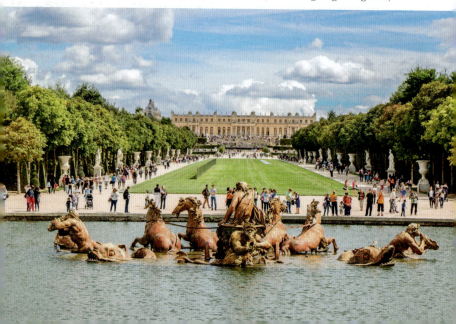

01.39.24.62.62, www.potager-du-roi.fr), and stables that now house the **Académie du Spectacle Equestre** (01.39.02.62.75, www. acadequestre.fr), which is responsible for the elaborate shows of tightly choreographed theatrics on horseback, run by the famous horse trainer Bartabas.

In the town of Versailles, grab a Historical Places brochure free from the **tourist office** (2bis av de Paris, 01.39.24.88.88, www.versailles-tourisme.com) and explore. The Quartier St-Louis opposite the Potager was developed by Louis XV around the Cathédrale St-Louis. Just off rue d'Anjou are the Carrés St-Louis, four market squares surrounded by 18th-century boutiques. North-east of the château is the Quartier Notre-Dame, part of the 'new town' designed by the Sun King himself. Eglise Notre-Dame is where members of the royal family were baptised and married. Around the corner is the Marché Notre-Dame, a market square dating back to 1671 and surrounded by restaurants and cafés.

Set in a building that dates back to the construction of the château, **Au Chapeau Gris** (7 rue Hoche, 01.39.50.10.81, www.auchapeau gris.com) is the oldest restaurant in Versailles, and serves up French country cuisine beneath ancient wooden beams. **Boeuf à la Mode** (4 rue au Pain, Marché Notre-Dame, 01.39.50.31.99, www.leboeufalamode-versailles.com) is an authentic 1930s brasserie serving steak and seafood. Another long-established restaurant is the traditional **Brasserie du Théâtre** (15 rue des Réservoirs, 01.39.50.03.21, www.brasserietheatre.com).

Château de Versailles.

★ Château de Versailles
78000 Versailles (01.30.83.78.00, advance tickets 08.92.68.46.94, www.chateauversailles.fr). **Open** *Apr-Oct* 9am-6.30pm Tue-Sun. *Nov-Mar* 9am-5.30pm Tue-Sun. *Garden* Apr-Oct 8am-8.30pm daily. *Park* 7am-8.30pm daily. *Garden & Park* Nov-Mar 8am-6pm daily. **Admission** €15; €13 reductions; free under-18s, under-26s (EU citizens), all 1st Sun of mth (Nov-Mar). PMP. **Grandes-Eaux Musicales** (*01.30.83.78.88*). **Open** *Apr-Oct* Sat, Sun. **Admission** €9; €7 reductions; free under-6s.

Artistic Retreats
AUVERS-SUR-OISE

This rural retreat, about an hour by train from Paris Gare du Nord, is where Vincent van Gogh spent his last weeks. His tiny attic room at the **Auberge Ravoux** is open to the public. Other Auvers residents included fellow artists Camille Pissarro, Paul Cézanne and Charles-François Daubigny. Today, you can explore the **Musée Daubigny** (Manoir des Colombières, rue de la Sansonne, 01.30.36.80.20, www.musee daubigny.com) and his **studio** (61 rue Daubigny, 01.30.36.60.60, www.atelier-daubigny.com), which is still decorated with his murals. Another attraction is the **Musée de l'Absinthe** (44 rue Callé, 01.30.36.83.26, www.musee-absinthe.com), a rather modest collection of art and artefacts related to the notorious drink. Banned in France from 1915, the green concoction is once again legal. The local artistic legacy has not been overlooked by Auvers' main historical attraction, either. The 17th-century **Château d'Auvers** (rue de Léry, 01.34.48.48.48, www.chateau-auvers.fr) features a walk-through tour with an Impressionist theme. Auvers' **tourist office** is at Parc Van Gogh, 38 rue du Général de Gaulle (01.30.36.71.81, www.tourisme-auverssuroise.fr).

You can always do as Van Gogh might have done, and dine at the **Auberge Ravoux**. Otherwise, try **L'Impressionist' Café** (Château d'Auvers, rue de Léry, 01.34.48.48.56). The **Hostellerie du Nord** (6 rue Général-de-Gaulle, 01.30.36.70.74, www.hostelleriedunord.fr) has Joël Boilleaut running the kitchen.

Auberge Ravoux
1 pl de la Mairie, 95430 Auvers-sur-Oise (01.30.36.60.60, www.maisondevangogh.fr). **Open** *Mar-Oct* 10am-6pm Wed-Sun. **Admission** €6; €4 reductions; free under-12s.

GIVERNY

In 1883, Claude Monet moved his mistress and their eight children into a quaint pink-brick house he had rented in bucolic Giverny, less than an hour

Giverny.

ESCAPES & EXCURSIONS

from Paris (Gare St-Lazare to Vernon, then 5km taxi or bus ride), and spent as much time cultivating a beautiful garden here as painting the water lilies in it. The leader of the Impressionist movement thrived on outdoor scenes, whether along the Seine near Argenteuil or by the Thames in London. Having once seen the tiny village of Giverny from the window of a train, he was smitten. By 1890, he had bought his dream home and soon had a pond dug, bridges built and a tableau of greenery created. As Monet's eyesight began to fail, he produced endless impressions of his paradise, trying to capture how the leaves and water reflected light. He died here in 1926.

Of the hundreds of tourists who visit here every day, not all are art-lovers; there are none of his original paintings actually on display here (though you will see the 32 Japanese woodblock prints collected by the artist). Most visitors are simply here for the lilies, and a good photo opportunity. The garden is as much a masterpiece as any of Monet's paintings, its famous water-lily pond, weeping willows and Japanese bridge still remarkably intact from the master's day; and the charming house, the **Fondation Claude Monet**, is dotted with touching mementos.

Once you're back in the village, be prepared for some difficulty finding a table at one of the scarce eating places, and long queues of impatient tourists almost everywhere you turn. Get here early, or book ahead to eat at the famous **Hôtel Baudy** museum-restaurant (81 rue Claude-Monet, 02.32.21.10.03, www.restaurantbaudy. com), where Monet's American disciples (such as Willard Metcalf and Dawson-Watson) set up their easels for several decadent years, expanding the old hotel into an *art-atelier extraordinaire*, with ballroom, rose garden and tennis courts – Cézanne stayed here for a month. Up the road, the **Musée des Impressionnismes Giverny**

(99 rue Claude-Monet, 02.32.51.94.65, www. museedesimpressionnismesgiverny.com) houses works by the American Impressionist colony.

Fondation Claude Monet

84 rue Claude-Monet, 27620 Giverny (02.32.51.28.21, www.fondation-monet.com). **Open** *Apr-Oct* 9.30am-6pm daily. Closed Nov-Mar. **Admission** *House & garden* €9.50; €5.50 reductions; free under-7s.

MILLY-LA-FORÊT

As a revered poet, painter, playwright and filmmaker, Jean Cocteau has left an artistic legacy that pervades many aspects of French culture. Yet the man was always an elusive figure. But now, thanks to the hefty financial input of Pierre Bergé (partner of the late Yves Saint Laurent and a close friend of Cocteau's), his old country house in Milly-la-Forêt, less than an hour south-east of Paris (RER D to Maisse, then 7km taxi ride), is open as the **Maison de Jean Cocteau**. Cocteau moved to Milly-la-Forêt in 1947 to escape the glitz of the capital. Following his death from a heart attack at the age of 74, in 1963, his long-term partner Edouard Dhermite (who starred in Jean-Pierre Melville's 1950 film of Cocteau's 1929 novel *Les Enfants Terribles*) locked up the study, bedroom and living room, leaving more than 500 oil paintings, drawings, sculptures and photographs untouched for decades.

The three rooms have been faithfully restored, leaving one with the impression that Cocteau left only a few minutes earlier. The living room is wonderfully flamboyant, with antique furniture and gold palm trees framing a Bérard painting of Oedipus. The bedroom, meanwhile, with its four-poster bed and a mural of a castle, boasts a fairytale quality reminiscent of Cocteau's masterful 1946 romantic fantasy film *La Belle et la Bête*. Finally the study, with its leopard-print walls and erotic memorabilia, offers the most intimate glimpse into the artist's creative process, by turns both inspiring and provocative.

The rest of the house has been converted into exhibition space with two galleries: one houses a collection of portraits of Cocteau by such artists as Picasso, Warhol and Modigliani; the other is dedicated to temporary exhibitions. A projection room showing documentaries and Cocteau's films concludes the visit, but the adventure continues in the gardens, dotted with sculptures, where he used to enjoy strolling and writing.

Cocteau's body rests nearby, in the **Chapelle Saint-Blaise-des-Simples** (rue de l'Amiral de Graville, Milly-la-Forêt, 01.64.98.84.94, www. chapelle-saint-blaise.org, €3, open times vary). The interior, like a scaled-down Sistine Chapel, is covered in murals painted by Cocteau in 1960.

Maison de Jean Cocteau

15 rue du Lau, 91490 Milly-la-Forêt (01.64.98.11.50, www.maisoncocteau.net). **Open** *Mar-Oct* 2-7pm Wed-Sun. *Nov* 2-6pm Sat, Sun. Closed Dec-Feb. **Admission** €7.50; €6.50 reductions; free under-10s.

Champagne Country
REIMS & EPERNAY

Named after the region in which it's produced, champagne – nearly all 300 million bottles a year of it – comes from the towns of Reims (nasally pronounced 'Ranse') and Epernay, some 25km apart. At less than an hour by train from Paris Gare de l'Est, both are ideal destinations for a weekend break. A tour of a champagne cellar is a big part of most visits. Most cellars give detailed explanations of how the drink is produced – from the grape varieties to the strict name and quality controls – and guided tours finish with a sample.

Epernay developed during the 19th century as champagne houses moved from Reims to acquire more space. The best tours are at Mercier and Moët & Chandon. The **tourist office** is at 7 av de Champagne (03.26.53.33.00, www.ot-epernay.fr).

Some 7,000 tonnes of chalk were extracted to create the 18km (11 miles) of cellars at **Mercier**, opened in 1858. Note the 20-tonne champagne barrel at the entrance: it took 24 bulls and 18 horses to drag it from Epernay to Paris for the 1889 Exposition Universelle. The 45-minute underground tour takes place on a little train.

Moët & Chandon started life in 1743 as champagne supplier to Madame de Pompadour, mistress of Louis XV. It later supplied Napoleon and Alexander I of Russia. Since then it has kept pole position, with more than 250 global outlets. In the hour-long tour, visitors are led through a section of the 28km (17 miles) of tunnels.

In Reims, most of the major champagne houses are open by appointment only, including **Lanson** (03.26.78.50.50, www.lanson.fr) and **Veuve Clicquot** (03.26.89.53.90, www. veuve-clicquot.com). **Pommery** is set in an intriguing Elizabethan building. The visit takes place some 30m (98ft) underground, in 18km (11 miles) of tunnels linking 120 Gallo-Roman chalk quarries. The **tourist office** is at 2 rue Guillaume-de-Machault (03.26.77.45.00, www.reims-tourisme.com).

Home of the coronation church of most French monarchs since Clovis in 496, Reims was an important city even in Roman times. Begun in 1211, the current **Cathédrale Notre-Dame** (03.26.47.55.34, www.cathedrale-reims.com) has rich Gothic decoration that includes thousands

Champagne vineyards.

ESCAPES & EXCURSIONS

ESCAPES & EXCURSIONS

LEST WE FORGET

Remembering the horrors of the Great War.

Perhaps the place that best evokes World War I is **Vimy Ridge** (Chemin des Canadiens, 62580 Vimy, 03.21.50.68.68, www. veterans.gc.ca, open mid Jan-mid Dec 11am-5pm Mon, 9am-5pm Tue-Sun, free), just north of Arras. Here the ground is still full of pockmarks from shells and craters, and some of the trenches and tunnels have been preserved, a rare stretch of battlefield left as a memorial – the area, dotted with war cemeteries, was largely reconstructed after the devastation of the conflict. The sandbags are now moulded in concrete so that you can walk down the trenches and look out across No Man's Land, seeing just how close the front line was to the enemy. Guided tours are also available through the network of tunnels. The second part of the site, up the hill, is the towering white-stone Canadian memorial that dominates the ridge. A view of the mining slag heaps in the distance acts as a reminder of one of the reasons why control of northern France was so crucial.

A century after World War I, its memories are still continuing to evolve. The **Maison Forestière** (Bois Lévêque, 59360 Ors, 03.27.84.54.83, www.tourisme-lecateau.fr, open mid Apr-mid Nov 2-6pm Wed-Fri, 10am-1pm, 2-6pm Sat, 3-6pm 1st Sun of mth, free), the house in the woods where war poet and Second Lieutenant in the Manchester Regiment Wilfred Owen spent his last night, was recreated as a contemporary artwork in 2011 by British artist Simon Patterson.

The red-brick house was transformed with the help of architect Jean-Christophe Denise into a strikingly minimalist white shell, its roof recalling an open book. 'Strange Meeting' and other poems are projected on to the walls and read in both English (by Kenneth Branagh) and French (by Philippe Capelle) in what Patterson describes as a commemoration of Owen's work, while the cellar where the soldiers slept and Owen wrote his last letter to his mother has been left in its original state, reached by a spiralling white exterior ramp. The house forms the starting point of a trail taking in the nearby Canal de la Sambre, where Owen was shot down on 4 November 1918, a week before the Armistice, and the military section of the communal cemetery where he is buried.

The cemetery of **Notre-Dame de Lorette** is the largest necropolis of French troops killed here between October 1914 and September 1915, with some 45,000 graves situated around a neo-Byzantine basilica. It was joined in 2014 by the **Anneau de la Mémoire** (International Memorial Ring). Spread across the hillside beneath the cemetery, the polished bronze elliptical ring by architect Philippe Prost symbolises unity. The inside of the ring is engraved with the names of 579,606 soldiers in alphabetical order, regardless of their nationality, religion or rank, showing the extraordinary number of people who lost their lives in this region during the war.

Maison Forestière.

of figures on the portals. Look out, too, for stained-glass windows by Chagall. The statues damaged during shelling in World War I can be seen next door in the former archbishop's palace, the **Palais du Tau** (2 pl du Cardinal-Luçon, 03.26.47.81.79).

In Reims, countless cafés and brasseries line lively place Drouet d'Erlon. In Epernay, **La Cave à Champagne** (16 rue Léon Gambetta, 03.26.55.50.70, www.la-cave-a-champagne.com) does good traditional French food.

Mercier

68 av de Champagne, 51200 Epernay (03.26.51.22.22, www.champagnemercier.fr). **Open** *Feb-mid Nov* 9.30-11am, 2-4pm daily. *Mid Nov-mid Dec* 9.30-11am, 2-4pm Mon, Thur-Sun. Closed mid Dec-Jan. **Admission** (incl 1 glass) from €13.50; €6 reductions; free under-10s.

Moët & Chandon

20 av de Champagne, 51200 Epernay (03.26.51.20.20, www.moet.com). **Open** *Late Mar-late Jan* 9.30-11.30am, 2-4.30pm daily. *Late Jan-late Mar* 9.30-11.30am, 2-4.30pm Mon-Fri. Closed until 1 Oct 2015. **Admission** (incl 1 glass) from €21; €10 reductions; free under-10s.

Pommery

5 pl du Général-Gouraud, 51100 Reims (03.26.61.62.56, www.pommery.com). **Open** *Apr-Oct* 10am-6pm daily. *Nov-Mar* 10am-5pm daily. **Admission** (incl 1 glass) €13-€18; €7-€9 reductions; free under-10s.

World War I

MEAUX

The town of Meaux played a hugely significant role in the outcome of World War I. It was here, just 40km from Paris, that French and British forces defeated the Germans at the First Battle of the Marne, forcing them to abandon their push on the capital. So near, in fact, was it to Paris that many Allied soldiers were ferried to the front by taxi. The September 1914 battle, which resulted in 500,000 casualties, saved Paris. But it unleashed the horrific trench warfare that would continue for the next three years.

Watched over by the baleful eyes of an enormous monument erected in the 1930s by the Americans, the monolithic slab of the **Musée de la Grande Guerre du Pays de Meaux**, half an hour by train from Paris's Gare de l'Est, is cantilevered so that it appears to hover above the ground. As you pass beneath it, you're confronted by the distant rumble of war and realise that you're standing on a map of the battleground. The weight of history hangs heavy in the air.

It was this history that so fascinated Jean-Pierre Verney when, as a child, he spent holidays

Musée de la Grande Guerre du Pays de Meaux.

with his grandparents near the Chemin des Dames World War I battle site and met an endless stream of veterans passing by on their way to revisit the killing fields. He became obsessed with the war and built up a collection of 50,000 objects. Now owned by the municipality of Meaux, this trove of memorabilia forms the backbone of the museum, which opened on 11 November 2011.

The space has been designed to convey history on multiple levels. There is immersion – walking between rows of soldiers, going into a dugout, looking down on life-size trenches from the no-man's land that forms the central aisle. There is the suggestive – a montage of voices and images in a lightbox. There is the practical – a vehicle for transporting carrier pigeons, aircraft and an early tank. And then there are the side aisles containing personal objects, ranging from erotic sculptures carved from shell casings to improvised musical instruments. There are also sections tackling the origins of the war and its consequences, including recent troubles whose roots can be traced back to the Great War and its botched peace settlements.

Musée de la Grande Guerre du Pays de Meaux

Rue Lazare Ponticelli, 77100 Meaux (01.60.32.14.18, www.museedelagrandeguerre.eu). **Open** *May-Sept* 9.30am-6.30pm Mon, Wed-Sun. *Oct-Apr* 10am-5.30pm Mon, Wed-Sun. **Admission** €10; €5-€9 reductions; free under-8s.

History

Gauls, guillotines and grands projets.

TEXT: NATASHA EDWARDS

The earliest settlers seem to have arrived in Paris around 120,000 years ago. One of them lost a flint spear-tip on the hill now called Montmartre, and the dangerous-looking weapon is to be seen today in the Stone Age collection at the Musée des Antiquités Nationales. There was a Stone Age weapons factory underneath present-day Châtelet, and the redevelopment of Bercy in the 1990s unearthed ten neolithic canoes, five of which are now sitting high and dry in the Musée Carnavalet.

By 250 BC, a Celtic tribe known as the Parisii had put the place firmly on the map. The Parisii were river traders, wealthy enough to mint gold coins; the Musée de la Monnaie de Paris has an extensive collection of their small change. Their most important *oppidum*, a primitive fortified town, was located on an island in the Seine, which is generally thought to have been what is today's Ile de la Cité. A superb strategic location and the capacity to generate hard cash were guaranteed to grab the attention of the Romans.

ROMAN PARIS

Julius Caesar arrived in southern Gaul as proconsul in 58 BC, and soon used the pretext of dealing with invading barbarians to stick his Roman nose into the affairs of northern Gaul. Caesar had a battle on his hands, but eventually the Paris region and the rest of Gaul were in Roman hands. Roman Lutetia (as Paris was known) was a prosperous town of around 8,000 inhabitants. As well as centrally heated villas and a temple to Jupiter on the main island (the remains of both are visible in the Crypte Archéologique), there were the sumptuous baths (now the Musée National du Moyen Age) and 15,000-seater Arènes de Lutèce.

'Legend has it that when Denis of Athens was decapitated by Valerian on Mons Martis (Montmartre), he picked up his head and walked to what is now St-Denis, to be buried there.'

CHRISTIANITY

Christianity arrived in around 250 AD in the shape of Denis of Athens, who became the first bishop of Paris. Legend has it that when he was decapitated by Valerian on Mons Martis, the mount of the martyrs (today better known as Montmartre), Denis picked up his head and walked with it to what is now St-Denis, to be buried there. The event is depicted in Henri Bellechose's Retable de Saint-Denis, now exhibited in the Louvre.

Gaul was still a tempting prize. Waves of barbarian invaders began crossing the Rhine from 275 onwards. They sacked more than 60 cities in Gaul, including Lutetia, where the people were massacred and the buildings on the Montagne Ste-Geneviève were pillaged

and burned. The bedraggled survivors used the rubble to build a rampart around the Ile de la Cité and to fortify the forum.

It was at this time that the city was renamed Paris. Its main role was as a rear base for the Roman armies defending Gaul, and it was here in 360 that Julian was proclaimed emperor by his troops. Around 450, with the arrival of the Huns in the region, the people of Paris prepared once again to flee. They were dissuaded by the feisty Geneviève. Seeing the walls of the city defended against him, no less a pillager than Attila the Hun was forced to turn back; he was defeated soon afterwards.

CLOVIS

In 464, Paris managed to resist another siege, this time by the Francs under Childeric. However, by 486, after a further blockade lasting ten years, Geneviève had no option but to surrender the city to Childeric's successor, Clovis, who went on to conquer most of Gaul and founded the Merovingian dynasty. He chose Paris as capital of his new kingdom, and it stayed that way until the seventh century, in spite of conflicts among his successors. Under the influence of his wife, Clotilde, Clovis converted to Christianity. He founded, and was buried in, the basilica of the Saints-Apôtres, later rededicated to Ste Geneviève when the saviour and future patron saint of Paris was interred there in 512. All that remains of the basilica today is a pillar in the grounds of the Lycée Henri IV; but there's a shrine dedicated to Ste Geneviève and some relics in the fine Gothic church of St-Etienne-du-Mont next door.

Geneviève and Clovis had set a trend. The Ile de la Cité was still the heart of the city, but, under the Merovingians, the Left Bank was the up-and-coming area for fashion-conscious Christians, with 11 churches built here in the period (there were only four on the Right Bank and one on Ile de la Cité). Not everyone was sold on the joys of city living, though. From 614 onwards, the Merovingian kings preferred the *banlieue* at Clichy, or wandered the kingdom trying to keep rebellious nobles in check. When one of the rebels, Pippin 'the Short', decided to do away with the last Merovingian in 751, Paris was starting to look passé.

Pippin's son, Charlemagne, built his capital at Aix-la-Chapelle (now Aachen in Germany), and his successors, the Carolingian dynasty, moved from palace to palace, consuming the local produce. Paris, meanwhile, was doing nicely as a centre for Christian learning, and had grown to a population of 20,000 by the beginning of the ninth century. This was the high point in the political power of the great abbeys like St-Germain-des-Prés, where transcription of the Latin classics was helping to preserve much of Europe's Roman cultural heritage. Power in the Paris area was exercised by the counts of Paris.

PARIS FINDS ITS FEET

From 845, Paris had to fight off another threat – the Vikings. But after various sackings and seiges, the Carolingians were finally able to secure the city. The dynasty gave way to the Capetian dynasty in 987, when Hugues Capet was elected king of France. Under the Capetians, although Paris was now at the heart of the royal domains, the city did not yet dominate the kingdom. Robert 'the Pious', king from 996 to 1031, stayed more often in Paris than his father had done, restoring the royal palace on the Ile de la Cité, and Henri I (1031-60) issued more of his charters in Paris than in Orléans. In 1112, the abbey of St-Denis replaced St-Benoît-sur-Loire as principal monastery.

Philippe-Auguste, Place de la Nation.

Paris itself still consisted of little more than Ile de la Cité and small settlements under the protection of the abbeys on each bank. On the Left Bank, royal largesse helped to rebuild the abbeys of St-Germain-des-Prés, St-Marcel and Ste-Geneviève, although it took more than 150 years for the destruction wrought there by the Vikings to be repaired. The Right Bank, where mooring was easier, prospered from river commerce, and three boroughs grew up around the abbeys of St-Germain-l'Auxerrois, St-Martin-des-Champs and St-Gervais. Bishop Sully of Paris began building the cathedral of Notre-Dame in 1163. The reign of Philippe-Auguste (1180-1223) was a turning point in the history of Paris. Before, it was a confused patchwork of royal, ecclesiastical and feudal authorities. Keen to raise revenues, Philippe favoured the growth of guilds, especially the butchers, drapers, furriers, haberdashers and merchants; so the bourgeoisie's rise began.

Philippe also ordered the building of the first permanent market buildings at Les Halles, and a new city wall, first on the Right Bank to protect the commercial heart of Paris, and later on the Left Bank. At the western end of the wall, he built a castle, the Louvre, to defend the road from the ever-menacing Normandy, whose duke was also King of England.

A GOLDEN AGE

Paris was now the principal residence of the king and the uncontested capital of France. To accommodate the growing royal administration, the Palais de la Cité, site and symbol of power for the previous thousand years, was remodelled and enlarged. Work was begun by Louis IX (later St Louis) in the 1240s, and continued under Philippe IV ('le Bel'). This architectural complex, of which the Sainte-Chapelle and nearby Conciergerie can still be seen, was inaugurated with great pomp at Pentecost 1313.

The palace was quickly filled with functionaries, so the king spent as much of his time as he could outside Paris at the royal castles of Fontainebleau and, especially, Vincennes. The needs of the plenipotentiaries left behind to run the kingdom were met by a rapidly growing city population, piled into less chic buildings. Paris was also reinforcing its identity as a major religious centre: as well as the local clergy and dozens of religious orders, the city was home to the masters and

IN CONTEXT

students of the university of the Sorbonne (established in 1253). An influx of scholars from all over Europe gave the city a cultural and intellectual cachet it was never to lose.

By 1328, Paris was home to 200,000 inhabitants, making it the most populous city in Europe. However, that year was also notable for being the last of the medieval golden age: the dynasty of Capetian kings spluttered to an inglorious halt when Charles IV died without an heir. The English quickly claimed the throne for Edward III, the son of Philippe IV's daughter. Refusing to recognise his descent through the female line, the late king's cousin, Philippe de Valois, claimed the French crown as Philippe VI. So began the Hundred Years War between France and England, which would go on for 116 years.

Jeanne d'Arc

IN CONTEXT

'In 1431, Henry VI of England was crowned King of France in Notre-Dame. He didn't last. Five years later, Henry was driven back to Calais by the Valois king, Charles VII.'

TROUBLES AND STRIFE

To make matters worse, the Black Death (bubonic plague) ravaged Europe from the 1340s onwards. Citizens not finished off by plague had to contend with food shortages, increasing taxes, riots, repression, currency devaluations and marauding mercenaries. Meanwhile, in Paris, the honeymoon period for the king and the bourgeoisie was coming to an end. Rich and populous, Paris was expected to bear the brunt of the war burden; and as defeat followed defeat (notably a disaster at Crécy in August 1346), the bourgeoisie and people of the city were increasingly exasperated by the futility of the sacrifices they were making for the hideously expensive war. To fund the conflict, King Jean II tried to

introduce new tax laws – without success. When the king was captured by the English at Poitiers in 1356, his problems passed on to his 18-year-old son, Charles.

The Etats Généraux, consultant body to the throne, was summoned to the royal palace on the Ile de la Cité to discuss the country's woes. The teenage king was besieged with angry demands for reform from the bourgeoisie, particularly from Etienne Marcel, then provost of the local merchants. Marcel seized control of Paris and began a bitter power struggle with the crown; in 1357, fearing widespread revolt, Charles fled to Compiègne. But as he ran, he had Paris blockaded. Marcel called on the peasants, who were raging against taxes, but they were crushed. He then called on Charles 'the Bad' of Navarre, ally to the English, but his arrival in Paris made many of Marcel's supporters nervous. On 31 July 1358, Marcel was murdered, and the revolution was over. As a safeguard, the returning Charles built a stronghold to protect Paris: the Bastille.

By 1420, following the French defeat at Agincourt, Paris was in English hands; in 1431, Henry VI of England was crowned King of France in Notre-Dame. He didn't last. Five years later, Henry and his army were driven back to Calais by the Valois king, Charles VII. Charles owed his power to Jeanne d'Arc, who led the victorious French in the Battle of Orléans, only to be betrayed by her compatriots, who decided she was getting too big for her boots. She was captured and sold to the English, who had her burned as a witch.

By 1436, Paris was once again the capital of France. But the nation had been bled nearly dry by war and was still divided politically, with powerful regional rulers across France continuing to threaten the monarchy. Outside the French borders, the ambitions of the Austrian Habsburg dynasty represented a serious threat. In this general atmosphere of instability, disputes over trade, religion and taxation were all simmering dangerously.

RENAISSANCE AND REFORMATION

In the closing decades of the 15th century, the restored Valois monarchs sought to reassert their position. A wave of building projects was the public sign of this effort, producing such masterpieces as St-Etienne-du-Mont, St-Eustache and private homes like Hôtel de Cluny (which today houses the Musée National du Moyen Age) and the Hôtel de Sens, which now accommodates the Bibliothèque de Forney. The Renaissance in France had its peak under François I. As well as being involved in the construction of the magnificent châteaux at Fontainebleau, Blois and Chambord, François was responsible for transforming the Louvre from a fortress into a royal palace.

Despite burning heretics by the dozen, François was unable to stop the spread of Protestantism, launched in Germany by Martin Luther in 1517. Resolutely Catholic, Paris was the scene of some horrific violence against the Huguenots, as supporters of the new faith were called. By the 1560s, the situation had degenerated into open warfare. Catherine de Médicis, the scheming Italian widow of Henri II, was the real force in court politics. It was she who connived to murder prominent Protestants gathered in Paris for the marriage of the king's sister on St Bartholomew's Day (23 August 1572). Catherine's main aim was to dispose of her powerful rival, Gaspard de Coligny, but the situation got out of hand, and as many as 3,000 people were butchered. Henri III attempted to reconcile the religious factions and eradicate the powerful families directing the conflict, but the people of Paris turned against him and he was forced to flee. His assassination in 1589 brought the Valois line to an end.

THE BOURBONS

The throne of France being up for grabs, Henri of Navarre declared himself King Henri IV, launching the Bourbon dynasty. Paris was not impressed. The city closed its gates against the Huguenot king, and the inhabitants endured a four-year siege by supporters of the new ruler. Henri managed to break the impasse by having himself converted to Catholicism (and is supposed to have said, 'Paris vaut bien une messe' – Paris is well worth a mass).

Henri set about rebuilding his ravaged capital. He completed the Pont Neuf, the first bridge to span the whole Seine. He commissioned place Dauphine and the city's first enclosed residential square – the place Royale, now place des Vosges.

Henri also tried to reconcile his Catholic and Protestant subjects, issuing the Edict of Nantes in 1598, effectively giving each religion equal status. The Catholics hated the deal, and the Huguenots were suspicious. Henri was the subject of at least 23 attempted

Marie de Médicis. See p316.

assassinations by fanatics of both persuasions. Finally, in 1610, a Catholic by the name of François Ravaillac fatally stabbed the king in traffic on rue de la Ferronnerie.

TWO CARDINALS

Since Henri's son, Louis XIII, was only eight at the time of his father's death, his mother, Marie de Médicis, took up the reins of power. We can thank her for the Palais du Luxembourg and the 24 paintings she commissioned from Rubens, now part of the Louvre collection. Louis took up his royal duties in 1617, but Cardinal Richelieu, chief minister from 1624, was the man who ran France. Something of a schemer, he outwitted the king's mother, his wife (Anne of Austria) and a host of others. Richelieu helped to strengthen the power of the monarch, and he did much to limit the independence of the aristocracy.

The Counter-Reformation was at its height, and lavish churches such as the Baroque Val-de-Grâce were an important reassertion of Catholic supremacy. The 17th century was 'le Grand Siècle', a time of patronage of art and artists, even if censorship forced the brilliant mathematician and philosopher René Descartes into exile. The first national newspaper, La Gazette, hit the streets in 1631; Richelieu used it as a propaganda tool. The cardinal founded the Académie Française, which is still working, slowly, on the dictionary of the French language that he commissioned from them in 1634. Richelieu died in 1642; Louis XIII followed suit a few months later. The new king, Louis XIV, was five years old. Anne of Austria became regent, with the Italian Cardinal Mazarin, a Richelieu protégé, as chief minister. Rumour has it that Anne and Mazarin may have been married. Mazarin's townhouse is now home to the Bibliothèque Nationale de France – Richelieu.

Endless wars against Austria and Spain had depleted the royal coffers and left the nation drained by exorbitant taxation. In 1648, the royal family was chased out of Paris by a popular uprising, 'la Fronde', named after the catapults used by some of the rioters. Parisians soon tired of the anarchy that followed. When Mazarin's army retook the city in 1653, the boy-king was warmly welcomed. Mazarin died in 1661 and Louis XIV, now 24 years old, decided he would rule France without the assistance of any chief minister.

SHINE ON, SUN KING

The 'Roi Soleil', or Sun King, was an absolute monarch. 'L'état, c'est moi' (I am the State) was his vision of power. To prove his grandeur, the king embarked on wars against England, Holland and Austria. He also refurbished and extended the Louvre, commissioned place Vendôme and place des Victoires, constructed the Observatory and laid out the grands boulevards along the line of the old city walls. His major project was the palace at Versailles. Louis moved his court there in 1682.

Louis XIV owed much of his brilliant success to the work of Jean-Baptiste Colbert, who was nominally in charge of state finances, but eventually took control of all the important levers of the state machine. Colbert was the force behind the Sun King's redevelopment of Paris. The Hôtel des Invalides was built to accommodate the crippled survivors of Louis' wars, the Salpêtrière to shelter fallen women.

In 1702, Paris was divided up into 20 quartiers (not until the Revolution was it re-mapped into arrondissements). Colbert died in 1683, and Louis' luck on the battlefield ran out. Hopelessly embroiled in the War of the Spanish Succession, the country was devastated by famine in 1692. The Sun King died in 1715, leaving no direct heir. His five-year-old great-grandson, Louis XV, was named king, with Philippe d'Orléans as regent. The court moved back to Paris. Installed in the Palais-Royal, the regent set about enjoying his few years of power, hosting lavish dinners that degenerated into orgies. The state, meanwhile, remained chronically in debt.

THE ENLIGHTENMENT

Some of the city's more sober residents were making Paris the intellectual capital of Europe. Enlightenment thinkers such as Diderot, Montesquieu, Voltaire and Rousseau were active during the reign of Louis XV. Literacy rates were increasing – 50 per cent of French men could read, 25 per cent of women – and the publishing industry was booming.

The king's mistress, Madame de Pompadour, encouraged him to finance the building of the Ecole Militaire and the laying out of place Louis XV, known to us as place de la Concorde. The church of St-Sulpice was completed in 1776. Many of the great houses in the area bounded by rue de Lille,

THE FRENCH REVOLUTION

From conception to bloody execution.

In the winter of 1788-89, Louis XVI was losing grip on his country's problems. Wars had left the state almost bankrupt; harvests had failed and food prices soared. Discontent reigned, and with it came demands for an end to absolute monarchy and for wider participation in government. Under pressure, Louis allowed the formation of an Assemblée Nationale, which started work on a national constitution. But behind the scenes, he began gathering troops to force it to disband; and on 12 July, he dismissed the commoner's ally, finance minister Jacques Necker. On 14 July, a crowd stormed the Bastille prison in response. Only seven prisoners were inside but the symbolic victory was huge.

The establishment of the constitution forged ahead. Tax breaks for the nobility and clergy were abolished; Church property was seized. But the price of bread remained high. In October, a mob of starving women marched to Versailles and demanded that the king come to Paris. He promised to send them grain, an offer they rejected by decapitating some of his guards. Louis transferred to the Tuileries. In the months that followed, the Jacobins roused powerful Republican feeling. The king and his family tried to flee Paris on 20 June 1791, but were apprehended.

On 14 September, Louis accepted the constitution. But other monarchies were plotting to reinstate him. In 1792, Austrian and Prussian troops invaded France. The Republicans, correctly, suspected Louis of conspiracy, and raised an army to capture him. He and his family were incarcerated by the radical Commune de Paris, headed by Danton, Marat and Robespierre.

Then came a massacre. Republicans invaded the prisons and murdered 2,000 so-called traitors. The monarchy was abolished on 22 September; the king was executed on 21 January 1793. Headed by Robespierre, the Jacobins vowed to wage terror against all dissidents. The Great Terror of 1794 saw the guillotine slice through 1,300 necks in six weeks. Eventually there was no more stomach for killing. On 28 July 1794, Robespierre was executed and the bloodiest of revolutions was finally over.

IN CONTEXT

rue de Varenne and rue de Grenelle date from the first half of the 18th century. The private homes of aristocrats and wealthy bourgeois, these would become the venues for numerous salons, the informal discussion sessions often devoted to topics raised by Enlightenment questioning.

The Enlightenment spirit of rational humanism finally took the venom out of the Catholic–Protestant power struggle, and the increase in public debate helped to change views about the nature of the state and the place and authority of the monarchy. As Jacques Necker, Louis XVI's finance minister on the eve of the Revolution, put it, popular opinion was 'an invisible power that, without treasury, guard or army, gives its laws to the city, the court and even the palaces of kings'. Thanks to the Enlightenment, and a growing burden of taxation on the poorest strata of society to prop up the wealthiest, that power would eventually overturn the status quo.

THE FRENCH REVOLUTION

The great beneficiary of the French Revolution, Napoleon Bonaparte, once remarked that lucky generals were to be preferred over good generals. The same applies to kings, and the gods of fortune certainly deserted Louis XVI in 1789, when bad weather and worse debts brought France to its knees. But few would have predicted that the next five years would see the execution of the king and most of the royal family, terror stalking the streets in the name of revolution, and the steady rise of a young Corsican soldier. For an account of the Revolution, *see p317* **The French Revolution**.

NAPOLEON

Amid the post-Revolutionary chaos, power was divided between a two-housed Assembly and a Directory of five men. The French public reacted badly to hearing of England's attempts to promote more popular rebellion; when a royalist rising in Paris needed to be put down, a young officer from Corsica was the man to do it – Napoleon Bonaparte.

Napoleon quickly became the Directory's right-hand man. When they needed someone to lead a campaign against Austria, he was the man. Victory saw France – and Napoleon – glorified. After an aborted campaign to Egypt in 1799, Napoleon returned home to put down

another royalist plot, made himself the chief of the newly governing three-man Consul – and by 1804 was emperor.

After failing to squeeze out the English by setting up the Continental System to block trade across the Channel, Napoleon waged massive wars against Britain, Russia and Austria. On his way to the disaster of Moscow, Napoleon gave France the lycée educational system, the Napoleonic Code of civil law, the Legion of Honour, the Banque de France, the Pont des Arts, the Arc de Triomphe, the Madeleine church (he re-established Catholicism as the state religion), La Bourse and rue de Rivoli. He was also responsible for the centralised bureaucracy that still drives the French public mad today.

As Russian troops – who had chased Napoleon's once-mighty army all the way from Moscow and Leipzig – invaded France, Paris itself came under threat. Montmartre, then named Montnapoléon, had a telegraph machine at its summit, one that had given so many of the emperor's orders and transmitted news of so many victories. The hill fell to Russian troops. Napoleon gave the order to blow up the city's main powder stores, and thus Paris itself. His officer refused. Paris accommodated carousing Russian, Prussian and English soldiers while Napoleon was sent to exile in Elba. A hundred days later, he was back, leading an army against Wellington and Blücher's troops in the mud of Waterloo. A further defeat saw the end of him. Paris survived further foreign occupation. The diminutive Corsican died on the South Atlantic prison island of St Helena in 1821.

ANOTHER ROUND OF BOURBONS

Having sampled revolution and military dictatorship, the French were now ready to give monarchy a second chance. The Bourbons got back in business in 1815, in the person of Louis XVIII, Louis XVI's elderly brother. Several efforts were made to adapt the monarchy to the new political realities, though the new king's Charter of Liberties was not a wholly sincere expression of how he meant to rule.

When another brother of Louis XVI, Charles X, became king in 1824, he decided that enough royal energy had been wasted trying to reconcile the nation's myriad factions. It was time for a spot of old-fashioned

Napoleon Bonaparte.

who never went out without his umbrella, he was eminently acceptable to the newly powerful bourgeoisie. But the poor, who had risked their lives in two attempts to change French society, were unimpressed by the new king's promise to embrace a moderate and liberal version of the Revolutionary heritage.

THE NINETEENTH CENTURY

Philosopher Walter Benjamin declared Paris 'the capital of the 19th century', and he had a point. Though it was smaller than its global rival, London, in intellectual and cultural spheres it reigned supreme. On the demographic front, its population doubled to one million between 1800 and 1850. Most of the new arrivals were rural labourers, who had come to find work on the city's expanding building sites. Meanwhile, the middle classes were doing well, thanks to the relatively late arrival of the industrial revolution in France, and the solid administrative structures inherited from Napoleon. The poor were as badly off as ever, only now there were more of them. The back-breaking hours worked in the factories would not be curbed by legislation: 'Whatever the lot of the workers is, it is not the manufacturer's responsibility to improve it,' said one trade minister. In Left Bank cafés, a new bohemian tribe of students derided the materialistic government. Workers' pamphlets and newspapers, such as *La Ruche Populaire*, gave voice to the starving, crippled poor. A wave of ill feeling was building up against Louis-Philippe.

On 23 February 1848, hundreds of Parisians – men, women and students – moved along the boulevards towards a public banquet at La Madeleine. The king's minister, François Guizot, had forbidden any direct campaigning by opposition parties in the forthcoming election, so the parties held banquets instead of meetings.

One diarist of the time noted that some of the crowd had stuffed swords and daggers underneath their shirts, but the demonstration was largely peaceful – until the troops stationed on the boulevard des Capucines opened fire, igniting a riot.

As barricades sprang up all over the city, a trembling Louis-Philippe abdicated and a liberal provisional government declared a republic. The virtual epidemic of poverty and unemployment was stemmed by creating

absolutism. But the forces unleashed during the Revolution, and the social divisions that had opened as a result, were not to be ignored – and the people were happy to respond with some old-fashioned rebellion.

In the 1830 elections, the liberals won a hefty majority in the Chamber of Deputies, the legislative body. Charles's unpopular minister Prince Polignac, a returned émigré, promptly dissolved the Chamber, announced a date for new elections and curtailed the number of voters. Polishing off this collection of bad decisions was the 26 July decree abolishing the freedom of the press. The day after its issue, 5,000 print workers and journalists filled the streets and three newspapers went to press. When police tried to confiscate copies, they sparked a three-day riot, 'les Trois Glorieuses', with members of the disbanded National Guard manning the barricades. On 30 July, Charles dismissed Polignac, but it was too late. He had little choice but to abdicate, and fled to England. As French revolutions go, it was a brief affair.

Another leftover from the Ancien Régime was now winched on to the throne – Louis-Philippe, Duc d'Orléans, who had some Bourbon blood in his veins. A father of eight national *ateliers*, but such 'radical' reforms made the right very nervous. A conservative government took power in May 1848, and shut down the *ateliers*. A month later, the poor were back in the streets. Some 50,000 took part in the 'June Days' protests, which were quite comprehensively crushed by General Cavaignac's troops. In total, about 1,500 Parisians died and some 5,000 were deported. As the pamphleteer Alphonse Karr said of the revolution's aftermath, '*plus ça change, plus c'est la même chose*' (the more things change, the more they stay the same). In December 1848, Louis Bonaparte – nephew of Napoleon – was elected president. By 1852, he had moved into the Tuileries palace and declared himself Emperor Napoleon III.

THE SECOND EMPIRE

The emperor appointed a lawyer as *préfet* to mastermind the reconstruction of Paris. In less than two decades, prefect Georges-Eugène Haussmann had created the most magnificent city in Europe. His goals included better access to railway stations, better water supplies, and new hospitals, barracks, theatres and *mairies*. It was a vast project,

and it transformed the capital with a network of wide avenues that were more hygienic than the narrow streets they replaced.

Not everyone was happy. Haussmann's works destroyed thousands of buildings, including beautiful medieval monuments; on the whole of Ile de la Cité only Notre-Dame and a handful of houses survived. Entire residential areas were wiped off the map, and only the owners of the buildings were compensated; tenants were merely booted out. Writers and artists lamented the loss of the more quirky Paris they used to know, and criticised the unfriendly grandeur of the new city. But there was no going back.

At home, the rapid industrialisation of the city saw the rise of Socialism and Communism among the disgruntled working classes, and Napoleon III gave limited rights to trade unions. Abroad, though, the now constitutional monarch was a disaster. After the relatively successful Crimean War of the mid 1850s, he tried in vain to impose the Catholic Maximilian as ruler of Mexico. The Franco-Prussian war was his next misadventure. France was soon defeated. At Sedan, in September 1870, 100,000 French troops were forced to surrender to

The escape of Léon Gambetta.

The Eiffel Tower, Exposition Universelle 1889. *See p322.*

Bismarck's Prussians; Napoleon III himself was captured, never to return.

The war continued, and back in Paris a provisional government hastily took power. Elections gave conservative monarchists the majority, though the Paris vote was firmly Republican. Former prime minister Adolphe Thiers assumed executive power. Meanwhile, Prussian forces marched on Paris and laid siege to the city. Paris held out, starving, for four brave months, its citizens picking rats from the gutter for food. Léon Gambetta, a young politician, escaped in style (by hot-air balloon) but failed to raise an army in the south. In January 1871, the provisional government signed a bitter armistice that relinquished the industrial heartlands of Alsace and Lorraine and agreed to pay a five-million-franc indemnity. German troops would stay on French soil until the bill was paid.

But with occupying army camps stationed around their city, Parisians considered the treaty a dishonour and remained defiant. Thiers ordered his soldiers to enter the city and strip it of its cannons, but the insurgents cut them short. The new government scuttled off to the haven of Versailles, and on 26 March Paris elected its own municipal body, the Commune, so called in memory of the spirit of 1792. The 92 members of the Commune hailed from the left and working classes; their agenda was liberal (schools would be secularised, debts suspended) but war-like

(Germany must be defeated). Paris itself was given a little makeover: the column extolling Napoleonic glory on place Vendôme was pulled down, and statues of the great emperor were smashed all over town.

Thiers would not stand by and watch. Artillery fire picked at the Communards' sandbag barricades on the edges of Paris, and the suburbs fell by 11 April. In the sixth week of fighting, troops broke in through the Porte de St-Cloud and covered the springtime city in blood. The ill-equipped Communards faced a massacre: some 25,000 were killed in a matter of days. In revenge, around 50 hostages were taken and shot, including the Archbishop of Paris. The infamous *pétroleuses*, women wielding petrol bombs, burned off their anger, torching the Tuileries and the Hôtel de Ville. On the last day of *la semaine sanglante*, 28 May 1871, 147 Communards were trapped and shot in Père-Lachaise cemetery, against the 'Mur des Fédérés', still an icon of the Commune struggle. The dead were buried in the streets, the prisons crammed with 40,000 Communards; thousands were deported, many to penal colonies in New Caledonia.

THE THIRD REPUBLIC
Thanks mainly to the huge economic boost provided by colonial expansion in Africa and Indo-China, the horrors of the Commune were soon forgotten in the self-indulgent

materialism of the turn of the century and the Third Republic. The Eiffel Tower was built as the centrepiece of the 1889 Exposition Universelle. For the next Exposition Universelle, in 1900, the Grand Palais and Petit Palais, the Pont Alexandre III and the Gare d'Orsay (now the Musée d'Orsay) were built to affirm France's position as a world power, and the first line of the métro opened. The first film screening had been held (1895), and clubs like the Moulin Rouge were buzzing. The lurid life of Montmartre – and its cheap rents – would attract the world's artistic community.

THE GREAT WAR

On 3 August 1914, Germany declared war on France. Although the Germans never made it to Paris in World War I – German troops were stopped 20 kilometres (12 miles) short of the city thanks to the French victory in the Battle of the Marne – the artillery was audible. Paris, and French society as a whole, suffered terribly, despite ultimate victory.

The nations gathered at Versailles to make the peace, and established new European states. The League of Nations was formed. Artists responded to the horrors and absurdity of the conflict with Surrealism, a movement that was founded in Paris by André Breton, a doctor who had treated troops in the trenches and embraced Freud's theories of the unconscious. In 1924, Surrealism had a manifesto, a year later its first exhibition. Again, artists (and photographers) flocked to Paris. Montmartre was now too expensive for them, and Montparnasse became the hub of artistic life. The interwar years were a whirl of activity in artistic and political circles. Paris became the avant-garde capital of the world, recorded by Hemingway, F Scott Fitzgerald and Gertrude Stein.

Meanwhile, the Depression unleashed a wave of political violence, Fascists fighting Socialists and Communists for control. At the same time, many writers were leaving Paris for Spain to cover – and, indeed, to take part in – the Civil War. Across the German border, the contentious territories of Alsace-Lorraine – and the burden of the World War I peace agreements signed in Paris – became one of many bugbears held by the new chancellor, Adolf Hitler. As war broke out, France believed that its Maginot line would hold against the

German threat. When the Nazis attacked France in May 1940, they simply bypassed the fortifications and came through the Ardennes.

WORLD WAR II

Paris was in German hands by June. The city fell without a fight. A pro-German government was set up in Vichy, headed by Marshall Pétain, and a young army officer, Charles de Gaulle, went to London to organise the Free French opposition. For Frenchmen happy to get along with the German army, the period of the Occupation presented few hardships and, indeed, some good business opportunities. Food was rationed, and tobacco and coffee went out of circulation, but the black market thrived. For people who resisted, there were the Gestapo torture chambers at avenue Foch or rue Lauriston. The Germans further discouraged uncooperative behaviour with executions: one victim, whose name now adorns a métro station, was Jacques Bonsergent, a student caught fly-posting and shot because he refused to reveal the names of his friends who escaped.

The Vichy government was so eager to please the Germans, it organised anti-Semitic measures without prompting. From the spring of 1941, the French authorities deported Jews to the death camps, frequently via the internment camp at Drancy. Prime Minister Pierre Laval argued that it was a necessary concession to his Third Reich masters. In July 1942, 12,000 Jewish French citizens were rounded up in the Vélodrome d'Hiver, a sports complex on the quai de Grenelle, and then dispatched to Auschwitz.

THE LIBERATION

Paris survived the war practically unscathed, ultimately thanks to the bravery of one of its captors. On 23 August 1944, as the Allied armies of liberation approached the city, Hitler ordered his commander, Dietrich von Choltitz, to detonate the explosives that had been set all over town in anticipation of a retreat. Von Choltitz refused. On 25 August, French troops, tactfully placed at the head of the US forces, entered the city, and General de Gaulle led the parade down the Champs-Elysées. Writers and artists swept back into Paris to celebrate. Hemingway held court at the Ritz and Scribe hotels with the great journalists of the day, clinking glasses with veterans of

IN CONTEXT

German soldiers march down the Champs-Elysées in 1940.

the Spanish Civil War such as Robert Capa and George Orwell. Picasso's studio was besieged by well-wishers.

However, the Liberation was by no means the end of France's troubles. De Gaulle was the hero of the hour, but relations between the interim government he commanded and the Resistance – largely Communist – were still tricky. Orders issued to maquis leaders in the provinces were often ignored. The Communists wanted a revolution, and de Gaulle suspected them of hatching plans to seize Paris prior to August 1944. Meanwhile, de Gaulle knew that he had to commit every available French soldier to the march on Germany, or risk being sidelined by the other Allies after the war. He had to leave homeland security to the very people – the 'patriotic militias' – who were most likely to be at least sympathetic to the Communist cause; or, even more dubiously, gendarmes who had worked with the occupying power.

Recovery was slow. There were shortages of everything; indeed, many complained they had been better off under the Germans. Even in the ministries, paper was so scarce that correspondence had to be sent out on Vichy letterhead with the sender crossing out 'Etat Français' at the top and writing 'République Française' instead.

THE FOURTH REPUBLIC

On 8 May 1945, de Gaulle made a broadcast to the nation to announce Germany's surrender. Paris went wild, but the euphoria didn't last. There were strikes. And more strikes. Liberation had proved to be a restoration, not the revolution the Communists, now the most powerful political force in the land, had hoped for. The Communist Party was, in at least one respect, as pragmatic as everyone else: it did its utmost to turn parliamentary democracy to its advantage, to wit, getting as many of the top jobs as it could.

A general election was held on 21 October 1945. The Communists secured 159 seats, the Socialists got 146 and the Catholic Mouvement Républicain Populaire got 152. A fortnight later, at the Assemblée Nationale's first session, a unanimous vote was passed maintaining de Gaulle in his position as head of state – but he remained an antagonistic leader. His reluctance to take a firm grip on the disastrous economic situation alienated many intellectuals and industrialists who had once been loyal to him, and his characteristic aloofness only made the misgivings of the general populace worse. He, on the other hand, was disgusted by all the political chicanery. On 20 January 1946, de Gaulle resigned his post.

France, meanwhile, looked to swift industrial modernisation under an ambitious plan put forward by internationalist politician Jean Monnet. Although the economy and daily life remained grim, in 1947 brash new fashion designer Christian Dior put together a stunning collection of strikingly simple yet luxurious clothes: the New Look. Such extravagance horrified many locals, but the fashion industry boomed. Meanwhile, the divisions in Paris between its fashionable and run-down working-class areas became more pronounced. The northern and eastern edges – areas revived only in the late 20th century by a taste for retro, industrial decor and cheap rent – were forgotten about. Félix Gouin, the new Socialist premier, quickly nationalised the bigger banks and the coal industry. But the right wing was growing, and there was even a rise of royalist hopes. A referendum was held in May 1946 to determine the crucial tenet of the Fourth Republic's constitution: should the Assemblée Nationale have absolute or restricted power? The results were a narrow victory for people who, like de Gaulle, had insisted the Assemblée's power should be qualified. De Gaulle's prestige increased, but it was another 12 years, and a whole new constitution – the Fifth Republic – before he came back to power. He spent much of his '*passage du désert*' writing his memoirs.

THE ALGERIAN WAR AND MAY 1968

The post-war years were marked by the rapid disintegration of France's overseas interests and by her rapprochement with Germany to create what would become the European Community. When revolt broke out in Algeria in 1956, almost 500,000 troops were sent in to protect national interests. A protest by Algerians in Paris on 17 October 1961 led to the deaths of hundreds of people at the hands of the city's police force. The extent of the violence was officially concealed for decades, as was the use of torture against Algerians by French troops. Algeria became independent in 1962.

Meanwhile, the slow, painful discoveries of collaboration in World War II, often overlooked in the rush to put the country back on its feet, were also being faced. The younger generation began to question the motives of the older one. De Gaulle's Fifth Republic was felt by many to be grimly authoritarian. In the spring of 1968, students unhappy with overcrowded university conditions took to the streets of Paris at the same time as striking Renault workers. These *soixante-huitards* sprang the greatest public revolt in French living memory. Many students were crammed into universities that had been cheaply expanded to accommodate them. Political discourse grew across the campuses, turning against the government's stranglehold on the media and President de Gaulle's poor grasp of the economy. Ministers did indeed at the time have a sinister habit of leaning on the leading newspaper editors of the day, and television was dubbed 'the government in your dining room'. Inflation was high, and the gap between the working classes and the bourgeoisie was becoming a chasm. Still, de Gaulle echoed many when he said the events of May 1968 were '*incompréhensible*'. The touchpaper was lit at overcrowded Nanterre university, on the outskirts of Paris, where students had been protesting against the war in Vietnam and the tatty state of the campus.

On 2 May, exhausted by the protests, the authorities closed the university down and threatened to expel some of the students. The next day, a sit-in was held in sympathy at the Sorbonne. Police were called to intervene, but made things worse, charging into the crowd with truncheons and tear gas. The streets were soon flooded with thousands of student demonstrators, now officially on strike. The trade unions followed, as did the lycées. By mid May, nine million people were on strike. On 24 May, de Gaulle intervened. His speech warned of civil war and pleaded for people's support. It didn't go down well: riots broke out, with students storming the Bourse. Five days later, as street violence peaked, de Gaulle fled briefly to Germany and Prime Minister Pompidou sent tanks to the edges of Paris. But the crisis didn't materialise. Pompidou conceded pay rises of between seven and ten per cent and increased the minimum wage; France went back to work. An election was called for 23 June, by which time the right had gathered enough momentum to gain a safe majority.

MITTERRAND

Following the presidencies of right-wingers Georges Pompidou and Valéry Giscard d'Estaing, the Socialist François Mitterrand

BURNING THE BANLIEUE

When rioting ripped through the suburbs.

In November 2005, violent suburban riots in Paris sent shockwaves through the country and abroad. The run-down estates around the capital became the scene for explosive confrontations with the police, as warehouses, restaurants and thousands of cars were set ablaze. Before long, the violence spread to other French cities. The government called a state of emergency, imposing curfews and banning public meetings at the weekends. Nevertheless, it was almost three weeks before the worst of the rioting was over.

The trigger for this unprecedented outbreak of violence was the accidental death on 27 October of two North African teenagers, in the north-east Paris suburb of Clichy-sous-Bois. According to locals, Bouna Traore, 15, and Zyed Benna, 17, panicked when they saw other black youths being chased by the police, and sought shelter in an electrical substation. As they entered the site, they were electrocuted, plunging the town into a blackout. To make matters worse, the incident came just two days after then Interior Minister Nicolas Sarkozy had made inflammatory remarks about the need to rid the *banlieue* of the '*racaille*', a highly pejorative term that can be translated as 'rabble' or 'scum'.

If this chain of events formed an explosive catalyst for the riots, the root cause went much deeper. When the economy plummeted in the 1970s, the populations of these high-rise estates found themselves struggling with factory closures and unemployment. While the wealthier moved to more desirable areas, the remaining residents – mainly North African families – were effectively left stranded in a suburban desert.

Over the three weeks of violence, nearly 3,000 arrests were made, more than 10,000 cars were set ablaze, and 300 buildings were firebombed. Initially, the government seemed to take a liberal view of its immigrant population, voting in a number of equal opportunities measures. Yet just two months later, Sarkozy's immigration bill reintroduced a hard line, laying down much stricter terms for immigrants seeking residency.

IN CONTEXT

Nicolas Sarkozy, 2007.

took up the task in 1981. His *grands projets* had a big impact on Paris. Mitterrand commissioned IM Pei's Louvre pyramid, the Grande Arche de la Défense, the Opéra Bastille and the more recent Bibliothèque Nationale de France – François Mitterrand.

CHIRAC, BUSH AND IRAQ

France may still boast the world's fourth-largest economy, the nuclear deterrent and a permanent seat on the UN Security Council, but her influence on the world stage had been waning for years until President Chirac, flushed from re-election and aware he was on to a PR winner, stood up in 2003 to oppose the US-led invasion of Iraq. France's official disapproval of George W Bush culminated in the threat to use her Security Council veto against any resolution authorising the use of force without UN say-so. Chirac's stance brought him popularity at home and abroad. But his domestic popularity couldn't last.

Chirac's prime minister, Jean-Pierre Raffarin, and the centre-right government began attacking some of France's more prized national institutions with a programme of

reforms, starting with the state pension. This led to some of the largest protests France had seen since 1995, with striking métro staff, hospital and postal workers, teachers and rubbish collectors bringing the capital to a virtual standstill. Planned restrictions on the uniquely Gallic, exceptionally generous system of unemployment benefit for out-of-work performing-arts professionals led to a further round of protests, as well as the cancellation of the Avignon and Aix summer cultural festivals. Then came the official mismanagement and aloofness that characterised the two-week heatwave of August 2003, during which as many as 14,000 elderly people died. The national mood stayed gloomy through 2004, and the clouds darkened further in 2005, as Paris lost its Olympic bid.

Then, in October 2005, the accidental deaths of two North African teenagers in Clichy-sous-Bois sparked riots that spread through the *banlieue* like wildfire (*see p325* **Burning the Banlieue**). Eventually Chirac declared a state of emergency that was lifted only in January 2006. Then, in March, trouble flared once again, this time provoked by an unpopular new employment bill, the CPE – which, after three months of strikes and protests, the government had to withdraw.

PRESIDENT BLING-BLING

Despite his provocations during the riots, Nicolas Sarkozy was elected president in May 2007, beating the Socialist candidate Ségolène Royal. Aside from a few desultory Molotov cocktails hurled in place de la Bastille on the night of the election, the response on the Left to Sarkozy's victory was characterised more by bemusement than anger. For a few months, bemusement held sway in the population at large, especially when Sarkozy embarked on a very public whirlwind romance with chanteuse and ex-model Carla Bruni. But voters soon sickened of the spectacle, and of Sarkozy's parallel courtship of several tycoons; by the time 'Président Bling-Bling' married Bruni in February 2008, his popularity had plummeted to less than 35 per cent.

During the next couple of years, Sarkozy's popularity continued to decline, but 2011 brought about a reversal of fortune as the country geared up for the presidential elections in 2012. Pictures of himself and a pregnant Carla on the beach during the summer contrasted strongly with the coverage of his main rival on the left, Dominique Strauss-Kahn, who was fighting sexual assault charges in New York. This wholesome image, coupled with a boost from his high-profile role in the Libya crisis, saw his approval rating jump to 37 per cent by September 2011.

HOLLANDE TO THE FORE

With the scandal engulfing Strauss-Kahn, François Hollande came to the fore as the leading Socialist candidate, defeating rival Martine Aubry in a run-off for the party candidacy in October 2011 with 56 per cent of the vote. The first round of the presidential election took place on 22 April 2012. Hollande came in first place and faced Sarkozy in the second round run-off on 6 May 2012, when he was duly elected 24th President of the French Republic and the first Socialist president in almost two decades. But Hollande's post-election elation was short-lived and a flagging economy, sliding opinion polls and close media scrutiny of his love life meant Hollande's honeymoon period was short-lived. In a 2014 poll, his approval rating hit a new low of just 13%.

JE SUIS CHARLIE

On 7 January 2015, a date that's now forever etched into the history of France, two gunmen, Cherif and Said Kouachi, burst into the offices of satirical magazine *Charlie Hebdo*. The pair shot dead 12 people before fleeing to an industrial estate north of the capital, where they were shot dead by police on 9 January. But the killing spree didn't end there. On 8 January, a lone gunman with links to the brothers shot dead a policewoman in southern Paris, and on 9 January, a gunman took several people hostage at a kosher supermarket in the east of Paris, demanding the release of the Kouachi brothers. Police stormed the supermarket that afternoon, killing the gunman and freeing 15 hostages. Inside, they discovered the bodies of four hostages. The outcry following the attacks was immense, and an estimated 3.5 million people joined the unity marches across France on 11 January.

Hollande's deft handling of the attacks saw his approval rating rebound to 40 per cent, but that figure is already in steep decline. Meanwhile, all eyes are to the right as Sarkozy and Marine Le Pen prepare to challenge for the presidency in 2017.

IN CONTEXT

Unity march in the wake of the Charlie Hebdo attacks

Architecture

A city of monumental ambitions.

TEXT: NATASHA EDWARDS

Paris's rulers have always understood the key role of architecture in the exercise of power. Long before François Mitterrand made his presidential mark on the capital in the 1980s with his *grands projets* – including the Opéra Bastille, Grande Arche de la Défense, Louvre Pyramid and Ministry of Finance – Colbert had glorified Louis XIV with the place Vendôme, place des Victoires and a series of triumphal arches. Yet the city is also one of Europe's most densely inhabited and lived-in capitals. For all its apparent uniformity, caused in large part by the prevalence of golden stone, Paris has never ceased to evolve and experiment, with aristocratic mansions, Baroque churches and Haussmannian apartments existing happily alongside concrete avant-garde houses, industrial premises, the cast iron of the Eiffel Tower, the high-tech Centre Pompidou – and, since 2015, a trio of dramatic new arrivals: the Fondation Louis Vuitton (*pictured right*), Fondation Pathé and Philharmonie.

ROMANESQUE TO GOTHIC

Medieval Paris congregated on the Ile de la Cité and the Latin Quarter. Although the clusters of medieval housing around Notre-Dame were razed by Haussmann in the 19th century, much of the medieval street plan remains. A few churches still survive as examples of simple Romanesque architecture, including the tower of **St-Germain-des-Prés** (see p192) and **St-Julien-le-Pauvre** (see p175).

The Gothic trademarks of pointed arches, ogival vaulting and flying buttresses had their start at the **Basilique St-Denis** (see p236), begun in the 12th century and completed in the 13th by master mason Pierre de Montreuil. **Notre-Dame** (see p51) continued the style with its sculpted façade, rich, delicate rose windows and fine, tendon-like buttresses. Montreuil's **Sainte-Chapelle** (see p54), built 1246-48, represents the peak of Gothic design, reducing stonework to a minimum between the expanses of stained glass. The Flamboyant Gothic style that followed unleashed an orgy of decoration. **Eglise St-Séverin** (see p175), with its twisting spiral column, is particularly original. Civil architecture can be seen in the impressive vaulted halls of the **Conciergerie** (see p51). The **Tour Jean Sans Peur** (see p84) is a rare fragment of an early 15th-century mansion. The city's two finest medieval mansions are the Hôtel de Cluny (now the **Musée National du Moyen-Age**; see p175) and the **Hôtel de Sens**.

RENAISSANCE

Italianate town planning, with its ordered avenues and neat squares and public spaces, came rather late to Paris. It was instigated by François I, who installed Leonardo da Vinci at Amboise, brought over Primaticcio and Rosso to work on his palace at **Fontainebleau** (see p301), and began transforming the **Louvre** (see p63) with the Cour Carrée. The **Eglise St-Etienne du Mont** (see p181) and the massive **Eglise St-Eustache** (see p84) display a transitional style, adding the classical motifs of the Renaissance over an essentially Gothic structure. Aristocratic quarters were established in St-Germain-des-Prés and the developing Marais; the latter has the **Hôtel Carnavalet** (see p129) and the **Hôtel de Lamoignon** (24 rue Pavée, 4th), the finest examples of Renaissance mansions in Paris.

Sainte-Chapelle.

THE ANCIEN REGIME

Henri IV took control of Paris in 1594 after a long siege. He found a city knee-deep in bodies and rubble, and promptly organised public building projects. Half-timbering was banned for façades, to be replaced by brick and stone, and bridges over the Seine were cleared of houses and shops. **Place Dauphine** (1st) and **place des Vosges** (see p127) reflected Henri's taste for classicism; the latter is irresistibly elegant, with symmetrical design, red-brick vaulted galleries and steeply pitched roofs, reflecting the influence of northern Renaissance style as well as Italy.

The nouveaux riches flocked to build mansions in the Marais and on the Ile St-Louis. Those in the Marais follow a symmetrical U-shaped plan, with the main residence at the rear of an elegant *cour*

IN CONTEXT

d'honneur; look through the entrance archways of the **Hôtel de Sully** (*see p127*) or the **Hôtel Salé** (*see p127*), where façades are richly decorated, in contrast with the face they present to the street.

The **Palais du Luxembourg** (*see p200*), built in the 1620s by Salomon de Brosse in Italianate style for Marie de Médicis, combines classic French château design with the more dramatic rustication of the Pitti Palace in Marie's native Florence. The 17th century was a high point in French power, and the monarchy desired buildings that reflected its grandeur. Great architects emerged under court patronage: de Brosse, François Mansart, Libéral Bruand and André le Nôtre, who redesigned the Tuileries gardens, created the park and fountains at Versailles and planned the Champs-Elysées. The **Eglise du Val-de-Grâce** (*see p181*), designed by Mansart and finished by Jacques Lemercier, is a grand Baroque statement designed to promote the Catholic Counter-Reformation, with its painted dome and barley sugar columns. Hospitals got the royal treatment: Libéral Bruand created the grand classical façades and polygonal chapel at the **Salpêtrière** (*see p185*) and **Les Invalides** (*see p221*), with its grandiose galleried courtyard and domed double church. But even at **Versailles** (*see p301*), ultimate architectural symbol of royal absolutism in the scale and glittery reflections of the Hall of Mirrors, Baroque never reached the decorative excesses of Italy or Austria.

Under Colbert, Louis XIV's chief minister, the creation of stage sets to magnify the Sun King's power proceeded apace. The Louvre grew as Claude Perrault created the sweeping west wing; triumphal arches at **Porte St-Denis** and **Porte St-Martin** (*see p81*) commemorate military victories, while Hardouin-Mansart's circular **place des Victoires** (*see p74*) and **place Vendôme** (*see p65*), an elegant octagon, were designed to show off equestrian statues of the king.

ROCOCO AND NEOCLASSICISM

In the early 18th century, the Faubourg St-Germain overtook the Marais as the city's most fashionable quarter, as the nobility built smart mansions with tall windows and elegant wrought ironwork, such as the **Hôtel Matignon** (57 rue de Varenne, 7th) today

home of the French prime minister. However, the finest example of frivolous rococo decoration is the **Hôtel de Soubise** (60 rue des Francs-Bourgeois, 3rd), with panelling, plasterwork and paintings by celebrated decorators of the day, including Boucher, Restout and van Loo. In furniture-makers' **Faubourg St-Antoine**, a different sort of accommodation grew up, with workshops around courtyards and lodgings up above.

Under Louis XV, several sumptuous buildings were commissioned, among them La Monnaie (now **Musée de la Monnaie de Paris**; *see p195*), the **Panthéon** (*see p182*), the **Ecole de Droit** (place du Panthéon, 5th) and many new theatres. Soufflot's Panthéon, like Jacques-Ange Gabriel's neoclassical **place de la Concorde** (*see p64*), was inspired by ancient Rome, as were the toll gates put up in 1785 by Nicolas Ledoux, famed for his almost minimalist geometrical style (still visible at Nation, Denfert-Rochereau and Parc Monceau) for the Mur des Fermiers Généraux.

THE 19TH CENTURY

The street fighting of the Revolution left Paris in a dilapidated state. Napoleon redressed this situation with a suitably grandiose vision to make Paris the most beautiful city in the world. He confiscated land from the aristocracy and the Church, and ordered a massive building spree. As well as five new bridges and 56 ornamental fountains, he built the **Eglise de la Madeleine** (*see p76*), a mock Greek temple in honour of the Grande Armée, plus a rash of statues and arches, most notably the **Arc de Triomphe** (*see p90*) and the **Arc du Carrousel** (*see p58*).

In 1853, Bonaparte's nephew Louis Napoleon (Napoleon III) appointed Baron Haussmann as the *préfet* of Paris, with a brief to remake the city. A fearsome administrator rather than an architect, Haussmann faced problems of sanitation, sewage and traffic-clogged streets. He set about bringing order, cutting broad, long boulevards through the urban fabric. An estimated 27,000 houses were razed in the process. The Haussmannian apartment block has endured, setting a adaptable format that lasted well into the 20th century, its utilitarian lines set off by mansarded roofs and rows of wrought-iron balconies. Haussmann also introduced English-style public parks, such as the

IN CONTEXT

Petit Palais.

Buttes-Chaumont (see p168), along with prisons, hospitals, train stations and sewers. Amid the upheaval, one building epitomised the grand style of the Second Empire: Charles Garnier's sumptuous **Palais Garnier** (1862-75; see p283).

Haussmann could also be an innovator, persuading Baltard to build new market pavilions at Les Halles in lacy iron rather than stone. Iron frames had already been used by Henri Labrouste in his lovely reading room at the **Bibliothèque Ste-Geneviève** (1844-50; 10 place du Panthéon, 5th), and they became increasingly common: stations such as Hittorff's **Gare du Nord** (1861-65; see p161) and Laloux's Gare d'Orsay (now **Musée d'Orsay**; see p224) are simply shells around an iron frame, producing light-filled interiors. The most daring iron construction of all was the **Eiffel Tower** (see p229). When it was built in 1889, it was the tallest structure in the world. Stylistically, eclecticism ruled, from the neo-Renaissance **Hôtel de Ville** (see p126) to neo-Byzantine **Sacré-Coeur** (see p116).

EARLY 20TH CENTURY

An outburst of extravagance for the 1900 Exposition Universelle marked the beginning of the 20th century, notably the **Grand Palais** (see p94), with its massive glass and steel nave, and the **Petit Palais**, awash in sculptures, mosaics, marble and wrought iron. The **Train Bleu** brasserie in the Gare de Lyon (see p157) is an ornate example of the heavy,

florid Beaux Arts style of this period. Art nouveau at its most fluid and flamboyant can be seen in Hector Guimard's instantly recognisable métro stations and his 1901 **Castel Béranger** (see p107).

All this was a long way from the roughly contemporary work of Henri Sauvage, who created a large social housing project in rue des Amiraux (18th), tiled artists' studio flats in **rue La Fontaine** (16th), and the 1920s extension of **La Samaritaine** (19 rue de la Monnaie, 1st). Funded by philanthropists, social housing began to appear in the city.

THE MODERN MOVEMENT

After World War I, two people stand out by virtue of their innovation and influence: Auguste Perret, architect of the **Théâtre des Champs-Elysées** (see p285), and Le Corbusier. A third architect, Robert Mallet-Stevens, is unrivalled for his elegance, best seen in his villas on rue Mallet-Stevens.

Perret stayed largely within a classical aesthetic, but was a pioneer in the use of reinforced concrete. Le Corbusier tried out his ideas in private houses, such as the Villa La Roche in the 16th (now the **Fondation Le Corbusier**; see p107). His **Pavillon Suisse** at the **Cité Universitaire** (see p216) and **Armée du Salut** hostel (12 rue Cantagrel, 13th) can be seen as a mid point between these villas and his Villes Radieuses mass housing schemes, which became so influential after 1945.

Fondation Pathé.

Meanwhile, the new love of chrome, steel and glass found its way into art deco cafés such as **La Coupole** (see p214). As in the 19th century, world fairs provided an excuse for grandiose state architecture, with a return to monumental classicism in the **Palais de la Porte Dorée**, built for the 1931 Exposition Coloniale, and the **Palais de Chaillot** (see p95) and **Palais de Tokyo** (see p96), built for the 1937 Exposition Internationale.

POST-WAR PARIS

The aerodynamic aesthetic of the post-war era yielded the 1958 **UNESCO building** (see p231) by Bernard Zehrfuss, Pier Luigi Nervi and Marcel Breuer, and the beginnings of **La Défense** (see p236) with the same architects' **CNIT** building, then the largest concrete span in the world. In the 1960s and '70s, tower blocks sprouted in the suburbs and new towns to replace the bidonvilles (shanty towns) that had served as immigrant housing. Inside the city redevelopment was limited, but new regulations allowed taller buildings; in 1960, the 23-storey **33 rue Croulebarbe** marked Paris's first high-rise residential block.

President Georges Pompidou embraced modernity, too, disastrously in the case of the expressways along the Seine, and more benignly in the form of the **Centre Pompidou** (see p124), opened in 1977. But after the construction of the **Tour Montparnasse** (see p213), Pompidou's successor, Valéry Giscard d'Estaing, prevented the Paris horizon from rising any higher.

THE 1980S AND '90S

President François Mitterrand's grands projets dominated the 1980s and '90s, with Jean Nouvel's **Institut du Monde Arabe** (see p184), IM Pei's **Louvre Pyramid** (see p63) and Johan Otto Von Sprecklesen's **Grande Arche de la Défense** (see p236), as well as Carlos Ott's **Opéra Bastille** (see p283), Dominique Perrault's **Bibliothèque Nationale** (see p188) and Chemetov & Huidobro's Bercy finance ministry. The buzzword was 'transparency', from Pei's pyramid to Nouvel's **Fondation Cartier** (see p209).

THE 21ST CENTURY

Jacques Chirac managed to squeeze one last project into his reign with the completion of Nouvel's **Musée du Quai Branly** (see p229) in 2006, a highly colourful baroque structure. Younger architects have been making their mark too: Manuelle Gautrand was behind the revamp of the **Gaîté Lyrique** (see p128).

Other areas have also come up for a makeover recently: the much-maligned 1970s **Forum des Halles** (see p82) complex is being revamped with a new glass canopy and landscaped gardens, while plans to pedestrianise a 2.5km stretch along the banks of the Seine between the Musée d'Orsay and the Pont de l'Alma – **Les Berges** (see p230) – were finally realised in 2014.

Meanwhile, the city also continues to benefit from exciting new cultural buildings. After the 2012 opening of the dramatic Islamic Arts department in the **Cour Visconti** (see p63) at the Louvre, the last 12 months have seen the opening of Frank Gehry's cloudlike glass **Fondation Louis Vuitton** (see p107) in the Bois de Boulogne and Renzo Piano's egg-like **Fondation Pathé** (see p174) on avenue des Gobelins. And to top it all, Jean Nouvel's new **Philharmonie** concert hall at La Villette (see p284) opened in early 2015. Nouvel skipped the first night, complaining that the building was still unfinished, but the response of concertgoers has been resoundingly positive.

IN CONTEXT

Hotels

After a slew of new hotel openings in the last couple of years, the big news during 2014 was all about closures, with two of the city's most famous hotels shutting their doors for major renovations. The Ritz (www.ritzparis.com) and the Crillon (www.crillon.com) will be shut for business until late 2015 at the earliest, as they freshen themselves up to try to contend with the influx of Asian super-luxury from the likes of Shangri-La, Raffles, Mandarin Oriental and the newly opened Peninsula Paris. In the meantime, these new arrivals have taken service and design to a new level, although rack rates can be eye-watering. For something a little less luxe, the city's burgeoning boutique hotel selection means you can still afford good design, as long as you can make do without the uniformed doormen. And further down the scale, hostels are getting ever hipper, with new arrivals at Gare du Nord and the Canal St-Martin.

STAYING IN PARIS

Paris's poshest hotels continue to offer the ultimate luxury experience: at the **Bristol**, the **George V** and the newly refurbished **Plaza Athénée** uniformed flunkeys whisk you through the revolving doors to an otherworldly domain of tinkling china, thick carpets and concierges for whom your wish is their desire, for a generous tip. And the last few years have brought even more competition to the luxury sector with the completion of a new **Shangri-La** and a new

Peninsula in the 16th, the complete makeover of the **Royal Monceau** on avenue Hoche by Philippe Starck, plus the arrival of the **W Paris-Opéra** and **Mandarin Oriental** – one can only wonder why it took quite so long for Mandarin Oriental to set up in a city seemingly made for its brand of high-end, low-key chic.

If palaces are beyond your pocket, then opt for one of Paris's increasingly luxurious boutique hotels. You can be soothed by fine linen, marble baths and a dreamy pool and hammam at **Le Metropolitan**, walk through silk taffeta curtains to your own terrace at **Le Petit Paris**, fall into a deep sleep at the pure white technological marvel that is the **Hôtel Gabriel**, gaze across the Marais rooftops from the cool new **Jules et Jim**, and fraternise at the trendy cava bar of the Spanish-owned **Banke**. For those who like a bit more glitz, the sparkly **Opéra Diamond** and unabashedly sexy **Sublim Eiffel** use fibre optics to create your own starry galaxy. All of these hotels have made the smooth move of abandoning petty pay-per-hour Wi-Fi in favour of providing it free, and Nespresso machines and iPod docks are making an appearance in bedrooms too.

THE BEST PADS

For bedroom bling
Buddha Bar Hotel. *See p345.*

For hip hostelling
Generator Paris. *See p362.*

For Montmartre magic
Hôtel Particulier Montmartre. *See p351.*

Further down the scale, there is now a wide choice of moderately priced and even budget design hotels, especially in the trendy east and north-east of the city, such as the Starck-designed **Mama Shelter**, **Standard Design Hotel**, **20 Prieuré** and **Hôtel Crayon**. And shoestring travellers should consider **St Christopher's Inn** on the Canal d'Ourcq, whose façade is lit up like an art installation at night (or, more centrally, at their new outpost opposite the Gare du Nord). Or the brand new 950-bed **Generator Hostel**, which opened in 2015 in the 10th.

Hotels are graded according to an official star rating system designed to sort the deluxe from the dumps – but we haven't followed it in this guide, as the ratings merely reflect room size and amenities such as lifts or bars, rather than other important factors such as decor, staff or atmosphere. Instead, we've divided the hotels by area, then listed them in four categories, according to the standard prices (not including seasonal offers or discounts) for one night in a double room with en suite shower/bath. For **Deluxe** hotels, you can expect to pay more than €350; for properties in the **Expensive** bracket, €250-€350; for **Moderate** properties, allow €150-€250; while **Budget** rooms go for less than €150. For **gay hotels**, *see pp255-261*.

Note that all hotels in France charge a room tax (*taxe de séjour*) of around €1 per person per night, although this is sometimes included in the rate. Children under 12 often stay for free when sharing a room with parents (check when booking), and small pets usually cost between €10 and €20 extra per night.

THE ISLANDS

Expensive

★ Hôtel du Jeu de Paume

54 rue St-Louis-en-l'Ile, 4th (01.43.26.14.18, www.jeudepaumehotel.com). M° Pont Marie. **Map** p409 K7.

With a discreet courtyard entrance, 17th-century beams, a private garden and a unique timbered breakfast room that was once a real tennis court built under Louis XIII, this is a charming and romantic hotel. These days, it is filled with an attractive array of modern and classical art, and has a coveted billiards table. A dramatic glass lift and catwalks lead to the guestrooms as well as two self-catering apartments, which are simple and tasteful, the walls hung with Pierre Frey fabric.

Moderate

Hôtel des Deux-Iles

59 rue St-Louis-en-l'Ile, 4th (01.43.26.13.35, www.deuxiles-paris-hotel.com). M° Pont Marie. **Map** p409 K7.

Hôtel des Deux-Iles.

This peaceful 17th-century townhouse on the Ile St-Louis offers 17 rooms kitted out in toned-down stripes, *toile de Jouy* fabrics and neo-colonial style furniture. Its star features are a tiny courtyard off the lobby and a vaulted stone breakfast area. All the bedrooms and bathrooms were freshened up a few years ago (fortunately saving the lovely tiles on the bathroom walls).

▶ *The equally pleasant Hôtel de Lutèce (65 rue St-Louis-en-l'Ile, 01.43.26.23.52, www.paris-hotel-lutece.com) is run by the same team.*

Budget

Hospitel Hôtel Dieu

1 pl du Parvis-Notre-Dame, 4th (01.44.32.01.00, www.hotel-hospitel.com). M° Cité or Saint-Michel. **Map** p408 J7.

If the thought of sleeping in a working hospital doesn't put you off (half the rooms here are used by families of the Hôtel Dieu hospital's in-patients and staff), you can stay in one of 14 recently renovated, spotless rooms with colourful contemporary decor, right in the middle of Ile de la Cité. A medical smell is present but not strong, bathrooms are quite large, and you couldn't ask for a better sightseeing base.

Hôtel Henri IV

25 pl Dauphine, 1st (01.43.54.44.53, www.henri 4hotel.fr). M° Pont Neuf. **Map** p408 J6.

Located on tree-lined, triangular place Dauphine, which is surrounded by some of Paris's most expensive real estate on Ile de la Cité and a stone's throw from Notre-Dame, the Henri IV remains Paris's best-value budget hotel. You therefore need to book well ahead. The 15 rooms are simple and unadorned, but clean, and the three paupers' penthouses with balconies and rooftop views go first.

THE LOUVRE & PALAIS-ROYAL

Deluxe

Hôtel Costes

239 rue St-Honoré, 1st (01.42.44.50.00, www.hotelcostes.com). M° Concorde or Tuileries. **Map** p401 G5.

Attitude definitely counts in this temple of notoriety – a place so trendy its website contains an online boutique of its own *ultra-branché* products, and where innumerable A-listers still gravitate to the low-lit bar after all these years. The Costes boasts one of the best pools in Paris, a sybaritic, Eastern-inspired affair with an underwater music system. Rooms are a modern take on Napoleon III, designed by Jacques Garcia.

Hôtel Sofitel le Faubourg

15 rue Boissy-d'Anglas, 8th (01.44.94.14.14, www.sofitel.com). M° Concorde or Madeleine. **Map** p401 F4.

ESSENTIAL INFORMATION

Hôtel Westminster.

This hotel is close to all the major couture boutiques, which is no surprise, as it used to house the *Marie Claire* offices. The rooms have Louis XVI armchairs, large balconies, walk-in wardrobes and Roger & Gallet goodies in the bathrooms; for shopping widowers, there's a small gym and a hammam. It's quiet too: the street has been closed to traffic since 2001 because the American embassy is on the corner. **Other locations** Sofitel Arc de Triomphe, 14 rue Beaujon, 8th (01.53.89.50.50); Hôtel Scribe, 1 rue Scribe, 9th (01.44.71.24.24).

★ Le Meurice
228 rue de Rivoli, 1st (01.44.58.10.10, www. lemeurice.com). Mº Tuileries. **Map** p401 G5.
With its extravagant Louis XVI decor, mosaic-tiled floors and modish restyling by Philippe Starck, Le Meurice is looking even grander than ever. All 160 rooms are done up in distinct historical styles; the Belle Etoile suite on the seventh floor provides panoramic views of Paris from its terrace. You can relax in the Winter Garden to the strains of regular jazz performances; for more intensive intervention, head over to the lavish spa with treatments by Valmont.
▶ *Don't miss dinner at the hotel's three Michelin-starred restaurant, but come with plenty of euros – the Collection Menu is €380.*

Le Westin
3 rue de Castiglione, 1st (01.44.77.11.11, www. thewestinparis.com). Mº Tuileries. **Map** p401 G5.
In the heart of shopping HQ, the Westin mixes belle époque features with pale limestone walls, beautiful vintage-style furniture (inspired by the 1930s and '40s), a neoclassical fountain and a patio. Its sleek modern bedrooms, decked out with top-end gadgets and the award-winning Heavenly Bed, sport balcony views over the Tuileries gardens. The bathrooms are sumptuous, and some have their own balconies. There's an excellent restaurant, Le First, with a sleek, boudoir-like interior by Jacques Garcia.

Moderate

★ Hôtel Brighton
218 rue de Rivoli, 1st (01.47.03.61.61, www.esprit-de-france.com). Mº Tuileries. **Map** p401 G5.
With several rooms overlooking the Tuileries gardens, the Brighton is great value, so book well ahead for a room with a view. Recently restored, it has a classical atmosphere, from the high ceilings in the rooms to the faux-marble and mosaic downstairs.

Hôtel du Lion d'Or
5 rue de la Sourdière, 1st (01.42.60.79.04, www.hotel-louvre-paris.com). Mº Tuileries. **Map** p401 G5.
Simple, brightly coloured rooms and fully furnished studios (with kitchenettes) that can sleep up to five make the Golden Lion a popular choice for families and groups of friends.

Hôtel Mansart
5 rue des Capucines, 1st (01.42.61.50.28, www. esprit-de-france.com). Mº Madeleine or Opéra. **Map** p401 G4.
This spacious hotel has real style, with a light, roomy lobby decorated with murals inspired by formal gardens. The 57 bedrooms feature pleasant fabrics, antiques and paintings; five of the rooms have an excellent view of place Vendôme.

Hôtel des Tuileries
10 rue St-Hyacinthe, 1st (01.42.61.04.17, www.hotel-des-tuileries.com). Mº Tuileries. **Map** p401 G5.
The fashion pack adores this 18th-century hotel (the staircase is listed), which is located in prime Right Bank shopping territory. The hotel recently reopened after a major modernisation, and the 24 comfy, clutter-free bedrooms now feature couture details aplenty.

Le Relais du Louvre
19 rue des Prêtres St-Germain-l'Auxerrois, 1st (01.40.41.96.42, www.relaisdulouvre.com). Mº Pont Neuf or Louvre-Rivoli. **Map** p402 H6.
The cellar of this characterful hotel, with its antiques and wooden beams, was once used by revolutionaries to print anti-royalist literature. It also inspired Puccini's Café Momus in *La Bohème*. The rooms are decorated in floral fabrics, and the front ones look out on to St-Germain-l'Auxerrois church. There's also a top-floor apartment with space for up to five people.

OPERA TO LES HALLES
Deluxe

Hotel W Paris-Opéra
4 rue Meyerbeer, 9th (01.77.48.94.94, www.wparis opera.fr). Mº Opéra/RER Auber. **Map** p401 H4.
The Starwood hotel group's latest venture took two and a half years to finish, but it was worth the wait, with 91 rooms that ooze NYC style from every nook and cranny. For an all-out treat, the 'Extreme Wow' suite will set you back a whopping €2,300 (don't worry, standard doubles start at €340), but you'll get 88sq m of smart modern design all to yourself, and the feeling that you've walked on to the set of a James Bond movie.

Hôtel Westminster
13 rue de la Paix, 2nd (01.42.61.57.46, www. warwickwestminsteropera.com). Mº Opéra/RER Auber. **Map** p401 G4.
This luxury hotel near place Vendôme has more than a touch of British warmth about it, no doubt owing to the influence of its favourite 19th-century guest, the Duke of Westminster (after whom the hotel was named). The hotel fitness centre has a top-floor location, with a tiled steam room and views over the

ESSENTIAL INFORMATION

city, and the cosy bar features deep leather chairs, a fireplace and live jazz at weekends.

★ InterContinental Paris Le Grand
2 rue Scribe, 9th (01.40.07.32.32, www.intercontinental.com). M° Opéra. **Map** p401 G4.
This 1862 hotel is the chain's European flagship – but, given its size, perhaps 'mother ship' would be more appropriate: this landmark establishment occupies the entire block (three wings, almost 500 rooms) next to the opera house; some 80 of the honey-coloured rooms overlook the Palais Garnier. The space under the vast *verrière* is one of the best oases in town, and the hotel's restaurant and coffeehouse, the Café de la Paix, is overseen by the hotel's head chef, Christophe Raoux. For a relaxing daytime break, head to the I-Spa by Algotherm for a seawater treatment.

Mandarin Oriental
251 rue St-Honoré, 1st (01.70.98.78.88, www.mandarinoriental.com). M° Tuileries. **Map** p401 G4.
Set in a 1930s building on rue St-Honoré, the Mandarin Oriental has a wonderfully indulgent location – and the interior doesn't disappoint either, with 138 luxurious rooms, fusion restaurants, a vast interior garden, and smart spa with pool and seven spa suites with private hammams. Decor-wise, think art deco meets oriental boudoir with chic, kitschy touches throughout. In the lobby, fake diamonds decorate the curtain holders and the imposing grey walls are encrusted with stripes of jewels. The boudoir theme continues into the bedrooms, where steely grey, gold or white walls are contrasted with plum-pink cushions and trimmings. Back on the ground floor, the main draw is the choice of eateries, all managed by top chef Thierry Marx. Marx's gastronomic offering is the Sur Mesure restaurant, an all-white affair where the chef creates Asian-influenced delights. Next door sits Bar 8, replete with a theatrical marble bar, walls inlaid with raindrop Lalique crystals, and snazzy cocktails. It's a top spot for a sophisticated slurp, especially in summer when tables spill out into the gardens.

Expensive

Hilton Paris Opéra
108 rue St-Lazare, 8th (01.40.08.44.44, www.hilton.com). M° St-Lazare. **Map** p401 G3.
Guests are cocooned in soundproofed luxury at this hotel, which was recently renovated and rebranded under the Hilton banner. The 19th-century Eiffel-inspired lobby with jewel-encrusted pink granite columns is a historic landmark. Rooms are spacious, with double entrance doors and exclusive Annick Goutal toiletries; the belle époque brasserie, Café Terminus, and sexy Golden Black Bar were designed by Sonia Rykiel. Guests have access to a nearby fitness centre.

★ Hôtel Chavanel
22 rue Tronchet, 8th (01.47.42.26.14, www.hotelchavanel.com). M° Madeleine. **Map** p401 G3.
The Chavanel is a dreamy place to lay your head. Twenty-five rooms are arranged across five floors, with two suites in the eaves, including one with a circular bed. The exquisite bathrooms feature tiles by Porcelanosa that resemble crushed silk, and all rooms – even the smallest – come with robes and slippers. Despite all these indulgent luxuries, Wi-Fi is free and the minibar reasonable. Breakfast is all-organic, including smoked salmon, and an astonishing array of cereals and breads. Located just a few steps away from place de la Madeleine and the Palais Garnier opera house, the Chavanel is superbly positioned for high-end shopping and highbrow culture. *Photos p342.*

Paris Marriott Opera Ambassador Hotel
16 bd Haussmann, 9th (01.44.83.40.40, www.marriott.com). M° Chaussée d'Antin or Richelieu Drouot. **Map** p401 H4.
If you're looking for some vintage style but can't face another gilded Louis XIV interior, check into this historic, Haussmann-era hotel, which sets traditional furniture against contemporary decor in each of the 294 bedrooms. The low-lit Lindbergh Bar is named after the pilot, who dropped in for a celebratory drink and cigar after his solo transatlantic flight in 1927. The hotel is perfect for the *grands magasins*.

Moderate

Hôtel Amour
8 rue Navarin, 9th (01.48.78.31.80, www.hotelamourparis.fr). M° St-Georges. **Map** p402 H2.
Opened back in 2006, this boutique hotel is a real hit with the in crowd. Each of the 20 rooms is unique, decorated on the theme of love or eroticism by a coterie of contemporary artists and designers, such as Marc Newson, M&M, Stak, Pierre Le Tan and Sophie Calle. Seven of the rooms contain artists' installations, and two others have their own private bar and a large terrace on which to hold your own party. The late-night brasserie has a coveted outdoor garden, and the crowd is young and beautiful and loves to entertain. *Photos p343.*

Hôtel Arvor Saint Georges
8 rue Laferrière, 9th (01.48.78.60.92, www.arvorhotel-paris.com). M° St-Georges. **Map** p402 H2.
Don't be put off by the slightly austere façade; the owner intended it this way to contrast with the homely atmosphere that reigns inside. Although you're right in the middle of the city, the hotel has the feel of a quiet country house. The decor is delicate and uncluttered, and most of the 30 spacious rooms, including six suites, overlook the rooftops (no.503 has the best view of the Eiffel Tower). The small terrace is the ideal spot to take a break the buzz.

Hôtel Chavanel. See p341.

Hôtel Britannique
20 av Victoria, 1st (01.42.33.74.59, www.hotel-britannique.fr). M° Châtelet/RER Châtelet les Halles. **Map** p408 J6.
Smiling staff in stripy waistcoats welcome you to this adorable hotel, where guest areas and rooms are cocooned in thick drapes, luscious carpets and a mishmash of British colonial-style furniture that make you feel like you've stepped into an English country cottage. Enjoy deeply delicious pastries in the warm, rustic breakfast room, or book a top-floor *chambre* and eat them on your plant-filled balcony – a rare oasis of greenery for such a central and reasonably priced hotel.

★ Hôtel Crayon
25 rue du Bouloi, 1st (01.42.36.54.19, www.hotelcrayon.com). M° Les Halles. **Map** p402 H5.
Brilliantly situated near the Louvre in a neighbourhood full of great restaurants, Hôtel Crayon offers colour therapy with rooms painted top to toe in a choice of 16 hues. Each also features a life-size hand-drawn nude pencilled on the wall in a Matisse style, a white bathroom with colour accents where vintage furniture has been adapted to support contemporary sinks, silky smooth cotton bedlinen and random vintage holiday snaps collected from flea markets and mounted in frames. You can order a selection of meals via room service, and a copious breakfast is served in the vaulted breakfast room. The ground floor also has an honesty bar decked out with 1950s furniture. For the same price as a run-of-the-mill three-star, this boutique hotel offers a wonderful experience in a great location.

Hôtel Langlois
63 rue St-Lazare, 9th (01.48.74.78.24, www.hotel-langlois.com). M° Trinité. **Map** p401 H3.
Built as a bank in 1870, this belle époque building became the Hôtel des Croisés in 1896. In 2001, after featuring in the Jonathan Demme film *Charade*, it changed its name to Hôtel Langlois in honour of the founder of the Cinémathèque Française. Its 27 spacious, air-conditioned bedrooms are decorated in art nouveau style; the larger ones have delightful hidden bathrooms.

Hotel Odyssey
19 rue Hérold, 1st (01.42.36.04.02, www.hotel odysseyparis.com). M° Palais Royal-Musée du Louvre or Les Halles. **Map** p402 J5.
The name may have changed, but otherwise the former Hotel O is as before – a sleek, 29-room venture that adds some welcome hip to the arrondissement accommodation options. Rooms (styled by cool young design company Ora-Ito, hence the 'O' in the hotel's name) are small but exquisitely done out, with retro-futuristic features that make you feel like you're on board a 1970s spaceship, with clean lines, gracious curves and blocks of pink, grey, purple and dark turquoise.

Budget

Hôtel Chopin

10 bd Montmartre (46 passage Jouffroy), 9th (01.47.70.58.10, www.hotel-chopin.com). M° Grands Boulevards. **Map** p402 J4.

Handsomely set in a historic, glass-roofed arcade next door to the Grévin museum in the heart of the Grands Boulevards, the Chopin's original 1846 façade adds to its old-fashioned appeal. The 36 rooms are quiet and functional, done out in an assortment of salmons, greens, yellows and blues.

▶ *For details of the Grévin, see www.grevin.com.*

Hôtel du Cygne

3 rue du Cygne, 1st (01.42.60.14.16, www.hotel ducygne.fr). M° Etienne Marcel/RER Châtelet Les Halles. **Map** p402 J5.

This traditional hotel located in a handsome 17th-century building has 20 compact, cosy and simple rooms embellished with touches such as antiques and home-made furnishings. It's on a pedestrianised street in the bustling Les Halles district, so light sleepers might prefer to book one of the rooms overlooking the courtyard.

Résidence Hôtel des Trois Poussins

15 rue Clauzel, 9th (01.53.32.81.81, www.les 3poussins.com). M° St-Georges. **Map** p402 H2.

Set just off the beaten track in a pleasant *quartier*, and within walking distance (uphill) of Montmartre, the Résidence Hôtel des Trois Poussins offers 40 brightly decorated en suite rooms overlooking the courtyard or quiet street. Two of the rooms feature terraces with splendid rooftop views. There's a patio for breakfast during the summer months.

Hôtel Amour. *See p341.*

LE MARCEAU BASTILLE ★★★★

Hôtel-Gallery
13 rue Jules César
75012 Paris
Tél: 00.33(0)1 43 43 11 65
Fax: 00.33(0)1 43 41 67 70
infos@hotelmarceaubastille.com
Géneral Manager: Christophe Diallo

Le Marceau Bastille – Hotel gallery is a charming and contemporary 4 stars hotel, located nearly a few steps away from the Bastille square, as well as the "Gare de Lyon" train station and the historic Marais neighbourhood. The hotel interiors denote a characteristically contemporary style.

Le Marceau Bastille Hotel offers 55 rooms of two kinds: First, the "urban" option guarantees a cozy and resolutely avant-garde type atmosphere swathed in vibrant color, still seeped in elegance. The "ecological" option provides calm and sunny rooms set off by bright yet soft tones, natural materials, organic forms and sleek lines. The furnishings are contemporary and combine delicacy with modern technology. The living room and the restaurant walls are dedicated to the Art with the permanent collections of contemporary artists.

Hotel Facilities

General
Bar, 24-Hour Front Desk, Newspapers, Non-Smoking Rooms, Rooms/Facilities for Disabled Guests, Elevator, free Safety Deposit Box, Heating, Design Hotel, Luggage Storage, Air-conditioning, Fitness room.

Services

Massage Room Service, Laundry, Dry Cleaning, Breakfast in the Room, Fax/Photocopying.
Free! All children under 2 years stay free of charge for cots.
Free! Wi-Fi is available in the entire hotel and is free of charge.
Free! Pets are allowed on request. No extra charges.
Extra beds are available on request only. Any type of extra bed or baby cot is upon request and needs to be confirmed by the hotel. Public parking is possible at a location nearby with preferential rates for clients of the hotel.

Hotel Policies

Check-in 13:00 & Check-out 12:00
Accepted credit cards
American Express, Visa, Euro/MasterCard, Carte Bleue, Diners Club, JCB
Area Information
Architect, Historic and Art Area.
Place de la Bastille - L'Opéra Bastille - L'Hôtel Sully - L'Hôtel Carnavalet - L'Institut du Monde Arabe et la Mosquée de Paris - Le Pavillon de l'Arsenal. Le Quartier du Marais - La Place des Vosges - Cour Saint - Emilion
Stroll and Walk Area
La Promenade Plantée - Le Port de Plaisance de Paris Arsenal - Le Jardin des Plantes and Muséum National d'Histoire Naturelle - L'Ile Saint Louis

Hôtel Daniel.

CHAMPS-ELYSEES & WESTERN PARIS

Deluxe

Buddha Bar Hotel

4 rue d'Anjou, 8th (01.83.96.88.88, www. buddhabarhotelparis.com). M° Concorde or Madeleine. **Map** p401 F4.

This latest instalment in the Buddha Bar empire is a wonderful mix of French style and neo-Asian extravagance set in a handsome 18th-century *hôtel particulier*. The Le Vraymonde restaurant is headed by acclaimed Senegalese chef Rougui Dia.

▶ *See also p346* **Excess All Areas**.

★ Four Seasons George V

31 av George V, 8th (01.49.52.70.00, www. fourseasons.com/paris). M° Alma Marceau or George V. **Map** p400 D4.

There's no denying that the George V is serious about luxury: chandeliers, marble and tapestries; glorious flower arrangements; divine bathrooms; and ludicrously comfortable beds in some of the largest rooms in all of Paris. The Versailles-inspired spa includes whirlpools, saunas and a menu of treatments for an unabashedly metrosexual clientele; non-guests can now reserve appointments. If you can afford it, it's worth every euro.

Hôtel le A

4 rue d'Artois, 8th (01.42.56.99.99, www. paris-hotel-a.com). M° Franklin D Roosevelt or St-Philippe-du-Roule. **Map** p401 E4.

The black-and-white decor of this designer boutique hotel provides a fine backdrop for the models, artists and media types hanging out in the lounge bar area; the only splashes of colour come from graffiti-like artworks by conceptual artist Fabrice Hybert. The 26 rooms all have granite bathrooms, and the starched white furniture slip covers, changed after each guest, make the smallish spaces seem larger than they are. The dimmer switches are a nice touch – as are the lift lights changing colour at each floor.

Hôtel le Bristol

112 rue du Fbg-St-Honoré, 8th (01.53.43.43.00, www.hotel-bristol.com). M° Champs-Elysées Clémenceau. **Map** p401 E4.

Set on the exclusive rue du Faubourg St-Honoré, near supremely luxury boutiques such as Christian Lacroix, Azzaro, Salvatore Ferragamo, Givenchy and Dolce & Gabbana, the Bristol is a luxurious 'palace' hotel with a loyal following of fashionistas and millionaires drawn by the location, impeccable service, larger than average rooms, sixth-floor pool and sundeck, and a three Michelin-starred restaurant, Epicure, with Eric Fréchon at the helm; in summer, tables are laid outside in the formal garden.

Hôtel Daniel

8 rue Frédéric-Bastiat, 8th (01.42.56.17.00, www.hoteldanielparis.com). M° Franklin D Roosevelt or St-Philippe-du-Roule. **Map** p401 E4.

A romantic hideaway close to the monoliths of the Champs-Elysées, this Relais & Châteaux property is decorated in chinoiserie and a palette of rich colours, with 26 rooms cosily appointed in *toile de Jouy* and an intricately hand-painted restaurant that feels like a courtyard. The gastronomic restaurant is a good deal for this neighbourhood; the bar menu is served at all hours.

EXCESS ALL AREAS

Take it to the max at the blingtastic Buddha Bar Hotel.

Minimalism seems to be the *mot du jour* among the city's high-end hoteliers, but happily the team behind the **Buddha Bar Hotel** (*see p345*) have no truck with such notions. Opened in June 2013, this five-star is a paean to decorative excess, with opulent, Franco-Asian decor and a palette of rich red and gold.

The scale and splendour of the chosen site, a grand historic mansion on rue d'Anjou, made its ambitions clear. Behind the dignified façade, the fantasy unfurls: a riot of writhing dragons and rich silks. For wining and dining there's a pricey pan-Asian restaurant, housed in the former stables; in summer, tables spill out on to the lantern-lit interior courtyard. Still more glowing red silk lanterns lead the way to cocktail bar Le Qu4tre – an intimate, seductively lit hideout, with properly potent cocktails. Drink too many and there's always the hammam, with its mosaic-tiled steam room. (Or, for the truly penitent, the compact fitness room).

The same maximalist spirit prevails through the 56 rooms and suites, which centre on enormous beds with latticed, Japanese-style headboards. Red and black calligraphy-printed rugs soften the parquet floors, while thoughtful touches run from pillow menus and plush bathrobes to well-stocked Nespresso machines. Bathrooms are equally dramatic, with huge showers, glimmering mosaic tiles and double-ended, gold dragon-painted baths. Nothing is understated here, right down to the 'do not disturb' signs – which take the form of over-sized, resplendent red silk tassels. Is it kitsch? Perhaps just a little – but that's all part of the glorious charm.

Hôtel Fouquet's Barrière

46 av George V, 8th (01.40.69.60.00, www.fouquets-barriere.com). M° George V. **Map** p400 D4.

This grandiose five-star hotel is built around the famous *fin-de-siède* brasserie Le Fouquet's. Five buildings form the hotel complex, housing 81 rooms (including 33 suites), upmarket restaurant Le Diane, the U Spa, an indoor pool and a rooftop terrace for hire. Jacques Garcia, of Hôtel Costes and Westin fame, was responsible for the interior design, which retains the Empire style of the exterior while incorporating luxurious touches inside – flatscreen TVs and mist-free mirrors as standard in the marble bathrooms. And, of course, it's unbeatable in terms of location: right at the junction of avenue George V and the Champs-Elysées.

Hôtel Plaza Athénée

25 av Montaigne, 8th (01.53.67.66.65, www.plaza-athenee-paris.com). M° Alma Marceau. **Map** p400 D5.

This palace is ideally placed for power shopping at Chanel, Louis Vuitton, Dior and other avenue Montaigne boutiques. Material girls and boys will enjoy the high-tech room amenities, such as remote-controlled air con, internet and video-game access on the TV via infrared keyboard, and mini hi-fi. Gourmands will enjoy dinner at Alain Ducasse's restaurant, as long as budget isn't an issue – some of the starters will set you back more than a mid-priced hotel room elsewhere. The hotel reopened in August 2014 after a year-long renovation.

Hôtel de Sers

41 av Pierre-1er-de-Serbie, 8th (01.53.23.75.75, www.hoteldesers.com). M° Alma Marceau or George V. **Map** p400 D4.

Behind its stately 19th-century façade, the Hôtel de Sers calls itself a baby palace, displaying an ambitious mix of minimalist contemporary furnishings, with a few pop art touches. Original architectural details, such as the grand staircase and reception, complete the picture. The large top-floor apartment affords dreamy views over Paris's rooftops.

★ Hôtel de la Trémoille

14 rue de la Trémoille, 8th (01.56.52.14.00, www.hotel-tremoille.com). M° Alma-Marceau. **Map** p400 D4.

The opening of a new restaurant-bar-lounge and improved spa and fitness facilities have made the Trémoille a serious competitor to the other palaces nearby. The 93 rooms are decorated to evoke no fewer than 31 different 'atmospheres', and the bathrooms are filled with Molton Brown products. A unique feature is the 'hatch', which enables room service to deliver your meal without disturbing you.

Hôtel de Vigny

9-11 rue Balzac, 8th (01.42.99.80.80, www.hotel devigny.com). M° George V. **Map** p400 D3.

This hotel has the feel of a private, plush townhouse. Although it's just off the Champs-Elysées, the Vigny pulls in a discerning, low-key clientele. Its 37 bedrooms and suites are decorated in tasteful stripes or florals, with marble bathrooms. Enjoy the sumptuous cuisine of Italian chef Alberico Penatti in the art deco Penati al Baretto restaurant.

★ Jays Paris

6 rue Copernic, 16th (01.47.04.16.16, www.jays-paris.com). M° Kléber or Victor Hugo. **Map** p400 C4.

Jays is a luxurious *boutique-apart* hotel that trades on a clever blend of antique furniture, modern design and high-tech equipment. The marble staircase, lit entirely by natural light filtered through the glass atrium overhead, gives an instant feeling of grandeur, and leads to five suites, each with a fully equipped kitchenette. A cosy salon is available to welcome in-house guests and their visitors.

Opéra Diamond

4 rue de la Pépinière, 8th (01.44.70.02.00, www.hotel-opera-diamond.com). M° St-Lazare. **Map** p401 F3.

This sparkling Best Western Premier hotel lives up to its name with a night-sky decor made up of black granite resin punctuated with crystals and LEDs. The 30 rooms are equally splendid, with Swarovski crystal touches to the furniture, black bathrooms and satin curtains that close to become a huge photomontage of a female nude crossed with architectural imagery. The Executive rooms on the fifth floor have iPod stations, Nespresso machines, and speakers in the bathrooms. A grassy courtyard with a fountain adds to the appeal. Unashamedly bling, but rather magical when night falls.

Peninsula Paris

19 av Kléber, 16th (01.58.12.28.88, www.peninsula.com). M° Kléber or Charles de Gaulle-Etoile. **Map** p400 C4.

See p354 **Nap of Luxury**.

Pershing Hall

49 rue Pierre-Charron, 8th (01.58.36.58.00, www.pershinghall.com). M° George V. **Map** p400 D4.

The refreshing mix of 19th-century grandeur and contemporary comfort makes Pershing Hall feel quite large, but this luxury establishment is really a cleverly disguised boutique hotel with just 26 rooms. Fashionable locals frequent the stylish bar and restaurant terrace. Designed by Andrée Putman, the neat bedrooms emphasise natural materials, with stained grey oak floors and fine mosaic-tiled bathrooms with geometric styling and copious towels. There's also a small spa and gym.

Renaissance Paris Arc de Triomphe

39 av de Wagram, 17th (01.55.37.55.37, www.marriott.com). M° Ternes. **Map** p400 C3.

LE CINQ CODET

Located in the heart of the elegant 7th arrondissement, just steps away from Les Invalides, the challenge behind Le Cinq Codet Hotel was a daring one: how to transform the former 1930s telephone exchange building into a hotel? From the inspired vision of Jean-Philippe Nuel, it is now a must-have address, designed as a Parisian home-from-home, as atypical as it is seductive.

Hotel Le Cinq Codet ★ ★ ★ ★ ★
5 rue Louis Codet, 75007 Paris
www.le5codet.com
contact@le5codet.com
+33 (0)1 53 85 15 60
+33 (0)1 53 85 83 96

You can't miss it. This six-storey undulating glass façade on avenue de Wagram is like no other part of the neighbourhood. All rooms are stylishly done out in pale greys, charcoals and dark wood, with Eames-style furniture. Nice high-tech touches include an iPod dock on the bedside radio and a large flatscreen TV with Wi-Fi keyboard. Bathrooms are a glory of polished metal, tasteful tiles and gleaming glass. The Makassar restaurant serves delicate and delicious Franco-Asian fusion food.

Royal Monceau
37 Avenue Hoche, 8th (01.42.99.88.00, www. leroyalmonceau.com). M° Charles de Gaulle Etoile. **Map** p400 D3.
This Starck-designed incarnation of the legendary old grande dame opened to the public (or at least those who could afford it) in 2010, offering everything from cosy studio rooms to the 190sq m Royal Monceau suite. In 2013, it was granted 'palace status', joining an elite group. With no fewer than three restaurants (two of which have recently been awarded a Michelin star each), desserts from star pastry chef Pierre Hermé and an indoor pool and spa, the Royal Monceau is back in the big league.

Le Sezz
6 av Frémiet, 16th (01.56.75.26.26, www.hotel sezz.com). M° Passy. **Map** p404 B6.
Le Sezz opened its doors in 2005 with 27 deluxe rooms and suites – the work of acclaimed French furniture designer Christophe Pillet. The understated decor represents a refreshingly modern take on luxury, with black parquet flooring, rough-hewn stone walls and bathrooms partitioned off with sweeping glass façades. The bar and public areas are equally chic.

Shangri-La Paris
10 av d'Iéna, 16th (01.53.67.19.98, www. shangri-la.com). M° Iéna. **Map** p404 C5.
Pierre-Yves Rochon's design at the Shangri-La is an ode to French imperialism, with lavish colonial-style paintings, knick-knacks and light fittings, artfully mixed with century-old marble floors, stained-glass windows and thick velveteen fabrics. Half of the 81 rooms and suites look out on to Eiffel's filigree tower, and the top-floor suite provides what could be Paris's best panorama over the Left Bank. Shangri-La may be a Chinese company, but it has gone out of its way to ensure that the building's 'French' architectural heritage remains intact: the mansion, built in 1896, drips in Napoleonic carvings and gilding; and there's a Louis XIV-style salon, the splendour of which rivals Versailles. The 15-metre indoor pool is stunning too.

Expensive

Hôtel Keppler
10 rue Keppler, 16th (01.47.20.65.05, www. keppler.fr). M° George V or Charles de Gaulle Etoile. **Map** p400 C4.
This newly renovated boutique hotel is a family-run treasure, decorated with striped wallpaper, funky mirrors, animal prints and various knick-knacks. None of the 39 rooms is huge, but all are cleverly thought through, so that lack of space is never an issue and the whole experience is pleasantly cosy. The top-floor suites have their own (large) balcony – perfect for an alfresco breakfast – and views over Paris's rooftops towards the Eiffel Tower.

Hôtel La Maison Champs Elysées
8 rue Jean Goujon, 8th (01.40.74.64.65, www. lamaisonchampselysees.com). M° Franklin D. Roosevelt. **Map** p401 E5.
See p361 **Chic Sleep**.

Hôtel Pergolèse
3 rue Pergolèse, 16th (01.53.64.04.04, www. pergolese.com). M° Argentine. **Map** p400 B3.
The Pergolèse was one of the first designer boutique hotels in town, but still looks contemporary a decade or so after being kitted out by Rena Dumas-Hermès with art deco-style furniture by Philippe Starck and rugs by Hilton McConnico. Rooms feature pale wood details and cool, white-tiled bathrooms, and there's also a large, two-bedroom family apartment.

★ Hôtel Regent's Garden
6 rue Pierre-Demours, 17th (01.45.74.07.30, www.hotel-regents-paris.com). M° Charles de Gaulle Etoile or Ternes. **Map** p400 C2.
This elegant hotel – built for Napoleon III's physician – features Second Empire high ceilings and plush upholstery, and a lounge overlooking a lovely walled patio. There are 39 large bedrooms, some with gilt mirrors and fireplaces. It's an oasis of calm just ten minutes from the Champs-Elysées, and was the first hotel in Paris to receive an Ecolabel, for its recycling and energy- and water-saving efforts.

Hôtel Square
3 rue de Boulainvilliers, 16th (01.44.14.91.90, www.hotelsquare.com). M° Passy/RER Avenue du Pdt Kennedy. **Map** p404 A7.
This courageously modern hotel has a dramatic yet welcoming interior, and attentive service that comes from having to look after only 22 rooms. They're decorated in amber, brick or slate colours, with exotic woods, quality fabrics and bathrooms seemingly cut from one huge chunk of Carrara marble. View the exhibitions in the atrium gallery or mingle with the media types at the Zebra Square restaurant/bar.

Les Jardins de la Villa
5 rue Bélidor, 17th (01.53.81.01.10, www.jardins delavilla.com). M° Porte Maillot. **Map** p400 B2.
Behind a sober frontage, this 33-room boutique hotel is an unexpectedly playful affair, with a couture theme and a penchant for fuchsia pink. It's dotted with surreal touches – not least the high heel-shaped

couch in reception. Beautifully appointed rooms pair modern luxuries (Nespresso machines, free Wi-Fi, sleek flatscreen TVs) with old-fashioned attention to detail (proper soundproofing and thick, light-blocking curtains). The location is off the tourist trail, though close to the métro.

★ Le Metropolitan

10 pl de Mexico, 16th (01.56.90.40.04, www. radissonblu.com). Mᵒ Trocadero. **Map** p400 B5.
This 48-room offering from Radisson Blu is supremely sleek. The discreet entrance is only a few metres wide, but once inside the triangular structure opens out into surprising volumes, with a monumental art deco-style fireplace, and cream leather and black granite reminiscent of New York in the 1930s. The first floor contains a swank insiders'

cocktail bar, but the biggest surprise of all is the breathtaking view of the Eiffel Tower from the front façade, best enjoyed through the huge oval window while lying on the four-poster bed of the sixth-floor suite. All rooms exude *luxe, calme et volonté* with solid oak floors, linen curtains and baths or showers carved from black or cream marble. Below ground is a sublime pool and hammam reserved for guests.

Moderate

Hôtel Elysées Ceramic

34 av de Wagram, 8th (01.42.27.20.30, www. elysees-ceramic.com). Mᵒ Charles de Gaulle Etoile. **Map** p400 D3.
Situated between the Arc de Triomphe and place des Ternes, this comfortable hotel has one of Paris's

Les Jardins de la Villa. *See p349.*

finest art nouveau ceramic façades, dating from 1904; inside, the theme continues with a ceramic cornice around the reception. All 57 rooms have been renovated in sophisticated chocolate or pewter tones with modern, art nouveau-inspired wallpaper and light fixtures. Outside is a terrace garden perfect for taking afternoon tea or evening cocktails.

MONTMARTRE & PIGALLE

Deluxe

★ Hôtel Particulier Montmartre

23 av Junot, 18th (01.53.41.81.40, www.hotel-particulier-montmartre.com). M° Lamarck Caulaincourt. **Map** p401 H1.
Visitors lucky (and wealthy) enough to manage to book a suite at the Hôtel Particulier Montmartre will find themselves in one of the city's hidden gems. Nestled in a quiet passage off rue Lepic, in the heart of Montmartre and opposite a mysterious rock known as the Rocher de la Sorcière (witch's rock), this sumptuous Directoire-style house is dedicated to art, with each of the five luxurious suites personalised by an avant-garde artist. The private garden conceived by Louis Bénech (famous for the Tuileries renovation) adds the finishing touch.

Expensive

Hôtel Banke

20 rue La Fayette, 9th (01.55.33.22.22, www. derbyhotels.com). M° Le Peletier. **Map** p401 H3.
The Banke may well have the most eye-popping lobby in the city, a huge two-storey space done in outrageous belle époque style, all crimson, black pillars and gold leaf beneath a whopping glass roof. After such opulence, the rooms are perhaps something of a let-down; but they are stylish and comfortably equipped. The mezzanine bar partakes of the lobby's luxe, and the Josefin restaurant serves nouvelle Med cuisine. There's also a gym and hammam for a post-sightseeing wind-down.

Kube Hotel

1-5 passage Ruelle, 18th (01.42.05.20.00, www. kubehotel.com). M° La Chapelle. **Map** p402 K1.
Kube sits behind an unremarkable façade in an unlikely neighbourhood – the Goutte d'Or. The Ice Kube bar serves up vodka glasses that, like the bar itself, are carved from ice; drinkers pay €29 to down four vodka cocktails in 25 minutes. Also on the menu, innovative cuisine at La Table du Cube. Access to the 41 rooms is by fingerprint technology.

Moderate

Hôtel des Arts

5 rue Tholozé, 18th (01.46.06.30.52, www. arts-hotel-paris.com). M° Abbesses or Blanche. **Map** p401 H1.

This Montmartre gem is pleasantly decorated with oriental rugs, wooden bookcases and Provençal-style furniture. The rooms here are simple but inviting, some affording pleasant views of the hidden roof gardens and windmills of the Butte. Art by local artists is displayed in the basement breakfast room.

Hôtel Royal Fromentin

11 rue Fromentin, 9th (01.48.74.85.93, www. hotelroyalfromentin.com). M° Blanche or Pigalle. **Map** p401 H2.
Wood panelling, art deco windows and a vintage glass lift echo the hotel's origins as a 1930s cabaret hall; its theatrical feel attracted Blondie and Nirvana. It's just down the road from the Moulin Rouge, and many of its 47 rooms overlook Sacré-Coeur. Rooms have been renovated in French style, with bright fabrics and an old-fashioned feel.

Terrass Hotel

12-14 rue Joseph-de-Maistre, 18th (01.46.06.72.85, www.terrass-hotel.com). M° Place de Clichy. **Map** p401 H1.
There's nothing spectacular about this classic hotel, but for people willing to pay top euro for the best views in town, it fits the bill. Ask for room 704 and you can lie in the bath and look at the Eiffel Tower. In decent weather, head up for brunch on the seventh-floor terrace, open from June to September.

Timhotel Montmartre

11 rue Ravignan, 18th (01.42.55.74.79, www. timhotel.fr). M° Abbesses or Pigalle. **Map** p401 H1.
The location adjacent to picturesque place Emile-Goudeau makes this one of the most popular hotels in the Timhotel chain. It has 59 rooms, comfortable without being plush; try to bag one on the fourth or fifth floor for stunning views.

Budget

Hôtel Eldorado

18 rue des Dames, 17th (01.45.22.35.21, www.eldoradohotel.fr). M° Place de Clichy. **Map** p401 G1.
This eccentric hotel is decorated with flea market finds. The Eldorado's winning features include a wine bar, one of the best garden patios in town and a loyal fashionista following. The cheapest rooms have shared bathrooms and toilets.

Hôtel Ermitage

24 rue Lamarck, 18th (01.42.64.79.22, www.ermitagesacrecoeur.fr). M° Lamarck Caulaincourt. **No credit cards. Map** p402 J1.
This 12-room townhouse hotel stands on the calm, non-touristy north side of Montmartre, only five minutes from Sacré-Coeur. The bedrooms are large and endearingly overdecorated, with bold floral wallpaper; those higher up have fine views.

ESSENTIAL INFORMATION

BEAUBOURG & THE MARAIS
Expensive

Hôtel Bourg Tibourg
19 rue du Bourg-Tibourg, 4th (01.42.78.47.39, www.hotelbourgtibourg.com). M° Hôtel de Ville. **Map** p409 K6.

The Bourg Tibourg has the same owners as Hôtel Costes (*see p338*) and the same interior decorator – but don't expect this jewellery box of a boutique hotel to be a miniature replica. Aside from its enviable location in the heart of the Marais and its fashion-pack fans, here it's all about Jacques Garcia's neo-Gothic-cum-Byzantine decor – impressive and imaginative. Scented candles, mosaic-tiled bathrooms and luxurious fabrics in rich colours create the perfect escape. There's no restaurant or lounge – posing is done in the neighbourhood bars.

Moderate

★ Hôtel de la Bretonnerie
22 rue Ste-Croix-de-la-Bretonnerie, 4th (01.48.87.77.63, www.bretonnerie.com). M° Hôtel de Ville. **Map** p409 K6.

With wrought ironwork, exposed stone and wooden beams, the labyrinth of corridors in this 17th-century *hôtel particulier* is full of atmosphere. Tapestries, rich colours and the occasional four-poster bed give the 29 rooms individuality. Location is convenient too.

Hôtel Duo
11 rue du Temple, 4th (01.42.72.72.22, www.duoparis.com). M° Hôtel de Ville. **Map** p406 K6.

An unbeatable location, designer decor, a gym with sauna and a convivial cocktail bar make this a popular choice for laptop-wielding young professionals. Its Jean-Philippe Nuel decor is so striking that passers-by sometimes enquire about the price of the outsize lampshades and mustard-coloured armchairs in the huge lounge lobby, which also has a bamboo courtyard garden. Based on a palette of brown with contrasting turquoise, mustard, lime green, pink or blue, each room is different and you can request a balcony, beams, wallpaper, a bath, separate loo, and road or courtyard preference.

Hôtel Jules et Jim
11 rue des Gravilliers, 4th (01.44.54.13.13, www.hoteljulesetjim.com). M° Arts et Métiers. **Map** p409 K5.

Located in the heart of the Marais, this modern hotel is surrounded by two paved courtyards and has lovely rooftop views. Guest rooms are comfortable, with all mod cons (iPod dock, flatscreen TV), while a continental buffet breakfast is served in the chic dining area. Guests can enjoy cocktails at the bar or on the terrace.

ESSENTIAL INFORMATION

IN THE KNOW NO VACANCIES

Hotels are often booked solid and cost more during the major trade fairs (January, May, September), and it's also hard to find a good room during Fashion Weeks. At quieter times, hotels can often offer special deals at short notice; phone ahead or check their websites.

★ Hôtel du Petit Moulin
29-31 rue de Poitou, 3rd (01.42.74.10.10, www.hoteldupetitmoulin.com). M° St-Sébastien Froissart. **Map** p409 L5.

Within striking distance of the hip shops around rue Charlot, this turn-of-the-century façade masks what was once the oldest *boulangerie* in Paris, lovingly restored as a boutique hotel by Nadia Murano and Denis Nourry. The couple recruited no lesser figure than Christian Lacroix for the decor, and the result is a riot of colour, trompe l'oeil effects and a savvy mix of old and new. Each of its 17 exquisitely appointed rooms is unique, and the walls in rooms 202, 204 and 205 feature drawings and scribbles taken from Lacroix's sketchbook.

Hôtel St-Louis Marais
1 rue Charles V, 4th (01.48.87.87.04, www.saintlouismarais.com). M° Bastille or Sully Morland. **Map** p409 L7.

Built as part of a 17th-century Célestin convent, this peaceful hotel had its bathrooms redone and Wi-Fi access installed a few years ago. Rooms are compact and cosy, with wooden beams, tiled floors and simple, traditional decor.

Les Jardins du Marais
74 rue Amelot, 11th (01.40.21.20.00, www.lesjardinsdumarais.com). M° Bastille. **Map** p409 L5.

The centrepiece of this ultra-swish hotel is a vast courtyard, filled with tables, potted plants and lampposts that wouldn't look out of place in Narnia. Inside, it's smart and modern; the lobby looks tastefully trendy in its steely black and white marble, with purple furnishings and Philippe Starck chairs.

Budget

Grand Hôtel Jeanne d'Arc
3 rue de Jarente, 4th (01.48.87.62.11, www.hoteljeannedarc.com). M° Chemin Vert or St-Paul. **Map** p409 L6.

The Jeanne d'Arc's strong point is its great location on a quiet road close to pretty place du Marché-Ste-Catherine. A recent refurbishment has made the reception area striking, with a huge mirror adding the illusion of space. The bedrooms are colourful and comfortable.

Hôtel Paris France

72 rue de Turbigo, 3rd (01.42.78.00.04, www.paris-france-hotel.com). Mº Temple. **Map** p402 L5.

A great central location, sweet lift, spruce staff and clean, pleasant rooms are on offer here. The attic has views of Montmartre and (if you lean out far enough) the Eiffel Tower.

BASTILLE & EASTERN PARIS

Deluxe

Hôtel Marceau Bastille

13 rue Jules César, 12th (01.43.43.11.65, www.hotelmarceaubastille.com). Mº Bastille. **Map** p409 M7.

This slick boutique hotel has 55 rooms divided into three different styles: urban, *écolo* (eco-friendly) or *privilège*, some with a balcony. The bar-lounge, overlooking a pleasant, bamboo-planted patio, is surrounded by a gallery that exhibits works by contemporary artists.

Moderate

Auberge Flora

44 bd Richard Lenoir, 11th (01.47.00.52.77, www.aubergeflora.fr). Mº Richard Lenoir. **Map** p407 M6.

Flora Mikula, the hugely talented chef behind Les Olivades and Les Saveurs de Flora, left the smart 8th for the more boho 11th to pursue her dream of creating an urban inn – the Auberge Flora. The 21 rooms are spread across three floors and themed around *bohème* (brocade throws, fringed lampshades, vivid colours), *potager* (kitchen garden; aubergine-coloured walls, vast pumpkin pictures as headboards), and *nature* (stone sinks, mirrors framed with tiny rounds of wood). All the rooms have iPod docks and flatscreen TVs, and the top two categories offer bathrobes too. As you would expect, breakfast is a treat.

Hi Matic

71 rue de Charonne, 11th (01.43.67.56.56, www.hi-matic.net). Mº Charonne. **Map** p407 N7.

The decor at the eco-friendly Hi Matic hotel near Bastille is positively multicoloured: every inch of wall space is either blue, lime, purple or yellow. The rooms are titchy but multitask, so you can whip out your duvet at night and roll it back up in the day. Breakfast is organic, and a masseur will come to your room if you fancy a well-being massage (€85). The hotel is scheduled to close for renovations (and a name change) in late 2015.

Le Pavillon Bastille

65 rue de Lyon, 12th (01.43.43.65.65, www.pavillonbastille.com). Mº Bastille. **Map** p407 M7.

The best thing about this hotel is its location between the Bastille opera and the Gare de Lyon. The 25 rooms may be small, but you're a stone's throw from the Viaduc des Arts.

Standard Design Hotel

29 rue des Taillandiers, 11th (01.48.05.30.97, www.standard-design-hotel-paris.com). Mº Ledru Rollin. **Map** p407 M6.

Hôtel Bourg Tibourg.

ESSENTIAL INFORMATION

NAP OF LUXURY

The Peninsula is a gloriously glam addition to the palace hotel club.

While the Crillon and the Ritz were closed for renovation, a new palace swept on to the scene in August 2014 in a swathe of creamy marble and falling crystal leaves. The **Peninsula Paris** (*see p347*) is all about drama – at the public entrance on avenue Kléber, two snow-white lions flank the steps beneath a contemporary glass awning that takes you straight into the Lobby restaurant. The other, more discreet, entrance is on avenue des Portugais, where the hotel's dark green Rolls-Royce awaits. White-clad bellhops rush to help new arrivals with their luggage, black-clad reception staff stand to attention behind a long black desk, and in the centre is the falling leaf sculpture, with a magnificent black and gilded staircase as its backdrop.

The hotel is the tenth in the world for the Hong Kong chain, and its first in Europe, the result of a long search and painstaking restoration. Built as a hotel in 1908, it became the UNESCO HQ after World War II, then was used by the French Foreign Ministry. The agreement ending the Vietnam War was signed in what is now the clubby Kléber bar.

All of the 200 rooms have the same features, on different scales. These include a private dressing room, an oval bath, a nail-polish dryer and a valet hatch. A mobile tablet lets you control everything from the comfort of your bed, from dimming the lights to ordering room service. A serene spa includes a cascade mosaic behind the 20-metre pool.

With room rates starting at €795 a night, the Peninsula Paris won't suit everyone's holiday budget, but there are other ways to experience its magic. The Lobby offers a lunch menu for €45 beneath a gilded ceiling, or afternoon tea with a pianist tinkling on the grand piano; the opulent LiLi restaurant serves high-end Cantonese cuisine in surroundings inspired by Chinese opera; and on the sixth floor, the glass-ceilinged L'Oiseau Blanc restaurant remembers the tragic French attempt at a first Atlantic crossing by air with a full-scale replica of the plane and pilot suspended above the courtyard. The terrace, with views of just about every Paris monument, is also open for drinks during the summer months.

The Standard Design's black and white interior, with the occasional splash of colour, is a winner with visitors looking for a break from the sometimes rather heavy atmosphere of more traditional hotels. The rooms have all mod cons, the breakfast room awakens the senses with bold stripes, and you can roll into bed after a night out in Bastille's cool bars and restaurants.

Budget

★ Mama Shelter
109 rue de Bagnolet, 20th (01.43.48.48.48, www.mamashelter.com). M° Alexandre Dumas, Maraîchers or Porte de Bagnolet.
The Philippe Starck-designed Mama Shelter is set a stone's throw east of Père Lachaise, and its decor appeals to the young-at-heart with Batman and Incredible Hulk light fittings, dark walls, polished wood and splashes of bright fabrics. Every room comes equipped with an iMac computer, TV, free internet access and a CD and DVD player; and when hunger strikes, there's a decent brasserie with a romantic terrace.

★ Le Quartier Bercy Square
33 bd de Reuilly, 12th (01.44.87.09.09, www.lequartierhotelbs.com). M° Daumesnil or Dugommier. **Map** p407 P9.
You'd never think that lime green and brown stripes would match bold silver and white replica 19th-century wallpaper, but it does at the boutique Quartier Bercy Square in the trendy 12th arrondissement. Rooms are small but inviting, often using coloured light to create atmosphere.

NORTH-EAST PARIS

Moderate

Le 20 Prieuré Hôtel
20 rue du Grand Prieuré, 11th (01.47.00.74.14, www.hotel20prieure.com). M° République. **Map** p402 M5.
This young, funky place benefits from particularly welcoming staff. Each bedroom features an enormous blow-up of a Paris landmark covering the entire wall behind the bed, giving you the illusion that you are sleeping halfway up the Eiffel Tower, or on Bir-Hakeim bridge as the métro speeds by (great for *Last Tango in Paris* fans). Bathrooms are mundane in comparison, but things brighten up again in the breakfast room, with pop art portraits.

Hôtel Gabriel
25 rue du Grand Prieuré, 11th (01.47.00.13.38, www.gabrielparismarais.com). M° République. **Map** p402 M5.
This hotel is a shrine to good-quality kip. The air-conditioned rooms are not short on techno wizardry: there's an iPod station, free Wi-Fi, and the *sine*

Mama Shelter.

qua non of sleep aids, the NightCove device. This white box is easily programmed to emit sounds and light that stimulate melatonin: choose between sleep, nap or wake-up programmes. If you're still feeling run-down, grab a detox massage courtesy of Franco-Japanese masseuse Mitchiko and her colleagues. A partner gym, jogging routes and green taxis complete the healthy vibe. *Photo p357.*

Hôtel Le Général
5-7 rue Rampon, 11th (01.47.00.41.57, www.legeneralhotel.com). M° République. **Map** p402 L5.
A fashionable find near the nightlife action, Le Général was one of Paris's first boutique bargains when it opened a decade ago. It is still notable for its moderate rates and sleek, neutral-toned interior.

Budget

Hôtel Beaumarchais
3 rue Oberkampf, 11th (01.53.36.86.86, www.hotelbeaumarchais.com). M° Filles du Calvaire or Oberkampf. **Map** p409 L5.

Made with

100% locally sourced ingredients

2015 guidebook on sale now
Written by local experts

This contemporary hotel is located in the heart of the Oberkampf area. Its 31 rooms are brightly decorated with colourful walls, bathroom mosaics and wavy headboards; breakfast is served on the tiny garden patio or in your room.

Hôtel Garden Saint-Martin

35 rue Yves Toudic, 10th (01.42.40.17.72, www. hotel-gardensaintmartin-paris.com). M° Jacques Bonsergent. **Map** p402 L4.
The shops, cafés and bars along the Canal St-Martin draw visitors to this hotel, where creature comforts are guaranteed at an excellent rate. No prizes will be won for the ordinary decor, but there is a very pleasant patio garden, and the staff are helpful.

THE LATIN QUARTER & THE 13TH

Expensive

★ Le Petit Paris

214 rue St-Jacques, 5th (01.53.10.29.29, www. hotelpetitparis.com). M° Maubert Mutualité/ RER Luxembourg. **Map** p408 J8.
This Latin Quarter venture is a dynamic exercise in taste and colour. The 20 rooms, designed by Sybille de Margerie, are arranged by era, running from the puce and purple of the medieval rooms to the wildly decadent orange, yellow and pink of the swinging '60s rooms, replete with specially commissioned sensual photographs of Paris monuments. Luxury abounds with finest silks, velvets and taffetas. Some of the rooms have small terraces, and those with baths have a TV you can watch while soaking. An honesty bar in the lounge and ultra-modern jukebox encourage conviviality.

Moderate

★ Five Hôtel

3 rue Flatters, 5th (01.43.31.74.21, www.the fivehotel.com). M° Les Gobelins or Port Royal. **Map** p406 J9.
The rooms in this stunning boutique hotel may be small, but they're all exquisitely designed. Fibre optics built into the walls create the illusion of sleeping under a starry sky, and you can choose from four different fragrances to subtly perfume your room (the hotel is entirely non-smoking). Guests staying in the suite have access to a private garden with a jacuzzi.

Hôtel la Demeure

51 bd St-Marcel, 13th (01.43.37.81.25, www. hotel-paris-lademeure.com). M° Les Gobelins. **Map** p406 K9.
This comfortable, modern hotel has 43 air-conditioned rooms, plus suites with sliding doors to separate sleeping and living space. The wraparound balconies of the corner rooms offer delightful

Hôtel Gabriel. See p355.

views across the city, and bathrooms feature either luxurious tubs or shower heads with elaborate massage possibilities.

Hôtel Résidence Henri IV

50 rue des Bernardins, 5th (01.44.41.31.81, www.residencehenri4.com). M° Cardinal Lemoine. **Map** p406 K7.
This belle-époque-style hotel has a mere eight rooms and five apartments, so guests are assured of the staff's full attention. The four-person apartments come with a handy mini-kitchen featuring a hob, fridge and microwave.

★ Hôtel de la Sorbonne

6 rue Victor-Cousin, 5th (01.43.54.58.08, www. hotelsorbonne.com). M° Cluny La Sorbonne/ RER Luxembourg. **Map** p408 J8.
It's out with the old at this charming, freshly renovated hotel, with bold, designer wallpapers, floral prints, lush fabrics and quotes from French literature woven into the carpets. Rooms are all equipped with iMac computers.

Select Hôtel

1 pl de la Sorbonne, 5th (01.46.34.14.80, www.selecthotel.fr). M° Cluny La Sorbonne. **Map** p408 J8.

Located at the foot of the Sorbonne, this 68-room hotel delivers pure, understated chic with its clever blend of modern art deco features, traditional stone walls and wooden beams. The winter garden and airy common areas have recently been redone in a sleek, contemporary style.

Budget

Familia Hôtel

11 rue des Ecoles, 5th (01.43.54.55.27, www. hotel-paris-familia.com). M° Cardinal Lemoine or Jussieu. **Map** p406 K8.

This old-fashioned Latin Quarter hotel has balconies hung with tumbling plants and walls draped with replica French tapestries. Owner Eric Gaucheron extends a warm welcome, and the 30 rooms have personalised touches such as sepia murals, cherry-wood furniture and stone walls.

▶ *The Gaucherons also own the Hôtel Minerve next door.*

★ Hôtel les Degrés de Notre-Dame

10 rue des Grands-Degrés, 5th (01.55.42.88.88, www.lesdegreshotel.com). M° Maubert-Mutualité or St-Michel. **Map** p406 J7.

On a tiny street across the river from Notre-Dame, this vintage hotel is an absolute gem. Its ten rooms are full of character, with original paintings, antique furniture and exposed beams (nos.47 and 51 have views of the cathedral). It has an adorable restaurant and, a few streets away, two studio apartments that the owner rents out to preferred customers only.

Hôtel Résidence Gobelins

9 rue des Gobelins, 13th (01.47.07.26.90, www.hotelgobelins.com). M° Les Gobelins. **Map** p406 K10.

A tiny lift leads to colourful rooms, all equipped with satellite TV and telephone. The breakfast room overlooks a private garden, and there's free internet use available at the reception.

ST-GERMAIN-DES-PRES & ODEON

Deluxe

★ L'Hôtel

13 rue des Beaux-Arts, 6th (01.44.41.99.00, www.l-hotel.com). M° Mabillon or St-Germain-des-Prés. **Map** p408 H6.

Guests at the sumptuously decorated L'Hôtel these days are more likely to be models and film stars than the starving writers who frequented the place during Oscar Wilde's last days (the playwright died here in November 1900). Under Jacques Garcia's careful restoration, each room has its own special theme: Mistinguett's *chambre* retains its art deco mirror bed, while Oscar's tribute room is appropriately clad in green peacock murals. Don't miss out on dinner in

Artus Hotel.

the fabulously decadent restaurant or on the hotel's glorious underground swimming pool, which you can reserve by the hour for private relaxation.

Expensive

Artus Hotel
34 rue de Buci, 6th (01.43.29.07.20, www.artus hotel.com). M° Mabillon. **Map** p408 H7.
The recently renovated Artus Hotel is the ideal spot for a classic taste of Paris – you couldn't be any closer to the heart of the Left Bank action if you tried. Inside, the look is chic boutique, with 27 individually designed rooms and suites, ranging from cosy to capacious. Staff are eager to help and full of local tips. The cocktail bar, Playtime, is handy for an *apéro* before stepping out into the bright lights of St-Germain.

Hôtel de l'Abbaye Saint-Germain
10 rue Cassette, 6th (01.45.44.38.11, www.hotel abbayeparis.com). M° Rennes or St-Sulpice. **Map** p405 G7.
A monumental entrance opens the way through a courtyard into this tranquil hotel, which was originally part of a convent. Wood panelling, well-stuffed sofas and an open fireplace in the drawing room make for a relaxed atmosphere, but, best of all, there's a surprisingly large garden. The 43 rooms and duplex apartments (some with terrace) are tasteful and luxurious.

★ Relais Saint-Germain
9 carrefour de l'Odéon, 6th (01.44.27.07.97, www.hotel-paris-relais-saint-germain.com). M° Odéon. **Map** p408 H7.
The rustic, wood-beamed ceilings remain intact at the Relais Saint-Germain, a 17th-century hotel bought and renovated by much-acclaimed chef Yves Camdeborde (originator of the *bistronomique* dining trend) and his wife Claudine. Each of the 22 rooms has a different take on eclectic Provençal charm, and the marble bathrooms are positively huge by Paris standards.
▶ *Hotel guests get an added bonus – first dibs on a sought-after seat in Le Comptoir restaurant next door; see p201.*

La Villa
29 rue Jacob, 6th (01.43.26.60.00, www.villa-saintgermain.com). M° St-Germain-des-Prés. **Map** p408 H6.
The charismatic La Villa features cool faux crocodile skin on the bedheads and crinkly taffeta over the taupe-coloured walls. Wonderfully, your room number is projected on to the floor outside your door; very useful for any drunken homecomings.

Villa d'Estrées
17 rue Gît-le-Coeur, 6th (01.55.42.71.11, www. villadestrees.com). M° St-Michel. **Map** p408 J7.

Jewel colours, sumptuous fabrics, stripes and patterns are the hallmarks of this polished boutique hotel; there's nothing at all minimalist about Villa d'Estrées, which was designed by Jacques Garcia. Each of the ten rooms and suites is individually decorated, all with a nod to Empire style and a crisp, slightly masculine feel.

Moderate

Le Clos Médicis
56 rue Monsieur-le-Prince, 6th (01.43.29.10.80, www.dosmedicis.com). M° Odéon/RER Luxembourg. **Map** p408 H8.
More like a stylish, private townhouse than a hotel, Le Clos Médicis is located by the Luxembourg gardens. Decor is refreshingly modern, with rooms done out with taffeta curtains and chenille bedcovers, and antique floor tiles in the bathrooms. The cosy lounge has a working fireplace.

Grand Hôtel de l'Univers
6 rue Grégoire-de-Tours, 6th (01.43.29.37.00, www.hotel-paris-univers.com). M° Odéon. **Map** p408 H7.
Making the most of its 15th-century origins, this hotel features exposed wooden beams, high ceilings, antique furnishings and toile-covered walls. Manuel Canovas fabrics lend a posh touch, but there are also useful services such as a laptop for hire.

Hôtel des Saints-Pères
65 rue des Sts-Pères, 6th (01.45.44.50.00, www. espritfrance.com). M° St-Germain-des-Prés. **Map** p405 G7.
Built in 1658 by one of Louis XIV's architects, this hotel has an enviable Left Bank location near St-Germain-des-Prés' designer boutiques. It boasts a charming garden and a sophisticated, if small, bar. The most coveted room here is no.100, with its fine 17th-century ceiling by painters from the Versailles School; it also has an open bathroom, so you can gaze at scenes from the myth of Leda and the Swan while you scrub.

Hôtel Villa Madame
44 rue Madame, 6th (01.45.48.02.81, www. hotelvillamadameparis.com). M° St-Sulpice. **Map** p408 G7.
This revamped hotel (formerly the Regents) located in a quiet street is a lovely surprise, its courtyard garden used for breakfast in the summer months. Honey- and chocolate-coloured woods mix with warm-toned velvets to make the rooms (all with plasma screens) feel cosy and inviting; some even have small balconies with loungers.

Le Placide
6 rue St-Placide, 6th (01.42.84.34.60, www. leplacidehotel.com). M° Sèvres-Babylone, St-Placide or Vanneau. **Map** p405 G7.

ESSENTIAL INFORMATION

Le Bellechasse.

With only 11 rooms, the Placide is just about as bijou as it gets. White, chrome and neutral tones reign throughout (as does bark- or bamboo-inspired wallpaper), broken only by the occasional funky cushion and throw. Rooms are spacious: all have large bathrooms as well as their own sitting area. The stylish ground-floor duplex has been designed for disabled guests.

MONTPARNASSE
Expensive

★ **Hôtel Aviatic**
105 rue de Vaugirard, 6th (01.53.63.25.50, www.aviatichotel.com). M° Duroc, Montparnasse Bienvenüe or St-Placide. **Map** p405 F8.
This historic hotel has masses of character, from the Empire-style lounge and garden atrium to the bistro-style breakfast room and polished marble floor in the lobby. New decoration throughout, in beautiful steely greys, warm reds, elegant, striped velvets and *toile de Jouy* fabrics, lends an impressive touch of glamour, and the service is consistently with a smile.

Moderate

Hôtel des Académies et des Arts
15 rue de la Grande Chaumière, 6th (01.43.26.66.44, www.hotel-des-academies.

com). M° Notre-Dame des Champs, Raspail or Vavin. **Map** p405 G8.
This small boutique hotel scores highly on style. There are cosy salons, fireplaces and an extensive collection of art books. The 20 immaculate rooms are individually designed around four *ambiances* (Paris Rive Gauche, Comédienne, Man Ray or Rulhmann), and offer wonderful views across the rooftops or down on to the spectacular Jérôme Mesnager mural in the courtyard.

Hôtel Delambre
35 rue Delambre, 14th (01.43.20.66.31, www.delambre-paris-hotel.com). M° Edgar Quinet or Vavin. **Map** p405 G9.
Occupying a narrow slot in a small street between Montparnasse and St-Germain, this hotel was home to Surrealist André Breton in the 1920s. Today it's modern and friendly, with cast-iron details in the 13 rooms and newly installed air-conditioning. The mini suite in the attic, comprising two separate rooms, is particularly pleasant and sleeps up to four.

Budget

Hôtel Istria Saint-Germain
29 rue Campagne-Première, 14th (01.43.20.91.82, www.hotel-istria-paris.com). M° Raspail. **Map** p405 G9.
Behind this unassuming façade is the place where the artistic royalty of Montparnasse's heyday – the likes of Man Ray, Marcel Duchamp and Louis Aragon – once lived. The Istria Saint-Germain has been modernised since then, but it still has plenty of charm, with 26 bright, simply furnished rooms.
▶ *Film fans take note: the artists' studios next door featured in Godard's A Bout de Souffle.*

Solarhôtel
22 rue Boulard, 14th (01.43.21.08.20, www.solar hotel.fr). M° Denfert Rochereau. **Map** p405 G10.
This hotel has managed to strike a great balance between price and sustainability. The simple en suite bedrooms are all equipped with low-energy lamps, and corridors are fitted with sensor-operated lights. Clients and staff are encouraged to recycle, with separate bins for plastics, paper, glass and batteries, and biodegradable waste from the organic breakfast gets turned into compost in a barrel in the garden.

THE 7TH & WESTERN PARIS
Deluxe

★ **Le Bellechasse**
8 rue de Bellechasse, 7th (01.45.50.22.31, www. lebellechasse.com). M° Assemblée Nationale or Solférino/RER Musée d'Orsay. **Map** p405 F6.
A former *hôtel particulier*, the Bellechasse fell into the hands of Christian Lacroix, already responsible for the makeover of the Hôtel du Petit Moulin (*see*

CHIC SLEEP
Maison Martin Margiela's stunning new hotel.

Belgian designer Martin Margiela, the Howard Hughes of fashion, vanished from his brand in 2009, leaving a strictly anonymous collective to continue his avant-garde work. It is this talented crew who are behind the design of Maison Martin Margiela's first couture hotel, the **Hôtel La Maison Champs Elysées** (*see p349*). Beyond the cream stone façade in a quiet street between the Grand Palais and Avenue Montaigne awaits an *Alice Through the Looking Glass* world.

Black cabochons on the cream marble floor seem to have been scattered by the wind as you enter the lobby. To the right is the White Lounge with its grand piano, illusional mirrors, and rows of hanging bulbs and stuffed flamingos in a glass case. To the left is the cigar bar, done out in burnt black wood with leather chairs. Black-clad tailor's dummies line the way to the Table du 8 restaurant and the secret urban garden beyond. The numerous young staff are professional but relaxed, making this hotel feel more like Los Angeles than the Golden Triangle.

The building was once the private club of the 'Centraliens' (graduates of the Ecole Centrale des Arts et Manufactures), and a gilded staircase leads to a series of magnificent Napoleon III salons that can be booked for weddings or other gatherings.

The main building has 11 rooms and six couture suites. The black Curiosity Case suite hosts revolving exhibitions in its floor-to-ceiling glass cabinet; the Gilded Lounge suite features Napoleon III reproduction mouldings on the walls and a library of classic literature just behind the bed. Through a silver corridor that feels like the entrance to an exclusive club are the other 40 'boutique' rooms with fantastic all-white bathrooms and plenty of high-tech minimalist cool – the only downside is working out how to switch off the lights.

p352). It reopened in July 2007, duly transformed into a trendy boutique hotel. It offers 34 splendid – though rather small – rooms.

Expensive

Hôtel La Bourdonnais
111-113 av de La Bourdonnais, 7th (01.47.05.45.42, www.hotellabourdonnais.com). Mº Ecole Militaire. **Map** p404 D7.
The Bourdonnais feels more like a traditional French bourgeois townhouse than a hotel, with 53 bedrooms decorated in rich colours, antiques and Persian rugs. The lobby opens on to a winter garden. The hotel was completely renovated in 2014.

Hôtel Duc de Saint-Simon
14 rue de St-Simon, 7th (01.44.39.20.20, www.hotelducdesaintsimon.com). Mº Rue du Bac. **Map** p405 G6.
A lovely courtyard leads the way into this popular hotel situated on the edge of St-Germain-des-Prés. Of the 34 romantic bedrooms, four have terraces over a closed-off, leafy garden. It's perfect for lovers, though if you can do without a four-poster bed there are more spacious rooms than the Honeymoon Suite.

★ Le Montalembert
3 rue Montalembert, 7th (01.45.49.68.68, www.hotel-montalembert.fr). Mº Rue du Bac. **Map** p405 G6.
Grace Leo-Andrieu's impeccable boutique hotel is a benchmark of quality. It has everything that *mode* maniacs (who flock here for Fashion Week) could want: bathrooms stuffed with Molton Brown toiletries, a set of digital scales and plenty of mirrors with which to keep an eye on their figure. Clattery stairwell lifts are a nice nod to old-fashioned ways in a hotel that is otherwise *tout moderne*.

Moderate

Hôtel Lenox
9 rue de l'Université, 7th (01.42.96.10.95, www.lenoxsaintgermain.com). Mº St-Germain-des-Prés. **Map** p405 G6.
This is a venerable literary and artistic haunt. The art deco-style Lenox Club Bar, open to the public, features comfortable leather club chairs and jazz instruments on the walls. Bedrooms, reached by an astonishing glass lift, have more traditional decor and city views.

Sublim Eiffel
94 bd Garibaldi, 15th (01.40.65.95.95, www.sublimeiffel.com). Mº Sèvres-Lecourbe. **Map** p405 E8.
Some Barry White on your iPod is essential for this luuurve hotel not far from the Eiffel Tower. Carpets printed with paving stones and manhole covers lead to the rooms, where everything has been put in place for steamy nights. It's all to do with the lighting effects, which include a starry Eiffel Tower or street-scene lights above the bed and sparkling LEDs in the showers, filtered by coloured glass doors. Lovers should head for the suite, with its jacuzzi, huge shower, bathrobes and DVDs, and book the Romance package (rose petals on the bed and champagne). All guests get the use of the mini-gym and hammam, and there is a massage room too. The bar adds a bit of jazz to an area in need of some action.

Budget

Hôtel Eiffel Rive Gauche
6 rue du Gros-Caillou, 7th (01.45.51.51.51, www.hotel-eiffel.com). Mº Ecole Militaire. **Map** p404 D6.
The Provençal decor and warm welcome make this a pleasant retreat. For the quintessential Paris view at a bargain price, ask to stay on one of the upper floors: you can see the Eiffel Tower from nine of the 29 rooms. All of them feature Empire-style headboards and modern bathrooms. Outside, there's a tiny, tiled courtyard.

YOUTH ACCOMMODATION

Auberge Internationale des Jeunes
10 rue Trousseau, 11th (01.47.00.62.00, www.aijparis.com). Mº Ledru-Rollin. **Map** p407 N7.
Cleanliness is a high priority at this large, 120-bed hostel close to Bastille. Rooms accommodate between two and four people, and the larger ones have their own shower and toilet. With the lowest hostel rates in central Paris, the place does tend to fill up fast during the summer months, but advance reservations can be made. Although the hostel is open all hours without any curfew, the rooms are closed for cleaning (11am-3pm). Under-35s only.

Auberge Jules-Ferry
8 bd Jules-Ferry, 11th (01.43.57.55.60, www.hihostels.com). Mº République. **Map** p402 M4.
This friendly IYHF hostel has 100 beds in rooms for two to six. There's no curfew, though rooms are closed between 10am and 2pm.

BVJ Paris/Quartier Latin
44 rue des Bernardins, 5th (01.43.29.34.80, www.bvjhotel.com). Mº Maubert Mutualité. **No credit cards**. **Map** p406 J7.
The BVJ hostel has 121 beds in clean but bare modern dorms (accommodating up to ten), and rooms with showers. There's also a TV lounge and a work room.
Other location BVJ Paris/Louvre, 20 rue Jean-Jacques-Rousseau, 1st (01.53.00.90.90).

Generator Paris
9-11 place du Colonel Fabien, 10th (01.70.98.84.00, www.generatorhostels.com). Mº Colonel Fabien. **Map** p403 M3.

Generator Paris.

Hostel life went from grimy to grand with the opening of this 920-bed hostel in February 2015. Housed in an impressive eight-storey building, the Generator styles itself as an affordable but quality place to stay, with an exceptionally lively vibe. What's more, it's located just a short walk from the bustling bars of Belleville and the Canal St-Martin. The hostel offers a métro-themed bar, a large Turkish-style lounge room, and a homely café with a bright conservatory dining area. Dorm rooms (with showers) start at €25 per person and private rooms at €98 (add €30 for a room with a private terrace). Book a room on the fifth floor or above to wake up to a gorgeous view of the city – or splash out on the penthouse suite. Multilingual staff and a travel desk are a bonus.

★ MIJE

6 rue de Fourcy, 4th (01.42.74.23.45, www.mije. com). M° St-Paul. **No credit cards**. Map p409 L6. MIJE runs three 17th-century Marais residences – one is a former convent – that provide the most attractive hostel sleeps in Paris. Its plain, clean rooms have snow-white sheets and sleep up to eight people; all have a shower and basin.
Other locations (same phone) 12 rue des Barres, 4th; 11 rue du Fauconnier, 4th.

St Christopher's Inn

159 rue de Crimée, 19th (01.40.34.34.40, www. st-christophers.co.uk/paris-hostels). M° Crimée, Jaurès, Laumière or Stanlingrad. Map p403 N1.
If you don't mind bunking up with others, you could try this branch of the youth hostel chain on the Canal de l'Ourcq. The decor in the bedrooms has a sailor's cabin feel, with round mirrors, bubble-pattern wallpaper and 1950s-inspired cabin furniture. The hostel comes into its own in its bar Belushi's, where the backpack brigade are joined by Parisians bent on taking advantage of the canal setting. *Photos p364.*
► *The company has recently opened a second, more central hostel right opposite Gare du Nord (same website as above).*

BED & BREAKFAST

Alcove & Agapes

(01.44.85.06.05, www.bed-and-breakfast-in-paris.com).
This B&B booking service offers over 100 *chambres d'hôtes* (€80-€320 for a double, including breakfast; three-, four- and five-bed rooms available too) with hosts who range from artists to grannies. Extras can include anything from dinner to cooking classes.

Good Morning Paris

43 rue Lacépède, 5th (01.47.07.28.29,
www.goodmorningparis.fr).
This company has 100 rooms in the city. Prices range from €89 to €134 for doubles, and from €121 for an apartment that sleeps two to four people. There's a minimum stay of two nights.

APART-HOTELS & FLAT RENTAL

A deposit is usually payable on arrival. Small ads for private short-term lets run in fortnightly anglophone mag *FUSAC* (www.fusac.fr); or check out www.frenchconnections.co.uk, which has a selection of furnished apartments for four or more people, and www.apartmentservice.com.

Citadines Apart'hotel

01.41.05.79.05, www.citadines.com.
The 16 modern Citadines complexes across Paris tend to attract a mainly business clientele. Room sizes vary from slightly cramped studios to quite spacious two-bedroom apartments.

Paris Address

01.43.20.91.57, www.parisaddress.com.
Paris Address has more than 280 apartments for rent in the heart of Paris and offers a friendly reception service – it makes a great alternative to staying in a hotel.

Paris Appartements Services

20 rue Bachaumont, 2nd (01.40.28.01.28, www.
paris-apts.com). M° Sentier. **Open** 9am-6pm
Mon-Fri. *Key pick-up* 24hrs.
This organisation specialises in short-term rentals, offering furnished studios and one-bedroom flats in the first to fourth arrondissements.

Swell Apartments

11 rue Duhesme, 18th (+44 (0)7725 056 421,
www.swell-apartments.co.uk). M° Lamarck
Caulincourt. **Map** p401 H1.
Don't be put off by the rather tatty entrance; this flat located on the north side of Montmartre (sleeping two) is delightful inside. The bedroom, with blue and white walls, has a crystal chandelier and marble fireplace.

St Christopher's Inn. *See p363.*

ESSENTIAL INFORMATION

Getting Around

ARRIVING & LEAVING

By air

Roissy-Charles-de-Gaulle airport
39.50, www.adp.fr.
Most international flights use Roissy-Charles-de-Gaulle airport, which is situated 30km (19 miles) north-east of Paris. Its three main terminals are some way apart, so check which one you need for your return flight. The terminals are linked by the free CDGVAL driverless train.

The **RER B** (RATP helpline, 36.58, www.transilien.com) is the quickest way to central Paris (about 25mins to Gare du Nord; 30mins to RER Châtelet-Les Halles; €9.75 single). RER trains run every 10-15mins, 4.56am-11.56pm daily from the airport to Paris.

Air France buses (08.92.35.08.20, www.cars-airfrance. com; €15 single, €24 return, €7.50 under-11s, free under-2s) leave every 20-30mins, 6am-11pm daily, from terminals, and stop at porte Maillot and place Charles-de-Gaulle (35-50min trip). Air France buses also run to Gare Montparnasse and Gare de Lyon (€16.50 single, €27 return, €8 under-11s, free under-2s) every 30mins (45-60min trip), 6am-10pm daily; there's a shuttle bus between Roissy and Orly (€19 single, €9.50 under-11s, free under-2s) every 30mins, 5.55am-10.30pm daily from Roissy; 6.30am-10.30pm Mon-Fri, 7am-10.30pm Sat, Sun from Orly.

The **RATP RoissyBus** (32.46, www.ratp.fr; €11.60) runs every 15-30mins, 5.45am-11pm daily, between the airport and the corner of rue Scribe/rue Auber (60mins); buy tickets on the bus.

Paris Airports Service is a door-to-door minibus service between airports and hotels. The more passengers on board, the less each one pays. Roissy prices go from €28 for one person to €104 for eight people, 6am-7pm (minimum €43, 4-6am, 7-10pm); book on 01.55.98.10.80, www. parisairportservice.com.

A **taxi** to central Paris takes 30-60mins depending on traffic conditions. Expect to pay approx €40-€50, plus €1 for each item of luggage.

Orly airport
39.50, www.adp.fr.
Domestic and international flights use Orly, 18km (11 miles) south of the city. It has two terminals: Orly-Sud (mainly international) and Orly-Ouest (mainly domestic).

Air France buses (08.92.35.08.20, www.cars-airfrance.com; €11.50 single, €18.50 return, €5.50 under-11s, free under-2s) leave both terminals every 20-30mins, 6am-11.40pm daily, and stop at Invalides and Montparnasse (30-45mins).

The **RATP Orlybus** (32.46, www.ratp.fr; €8.25) runs between the airport and Denfert-Rochereau every 15mins, 5.35am-11.40pm daily (30min trip); buy tickets on the bus.

The high-speed **Orlyval** (www.orlyval.fr) shuttle train runs every 4-7mins (6am-11pm daily) to RER B station Antony (€12.85 to Châtelet-les-Halles); getting into central Paris takes about 35mins.

You could also catch the **Paris par le train bus** (€6.45, www. parisparletrain.fr) to Pont de Rungis, where you can take the RER C into central Paris. Buses run every 15mins, 4.40am-1am daily from Orly-Sud; 35min trip.

Orly prices for the **Paris Airports Service** door-to-door facility (*see left*) are the same as for Roissy-Charles-de-Gaulle.

A **taxi** into town takes 20-40mins and costs €16-€26, plus €1 for each piece of luggage.

Paris Beauvais airport
08.92.68.20.66, www. aeroportbeauvais.com. Beauvais, 70km (44 miles) from Paris, is served by budget airlines such as **Ryanair** (08.92.78.02.10, www.ryanair.com). Buses (€17) leave for Porte Maillot 20mins after each arrival; buses the other way leave 3hrs before each departure. Get tickets from arrivals lounge or buy them on the bus.

Major airlines

Aer Lingus
*08.21.23.02.67,
www.aerlingus.com.*

Air France
36.54, www.airfrance.fr.

American Airlines
*08.26.46.09.50, www.
americanairlines.fr.*

British Airways
*08.25.82.54.00,
www.britishairways.fr.*

Continental
*01.71.23.03.35,
www.continental.com.*

Easyjet
08.20.42.03.15, www.easyjet.com.

KLM & NorthWest *08.92.70.26.08,
www.klm.com.*

United
08.10.72.72.72, www.united.fr.

By car

Options for crossing the Channel with a car include: **Eurotunnel** (08.10.63.03.04, www.eurotunnel. com); **Brittany Ferries** (08.25.82.88.28, www.brittanyferries. com); **P&O Ferries** (03.66.74.03.25, www.poferries.com); and **My Ferry Link** (08.11.65.47.65, www.myferrylink.com).

Shared journeys

Bla Bla Car
www.covoiturage.fr.
Find your ride online and book via the website. For example, a Paris-Lyon trip will cost approx €30 per traveller.

By coach

International coach services will deposit you at the Gare Routière Internationale Paris-Gallieni at Porte de Bagnolet, 20th. For reservations (in English), call **Eurolines** on 08.92.89.90.91 (€0.34 per min) or 01.41.86.24.21 from abroad, or visit www.eurolines.fr. Fares start from as little as £19 for a single ticket from London to Paris.

By rail

From London, Eurostar services (UK: 0044.3432.186186, www. eurostar.com) to Paris depart from the dedicated terminal at St Pancras International. Thanks to the new high-speed track, the journey from London to Paris now takes 2hrs 15mins direct, slightly longer for trains stopping at Ashford and Lille. Eurostar services from the new terminal at Ebbsfleet International,

ESSENTIAL INFORMATION

near junction 2 of the M25, take 2hrs 5mins direct. Fares start at £72 for a London-Paris return ticket. Passengers must check in at least 30mins before departure time. Trains arrive at Gare du Nord (www.sncf.fr), with easy access to public transport and taxi ranks.

Cycles can be taken as hand luggage if they are dismantled and carried in a bike bag. You can also check them in at the EuroDespatch depot at St Pancras (Esprit Parcel Service, 0844 822 5822) or the Geoparts depot at Gare du Nord (01.55.31.58.33). Check-in should be done at least 24 hours ahead; a Eurostar ticket must be shown. The service costs £25/€29.

MAPS

Free maps of the métro, bus and RER systems are available at airports and métro stations. Other brochures from métro stations are *Paris Visite – Le Guide*, with details of transport tickets and a small map, and *Plan de Paris*, a fold-out one showing Noctambus night bus lines. A Paris street map (Plan de Paris) can be bought from newsagents. The blue *Paris Pratique* is clear and compact.

PUBLIC TRANSPORT

Almost all of the Paris public transport system is run by the **RATP** (Régie Autonome des Transports Parisiens; 32.46, www. ratp.fr): the bus, métro (underground) and suburban tram routes, as well as lines A and B of the RER (Réseau Express Régional) suburban express railway, which connects with the métro within the city centre. National rail operator **SNCF** (36.35, www. sncf.com) runs RER lines C, D and E, and serves the Paris suburbs (Banlieue), as well as French regions and international destinations (Grandes Lignes).

Fares & tickets

Paris and suburbs are divided into six travel zones; zones 1 and 2 cover the centre. RATP tickets and passes are valid on the métro, bus and RER. Tickets and *carnets* can be bought at métro stations, tourist offices and *tabacs* (tobacconists); single tickets can also be bought on buses. Hold on to your ticket in case of spot checks; you'll also need it to exit RER stations.

● A single ticket T+ costs €1.80, but it's more economical to buy a *carnet* of ten for €14.10.

● A one-day Mobilis pass costs from €7 for zones 1 and 2 to €16.60 for zones 1-5.

● A one-day Paris Visite pass for zones 1-3 is €11.15; a five-day pass is €35.70, with discounts on some attractions.

● One-week or one-month passes (passport photo needed) offer unlimited travel in the relevant zones; if bought in zones 1 or 2, each is delivered as a Navigo swipe card. A *forfait mensuel* (monthly pass valid from the first day of the month) for zones 1 and 2 costs €70; a weekly *forfait hebdomadaire* (weekly pass valid Mon-Sun inclusive) for zones 1 and 2 costs €21.25 and is better value than Paris Visite passes.

Métro & RER

The Paris **métro** is the fastest and cheapest way of getting around the city. Trains run 5.30am-12.40am Mon-Thur, 5.30am-1.30am Fri-Sun. Individual lines are numbered, with each direction named after the last stop. Follow the orange *Correspondance* to change lines. Be prepared for the fact that some interchanges, such as Châtelet-Les-Halles, Montparnasse-Bienvenüe and République, involve long walks. The exit (*Sortie*) is indicated in blue. The driverless line 14 runs from Gare St-Lazare to Olympiades. Pickpockets and bag-snatchers are rife on the network – pay special attention as the doors are closing.

The five **RER** lines (A, B, C, D and E) run 5.30am-1am daily through Paris and into the suburbs. Within Paris, the RER is useful for faster journeys – Châtelet-Les-Halles to Gare du Nord is one stop on the RER, and six on the métro. Métro tickets are valid for RER journeys within zones 1 and 2.

Buses

Buses run 6.30am-8.30pm, with some routes continuing until 12.30am, Mon-Sat; limited services operate on selected lines on Sunday and public holidays. You can use a métro ticket, a ticket bought from the driver (€2) or a travel pass to travel on the bus. Tickets should be punched in the machine next to the driver; passes should be shown to the driver. When you want to get off, press the red request button.

Night buses

After the métro and normal buses stop running, the only public

transport – apart from taxis – are the 47 **Noctilien** lines, running between place du Châtelet and the suburbs (hourly 12.30am-5.30am Mon-Thur; half-hourly 1am-5.35am Fri, Sat); look out for the Noctilien logo on bus stops or the N in front of the route number. A ticket costs €1.70 (€2 from the driver); travel passes are valid.

River transport

Batobus (08.25.05.01.01, *www.batobus.com*).
River buses stop every 20-25mins at: Eiffel Tower, Musée d'Orsay, St-Germain-des-Prés (quai Malaquais), Notre-Dame, Jardin des Plantes, Hôtel de Ville, Louvre, Champs-Elysées (Pont Alexandre III). They run early Sept-late Mar 10am-5pm Mon-Thur; 10am-7pm Fri-Sun; late Mar-late Apr 10am-7pm Mon-Thur; 10am-9.30pm Fri-Sun; late Apr-early Sept 10am-9.30pm daily. A one-day pass is €16 (€7, €10 reductions); two-day pass €19 (€10, €13 reductions); annual pass €60 (€38 reductions). Tickets can be bought at Batobus stops, online at www.batobus.com, RATP ticket offices and the Office de Tourisme (*see p378*).

Trams

Three modern tram lines (www.ratp. fr) operate in the suburbs. They connect with the métro and RER; fares are the same as for buses. The network is set to grow to seven lines and nearly 100km of track by 2016, making it the third largest in Europe in terms of passenger numbers.

RAIL TRAVEL

Suburban destinations are served by the RER. Other locations farther from the city are served by the SNCF railway; the TGV high-speed train has slashed journey times and is being extended to all the main regions. There are few long-distance bus services. Tickets can be bought at any SNCF station (not just the one from which you'll travel), SNCF shops and travel agents. If you reserve online or by phone, you can pay and pick up your tickets from the station or have them sent to your home. SNCF automatic machines (*billeterie automatique*) only work with French credit/debit cards. Regular trains have full-rate White (peak) and cheaper Blue (off-peak) periods. You can save on TGV fares by buying special cards. The Carte 12/25 gives under-26s a 25-50 per cent reduction; even without it, under-26s are entitled to 25 per cent off. Buy tickets in advance to secure the cheaper fare. Before you board any train, stamp your ticket in the orange *composteur* machines located on the platforms, or you might have to pay a hefty fine. *See also p374* **Lost Property**.

SNCF reservations & tickets

National reservations & information 36.35 (€0.34 per min), www.sncf. com. **Open** 7am-10pm daily.

Mainline stations

Gare d'Austerlitz
Central and south-west France and Spain.

Gare de l'Est
Alsace, Champagne and southern Germany.

Gare de Lyon
Burgundy, the Alps, Provence and Italy.

Gare Montparnasse
West France, Brittany, Bordeaux, the south-west.

Gare du Nord
Eurostar, Channel ports, north-east France, Belgium and the Netherlands.

Gare St-Lazare
Normandy.

TAXIS

Paris taxi drivers are not known for their flawless knowledge of the Paris street map; if you have a preferred route, say so. Taxis can also be hard to find, especially at rush hour or early in the morning. Your best bet is to find a taxi rank (station de taxis, marked with a blue sign) on major roads, crossroads and at stations. A white light on a taxi's roof indicates the car is free; an orange light means the cab is busy. Rates (low to high) are based on zone and time of day: **A** (10am-5pm Mon-Sat central Paris); **B** (5pm-10am Mon-Sat, 7am-midnight Sun central Paris; 7am-7pm Mon-Sat inner suburbs and airports); **C** (midnight-7am Sun central Paris; 7pm-7am Mon-Sat, all day Sun inner suburbs and airports; all times outer suburbs). Most journeys in central Paris cost €7-€15; there's a minimum charge of €7, plus €1 for more than one piece of luggage over 5kg or bulky objects, and a surcharge from

mainline stations. Most drivers will not take more than three people, but they should take a couple and two children. There is a charge of €3 for a fourth adult passenger.

Don't feel obliged to tip, although rounding up to the nearest euro is polite. Taxis are not allowed to refuse rides if they deem them too short and can only refuse to take you in a certain direction during their last half-hour of service (both rules are often ignored). If you want a receipt, ask for *un reçu* or *la note*. Complaints should be made to the **Bureau des Taxis et des Transports Publics**, 36 rue des Morillons, 75732 Paris Cedex 15 (01.55.76.20.05). *See also p374* **Lost Property**.

Phone cabs

These firms take phone bookings 24/7; you also pay for the time it takes your taxi to reach you. If you wish to pay by credit card, mention this when you order.

Alpha
*01.45.85.85.85,
www.alphataxis.fr.*

G7
36.07, www.taxis-g7.fr.

Taxis Bleus
36.09, www.taxis-bleus.com.

DRIVING

If you bring your car to France, you must bring its registration and insurance documents.

As you come into Paris, you will meet the Périphérique, the giant ring road that carries traffic into, out of and around the city. Intersections, leading on to other main roads, are called *portes* (gates). Driving on the Périphérique is not as hair-raising as it might look, though it's often congested. Some hotels have parking spaces that are payable by the hour or day.

In peak holiday periods, the organisation Bison Futé hands out brochures at motorway *péages* (toll gates), suggesting less crowded routes. French roads are categorised as Autoroutes (motorways, with an 'A' in front of the number), Routes Nationales (national 'N' roads), Routes Départementales (local, 'D' roads) and rural Routes Communales ('C' roads). Autoroutes are toll roads; some sections, including most of the area around Paris, are free.

Infotrafic *08.92.70.77.66 (€0.34 per minute), www.infotrafic.fr.*

Bison Futé
08.00.10.02.00, www.bison-fute. equipement.gouv.fr.

Breakdown services

Beaking down in France can be an expensive business, so it's advisable to take out additional breakdown insurance cover before you travel, for example with a company such as the **AA** (www.theaa.com) or **Green Flag** (www.greenflag.com). **Dan Dépann Auto** (08.00.25.10.00, www. dandepann.fr) operates a 24-hour breakdown service in the Paris area.

Driving tips

● At junctions where no signposts indicate right of way, the car coming from the right has priority. Many roundabouts now give priority to those on the roundabout. If this is not indicated (by road markings or a sign with the message *Vous n'avez pas la priorité*), priority is for those coming from the right.

● Drivers and all passengers must wear seat belts.

● Under-tens are not allowed to travel in the front of a car, except in baby seats facing backwards.

● You should not stop on an open road; you must pull off to the side.

● When drivers are flashing their lights at you, this often means they will not slow down and are warning you to keep out of the way.

Parking

If you park illegally, you risk getting your car clamped or towed away. It's forbidden to park in zones marked for deliveries (*livraisons*) or taxis. Parking meters have now been replaced by *horodateurs*, pay-and-display machines, which take a special card (*carte de stationnement* at €15 or €40, available from *tabacs*). Many also now accept payment by credit/debit cards. Parking is often free at weekends, after 7pm and in August.

Car hire

To hire a car, you must be 25 or over and have held a licence for at least a year. Some agencies accept drivers aged 21-24, but a supplement is usually payable. Take your licence and passport with you. Bargain firms may have an extremely high charge for damage: make sure you read the small print.

Hire companies

Ada
www.ada.fr.

Avis
08.21.23.07.60, www.avis.fr.

Budget
08.25.00.35.64, www.budget.fr.

EasyCar *www.easycar.com.*

Europcar
08.25.35.83.58, www.europcar.fr.

Hertz
01.55.31.93.21, www.hertz.fr.

Rent-a-Car
08.91.70.02.00, www.rentacar.fr.

Chauffeur-driven cars

Chauffeur Services Paris
(01.80.40.00.86, www.csparis.com). **Open** 24hrs daily. **Prices** from €105 airport transfer; €240 for 4 hours.

CYCLING

In 2007, the mayor launched a municipal bike hire scheme, **Vélib** (www.velib.paris.fr), which has become a model for similar projects around the world. There are now more than 20,000 bicycles available 24 hours a day, at nearly 1,800 'stations' across the city. Just swipe your travel card to release the bikes from their stands. The *mairie* actively promotes cycling in the city and the Vélib scheme is complemented by the 400km (250 miles) of bike lanes snaking their way around Paris.

The Itinéraires Paris-Piétons-Vélos-Rollers – scenic strips of the city that are closed to cars on Sundays and holidays – continue to multiply; www.paris.fr can provide an up-to-date list of routes and a downloadable map of cycle lanes. A free Paris à Vélo map can be picked up at any *mairie* or from bike shops. Cycle lanes (pistes cyclables) run mostly N–S and E–W. N–S routes include rue de Rennes, av d'Italie, bd Sébastopol and av Marceau. E–W routes take in the rue de Rivoli, bd St-Germain, bd St-Jacques and av Daumesnil. You could be fined if you don't use them. Cyclists are also entitled to use certain bus lanes (especially the new ones, set off by a strip of kerb stones); look out for traffic signs with a bike symbol. Don't let the locals' blasé attitude to helmets and lights convince you it's not worth using them.

Cycles & scooters for hire

Bike insurance may not cover theft; check when you book.

Freescoot
63 quai de la Tournelle, 5th (01.44.07.06.72, www.freescoot.fr). Mº Maubert Mutualité or St-Michel. **Open** 9am-1pm, 2-7pm daily; closed Sun Oct-mid May. Hires out bicycles (from €15 per day) and scooters (from €45 per day).

Left Bank Scooters
(06.82.70.13.82, www.leftbankscooters.com).
This company hires out vintage-style Vespas (from €70 per day), with delivery and collection from your apartment or hotel. Various tours also available.

WALKING

Walking is easily the best way to explore Paris; just remember to remain vigilant at all times. Brits should be aware that traffic will be coming from the 'wrong' direction and that zebra crossings mean very little. By law, drivers are only obliged to stop at a red traffic light – even then, many will take a calculated risk.

TOURS

Bus tours

The following companies offer hop-on, hop-off bus tours of the city with commentary available in a variety of languages.

Les Cars Rouges
01.53.95.39.53, www.carsrouges.com. **Tickets** €31; €15 4-11s. Tours leave every 7-15mins and the round trip takes 2hrs 15mins. You can hop on and off along the way and tickets are valid for two consecutive days.

Paris City Vision
01.44.55.61.00, www.pariscityvision.com. **Tickets** €31; €16 4-11s. Choose beetween four different Open Tour routes around Paris.

Bike tours

Fat Tire Bike Tours
01.56.58.10.54, http://fattirebiketours.com/paris. **Tickets** €30; €28 reductions.
Offers various bike tours of the city, with the main tour starting at the south leg of the Eiffel Tower. Tours run daily at 11am, with a 3pm tour added in summer. Check online for more details.

Boat tours

Cruising along the River Seine is a delightful way to see Paris. The companies below all run a variety of tours on the river. Most boats depart from the quays in the 7th and 8th arrondissements, and proceed to go on a circuit around the islands. Check online for full tour details and times: many companies operate more than one type of tour, though the basic tour usually runs every 20-60mins in summer. Rates are for one day only, though other tickets may be available (and there are sometimes reductions for booking online in advance).

Bateaux-Mouches
Pont de l'Alma, 8th (01.42.25.96.10, www.bateaux-mouches.fr). Mº Alma-Marceau. **Tickets** €12.50; €5.50 reductions; free under-4s.

Bateaux Parisiens
Port de la Bourdonnais, 7th (www.bateauxparisiens.com). RER Champ de Mars. **Tickets** €13; €5 reductions; free under-3s.

Batobus Tour Eiffel
Various stops (08.25.05.01.01, www.batobus.com). **Tickets** €15; €7 reductions.

Vedettes de Paris
Port de Suffren, 7th (01.44.18.19.50, www.vedettesdeparis.com). Mº Bir-Hakeim. **Tickets** €13; €5 reductions; free under-4s.

Vedettes du Pont-Neuf
Sq du Vert-Galant, 1st (01.46.33.98.38, www.vedettesdupontneuf.com). Mº Pont-Neuf. **Tickets** €13; €7 under-12s; free under-4s.

Walking tours

Paris Walking Tours
01.48.09.21.40, www.paris-walks.com. **Tickets** €12; €8-€10 reductions.
Led by long-term resident expats, these daily two-hour walking tours (times vary by season) explore various city locales.

Visites Spectacles
01.48.58.37.12, www.visites-spectacles.com. **Tickets** €16-€26; €18-€22.50 reductions; free under-4s.
Combining historical tours with interactive theatre performances, Visites Spectacles' themed treats range from the Spirit of Montmartre to Eiffel Tower Romance.

Resources A-Z

ADDRESSES

Paris *arrondissements* are indicated by the last two digits of the postal code: 75002 denotes the second, 75015 the 15th, and so on. The 16th arrondissement is divided into two sectors, 75016 and 75116. Some business addresses have a more detailed postcode, followed by a Cedex number, which indicates the arrondissement; *bis* or *ter* is the equivalent of 'b' or 'c' after a building number.

AGE RESTRICTIONS

For heterosexuals and homosexuals, the age of consent is 15. You must be 18 years old to drive, and to consume alcohol in a public place. You must be 16 years old to buy cigarettes.

ATTITUDE & ETIQUETTE

Parisians take manners seriously and are generally more courteous than their reputation may have led you to believe. If someone brushes you accidentally when passing, they will more often than not say '*pardon*'; you can do likewise, or say '*c'est pas grave*' (don't worry). In shops it is normal to greet the assistant with a '*bonjour madame*' or '*bonjour monsieur*' when you enter, and say '*au revoir*' when you leave. The business of '*tu*' and '*vous*' can be tricky for English speakers. Strangers, people significantly older than you and professional contacts should be addressed with the respectful '*vous*'; friends, relatives, children and pets as '*tu*'. When among themselves, young people will often launch straight in with '*tu*'.

BUSINESS

The best first stop for initiating business is the CCIP (Chambre de Commerce et d'Industrie de Paris; *see p370*). Banks can refer you to lawyers, accountants and tax consultants.

Conventions & conferences

CNIT *2 pl de la Défense, BP 321, 92053 Paris La Défense (01.40.68.22.22, www.viparis.com).* M°/RER Grande Arche de La Défense. Mainly computer fairs.
Palais des Congrès *2 pl de la Porte-Maillot, 17th (01.40.68.22.22, www.viparis.com).* M° Porte-Maillot.
Parc des Expositions de Paris-Nord Villepinte *Zac Paris Nord 2, 93420 Villepinte (01.40.68.22.22, www.viparis.com).* RER Parc des Expositions.
Trade fair centre near Roissy.
Paris-Expo *1 pl de la Porte de Versailles, 15th (01.40.68.22.22, www.paris-expoportedeversailles. com).* M° Porte de Versailles.
The city's biggest expo centre.

Courier services

ATV *08.11.65.56.05, www. coursiers.com.* **Open** 24hrs daily.
Bike or van messengers 24/7. Rates rise after 8pm and at weekends.
Chronopost *08.25.80.18.01, 09.69.39.13.91, www.chronopost.fr.* **Open** 9am-8pm Mon-Fri; 9am-1pm Sat (in post offices).
This overnight delivery offshoot of the state-run post office is the most widely used service for parcels.
UPS *08.21.23.38.77, www.ups. com.* **Open** 8am-7pm Mon-Fri; 8am-1pm Sat.
International courier services.

Secretarial services

SPRING *57-59 bd Malesherbes, 8th (01.77.69.12.12, www.spring france.com).* M° St-Augustin.
Open 8am-8pm Mon-Fri.
Employment agency specialising in bilingual secretaries and staff.
Other locations throughout the city.

Translators & interpreters

Documents such as birth certificates, loan applications and so on must be translated by certified legal translators, listed at the **CCIP** (*see p370*) or embassies. For business translations there are dozens of reliable independents.

Association des Anciens Elèves de l'Esit *01.44.05.41.46, www. aaeesit.com.* **Phone enquiries** 8am-8pm Mon-Fri; 8am-6pm Sat.
Booking (via email only) at mdttraducteurs@aaeesit.com.
A translation and interpreting co-operative whose 900 members are graduates of the Ecole Supérieure d'Interprètes et de Traducteurs.
International Corporate Communication *3 rue des Batignolles, 17th (01.43.87.29.29, www.iccparis.com).* M° Place de Clichy. **Open** 9am-6pm Mon-Fri.
Translators of financial and corporate documents, plus simultaneous translation.

Useful organisations

American Chamber of Commerce *77 rue de Miromesnil, 8th (01.56.43.45.67, www.amcham france.org).* M° Miromesnil.
Closed to the public, calls only.
British Embassy Commercial Library *35 rue du Fbg-St-Honoré, 8th (01.44.51.31.00, www.ukin france.fco.gov.uk).* M° Concorde.
Open by appointment 9.30am-1pm, 2.30-6pm Mon-Fri.
Stocks trade directories, and assists British companies that wish to develop or set up in France.

ESSENTIAL INFORMATION

CCIP (Chambre de Commerce et d'Industrie de Paris) *27 av de Friedland, 8th (08.20.01.21.12, www.ccip.fr). M° Charles de Gaulle Etoile.* **Open** 8.30am-6.30pm Mon-Fri.

A variety of services for people doing business in France, and very useful for small businesses. Pick up the free booklet *Discovering the Chamber of Commerce* from its head office.

Other locations Bourse du Commerce, 2 rue de Viarmes, 1st (has a free library and bookshop); 2 rue Adolphe-Jullien, 1st (support for businesses wishing to export goods and services to France).

US Commercial Service *Postal address: US Embassy, 2 av Gabriel, 8th. Visit: US Commercial Service, NEO Building, 14 bd Haussmann, 9th (01.43.12.71.28, www.buyusa. gov/france). M° Richelieu Drouot.* **Open** by appointment 9am-6pm Mon-Fri.

Helps American companies looking to trade in France.

CONSUMER

In the event of a serious problem, try one of the following:

Direction Départementale de la Concurrence, de la Consommation et de la Répression des Fraudes *8 rue Froissart, 3rd (01.40.27.16.00, www.economie.gouv.fr/dgccrf). M° St-Sébastien Froissart.* **Open** 9am-noon, 2-5pm Mon-Fri.

Come here to file a consumer complaint concerning problems with Paris-based businesses.

Institut National de la Consommation *80 rue Lecourbe, 15th (01.45.66.20.20, www.conso. net). M° Sèvres Lecourbe.* **Open** by phone 9am-12.30pm, 1.30-4.30pm Mon-Fri; recorded information at other times.

Deals with questions on housing, consumer, regulatory and administrative issues.

CUSTOMS

Customs declarations are not usually necessary if you arrive from another EU country and are carrying legal goods for personal use. The amounts given below are a guide only: if you come close to the maximums in several categories, you may still have to explain your personal habits to customs.

● 1,000 cigarettes, 400 small cigars, 200 cigars or 1kg loose tobacco.

● 10 litres of spirits (more than 22% alcohol), 90 litres of wine (of which 60 litres sparkling wine) or 110 litres of beer.

Coming from a non-EU country, you can bring:
● 200 cigarettes, 100 small cigars, 50 cigars or 250g tobacco.
● 1 litre of spirits (more than 22% alcohol; 2 litres if less than 22% alcohol), 4 litres of wine or 16 litres of beer.
● 50g (1.76oz) of perfume.

Tax refunds

Non-EU residents can claim a refund or *détaxe* (around 12 per cent) on VAT if they spend over €175 in any one day in one shop and if they live outside the EU for more than six months in the year. At the shop concerned ask for a *bordereau de vente à l'exportation*, and when you leave France have it stamped by customs. Then send the stamped form back to the shop. *Détaxe* does not cover food, drink, antiques, services or works of art.

Customs Information Centre *(08.11.20.44.44, www.douane. gouv.fr).* **Open** 8.30am-6.30pm Mon-Fri.

DISABLED

It's always wise to check up on a site's accessibility and provision for disabled access before you visit. There is information (in French) on the Secrétaire d'Etat aux Personnes Handicapées website: www. handicap.gouv.fr, call 01.40.56.60.00.

Association des Paralysés de France *13 pl de Rungis, 13th (01.53.80.92.97, www.apf.asso.fr). M° Place d'Italie.* **Open** 9am-12.30pm, 1.30-5.30pm Mon-Thur; 9am-12.30pm, 1.30-5pm Fri. Publishes *Guide 98 Musées, Cinémas* (€3.81) listing accessible museums and cinemas, and also has a guide to restaurants and sights.

Fédération APAJH (Association pour Adultes et Jeunes Handicapés) *29th Floor, Tour Montparnasse, 33 av du Maine, 15th (01.44.10.23.40, www.apajh. org). M° Montparnasse Bienvenüe.* Advice for disabled people living in France.

Maison Départementale des Personnes Handicapées de Paris *69 rue de la Victoire, 9th (08.05.80.09.09, 01.53.32.39.39, www.mdph.fr).* **Open** 9am-4pm Mon-Fri.

Advice available in French to disabled persons living in or visiting Paris. The Office de Tourisme website (www.parisinfo.com) also provides plenty of useful information for disabled visitors.

Getting around

The métro and buses are not wheelchair-accessible, with the exception of métro line 14 (Méteor), stations Barbès-Rochechouard (line 2) and Esplanade de la Défense (line 1), and bus lines 20, 21, 22, 24, 26, 27, 28, 29, 30, 31, 32, 38, 39, 42, 43, 46, 47, 48, 52, 53, 54, 56, 57, 58, 60, 61, 62, 63, 64, 65, 66, 67, 68, 69, 70, 72, 73, 74, 75, 76, 80, 81, 82, 83, 84, 85, 86, 87, 88, 89, 91, 92, 93, 94, 95, 96 and PC (Petite Ceinture) 1, 2 and 3. Forward seats on buses are intended for people with poor mobility. RER lines A, B, C, D and some SNCF trains are wheelchair-accessible in parts. For a full list of wheelchair-accessible stations: 09.70.81.83.85, www. infomobi.com. All Paris taxis are obliged by law to take passengers in wheelchairs.

DRUGS

French police have the power to stop and search anyone. It's wise to keep prescription drugs in their original containers and, if possible, to carry copies of the original prescriptions. If you're caught in possession of illegal drugs, you can expect a prison sentence and/or a fine. *See also p371* Health.

ELECTRICITY

Electricity in France runs on 220V. Visitors with British 240V appliances can change the plug or use an adaptor (*adaptateur*). For US 110V appliances, you'll need to use a transformer (*transformateur*), available at BHV, Fnac and Darty.

EMBASSIES & CONSULATES

For a full list of embassies and consulates, see the *Pages Jaunes* (www.pagesjaunes.fr) under the 'Ambassades et Consulats' section. Consular services (passports, etc) are for citizens of that country only.

Australian Embassy *4 rue Jean-Rey, 15th (01.40.59.33.00, www. france.embassy.gov.au). M° Bir-Hakeim.* **Open** *Consular services* 9am-noon, 2-4pm Mon-Fri.

British Embassy *35 rue du Fbg-St-Honoré, 8th (01.44.51.31.00, www.ukinfrance.fco.gov.uk). Mº Concorde. Consular services: 18bis rue d'Anjou, 8th. Mº Concorde.* **Open** by appointment 9.30am-12.30pm Mon-Fri.
British citizens wanting to use consular services (new passports, etc) should ignore the long queue that stretches along rue d'Anjou (this is for the visa department), and instead walk straight in at no.18bis.

Canadian Embassy *35 av Montaigne, 8th (01.44.43.29.00, www.amb-canada.fr). Mº Franklin D. Roosevelt.* **Open** 9am-noon, 2-5pm Mon-Fri. *Consular services: 01.44.43.29.02.* **Open** 9am-noon Mon-Fri. *Visas: 37 av Montaigne, 8th (01.44.43.29.16).* **Open** 8.30-10.30am Mon-Fri.

Irish Embassy *12 av Foch, 16th. Consulate: 4 rue Rude, 16th (01.44.17.67.00, www.embassyofireland.fr). Mº Charles de Gaulle Etoile.* **Open** *Consular/visas* 9.30am-noon Mon-Fri; by phone 9.30am-1pm, 2.30-5.30pm Mon-Fri.

New Zealand Embassy *7ter rue Léonard-de-Vinci, 16th (01.45.01.43.43, www.nzembassy.com/france). Mº Victor Hugo.* **Open** 9am-1pm Mon-Fri.

South African Embassy *59 quai d'Orsay, 7th (01.53.59.23.23, www.afriquesud.net). Mº Invalides.* **Open** 8.30am-5.15pm Mon-Fri. *Consulate & visas: 01.47.53.99.70.* **Open** 9am-noon Mon-Fri.

US Embassy *2 av Gabriel, 8th (01.43.12.22.22, http://france.usembassy.gov). Mº Concorde. Consulate & visas: 4 av Gabriel, 8th (08.10.26.46.26). Mº Concorde.* **Open** *Consular services* 9am-12.30pm, 1-3pm Mon-Fri. *Visas 08.92.23.84.72 or check the website for non-immigration visas.*

EMERGENCIES

Most of the following services operate 24 hours a day. In a medical emergency, such as a road accident, you should phone the Sapeurs-Pompiers, who have trained paramedics. *See also* **Health: Accident & Emergency; Doctors; Helplines**; and **Police**.

Ambulance (SAMU) 15
Police 17
Fire (Sapeurs-Pompiers) 18
Emergency (from a mobile phone) 112

Centre anti-poison
01.40.05.48.48

GAY & LESBIAN

For information on HIV and AIDS, *see below* **Health**. *See also pp255-261* **Gay & Lesbian**.

HEALTH

Nationals of non-EU countries should take out insurance before leaving home. EU nationals staying in France can use the French Social Security system, which refunds up to 70 per cent of medical expenses. UK residents travelling in Europe require a European National Health Insurance Card (EHIC). This allows them to benefit from free or reduced-cost medical care when travelling in a country belonging to the European Economic Area (EEA) or Switzerland. The EHIC is free of charge. For further information, refer to www.dh.gov.uk/travellers.

If you're staying for longer than three months, or working in France but still making National Insurance contributions in Britain, you will need form E128 filled in by your employer and stamped by the NI contributions office in order to get a French medical number. Consultations and prescriptions have to be paid for in full on the spot, and are reimbursed on receipt of a completed *fiche*. If you undergo treatment, the doctor will give you a prescription and a *feuille de soins* (bill of treatment). Stick the small stickers from the medication boxes on to the *feuille de soins*. Send this, together with the prescription and details of your EHIC card, to the local Caisse Primaire d'Assurance Maladie for a refund. For those resident in France, more and more doctors now accept the Carte Vitale, which lets them produce a digital *feuille de soins* and allows you to pay only the non-reimbursable part of the bill. Information on health insurance can be found at www.ameli.fr, where you can also track refunds online. See also the Ministry of Health's website at www.sante.gouv.fr.

Accident & emergency

Hospitals specialise in one type of emergency or illness – refer to the Assistance Publique's website (www.aphp.fr). In a medical emergency, call the Sapeurs-Pompiers or SAMU (*see left* **Emergencies**). The following (in order of district) have 24-hour accident and emergency services:

ADULTS
Hôpital Hôtel-Dieu *1 pl du Parvis Notre-Dame, 4th (01.42.34.82.34). Mº Cité.*
Hôpital St-Louis *1 av Claude-Vellefaux, 10th (01.42.49.49.49). Mº Goncourt.*
Hôpital St-Antoine *184 rue du Fbg-St-Antoine, 12th (01.49.28.20.00). Mº Faidherbe-Chaligny.*
Hôpital de la Pitié-Salpêtrière *47-83 bd de l'Hôpital, 13th (01.42.16.00.00). Mº Saint-Marcel.*
Hôpital Cochin *27 rue du Fbg-St-Jacques, 14th (01.58.41.41.41). RER Port Royal.*
Hôpital Européen Georges Pompidou *20 rue Leblanc, 15th (01.56.09.20.00). RER Pont du Garigliagno.*
Hôpital Bichat-Claude Bernard *46 rue Henri-Huchard, 18th (01.40.25.80.80). Mº Porte de Saint-Ouen.*
Hôpital Tenon *4 rue de la Chine, 20th (01.56.01.70.00). Mº Porte de Bagnolet.*

CHILDREN
Hôpital Armand Trousseau *26 av du Dr Arnold-Netter, 12th (01.44.73.74.75). Mº Bel Air.*
Hôpital Necker *149 rue de Sèvres, 15th (01.44.49.40.00). Mº Duroc.*
Hôpital Robert Debré *48 bd Sérurier, 19th (01.40.03.20.00). Mº Pré Saint Gervais.*

PRIVATE HOSPITALS
American Hospital in Paris *63 bd Victor-Hugo, 92200 Neuilly (01.46.41.25.25, www.american-hospital.org). Mº Porte Maillot, then bus 82.* **Open** 24hrs daily. English-speaking hospital. French Social Security refunds only a small percentage of the total treatment costs.
Hertford British Hospital (Hôpital Franco-Britannique) *3 rue Barbès, 92300 Levallois-Perret (01.46.39.22.22, www.british-hospital.org). Mº Anatole-France.* **Open** 24hrs daily. Most of the staff at the Hertford speak English.

Contraception & abortion

To get the pill (*la pilule*) or coil (*stérilet*), you need a prescription, available on appointment from the two places listed below, from a *médecin généraliste* (GP) or from a gynaecologist. The morning-after pill (*la pilule du lendemain*) can be had from pharmacies without prescription but is not reimbursed.

ESSENTIAL INFORMATION

Condoms (*préservatifs*) and spermicides are sold in pharmacies and supermarkets, and there are condom machines in most métro stations, club lavatories and on some street corners.

Centre de Planification et d'Education Familiales *27 rue Curnonsky, 17th (01.48.88.07.28, www.sante.gouv.fr). M° Porte de Champerret.* **Open** 9am-5pm Mon-Fri.
Free consultations on family planning and abortion.

MFPF (Mouvement Français pour le Planning Familial) *10 rue Vivienne, 2nd (01.42.60.93.20, www.planning-familial.org). M° Bourse.* **Open** 2-7pm Mon; 11am-1pm Tue; by appointment Wed, Thur.
Phone for an appointment for prescriptions and contraception advice. For abortion advice, turn up at the centre at one of the designated time slots.

Dentists

Dentists can be found by looking in the *Pages Jaunes* under *Dentistes*. For emergencies, contact one of the following:

Hôpital de la Pitié-Salpêtrière *(see p371)* also offers 24hr emergency dental care.
SOS Dentaire *87 bd Port-Royal, 13th (01.43.37.51.00, 01.43.36.36.00). M° Les Gobelins/ RER Port-Royal.* **Open** by phone for appointment after 6pm.
A telephone service for emergency dental care.

Doctors

You'll find a list of GPs in the *Pages Jaunes* under *Médecins: Médecine générale.* For a social security refund, choose a doctor or dentist who is *conventionné* (state registered). Consultations cost €23 or more, of which part can be reimbursed.

Centre Médical Europe *44 rue d'Amsterdam, 9th (01.42.81.93.33, www.centre-medical-europe.com). M° St-Lazare.* **Open** *With appointment* 8am-7pm Mon-Fri; 8am-6pm Sat. Practitioners in all fields; modest consultation fees.

SOS Médecins *36.24, www.sosmedecins.com.* House calls cost approx €33 before 7pm weekdays; from €53 at weekends; from €69 after 7pm and during holidays; prices will be higher if you don't have French social security.

Opticians

Branches of Alain Afflelou (www.alainafflelou.com) and Lissac (www.lissac.fr) stock hundreds of frames and can make up prescription glasses within the hour. For an eye test, you'll need to go to an *ophtalmologiste* – ask the optician for a list. Contact lenses can be bought over the counter if you have your prescription details with you.

Hôpital des Quinze-Vingts *28 rue de Charenton, 12th (01.40.02.15.20).*
Specialist eye hospital offers on-the-spot consultations for eye problems.
SOS Optique *01.48.07.22.00, www.sosoptique.com.*
Offers a 24-hour repair service for glasses.

Pharmacies

French *pharmacies* sport a green neon cross. A rota of *pharmacies de garde* operate at night and on Sundays; see below for a list of these night pharmacies. If closed, a pharmacy will have a sign indicating the nearest one open. Staff can provide basic medical services such as bandaging wounds (for a small fee) and will indicate the nearest doctor on duty. *Parapharmacies* sell almost everything *pharmacies* do but cannot dispense prescription medication. Toiletries and sanitary products are often less expensive in supermarkets.

Grande Pharmacie de la Nation *13 pl de la Nation, 11th (01.43.73.24.03). M° Nation.* **Open** 8am-9pm daily.
Matignon *1 av Matignon, 8th (01.43.59.86.55, www.pharmaciematignon.com). M° Franklin D. Roosevelt.* **Open** 8.30am-2am daily.
Pharmacie des Champs-Elysées *84 av des Champs-Elysées, 8th (01.45.62.02.41). M° George V.* **Open** 24hrs daily.
Pharmacie Européene de la Place de Clichy *6 pl de Clichy, 9th (01.48.74.65.18). M° Place de Clichy.* **Open** 24hrs daily.
Pharmacie des Halles *10 bd de Sébastopol, 4th (01.42.72.03.23). M° Châtelet.* **Open** 8am-9pm daily.
Pharmacie d'Italie *61 av d'Italie, 13th (01.44.24.19.72). M° Tolbiac.* **Open** 8am-9pm daily.
Pharma Presto *01.61.04.04.04, www.pharma-presto.com.* **Open** for emergencies 24hrs daily. Delivery (€38 8am-6pm; €45 6pm-8am & during weekends) of medication.

STDs, HIV & AIDS

Cabinet Médico-Social Municipal Figuier *2 rue Figuier, 4th (01.49.96.62.70). M° Pont-Marie.* **Open** *HIV test walk-in* 1.30-6.30pm Mon, Wed, Thur; 9.15am-noon Sat. *With appointment* 9am-12.15pm, 1.30-6.30pm Mon, Fri; 1.30-6.30pm Tue.
Free, anonymous tests (*dépistages*) for HIV, hepatitis B and C and syphilis (wait one week for results). Good counselling service, too.
Le Kiosque Infos Sida-Toxicomanie *48 rue François Miron, 4th (01.44.78.00.00, www.lekiosque.org). M° St-Paul.* **Open** *Walk-in* 10am-7pm Mon-Fri.
Youth association offering information and counselling on AIDS, sexuality and drugs, and fast AIDS tests for gay men. Also works with Checkpoint (36 rue Geoffroy l'Asnier, 4th, 01.44.78.24.44).
SIDA Info Service *08.00.84.08.00, www.sida-info-service.org.* **Open** 24hrs daily.
Confidential AIDS information in French.

HELPLINES

Alcoholics Anonymous in English *01.46.34.59.65, www.aaparis.org.*
A 24hr recorded message gives details of AA meetings at the American Cathedral or American Church (*see p375*).
Allô Service Public *39.39, www.service-public.fr.* **Open** 8.30am-7pm Mon-Fri.
A source of information and contacts for all aspects of tax, work and administration matters. They even claim to be able to help out if you have problems with neighbours. The catch: operators speak only French. Foreigners can call Info Migrants on 01.53.26.52.82 (open 9am-1pm, 2-4pm Mon-Fri).
Counseling Center *01.47.23.61.13, www.americancathedral.org.* There's a walk-in clinic 11am-1pm 1st & 3rd Thur of mth.
English-language counselling, based at the American Cathedral.
Drogues Info Service *08.00.23.13.13, Ecoute Alcool 08.11.91.30.30, Tabac Info Service 39.89, www.drogues.gouv.fr.*
Phone service, in French, for help with drug, alcohol and tobacco problems.
Narcotics Anonymous *01.43.72.12.72, www.narcotiquesanonymes.org.*
The helpline is open daily 10am-10pm. Meetings in English are held every week.

ESSENTIAL INFORMATION

SOS Dépression *01.40.47.95.95,
http://sos.depression.free.fr.*
Open 24hrs daily.
People listen and/or give advice to
those suffering from depression.
SOS Dépression can send round
a counsellor or psychiatrist in case
of a crisis.
SOS Help *01.46.21.46.46, www.
soshelpline.org.* **Open** 3-11pm daily.
English-language helpline.

ID

French law requires that some form
of identification be carried at all
times. You should be prepared to
produce your passport or EHIC
card (*see p371*).

INSURANCE

See p371 **Health**.

INTERNET

ISPs

Free *10.44, www.free.fr.*
Open 24hrs daily.
SFR *10.23, www.sfr.fr.*
Open 8am-10pm daily.
Orange *39.00, www.orange.fr.*
Open 24hrs daily.
Bouygues *10.34, www.bouygues
telecom.fr.* **Open** 8am-8pm
Mon-Sat.

Internet access

An increasing number of public
spaces now offer Wi-Fi hotspots.

Milk *31 bd de Sébastopol, 1st
(01.42.33.68.17, www.milklub.
com).* *M° Châtelet/RER Châtelet
Les Halles.* **Open** 24hrs daily.
The biggest internet café in Paris.
Other locations 5 rue d'Odessa,
14th (01.43.20.10.37).

LANGUAGE

See pp379-381 **Vocabulary**.

LEFT LUGGAGE

Gare du Nord

There are self-locking luggage
lockers (6.15am-11.15pm daily)
situated on Level -1 under the
main station concourse.

Roissy-Charles-de-Gaulle airport

Bagages du Monde
*(01.34.38.58.90, www.
bagagesdumonde.com).*

Terminal 1 *Niveau Départ,
Porte 14 (01.34.38.58.82).* **Open**
9.15am-1.30pm, 3.30-7pm daily.
Between Terminal 2C & 2E *Gare
TGV Niveau 4 (01.34.38.58.90).*
Open 6am-9.30pm daily.
Company with counters in Roissy-
Charles-de-Gaulle and an office in
Paris (102 rue de Chemin-Vert, 11th,
01.34.38.58.96, open 9am-noon,
2-6pm Mon-Fri). Can ship baggage
worldwide or store it.

LEGAL HELP

Mairies can answer some legal
enquiries; ask for times of their
free *consultations juridiques.*
See also p370 **Embassies**.

**Direction Départementale
de la Concurrence, de la
Consommation et de la
Répression des Fraudes** *8 rue
Froissart, 3rd (01.40.27.16.00).*
M° St-Sébastien Froissart. **Open**
9am-noon, 2-5pm Mon-Fri.
Part of the Ministry of Finance;
deals with consumer complaints.
**Palais de Justice Galerie de
Harlay** *Escalier S, 4 bd du Palais,
4th (01.44.32.52.52).* *M° Cité.*
Open 9.30am-noon Mon-Fri.
Free legal consultation. Make sure
you arrive early and obtain a ticket
for the queue.
SOS Avocats *08.25.39.33.00,
www.avocatparis.org.* **Open**
7-11.30pm Mon-Fri.
Free legal advice by phone.

LIBRARIES

Every *arrondissement* has a free
public library. To get a library card,
you need to provide ID and evidence
of a fixed address in Paris.

American Library *10 rue du
Général-Camou, 7th (01.53.59.
12.60, www.americanlibraryinparis.
org).* *M° Ecole-Militaire/RER Pont
de l'Alma.* **Open** 10am-7pm Tue,
Wed, Fri, Sat; 10am-10pm Thur;
1-7pm Sun (shorter hours in Aug).
Admission day pass €15; €10
reductions; annual €120.
A useful resource: this is the largest
English-language lending library
on the continent. It receives 400
periodicals, as well as popular
magazines and newspapers.
**Bibliothèque Historique de la
Ville de Paris** *Hôtel Lamoignon,
24 rue Pavée, 4th (01.44.59.29.40).*
M° St-Paul. **Open** 10am-6pm
Mon-Sat. **Admission** free (bring
passport photo and ID).
A decent range of books and
documents on Paris history.

**Bibliothèque Marguerite
Durand** *79 rue Nationale, 13th
(01.53.82.76.77).* *M° Tolbiac.* **Open**
2-6pm Tue-Sat. **Admission** free.
This library holds some 40,000 books
and 120 periodicals on women's
history. The feminism collection
includes letters of Colette and
Louise Michel.
**Bibliothèque Nationale de
France François Mitterrand**
*quai François-Mauriac, 13th
(01.53.79.59.59, www.bnf.fr).*
M° Bibliothèque. **Open** 2-7pm
Mon; 9am-7pm Tue-Sat; 1-7pm Sun.
Closed 2wks Sept & bank holidays.
Admission day pass €3.50; annual
€38; €20 reductions.
Books, papers and periodicals, plus
titles in English. An audio-visual
room lets you browse photo, film
and sound archives.
**Bibliothèque Publique
d'Information (BPI)** *Centre
Pompidou, 4th (01.44.78.12.33,
www.bpi.fr).* *M° Hôtel de Ville/
RER Châtelet Les Halles.* **Open**
noon-10pm Mon, Wed-Fri; 11am-
10pm Sat, Sun. Closed 1 May.
Admission free.
Now arranged across three levels,
the Centre Pompidou's vast library
has a huge global press section,
reference books and language-
learning facilities.
BIFI (Bibliothèque du Film) *51
rue de Bercy, 12th (01.71.19.33.33,
www.cinematheque.fr).* *M° Bercy.*
Open 10am-7pm Mon, Wed-Sat;
10am-8pm Sun. Closed 2wks Aug.
Admission €3.50 day pass; €34
annual; €15 reductions.
Housed in the same building as the
Cinémathèque Française, this world-
class researchers' and film buffs'
library offers books, magazines,
film stills and posters, as well as
films on video and DVD.
Documentation Française *29-31
quai Voltaire, 7th (01.40.15.71.10,
www.ladocumentationfrancaise.fr).*
M° Rue du Bac. **Open** 10am-1pm,
2-6pm Mon-Fri. Closed Aug &
1st wk Sept.
The official government archive
and central reference library has
information on French politics and
economy since 1945.

LOCKSMITHS

There are many round-the-clock
repair services in the capital
handling locks, plumbing and,
sometimes, car repairs. Most of
them charge a minimum €18-€20
call-out (*déplacement*) and €30 per
hour, plus the cost of parts. Charges
are inevitably higher on Sunday
and at night.

Allô Serrurerie *01.40.29.44.68,*
www.alloserrurerie.com.
SOS Dépannage *08.20.22.23.33,*
www.okservice.fr.
SOS Dépannage is double the price
of most services, but claims to be
twice as reliable.

LOST PROPERTY

Bureau des Objets Trouvés
36 rue des Morillons, 15th
(08.21.00.25.25, www.prefecture
depolice.interieur.gouv.fr). M°
Convention. **Open** 8.30am-5pm
Mon-Thur; 8.30am-4.30pm Fri.
Visit in person to fill in a form
specifying details of the loss. This
may have been the first lost property
office in the world, but it is far from
the most efficient. Huge delays in
processing claims mean that if your
trip to Paris is short, you may need
to nominate a proxy to collect found
objects after you leave, although
small items can be posted. If your
passport was among the items lost,
you'll need to go to your consulate
to get a single-entry temporary
passport in order to leave the country.

SNCF lost property
Some mainline SNCF stations have
their own lost property offices.
See also p367.

MONEY

The amount of currency visitors
may carry is not limited. However,
sums worth over €10,000 must be
declared to customs when entering
or leaving the country.

The euro

Non-French debit and credit cards
can be used to withdraw and pay in
euros, and currency withdrawn in
France can be used subsequently all
over the euro zone. Daylight robbery
occurs, however, if you try to deposit
a euro cheque from any country other
than France in a French bank: they
currently charge around €15 for this
service, and the European parliament
has backed down on its original
decision that cross-border payments
should be in line with domestic
ones across the euro zone. This is
good news for the British, though:
if you transfer money from the UK
to France in euros, you will pay the
same charges as if Britain were
within the euro zone.

ATMs

Withdrawals in euros can be made
from bank and post office automatic

cash machines. The specific cards
accepted are marked clearly on
each machine, and most can give
instructions in English. Credit card
companies charge a fee for cash
advances, but rates are often better
than at banks.

Banks

French banks usually open 9am-
5pm Mon-Fri (some close during
lunchtime); some banks also open on
Sat. All are closed on public holidays,
and from noon on the previous day.
Note that not all banks have foreign
exchange counters. The commission
rates vary between banks; the state-
owned Banque de France usually
offers good rates. Most banks will
accept travellers' cheques, but may
be reluctant to accept personal
cheques even with the Eurocheque
guarantee card, which is not widely
used in France.

Bank accounts

To open an account (*ouvrir un
compte*), French banks require proof
of identity, address and your income
(if any). You'll probably be required
to show your passport, an electricity,
gas or phone bill in your name and a
payslip/letter from your employer.
Students need a student card and
may need a letter from their parents.
Of the major national banks (BNP,
Crédit Lyonnais, Société Générale,
Banque Populaire, Crédit Agricole),
Société Générale tends to be the most
foreigner-friendly. Most banks don't
hand out a Carte Bleue/Visa card
until several weeks after you've
opened an account. A chequebook
(*chéquier*) is usually issued in about
a week. Payments made with a Carte
Bleue are debited directly from your
current account, but you can arrange
for purchases to be debited at the
end of every month. French banks
are tough on overdrafts, so try to
anticipate any cash crisis in advance
and work out a deal for an authorised
overdraft (*découvert autorisé*) or you
risk being blacklisted as '*interdit
bancaire*' – forbidden from having
a current account – for anything up
to ten years. Depositing foreign
currency cheques can be slow, so try
to use wire transfer or a bank draft in
euros to receive funds from abroad.

Bureaux de change

If you happen to be arriving in Paris
early in the morning or late at night,
you will be able to change money at
the **Travelex** bureaux de change in
Roissy terminals 1 (7.30am-8pm

Mon-Sat, 7am-2.30pm Sun), 2A
(7am-5pm & 6am-10.30pm), 2C
(6am-10.30pm), 2D (7am-9.30pm),
2E (7am-9.30pm), and 3 (6.30am-
9.30pm), and at Orly Sud. Travelex
also has bureaux de change at the
following stations:

Gare Montparnasse
01.42.79.03.88. **Open** 8am-7pm
Mon-Sat; 10am-4pm Sun.
Gare du Nord *01.40.82.96.59.*
Open 6.30am-10.30pm Mon-Sat;
7.30am-10.30pm Sun.
Gare St-Lazare *01.42.93.74.58.*
Open 8am-7pm Mon-Sat; 10am-
4pm Sun.

Credit cards

Major international credit cards are
widely used in France; Visa (which
is more commonly known in France
as Carte Bleue) is the most readily
accepted. French-issued credit cards
have a security microchip (*puce*) in
each card. The card is slotted into a
reader, and the holder then keys in a
PIN to authorise the transaction. In
case of credit card loss or theft, call
one of the following 24hr services
with English-speaking staff on
hand to help:

American Express *01.44.77.72.00.*
Diners Club *08.10.31.41.59.*
MasterCard *08.00.90.13.87.*
Visa *08.92.70.57.05.*

Foreign affairs

American Express *11 rue Scribe,
9th (01.47.77.70.00, www.
americanexpress.com).* M° Opéra.
Open 9am-6.30pm Mon-Sat.
Travel agency, bureau de change,
poste restante (you can leave
messages for other card holders),
card replacement, travellers' cheque
refund service, money transfers and
cash machine for AmEx cardholders.
Barclays *6 rond-point des Champs-
Elysées, 8th (01.44.95.13.80, www.
barclays.fr).* M° Franklin D. Roosevelt.
Open 9.15am-5.30pm Mon-Fri.
Barclays' international Expat
Service handles direct debits,
international transfer of funds,
and so on.
Citibank *1-5 rue Paul Cézanne, 8th
(01.70.75.50.00, www.citibank.fr).*
M° St-Philippe-du-Roule. **Open**
8am-6pm Mon-Fri.
Bank clients get good rates for
international money transfers,
preferential exchange rates and
commission-free travellers' cheques.
Travelex *52 av des Champs-Elysées,
8th (01.42.89.80.33, www.travelex.
com/fr).* M° Franklin D. Roosevelt.

Open 9am-10.30pm Mon-Sat;
10am-9.30pm Sun.
Travelex issues travellers' cheques
and insurance and also deals with
bank transfers.

Western Union Money Transfer
www.westernunion.com. Many
post offices in the city (*see right*)
provide Western Union services.
Transfers from abroad should arrive
within 15 minutes; charges paid
by sender.

Tax

French VAT (*taxe sur la valeur
ajoutée* or TVA) is arranged in four
bands: 2.1 per cent for items of
medication and newspapers; 5.5 per
cent for food, books, CDs and DVDs;
10 per cent for restaurant meals; and
20 per cent for all other types of
goods and services.

NATURAL HAZARDS

Paris has no natural hazards as such,
though in recent years the town hall
has produced evacuation plans to
cover flooding.

OPENING HOURS

Standard opening hours for shops
are 9 or 10am to 7 or 8pm Monday to
Saturday. Some shops are closed on
Monday. Shops and businesses often
close at lunchtime, usually 12.30-
2pm; many shops close in August.
Sunday opening is found in the
Marais, on the Champs-Elysées, at
Bercy Village and in the Carrousel
du Louvre. Most areas have a local
grocer that stays open into the night
and will often open on Sundays and
public holidays too.

24hr florist Elyfleur *82 av de
Wagram, 17th (01.47.66.87.19,
www.elyfleurs.com). M° Wagram.*
24hr garage Shell *6 bd Raspail, 7th
(01.45.48.43.12). M° Rue du Bac.*
This garage has an extensive array
of everyday supermarket products
on sale from the Casino chain.
No alcohol is sold 10pm-8am.
24hr newsagents include: *33 av des
Champs-Elysées, 8th, M° Franklin D.
Roosevelt. 2 bd Montmartre, 9th,
M° Grands Boulevards. 13 pl de la
Bourse, 2nd, M° Bourse. 14-16 bd
de la Madeleine, 9th, M° Opéra.
16 bd de Clichy, 18th, M° Pigalle.*
Late-night tabacs Le Brazza
*86 bd du Montparnasse, 14th
(01.43.35.42.65). M° Montparnasse-
Bienvenüe. Open 7am-12.30am
daily.* La Favorite *3 bd St-Michel,
5th (no phone). M° St-Michel. Open
8am-2am daily.*

POLICE

The French equivalent of 999 or 911
is 17 (112 from a mobile), but don't
expect a speedy response. That
said, the Préfecture de Police has no
fewer than 94 outposts in the city. If
you're assaulted or robbed, report the
incident as soon as possible. You'll
need to make a statement (*procès
verbal*) at the *point d'accueil* closest
to the site of the crime. To find the
nearest, call the **Préfecture
Centrale** (01.53.71.53.71,
01.53.73.53.73, open 24hrs daily)
or go to www.prefecturedepolice.
interieur.gouv.fr. Stolen goods
are unlikely to be recovered, but
you'll need a police statement
for insurance. *See also p371*
Emergencies.

POSTAL SERVICES

Post offices (*bureaux de poste*) are
mostly open 8am-8pm Mon-Fri;
9am-1pm Sat, apart from the 24-hour
post office listed below. Details of all
branches are included in the phone
book: under 'Administration des
PTT' in the *Pages Jaunes*; under
'Poste' in the *Pages Blanches*. Most
post offices contain automatic
machines (in French and English)
that weigh your letter, print out a
stamp and give change, saving you
from wasting time in an enormous
queue. You can also usually buy
stamps and sometimes envelopes
at a tobacconist (*tabac*). For more
information refer to www.laposte.fr.

Main Post Office *52 rue du
Louvre, 75001 Paris, 1st (36.31,
www.laposte.fr). M° Les Halles or
Louvre Rivoli.* **Open** 7.30am-6am
Mon-Sat; 24hrs daily for poste
restante, telephones, stamps, faxes,
photocopying and a modest amount
of banking operations. This is the
best place to arrange to have your
mail sent to if you haven't got a fixed
address in Paris. Mail should be
addressed to you in block capitals,
followed by Poste Restante, then the
post office's address. There will be a
charge of approximately €0.50 for
each letter received.

RECYCLING & RUBBISH

The city has a system of colour-
coded domestic recycling bins. A
yellow-lidded bin can take paper,
cardboard cartons, tins and small
electrical items; a white-lidded bin
takes glass. All other rubbish goes in
the green-lidded bins, except for used
batteries (shops that sell batteries

should accept them), medication
(take it back to a pharmacy), toxic
products (call 01.43.61.57.36 to have
them picked up) or car batteries
(take them to an official tip or return
to garages exhibiting the 'Relais
Verts Auto' sign). Green, hive-
shaped bottle banks can be found
on many street corners. More
information is available at www.
environnement.paris.fr.

RELIGION

You can find churches and religious
centres listed in the *Pages Jaunes*
under 'Eglises' and 'Cultes'. The
French capital has several English-
speaking churches.

American Cathedral *23 av
George V, 8th (01.53.23.84.00,
www.americancathedral.org).
M° George V.*
American Church in Paris *65 quai
d'Orsay, 7th (01.40.62.05.00, www.
acparis.org). M° Invalides.*
**Emmanuel International Church
of Paris** *56 rue des Bons Raisins,
Rueil-Malmaison (01.47.51.29.63,
www.eicparis.org). RER Reuil-
Malmaison, then bus 244.*
Kehilat Gesher *10 rue de Pologne,
78100 St-Germain-en-Laye
(01.39.21.97.19, www.kehilatgesher.
org). RER St-Germain-en-Laye.*
The Liberal English-speaking
Jewish community has services in
Paris and the western suburbs.
La Mosquée de Paris *2bis
pl du Puits de l'Ermite, 5th
(01.45.35.97.33, www.mosquee-
de-paris.org). M° Place Monge.*
St George's Anglican Church
*7 rue Auguste-Vacquerie,
16th (01.47.20.22.51, www.
stgeorgesparis.com). M° Charles
de Gaulle Etoile.*
**St Joseph's Roman Catholic
Church** *50 av Hoche, 8th
(01.42.27.28.56, www.stjoeparis.
org). M° Charles de Gaulle Etoile.*
St Michael's Church of England
*5 rue d'Aguesseau, 8th (01.47.42.
70.88, www.saintmichaelsparis.org).
M° Madeleine.*

RENTING A FLAT

Rental apartments are generally
cheapest in northern, eastern and
south-eastern Paris. You can expect
to pay approximately €20 per square
metre per month (which works out as,
for example, €700 per month for a
modest 35sq m apartment). Studios
and one bedroom flats fetch the
highest prices proportionally; the
provision of lifts and cellars will
also boost the rent.

ESSENTIAL INFORMATION

ESSENTIAL INFORMATION

Flat-hunting

Given the scarcity of housing stock in Paris, it's a landlord's world; you'll need to search actively, or even frenetically, in order to find an apartment. The internet is a decent place to start: www.explorimmo.fr lists rental ads from *Le Figaro* and specialist real estate magazines; you can place a classified ad or check lettings on www.avendrealouer.fr. Thursday morning's *De Particulier à Particulier* (www.pap.fr) is a must for those who want to rent directly from the owner, but be warned – most flats go within hours. Fortnightly *Se Loger* (www.seloger.com) is also worth getting, though most of its ads are placed by agencies.

Landlords keen to let to foreigners advertise in the English-language *FUSAC* (www.fusac.fr); rents tend to be higher than in the French press. There are also assorted free ad brochures that can be picked up from agencies. Private landlords often set a visiting time; prepare to meet hordes of other flat-seekers and have your documents and cheque book to hand.

There's also the option of flat-sharing – one that's been growing in popularity in recent years. To look for housemates, pick up a copy of *FUSAC* or browse the 3,000-odd weekly announcements that can be found at www.colocation.fr, which also organises monthly soirée Le Jeudi de la Colocation, a chance to meet potential flatmates in the flesh.

Rental laws

The minimum lease (*bail de location*) on an unfurnished flat is three years (though the tenant can give notice and leave before this period is up); furnished flats are generally let on one-year leases. During this period the landlord can raise the rent only by the official construction inflation index. At the end of the lease, the rent can be adjusted, but tenants can object before a rent board. Tenants can be evicted for non-payment, or if the landlord wishes to sell the property or use it as his own residence. It is illegal to throw people out in winter.

Landlords will probably insist you present a dossier with pay slips (*fiches de paie/bulletins de salaire*) showing income equivalent to three to four times the monthly rent, and for foreigners in particular, provide a financial guarantor (someone who will sign a document promising to pay the rent if you abscond). When taking out a lease, payments usually include the first month's rent, a deposit (*caution*) of the equivalent of two months' rent, and an agency fee, if applicable.

It's customary to have an inspection of the premises (*état des lieux*) at the start and end of the rental, the cost of which (around €150) is shared by landlord and tenant. Landlords may try to rent their flats *non-declaré* – in other words, without a written lease – and get rent in cash. This can make it difficult for tenants to establish their rights – which is one reason why landlords do it.

SAFETY & SECURITY

Beware of pickpockets, especially around the city's crowded tourist hotspots and métro stations. See also *p366* **Métro & RER** and *p375* **Police**.

SHIPPING SERVICES

Hedley's Humpers *6 bd de la Libération, 93284 St-Denis (01.48.13.01.02, www.hedleys humpers.com). M° Carrefour Pleyel.* **Open** 9am-1pm, 2-6pm Mon-Fri. Closed 2wks Aug. Specialist in transport of furniture and antiques. In UK: 3 St Leonards Road, London NW10 6SX (020 8965 8733). In USA: 271 Scholes Street, Brooklyn, New York NY 11101 (1-718 433 4005).

SMOKING

Although smoking seems to be an essential part of French life (and death), the French state and public health groups have recently waged war against the cigarette on several fronts. Smoking is now completely banned in all enclosed public spaces, including bars, cafés, clubs, restaurants, hotel foyers and shops, as well as on public transport. Many bars, cafés and clubs offer smoking gardens or terraces. There are also increasingly strident anti-smoking campaigns in France. Prices have also soared during the last few years.

For information about stopping smoking, contact the **Tabac Info Service** (39.89, www.tabac-info-service.fr). If you're a dedicated smoker, you'll soon learn that most *tabacs* in Paris close at 8pm (for a few that don't, *see p375* **Opening hours**). Some bars sell cigarettes behind the counter, but generally only to customers who have a drink.

STUDY

Language

Most of the large multinational language schools, such as **Berlitz** (01.40.74.00.17, www.berlitz.fr), have at least one branch in Paris.

Alliance Française *101 bd Raspail, 6th (01.42.84.90.00, www.alliancefr.org). M° St-Placide.* The Alliance Française is a non-profit French-language school. Beginner and specialist courses start every month.
Institut Catholique de Paris *21 rue d'Assas, 6th (01.44.39.52.68, www.icp.fr/ilcf). M° St-Sulpice.* Courses offered in French culture and language. You must hold a baccalauréat-level qualification and be 18 or over (but you don't have to be Catholic).
La Sorbonne – Cours de Langue et Civilisation *47 rue des Ecoles, 5th (01.44.10.77.00, www.ccfs-sorbonne.fr). M° Cluny-La Sorbonne/ RER Luxembourg.* Classes for foreigners ride on the name of this eminent institution. Teaching is grammar-based.
University of London Institute in Paris *9-11 rue Constantine, 7th (01.44.11.73.83, www.ulip. lon.ac.uk). M° Invalides.* Linked to the University of London, this 4,000-student institute offers English courses for Parisians, as well as French courses at university level.

Specialised

Many of the prestigious Ecoles Nationales Supérieures (including film schools La FEMIS and ENS Louis Lumière) offer a range of summer courses in addition to their full-time degree courses – ask for *formation continue.*

Adult education courses *www.paris.fr or your local mairie.* A huge range of inexpensive adult education classes is run by the city of Paris, including French as a foreign language, computer skills and applied arts.
American University of Paris *6 rue du Colonel Combes, 7th (01.40.62.07.20, www.aup.edu). M° Ecole-Militaire/RER Pont de l'Alma.* International college awarding four-year American liberal arts degrees (BA/BSc).
Cordon Bleu *8 rue Léon-Delhomme, 15th (01.53.68.22.50, www. cordonbleu.edu). M° Vaugirard.*

Courses range from three-hour sessions on classical and regional cuisine to a nine-month diploma for those starting a culinary career.
Ecole du Louvre *Palais du Louvre, porte Jaujard, place du Carrousel, 1st (01.55.35.18.00, www.ecole dulouvre.fr). M° Palais Royal Musée du Louvre.*
Offers art history and archaeology courses. Foreign students not wanting to take a degree can attend lectures.
INSEAD *bd de Constance, 77305 Fontainebleau (01.60.72.40.00, www.insead.edu).*
Highly regarded international business school offering a ten-month MBA course in English as well as PhDs in a wide range of business subjects.
Parsons School of Design *45 rue Saint Roch, 1st (01.76.21.76.40, www.newschool. edu/parsons-paris). M° Pyramides.*
Subsidiary of the New York art college offering BFA programmes in fine art, photography, fashion, marketing and interior design.
Ritz-Escoffier Ecole de Gastronomie Française *38 rue Cambon, 1st (01.43.16.30.50, www.ritzparis.com). M° Madeleine.*
Everything from afternoon demonstrations in the Ritz kitchens to diplomas. Courses in French with English translation.

TELEPHONES
Mobile phones

A subscription (*abonnement*) will normally get you a free phone if you sign up for at least one year. Two hours' calling time a month costs about €35 per month. International calls are normally charged extra – a lot extra.

Remember that using your UK mobile phone in France can cost considerably more than at home, especially if you use data roaming, although rates are considerably lower nowadays.

Bouygues Télécom *10.64, www.bouyguestelecom.fr.*
Orange *39.70, www.orange.fr.*
SFR *10.23, www.sfr.fr.*
Virgin Mobile *10.05, www.virginmobile.fr.*

Dialling & codes

All French phone numbers have ten digits. Paris and Ile-de-France numbers begin with 01; the rest of France is divided into four zones (02-05). Mobile phone numbers start

with 06. 08 indicates a special rate; numbers beginning with 08 can only be reached from inside France. If you are calling France from abroad, leave off the 0 at the start of the ten-digit number. The country code is 33. To call abroad from France dial 00, then the country code, then the number.

Operator services

Operator assistance, French directory enquiries *(renseignements) 12.* To make a reverse-charge call within France, ask to make a call *en PCV*.
Airparif *01.44.59.47.64, www.airparif.asso.fr.*
Information about pollution levels and air quality in Paris and Ile-de-France: an invaluable resource for asthmatics.
Telegram all languages, international *08.00.35.36.55*; within France *36.55.*
Telephone engineer *10.13.*
Time *36.99.*

Public phones

Most public phones in Paris use *télécartes* (phonecards), which are sold at post offices, *tabacs*, airports and train and métro stations. For cheap international calls, you can also buy a *télécarte à puce* (card with a microchip) or a *télécarte pré-payée*, which features a numerical code you dial before making a call; these can be used on domestic phones too. Travelex's International Telephone Card can be used in more than 80 countries (available from **Travelex** agencies, *see p374*). Cafés have coin phones, while post offices usually have card phones. In a phone box, the display screen will read '*Décrochez*'. Pick up the phone. When '*Introduisez votre carte*' appears, put your card into the slot; the screen should read '*Patientez SVP*'. '*Numérotez*' is your signal to dial. '*Crédit épuisé*' means you have no more units left. Hang up ('*Raccrochez*') – and don't forget your card. Some public phones take credit cards. If you're using a credit card, insert the card, enter your PIN number and '*Patientez SVP*' will appear.

Telephone directories

Telephone books can be found in all post offices and most cafés. The *Pages Blanches* (White Pages) list people and businesses alphabetically; the *Pages Jaunes* (Yellow Pages) list businesses and services by category order.

Online versions can be found at www.pagesjaunes.fr.

Telephone charges

All local calls in Paris and Ile-de-France (to numbers beginning with 01) cost €0.08/call.
International destinations are divided into 16 zones. Reduced-rate periods for calls within France and Europe are 7pm-8am during the week and all day Saturday and Sunday. Reduced-rate periods for the US and Canada are 7pm to 1pm Monday to Friday and all day Saturday and Sunday.

Cheap providers

Getting wise to the market demand, the smaller telephone providers are becoming increasingly popular, as rates from Orange (formerly France Télécom) are not exactly at bargain-basement levels. The following can offer alternative rates – although you will still need to rent your telephone line from Orange:
AT&T Direct *(local access)* *08.00.99.00.11.*
Free *10.44, www.free.fr.*
With the Freebox (Free's modem for ADSL connection), €29.99 per month gets you ten hours of free calls to landlines (additional calls cost €0.01 per minute), €0.19 per minute to mobiles and €0.03 per minute for most international calls.
Onetel *08.05.92.51.51, www.onetel.fr.*

Special-rate numbers

0800 Numéro Vert Freephone.
0810 Numéro Azur €0.06/min (landline), €0.15/min (mobile).
0820 Numéro Indigo €0.12/min.
0825 Numéro Indigo II €0.15/min.
0836.64/0890.64/ 0890.70 €0.112/min.
0890.71 €0.15/min.
0891.67/0891.70 €0.80/min.
0836/0892 €0.34-€0.56/min.
This line is for the likes of ticket agencies, cinema and transport information.
10.14 Orange information; free (except if calling from mobile phones).

TIME

France is one hour ahead of Greenwich Mean Time (GMT). France uses the 24hr system (for example, 18h means 6pm).

THE LOCAL CLIMATE

Average temperatures and monthly rainfall in Paris.

	High (°C/°F)	Low (°C/°F)	Rainfall (mm/in)
Jan	7 / 45	2 / 36	53 / 2.1
Feb	10 / 50	2 / 36	43 / 1.7
Mar	13 / 55	4 / 39	49 / 1.9
Apr	17 / 63	6 / 43	53 / 2.1
May	20 / 68	9 / 48	65 / 2.6
June	23 / 73	12 / 54	54 / 2.1
July	25 / 77	15 / 59	62 / 2.4
Aug	26 / 79	16 / 61	42 / 1.7
Sept	23 / 73	12 / 54	54 / 2.1
Oct	20 / 68	8 / 46	60 / 2.4
Nov	14 / 57	4 / 39	51 / 2.0
Dec	7 / 45	3 / 37	59 / 2.3

TIPPING

A service charge of ten to 15 per cent is legally included in your bill at all restaurants, cafés and bars. However, it is polite either to round up the final amount for drinks, or to leave a cash tip of €1-€2 or more for a meal, depending on the restaurant and, of course, the quality of the service you receive.

TOILETS

The city's automatic street toilets are not really as terrifying as they first appear. Each loo is completely washed down and disinfected after use. If a space age-style lavatory experience doesn't appeal, you can nip into the toilets of a café; although theoretically reserved for customers' use, a polite request should win sympathy with the waiter – and you may find you have to put a €0.20 coin into a slot in the door-handle mechanism, customer or not. Fast-food chain toilets often have a code on their toilet doors that is made known to paying customers only.

TOURIST INFORMATION

Office de Tourisme et des Congrès de Paris *25 rue des Pyramides, 1st (08.92.68.30.00 recorded information available in English & French, www.paris info.com). M° Pyramides.* **Open** *Summer* 9am-7pm daily. *Winter* 10am-7pm daily.
Provides information on Paris and the suburbs, plus services such as a shop, bureau de change, hotel reservations, phonecards, museum cards, travel passes and tickets. Multilingual staff.
Other locations *Gare de Lyon* 20 bd Diderot, 12th. M° Gare de Lyon.

Open 8am-6pm Mon-Sat. *Gare du Nord* 18 rue de Dunkerque, 10th. M° Gare du Nord. **Open** 8am-6pm daily. *Anvers* 72 bd Rochechouart, 18th. M° Anvers. **Open** 10am-6pm daily. *Porte de Versailles* 1 pl de la Porte de Versailles, 15th. **Open** 11am-7pm during trade fairs.

VISAS & IMMIGRATION

EU nationals don't need a visa to enter France, nor do US, Canadian, Australian, New Zealand or South African citizens for stays of up to three months. Nationals of other countries should enquire at the nearest French embassy or consulate before leaving home. If they are travelling to France from one of the countries in the Schengen agreement (most of the EU, but not Britain or Ireland), the visa from that country should be sufficient.

EU citizens may stay in France for as long as their passport is valid. Non-EU citizens who wish to stay for longer than three months must apply to the French embassy or consulate in their own country for a long-term visa. For more information, contact:

CIRA (Centre Interministeriel de Renseignements Administratifs) *39.39, www. service-public.fr.* **Open** 8am-7pm Mon-Fri.
The CIRA gives advice on most French administrative procedures via its local-rate phone line.
Préfecture de Police de Paris Service Etrangers *7-9 bd du Palais, 4th (01.56.95.26.80, www.prefecturedepolice.interieur. gouv.fr). M° Cité.* **Open** 9am-3.45pm Mon-Fri.
This office can provide information on residency, along with work permits for foreigners.

WEIGHTS & MEASURES

France uses only the metric system; remember that all speed limits are in kilometres per hour. One kilometre is equivalent to 0.62 miles (1 mile = 1.6km). Petrol, like other liquids, is measured in litres (one UK gallon = 4.54 litres; 1 US gallon = 3.79 litres).

WHAT TO TAKE

Binoculars for studying high-altitude details of monuments, a pocket knife with corkscrew (for improvised picnics) and – vital for getting around the city on foot – comfortable shoes.

WHEN TO GO

In July and August, during the long school holidays, there are often great deals to be had on hotels and a good range of free events laid on by the city (such as Paris-Plages), but many family-run restaurants and shops close as the local   s go off *en vacances*. Avoid October, with its fashion weeks and trade shows.

WOMEN

Although Paris is not an especially threatening city for women, the precautions you would take in any major metropolis apply here: be careful at night in certain areas, including Pigalle, the rue St-Denis, Stalingrad, La Chapelle, Château Rouge, Gare de l'Est, Gare du Nord, the Bois de Boulogne and Bois de Vincennes. If you receive unwanted attention, a politely scathing *N'insistez pas!* (Don't push it!) will make your feelings abundantly clear. If things get too heavy, go into the nearest shop or café.

CIDFF (Centre d'Information sur les Droits des Femmes et des Familles) *17 rue Jean Poulmarch, 10th (01.83.64.72.01, www.info femmes.com). M° Porte de Pantin.* **Open** 10am-12.30pm, 1.30-5.30pm Mon-Thur; 10am-12.30pm Fri.
The CIDFF offers plenty of health, legal and professional advice for women.
Violence Conjugale: Femmes Info Service *39.19.* **Open** 9am-10pm Mon-Fri; 9am-6pm Sat, Sun.
A hotline for the victims of domestic violence, directing them to medical aid, shelters and other services.
Viols Femmes Informations *08.00.05.95.95.* **Open** 10am-7pm Mon-Fri. Freephone service.
Help and advice available, in French, to rape victims.

Vocabulary

In French, the second person singular (you) has two forms. Phrases here are given in the more polite *vous* form. The *tu* form is used with family, friends, children and pets; you should be careful not to use it with people you do not know sufficiently well. Courtesies such as *monsieur*, *madame* and *mademoiselle* are used more than their English equivalents.

GENERAL

Good morning/afternoon, hello bonjour; **good evening** bonsoir; **goodbye** au revoir; **OK** d'accord; **yes** oui; **no** non; **how are you?** comment allez vous?/vous allez bien?; **how's it going?** comment ça va?/ça va? (familiar)

Sir/Mr monsieur (M.); **madam/Mrs** madame (Mme); **miss** mademoiselle (Mlle); **please** s'il vous plaît; **thank you** merci; **sorry** pardon; **excuse me** excusez-moi; **I am going to pay** je vais payer

Do you speak English? parlez-vous anglais?; **I don't speak French** je ne parle pas français; **I don't understand** je ne comprends pas; **speak more slowly, please** parlez plus lentement, s'il vous plaît

It is c'est; **it isn't** ce n'est pas; **good** bon/bonne; **bad** mauvais/mauvaise; **small** petit/petite; **big** grand/grande; **beautiful** beau/belle; **well** bien; **badly** mal; **a bit** un peu; **a lot** beaucoup; **very** très

With avec; **without** sans; **and** et; **or** ou; **because** parce que; **who?** qui?; **when?** quand?; **what?** quoi?; **which?** quel?; **where?** où?; **why?** pourquoi?; **how?** comment?; **at what time/when?** à quelle heure?

Forbidden interdit/défendu; **out of order** hors service (HS)/en panne; **daily** tous les jours (TLJ)

ON THE PHONE

Hello allô; **who's calling?** c'est de la part de qui?/qui est à l'appareil?; **this is… speaking** c'est à l'appareil; **I'd like to speak to…** j'aurais voulu parler à ; **hold the line** ne quittez pas; **please call back later** rappelez plus tard

s'il vous plaît; you must have the wrong number vous avez dû composer un mauvais numéro

GETTING AROUND

Where is the (nearest) métro? où est le métro (le plus proche)?; **when is the next train for…?** c'est quand le prochain train pour… ?; **ticket** un billet; **station** la gare; **platform** le quai; **entrance** entrée; **exit** sortie; **left** gauche; **right** droite; **straight on** tout droit; **far** loin; **near** pas loin/près d'ici

SIGHTSEEING

Museum un musée; **church** une église; **exhibition** une exposition; **ticket** (*museum*) un billet; (*theatre, concert*) une place; **open** ouvert; **closed** fermé; **free** gratuit; **reduced price** un tarif réduit

ACCOMMODATION

Do you have a room (for this evening/for two people)? avez-vous une chambre (pour ce soir/pour deux personnes)?; **full** complet; **room** une chambre; **bed** un lit; **double bed** un grand lit; **(a room with) twin beds** (une chambre à) deux lits; **with bath(room)/shower** avec (salle de) bain/douche; **breakfast** le petit déjeuner

SHOPPING

Cheap pas cher; **expensive** cher; **how much?/how many?** combien?; **have you got change?** avez-vous de la monnaie?; **I'll take it** je le prends; **I would like…** je voudrais…; **may I try this on?** est-ce que je pourrais essayer cet article?; **do you have a smaller/larger size?** auriez-vous la taille en-dessous/au dessus?; **I'm a size 38** je fais du 38

STAYING ALIVE

Be cool restez calme; **I don't want any trouble** je ne veux pas d'ennuis; **I only do safe sex** je ne pratique que le safe sex

NUMBERS

0 zéro; 1 un, une; 2 deux; 3 trois; 4 quatre; 5 cinq; 6 six; 7 sept; 8 huit;

9 neuf; 10 dix; 11 onze; 12 douze; 13 treize; 14 quatorze; 15 quinze; 16 seize; 17 dix-sept; 18 dix-huit; 19 dix-neuf; 20 vingt; 21 vingt-et-un; 22 vingt-deux

30 trente; 40 quarante; 50 cinquante; 60 soixante; 70 soixante-dix; 80 quatre-vingts; 90 quatre-vingt-dix; 100 cent

1,000 mille; 10,000 dix mille; 1,000,000 un million

DAYS, MONTHS & SEASONS

Monday lundi
Tuesday mardi
Wednesday mercredi
Thursday jeudi
Friday vendredi
Saturday samedi
Sunday dimanche

January janvier
February février
March mars
April avril
May mai
June juin
July juillet
August août
September septembre
October octobre
November novembre
December décembre

Spring le printemps
Summer l'été
Autumn l'automne
Winter l'hiver

EATING OUT

Except for the very simplest restaurants, it's wise to book ahead. This can usually be done on the same day as your intended visit, although really top-notch establishments require bookings weeks or months in advance. Many venues close in August, and some also close at Christmas. All bills include a service charge, but an additional tip of a few euros (for the whole table) is polite unless you're unhappy with the service.

I'd like to book a table (for three/at 8pm) je voudrais réserver une table (pour trois personnes/à vingt heures); **lunch** le déjeuner; **dinner** le dîner; **coffee** (espresso)

un café; **tea** un thé; **wine** le vin; **beer** une bière; **mineral water** eau minérale; **tap water** une carafe d'eau; **the bill, please** l'addition, s'il vous plaît

Preparation (la préparation)

en croûte in a pastry case. **farci** stuffed. **au four** baked. **flambé** flamed in alcohol. **forestière** with mushrooms. **fricassé** fried and simmered in stock, usually with creamy sauce. **fumé** smoked. **garni** garnished. **glacé** frozen or iced. **gratiné** topped with breadcrumbs or cheese and grilled. **à la grècque** vegetables served cold in the cooking liquid with oil and lemon juice. **grillé** grilled. **haché** minced. **julienne** (vegetables) cut into matchsticks. **lamelle** very thin slice. **mariné** marinated. **pané** breaded. **en papillote** cooked in a packet. **parmentier** with potato. **pressé** squeezed. **râpé** grated. **salé** salted.

Cooking type (la cuisson)

cru raw. **bleu** practically raw. **saignant** rare. **rosé** (of lamb, duck, liver, kidneys) pink. **à point** medium rare. **bien cuit** well done.

Basics (essentiels)

ballotine stuffed, rolled-up piece of meat or fish. **crème fraîche** thick, slightly soured cream. **épices** spices. **feuilleté** 'leaves' of (puff) pastry. **fromage** cheese. **fruits de mer** shellfish. **galette** round flat cake of flaky pastry, potato pancake or buckwheat savoury crêpe. **gelée** aspic. **gibier** game. **gras** fat.

légume vegetable. **maison** of the house. **marmite** small cooking pot. **miel** honey. **noisette** hazelnut; small, round portion of meat. **noix** walnut. **noix de coco** coconut. **nouilles** noodles. **oeuf** egg; **– en cocotte** baked egg; **– en meurette** egg poached in red wine; **– à la neige** see *île flottante*. **parfait** sweet or savoury mousse-like mixture. **paupiette** slice of meat or fish, stuffed and rolled. **timbale** dome-shaped mould, or food cooked in one. **tisane** herbal tea. **tourte** covered pie or tart, usually savoury.

Meat (viande)

agneau lamb. **aloyau** beef loin. **andouillette** sausage made from pig's offal. **bavette** beef flank steak. **biche** venison. **bifteck** steak. **boudin noir/blanc** black (blood)/ white pudding. **boeuf** beef; **– bourguignon** beef cooked Burgundy style, with red wine,

onions and mushrooms; **– gros sel** boiled beef with vegetables. **carbonnade** beef stew with onions and stout or beer. **carré d'agneau** rack of lamb. **cassoulet** stew of white haricot beans, sausage and preserved duck. **cervelle** brains. **châteaubriand** thick fillet steak. **chevreuil** young roe deer. **civet** game stew. **cochon de lait** suckling pig. **contre-filet** sirloin steak. **côte** chop; **– de boeuf** beef rib. **croque-madame** sandwich of toasted cheese and ham topped with an egg. **croque-monsieur** sandwich of toasted cheese and ham. **cuisses de grenouille** frogs' legs. **daube** meat braised in red wine. **entrecôte** beef rib steak. **escargot** snail. **estouffade** meat that's been marinated, fried and braised. **faux-filet** sirloin steak. **filet mignon** tenderloin. **foie** liver; **– de veau** calf's liver. **gigot d'agneau** leg of lamb. **hachis parmentier** shepherd's pie. **jambon** ham; **– cru** cured raw ham. **jarret** ham shin or knuckle. **langue** tongue. **lapin** rabbit. **lard** bacon. **lardon** small cube of bacon. **lièvre** hare. **marcassin** wild boar. **merguez** spicy lamb/beef sausage. **mignon** small meat fillet. **moelle** bone marrow; **os à la –** marrowbone. **navarin** lamb and vegetable stew. **onglet** cut of beef, similar to bavette. **pavé** thick steak. **petit salé** salt pork. **pied** foot (trotter). **porc** pork. **porcelet** suckling pig. **pot-au-feu** boiled beef with vegetables. **queue de boeuf** oxtail. **ragoût** meat stew. **rillettes** potted pork or tuna. **ris de veau** veal sweetbreads. **rognons** kidneys. **rôti** roast. **sang** blood. **sanglier** wild boar. **saucisse** sausage. **saucisson sec** small dried sausage. **selle** (*d'agneau*) saddle (of lamb). **souris d'agneau** lamb knuckle. **tagine** slow-cooked North African stew. **tartare** raw minced steak (also tuna or salmon).

ESSENTIAL INFORMATION

tournedos small slices of beef fillet, sautéed or grilled. **travers de porc** pork spare ribs. **veau** veal.

Poultry (volaille)

aiguillettes (*de canard*) thin slices (of duck breast). **blanc** breast. **caille** quail. **canard** duck; **confit de** – preserved duck. **coquelet** baby rooster. **dinde** turkey. **faisan** pheasant. **foie gras** fattened goose or duck liver. **gésiers** gizzards. **magret** duck breast. **oie** goose. **perdrix** partridge. **poulet** chicken. **suprême** (*de poulet*) fillets (of chicken) in a cream sauce.

Fish & seafood (poissons & fruits de mer)

anguille eel. **bar** sea bass. **belon** smooth, flat oyster. **bisque** shellfish soup. **bouillabaisse** Mediterranean fish soup. **brochet** pike. **bulot** whelk. **cabillaud** fresh cod. **carrelet** plaice. **colin** hake. **coquille** shell. **coquilles St-Jacques** scallops. **crevettes** prawns (UK), shrimp (US). **crustacé** shellfish. **daurade** sea bream. **eglefin** haddock. **escabèche** sautéed and marinated fish, served cold. **espadon** swordfish. **fines de claire** crinkle-shelled oysters. **flétan** halibut. **hareng** herring. **homard** lobster. **huître** oyster. **langoustine** Dublin Bay prawns, scampi. **limande** lemon sole. **lotte** monkfish. **maquereau** mackerel. **merlan** whiting. **merlu** hake. **meunière** fish floured and sautéed in butter. **moules** mussels; **– à la marinière** cooked with white wine and shallots. **morue** dried, salted cod; **brandade de** – cod puréed with potato. **oursin** sea urchin. **palourde** type of clam. **poulpe**

octopus. **raie** skate. **rascasse** scorpion fish. **rouget** red mullet. **St-Pierre** John Dory. **sandre** pike-perch. **saumon** salmon. **seiche** squid. **truite** trout.

Vegetables (légumes)

aligot mashed potatoes with melted cheese and garlic. **asperge** asparagus. **céleri** celery. **céleri rave** celeriac. **cèpe** cep mushroom. **champignon** mushroom; **– de Paris** button mushroom. **chanterelle** small, trumpet-like mushroom. **choucroute** sauerkraut; **– garnie** with cured ham and sausages. **ciboulette** chive. **citronelle** lemongrass. **coco** large white bean. **cresson** watercress. **échalote** shallot. **endive** chicory (UK), Belgian endive (US). **épinards** spinach. **frisée** curly endive. **frites** chips (UK), fries (US). **gingembre** ginger. **girolle** small, trumpet-like mushroom. **gratin dauphinois** sliced potatoes baked with milk, cheese and garlic. **haricot** bean;

– **vert** green bean. **mâche** lamb's lettuce. **morille** morel. **navet** turnip. **oignon** onion. **oseille** sorrel. **persil** parsley. **pignon** pine nut. **poivre** pepper. **poivron** red or green (bell) pepper. **pomme de terre** potato. **pommes lyonnaises** potatoes fried with onions. **riz** rice. **truffes** truffles.

Fruit (fruits)

ananas pineapple. **cassis** blackcurrants. **citron** lemon; – **vert** lime. **fraise** strawberry. **framboise** raspberry. **groseille** redcurrant; – **à maquereau** gooseberry. **myrtille** blueberry. **pamplemousse** grapefruit. **pomme** apple. **prune** plum. **pruneau** prune. **quetsche** damson.

Desserts & cheese (desserts & fromage)

bavarois moulded cream dessert. **beignet** fritter or doughnut. **chèvre** goat; goat's cheese. **clafoutis** baked batter filled with fruit. **crème brûlée** creamy custard dessert with caramel glaze. **crème chantilly** sweetened whipped cream. **fromage blanc** smooth cream cheese. **glace** ice-cream. **île flottante** whipped egg white floating in vanilla custard. **réglisse** liquorice. **tarte aux pommes** apple tart. **tarte tatin** warm, caramelised apple tart cooked upside down.

Soups & sauces (soupes & sauces)

aïoli garlic mayonnaise. **anchoïade** spicy anchovy and olive paste. **béarnaise** sauce of butter and egg yolk. **blanquette** 'white' stew made with eggs and cream. **potage** soup. **velouté** stock-based white sauce; creamy soup. **vichyssoise** cold leek and potato soup.

Further Reference

BOOKS

Non-fiction

Robert Baldick *The Siege of Paris* A gripping account of the Paris Commune of 1871.
Antony Beevor & Artemis Cooper *Paris after the Liberation* Rationing, freedom, Existentialism.
NT Binh *Paris au cinéma* Attractively illustrated hardback round-up of Paris sights on film.
Henri Cartier-Bresson *A propos de Paris* Classic black-and-white shots by a giant among snappers.
Vincent Cronin *Napoleon* A fine biography of the emperor.
Léon-Paul Fargue *Le Piéton de Paris* The city anatomised, just before World War II.
Jean-Marie Gourio *Brèves de comptoir* An anthology of wisdom and weirdness overheard at café counters. A French classic.
Alastair Horne *The Fall of Paris* Detailed chronicle of the Siege and Commune 1870-71.
J-K Huysmans *Croquis Parisiens* The world that Toulouse-Lautrec painted.
Ian Littlewood *Paris: Architecture, History, Art* Paris's history and its treasures.
Henri Michel *Paris Allemand; Paris Résistant* Detailed, two-volume account of life in Paris during the Occupation.
Noel Riley Fitch *Literary Cafés of Paris* Who drank what, where.
Virginia Rounding *Les Grandes Horizontales* Entertaining lives of four 19th-century courtesans.
Simon Schama *Citizens* Epic, readable account of the Revolution.
Thibaut Vandorselaer *Paris BD* A lovely series of walking trails around the city, illustrated entirely with 'BD' (cartoon) panels.

Fiction & poetry

Honoré de Balzac *Illusions perdues; La Peau de chagrin; Le Père Goriot; Splendeurs et misères des courtisanes* Much of the 'Comédie Humaine' cycle of novels is set in Paris.
Charles Baudelaire *Le Spleen de Paris* Prose poems, Paris settings.
Louis-Ferdinand Céline *Mort à crédit* Vivid, splenetic account of an impoverished Paris childhood.

Victor Hugo *Notre Dame de Paris* Romantic vision of medieval Paris. Quasimodo! Esmeralda! The bells!
W Somerset Maugham *Christmas Holiday* Young Brit spends Christmas with a prostitute in Paris.
Gérard de Nerval *Les Nuits d'octobre* Late-night Les Halles and environs, mid 19th century.
Georges Perec *La Vie, mode d'emploi* Cheek-by-jowl life in a Haussmannian apartment building.
Raymond Queneau *Zazie dans le Métro* Paris in the 1950s: bright and very *nouvelle vague*.
Nicolas Restif de la Bretonne *Les Nuits de Paris* The sexual underworld of Louis XV's Paris.
Georges Simenon *Rue Pigalle; Maigret et les braves gens*, etc. Many of the famous Maigret books are set in Paris.
Emile Zola *L'Assommoir; Nana; Le Ventre de Paris* Accounts of the underside of the Second Empire from the master Realist.

The ex-pat angle

Janet Flanner *Paris Journal* Three volumes of reports on post-war Paris arts and politics, written for the *New Yorker*.
Henry Miller *Tropic of Cancer* Love and low life: lusty and funny.
George Orwell *Down and Out in Paris and London* Work in a Paris restaurant, hunger in a Paris hovel, suffering in a Paris hospital.

FILM

Jacques Audiard *The Beat that My Heart Skipped* Audiard turns the story of Tom, a petty Parisian crook specialising in real-estate swindles and classical piano, into a study of alienation and reinvention.
Luc Besson *Subway* Christophe Lambert goes underground.
Marcel Carné *Hôtel du Nord* Arletty stars in this poetic slice of life by the Canal St-Martin.
René Clair *Paris qui dort* Clair's surrealist silent comedy is one of the best Paris films ever made.
Jean-Luc Godard *A Bout de Souffle* Belmondo, Seberg, Godard, the Champs-Elysées, the attitude, the famous ending. Essential.
Michel Hazanavicius *The Artist* Silent black-and-white blockbuster that won five Oscars, including best actor for Jean Dujardin.

Abdellatif Kechiche *La Vie d'Adèle* An explicit portrait of two young women falling in love.
Richard Linklater *Before Sunset* It looks like a walk in the park – and a float down the Seine – but Linklater's magic-hour impromptu lights up passions and possibilities.
Edouard Molinaro *Un Témoin dans la ville* Lino Ventura on the run in 1950s Paris. Superb *noir*.
François Truffaut *Les 400 Coups* The first of the Antoine Doinel cycle.
Agnès Varda *Cléo de 5 à 7* The *nouvelle vague* heroine spends an anxious afternoon in the city.

MUSIC

Miles Davis *Ascenseur pour l'échafaud* The soundtrack to Louis Malle's film is superb after-dark jazz.
Baptiste Trotignon *Song Song Song* Jazz-chanson from this supremely talented pianist.
Fréhel *1930-1939* The immortal Fréhel sings of love, drugs and debauchery in true *chanson réaliste* style.
Naive New Beaters *Wallace* Great pop from a hot Paris band.
Sebastien Tellier *My God is Blue* Transgressive electro pop.
Serge Gainsbourg *Le Poinçonneur des Lilas* Classic early Gainsbourg.

WEBSITES

www.parisinfo.com Official site of the Office de Tourisme.
www.ratp.fr Everything you'll need to know about using the buses, métro, RER and trams.
www.timeout.fr Your critical guide to arts, culture and going out in Paris (English and French).
www.velib.paris.fr All you need to know about using Velib'.

APPS

Time Out (free) The ultimate guide to the capital's culture.
Patrimap (free) Pinpoints nearby monuments along with potted descriptions, and also features a series of itineraries.
RATP (free) Access a wide range of Paris transport maps.
Vélib' (free) Tells you where bikes are available around the city.
Louvre (free) All you need to know before you visit the Louvre.

Index

3W Café, Le 261
6 Paul Bert, Le 145
7th arrondissement
  218-233
9b, Le 169
20 Prieuré Hôtel, Le 355
21, Le 195
104 161
114, Le 150
144 Petrossian, Le 231

A

A la Biche au Bois 157
A la Civette 58
A la Petite Reine 300
A La Providence
  (Quincaillerie
  Leclercq) 155
A Noste 74
AB33 137
Abbey Bookshop 179
Abeilles, Les 187
Abercrombie &
  Fitch 99
Abricadabra Péniche-
  Antipode 248
Absinthe Museum 303
Académie de la Grande-
  Chaumière 208
Académie du Spectacle
  Equestre 303
Accattone 252
accident & emergency
  371
accommodation 336-364
Action 252
Adam Mickiewicz
  library-museum 55
addresses 369
Adöm 28
Adrenaline 203
Afaria 217
Africolor 39
age restrictions 369
Agnès b 87
Air de Paris 189
airports & air travel 365
  left luggage 373
Alain Ducasse au Plaza
  Athénée 96
Alain Mikli 227
Album 179
Alcazar, L' 192
Alcove & Agapes 363
Alexander Nevsky
  Cathedral 103
Alice Cadolle 68
Alimentation Générale,
  L' 169, 262
Alléosse 100
Ambassade
  d'Auvergne, L' 131
ambulance 371

American Apparel 69
American Cemetery 239
Ami Jean, L' 231
Andy Wahloo 135, 262
Angelina 67
Anikalena Skärström
  137
Anne et Valentin 138
Anne Sémonin 69
Anneau de la Mémoire
  306
Années Scooter, Les 28
Antoine et Lili 166
APC 204
apartment rental 375-376
  apart-hotels & holiday
  lets 364
Appartement 217 69
Apple Store 79
April 77 138
Aquaboulevard 248
aquariums 247
Arc de Triomphe 90
Arc du Carrousel 58
architecture 328-333
Ardoise, L' 65
Arènes de Lutèce 183
Armistice Day 39
Arnaud Delmontel 121
Arnaud Larher 117
Arobase L' 188
Arpège, L' 225
Art St-Germain-
  des-Prés 34
Artisan Parfumeur, L'
  227
Arts Florissants, Les 280
Artus Hotel 359
Arty Dandy 198
Assemblée Nationale 220
Astier 29
Astier de Villatte 69
Astrance 109
Atao 104
Atelier Brancusi 124
Atelier de l'Eclair, L' 84
Atelier de Paris –
  Carolyn Carson 289
Atelier Maître Albert 178
Ateliers de Charonne 277
Au Bon Accueil 231
Au Chapeau Gris 303
Au Chien Jaune 299
Au Délice Impérial 301
Au Duc des Lombards
  278
Au Général Beuret 215
Au Lapin Agile 270
Au Magique 279
Au Nom de la Rose 138
Au Passage 149, 153
Au Pied de Cochon 25
Au Rendez-vous des
  Amis 117

Au Vieux Chêne 150
Auberge du 15, L' 187
Auberge Flora 353
Auberge Internationale
  des Jeunes 362
Auberge Jules-Ferry 362
Auberge Ravoux 303
Auditorium du
  Louvre 251, 283
Auteuil 107
Autobus Impérial, L' 85
Autour de Midi-
  Minuit 277
Auvers-Sur-Oise 303
Aux Merveilleux
  de Fred 84
Ave Maria 151
Azzedine Alaïa 138

B

ba&sh 138
babysitting 243
Badaboum 263
Bains du Marais, Les 126
Baiser Salé 278
Balenciaga 100
Balmain 100
Ballroom du Beefclub,
  Le 86
Balzac, Le 252
Bambou, Le 187
Banana Café 256
banks 374
Banlieues Bleues 32
Bar à Manger (BAM),
  Le 258
Bar à Sushi Izimi 104
Bar Dix, Le 202
Bar du Marché, Le 197
Bar Ourcq 165
Baratin, Le 168
Barav, Le 132
Baromètre, Le 135
Baron Rouge, Le 151
Baron, Le 263
bars see cafés & bars
Basilique St-Denis 236
Bastille 142-155
Bastille Day (Le
  Quatorze Juillet) 35
Bataclan, Le 272
Bateaux-Mouches 368
Bateaux Parisens 368
Batignolles 103
Batobus Tour Eiffel 368
Batofar 268, 279
Bear's Den, Le 256
Beaubourg 124-127
bed & breakfasts 363
Bellechasse, Le 360
Belleville 167-171
Bellevilloise, La 170, 265
Bercy 155-157

Berges, Les 230
Berthillon 55
BHV Marais 127
Bibliothèque Historique
  de la Ville de Paris 127
Bibliothèque Nationale
  de France François
  Mitterrand 188
Bibliothèque Nationale
  de France – Richelieu
  & Musée du Cabinet
  des Médailles 74
Bières Cultes 117
Big Fernand 81
Birdland 199
Bistro, Le 231
Bistro du Peintre, Le 28
Bistrot Napolitain, Le 96
Bistrot Paul Bert, Le 145
Bistrot Victoires 74
Blancs Manteaux,
  Les 270
Blend 85
Blueberry 201
boat tours 368
Boeuf à la Mode 303
Bofinger 132
Bogato 215
Bois de Boulogne 107
Bois de Vincennes 156
Bon Marché, Le 227
Bones 145, 153
Bonton 227
Boucheron 69
Bouillon Racine 201
Boulanger de Monge,
  Le 185
Boule Noire, La 273
boulevard St-Germain
  192
Boulogne-Billancourt
  237
Bourse, The 73-79
Bourse de Commerce 84
Brasserie Balzar 180
Brasserie de l'Ile
  St-Louis 55
Brasserie du Théâtre
  303
Brasserie Lipp 192
Brasserie Vagenende 192
Bread & Roses 201
breakdown services 367
Brébant, Le 82
Breizh Café 133
Broken Arm 135
Buddha Bar Hotel 345
Buisson Ardent, Le 185
Bunker, Le 259
bureaux de change 374
buses 366
  to and from airports
  365
  tours 368

Bus Palladium, Le 273
business services 369-370
Butte-aux-Cailles 186
Buvette Gastrothèque 119
BVJ Paris/Quartier Latin 362
By Terry 69

C

cabaret 269-271
Cabaret Sauvage, Le 265
Café Aouba 151
Café Arena, Le 256
Café Charbon 170
Café Charlot 135
Café Chéri(e) 170
Café Cox 256
Café de Flore 197
Café de la Gare 271
Café de la Paix 77
Café de la Presse 151
Café des Initiés, Le 67
Café des Sports, Le 170
Café du Marché, Le 233
Café Livres 126
Café Marly 67
Café Matisse 118
Café Milou 215
Café Suédois 135
Café Titon 151
Caféothèque, La 135
cafés & bars:
  By area:
    Bastille & Eastern Paris 150-154
    Beaubourg & the Marais 126, 135-137
    Champs-Elysées & Western Paris 99, 106,
    The Latin Quarter & the 13th 179, 182, 187, 188-189
    Montmartre & Pigalle 116-117, 120-121
    Montparnasse & Beyond 215
    North-east Paris 165-166, 169-171
    Opéra to Les Halles 67-68, 75-76, 77-79, 82, 86-87
    St-Germain-des-Prés & Odéon 197-198, 202-203
    The 7th & Western Paris 226-227, 233
  By type:
    gay & lesbian 256-258, 261
café-théâtre 269-271
Calbar, Le 151
Cale Sèche, La 170
Cambodge, Le 168
Caméléon 201
Canal St-Martin 160
Candelaria 135

Cantine du Troquet, La 213
Cantine Merci 133
Caravane Chambre 19 154
cars
  driving in Paris 367
  ferries 365
  hire 367-368
Cartel Club 265
Cartier 79
Cartoucherie de Vincennes 289
Castel Béranger 107
Catacombes, Les 216
Cathédrale de Chartres 300
Cathédrale Notre-Dame de Paris 51
Cathédrale Notre-Dame, Reims 305
Cathédrale St-Gatien, Tours 297
Causses 121
Cave à Champagne, La 307
Cave à Michel, La 170
Cave des Papilles, La 215
Caveau de la Huchette 279
Caveau des Oubliettes 279
Caves Augé, Les 100
Caves de Prague, Les 151
Caves Populaires, Les 106
Caves Taillevent, Les 100
Centre de Danse du Marais 288
Centre Gai et Lesbien 255
Centre National de la Danse 287
Centre Pompidou (Musée National d'Art Moderne) 124-125
  film 252
  Galerie des Enfants 243
Centre Pompidou Metz 298
Cerisaie, La 213
Chacha Club 262
Chambelland 153, 154
Champmeslé, La 261
Champo, Le 252
Champs-Elysées 90
Chanel 69
Chanel Joaillerie 69
Chantelivre 203
Chantilly 299
Chapelle de la Médaille Miraculeuse 221
Chapelle des Lombards, La 265
Chapelle du Martyr 112
Chapelle Expiatoire 91
Chapelle-Saint-Blaise-des-Simples 305

Chapelle St-Louis de-la-Salpêtrière 185
Chaplin Denfert, Le 252
Charlie Birdy 99
Chartier 243
Chartres 299-300
Château d'Auvers 303
Château de Chantilly 299
Château de Fontainebleau 301
Château de Malmaison 239
Château de Vaux-le-Vicomte 301
Château de Versailles 301-303
Château de Vincennes 237
Chateaubriand, Le 153, 168
Châtelet – Théâtre Musical de Paris 283
Chemin de la Croix, Le 32
Chez Adel 276
Chez Georges 202
Chez Gladines 187
Chez Hanna 133
Chez Jeannette 165
Chez Jenny 133
Chez Julien 133
Chez Michou 270
Chez Miki 74
Chez Moune 265
Chez Omar 133
Chez Paul 144
Chez Prosper 151
Chez Prune 165
Chez Régine 265
Chez Vong 85
children 242-249
  aquariums & zoos 247
  babies & toddlers 243
  babysitting 243
  eating out 243
  museums & sightseeing 243-247
  parks & theme parks 248-249
  performing arts 248
  swimming & skating 248-249
China 152
Chinatown 186
Choux d'Enfer 84
Christian Constant 203
Christian Liaigre 227
Christian Louboutin 69
Christmas (Noël) 39
Christophe Lemaire 138
Ciel 84, 182
Cigale, La/Boule Noire, La 273
Cimetière de Montmartre 115
Cimetière de Passy 91
Cimetière de Picpus 156
Cimetière des Batignolles 103

Cimetière du Montparnasse 209
Cimetière du Père-Lachaise 144, 148
Cinéaqua 91, 247
Cinéma au Clair de Lune 254
Cinéma des Cinéastes, Le 252
Cinéma du Panthéon, Le 252
Cinéma en Plein Air, Le 36
cinemas 251-254
Cinémathèque Française 252
Cinquante, Le 165
circuses 248
Cirque d'Hiver Bouglione 248
Cirque Pinder 248
Citadines Apart'hotel 364
Cité de l'Architecture et du Patrimoine 94, 244
Cité de la Mode et du Design 188
Cité de la Musique 283
Cité des Sciences et de l'Industrie, La 161
Cité du Cinéma 250
Cité Nationale de l'Histoire de l'Immigration 156
Cité Universitaire 216
climate 378
Clos Médicis, Le 359
Closerie des Lilas, La 208
Clover 225, 226
Club 18, Le 258
clubs 262-269
  gay 258-259, 261
coach travel 365
Cobéa 213
Cochon à l'Oreille, Le 86
Cocotte, La 154
Cocottes, Les 232
Coffee Parisien 201
Colette 69
Collection 1900, La 59
Collège de France 181
Comédie Française 289
comedy 269-271
Comedy Club, Le 271
Comme à Lisbonne 136
Comme des Garçons 100
Compagnie des Vins Surnaturels 202
Comptoir, La 201
Conciergerie, La 51
conference centres 369
Confluences 293
Conserverie, La 75
consumer rights 370
contraception 371
convention centres 369
CopperBay, Le 165
Coq Rico, Le 115

COS 138
Côté Court 254
Coupole, La 214
courier services 369
Coutume Café, Le 226
Couvent des Récollets 161
Crazy Horse Saloon 269
credit cards 374
Crêperie Bretonne Fleurie de l'Epouse du Marin, La 145
Crocodile, Le 182
Crocodisc 182
Cru 133
Crypte Archéologique, La 54
CUD Bar, Le 258
Culture(s) 167
customs regulations 370
cycling 368

D

Da Zavola 179
Dada, Le 99
Dame de Canton, La 269
Dammann Frères 138
dance 286-288
Daumesnil 155-157
Dauphin, Le 168
David Toutain 232
D'Chez Eux 232
Dédé la Frite 75
Défense, La 236
Delaville Café 166
Delfonics 70
Délices d'Orient, Les 233
Denfert-Rochereau 216-217
dentists 372
Dépot, Le 259
Dernier Bar Avant la Fin du Monde, Le 67
Derrière 134
Dessous d'Apollon, Les 260
Détaille 1905 121
Deux Magots, Les 197
Deyrolle 227
Didier Ludot 70
Dior 100
Dior Joaillerie 70
Diptyque 179
Dirty Dick 120
disabled access 370
Disneyland Paris/Walt Disney Studios Park 249
Disquaires, Les 273
Divan du Monde, Le 265
Djoon, Le 269
Docks en Seine 188
doctors 372
Dollhouse 261
Dôme, Le 208
Dong Huong 168
DPAM 154
driving 365, 367
Drouant 77

drugs 370
Drugstore Publicis 100
Du Pain et des Idées 167
Duplex, Le 256

E

E Dehillerin 87
Eau et les Rêves, L' 167
Eclair de Génie, L' 84
Eclaireur, L' 138
Ecole Ferrandi 201
Ecole Militaire 228
Ecole Nationale Supérieure des Beaux-Arts (Ensb-a) 192
Ecole Normale Supérieure 180
Ecurie, L' 180
Editeurs, Les 203
Editions de Parfums Frédéric Malle 227
Eglé Bespoke 70
Eglise de la Madeleine 76
Eglise de la Trinité 118
Eglise du Saint-Esprit 156
Eglise du Val-de-Grâce 181
Eglise St-Augustin 76
Eglise St-Étienne-du-Mont 181
Eglise St-Eustache 84
Eglise St-Germain-des-Prés 192
Eglise St-Germain-l'Auxerrois 59
Eglise St-Gervais-St-Protais 128
Eglise St-Julien-le-Pauvre 175
Eglise St-Laurent 160
Eglise St-Louis-en-l'Ile 55
Eglise St-Médard 181
Eglise St-Nicolas du Chardonnet 175
Eglise St-Paul-St-Louis 128
Eglise St-Roch 59
Eglise St-Séverin 175
Eglise St-Sulpice 200
Eglise St-Vincent-de-Paul 161
Eiffel Tower 228, 229
EKO 265
electricity 370
embassies 370-371
emergencies 371
Encrier, L' 145
Endroit, L' 106
Ensemble Intercontemporain 281
Entr'acte, L' 67
Entrée des Artistes, L' 152
Entrepôt, L' 215, 254
Epernay 305-307
Epicerie du Père Claude, L' 233

Epicerie Générale 227
Epicerie Musicale, L' 167
Epigramme, L' 195
Epiphany (Fête des Rois) 39
Erès 100
Escapes & Excursions 296-307
Auvers-Sur-Oise 303
Chantilly 299
Chartres 299-300
Epernay 305-307
Fontainebleau 300-301
Giverny 303-304
Milly-la-Forêt 304-305
Reims 305-307
Tours 296-299
Vaux-le-Vicomte 301
Versailles 301-303
Escargot Montorgueil, L' 83
Espace B 273
Espace Chapiteaux 248
Espace Dali 112
Espace Fondation EDF 221
Estaminet, L' 136
Etamine Café 257
Etés de la Danse, Les 35
Etoile du Nord, L' 288
Etoile Lilas 251
Etoile Manquante, L' 136
Etoile Paris 265
Etoiles du Rex 244
Etrange Festival, L' 254
Eurostar 365

F

Familia Hôtel 357
Fantôme, Le 166
Fargo 154
Fashion Week 31
Fat Tire Bike Tours 368
Faubourg St-Germain, the 220-228
Fauchon 100
Fausse Boutique, La 121
Favela Chic 265
Feeling Bar, Le 257
Ferrandaise, La 202
Festival Chopin à Paris 35
Festival Classique au Vert 36
Festival d'Automne 38
Festival de l'Imaginaire, l' 37
Festival de St-Denis 34
Festival des Inrockuptibles 39
Festival International de Films de Femmes 254
Festival Jazz à Saint-Germain-des-Prés 33
Festival Paris Ile-de-France 38
Fête de la Gastronomie 38
Fête de la Musique 34
Fête de l'Assomption 37

Fête des Rois (Epiphany) 39
Fête des Vendanges de Montmartre 38
Fête du Beaujolais Nouveau 39
Fête du Travail 33
Fête du Vélo 34
FIAC 38
Fifi Chachnil 72
Film 250-254
festivals 254
Fils à Maman, Les 82
Fines Gueules, Les 75
Finger in the Nose 138
Finkelsztajn 139
fire service 371
Five Hôtel 357
Flamboire, Le 119
flats see apartment rental
Flèche d'Or, La 273
Fleurs, Les 154
Fnac Forum 87
Fnac Junior 204
Foire de Paris 32
Foire du Trône 32
Folies-Bergère 81
Follivores & les Crazyvores, Les 258
Fondation Cartier pour l'Art Contemporain 209
Fondation Claude Monet 304
Fondation d'Enterprise Paul Ricard 94
Fondation Dubuffet 200
Fondation Henri Cartier-Bresson 209
Fondation Le Corbusier 107
Fondation Louis Vuitton 107, 108
Fondation Nationale des Sciences-Politiques 220
Fondation Pierre Bergé Yves Saint Laurent 94
Fontaine des Innocents 83
Fontainebleau 300-301
Forum des Halles 87
Forum des Images 252
Four Seasons George V 345
Fourmi, La 116, 263
FR66 127
Free 'P' Star 139
Freescoot 368
French Tennis Open 34
French Touche 106
Frenchie 85
Frenchie Bar à Vins 86
Fromagerie Barthélémy 301
Fromagerie Dubois et Fils 106
Fromagerie Quatrehomme 227
Full Metal 259

See Venice

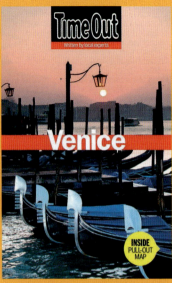

Time Out
Written by local experts

Venice

INSIDE
PULL-OUT
MAP

2015 guidebook on sale now
Written by local experts

like a local

Fumoir, Le 68
Furieux, Les 152

G

Gabrielle Geppert 70
Gai Moulin, Le 258
Gaîté Lyrique 128
Galerie Ching Tsai Too
103
Galerie du Carrousel du
Louvre, La 70
Galerie Emmanuel
Perrotin 139
Galerie Fatiha Selam 139
Galerie Patrick Seguin
154
Galeries Lafayette 82
Galeries Nationales du
Grand Palais 94
Galignani 70
Gallopin 73
Galopin, Le 169
Garance 225
Gare au Gorille 105
Gare du Nord 161
Garde Robe, La 75
Garde-Temps, Le 120
Gâteaux Thoumieux
228, 230
Gauloise, La 232
gay & lesbian 255-261
bars & cafés 256-258
clubs 258-259
information &
resources 255-256
restaurants 258
sex clubs & saunas
259-260
shops & services
260-261
Gay Pride 255
Gaya Rive Gauche 225
Gazzetta, La 149
Generator Paris 362
Géode, La 251
Gérard Mulot 204
Germain 195
Gibert Joseph 204
Gibus, Le 266
Givenchy 100
Giverny 303-304
Glaz'art, Le 266
Glou 134
Glup's 100
Gobelins, Les 185-186
GoldyMama 171
Good Morning Paris
364
Goutte d'Or 112
Gouttière, La 170
Grand Hôtel de
l'Univers 359
Grand Hôtel Jeanne
d'Arc 352
Grand Pan, Le 214
Grand Rex, Le 251
Grand Véfour, Le 65
Grande Arche de La
Défense, La 236

Grande Galerie de
l'Evolution 183
Grands Boulevards, the
79-82
Granterroirs 97
Grenier, Le 270
Grévin 244
Guerlain 101

H

Haï Kaï 169
Haili 215
Halles, Les 82-87
Hammam de la Grande
Mosquée 185
Hammam Medina
Centre 171
Hangar, Le 134
Harry's New York Bar 79
Hazar & Co 215
health 371-372
Hédiard 101
helplines 372
Hermès 198
Hervé Chapelier 204
Hervé Léger 70
Hi Matic 353
Hide, Le 97
Higuma 65
Hilton Paris Opéra 341
History 310-323
HIV & AIDS 372
Hobo Club 266
Hokkaido 75
Hospitel Hôtel Dieu 338
hospitals 371
Hostellerie du Nord 303
Hôtel, L' 358
Hôtel Amour 341
Hôtel Arvor Saint
Georges 341
Hôtel Aviatic 360
Hôtel Banke 351
Hôtel Baudy 304
Hôtel Beaumarchais 355
Hôtel Boisgelin 220
Hôtel Bourg Tibourg 352
Hôtel Brighton 339
Hôtel Britannique 342
Hôtel Chavanel 341
Hôtel Chopin 343
Hôtel Costes 338
Hotel Crayon 342
Hôtel Daniel 345
Hôtel d'Avaray 220
Hôtel de l'Abbaye Saint-
Germain 359
Hôtel de la Bretonnerie
352
Hôtel de la Sorbonne 357
Hôtel de la Trémoille 347
Hôtel de Monaco 220
Hôtel de Sers 347
Hôtel de Vigny 347
Hôtel de Ville 124, 126
Hôtel de Villeroy 220
Hôtel Delambre 360
Hôtel des Académies
et des Arts 360

Hôtel des Arts 351
Hôtel des Deux-Iles 337
Hôtel des Grands
Hommes 180
Hôtel des Saints-Pères
359
Hôtel des Tuileries 339
Hôtel d'Estrées 220
Hôtel Drouot 81
Hôtel du Cygne 343
Hôtel du Jeu de Paume
337
Hotel du Lion d'Or 339
Hôtel du Petit Moulin 352
Hôtel Duc de Saint-
Simon 362 Hôtel Duo
352
Hôtel Eiffel Rive
Gauche 362
Hôtel Eldorado 351
Hôtel Elysées Ceramic
350
Hôtel Ermitage 351
Hôtel Fouquet's Barrière
347
Hôtel Gabriel 355
Hôtel Garden Saint-
Martin 357
Hôtel Henri IV 338
Hôtel Istria Saint-
Germain 360
Hôtel Jules et Jim 352
Hôtel Keppler 349
Hôtel La Bourdonnais
362
Hôtel la Demeure 357
Hôtel La Louisiane 192
Hôtel La Maison Champs
Elysées 349, 361
Hôtel Langlois 342
Hôtel le A 345
Hôtel le Bristol 345
Hôtel Le Général 355
Hôtel Lenox 362
Hôtel les Degrés de
Notre-Dame 358
Hôtel Mansart 339
Hôtel Marceau Bastille
353
Hôtel Matignon 220
Hôtel Napoléon 301
Hotel Odyssey 342
Hôtel Paris France 353
Hôtel Particulier
Montmartre 351
Hôtel Pergolèse 349
Hôtel Plaza Athénée 347
Hôtel Regent's Garden
349
Hôtel Résidence Gobelins
358
Hôtel Résidence Henri IV
357
Hôtel Royal Fromentin
351
Hôtel St-Louis Marais
352
Hôtel Sofitel le Faubourg
338
Hôtel Square 349

Hôtel Villa Madame 359
Hotel W Paris-Opéra 339
Hôtel Westminster 339
hotels 336-364
apart-hotels & flat
rental 364
bed & breakfast 363
youth accommodation
362
Hugo Boss 101
Huilerie Artisanale
Leblanc 198
Huîtrerie Régis 202
Hune, La 198

I

I Love My Blender 127
ID 373
IDM 259
IEM 260
Ile de la Cité 51-54
Ile St-Louis 54-55
Ilot, L' 134
Impact 259
Impressionist'Café L'
303
Institut Catholique 199
Institut de France 195
Institut du Monde Arabe
184, 279
insurance (health) 371
InterContinental Paris Le
Grand 341
Inter-LGBT 256
International, L' 273
internet 373
Invalides & Musée de
l'Armée, Les 220, 221
IRCAM 283
Iris 228
Iro 139
Isabel Marant 154
Izraël 139

J

Jabugo Ibérico & Co 101
Jacadi 216
Jacasses, Les 261
Jacenko 139
Jacques Génin 139
Jadis 217
Jardin & Palais du
Luxembourg 200
Jardin Atlantique 208
Jardin d'Acclimatation
249
Jardin des Plantes 183,
184
Jardin des Serres
d'Auteuil, Le 107
Jardin des Tuileries 59
Jardin du Luxembourg
249
Jardin du Musée de la Vie
Romantique 120
Jardin Tino Rossi (Musée
de la Sculpture en Plein
Air) 184

INDEX

Jardins de la Villa, Les 349
Jardins du Marais, Les 352
Java, La 266
Jay Ahr 71
Jays Paris 347
jazz & blues 277-279
Jazz à la Villette 36
Jazz Club Etoile 278
Jean-Charles Rochoux 204
Jean-Paul Hévin 204
Jeu de Paume 63
Jimmy Fairly 140
Joseph 198
Joséphine Chez Dumonet 202
Josselin 214
Journées du Patrimoine 38
Jules Verne 232

K

K Jacques 140
Kenzo 204
Kibélé, Le 277
Kiliwatch 87
Kitsuné 71
Kokon To Zai 87
Kremlin, Le 116
KriZa Bar 215
Kube Hotel 351

L

Laboratoires d'Aubervilliers, Les 293
Ladurée 99
language 379-381
Lanson 305
Lanvin 101
Lapérouse 195
Lasserre 97
Latin Quarter, the 172-185
Laurent 90
Lavinia 79
Lazare 105
LE66 102
Lefranc.ferrant 198
Left Bank Scooters 368
left luggage 373
legal help 373
Legay Choc 260
Legrand Filles et Fils 76
lesbian Paris see gay & lesbian
libraries 373
Lido, Le 270
Limonaire, Le 277
Little Breizh 196
Liza 75
Lizard Lounge 136
LMDW 204
Lock Groove, Le 215
locksmiths 373
Lockwood, Le 86

Loge, La 288
Loir dans la Théière, Le 136
Longchamp 102
lost property 374
Louis Vuitton 102
Loulou Addict 155
Louvre, the see Musée du Louvre
Louvre des Antiquaires 71
Louxor, Le 254
Lucernaire, Le 292
Luxembourg, the 198-205

M

Ma Cocotte 115
Mac Mahon, Le 254
Machine du Moulin Rouge, La 266
Mâchon d'Henri 199
MAC/VAL 237
Madame de 216
Madonnina, La 169
Magnifique, Le 267
Mains d'Oeuvres 275
Maison de Balzac 109
Maison de Jean Cocteau 304-305
Maison de la Culture du Japon 29
Maison de Radio France 283
Maison de Victor Hugo 129
Maison des Arts de Créteil 287
Maison des Bonbons, La 216
Maison DoDuDinDon 167
Maison du Chocolat, La 109
Maison Européenne de la Photographie 129
Maison Fabre 71
Maison Forestière 306
Maison Mère, La 120
Maison Rouge – Fondation Antoine de Galbert, La 145
Mama Shelter 355
Mam'Zelle Swing 29
Mandarin Oriental 341
Manoush 71
Mansart, Le 120
Manufacture Nationale des Gobelins 186
Marais, The 127-141
Marathon de Paris 32
Marc by Marc Jacobs 71
Marché Anvers 121
Marché aux Puces d'Aligre 155
Marché aux Puces de St-Ouen 117
Marché aux Puces de Vanves 116

Marché Bastille 155
Marché Batignolles 106
Marché Beauvau 155
Marche des Fiertés 35
Marché Monge 185
Marché Président-Wilson 102
Marché St-Pierre 112
Marie-Anne Cantin 233
Marie-Hélène de Taillac 204
Marie Mercié 205
Marks & Spencer 102
Marlusse et Lapin 116
Maroquinerie, La 170, 275
Martin Grant 140
Martin Margiela 72
Mass for Louis XVI 39
Matières à Reflexion 28
Max Linder Panorama 251
MC93 Bobigny 293
Mécanique Ondulatoire, La 275
Méditerranée 199
Mémorial de la France Combattante 239
Mémorial de la Shoah, Le 129
Mémorial des Martyrs de la Déportation 54
Mémorial du Maréchal Leclerc de Hauteclocque et de la Libération de Paris & Musée Jean Moulin 212
Ménagerie de Verre 288
Ménagerie du Jardin des Plantes 247
Ménilmontant 167-171
Merci 140
Mercier 305, 306
Merle Moqueur, Le 187
métro 366
Metropolitan, Le 350
Meurice, Le 339
    restaurant 90
Michel Chaudun 233
Michi 75
MIJE 363
Millimètres 121
Milly-la-Forêt 304-305
Miroir, Le 115
Miss Kô 98
Missiessy 205
MG Road 134
MK2 Bibliothèque 251
Moët & Chandon 305, 307
Moisan 155
Mon Vieil Ami 55
Mona Bismarck American Center for Art & Culture 95
Monceau 103
Mondial de l'Automobile 38
money 374-375

Monnaie de Paris 195
Monseigneur 267
Monster Melodies 87
Montagne Ste-Geneviève 179
Montalembert, Le 362
Monte-en-l'air, Le 171
Montmartre 110-117
Montparnasse 206 216
Montsouris 216-217
Moonshiner 152
Moose 203
Mosquée de Paris, La 184, 375
Motel, Le 152, 275
Mots à la Bouche, Les 260
Mouffetard 179
Moulin de la Galette, Le 116
Moulin Rouge 270
Mouton à Cinq Pattes 205
Musée Albert Kahn 239
Musée Art Ludique 188, 189
Musée-Atelier Adzak 212
Musée Belmondo 239
Musée Bourdelle 212
Musée Carnavalet 129
Musée Cernuschi 104
Musée Cognacq-Jay 131
Musée Dapper 95
Musée d'Archéologie Nationale 239
Musée d'Art et d'Histoire du Judaïsme 129
Musée d'Art Halle St-Pierre 115
Musée d'Art Moderne de la Ville de Paris 95
Musée Daubigny 303
Musée de la Chasse et de la Nature 131
Musée de la Contrefaçon 95
Musée de la Franc-Maçonnerie 77
Musée de la Grande Guerre du Pays de Meaux 307
Musée de la Magie 246
Musée de la Mode et du Textile 63
Musée de la Musique 164, 246
Musée de la Poste 213
Musée de la Poupée 246
Musée de la Préfecture de Police 178
Musée de la Publicité 64
Musée de la Sculpture en Plein Air (Jardin Tino Rossi) 185
Musée de la Vie Romantique 118
Musée de l'Absinthe 303
Musée de l'Air et de l'Espace 236
Musée de l'Armée 220, 221

Musée de l'Erotisme 118
Musée de l'Histoire de
France 131
Musée de l'Opéra 79
Musée de l'Orangerie 63
Musée de Montmartre
115, 116
Musée des Années 30
237, 239
Musée des Archives
Nationales 131
Musée des Arts
Décoratifs 63
Musée des Arts et
Métiers 129, 244
Musée des Arts Forains
157
Musée des Beaux Arts,
Chartres 300
Musée des Beaux Arts,
Tours 297
Musée des Egouts
229, 244
Musée des
Impressionnismes
Giverny 304
Musée des Lettres et
Manuscrits 200
Musée d'Orsay 224
concerts 286
Musée du
Compagnonnage,
Tours 297
Musée du Louvre 63, 80
Musée du Louvre-
Lens 298
Musée du Luxembourg
200
Musée du Quai Branly
229
Musée du Service de
Santé des Armées 181
Musée du Vin 109
Musée Edith Piaf 168
Musée Fragonard 237
Musée Gourmand du
Chocolat 244
Musée Guimet 277
Musée Jacquemart-
André 104
Musée Jean Moulin 212
Musée Maillol 224
Musée Marmottan –
Claude Monet 109
Musée National d'Art
Moderne (Centre
Pompidou 124-125
Musée National de la
Légion d'Honneur
et des Ordres de
Chevalerie p220
Musée National de la
Marine 95, 246
Musée National de la
Renaissance 236
Musée National
Delacroix 195
Musée National des
Arts Asiatiques –
Guimet 95

Musée National du
Moyen Age – Thermes
de Cluny 175
concerts 286
Musée National Gustave
Moreau 118
Musée National Jean-
Jacques Henner 104
Musée National Picasso
131, 132
Musée National Rodin
220, 224
Musée Nissim de
Camondo 104
Musée Pasteur 212
Musée Valentin Haüy
231
Musée Zadkine 200
Musées des Parfumeries-
Fragonard 77
Muséum National
d'Histoire Naturelle 246
music
chanson 276-277, 279
classical music &
opera 280-286
festivals 30-39
jazz & blues 277-279
rock & pop 272-276, 279
world & traditional
277, 279

N

Nature et Découvertes 72
Nauti Store 102
New Morning 267
New Year's Eve/
New Year's Day 39
Next 259
nightlife 262-279
cabaret, comedy &
café-théâtre 269-271
clubs 262-269
gay & lesbian 258-259,
261
music 272-279
Nodus 140
Noël (Christmas) 39
Noir Kennedy 28
Nomade Shop 140
Notre-Dame Cathedral
see Cathédrale Notre-
Dame de Paris
Notre-Dame de
Lorette 306
Nouveau Casino 267
Nouveau Latina, Le 254
Nouvel An Chinois 39
Nouvelle Athènes, La 118
Nouvelles Frontières 72
Nüba 269
Nuit Blanche 38
Nuit des Musées, La 33

O

O Château 76
Observatoire de
Paris 213

Occitane en Provence, L'
54
Odéon 190-205
Odéon, Théâtre de
L'Europe 292
Ofr. 140
Olympia 275
Olympia Le-Tan 72
Ombres, Les 232
Onze, Le 278
Open Café 257
opening hours 375
opera 280-286
Opéra 76-79
Opéra Bastille 144
Opéra Diamond 347
Opéra National de Paris,
Bastille 283
Opéra National de Paris,
Palais Garnier 283
Opportun, L' 214
opticians 372
Orchestre Colonne 281
Orchestre de Chambre de
Paris 281
Orchestre de Paris 281
Orchestre Lamoureux
281
Orchestre National de
France 281
Orchestre Pasdeloup 281
Orchestre
Philharmonique de
Radio France 283
Orly airport 365
O'Sullivans by the
Mill 276

P

Pagode, La 254
Palais de Chaillot 95
Palais de Justice 81
Palais de la Découverte
95
Palais de la Porte
Dorée Aquarium
Tropical 247
Palais de Tokyo: Site
de Création
Contemporaine 96
Palais des Congrès 276
Palais Galliera – Musée
de la Mode 96
Palais Garnier 287
Palais Omnisports de
Paris-Bercy 276
Palais-Royal 64
Palette, La 197
Panic Room 263
Pantalon, Le 183
Panthéon, Le 180, 182
Pantin 238
Paperdolls 117
Papilles, Les 182
Paradis Latin 271
Parc André Citroën 231
Parc Astérix 249
Parc de Belleville 167
Parc de Bercy 157

Parc de la Villette
164, 249
Parc de Thoiry 247
Parc des Buttes-
Chaumont 168, 249
Parc des Expositions
de Paris-Nord
Villepinte 369
Parc Georges
Brassens 217
Parc Monceau 103, 104
Parc Montsouris 217
Parc Zoologique de Paris
248
Paris Address 364
Paris Appartements
Services 364
Paris Beauvais airport
365
Paris Cinéma 35
Paris Face Cachée 31
Paris Jazz Festival 35
Paris Marriott Opera
Ambassador Hotel 341
Paris-Plages 36
Paris Quartier d'Eté 36
parking 367
Passy 107
Patinoire Sonja Henie
248
Pâtisserie Cyril Lignac
84
Pâtisserie des Rêves 109
Pâtisserie Stohrer 83
Patrick Roger 198
Paul & Joe 228
Paul Smith 102
Paulé Ka 72
Pause Café 152
Pavillon Bastille, Le 353
Pavillon de l'Arsenal 131
Pavillon de l'Hermitage
144
Pavillon Ledoyen 90
Peggy Kingg 205
Péniche Opéra 284
Peninsula Paris 347, 354
Pères Populaires, Les 152
performing arts 280-293
classical music &
opera 280-286
dance 286-288
theatre 289-293
for children 248
Perle, La 137
Perraudin 180
Pershing Hall 347
Petit Bain 188
Petit Fer à Cheval,
Le 137
Petit Journal
Montparnasse, Le 279
Petit Paris, Le 357
Petit Patrimoine, Le 299
Petite Table, La 137
Pétrelle 120
Pharamond, Le 85
pharmacies 372
Philharmonie de
Paris 284

INDEX

Pho 14 187
Pierre Gagnaire 98
Pierre Hardy 72
Pierre Hermé 205
Pierre Sang on Gambey 153
Pigalle 117-121
Pinacothèque 96
Pink Flamingo 168
Pirouette 85
Piscine Butte-aux-Cailles 249
Piscine Josephine-Baker 249
Pizza Chic 202
place de la Concorde 64
place de la République 130
place des Victoires 74
place des Vosges 127, 131
place Vendôme 65
Placide, Le 359
Plomb du Cantal, Le 214
Plus Que Parfait 260
Poilâne 205
Point Ephémère 267, 276
Point Virgule, Le 271
police 375
Polidor 200
Polka Galerie 140
Pommery 305, 307
Pont Alexandre III 48
Pont Charles-de-Gaulle 48
Pont de la Concorde 48
Pont de l'Alma 48
Pont des Arts 48
Pont Neuf 48
Popelini 84
Porte 12 165, 166
Porte St-Denis 81, 160
Porte St-Martin 81
postal services 375
Potager du Marais, Le 134
Potager du Roi 302
Potemkine 167
Pozzetto 141
Prada 103
Prairies de Paris, Les 141
Pré Verre, Le 178
Première Pression Provence 121
Prescription Cocktails Club 198
Printemps 82
Printemps des Poètes, Le 31
Printemps des Rues, Le 32
Printemps du Cinéma 31
Prix de Diane 34
Prix de l'Arc de Triomphe 38
P'tit Bar, Le 152
public holidays 33
public transport 366-367
Puces du Design, Les 39
Pull-In Underwear 87

Pulpéria, La 149
Pylones 55

Q

Quartier Bercy Square, Le 355
Quatorze Juillet (Bastille Day), Le 35
Queen 258, 268
Quetzal, Le 257
Quinzaine des Réalisateurs 34

R

Racines 82
Racines 2 66
Raidd Bar 257
rail travel 366-367
  Gare du Nord 161
  left luggage 373
  to and from airports 365
Rech 98
Recyclerie 116, 119
recyling 375
Red House, Le 154
Regard du Cygne 288
Reims 305-307
Relais du Louvre, Le 339
Relais Saint-Germain 359
religion 375
Renaissance Paris Arc de Triomphe 347
Réparate, Le 157
Repetto 79
République, Le 271
Requin Chagrin, Le 182
RER 366
RER B 365
Reservoir, Le 276
Résidence Hôtel des Trois Poussins 343
Restaurant, Le 196
Restaurant Boucherie les Provinces 149
Restaurant du Palais-Royal 66
Restaurant L'Entredgeu 98
restaurants
  By area:
  Bastille & Eastern Paris 145-150, 157
  Beaubourg & the Marais 131-134
  Champs-Elysées & Western Paris 96-99, 104-105, 109
  The Latin Quarter & the 13th 178-179, 182, 185, 187
  Montmartre & Pigalle 115-116, 119-120
  Montparnasse & Beyond 213-214, 217
  North-east Paris 164-165, 168-169

Opéra to Les Halles 65-66, 74-75, 77, 81-82, 85-86
St-Germain-des-Prés & Odéon 195-197, 201-202
The 7th & Western Paris 225, 231-233
  By type:
  children 243
  gay & lesbian 258
Restaur'Bronze 28
Rex 268
Ribouldingue 178
Richart 228
Rick Owens 72
Rive Gauche, Le 261
river transport 366
Roca 98
Rock en Seine 36
Roger Vivier 103
Roissy-Charles-de-Gaulle airport 365
Rosa Bonheur 261
Rosa Bonheur sur Seine 226
Rose Bakery 120
Rosie, La 117
Rostand, Le 203
Rotonde, La 208
Rouge Passion 120
Rouleau de Printemps, Le 169
Royal Cheese 87
Royal Monceau 349
Ruche, La 217
Ryst Dupeyron 228

S

Sabbia Rosa 205
Sacré-Coeur 116
Salle Cortot 284
Salle Gaveau 284
Salle Pleyel 284
Salle Richelieu 289
Salons du Palais-Royal Shiseido 72
Sancerre, La 117
St Christopher's Inn 363
St-Denis 236
St-Germain-des-Prés 192-198
St-Germain-en-Laye 239
St-Jean-de-Montmartre 112
St-Julien-le-Pauvre 174
  Église St-Julien-le-Pauvre 175
St-Pierre-de-Montmartre 112
St-Séverin 174
  Église St-Séverin 175
St-Sulpice 198-205
  Église St-Sulpice 200
Sainte-Chapelle 54
Sancerre, Le 117
Sardine, La 171
Saturne 75
Saut du Loup, Le 68

Scream 258
Secteur X 260
Seine, the 46-48 boat tours 368
  river transport 366
Select, Le 203
Select Hôtel 357
Semilla 196
Sennelier 228
Sentier 83-87
Sentier des Halles 277
Sentou Galerie 228
Sephora 103
Septime 150, 153
Sergent Recruteur, Le 55
Severo 214
Sezz, Le 349
Shakespeare & Company 179
Shangri-La Paris 349
shipping services 376
shopping
  By area:
  Bastille & Eastern Paris 154-155
  Beaubourg & the Marais 126-127, 137-141
  Champs-Elysées & Western Paris 99-102, 106, 109
  The Latin Quarter & the 13th 179, 183, 187, 189
  Montmartre & Pigalle 121
  Montparnasse & Beyond 215
  North-east Paris 215-216
  Opéra to Les Halles 68-73, 76, 82, 87
  St-Germain-des-Prés & Odéon 198, 203-205
  The 7th & Western Paris 227-228, 233
Showcase 268
Shu 196
Silencio 268
Silvera 155
Sir Winston 99
Six Nations 31
skating 248
smoking 376
So What!, Le 261
Social Club, Le 268
Solarhôtel 360
Solidays 35
Sonia Rykiel 198
Sorbonne, La 179, 182
SOS Homophobie 256
Souffle Continu 155
Souffleurs, Les 257
Souk, Le 150
Spa Nuxe 87
Space Hair 260
Spring 66
Sputnik 187
Spyce Bar, Le 258
Stade de France 237, 247

Standard Design
 Hotel 353
STDs 372
Stella McCartney 72
Stolly's 137
Storie 216
Studio 28 254
Studio Galande 254
Studio Harmonic 288
Studio-Théâtre 289
study 376-377
Sublim Eiffel 362
Sun City 260
Sunset/Le Sunside,
 Le 279
Suresnes 239
Surface 2 Air 141
Swan Bar, Le 279
Swell Apartments 364
swimming 248-249
synagogue 375

T

Table Lauriston, La 99
Taillevent 99
Talents – Création
 Contemporaine 79
Tambour, Le 87
Tango (La Boîte à
 Frissons), Le 258
Tape Bar 154
Tarmac, Le 293
taxis 367
Techno Parade 38
telephones 377
Télescope Café 68
Temps des Cerises, Le
 137
Terrass Hotel 351
Tête dans les Olives,
 La 171
TGV 366
Thaïm 66
theatre 289-293
Théâtre de la Bastille 288
Théâtre de la Cité
 Internationale 292
Théâtre de la Huchette
 292
Théâtre de la Madeleine
 291
Théâtre de la Tempête
 289
Théâtre de la Ville 277,
 285, 287, 292
Théâtre de l'Aquarium
 289
Théâtre de l'Atelier 112
Théâtre de l'Epée de
 Bois 289
Théâtre des Abbesses
 292
Théâtre des Bouffes du
 Nord 285, 289
Théâtre des Champs-
 Elysées 285
Théâtre des Variétés 81
Théâtre d'Ivry Antoine
 Vitez 293

Théâtre du Châtelet 279,
 287, 291
Théâtre du Rond Point
 291
Théâtre du Soleil 289
Théâtre du Vieux
 Colombier 289
Théâtre Dunois 248
Théâtre Gérard-Philipe
 293
Théâtre Marigny 291
Théâtre Nanterre
 Amandiers 293
Théâtre National de
 Chaillot 287, 291
Théâtre National de
 l'Opéra Comique 285
Théâtre Paris Villette
 290, 291
theme parks 249
Thomas Cook 106
Tienda Esquipulas 117
time 377
Timhotel Montmartre
 351
tipping 378
toilets 378
Torréfacteur Verlet 72
Tour d'Argent, La 185
Tour de France, Le 35
Tour de Montlhéry (Chez
 Denise), La 85
Tour Eiffel see Eiffel
 Tower
Tour Jean Sans Peur 84
Tour Montparnasse 208,
 213
Tour St-Jacques 126
tourist information 378
tours 368
Tours 296-299
Trac, Le 189
translators 369
Train Bleu, Le 157
trains 365, 366
trams 366
Trois Arts, Les 171
Trois Baudets, Les 277
Troquet des Glaces, Le
 171
Truskel, Le 76, 263

U

UGC Ciné Cité Bercy 251
Un Dimanche à Paris 197
UNESCO 231
Unico 150

V

Vanessa Bruno 205
Vaudeville, Le 73
Vaux-le-Vicomte 301
Vedettes du Pont-
 Neuf 368
Verjus 66
Verre Volé, Le 165
Versailles 301-303
Veuve Clicquot 305

Viaduc d'Austerlitz 48
Viaduc des Arts, Le 157
Vieux Belleville, Le 277
Vignoles, Les 141
Villa, La 359
Villa d'Estrées 359
Village Joué Club 76
Village St-Paul, Le 141
Village Suisse 231
Villette, La 160
Vimy Ridge 306
Vin en Tête 106
Vincennes 237
Vino, Il 233
Vintage Bar 141
visas & immigration 378
Viveka Bergström 171
vocabulary 379-381

W

WAIT 141
walking 368
 Père-Lachaise 148
Wanderlust 269
We Love Green Festival
 34
weights & measures 378
Westin, Le 339
WH Smith 72
women 378

Y

Yohji Yamamoto 72
youth accommodation
 362
Yves Saint Laurent 205

Z

ZAC Rive Gauche 188
Zadig & Voltaire 141
Zèbre O Grenier, Un 171
Zen 66
Zénith 276
Zenzoo 76
Ze Restoo 258
zoos 247-248

INDEX

Bags packed, milk cancelled, house raised on stilts.

You've packed the suntan lotion, the snorkel set, the stay-pressed shirts. Just one more thing left to do – your bit for climate change. In some of the world's poorest countries, changing weather patterns are destroying lives.

You can help people to deal with the extreme effects of climate change. Raising houses in flood-prone regions is just one life-saving solution.

Climate change costs lives. Give £5 and let's sort it *Here & Now*

www.oxfam.org.uk/climate-change

Oxfam is a registered charity in England and Wales (No.202918) and Scotland (SCO039042). Oxfam GB is a member of Oxfam International.

Be Humankind ⚥ Oxfam

Advertisers' Index

Please refer to the relevant pages for contact details.

Galeries Lafayette	**IFC**
Le Lido	**14**
Vedettes de Paris	**26**

Explore

Batobus	**50**
Bateaux Parisiens	**62**
Fauchon	**78**
Bouillon Racine	**194**
Pharamond	**194**

Arts & Entertainment

Moulin Rouge	**282**

Essential Information

Paris Address	**340**
Hôtel Marceau Bastille	**344**
Hôtel Le Cinq Codet	**348**

Maps

MAPS

Paris Arrondissements

MAPS

MAPS

MAPS

MAPS

Latin Quarter

MAPS

MAPS

Street Index

4 Fils, r. des - p402 K5/L6, p406 K5/L6, p409 K5/L5/6
4 Septembre, r. du - p401 H4
8 Mai 1945, r. - p402 K3/L3
29 Juillet, r. du - p401 G5, p405 G5

Abbaye, r. de l' - p405 H7, p408 H7
Abbe de l'Epee, r. de l' - p408 H8/J8
Abbe-Gregoire, r. de l' - p405 F7/G7/8
Abbé, r. de l' - p404 C9/D9/10
Abbesses, pl. des - p402 H1/2
Abbesses, r. des - p401 H1, p402 H1/2
Abbeville, r. d' - p402 J2/K3
Abel-Hovelacque, r. - p406 K10
Abel, r. - p407 M8
Aboukir, r. d' - p402 J4/K4
Acacias, r. des - p400 C3
Adour, Villa de l' - p403 P3
Affre, r. - p402 K1
Aguesseau, r. - p401 F4
Alain-Chartier, r. - p404 C9
Alain, r. - p405 F9/10
Alasseur, r. - p404 D7
Albert 1er, Cours - p401 D5/E5, p405 D5/E5
Albert-de-Lapparent, r. - p405 E8
Albert-de-Mun, av - p400 C5, p404 C5
Albert-Thomas, r. - p402 L4
Alboni, Sq - p404 B6
Alencon, r. d' - p405 F8
Alesia, r. d' - p405 E10/F10
Alexandre-Charpentier, r. - p400 B2
Alexandre-Dumas, r. - p407 P7/Q6/7
Alexandre III, Pont - p401 E5, p405 E5
Alexandre-Parodi, r. - p402 L2
Alexandrine, pge - p407 P6
Alexandrine, pl. - p403 P6
Alfred-Bruneau, r. - p400 A6, p404 A6
Alibert, r. - p402 L4
Aligre, r. d' - p407 N7/8
Alleray, pl. d' - p405 D10/E10
Alleray, r. d' - p404 D9, p405 E10
Alma, Pont de l' - p400 D5, p404 D5
Alouettes, r. des - p403 N3
Alphonse-Baudin, r. - p403 M5/6, p407 M5/6
Alphonse-Bertillon, r. - p405 E10
Alphonse-de-Neuville, r. - p400 D1
Alsace, r. d' - p400 C1, p402 K2/3
Amandiers, r. des - p403 P4/5
Ambroise-Paré, r. - p402 K2
Amélie, r. - p401 E6, p405 E6
Amelot, r. - p402 L5/M6, p406 L5/M6, p409 L5
Amiral-Bruix, bd de l' - p400 A3/A/B3
Amiral-d'Estaing, r. de l' - p400 C4/5
Amiral-Roussin, r. de l' - p404 D8/9
Ampère, r. - p400 D1, p401 D1
Amsterdam, r. d' - p401 G2/3
Anatole-de-la-Forge, r. - p400 C3

Anatole-France, quai - p401 F5/G5, p405 F5/G5/6
Anatole-France, r. - p400 B1/C1
André-Citroën, quai - p404 A8/9/B7
André-del-Sarte, r. - p402 J1
André-Gide, r. - p405 E9/10
André-Maillot, bd - p400 A3
Anjou, quai d' - p406 K7/L7, p409 K7/L7
Anjou, r. de - p401 F3/4
Ankara, r. d' - p404 B6/7
Annam, r. d' - p403 Q4
Annonciation, r. de l' - p404 A6
Antoine-Bourdelle, r. - p405 F8
Aqueduc, r. d' - p402 L2
Arago, bd - p405 H10, p406 H10/J10
Arbalete, r. de l' - p406 J9/K9
Arbre-Sec, r. de l' - p402 J6, p406 J6
Arc-de-Triomphe, r. de l' - p400 C3
Arcade, r. de l' - p401 F4/G3
Archeveche, Pont de - p406 K7
Archives, r. des - p402 K5/6/L5, p406 K5/6/L5, p409 K5/6/L5
Arcole, Pont d' - p402 K6, p406 K6
Arcole, r. d' - p406 J6/7
Ardennes, r. des - p403 N1
Arènes, r. des - p406 K8
Aristide-Briand, r. - p401 F5/6, p405 F5/6
Aristide, r. - p400 B1
Armand-Carrel, r. - p403 M2/N2
Armand-Moisant, r. - p405 F9
Arquebusiers, r. des - p402 L6, p406 L6, p409 L6
Arsenal, r. de l' - p406 L7
Arsonval, r. d' - p405 E9
Arthur-Groussier, r. - p403 M4
Artois, r. d' - p401 D3/E3/4
Arts, Pont des - p401 H6, p402 H6, p405 H6, p406 H6, p408 H6
Assas, r. d' - p405 G7/8/H8/9, p408 G8/H8/9
Asseline, r. - p405 F10
Assomption, r. de l' - p404 A7
Astorg, r. d' - p401 F3/4
Athènes, r. d' - p401 G3
Atlas, r. de l' - p403 M3
Auber, r. - p401 G3/4
Aubervilliers, r. d' - p402 L1
Aubriot, r. - p409 K6
Aubry, Cité - p403 Q6, p407 Q6
Augereau, r. - p400 D6, p404 D6
Auguste-Comte, r. - p405 H8, p406 H8, p408 H8
Auguste-Vitu, r. - p404 A8
Augustin-Thierry, r. - p403 P3
Aumale, r. de - p401 H3, p402 H3
Austerlitz, Pont d' - p406 L8
Austerlitz, quai d' - p406 L8/9/M9, p407 M9
Avre, r. de l' - p404 D8
Avron, r. d' - p407 Q7

Babylone, r. de - p405 F7/G7
Bac, r. du - p405 F7/G6/7
Bachelet, r. - p402 J1
Bachaumont, r. - p402 J5, p406 J5

Bagnolet, r. de - p403 Q6, p407 Q6
Balard, r. - p404 A8/9
Ballu, r. - p401 G2
Balzac, r. - p400 D3
Banque, r. de la - p402 H4/5
Banquier, r. du - p406 K10
Barbès, bd - p402 J1
Barbet-de-Jouey, r. - p405 F6/7
Barbette, r. - p402 L6, p406 L6, p409 L6
Baron-Le-Roy, r. - p407 P10
Barque, r. - p405 E9
Barres, r. des - p402 K6, p406 K6, p409 K6
Basfroi, r. - p407 N6/7
Bassano, r. de - p400 C4/D4
Bassou, r. de - p400 C4/D4
Bastille, bd de la - p406 L8/M7, p409 M7
Bastille, pl. de la - p407 M7, p409 M7
Bastille, r. de la - p409 L7/M7
Batignolles, r. des - p401 F1/2
Batignolles, sq des - p401 E1/F1
Bauches, r. des - p400 A6, p404 A6
Baume, r. de la - p401 E3
Bausset, r. - p404 D9
Bayard, r. - p401 E4/5, p405 E5
Bayen, r. - p400 C2
Béarn, r. de - p409 L6
Beaubourg, r. - p402 K5, p409 K5
Beauce, r. de - p409 L5
Beauharnais, Cité - p407 P7
Beaujon, r. - p400 C3/D3
Beaumarchais, bd - p402 L5/6, p406 L5/6/M6, p409 L5/6/M6
Beaune, r. de - p401 G6, p405 G6
Beauregard, r. - p402 J4
Beaurepaire, r. - p402 L4
Beautreillis, r. - p406 L7, p409 L7
Beaux-Arts, r. des - p405 H6, p408 H6
Beccaria, r. - p407 N7/8
Becquerel, r. - p402 J1
Bel-Air, av du - p407 Q8
Belfort, r. de - p403 N6, p407 N6
Bellechasse, r. de - p401 F6, p405 F6
Bellefond, r. - p402 J3
Belles-Feuilles, r. des - p400 A4/B4/5
Belleville, bd de - p403 N4
Belleville, r. de - p403 N3/P3/Q3
Bellor, r. - p402 L1
Belzunce, r. de - p402 J2/K2
Bénard, r. - p405 F10
Béranger, r. - p402 L4/5, p406 L5, p409 L5
Berbier-du-Mets, r. - p406 K10
Bercy, bd de - p407 N9/P9
Bercy, Pont de - p407 M9
Bercy, quai de - p407 N9/10
Bercy, r. de - p406 M8, p407 M8/9/N9/P10
Berger, r. - p402 J5, p406 J5
Bergère, Cité - p402 J4
Bergère, r. - p402 J3/4
Bergers, r. des - p404 B8/9
Bernardins, r. des - p406 J7/8/K7
Berne, r. de - p401 F2

Bernoulli, r. - p401 F2
Berri, r. de - p400 D4, p401 D3/E3
Berteaux-Dumas, r. - p400 A2
Berthe, r. - p402 H1
Berthie-Albrecht, av - p400 D3
Berthier - p400 C1/D1
Berthollet, r. - p406 J9
Berton, r. - p404 B6
Beslay, pge - p403 M5, p407 M5
Béthune, quai de - p406 K7, p409 K7
Bichat, r. - p402 L3/4/M4
Bidassoa, r. de la - p403 P4/Q5
Bienfaisance, r. de la - p401 E3/F3
Bièvre, r. de - p406 J7/K7
Bineau, bd - p400 A1
Biot, r. - p401 G2
Birague, r. de - p406 L6, p409 L6/7
Bir-Hakeim, Pont de - p400 B6, p404 B6
Bisson, r. - p403 N4
Bixio, r. - p405 E7
Blanche, r. - p401 G2/3
Blancs-Manteaux, r. des - p402 K6, p406 K6, p409 K6
Bleue, r. - p402 J3
Blomet, r. - p404 C9/D9, p405 D9/E8
Bluets, r. des - p403 N5, p407 N5
Boccador, r. du - p400 D4/5
Boétie, r. la - p401 D4/E3/4/F3
Boissière, r. - p400 B4/C4/5, p404 C5
Boissonade, r. - p405 G9/G9
Boissy-d'Anglas, r. - p401 F4/5
Bonne-Nouvelle, bd - p402 J4/K4
Bonaparte, r. - p401 H6, p405 H6/7, p408 H6/7
Bonne, r. de la - p402 J1
Borghèse, r. - p400 A1
Borrégo, r. du - p403 Q3
Bosquet, av - p400 D5/6, p404 D5/6
Botzaris, r. - p403 N2/3
Bouchardon, r. - p402 K4
Boulainvilliers, r. de - p404 A6/7
Boulangers, r. des - p406 K8
Boulard, r. - p405 G10
Boulets, r. des - p407 P7
Bouquet-de l'Champ, r. du - p400 C5, p404 C5
Bourbon, quai de - p406 K7, p409 K7
Bourdon, bd - p406 L7/8/M7, p409 L7/M7
Bourdonnais, av de la - p400 D6, p404 C6/D6
Bourdonnais, r. des - p402 J6, p406 J6
Bouret, r. - p403 M2
Bourg-Tibourg, r. du - p409 K6
Bourgogne, r. de - p405 F5
Boursault, r. - p401 F1/2
Bourseul, r. - p404 D9
Bouvier, Imp - p407 P7
Bouvines, av de - p407 Q7
Boyer-Barret, r. - p405 F10
Boyer, r. - p403 P4
Brady, pge - p402 K4
Brancion, r. - p404 D10, p405 D10/E10

Branly, quai - p400 C5/6/D5, p404 C5/6/D5
Braque, r. - p402 K5, p406 K5, p409 K5
Brèche-aux-Loups, r. de la - p407 P9/10/Q9
Bréguet, r. - p403 M6/N6, p407 M6
Bretagne, r. de - p402 L5, p406 L5, p409 L5
Breteuil, av de - p405 E7/8
Brey, r. - p400 C3
Brézin, r. - p405 G10
Broca, r. - p406 J9/10
Brochant, r. - p401 F1
Brown-Séquard, r. - p405 F9
Bruant, r. - p406 L10
Brun, r. le - p406 K9/10
Brunel, r. - p400 B3
Brunetière, av - p400 D1
Bruxelles, r. de - p401 G2
Bruyère, r. la - p401 G2/H2
Buci, r. de - p406 H7, p408 H7
Budapest, r. de - p401 G3
Buffon, r. - p406 K9/L8/9
Bugeaud, av - p400 A4/B4
Buisson-St-Louis, r. de - v M3/4
Bureau, pge du - p407 P6, p407 Q7
Burnouf, r. - p403 M3
Burq, r. - p401 H1, p402 H1
Buzenval, r. de - p407 Q7

Cadet, r. - p402 J3
Caffarelli, r. - p409 L5
Cail, r. - p402 L2
Caire, r. du - p402 J4/K4
Calais, r. de - p401 G2
Cambacérès, r. - p401 F3/4
Cambon, r. - p401 G4
Cambronne, r. - p404 D8/9
Campagne-Première, r. - p405 G9/G9
Campo-Formio, r. de - p406 L10
Canettes, r. des - p408 H7
Capri, r. de - p407 Q10
Capron, r. - p401 G1
Capt-Ménard, r. du - p404 A8/B8
Capucines, bd des - p401 G4
Capucines, r. des - p401 G4
Cardinal-Lemoine, r. du - p406 K7/8
Cardinet, r. - p400 D2, p401 E1/2/F1
Carmes, r. des - p406 J7/8, p408 J7/8
Carnot, av - p400 C3, p400 B1/C1
Carrière-Mainguet, Imp - p403 P6, p407 P6
Carrousel, pl. du - p401 H5, p405 H5
Carrousel, Pont du - p401 G6/G6, p405 G6/H6
Cascades, r. des - p403 P3/4
Casimir-Périer, r. - p401 F6, p405 F6
Cassette, r. - p405 G7
Cassini, r. - p405 H9, p406 H9
Castagnary, r. - p405 E10
Castellane, r. de - p401 G4
Castex, r. - p406 L7, p409 L7
Castiglione, r. de - p401 G5
Catalogne, pl. - p405 F9
Cauchy, r. - p404 A8/9
Caulaincourt, r. - p401 G1/H1, p402 H1/J1
Caumartin, r. de - p401 G3/4
Cave, r. - p402 K1
Cavendish, r. - p403 N2
Célestins, quai de - p406 K7/L7, p409 K7/L7
Cels, r. - p405 G10
Cendriers, r. des - p403 N5/P5
Censier, r. - p406 K9

Cerisaie, r. de la - p406 L7, p409 L7
Cernuschi, r. - p401 E1
César-Franck, r. - p405 E8
Cévennes, r. des - p404 A8/B9
Chabrol, r. de - p402 J3/K3
Chaillot, r. de - p400 C4/5/D4
Chaise, r. de la - p405 G7
Chalet, r. du - p403 M3
Chalgrin, r. - p400 B3/C3
Chaligny, r. - p407 N7/8
Chalon, r. de - p407 M8/N8
Champ-de-Alouette, r. du - p406 J10
Champ-de-Mars, r. - p401 D6/E6
Champs-Elysées, av des - p400 C3/D4, p401 D4/E4/F4/5
Change, Pont au - p402 J6, p406 J6, p408 J6
Chanoinesse, r. - p406 K7
Chantier, pge du - p407 M7
Chanzy, r. - p407 N7/P7
Chapelle, bd de la - p402 K2/L2
Chapon, r. - p402 K5, p406 K5, p409 K5
Chappe, r. - p402 H1/2
Chaptal, r. - p400 B1
Charcot, r. - p407 M10
Chardin, r. - p400 B6, p404 B6
Charenton, r. de - p407 M7/8/N8/P9/10/Q10
Charlemagne, r. - p406 L7, p409 L7
Charles-Baudelaire, r. - p407 M7/N7
Charles-Dallery, pge - p407 N6/7
Charles de Gaulle, av - p400 A2/3
Charles-de-Gaulle, pl. - p400 C3
Charles-de-Gaulle, Pont - p406 M8/9
Charles-de-Mars, r. du - p404 D6, p405 D6/E6
Charles-Delescluze, r. - p407 N7
Charles-Divry, r. - p405 G10
Charles-Fillion, pl. - p401 F1
Charles-Floquet, av - p404 C6/7/D7
Charles-Laffitte, r. - p400 A2/3
Charles-Lecocq, r. - p404 C9
Charles-Nicolle, r. - p407 N8/P8
Charles-Nodier, r. - p402 J1
Charles-Risler, av - p404 D6/7
Charles, r. - p406 L7, p409 L7
Charlot, r. - p402 L5, p406 L5, p409 L5
Charolais, r. du - p407 N8/9/P9/10
Charonne, bd de - p403 P6/Q6, p407 P6/Q6/7
Charonne, r. de - p403 P6, p407 M7/N7/P6/Q6
Chartres, r. de - p400 A2, p402 K1/2
Chateau-d'Eau, r. du - p402 K4/L4
Chateau-Landon, r. du - p402 L2
Chateau, r. du - p405 F10
Chateaudun, r. de - p401 G3/H3, p402 H3
Châtelet, pl. du - p402 J6, p406 J6, p408 J6
Chaudron, r. - p402 L2
Chaussée-d'Antin, r. de la - p401 G3/H3/4
Chavaleret, r. du - p406 M8
Chazelles, r. de - p400 D2, p401 D2

Chemin-Vert, r. du - p403 M6/N5/6, p407 M6/N5/6, p409 M6
Cherche-Midi, r. du - p405 F8/G7/8
Chernoviz, r. - p400 B6, p404 B6
Chevalier-de-la-Barre, r. de - p402 J1
Chevalier, r. - p405 G7, p408 G7
Chevert, r. - p401 E6, p405 E6/7
Chine, r. de la - p403 Q4/5
Choiseul, pge - p401 H4
Choiseul, r. de - p401 H4, p402 H4
Chomel, r. - p405 G7
Christine, r. - p408 H7
Cimarosa - p400 C4
Cino-del-Duca, r. - p400 B1/2
Cinq-Martyrs-du-Lycée-Buffon, pl des - p405 E9/F9
Cirque, r. du - p401 E4
Cité, r. de la - p406 J6/7, p408 J6/7
Citeaux, r. de - p407 N7/8
Clairaut, r. - p401 F1
Claude-Bernard, r. - p406 J9
Claude-Decaen, r. - p407 Q9/10
Claude-Tillier, r. - p407 P7/8
Claude-Vellefaux, av - p403 M3
Clauzel, r. - p401 H2, p402 H2
Clavel, r. - p403 N3
Clef, r. de la - p406 K8/9
Clément-Marot, r. - p400 D4
Clément, r. - p408 H7
Cler, r. - p401 D6/E6, p405 D6/E6
Cléry, r. - p402 J4
Clichy, av de - p401 F1/G1/2/3
Clichy, bd de - p401 G2/H2
Clichy, pl. de - p401 G2
Clignancourt, r. de - p402 J1/2
Clisson, r. - p406 L10/M10
Cloître-Notre-Dame, r. du - p406 J7/K7
Clos-Feuquières, r. du - p404 C9/10
Clotilde, r. - p406 J8, p408 J8
Clovis, r. - p406 J8
Cognacq-Jay, r. - p400 D5, p404 D5
Colbert, r. - p402 H4
Colisée, r. du - p401 E4
Collégiale, r. de la - p406 K9
Colonel-Driant, r. du - p402 H5, p406 H5
Colonel-Fabien, pl. du - p403 M3
Colonel-Moll, r. du - p400 C3
Colonel-Rozanoff, r. du - p407 P8
Colonnes-du-Trône, r. du - p407 Q8
Comète, r. de la - p401 E6, p405 E6
Commandant-René-Mouchotte, r. du - p405 F9
Commerce, pl. du - p404 C8
Commerce, r. du - p404 C8
Commines, r. - p409 L5
Concorde, pl. de la - p401 F5, p405 F5
Concorde, Pont de la - p401 F5, p405 F5
Condamine, r. la - p401 F1/2
Condé, r. de - p405 H8, p406 H7, p408 H7
Condorcet, r. - p402 J2
Constantine, r. de - p401 E6, p405 E6
Constantinople, r. de - p401 F2
Conti, quai de - p402 H6, p406 H6, p408 H6

Contrescarpe, pl. de la - p406 J8
Convention, r. de la - p404 A8/B8/9/C9
Copernic, r. - p400 B4/C4
Copreaux, r. - p405 E9
Coquillière, r. - p402 H5/J5, p406 H5/J5
Cordelières, r. des - p406 J10
Coriolis, r. - p407 P9/10
Corse, quai de la - p402 J6, p406 J6, p408 J6
Cortambert, r. - p400 A5/6/B5
Corvisart, r. - p406 J10
Costa-Rica, pl. de - p400 B6, p404 B6
Cotentin, r. du - p405 E9/F9
Cotte, r. de - p407 N7
Courcelles, bd de - p400 D2/3, p401 D2/E2/F2
Courcelles, r. de - p400 C1/D2, p401 D3/E3
Cour-des-Noues, r. de la - p403 Q5, p407 Q5
Couronnes, r. des - p403 N4/P3/4
Courtois, pge - p403 P6, p407 P6
Coustou, r. - p401 H2
Coypel, r. - p406 K10
Crémieux, r. - p407 M8
Crespin-du-Gast, r. - p403 N5, p407 N5
Crillon, r. - p406 L7/8, p409 L7
Crimée, r. de - p403 N1/2
Croissant, r. du - p402 J4
Croix-des-Petits-Champs, r. - p402 H5, p406 H5
Croix-Nivert, r. de la - p404 C8/9/10/D8
Croix-Nivert, villa de la - p404 D8
Cronstadt, r. de - p404 D10
Croulebarbe, r. de - p406 J10/K10
Crozatier, r. - p407 N7/8
Crussol, r. de - p402 L5/M5, p403 M5, p406 L5/M5, p407 M5, p409 L5/M5
Cujas, r. - p406 J8, p408 J8
Custine, r. - p402 J1
Cuvier, r. - p406 K8/L8

Dagorno, r. - p407 Q8/9
Daguerre, r. - p405 G10
Dalou, r. - p405 E8/9
Dames, r. des - p401 F2/G1
Damrémont, r. - p401 G1/H1
Daniel-Stern, r. - p404 C7
Danielle-Casanova, r. - p401 G4
Dante, r. - p406 J7, p408 J7
Danton, r. - p400 B1, p406 H7/J7, p408 H7/J7
Dantzig, r. de - p404 C10/D10
Darboy, r. - p403 M4
Darcet, r. - p401 G2
Dareau, r. - p405 H10, p406 H10
Daru, r. - p400 D3
Daubenton, r. - p406 K9
Daubigny, r. - p401 E1/2
Daumesnil, av - p407 M7/8/N8/P9/Q9
Daunou, r. - p401 G4
Dauphine, pl. - p406 J6, p408 J6
Dauphine, r. - p406 H6/7, p408 H6/7
Dautancourt - p401 F1/G1
Daval, r. - p407 M6/7
Débarcadère, r. du - p400 B3
Debelleyme, r. - p402 L5, p406 L5, p409 L5
Decamps, r. - p400 A5/B5, p404 A5/B5
Decrès, r. - p405 E10/F10

STREET INDEX

Degas, r. - p404 A7/8
Delaitre, r. - p403 P4
Delambre, r. - p405 G9
Delépine, Imp - p407 P7
Delessert, bd - p400 B6, p404 B6
Delouvain, r. - p403 P3
Delta, r. du - p402 J2
Demarquay, r. - p402 K2/L2
Denfert-Rochereau, pl. - p405 H10
Denfert-Rochereau, av - p405 H9/10
Départ, r. du - p405 F9/G8
Département, r. du - p402 L1
Desaix, r. - p404 C7
Desbordes-Valmore, r. - p400 A5/6
Desbordes, r. - p404 A6
Descartes, r. - p406 J8, p408 J7/8
Désir, pge du - p402 K3
Desnouettes, r. - p404 B10/C10
Deux-Ponts, r. des - p406 K7, p409 K7
Diderot, bd - p407 M8/N8/P8
Didot, r. - p405 F10
Dixmude, bd de - p400 B2
Dr-Finlay, r. du - p404 B7/C7
Dr-Goujon, r. du - p407 Q9
Dr-Lancereaux, r. du - p401 E3
Dr-Roux, r. du - p405 E9
Domat, r. - p408 J7
Dombasle, r. - p404 C10/D10
Dorian, av - p407 P8/Q8
Dorian, r. - p407 P8
Douai, r. de - p401 G2
Double, Pont au - p406 J7
Doudeauville, r. - p402 J1/K1
Dragon, r. du - p405 G7
Drouot, r. - p402 H3/4
Duban, r. - p400 A6, p404 A6
Duée, r. de la - p403 Q4
Dufrénoy, r. - p400 A5, p404 A5
Dugommier, r. - p407 P9
Dulong, r. - p401 E1/F1/2
Dumas, pge - p407 P7
Dumeril, r. - p406 K9/10
Dumont-d'Urville, r. - p400 C4
Dunkerque, r. de - p402 J2/K2
Dunois, r. - p406 L10/M10
Duperré, r. - p401 H2
Dupetit-Thouars, r. - p402 L5, p406 L5, p409 L5
Duphot, r. - p401 G4
Dupin, r. - p405 G7
Dupleix, pl. - p404 C7
Dupleix, r. - p404 C7/D7
Dupuis, r. - p402 L5, p406 L5
Duquesn, av - p405 E7e
Durance, r. de la - p407 P9/Q9
Duranti, r. - p403 N5/6, p407 N5/6/P6
Duranton, r. - p404 B9
Duret, r. - p400 B3
Duris, r. - p403 P4/5, p407 P5
Duroc, r. - p405 E8
Dutot, r. - p405 E9
Dutruit, av - p401 F4/5, p405 F5
Duvivier, r. - p401 E6, p405 E6

E. Clichy, pge - p401 G1/2
E. Delaunay, pge - p403 P6, p407 P6
Eblé, r. - p405 E7/8
Echiquier, r. de l' - p402 J4/K4
Ecluses-St-Martin, r. des - p402 L3/M3
Ecole-de-Medecine, r. de l' - p406 H7/J7, p408 H7/J7
Ecoles, r. des - p406 J7/8/K8, p408 J7
Ecouffes, r. des - p402 K6, p406 K6, p409 K6

Edgar-Quinet, bd - p405 G9
Edimbourg, r. d' - p401 F2
Edmond-Flamand, r. - p407 M9
Edmond-Rostand, pl. - p406 H8, p408 H8
Edmond-Valentin, r. - p400 D6, p404 D6
Edouard-Jacques, r. - p405 F10
Edouard-Manet, r. - p406 K10
Edouard-Pailleron, r. - p403 M2/N2
Edouard-Robert, r. - p407 Q9
Edward-Tuck, av - p401 F5, p405 F5
Eglise, r. de l' - p404 B8/C8/9
Elisa-Borey, r. - p403 P4/5
Elisée-Reclus, av - p404 D6
Elysée, r. de l' - p401 F4
Elzévir, r. - p402 L6, p406 L6, p409 L6
Emeriau, r. - p404 B7/8
Emile-Acollas, av - p404 D7
Émile-Augier, bd - p400 A5/6
Emile-Deschanel, av - p400 D6, p404 D6
Emile-Dubois, r. - p405 H10, p406 H10
Emile-Lepeu, r. - p403 P6, p407 P6
Emile-Ménier, r. - p400 A4
Émile-Zola, av - p404 A8/B8/C8
Enghien, r. d' - p402 J4/K4
Entrepreneurs, r. des - p404 B8/C8
Envierges, r. des - p403 P3/4
Eperon, r. de l' - p408 H7
Erard, r. - p407 N8/P8
Erasme, r. - p406 J9, p408 J9
Ermitage, r. de l' - p403 P3/4
Ermitage, villa de l' - p403 P4
Ernest-Cresson, r. - p405 G10
Ernest-Psichari, r. - p401 E6, p405 E6
Ernest-Renan, r. - p405 E8/9
Ernestine, r. - p402 K1
Esquirol, r. - p406 L10
Est, r. de l' - p403 P4/Q4
Estrapade, r. de l' - p406 J8, p408 J8
Estrées, r. d' - p405 E7
Etats-Unis, pl. des - p400 C4
Etex, r. - p401 G1
Étienne-Dolet, r. - p403 N4/P4
Etienne-Marcel, r. - p402 J5
Etoile, r. de l' - p400 C3
Eugène-Carrière, r. - p401 G1
Eugène-Gibez, r. - p404 C10
Eugène-Manuel, r. - p400 A6/B6, p404 B6
Eugène-Millon, r. - p404 C9
Eugène-Varlin, r. - p402 L2/3
Euler, r. - p400 D4
Eupatoria, r. d' - p403 P4
Euryale-Dehaynin, r. - p403 N1
Exposition, r. de l' - p400 D6, p404 D6

F. Delorme, r. - p400 D1
Fabert, r. - p401 E5/6
Fabert, r. - p405 E5/6
Fabre-d'Eglantine, r. - p407 Q8
Fagon, r. - p406 K10
Faidherbe, r. - p407 N7
Faisanderie, r. de la - p400 A4/5
Falguiere, r. - p405 E9/F8/9
Fallempin, r. - p404 C7/8
Faubourg-du-Temple, r. du - p402 L4/M4, p403 M4
Faubourg-Montmartre, r. du - p402 H3/J3/4
Faubourg-Poissonnière, r. du - p402 J2/3/4
Faubourg-St-Antoine, r. du - p407 M7/N7/P7

Faubourg-St-Denis, r. du - p402 K2/3/4
Faubourg-St-Jacques, r. du - p405 H10, p406 H9/10
Faubourg-St-Honoré, r. du - p400 D3, p401 D3/E3/4/F4
Faubourg-St-Martin, r. du - p402 K3/4/L2/3
Fauvet, r. - p401 G1
Favorites, r. des - p404 D9, p405 D9/10
Fayette, r. la - p401 H3, p402 H3/J3/K2/3/L2/M2
Fécamp, r. de - p407 Q9/10
Fédération, r. de la - p404 C7
Félix-Eboué, pl. - p407 Q9
Félix-Faure, av - p404 A9/B9/C9
Fer-à-Moulin, r. du - p406 K9
Ferdinand-Duval, r. - p409 K6/L6
Ferdinand-Fabre, r. - p404 C9
Fernand-Léger, r. - p403 P5, p407 P5
Fessart, r. - p403 N3
Feuillantines, r. des - p408 H9/J9
Feydeau, r. - p402 H4
Filles-du-Calvaire, r. des - p402 L5, p406 L5, p409 L5
Firmin-Gillot, r. - p404 C10
Flandre, pge de - p403 M1
Flandre, r. de - p403 M1
Flandrin, bd - p400 A4, p404 A4
Fleurs, quai aux - p406 K7
Fleurus, r. de - p405 G7/8
Foch, av - p400 A4/B3/4/C3
Folie-Méricourt, r. de la - p402 L4/M4, p403 M5, p407 M5
Folie-Regnault, pge de la - p403 P5
Folie-Regnault, r. de la - p403 P6, p407 P5/6
Folie, r. de la - p403 P5/6
Fondary, r. - p404 C8
Fontaine-au-Roi, r. de la - p403 M4/N4
Fontaine, r. - p401 H2
Fontaine, r. la - p404 A7
Fontarabie, r. de - p403 Q6, p407 Q6
Fontenoy, pl. de - p405 D7/E7
Forest, r. - p401 G1
Forge-Royale, r. de la - p407 N7
Fortuny, r. - p401 D2/E2
Fossés-St-Bernard, r. des - p406 K7/8, p409 K7/8
Four, r. du - p405 H7, p408 G7/H7
Fourcroy, r. - p400 C2
Fourcy, r. de - p406 K7/L6, p409 K6/7/L6
Francois-1er, r. - p400 D4, p401 E5, p405 D5
François-Bonvin, r. - p405 D8
François-Mauriac, quai - p407 M10/N10
Francois-Miron, r. - p402 K6, p406 K6, p409 K6/L6
François-Mitterrand, quai - p401 F5/G5
François-Truffaut, r. - p407 N10/P10
Francs-Bourgeois, r. des - p402 L6, p406 L6, p409 K6/L6
Franklin-D.-Roosevelt, av - p401 E3/4/5
Franklin, r. - p400 B5/6, p404 B5/6
Frédéric-Bastiat, r. - p401 E3/4
Frédéric-Le Play, av - p404 D6/7
Frédérick-Lemaître, r. - p403 P3
Frémicourt, r. - p404 C8/D8
Frères-Morane, r. des - p404 C8/9

Fresnel, r. - p400 C5, p404 C5
Friedland, av de - p400 C3/D3
Froidevaux, r. - p405 G9/10
Froment, r. - p403 M6, p407 M6
Fulton, r. - p407 M9

Gabriel-Laumain, r. - p402 J3
Gabriel-Péri, r. - p400 C1
Gabriel, av - p401 E4/F4
Gabriel, r. - p407 P10
Gabrielle, r. - p402 H1
Gaillon, r. - p401 H4
Gaîté, r. de la - p405 F9/G9
Galande, r. - p406 J7, p408 J7
Galilée, r. - p400 C4/D4
Galvani, r. - p400 C2
Gambetta, av - p403 P5/Q4/5, p407 P5/Q5
Gambetta, pge - p403 Q3/4
Gambetta, pl. - p403 Q5
Ganneron, r. - p401 G1
Garancière, r. - p405 H7, p406 H7, p408 H7
Gare-de-Reuilly, r. de la - p407 Q9
Gare, quai de la - p407 M9/10
Garibaldi, bd - p405 D8/E8
Garreau, r. - p401 H1, p402 H1
Gassendi, r. - p405 G10
Gâtines, r. de - p403 Q4/5, p407 Q5
Gay-Lussac, r. - p406 H8/J8/9, p408 H8/J8/9
Général-Bertrand, r. du - p405 E8
Général-Camou, r. du - p400 D6, p404 D6
Général-Eisenhower, av du - p401 E4
Général-Foy, r. de - p401 F2/3
Général-Leclerc, av du - p405 G10
Général-Lucotte, r. du - p404 A10
Général-Martial-Valin, bd - p404 A9/10/B10
Général-Michel-Bizot, av de - p407 Q10
Général-San Martin, av du - p403 N2/3
Génie, pl. du - p407 P7/8
Geoffroy-l'Asnier, r. - p406 K6, p409 K6
Geoffroy-St-Hilaire, r. - p406 K8/9
George-V, av - p400 D4/5
Georges-Bizet, r. - p400 C4/D4/5
Georges-Mandel, av - p400 A5/B5, p404 A5/B5
Georges-Pompidou, voie - p406 K7/J7, p409 K7/L7
Gerbier, r. - p403 P6, p407 P6
Gergovie, r. de - p405 E10/F10
Germain-Pilon, r. - p401 H1/2, p402 H1/2
Gesvres, quai de - p402 J6, p406 J6
Ginoux, r. - p404 B8
Girardon, r. - p401 H1, p402 H1
Gît-le-Couer, r. - p408 J7
Glacière, r. de la - p406 J9/10
Gobelins, av des - p406 K9/10
Godefroy-Cavaignac, r. - p403 N6, p407 N6/7
Godin, Villa - p403 Q6, p407 Q6
Godot-de-Mauroy, r. - p401 G3/4
Goethe, r. - p400 D5, p404 D5
Gounod, r. - p400 D2
Gourgaud, av - p400 C1
Goutte-d'Or, r. de la - p402 K1
Gouvion-St-Cyr, bd - p400 B2/C1/2
Gracieuse, r. - p406 K8/9
Gramme, r. - p404 C8

Gramont, r. de - p401 H4, p402 H4
Grand-Cerf, pge du - p402 J5, p406 J5
Grande-Armée, av de la - p400 B3/C3
Grands-Augustins, quai des - p406 H6/J6/7, p408 H6/J6/7
Grands-Augustins, r. des - p408 H6/7
Grands-Champs, r. des - p407 Q7
Grange-aux-Belles, r. de la - p402 L3
Grange-Batalière, r. de la - p402 H3/J3
Gravelle, r. de - p407 Q9/10
Gravilliers, r. des - p402 K5, p406 K5, p409 K5
Grégoire-de-Tours, r. - p408 H7
Grenelle, bd de - p404 C7/D8
Grenelle, Pont de - p404 A7/B7
Grenelle, quai de - p404 B7
Grenelle, r. de - p401 F6/G6, p404 D6, p405 D6/E6/F6/G6/7
Greneta, r. - p402 J5/K5, p406 J5/K5
Gros, r. - p404 A7
Guénégaud, r. - p400 H6, p408 H6
Guersant, r. - p400 B1/C1
Guillaume-Tell, r. - p400 C2
Guilleminot, r. - p405 F10
Guisarde, r. - p405 H7, p408 H7
Gustav-Charpentier, r. - p400 B2
Gustave-Eiffel, av - p400 C6, p404 C6
Gustave-Lepeu, pge - p403 P6, p407 P6
Gutenberg, r. - p404 A9/B8
Guynemer, r. - p405 G8, p408 G8/H8

Haies, r. des - p407 Q7
Halévy, r. - p401 G4
Halles, r. des - p402 J5/6, p406 J5/6
Hameau, r. du - p404 B10/C10
Hamelin, r. - p400 C4/5
Harpe, r. de la - p406 J7, p408 J7
Haussmann, bd - p401 D3/E3/F3/G3/H3/4
Hautefeuille, r. - p406 J7, p408 J7
Hauteville, r. de - p402 J3/4/K3
Helder, r. de - p401 H4
Henri-Barbusse, r. - p406 H9, p408 H8/9
Henri-Chevreau, r. - p403 P4
Henri-IV, bd - p406 L7, p409 K7/L7/M7
Henri-IV, quai - p406 L7/8, p409 L7
Henri-Martin, av - p400 A5, p404 A5
Henri-Poincaré, r. - p403 Q4
Henri-Rochefort, r. - p401 E2
Henri-Turot, r. - p403 M3
Henry-Mounier, r. - p401 H2, p402 H2
Herold, r. - p402 H5/J5, p406 H5/J5
Hittorff, r. - p402 K4
Hoche, av - p400 D3
Homond, r. - p406 J8/9
Hôpital-St-Louis, r. de l' - p402 L3
Hôpital, bd de l' - p406 K10/L8/9/10

Horloge, quai de l' - p402 J6, p406 J6, p408 J6
Hôtel-de-Ville, quai de l' - p406 K6/7, p409 K6/7
Hôtel-de-Ville, r. de l' - p406 K6/7, p409 K6/7
Houdart, r. - p403 P5, p407 P5
Houdon, r. - p401 H2, p402 H2
Huchette, r. de la - p406 J7, p408 J7
Humblot, r. - p404 C7
Huyghens, r. - p405 G9

Iéna, av d' - p400 C4/5, p404 C5
Iéna, Pont d' - p400 C6, p404 C6
Ile-de-la-Réunion, pl. de l' - p407 Q8
Ingénieur, r. de l' - p404 B8
Inkermann, bd d' - p400 A1/2
Invalides, bd des - p401 E6/F6, p405 E6/7/F8
Invalides, pl. des - p401 E6, p405 E6
Invalides, Pont des - p401 E5, p405 E5
Italie, pl. d' - p406 K10
Italiens, bd des - p401 H4, p402 H4

Jacob, r. - p401 G6/H6, p405 G6/H6, p408 G6/H6
Jacques-Callot, r. de - p408 H6
Jacques-Hillairet, r. - p407 P8/9
Jacques-Ibert, r. - p400 B1/C1
Jacques-Louvel-Tessier, r. - p402 M4
Japon, r. du - p403 Q5, p407 Q5
Jardiniers, r. des - p407 Q10
Jardins, r. des - p409 L7
Jarente, r. de - p409 L6
Jaucourt, r. - p407 P8
Javel, r. de - p404 A8/B8/C9
Jean-Aicard, av - p403 N5, p407 N5
Jean-Baptiste-Dumas, r. - p400 C2
Jean-Calvin, r. - p406 J9
Jean-de-Beauvais, r. - p408 J8
Jean-Dolent, r. - p406 H10
Jean-Ferrandi, r. - p405 F8
Jean-Formigé, r. - p404 C9
Jean-François-Lépine, r. - p402 K1
Jean-Giraudoux, r. - p400 C4/D4
Jean-Goujon, r. - p400 D5, p401 D5/E5, p405 D5/E5
Jean-Jacques-Rousseau, r. - p402 J5, p406 J5
Jean-Jaurès, av - p403 M2/N1
Jean-Maridor, r. - p404 B9
Jean-Mermoz, r. - p401 E4
Jean-Nicot, r. - p401 E5/6, p405 E5/6
Jean-Oestreicher, r. - p400 B1/C1
Jean-Pierre-Timbaud, r. - p402 L5/M5, p403 M4/5/N4
Jean-Rey, r. - p400 C6, p404 C6
Jean-Zay, r. - p405 F9
Jeanne-d'Arc, r. - p406 K9/L10
Jemmapes, quai de - p402 L2/3/4/M2
Jenner, r. - p406 L10
Jessaint, r. de - p402 K1
Jeûneurs, r. des - p402 J4
Joseph-Bara, r. - p405 H9, p408 H9
Joseph-Bouvard, av - p400 C6/D6, p404 C6/D6
Joseph-de-Maistre, r. - p401 G1/H1

Joseph-Kessel, r. - p407 N10
Joseph-Liouville, r. - p404 C8/D8
Jouffroy, pl. - p402 J4
Jouffroy, r. - p400 D2, p401 D1/2/E1/2
Jour, r. du - p402 J5, p406 J5
Jourdain, r. du - p403 P3
Jouy, r. de - p406 K6, p409 K6
Juge, r. - p404 C7
Juillet, r. - p403 P4
Jules-Bourdais, r. - p400 D1
Jules-César, r. - p406 M7, p407 M7
Jules-Chaplain, r. - p405 G8
Jules-Dumien, r. - p403 Q4
Jules-Ferry, bd - p402 L4/M4/5
Jules-Romains, r. - p403 N3
Julien-Lacroix, r. - p403 N3/4/P4
Juliette-Dodu, r. - p402 M3, p403 M3
Juliette-Lamber, r. - p401 D1
Junot, av - p401 H1, p402 H1
Jura, r. du - p406 K9
Jussieu, pl. - p406 K8
Jussieu, r. - p406 K8

Keller, r. - p404 B8, p407 M6/7/N7
Képler, r. - p400 C4/D4
Kléber, av - p400 B5/C4/5, p404 B5/C5

Labat, r. - p402 J1
Laborde, r. de - p401 F3
Labrouste, r. - p405 D10/E10
Lacépède, r. - p406 K8
Lacharrière, r. - p403 M5/N5, p407 M5/N5
Lacordaire, r. - p404 B8/9
Lacretelle, r. - p404 C10
Lacuée, r. - p407 M7, p409 M7
Laffitte, r. - p401 H3/4
Lagarde, r. - p406 J9
Laghouat, r. de - p402 K1
Lagny, r. de - p407 Q7
Lagrange, r. - p406 J7
Lakanal, r. - p404 C8
Lalande, r. - p405 G10
Lalo, r. - p400 A3/B3
Lamarck, r. - p401 H1, p402 H1/J1
Lamartine, r. - p402 H3/J3
Lamballe, av de - p404 A7/B7
Lamblardie, r. - p407 Q9
Lancette, r. de la - p407 P9/Q9
Lancry, r. de - p402 L4
Landrieu, pge - p400 D6, p404 D6
Langeac, r. de - p404 C10
Lannes, bd - p400 A3
Laos, r. du - p404 D7/8
Lapl.., r. - p406 J8, p408 J8
Lappe, r. de - p407 M7
Larrey, r. - p406 K9
Latran, r. - p408 J7
Laugier, r. - p400 C1/2/D2
Laumière, av de - p403 N1/2
Laurence-Savart, r. - p403 P4/Q4
Lauriston, r. - p400 B4/5/C4
Lauzin, r. - p403 N3
Leblanc, r. - p404 A9/10
Lecluse, r. - p401 G2
Lecourbe, r. - p404 B9/10/C9/D9, p405 D8/E8
Ledru-Rollin, av - p406 L8/M8, p407 M7/8/N6/7
Lefebvre, bd - p404 C10
Legendre, r. - p401 E2/F1/G1
Lemercier, r. - p401 F1
Léo-Delibes, r. - p400 B4/5/C5
Léon-Frot, r. - p403 N6/P6, p407 N6/P6
Léon-Giraud, r. - p403 N1

Léon-Jost, r. - p400 D2
Léon-Jouhaux, r. - p402 L4
Léon-Lhermitte, r. - p404 C9/D9
Léon-Maurice-Nordmann, r. - p406 J10
Léon, r. - p402 K1
Leonard-de-Vinci, r. - p400 B4
Léon-Blum, pl. - p403 N6, p407 N6
Léopold-Bellan, r. - p402 J4/5
Lepage, cité - p403 M2
Lepic, r. - p401 G2/H1, p402 H1
Leriche, r. - p404 C10
Leroux, r. - p400 B4
Lesdiguières, r. - p409 L7
Lesseps, r. de - p403 Q6, p407 Q6
Letellier, r. - p404 C8
Levert, r. - p403 P3
Lévis, r. de - p401 E1/2/F2
Lhomond, r. - p408 J8
Liancourt, r. de - p405 G10
Liège, r. de - p401 G2
Ligner, r. - p403 Q6, p407 Q6
Lille, r. de - p401 F5/6/G6, p405 F5/6/G6
Lincoln, r. - p400 D4
Linné, r. - p406 K8
Linois, r. - p404 B7/8
Lions-St-Paul - p406 L7, p409 L7
Lisbonne, r. de - p401 E3
Littre, r. - p405 F8/G8
Lobau, r. de - p402 K6, p406 K6
Lobineau, r. - p405 H7, p408 H7
Lodi, r. du - p408 H6
Logelbach, r. de - p401 E2
Loire, quai de la - p403 M1/2/N1
Lombards, r. des - p402 J6/K6, p406 J6/K6
Londres, r. de - p401 G3
Longchamp, allée de - p400 A3
Longchamp, r. de - p400 A4/B5/C5, p404 B5/C5
Lord-Byron, r. - p400 D3
Louis-Blanc, r. - p402 L2/M2
Louis-Bonnet, r. - p403 M4/N4
Louis-David, r. - p400 B5, p404 B5
Louis-le-Grand, r. - p401 G4/H4
Louis-Nicolas-Clérambault, r. - p403 P5, p407 P5
Louis-Philippe, pge - p407 M6
Louis-Philippe, Pont - p406 K7, p409 K7
Louise-Weiss, r. - p407 M10
Lourmel, r. de - p404 B8/9/10/C7/8
Louvois, r. de - p401 H4, p402 H4
Louvre, quai du - p401 G6/H6, p402 H6, p405 G6/H6, p406 H6
Louvre, r. du - p402 H5/J4/5, p406 H5/J5
Lowendal, av - p404 D5/D7/E7
Lowendal, sq - p404 D8
Lübeck, r. de - p400 C4/5
Lucien-Sampaix, r. - p402 L3/4
Lune, r. de la - p402 J4
Lutèce, r. de - p402 J6, p406 J6, p408 J6
Lyon, r. de - p407 M7/8
Lyonnais, r. des - p406 J9

Mabillon, r. - p408 H7
Mac-Mahon, av - p400 C3
Madame, r. - p405 G7/8, p408 G7/8
Madeleine-Michelis, r. - p400 A2
Madeleine, bd de la - p401 G4

STREET INDEX

Madeleine, pl. de la - p401 F4/G4
Mademoiselle, r. - p404 C8/D8
Madrid, r. de - p401 F3
Magdebourg, r. de - p400 C5, p404 C5
Magellan, r. - p400 D4
Magenta, bd de - p402 J2/K2/3/L4
Mail, r. du - p402 J4
Main-d'Or, pge de la - p407 N7
Maine, av du - p405 F8/9/10/G10
Maine, r. du - p405 F9
Maire, r. au - p402 K5, p406 K5, p409 K5
Maître-Albert, r. - p406 J7
Malakoff, av de - p400 B3/4
Malaquais, quai - p405 H6, p408 H6
Malar, r. - p401 D5/6, p405 D5/6
Malesherbes, bd - p400 D1, p401 D1/E1/2/F2/3/4
Malher, r. - p402 L6, p406 L6, p409 L6
Mal-Juin, pl. du - p400 C1/2
Malte, r. de - p402 L4/5, p409 M5
Mander, r. - p402 J5, p406 J5
Manin, r. - p403 N2
Manutention, r. de la - p400 C5, p404 C5
Marais, pge des - p402 L4
Marbeau, r. - p400 B3
Marbeuf, r. - p400 D4, p401 D4
Marceau, av - p400 C3/4/D4/5
Marcel-Proust, av - p400 B6, p404 B6
Marché-St-Honoré, pl. du - p401 G4
Mare, r. de la - p403 P3/4
Maréchal-de-Lattre-de-Tassigny, pl. du - p400 A4
Maréchal-Gallieni, av du - p401 E5/6, p405 E5/6
Margueritte, r. - p400 D2
Marie-Stuart, r. - p402 J5, p406 J5
Marie, Pont - p406 K7, p409 K7
Marignan, r. de - p401 D4/E4
Marigny, av de - p401 E4/F4
Mario-Nikis, r. - p404 D8
Marius-Aufan, r. - p400 B1
Marivaux, r. de - p401 H4, p402 H4
Marne, quai de la - p403 N1
Maroc, r. du - p402 L1/M1, p403 M1
Maronites, r. des - p403 N4/P/4
Marronniers, r. des - p404 A7
Martel, r. - p402 K3
Martyrs, r. des - p402 H2/3
Marx-Dormoy, r. - p402 K1/L1
Massenet, r. - p400 A6, p404 A6
Mathurin-Moreau, av - p403 M2/3
Mathurin-Régnier, r. - p405 E9
Mathurins, r. des - p401 F3/G3
Matignon, av - p401 E4
Maubeuge, r. de - p402 H3/J2/3/K2
Maublanc, r. - p404 D9
Maurice-Ripoche, r. - p405 F10/G10
Mayet, r. - p405 F8
Mazagran, r. de - p402 K4
Mazarine, r. - p405 H6/7, p406 H6/7, p408 H6/7
Mazas, pl. - p406 L8
Meaux, r. de - p403 M2/N1/2
Méchain, r. - p406 H10
Médéric, r. - p400 D2

Médicis, r. de - p406 H8, p408 H7/8
Mégisserie, quai de la - p402 J6, p406 J6, p408 J6
Meissonier, r. - p400 D2
Mélingue, r. - p403 P3
Ménilmontant, bd de la - p403 N4/5/P5/6, p407 N5/P5/6
Ménilmontant, r. de - p403 P4/Q4
Merlin, r. - p403 N5/P6, p407 N5/P6
Mesnil, r. - p400 B4
Messageries, r. des - p402 J3/K3
Messeran, r. - p405 E8
Messine, av de - p401 E3
Metz, r. de - p402 K4
Meuniers, r. des - p407 Q10
Meynadier, r. - p403 N1/2
Mezlay, r. - p402 K4/K4
Michel-le-Comte, r. - p402 K5, p406 K5, p409 K5
Michelet, r. - p405 H9, p408 H9
Milan, r. de - p401 G2/3
Milton, r. - p402 H2/3/J2
Minimes, r. des - p402 L6, p406 L6, p409 L6
Miollis, r. - p404 D8
Mirabeau, Pont - p404 A8
Mirbel, r. de - p406 K9
Miromesnil, r. de - p401 F3/4
Molière, r. - p401 H5, p405 H5
Monbel, r. de - p401 E1
Monceau, r. de - p401 D3/E2/3
Moncey, r. - p401 G2
Monge, r. - p406 K8/9
Monnaie, r. de la - p402 J6, p406 J6
Monsieur-le-Prince, r. - p406 H7/8, p408 H7/8
Monsieur, r. - p405 F7
Monsigny, r. - p401 H4
Monsoreau, sq - p407 Q6
Mont Cenis, r. du - p402 H1/J1
Montaigne, av - p400 D5, p401 D4/5/E4, p404 D5
Montalivet, r. - p401 F4
Montebello, quai de - p406 J7
Monte-Cristo, r. - p407 Q6/7
Montgallet, r. - p407 P8
Mont-Louis, r. de - p403 P6, p407 P6
Montmartre, bd - p402 H4
Montmartre, r. - p402 J4/5
Montmorency, r. de - p402 K5, p406 K5, p409 K5
Montorgueil, r. - p402 J4/5, p406 J5
Montparnasse, bd du - p405 F8/G8/9/H9
Montparnasse, r. du - p405 G8/9
Montreuil, r. de - p407 P7/Q7
Mont-Rosier, r. - p400 A2
Monttessuy, r. de - p400 D6, p404 D6
Mont-Thabor, r. du - p401 G4/5
Montyon, r. de - p402 J3
Morand, r. - p403 M4/N4
Moreau, r. - p407 M7
Moret, r. - p403 N4
Morillons, r. des - p404 C10/D10
Morland, bd - p406 L7/8, p409 L7/8
Mornay, r. - p406 L7, p409 L7
Moscou, r. de - p401 F2/G2
Moselle, r. de la - p403 M1
Motte-Picquet, av de la - p404 D7, p405 D7/E6
Mouffetard, r. - p406 J8/9
Moufle, r. - p403 M6, p407 M6
Moulin-Joly, r. du - p403 N4
Mousset, imp - p407 P8

Mouton-Duvernet, r. - p405 G10
Moynet, cité - p407 P8
M'tage Ste Genevieve - p406 J7/8
Muller, r. - p402 J1
Murillo, r. - p401 E2
Myrha, r. - p402 J1/K1

Nancy, r. de - p402 K4
Nanettes, r. des - p403 N5, p407 N5
Naples, r. de - p401 F2
Nation, pl. de la - p407 Q7/8
Nationale, r. - p406 L10
Nations-Unies, av des - p400 B6/C5/6, p404 C5/6
Navarin, r. de - p401 H2
Nélaton, r. - p404 B7
Nesle, r. de - p408 H6
Neuf, Pont - p402 H6/J6, p406 H6/J6, p408 H6/J6
Neuve-des-Boulets, r. - p407 P7
Neuve-St-Pierre, r. - p406 L7, p409 L7
Nevers, r. de - p406 H6, p408 H6
New-York, av de - p400 C5/6/D5, p404 C5/D5
Nice, r. de - p403 P6, p407 P6
Nicolaï, r. - p407 P10/Q9/10
Nicolas Chuquet, r. - p400 D1
Nicolet, r. - p402 J1
Nicolo, r. - p400 A5/6/B6, p404 A6/B6
Niel, av - p400 C2
Niepce, r. - p405 F10
Nollet, r. - p401 F1
Norvins, r. - p402 H1
Notre-Dame-de-Lorette, r. - p401 H2/3, p402 H2/3
Notre-Dame-de-Nazareth, r. - p402 K4/K4
Notre-Dame-des-Champs, r. - p405 G8/9/H9
Notre-Dame-des-Victoires, r. - p402 H4
Notre-Dame, Pont - p402 J6, p406 J6, p408 J6
Nôtre, r. le - p400 B6, p404 B6

Oberkampf, r. - p402 L5/M5, p403 M5/N4/5, p406 L5/M5, p407 M5/N5, p409 L5/M5
Octave-Gréard, av - p400 C6, p404 C6
Odéon, r. de l' - p406 H7, p408 H7
Odessa, r. d' - p405 G9
Oise, quai de l' - p403 N1
Olivier-de-Serres, r. - p404 C10
Olivier-Métra, r. - p403 P3/Q3/4
Olivier-Noyer, r. - p405 F10
Opéra, av de l' - p401 G4/H4/5, p405 H5
Opéra, pl. de - p401 G4
Oran, r. d' - p402 K1
Orfèvres, quai des - p406 J6, p408 J6
Orfila, r. - p403 Q4/5, p407 Q5
Orillon, r. de l' - p403 M4/N4
Orléans, quai d' - p406 K7, p409 K7
Ormeaux, r. - p407 Q7
Ormesson, r. de - p409 L6
Orsay, quai d' - p400 D5, p401 D5/E5, p405 D5/E5, p404 D5
Orsel, r. d' - p402 H2/J2
Orteaux, r. des - p403 Q6, p407 Q6
Ortolan, r. - p406 J8/K8
Oscar-Roty, r. - p404 B9
Oudinot, r. - p405 F7
Ourcq, r. de l' - p403 N1

Paix, r. de la - p401 G4
Pajol, r. - p402 L1
Palais-Royal, pl. du - p401 H5, p402 H5, p405 H5, p406 H5
Palais, bd du - p406 J6/7, p408 J6
Palestine, r. de - p403 P3
Pali-Kao, r. de - p403 N4
Panoyaux, r. des - p403 P4
Paradis, r. de - p402 J3/K3
Parc-Royal, r. du - p402 L6, p406 L6, p409 L6
Parmentier, av - p403 M4/5/N5/6, p407 M5/N5/6
Parmentier, r. - p400 B1/2
Parrot, r. - p407 M8
Partants, r. des - p403 P5, p407 P5
Pascal, r. - p406 J9/10
Pasquier, r. - p401 F3/4
Passy, r. de - p400 A6, p404 A6/B6
Pasteur, bd - p405 E8/9
Pasteur, r. - p403 M5, p407 M5
Pastourelle, r. - p402 K5/L5, p406 K5/L5, p409 K5/L5
Paul-Albert, r. - p402 J1
Paul-Barruel, r. - p404 D9, p405 D9
Paul-Baudry, r. - p401 E4
Paul-Bert, r. - p407 N7
Paul-Doumer, av - p400 A6/B5/6, p404 A6/B5/6
Paul-Feval, r. - p402 H1
Paul-Lelong, r. - p402 H4/J4
Paul-Valéry, r. - p400 B4/C4
Pelée, r. - p403 M6, p407 M6, p409 L6/M6
Peletier, r. le - p402 H3
Pelleport, r. - p403 Q3/4
Penthièvre, r. de - p401 E4/F3
Pépinière, r. de la - p401 F3
Perdonnet, r. - p402 L2
Père-Lachaise, av du - p403 Q5
Pereire, bd - p400 B2/3/C2/D1, p401 D1/E1
Pergolèse, r. - p400 B3
Perle, r. de la - p402 L6, p406 L6, p409 L6
Pernety, r. - p405 F10
Pérouse, r. la - p400 C4
Perrée, r. - p402 L5, p406 L5, p409 L5
Perronet, r. - p400 A1
Pershing, bd - p400 B2
Petel, r. - p404 D9
Pétion, r. - p403 N6, p407 N6
Petit-Musc, r. du - p406 L7, p409 L7
Petit-Pont - p406 J7, p408 J7
Petit, r. - p403 N1
Petites-Ecuries, r. des - p402 J3/K3
Petits-Champs, r. des - p401 H4/5, p402 H4/5
Petits-Hôtels, r. des - p402 K3
Pétrelle, r. - p402 J2
Phalsbourg, r. de - p401 E2
Philippe-de-Girard, r. - p402 L1/2
Philippe-Auguste, av - p407 P6/7/Q7
Piat, r. - p403 N3/4
Picardie, r. de - p409 L5
Picpus, bd de - p407 Q8/9
Picpus, r. de - p407 P8/Q8/9
Pierre-1er-de-Serbie, av - p400 C5/D4/5, p404 C5
Pierre-Bayle, r. - p403 P6, p407 P6
Pierre-Bourdan, r. - p407 P8
Pierre-Charron, r. - p400 D4
Pierre-Demours, r. - p400 C2/D2
Pierre-Dupont, r. - p402 L2

Pierre-et-Marie-Curie, r. - p406 J8, p408 J8
Pierre-Leroux, r. - p405 F7/8
Pierre-Lescot, r. - p402 J5, p406 J5
Pierre-Levée, r. de la - p403 M4/5
Pierre-Nicole, r. - p406 H9, p408 H9
Pierre-Picard, r. - p402 J1
Pigalle, pl. - p401 H2, p402 H2
Pigalle, r. - p401 G3/H2, p402 H2
Pinel, r. - p406 K10/L10
Pirandello, r. - p406 K9/10
Pirogues, r. des - p407 P10
Pixérécourt, r. - p403 Q3/4
Plaine, r. de la - p407 Q7
Plaisance, r. de - p405 F10
Planchat, r. - p403 Q6, p407 Q6/7
Planche, r. de la - p405 G7
Plateau, r. du - p403 N3
Platon, r. - p405 E9
Plâtrières, r. des - p403 P4
Plélo, r. de - p404 B9
Point-des-Champs-Elysées, rond - p401 E4
Poirier, Villa - p404 D8
Poissonnière, bd - p402 J4
Poissonnière, r. - p402 J4
Poissy, r. de - p406 K7/8
Poitou, r. de - p402 L5, p406 L5, p409 L5
Poliveau, r. - p406 K9/L9
Polonceau, r. - p402 K1
Pommard, r. de - p407 N90/10/P10
Pompe, r. de - p400 A5/6/B4, p404 A5
Poncelet, r. - p400 C2/3/D2
Pondichéry, r. de - p404 C7
Poniatowski, bd - p407 Q10
Pont-aux-Choux, r. du - p402 L5, p406 L5, p409 L5
Pont-Neuf, r. du - p402 J5/6, p406 J6
Ponthieu, r. de - p401 D4/E4
Pontoise, r. de - p406 K7
Popincourt, r. - p403 M6/N6, p407 N6/N6
Port-Royal, bd de - p406 H9/J9
Portalis, r. - p401 F3
Porte-d'Issy, r. de la - p404 B10
Porte-de-Champerret, av de la - p400 B1/C1
Porte-de-Sèvres, av de la - p404 A10
Porte-de-Villiers, av de la - p400 B1/2
Porte-Maillot, pl. de la - p400 B3
Portefoin, r. - p409 L5
Poissonniers, r. des - p402 J1/K1
Pot-de-Fer, r. du - p406 J8/9, p408 J8/9
Poulet, r. - p402 J1
Poulletier, r. - p406 K7, p409 K7
Pradier, r. - p403 N3
Prairies, r. des - p403 Q5, p407 Q5
Président-Ecuries, cours des - p402 K3/4
Président-Kennedy, av du - p400 B6/C6, p404 A7/B6/7/C6
Président-Mithouard, pl. du - p405 E7
Président-Wilson, av du - p400 C5/D5, p404 C5/D5
Presles, r. de - p404 C7
Pressoir, r. du - p403 N4
Princesse, r. - p408 H7
Printemps, r. du - p401 E1
Procession, r. de la - p405 D9/E9/10

Prony, r. de - p400 D2, p401 D2/E2
Proudhon, r. - p407 P9
Provence, r. de - p401 G3/H3, p402 H3
Puteaux, r. - p401 F2
Pyramides, r. des - p401 G5/H5, p405 G5/H5
Pyrénées, r. des - p403 P3/4/Q4/5/6, p407 Q5/6

Quatre-Septembre, r. du - p402 H4
Quatrefages, r. de - p406 K8/9
Quentin, r. - p400 D4
Quessant, r. de - p404 C7/D7
Quest, r. de l' - p405 E10/F9/10
Quinault, r. - p404 D8
Quincampoix, r. - p402 J6/K5, p406 J5/6/K5
Quintinie, r. la - p404 D9, p405 D9

Racine, r. - p406 H7/J7, p408 H7/J7
Rambouillet, r. de - p407 N8
Rambuteau, r. - p402 K5/6, p406 K5/6, p409 K5/6
Ramey, r. - p402 J1
Rampal, r. - p403 N3
Rampon, r. - p402 L5/M5
Ramponeau, r. - p403 N4
Ramus, r. - p403 Q5, p407 Q5
Ranelagh, r. du - p404 A7
Rapée, quai de la - p406 L8/M8, p407 M8/9
Rapp, av - p400 D5/6, p404 D5/6
Raspail, bd - p405 G7/8/9/10
Raymond-Losserand, r. - p405 E10/F10
Raymond-Poincaré, av - p400 B4/5, p404 B5
Raynouard, r. - p400 B6, p404 A6/7/B6
Réaumur, r. - p402 J4/K5, p406 K5, p409 K5
Rébeval, r. - p403 M3/N3
Récollets, r. des - p402 L3
Regard, r. de - p405 G7/8
Regrattier, r. le - p406 K7, p409 K7
Reims, bd de - p400 C1/D1
Reine-Blanche, r. de la - p406 K9/10
Reine, cours la - p401 E5/F5, p405 E5
Renard, r. du - p402 K5/6, p406 K6
Renaudes, r. des - p400 C2/D2
Rendez-vous, r. du - p407 Q8
René-Boulanger, r. - p402 K4/L4
René-Coty, av - p405 H10
Rennequin, r. - p400 C2/D2
Rennes, r. de - p405 G7/8, p408 G7/H7
Repos, r. du - p403 P6, p407 P6
République, av de la - p402 L4/M5, p403 M5/N5, p407 M5/N5
République, pl. de la - p402 L4
Retaud, r. - p406 J9, p408 J9
Retrait, r. du - p403 P4/Q4
Reuilly, bd de - p407 P9/Q9
Reuilly, r. de - p407 P7/8/9/Q9
Réunion, r. de la - p403 Q6, p407 Q6
Rhin, r. du - p403 N1/2
Ribérolle, Villa - p403 Q6, p407 Q6
Ribot, cité - p403 N4
Richard-Lenoir, bd - p403 M5/6, p407 M5, p407 M6

Richard-Lenoir, r. - p403 N6, p407 N6
Richelieu, r. de - p401 H4/5, p402 H4/5, p405 H5, p406 H5
Richer, r. - p402 J3
Richerand, av - p402 L4
Richomme, r. - p402 K1
Rignard, r. - p400 A5, p404 A5
Rigoles, r. des - p403 P3/4/Q4
Riquet, r. - p402 L1, p403 M1
Riverin, cité - p402 K4
Rivoli, r. de - p401 G5/H5, p402 J6/K6, p405 G5/H5, p406 H5/J6/K6/L6
Rivoli, r. de - p409 K6/L6/7
Robert-Desnos, pl. - p402 L3/M3
Robert-Schuman, av - p401 D5/E5
Robineau, r. - p403 P5, p407 P5
Rochechouart, bd de - p402 H2/J2
Rochechouart, r. de - p402 J2/3
Rochefoucauld, r. de la - p401 H2/3
Rocher, r. du - p401 F2/3
Rocroy, r. de - p402 K2
Rodier, r. - p402 J2/3
Roger-Bacon, r. - p400 C2
Roi-de-Sicile, r. du - p402 K6/L6, p406 K6/L6, p409 K6/L6
Rollin, r. - p406 K8
Rome, r. de - p401 E1/F1/2/3/4
Rondeaux, r. des - p403 Q5, p407 Q5
Roquette, r. de la - p403 M6/N6, p407 M6/N6/P6
Rosenwald, r. - p405 D10/E10
Rosiers, r. des - p402 K6/L6, p406 K6/L6, p409 K6/L6
Rossini, r. - p402 H3
Rouelle, r. - p404 B7/C7
Roule, av du - p400 A2/B2
Roule, r. du - p402 J5/6, p406 J5/6
Rousselet, r. - p405 F7/8
Rouvray, r. de - p400 A1/B1
Royal, Pont - p401 G5, p405 G6
Royale, r. - p401 F4
Royer-Collard, r. - p408 J8
Rubens, r. - p406 K10

S. de Sacy, av - p400 C6, p404 C6
Sablière, r. de la - p405 F10
Sablons, r. des - p400 B5, p404 B5
Sablonville, r. de - p400 A2
Saïd, villa - p400 A3
Saïda, r. de la - p404 C10
St-Amand, r. - p405 E10
St-Ambroise, r. - p403
St-Andre-des-Arts, r. - p406 H7/J7, p408 H7/J7
St-Antoine, r. - p406 L6/7, p409 L6/7/M7
St-Augustin, pl. - p401 F3
St-Augustin, r. - p401 H4, p402 H4
St-Benoît, r. - p405 H6/7, p408 H6/7
St-Bernard, quai - p406 K7/8/L8
St-Bernard, r. - p407 N7
St-Charles, r. - p404 A9/B7/8/9/C7
St-Charles, sq - p407 P8
St-Chaumont, cité - p403 M3
St-Claude, r. - p402 L6, p406 L6, p409 L6
St-Denis, bd - p402 K4

St-Denis, r. - p402 J5/6/K4/5, p406 J5/6
St-Didier, r. - p400 B4/5, p400 B5, p404 B5
St-Dominique, r. - p400 D6, p401 D6/E6/F6, p404 D6, p405 D6/E6/F6
St-Eloi, Cour - p407 P8
St-Emilion, Cour - p407 P10
St-Fargeau, r. - p403 Q4
St-Ferdinand, r. - p400 B3/C3
St-Fiacre, r. - p402 J4
St-Georges, r. - p401 H3, p402 H3
St-Germain, bd - p401 F5/6/G6, p405 F5/6/G6/7/H7, p406 H7/J7/K7, p408 H7/J7
St-Gilles, r. - p402 L6, p406 L6, p409 L6
St-Guillaume, r. - p405 G6/7
St-Hippolyte, r. - p406 J10
St-Honoré, r. - p401 F4/G4/5, p402 H5/J5, p405 G5/H5, p406 H5/J5
St-Jacques, bd - p405 H10, p406 H10
St-Jacques, r. - p406 H9/J7/8/9, p408 H9/J7/8/9
St-Jean-Baptiste-de-la-Salle, r. - p405 F8
St-Joseph, r. - p402 J4
St-Julien-le-Pauvre, r. - p408 J7
St-Lambert, r. - p404 C9/10
St-Lazare, r. - p401 G3/H3, p402 H3
St-Louis-en-l'Ile, r. - p406 K7, p409 K7
St-Louis, Pont - p406 K7
St-Mandé, av de - p407 Q8
St-Marc, r. - p402 H4/J4
St-Marcel, bd - p406 K9/L9
St-Martin, bd - p402 K4/L4
St-Martin, r. - p402 J6/K4/5/6, p406 J6/K5/6
St-Maur, r. - p403 M3/4/N5/6, p407 N5/6, M5/N5
St-Médard, r. - p406 J8/K8
St-Merri, r. - p406 K6
St-Michel, bd - p405 H9, p406 H8/9/J7, p408 H8/J7
St-Michel, Pont - p406 J7, p408 J7
St-Michel, quai - p406 J7, p408 J7
St-Ouen, av de - p401 G1
St-Paul, r. - p406 L7, p409 L7
St-Petersbourg, r. de - p401 F2/G2
St-Pierre-Amelot, pge - p402 L5/M5, p403 M5, p406 M5, p407 M5, p409 M5
St-Pierre, pl. - p402 J2
St-Placide, r. - p405 G7/8
St-Roch, r. - p401 G5/H5, p405 G5/H5
St-Romain, r. - p405 F8
St-Sabin, r. - p402 M6, p403 M6, p406 M6, p407 M6, p409 M6
St-Saens, r. - p404 C7
St-Sauveur, r. - p402 J5, p406 J5
St-Sébastien, pge - p402 L5/M5, p403 M5, p406 M5, p407 M5, p409 M5
St-Sébastien, r. - p402 M5, p403 M5, p406 M5, p407 M5, p409 M5
St-Senoch, r. de - p400 C2
St-Séverin, r. - p406 J7, p408 J7
St-Simon, r. de - p401 F6/G6, p405 F6/G6
St-Sulpice, r. - p405 H7, p406 H7, p408 H7
St-Vincent, r. - p402 H1/J1

STREET INDEX

Ste-Anastase, r. - p409 L6
Ste-Anne, r. - p401 H4/5,
p402 H4
Ste-Apolline, r. - p402 K4
Ste-Cécile - p402 J3
Ste-Croix-de-la-Bretonnerie, r. -
p402 K6, p406 K6, p409 K6
Ste-Foy, r. - p402 K4
Ste-Marthe, r. - p403 M3
Saintonge, r. de - p402 L5,
p406 L5, p409 L5
Sts-Pères, r. des - p401 G6/H6,
p405 G6/7, p408 G6/H6
Sambre-et-Meuse, r. du -
p403 M3
Santé, r. de la - p406
H10/J9/J10
Santerre, r. - p407 Q8
Santeuil, r. de - p406 K9
Saulnier, r. - p402 J3
Saussaies, r. de - p401 F4
Saussure, r. de - p401 E1/F2
Savoie, r. de - p408 H7/J7
Saxe, av de - p405 E7/8
Scheffer, r. - p400 A5/B5,
p404 A5/B5
Schuman, r. - p405 D5/E5
Scipion, r. - p406 K9
Scribe, r. - p401 G4
Sébastien-Mercier, r. r. -
p404 A8/B8
Sébastopol, bd de - p402
J5/6/K4/5, p406 J5/6/K5
Secrétan, av - p403 M2
Sedaine, r. - p403 M6/N6,
p407 M6/N6
Sédillot, r. - p400 D6, p404 D6
Séguier, r. - p406 J7, p408 J7
Ségur, av de - p405 E7
Seine, quai de la - p403
M1/2/N1
Seine, r. de - p401 H6,
p405 H6/7, p406 H6/7,
p408 H6/7
Senlis, r. de - p400 C1
Sentier, r. du - p402 J4
Sergent-Bauchat, r. du -
p407 P8
Servan, r. - p403 N5/6,
p407 N5/6
Servandoni, r. - p405 H7,
p408 H7
Severo, r. - p405 F10/G10
Sévigné, r. de - p402 L6, p406
L6, p409 L6
Sèvres, r. de - p405 F7/8/G7
Siam, r. de - p400 A5
Simon-Bolivar, av - p403
M2/3/N3
Simon-Dereure, r. - p401 H1,
p402 H1
Simone-de-Beauvoir,
passerelle - p407 N10
Singer, r. - p400 A6, p404 A6
Sofia, r. de - p402 J1
Soleil, r. du - p403 Q3
Soleillet, r. - p403 P5, p407 P5
Solférino, passerelle -
p401 G5
Solferino, r. de - p401 F6,
p405 F6
Somme, bd de la - p400 C1
Sommerard, r. du - p406 J7
Sorbier, r. - p403 P4/5, p407
P5/Q5
Sorbonne, r. de la - p406 J7/8,
p408 J7/8
Soufflot, r. - p406 H8/J8,
p408 H8/J8
Sourdière, r. de la - p401 G5,
p405 G5
Souzy, cité - p407 P7
Spontini, r. - p400 A4/5
Staël, r. de - p405 E8/9
Stanislas, r. - p405 G8
Stendhal, r. - p403 Q5, p407 Q5

Stéphane-Mallarmé, av -
p400 C1
Stephen-Pichon, av - p406
K10/L10
Stephenson, r. - p402 K1
Strasbourg, bd de - p402 K3/4
Sueur, r. le - p400 B3
Suez, r. de - p402 K1
Suffren, av de - p400 C6, p404
C6/7/D7, p405 D8/E8
Suger, r. - p406 H7/J7,
p408 H7/J7
Sully, Pont de - p406 K7/L7,
p409 K7/L7
Sully, r. de - p406 L7, p409 L7
Surcouf, r. - p401 E5/6,
p405 E5/6
Surène, r. de - p401 F4

Taclet, r. - p403 Q4
Taillandiers, r. des -
p407 M6/7
Taillebourg, av de - p407 Q7
Taine, r. - p407 P9
Taitbout, r. - p401 H3
Tandou, r. - p403 N1
Tanger, r. de - p402 L1/M1,
p403 M1
Tanneries, r. des - p406 J10
Tasse, r. le - p400 B6, p404 B6
Taylor, r. - p402 K4/L4
Télégraphe, r. du - p403 Q3/4
Temple, bd du - p409 L5
Temple, r. du - p402 K5/6/L5,
p406 K5/6/L5, p409
K5/6/L5
Ternes, av des - p400 B2/C/3
Terrage, r. du - p402 L3
Terrasse, r. de la - p401 E2
Terre-Neuve, r. de - p407 Q6/7
Terroirs-de-France, av des -
p407 P10
Texel, r. du - p405 F9/10
Thann, r. de - p401 E2
Théâtre, r. du - p404 B7/8/C/8
Thénard, r. - p408 J7
Théodore-de-Banville, r. -
p400 D2
Théodore-Deck, r. - p404 C9
Théodule-Ribot, r. - p400 D2
Théophile-Gautier, av - p404 A7
Théophile-Roussel, r. -
p407 M7/N7
Théophraste-Renaudot, r. -
p404 C9
Thérèse, r. - p401 H5
Thermopyles, r. des - p405 F10
Thiéré, pge - p407 M7
Thierry-de-Martel, bd -
p400 A3/4
Thionville, r. de - p403 N1
Thouin, r. - p406 J8
Tholozé, r. - p401 H1
Thoréton, villa - p404 B9
Thorigny, r. de - p402 L6, p406
L6, p409 L6
Thouin, r. - p408 J8
Tiphaine, r. - p404 C7/8
Tiquetonne, r. - p402 J5,
p406 J5
Titon, r. - p407 P7
Tlemcen, r. de - p403 P5,
p407 P5
Tocqueville, r. de - p401 D1/
E1/2
Tolbiac, Pont de - p407 N10
Tolbiac, r. de - p407 N10
Torricelli, r. - p400 C1
Tour-d'Auvergne, r. de la -
p402 J2
Tour-Maubourg, bd de la - p401
E5/6, p405 E5/6/7
Tour, r. de la - p400 A5/B6,
p404 A5/B6
Tournefort, r. - p406 J8/9,
p408 J8

Tournelle, Pont de la - p406 K7,
p409 K7
Tournelle, quai de la - p406 K7,
p409 K7
Tournelles, r. des - p402 L6,
p406 L6/7, p409 L6/7
Tournon, r. de - p405 H7, p406
H7, p408 H7
Tourtille, r. de - p403 N4
Tourville, av de - p405 E7
Tracy, r. de - p402 K4
Transvaal, r. du - p403 P4
Traversière, r. - p407 M8
Treilhard, r. - p401 E3
Trémoille, r. de la - p400 D4/5
Trésor, r. du - p409 K6
Trévise, cité de - p402 J3
Trévise, r. de - p402 J3
Trocadéro et du 11-Novembre,
pl. du - p400 B5, p404 B5
Trois-Bornes, r. des - p403
M4/5
Trois-Frères, r. des - p402 H1/2
Tronchet, r. - p401 G3/4
Trône, av du - p407 Q8
Trousseau, r. - p407 N7
Truffaut, r. - p401 F1
Tuileries, quai des - p405
F5/G5/6
Tunis, r. de - p407 Q7
Turbigo, r. de - p402 J5/K5,
p406 J5/K5, p409 K5
Turenne, r. de - p402 L5/6,
p406 L5/6, p409 L5/6
Turin, r. de - p401 G2
Turquetil, pge - p407 P7

Ulm, r. d' - p406 J8/9,
p408 J8/9
Université, r. de - p400 D5/6,
p401 D5/E5/F5/6/G6,
p404 D5/6, p405 D5/E5/
F5/6/G6
Uzès, r. d' - p402 J4

Val-de-Grâce, r. du - p406 H9,
p408 H9
Valette, r. - p406 J8, p408 J8
Valhubert, pl. - p406 L8
Valmy, quai de - p402
L2/3/4/M2
Valois, r. de - p401 H5, p402
H5, p405 H5, p406 H5
Van-Gogh, r. - p407 M8
Van-Dyck, av - p401 D3/E2
Vaneau, cité - p405 F6/7
Vaneau, r. - p405 F7
Varenne, cité de - p405 F7
Varenne, r. de - p401 F6
Vasco-de-Gama, r. - p404
B9/10
Vauban, pl. - p405 E7
Vaucouleurs, r. de - P403 N4
Vaugelas, r. - p404 C10
Vaugirard, bd de - p405 F9
Vaugirard, r. de - p404 C9/10/
D9, p405 D9/E8/9/F8/
G8/H7/8, p406 H7, p408
G8/H7
Vauquelin, r. - p406 J9
Vavin, av - p405 G8, p408
G8/H8
Vavin, r. - p405 G8
Vendôme, pl. - p401 G4
Vercingétorix, r. - p405 E10/
F9/10
Verdun, av de - p402 L3
Verdun, r. de - p400 B2
Vergniaud, r. - p400 B1
Vernet, r. - p400 C4/D4
Verneuil, r. de - p401 G6,
p405 G6
Vernier, r. - p400 C2
Verniquet, r. - p400 D1
Véron, r. - p401 H1/2, p402 H2
Véronèse, r. - p406 K10

Verrerie, r. de la - p402 K6,
p406 K6, p409 K6
Verrier, r. le - p405 H9
Versailles, av de - p404 A7/8
Vertbois, r. du - p402 K4
Verte, allée - p403 M6,
p407 M6
Verzy, av de - p400 B2
Viala, r. - p404 C7
Vicq-d'Azir, r. - p403 M3
Victoire, r. de la - p401 G3/H3,
p402 H3
Victoires, pl. des - p402 H5/J5,
p406 H5
Victor, bd - p404 B10
Victor-Duruy, r. - p404 D9/10
Victor-Hugo, av - p400 A4/5/
B3/4
Victor-Hugo, bd - p400 A1/
B1/2
Victor-Hugo, pl. - p400 B4
Victor-Massé, r. - p401 H2
Victoria, av - p402 J6/K6, p406
J6, p408 J6
Vieille-du-Temple, r. - p402
L5/6, p406 L5/6, p409
L5/6
Vienne, r. de - p401 F3
Viète, r. - p401 D2/E2
Vigée-Lebrun, r. - p405 E9
Vignes, r. des - p404 A6/7
Vignoles, r. des - p407 Q6/7
Vignon, r. - p401 G4
Villaret-de-Joyeuse, r. - p400 C3
Villars, av de - p405 E7
Ville-l'Évêque, r. de la - p401 F4
Villedo, r. - p401 H5, p402 H5,
p406 H5
Villehardouin, r. - p409 L6
Villemain, av - p405 F10
Villette, bd de la - p402 M2,
p403 M2/3
Villiers-de-l'Isle-Adam, r. -
p403 Q4
Villiers, av de - p400 C1/D2,
p401 D2/E2, p400 A1/B1
Vinaigriers, r. des - p402 L3
Vincennes, cité de - p407 Q8
Vincent-Auriol, bd - p406 K10/
L10/M10, p407 M9/10
Vineuse, r. - p400 B5/6,
p404 B5/6
Violet, r. - p404 C7/8
Visconti, r. - p405 H6, p408 H6
Vital, r. - p400 A6, p404 A6
Vivienne, r. - p402 H4
Volney, r. - p401 G4
Volontaires, r. des - p405 E9
Volta, r. - p402 K4/5
Voltaire, bd - p402 L5/M5,
p403 M5/N6, p406
L5/M5, p407 M5/6/N6/P7,
p409 L5/M5
Voltaire, cité - p407 P7
Voltaire, quai - p401 G6/H6,
p405 G6, p408 G6/H6
Voltaire, r. - p407 P7
Vosges, pl. des - p402 L6, p406
L6, p409 L6
Vouillé, r. de - p404 D10, p405
D10/E10
Vulpin, r. - p406 J10

Wagram, av de - p400 C1/C2/
C3/D1/D2/D3
Wagram, pl. de - p400 D1
Wallons, r. des - p406 K9/L9
Washington, r. - p400 D3/4
Wattignies, r. de - p407 Q10
Weber, r. - p400 B3
Winston-Churchill, av -
p401 E4/5

Yser, bd de l' - p400 B1/2/C1
Yves-Toudic, r. - p402 L4